Modernization in Colombia

Florida A&M University, Tallahassee
Florida Atlantic University, Boca Raton
Florida Gulf Coast University, Ft. Myers
Florida International University, Miami
Florida State University, Tallahassee
University of Central Florida, Orlando
University of Florida, Gainesville
University of North Florida, Jacksonville
University of South Florida, Tampa
University of West Florida, Pensacola

Modernization in Colombia

The Laureano Gómez Years, 1889–1965

James D. Henderson

University Press of Florida

Gainesville · Tallahassee · Tampa · Boca Raton
Pensacola · Orlando · Miami · Jacksonville · Ft. Myers

Copyright 2001 by the Board of Regents of the State of Florida
Printed in the United States of America on acid-free paper
All rights reserved

06 05 04 03 02 01   6 5 4 3 2 1

Library of Congress Cataloging-in-Publication Data
Henderson, James D. 1942–
Modernization in Colombia: the Laureano Gómez years, 1889–1965 /
James D. Henderson.
p. cm.
Includes bibliographical references and index.
ISBN 0-8130-1824-2 (alk. paper)
1. Colombia–History–1886–1903. 2. Colombia–History–1903–1946.
3. Colombia–History–1946–1974. 4. Gómez, Laureano, 1889–1965.
I. Title.

F2276.5.H46 2001
986.106'2–dc21   00-051051

The University Press of Florida is the scholarly publishing agency
for the State University System of Florida, comprising Florida A&M
University, Florida Atlantic University, Florida Gulf Coast University,
Florida International University, Florida State University, University of
Central Florida, University of Florida, University of North Florida,
University of South Florida, and University of West Florida.

University Press of Florida
15 Northwest 15th Street
Gainesville, FL 32611–2079
http://www.upf.com

This book is dedicated to the memory of my parents,
James and Barbara Pardue Henderson

Contents

Illustrations

Acknowledgments

I am indebted to many people and institutions for their encouragement and support during my years of work on this book. My wife, Linda, my children, and my parents were especially understanding of my need to devote time and attention to "the Gómez study." My colleagues at Coastal Carolina University were supportive in many ways. Members of Coastal's Department of Politics and International Studies collegially supported my request for leave from teaching duties during 1990–91, when I wrote the first half of this volume. Our departmental administrative assistant, Bonnie Senser, was unfailingly helpful and good-humored. Faculty of the Reference Department at the university's Kimbel Library—Margaret Fain, Marchita Phifer, and Blake Deegan—helped me locate hard-to-find volumes on Colombian history via interlibrary loan. Tabby Shelton spent many hours reformatting the manuscript.

Colombianists Jane Rausch of the University of Massachusetts and Maurice Brungardt of Loyola University of New Orleans made invaluable suggestions in helping me ready the manuscript for publication.

A great many Colombians aided my research. Especially helpful were Alvaro Gómez Hurtado, Roberto Herrera Soto, Alberto Bermúdez, and staff of the Sala de Investigadores of the National Library in Bogotá.

Institutional support was provided by both the University of South Carolina and Coastal Carolina University, and by my previous employer, Grambling State University in Louisiana. The American Philosophical Society, the American Council of Learned Societies, the Council for International Exchange of Scholars, and the J. William Fulbright Foreign Scholarship Board provided generous assistance that allowed me to work a total of three years on this project in Colombia, between 1980 and 1993. I am deeply grateful to all these people and institutions.

Introduction

Colombia is a country best described in superlatives. Its mountains are South America's most verdant, its coffee the mildest, its red tape the most vexing, and its system of public transportation the world's cheapest and most accessible. Colombian history is the hemisphere's most confounding. And its transition to modernity has been the most abrupt. Over most of the present century its civil life has been the most consistently violent of any American republic. These things make Colombia an intriguing, compelling place, all the more so when one comes to know Colombians, their civility, their patience before adversity.

The extraordinary complexity of Colombia's recent past stands in sharp contrast to the unremarkable character of its nineteenth-century history. As elsewhere in Latin America, the country's social calm was regularly punctuated by civil wars in which members of the social and political elite led armies in contests whose goal was overthrow of the central government. During lapses between civil wars, Colombian society reverted to its sleepy premodern character. Campesino soldiers put aside their rifles and returned to the land. Like the rest of Latin America, Colombia was an intensely rural place whose people were locked in a seignorial system characterized by extreme social inequality, hierarchy, and networks of reciprocal interdependence. Kinship ties, and those of clientage, were the chief forces of cohesion in the premodern nation.

In the nineteenth century, before the rapid and violent social change that is the chief focus of this study, Colombia was more static than most other Latin American nations. Lacking lucrative exports—coffee not yet having loomed large in the national economy—foreigners and foreign capital kept their distance. Colombians traveled little, for there was little reason to do so. Not much money circulated, and there were few consumer goods to be had, even by those lucky enough to possess discretionary income. Inward looking and parochial, Colombians were shut away in a mountain fastness that separated them almost as effectively from one another as from the wider world.

The study that follows traces Colombia's transition from nineteenth-century social stasis, isolation, and poverty, to rapid integration into the global market economy during the first third of the twentieth century. Burgeoning coffee exports gave impetus to the physical development that national leaders had long sought. Thanks largely to coffee Colombia rapidly became a mobile and acquisitive society whose chief feature was an aggressive rural middle class.

Conservative Party politician Laureano Gómez stands at the center of the present work. Gómez's life spanned the era during which Colombian society became increasingly individualized and violent. Thoroughly schooled in his country's tradition of political polemic shaped intellectually by militant Spanish Jesuits, young Gómez was encouraged by his elders to become a crusader for religiously orthodox approaches to national affairs. First a newspaperman, then a politician, Laureano Gómez became his nation's greatest orator and parliamentarian at a moment when eloquence in representative bodies was prized above all else.

Laureano Gómez and his contemporaries, most notably Alfonso López Pumarejo (1886–1959) and Jorge Eliécer Gaitán (1898–1948), fought political battles during the 1930s and 1940s, while the masses looked on enthralled. The Conservative caudillo and his peers reveled in the politics of spectacle. Yet as men like Gómez dominated the public world, greater Colombia changed at an accelerating pace. Growing social pluralization coupled with an increasing spirit of individual self-interest were weakening popular loyalty to Colombia's traditional political elites. Laureano Gómez, leader of the Conservatives, along with his Liberal counterparts, wielded immense power and influence over a people rapidly outgrowing their quasi-democratic, oligarchic political system. Colombia's political elites, caught up in their bitter disputes, were on the way to becoming leaders with no followers. That dwindling of traditional loyalties became obvious during the eight years between 1949 and 1957, when greater society flourished in an ambience of political collapse and rural violence. That time of turmoil, the era of the Violencia, ultimately cost many thousand lives and destroyed the prestige of Colombia's traditional leadership class, especially that of Laureano Gómez, who was president during the most intense phase of the Violencia.

Colombia experienced an economic boom in the years after World War II. Scholars have termed that period the Golden Age of Colombian industry. They were also years when burgeoning coffee production coincided with historic high prices, which in turn expanded and strengthened the class of yeoman farmers who produced it. Social indicators changed in equally dramatic fashion over the period. Whereas 61 percent of all Colombians lived in the countryside in 1951, only a third of them did so a generation later. Levels of infant mortality and illiteracy declined rapidly, and average life expectancy increased. A growing proportion of Colombia's children enrolled in elementary school, their numbers doubling from 55 percent in 1950 to 80 percent in 1980.[1] Gross domestic product (GDP) increased an extraordinary 5.6 percent annually between 1946 and 1955, and at 5.15 percent annually during the quarter-century that followed.[2]

Great economic growth thus coincided with political collapse and rural violence. It was as if greater Colombia went about its business unconcerned that its once-revered public world was in ruin. The nation cheered when Laureano Gómez and his old Liberal foes reestablished amicable relations in 1957, and again when they launched the coalition National Front government a year later. But neither the Conservatives nor the Liberals recaptured their old constituencies, which together had once embraced the entire nation. By 1965, the time of Gómez's death, a politically alienated citizenry pursued its personal ends with indifference if not scorn for the nation's traditional institutions of governance. Gone was the old social tranquillity, gone was the once great public world. Colombian political arrangements no longer expressed the popular will. Over the remaining years of the century Colombian politicians struggled painfully toward creating a polity more responsive to the needs of their complex, pluralistic society, full of bellicose citizens.

The present volume surveys social, political, and economic change in Colombia from the latter nineteenth century through the first two-thirds of the twentieth century. The first chapter examines a nation isolated from the Western capitalist world, one whose people lived for the most part at subsistence level. Racked by constant civil war, the country of Laureano Gómez's extreme youth was a quaint and primitive place where the well-to-do traveled over malodorous city streets on horseback, in carriages, or in sedan chairs, and where the rest made their way on foot. Reaching the national capital from any point outside Colombia required energy, dedication, and resources that few foreigners were willing to expend. Colombia of the 1880s was physically much the same as it had been over the previous three centuries.

Turn-of-the-century elite culture and the process through which educated Colombians gained their political identities make up the bulk of chapter 2. Examined there are the high degree of cultural conformity within the elite, and the mechanism through which future political leaders—Laureano Gómez and Alfonso López among them—were politicized by men whose party allegiances had crystallized a half-century earlier. The implication of partisanship was strikingly revealed to schoolboys of the Generation of the Centenary during the War of the Thousand Days, a contest whose effects they witnessed in especially vivid ways. Chapter 2 also chronicles the process through which Colombia lost its province of Panama in 1903, and the impact of that loss on its citizenry.

Colombia's Republican era is the focus of chapter 3. Republicanism is defined here as a widely shared impulse among influential Colombians to work for national progress in a bipartisan fashion. Thus construed, national leaders from Rafael Reyes, whose term began in 1904, through Miguel Abadía Méndez, whose presidential term expired in 1930, can be seen as sharing a Republican mentality. Personal and ideological differences notwithstanding, presidents of the 1904–1930 period tried above all else to help Colombia achieve physical progress. Collateral goals were to dampen destructive political partisanship and to improve relations with the United States. Rafael Reyes and Carlos E. Restrepo were Conservatives who governed with significant Liberal support and collaboration. Marco Fidel Suárez, Pedro Nel Ospina, and Abadía Méndez, who held office between 1918 and 1930, looked to foreign nations, especially the United States, to provide the investment Colombia needed to lift it out of isolation and backwardness. Chapter 3 also explores the early political career of Conservative firebrand Laureano Gómez. An enemy of Republicanism, Gómez and his allies attacked Republican bipartisanship as a form of apostasy and tarred as antipatriotic and venal those national leaders who sought accommodation with the United States.

Chapter 4 examines the bourgeois cultural consensus prevailing in Colombia over the first quarter of the twentieth century. It finds great similarity between the attitudes of educated Colombians and attitudes of their counterparts in other parts of the Western world. The nation's leading thinkers were informed by deterministic social theory that had evolved from nineteenth-century positivism. They believed, consequently, that the social, ethnic, and sexual inequality present in Colombian society was the inevitable product of natural selection. Also figuring in chapter 4 is treatment of Colombia's incipient social modernization during the first quarter of the century. The chapter ends with discussion of the tempestuous early political career of Laureano Gómez. Between 1912 and 1916, Gómez combated what he saw as the pernicious National Conservatism of party leader Marco Fidel Suárez, eventually suffering a humiliating defeat at the hands of Suárez. Gómez persisted in his struggle against Suárez until 1921, when, aided by Liberal allies in Congress, he managed to drive his elderly adversary from the presidency.

The epochal arrival of money in Colombia is the subject of chapter 5, which begins with consideration of businessman President Pedro Nel Ospina's effort to place his nation on a sound fiscal footing. There follows discussion of the origins of Colombia's economic bonanza of the mid-1920s, and the uses to which it was put. Special attention is given to the impact of money on Colombia's social structure, as well as to the psychological changes wrought when formerly impoverished citizens achieved relative affluence. Laureano Gómez came to appreciate money and its power during the 1920s. Chapter 5 chronicles his role in the expenditure of Colombia's $25 million Panama indemnity, and it suggests the use to which he eventually put the inheritance his family received in 1925.

Chapter 6 examines both the immediate social consequences of Colombia's newfound wealth, and events surrounding Liberal victory in the presidential contest of 1930. Thoroughgoing economic change in Colombia intensified social inequalities that energized the nation's nascent labor movement. Hidebound Conservative regimes of the 1920s were threatened by organized labor, which they feared was suffused with a spirit of revolutionary socialism. Hence they discouraged labor organization and employed public force to break strikes, sometimes violently. The chapter concludes with discussion of Conservative loss of power in 1930, and the first two years of the Liberal Olaya Herrera presidency. It is shown that Olaya, who enjoyed Conservative support during the first half of his term, was successful in attenuating effects of the Great Depression in Colombia. At the same time neither he nor members of his Conservative coalition could contain political violence that attended the change of regime. In that sense the nation's political elites were as much victims of their highly politicized system as were humble Colombians, who suffered the violence of 1930–1932.

Chapter 7 treats political aspects of the 1930s, giving special attention to the Liberal Party reforms of that decade and to Conservative Party opposition to them. Chapter 8 takes up economic and social change during the 1930s and 1940s, and the passionate attack on Liberal Party rule led by Laureano Gómez.

Chapter 9 concerns the appearance of the Violencia, a breakdown of civil order heightened by the assassination of Liberal leader Jorge Eliécer Gaitán in April 1948. Chapter 10 takes up Colombian economic development and social change during the latter 1940s and 1950s. Politics during the 1950s is the subject of chapter 11. Chapter 12 deals with the National Front government and its operation during its first years. It also assesses national socioeconomic and cultural development between 1958 and 1965. The epilogue assesses the role of the Generation of the Centenary in Colombian history, and that of Laureano Gómez in particular.

I.

Toward Modernity,
1889–1932

I

Fin de Siècle Colombia

Colombia and the Wider World

Remarkable forces were afoot in the world as Laureano Gómez began his life in 1889. A historical process long under way in the West had raised Great Britain, Germany, France, and other nations of the European metropolis to the height of power and influence. Europeans had mastered all other peoples through conquest, colonization, and commerce. Now, at century's end, they dazzled the rest with wondrous inventions. Physicians announced cures for diseases that had ever afflicted humankind. Steam and internal combustion engines revolutionized transportation, and inventors were soon to successfully test the airplane. Telephones and undersea telegraph cables had been in operation for several decades, and in France the Curies were involved in their study of radioactivity. Abroad, Europeans were extending their civilization, by force where necessary, into Asia and Africa. They happily bore the "white man's burden" in the service of their respective fatherlands. This was the European Age, the Europe that held the world of young Laureano Gómez in its thrall.

If northern Europe stood atop the Western cultural and economic system in those years, Colombia languished near the bottom. As a former dependency of Spain, Catholic Europe's leader in combating the Protestant heresy in the sixteenth century and Enlightenment rationalism in the seventeenth and eighteenth, Colombia[1] had been intentionally isolated from the forces setting northern Europe on the path toward world domination. Colombians did not challenge the social, ideological, or economic structures implanted throughout Spanish America at the moment of discovery. Conformity and control were watchwords through the centuries that witnessed dramatic change in those parts of Europe that would lead the world into the modern industrial age.

Colombia's disadvantageous place in the Eurocentric world of the late nineteenth century is nowhere more clearly revealed than in the area of economic development. Looking eastward toward Africa and westward toward the Pacific, Colombia and the rest of Latin America were isolated and distant from major commercial centers. Even before the precious metals once important to Europe's expansion were exhausted, Latin America played a minor role in

CARIBBEAN SEA

PANAMA

VENEZUELA

Atrato River

Western Cordillera

Cauca River

Central Cordillera

Magdalena River

Eastern Cordillera

PACIFIC
OCEAN

Meta River

Eastern Llanos

Vichada River

Sumapaz

Guaviare River

Apaporis River

Amazon Watershed

ECUADOR

Caquetá River

BRAZIL

Putumayo River

PERU

AMAZON RIVER

1. Physical map of Colombia.

2. Political map of Colombia.

world commerce. Its share of global trade averaged but 11 percent throughout the eighteenth century, and declined sharply thereafter. No significant regional export appeared in the nineteenth century, with the result that by the 1880s the region's share in world trade was a paltry 5 percent of the global total, less than half that of Germany alone.[2] And this decline occurred over 100 years, during which global trade increased fiftyfold.[3]

Colombia was perhaps Latin America's least-favored large state during the century of explosive growth in world trade. Save for its tobacco, which enjoyed some success in international markets in the nineteenth century, the nation possessed little of interest to the metropolis. And owing to its broken terrain, poor roads, and stormy political climate, it was virtually inaccessible to foreign capital. Colombians would eventually seize on coffee as their lucrative export, but coffee would not dominate Colombia's economy until the twentieth century.

Educated Colombians complained about a national commercial "paralysis" that condemned citizens living in even the most favored parts of the country to a primitive existence entirely unbefitting the age in which they lived. As one writer put it, his fellow citizens were sunk in "an inertia and depressing status quo," dwelling in "sad and indolent thatched-roofed hamlets as in colonial times."[4]

People of the Andean nation had as much trouble internalizing the liberal ethos then dominant in the West as they did finding their place in the world economic system. Shortly before Laureano was born, Colombia settled into a spell of conservative rule destined to last for nearly half a century, ending only in 1930. Political liberalism, in control from 1853 and vigorous during the 1860s and '70s, lost its drive and confidence in the 1880s, defeated not so much because of the inferiority of their program as by the nation's inability to implement it. Colombia simply lacked the economic infrastructure to integrate itself into the world market or a social structure that could adapt to liberalism's egalitarian premises. Small gains made during the Liberal ascendance were wiped out by incessant civil wars. Such was hardly the case in Europe, where liberalism had long since triumphed. In Great Britain, Sweden, Norway, Germany—and even in eastern European countries such as Serbia—liberal parties and liberal constitutions were the norm. Church was being separated from state, and the status quo was successfully challenged in countless other ways.

As Colombians were signaling their inability to effect the program of nineteenth-century liberalism, whether economic, political, or social, Europeans were moving beyond liberalism. Socialist ideas were gaining currency among an urban proletariat that long had viewed the prevailing philosophy as a smoke screen masking their exploitation by the moneyed classes. Bismarck had become so concerned over the militancy of German workers that he attempted to outlaw socialism in 1876. Social democratic parties were founded in both Sweden and Great Britain in the year of Laureano Gómez's birth, and in the latter nation organized labor paralyzed industry in the great London dock strike of 1889. That same year the Second International was founded in Paris, and much farther eastward there were antimetropolitan rumblings of a related but distinct kind. East Indians were in open revolt against the Dutch, Indians met in their first National Congress, and Chinese revolutionary Sun Yat-sen laid the groundwork for his uprising against avaricious foreigners. In all these ways peoples of Europe and elsewhere heralded the great issues of the coming century.

In Colombia there were few portents of the coming era. There were no factories, no labor unions, no socialist parties, no urbanization. Colombia in the late 1880s was a place far from the modern world, sunk in a solitude that had lasted not one but four hundred years. Ambitious men were frustrated by that state of affairs, though there was little they could do about it. One such man was the father of Laureano Gómez. José Gómez, a tradesman of modest means, lived in Ocaña, in the department of Santander, lying not far from the Río Magdalena.

Ocaña to Bogotá

Ocaña was a provincial town on the road linking Cartagena with Caracas to the west, and with the mountainous interior of the country to the south. By the mid-nineteenth century Ocaña had lost the importance it had enjoyed in earlier times. More direct routes to Venezuela were opened, and steamboats made travel to Bogotá via the Río Magdalena infinitely preferable to the overland journey. As Ocaña drifted into the backwater of national history, ambitious residents like the merchant jeweler José Laureano Gómez grew restless and irritable.

It didn't take much to make José Gómez angry. People around Ocaña had learned to tell when the businessman was in one of his foul moods and did their best to avoid him on such days, sometimes crossing the street to do so. Family members knew even before he reached home when José Gómez's day had not gone well. Upon arriving home the irascible Ocañero was in the habit of announcing his presence by hurling his hat into the front patio ahead of him and stalking off to his private quarters. His wife, Dolores Castro, described as an intelligent and prudent woman, spared no effort in placating him. Knowing that her husband liked his eggs boiled to a certain firmness, for example, she went so far as to purchase hens whose eggs she thought would lend themselves to proper preparation.[5]

Conservative by family tradition, José Gómez shared the belief of economic liberals that Colombia, and his quiet hometown of Ocaña, should be much more prosperous than they were in 1888. In fact his bad temper may have been as much a function of Colombia's economic stagnation, incessant civil wars, and intractability before the forces of change, as of personal idiosyncrasy.

José Gómez's father was also an impatient man, and something of a visionary as well. Once he constructed a flying machine modeled on da Vinci's famous design. He built it of wood and cloth and had two slaves carry it to a nearby mountain where he attempted a spectacularly unsuccessful takeoff. Unfortunately the fabric used to cover the wings proved too heavy for the task at hand. As with so much in the Colombia of those times, vision and enthusiasm weren't sufficient to overcome errors of technique and lack of appropriate technology. It was a point hardly lost on the grandfather of Laureano Gómez as he limped home assisted by servants who were doubtless both chagrined and amused by their master's folly.

By mid-1888, Ocaña had become burdensome to José Laureano Gómez. His business, built around the sale of gold and silver filigree that he had fabricated in the river town of Mompós, was in decline. And there was nothing suggesting that Ocaña would ever regain its old prosperity. His family was growing too. The news that his wife was pregnant with their third child set the jeweler wondering whether he shouldn't reestablish his business elsewhere, perhaps in Bogotá, where he had commercial ties. His plan to leave crystallized on a day when Ocañeros were busy celebrating a fiesta whose high point was a parade of garish papier-mâché figures called *gigantes y cabezudos* (giants and big-heads). The figures were usually made in the likenesses of celebrated national and local figures, but local wits also liked to include caricatures of the town's more notable characters as well. Thus only one person was surprised to see included among the big-heads Ocaña's irascible jeweler, its painted green eyes bloodshot and bulging, the citizen wearing it ranting and cavorting in an altogether amusing manner. There is no record of José Gómez's reaction at the moment of self-recognition. But ever afterward family members relished recounting the story of his return home. His hat arrived first with unprecedented velocity. Summoning his wife and servants, his face flushed and his pale eyes bulging, he announced in stentorian tones, "We're moving to Bogotá. This town has become unbearable!"

Traveling as he was, with considerable luggage, his wife, children, and family retainers, José Gómez chose the more economical land route to Bogotá. It was a journey not to be taken lightly, for it extended 600 kilometers along trails winding ever higher into the eastern cordillera of the Colombian Andes. One could never be certain that accommodations were available at villages along the way, or even that accidents en route wouldn't force travelers to camp under the stars or in a freezing downpour. Landslides were an ever present danger, and when rivers and streams were swollen the traveler simply waited until they could be forded. Everyone rode armed because there was also the possibility of being waylaid along some lonely stretch of trail. Such were the realities of cross-country travel in late-nineteenth-century Colombia.

The party that departed Ocaña in mid-1888 first moved eastward across the piedmont of the cordillera over countless ridges and valleys. At one point the trail wound through a desolate 100-kilometer stretch, rising to an altitude of more than 2,500 meters. Then it descended until reaching the town of Cúcuta, not far from the Venezuelan border. From Cúcuta, capital of Santander del Norte, the road turned southward toward the town of Pamplona, two days' ride away.

Pamplona marked the beginning of the most arduous part of the trip. From there the road to Bogotá branched, with a longer though slightly easier route taking travelers westward through Bucaramanga, Socorro, and Barbosa. The more direct road ran due south over the Páramo de Almorzadero, down through arid canyons of the Río Chicamocha, and then up again into the highlands of Boyacá. Both roads finally converged in the city of Tunja, former center of Chibcha Indian culture. José Gómez chose the more difficult, more direct route.

Departing Pamplona, itself lying at an elevation of 2,300 meters, the travelers spent the first day climbing toward the *páramo*, a treeless plain swept by icy winds and rain, frequently obscured by blowing fog and mist. The Páramo de Almorzadero was part of the Sierra Nevada del Cocuy, which lay along its eastern edge. For two days they braved unending cold before finally descending into Málaga, a pleasant town in the valley of the Río Servitá. After resting in Málaga they set out for Sogamoso, five days' hard ride up the canyon of the Río Chicamocha, always skirting the massif of El Cocuy. It was on that leg of the trip that the party noticed riders following them at some distance. Fearing the worst, they left the trail and took refuge in a cave they found high on the valley wall, where they hid until the potential danger passed. The vignette was a favorite of Laureano Gómez, who liked to recall that there in the cave his father had discovered a rich vein of emerald-bearing rock. Carefully recording the cave's location by sighting the 5,000-meter snowcapped mountain El Cocuy to the northeast, he vowed someday to return and claim the treasure.

At length the party left their cave and the canyon, and emerged in the cool highlands of Boyacá. They had reached the Colombian heartland. In relatively quick succession they passed through the mountain towns of Paz del Río, Sogamoso, Duitama, and Paipa, at last entering Tunja, the capital of Boyacá, then populated by some 5,300 souls. The end of the journey was in sight. More than three weeks had passed, sixteen days of which had been spent on muleback. But still one more ordeal lay ahead. Two days' travel south of Tunja, over the battlefield where Bolívar insured Colombia's independence sixty-nine years earlier, past the market town of Ventaquemada, lay another páramo, that of Chocontá.

A French traveler of the same epoch recorded his impressions of that particular part of the route followed by José Gómez and his party in 1888. Explorer Gaspard Mollien was at once appalled by the roads of Boyacá and filled with admiration for the Colombians who braved them. He was particularly awed by the valor of several women in his party who carried small children in their arms. "In spite of the constant danger," he wrote, "they laughed and sang with the same joy as if they rode in the best carriages and on the best highways of France." Of the landscape itself he wrote: "It is cold on the páramo of Chocontá, and the wind blows with as much force as on the seashore. A fine, cold rain froze on our faces and hands. The soil is black, the land rolling, like dunes. The grass is so fine that footprints of travelers disappear as rapidly as in the sands of African deserts."[6]

The European marveled both at the "frightening cold" of highland Colombia, and at the hardiness of native populations who withstood it, all the while lightly dressed and scorning fires as detrimental to their health. In a vignette that might well have been told by José Gómez, Mollien described the happy ending of a páramo night that did not begin at all well. Although he was fully dressed, wrapped in several wool blankets, and occupying the most sheltered spot in the hut, he was "numb with cold," miserable, and unable to sleep. Fortunately, as he recalled it, "our host had the singular idea of raising a large number of cats and training them to sleep on the feet of travelers. Thus two of them climbed up on me and thanks to the heat from those small animals I was finally able to warm up."[7]

A month had passed since the Gómez family had set out from Ocaña, but at last Bogotá was close at hand. Descending from the páramo down through the village of Sesquilé, they entered the broad, fertile highland plain known as the Sabana de Bogotá. Some eighty kilometers from north to south and fifty from east to west, it was the first flat land they had seen since leaving Cúcuta. Slowly they rode among fields of corn, sesame, wheat, and barley, eventually reaching the village of Usaquén, fifteen kilometers from the capital. Another ten kilometers took them to a cluster of houses at the outskirts of the city, a place named Chapinero for the club-footed blacksmith whose shop once stood there. From there the steeple of Bogotá's cathedral was visible, and soon the red tile roofs of the city could be seen in the distance. In less than an hour their mules were clattering over the rude bridge spanning San Diego Creek (Quebrada de San Diego), near the church after which both bridge and stream were named. The mountains were close now, the city nestled against a range of 1,000-meter peaks rising just to the east. The San Diego, and its larger sister streams, the

San Francisco and San Agustín, a few blocks further south, flowed down from those mountains and through the city, joining the meandering Río Bogotá out on the Sabana.

The noise, congestion, and squalor greeting José Gómez's companions upon entering Colombia's capital that afternoon was probably shocking to them, following so closely their weeks of sylvan travel. Though it contained barely 100,000 residents, Bogotá consisted of a congested 193 blocks, arranged in a rough rectangle along the mountains. The city's population density, at more than 400 inhabitants per hectare, would never be greater than it was in Bogotá in the late nineteenth century.[8]

Traffic was by tradition heaviest in the city's major artery, the Calle Real, which ran north and south through Bogotá, and down which José Gómez and his party picked their way. Crowds of Bogotanos jostled for precedence in the dusty, ill-paved thoroughfare. Most of the pedestrians were short and somber, and both men and women bent under some burden. Their swarthy features bespoke Indian ancestry. Along the sidewalks street vendors hawked their wares, and beggars, some seated, some ambulatory, exhibited festering sores, or hands and feet ravaged by leprosy. Here and there drunks slept off effects of the popular indigenous brew called *chicha*.

Several plazas opened on the Calle Real. Those too teemed with humanity, for they were places where country people sold foodstuffs to the urban dwellers. Only recently had the practice of using the principal plazas as markets been banned as unhygienic and anti-aesthetic. Tiring of the garbage piled in the Parque Santander, near the center of town, some Bogotano adorned the statue of the revered Santander with a straw hat and ruana, and hung a sign around its neck reading, "If you don't clean this place up, I'm leaving."[9] City fathers responded to the threat, and when José and Dolores Gómez passed the park that afternoon in 1888, it was relatively clean and uncongested.

Adding to the difficulty of traveling the length of Bogotá's main street, filled as it was with human and animal traffic, was the fact that it was being excavated all along its length. The first of the iron tubes destined to bring drinking water to the center of the city were being laid, and clouds of dirt and dust hung in the air, unpleasant byproducts of urban development. Over the coming year nearly a third of the city would be served by underground water pipes, laid by the newly incorporated Compañía de Acueducto de Bogotá.[10]

Colombia's capital was, in short, everything that Ocaña was not. Its bustle suggested that it was the sort of place where an enterprising small-town businessman like José Gómez could make good. Musing on all this the father of Laureano Gómez led his group down the Calle Real, past the Plaza de Bolívar, past the presidential residence, and across the malodorous Río San Agustín. Ultimately they reached barrio Santa Bárbara, where a rented house awaited them. Dusk was falling. The city's street lights were just being lighted as the party from Ocaña reached its destination.

The Highways of Colombia

The trip from Ocaña to Bogotá had taken José Gómez and his family through the easternmost of three Andean ranges spreading through the country along north-south axes. Had they continued beyond Bogotá, they would have descended the eastern cordillera to the Río Magdalena valley, Colombia's river link with the outside world. Scattered along the upper reaches of the valley were Neiva, Ibagué, Girardot, and Honda, the latter town being the head of navigation for traffic moving upriver from the port of Barranquilla. Two other important population centers, Popayán and Cali, lay hard days' travel across the Central Cordillera in the upper Río Cauca valley. Medellín, Colombia's second city and center of rapidly spreading coffee cultivation, lay 460 kilometers north of Cali. A popular route to the capital of Antioquia was that up from Puerto Berrío, on the Magdalena. With the exception of towns on the Magdalena below Honda, virtually all inland population centers were reached only by horse- or muleback, or on foot. While Colombia did have a few scattered railroads in 1889, they were short lines, used chiefly to move freight to Río Magdalena ports.[11]

Colombia's broken terrain and constant civil wars had frustrated national economic development throughout the nineteenth century. That stagnation was evidenced not only in the relative absence of rail lines, but in the generally atrocious state of all the nation's roads. The lack of transportation links was a fact of life in Colombia that became increasingly galling as railroads revolutionized travel in other American republics. At the end of the century the United States had a staggering 300,000 kilometers of track, while Argentina had 20,000. Meanwhile, Colombia had a risible 565 kilometers. But Colombia's failure to build railroads wasn't for want of effort. In 1884 a major attempt was made to link Girardot with Bogotá. The Baldwin Locomotive Works in the United States was contracted to supply the rail and equipment, and Colombians prepared the roadbeds, cut crossties, and built station houses. All was in readiness, even down to the detail of tickets and ticket punches on counters in the stations, when word arrived that the rails arriving in Girardot were too heavy to transport by muleback. The decision was made to have smaller rails manufactured at the newly opened Subachoque ironworks. But civil war began early in 1885, causing what would lengthen to a twenty-four-year suspension of the project.[12]

Well into the nineteenth century Colombia's most important land route, that lying between the capital and Honda, had sections in such disrepair that human porters bore travelers over parts that were unsafe even on muleback. A North American engineer traveling what he referred to as the "so-called road from the capital to Honda" in the 1860s found that goods imported from the United States were frequently cheaper in Honda than were comparable items brought down from the Sabana de Bogotá.[13] Twenty years later a trade commissioner named William Elroy Curtis, sent south by U.S. President Chester A. Arthur "to bring our Spanish-American neighbors into closer commercial and political relations with us," described the way agricultural implements, carriages and other passenger vehicles, "all [having] been imported from the United States or England," were transported to Bogotá: "They [are] brought to Honda by the river steamers, packed in small sections, and thence lugged over the mountains piece by piece. One peon will carry a wheel, another an axle, a third a coupling-pole or single-tree, and the screws and bolts are packed in small boxes on cargo mules. The upper part or body of the vehicle is likewise taken to pieces and packed in sections. One man will sometimes be a month in carrying a wagon-wheel from Honda to the plain. His method is to carry it some 50 or 100 paces and then rest, making sometimes less than two miles a day."[14]

Yet another visitor, writing in the year of Laureano Gómez's birth, described the dire economic consequences of the nation's primitive transportation network: "Perhaps the chief impediment to the extension of trade in Colombia during the past year has been the terrible condition of the chief roads of the country. The road between Honda and Bogotá, certainly the most important in Colombia, has been allowed, through neglect, to fall into such a condition as to be almost impassable. . . . The time occupied in transporting goods over that short distance has been greater than that taken from Europe to Honda."[15]

The road itself was described by Curtis as "alternating between deep valleys and dizzying mountain peaks." There were places, he wrote, where it was "little else than a trail, not wide enough in many places for two mules to walk abreast, and so tortuous and precipitous as to be impassable except on the backs of animals trained to the road."[16] Curtis did admit that the inconveniences and hardships of the journey were compensated by the captivating scenery along the way. However, that was faint praise indeed, especially when it rang in the ears of men like José Laureano Gómez, and all the others impatient to see Colombia join the modern age.

Colombia in Regeneration

As the decade of Laureano Gómez's birth dawned, Colombian leaders despaired over their inability to achieve either order or progress. From the time the Liberal Party gained power in 1860, subsequently imposing on the nation a constitution notable for its extreme federalism and weak central government, the Rionegro Constitution of 1863, Colombia had drifted in a lethargy punctuated only by sporadic partisan clashes, one of which grew into a full-scale revolution. In the unsuccessful Conservative revolution of 1876, rebel soldiers marched with pictures of Jesus and Pope Pius IX, and banners proclaiming that they fought in the name of God. Members of the ecclesiastical community openly supported the uprising, which had as one of its causes Liberal legislation promoting secular education.[17]

Members of the Colombian elite were sincere in their political beliefs, Liberals stressing decentralization of state power, economic and personal liberty, and Conservatives defending prerogatives of the Church and opposing social secularization and weakening of social hierarchies. Still the Liberal-Conservative debate in Colombia had a certain artificiality about it. As members of the opposing bands fought for control of the state, shedding blood and expending scarce resources, they did so in a social setting virtually unchanged from colonial times. There was no emergent middle class in Colombia as there was in Europe, where triumphant bourgeois revolutionaries forced anciens régimes to free them from feudal restraints and to allow them a voice in government. The process of social diversification, born of the commercial revolution to which Europe owed its global dominance, had not yet taken place in Colombia. Political debate there was a "conversation among gentlemen," as one writer phrased it.[18] The debate over liberal and conservative principles was an intra-elite affair in which traditional leaders of society fought to impose their ideals as they marched at the head of peasant armies whose cadres were clients first and co-ideologists second.

Under such circumstances it is hardly surprising that by the 1880s, Colombian Liberals had not achieved the successes of their European counterparts. Not only was their movement severely weakened by the absence of a self-sufficient middle class, but their programs were constantly stymied by an articulate and aggressive Conservative Party that enjoyed considerable support among the peasantry. The Conservatives had been astute in turning the Liberals' vaunted federalism against them. As soon as the Constitution of 1863 was implemented, they wrested control of several important states away from the ruling party.

Especially galling to Liberals was their failure in the area of economics. For at least a hundred years it had been an article of faith among liberals everywhere in the Western world that the freeing of trade through the lowering of tariffs and other such artificial restraints would invigorate commerce. A nation like Colombia would act on its natural advantage in supplying products such as tobacco, quinine, and coffee to the world market, thus fixing itself securely in the Western commercial network. The theory was sound in the sense that raw materials enjoyed a comparative price advantage over manufactured goods throughout the late nineteenth century. Suggestive of that fact were the booms in Argentine beef, Canadian wheat, and Peruvian fertilizers that drew large quantities of foreign capital into those countries during the 1880s. Yet Colombia had been unable to profit from those favorable conditions. Tobacco and quinine prices were in decline by 1880, coffee exports had increased but slowly throughout the 1870s, and there was a severe scarcity of investment capital owing to laws permitting the export of bullion, adherence to a gold standard, and absence of a national banking system.

Confronted by the failure of Liberal political, economic, and social programs, influential members of the Colombian elite prepared to undertake a drastic restructuring of the state. That task, which came to be known as the Regeneration, fell to Liberal politician Rafael Núñez, who was elected president in 1880. Núñez had been active in politics for nearly thirty years, first serving in Conservative cabinets during the 1850s. Shortly after the Liberals seized power following the civil war of 1860, Núñez left Colombia to serve as commercial representative in the United States, and later in Le Havre and Liverpool. During his eleven years abroad he meditated on national politics while maintaining political visibility through essays published in Colombian newspapers. When he returned home in 1874, as civil war again approached, Núñez intensified his criticism of the political turmoil plaguing Colombia. The thrust of his writings was that economic progress and greater state control were inextricably linked. By 1878, Núñez led a reformist Liberal faction known as the Independents. In that year he delivered a speech in which he warned, "we have reached a point at which we are confronted by this specific dilemma: [either we achieve] fundamental administrative regeneration, or [we suffer] catastrophe."[19] In Núñez's view, actual dissolution of Colombia was a distinct possibility. "Rather than a great national boundary we have many local boundaries," he wrote. "Instead of an army, we have nine. And every two years at election time we hear talk of one state preparing military campaigns against another, or against the central government."[20]

When he won his first two-year term as president in 1880, Núñez undertook a program that within eight years would strengthen the central government at the expense of the states, renew and invigorate church-state links, and abandon extreme laissez-faire policies. Núñez's Liberal Independents were joined by moderate Conservatives, and the two factions would declare themselves the Nationalist Party in 1888.

Rafael Núñez's movement to the right reflected both his personal metamorphosis and the conservatizing of liberalism going on everywhere in the West during the latter nineteenth century. Among the forces accounting for this shift was the fear among elites that unless checked democracy would lead to mob rule. No less a personage than John Stuart Mill had become convinced by the 1870s that the masses must be reined in through such devices as granting a weighted vote to the moneyed classes. Colombia of course had no aggressive proletariat at the time Mill called for limits on British democracy. But the newfound conservatism of Mill and many other European liberals did make it easier for men like Núñez to find common ground with Conservatives, who had always mistrusted democracy.

Western liberals drew motive force for their rightward movement in the ideological complex known as positivism. Historian Charles Hale has explained that Latin American liberals found comfort in Auguste Comte's teaching that mankind was moving inexorably toward an era of generalized well-being characterized by rational, "scientific" management of politics and society.[21] Whether through institutional arrangements or imposition of a benevolent dictatorship, progressive-minded leaders were certain that they could force their nations into the modern age. In Mexico, Porfirio Díaz and his coterie of technocrats, the *científicos* (scientists), oversaw industrialization of the country. Brazil's development was directed by a military elite that went so far as to emblazon the Comtean slogan "order and progress" on their national banner. In Colombia it was the "Regenerator," Rafael Núñez, who laid the groundwork for progress in a new national constitution drawn up in 1886.

The Constitution of 1886 became a reality during Núñez's second term as president. Members of his party's left, or Radical wing, rose in rebellion against the government early in 1885, just six months after he had assumed office. They were angered at Núñez's betrayal of their cause, especially as manifested in his appointment of Conservatives to high office. The Radicals did themselves no favor, for in turning on their moderate copartisan they forced him into even greater reliance on the Conservatives. The uprising was crushed rather easily, and by September of that year Núñez could announce that the Liberal Rionegro Constitution had "ceased to exist." "Soon the people will give themselves a new one," he added, "one which will satisfy their true needs and will reflect the inclinations of the great majority of the Colombian people."[22]

The constitution drawn up by Núñez's constituent assembly and presented to the nation in mid-1886 reflected the statist, conservative shift in late-nineteenth-century Latin American political thought. It strengthened the central government, especially the office of the president. Many offices that had previously been elective became appointive. New restrictions were placed on the franchise, as well as on freedom of speech. Especially significant was the renewed emphasis given the Church as a leading institution of government. Himself a skeptic, Núñez took a functional view of religion, seeing it as an instrument for harmonizing class interests—the "knife fight between the masses and the socioeconomic elite" that he had observed during his years in Europe.[23] He advocated a practical Christianity that would fill the "moral vacuum" he perceived in modern society. It was in that spirit that he favored constitutional provisions making Roman Catholicism the state religion, and requiring that all public education in Colombia conform to Church doctrine. Within a year of the constitution's ratification, Colombia had signed a concordat with the Vatican giving the Church considerable freedom from state control, remitting national moneys to it for the support of its works, and returning to it property confiscated during the era of Liberal rule.

Núñez perceived himself as the man Colombia needed to reconcile and harmonize national institutions. By bringing together church and state and the two parties he saw himself playing a necessary role in smoothing the way for his country's evolution toward the stage of development already reached by nations like England and the United States. His was a Spencerian view that individuals were organic parts of greater society. Their personal advancement, and that of society at large, were necessarily achieved harmoniously rather than through struggle. Prudence, restraint, and morality were qualities that Núñez sought to make part of Colombian institutions. For philosophers, he wrote, "the six words justice, security, order, stability, liberty, and progress have a single and identical meaning."[24]

Three years before he was able to carry out his reform, Núñez wrote an essay in which he gave an economic justification for reform. Titled "Let Us Work Together," the piece began with a gloomy assessment of Colombia's economic backwardness: "We lack industry because we have neither machinery, nor technological skill, nor personal security, nor other indispensable things. We annually import goods valued at twelve million pesos, for which we cannot pay because costly and slow means of transportation place our export goods at a disadvantage with respect to similar goods from other countries." He pointed out that Mexico, Argentina, and Chile had entered a new era thanks chiefly to railroads that had helped bring both prosperity and peace. "For Colombia," he concluded, "the moment has come to enter the mainstream unless we want to find ourselves left behind, immobilized like stakes driven into the shore." Continuing the metaphor, he likened Colombia to "a ship tossed by a dangerous storm: Either we weather it or we go to the bottom."[25]

Economic reform figured prominently in the Regeneration. Among Núñez's first actions to stimulate the economy was the establishment of a national bank in 1881. At about the same time, he took Colombia off the gold standard and soon introduced the use of paper currency. He imposed tariffs to encourage infant industry, and imposed internal taxes that increased national revenues, although not enough to offset deficits. Núñez also did his best to promote railroad construction, though his early attempts were frustrated by the Liberal uprising of 1885. He continued his efforts, however, and by the end of the 1890s, there were some 650 kilometers of track in Colombia, more than double the amount laid in 1885.[26]

Modernizing Elites

The Regeneration was a series of measures through which modernizing elites rationalized the state to the end of achieving the progress they saw as desirable, necessary, and inevitable. It was part of a process of state making that continues today, though in an atmosphere less heady than that of the Eurocentric world of Núñez's day. Modern scholars point out that Núñez and his immediate successors failed to achieve a great deal through their reforms. Núñez was unable to raise much money with his protective tariff, his national bank seemed to cause nothing but inflation, and industrialization was thwarted because there was no infrastructure to support it. And before the Regenerator was ten years in his grave, a new series of disasters would befall the nation. Yet Colombians had no way of knowing that in the early 1890s. To them the future didn't appear so gloomy. In fact many of them were encouraged and pleased by the changes they saw taking place around them.

Typical of the optimistic Regeneration-era Colombian was eighteen-year-old Julio Palacio, who bragged of his "record-breaking" four-day trip from Bogotá to Barranquilla on the Caribbean coast in 1890. A ninety-kilometer leg of his journey, from Facatativá, on the Sabana, down to Honda, was made in an astonishing fourteen hours. That could only have been done on a trail markedly improved over the one existing there a decade earlier. In Honda, Palacio noted the "intense, almost feverish commercial activity" of the river port, an early consequence of the boom in coffee export that would revolutionize national finances in coming decades.[27] Coffee exports tripled over the eight years between 1887 and 1894, swelling from 111,000 to 338,000 sacks. By 1898 the total rose to more than half a million sacks.[28] In the opinion of Antonio Roldán, a prominent Nationalist politician of the day, it was Núñez's paper money regime that fueled the expansion of coffee cultivation. His only complaint was of the scarcity of labor caused by peasants who, encouraged by homestead laws passed in the 1870s and 1880s, poured into the cool coffee-producing highlands.[29]

There were other signs of the industrial progress that Colombian leaders yearned for. Both the National School of Mines and the Colombian Society of Engineers were founded in 1887. Two years later the United Fruit Company incorporated in Colombia, and in the same year a plant producing sulfuric acid was in production in Bogotá. In 1891 the Kopp Bavaria opened in the outskirts of Bogotá. The new brewery represented progress of a tangible and especially welcome sort. For the first time Colombians could drink a hygienically prepared beverage far safer than the fermented indigenous drink chicha, which was prepared under unsanitary conditions. The nation was, in short, slowly and painfully taking on the accouterments of modern life.

A clear indication that times were changing appeared in the form of newspaper advertisements touting new products of modern technology. Aware even in the 1890s that the endorsement of local celebrities would enhance sales, the marketers of new products prevailed upon well-known local figures to endorse their wares. Kopp Bavaria secured the support of Minister of Foreign Relations Marco Fidel Suárez. In Suárez they had one of the bright lights of Regeneration-era politics, a protégé of acting president Miguel Antonio Caro. Suárez obligingly supplied Kopp executives the following endorsement: "I certify that thanks to the use of Bavaria beer, there has been a marked improvement in the dyspepsia from which I've long suffered. Foreign beers do not help, and instead aggravate my condition."[30]

Suárez's endorsement prompted another literate Bogotano to respond in print chiding the minister for inelegance, even poor taste in writing "I suffer from dyspepsia," and warning Suárez that he jeopardized his well-earned reputation as a grammarian and literary stylist. The following day Suárez replied in a lengthy article replete with references to the classics, in which he amply demonstrated that it was perfectly appropriate to write "I suffer from dyspepsia."[31]

Such was the small-town atmosphere of Colombia's capital when Laureano Gómez was born there near the end of the century. At the time of the lively and literate exchange there were but 85,000 people living in Bogotá proper, and another 50,000 in the immediate environs.[32] And that population remained remarkably undifferentiated, as evidenced by several aspects of the Kopp advertising campaign. Most residents, some 80 percent of them, could not read Marco Fidel Suárez's praise of Bavaria beer. But that did not matter, as a majority of Colombia's lower class could afford neither newspapers nor expensive bottled beer. The size of the upper stratum of Colombian society is suggested by the fact that during the 1890s the average newspaper press run was just 1,000 copies. In a national capital whose literate population did not exceed 3,000, and whose intellectual elite numbered a few hundred high-ranking government officials well and properly cited the classics in defending their literary style. That was the sort of thing that led Bogotanos to call their city the Athens of South America.

Given the intimate character of the nineteenth-century Colombian elite it's not surprising that the celebrated Marco Fidel Suárez should be a friend of José Laureano Gómez, the irascible merchant jeweler recently arrived from Santander. Nor is it surprising that Suárez occasionally paid social visits to the first Gómez residence on Carrera 6 (Sixth Avenue), just a few blocks from the presidential residence and government ministries. Suárez was a bachelor, after all, only a few years removed from the provinces himself. And Suárez's office at the Foreign Ministry was just two blocks up the street and around the corner from the Gómez residence. Thus it was that future Colombian president Suárez came to meet future president Laureano Gómez when the latter was but two years old. As the years passed, and as Suárez became more important in Colombian politics, the two would see each other frequently. Indeed they would see each other too frequently for Suárez's liking.

The Birthplace of Laureano Gómez

Laureano Gómez was the third of six children born to José and Dolores Gómez.[33] When he was not yet a month old his parents took him to the church of barrio Santa Barbara, three blocks down Carrera 6, where he was baptized Laureano Eleuterio Gómez Castro. The young priest Carlos Cortés Lee conducted the ceremony. José Gómez did well in his business and soon was able to move his growing family from their modest one-story house on Carrera 6, to an imposing two-story structure on Carrera 7 (Seventh Avenue). The location of the new house was especially felicitous. Immediately behind their original residence, and accessible through a gate in a common rear wall, family possessions needed be moved but a few meters to their new resting places. Large and built in the colonial style, it stood on the city's principal avenue, known variously to Bogotanos as Calle Real, Calle de la Carrera, or simply as Séptima. Because it faced the plaza of historic San Agustín Church, their block was sometimes referred to by its colonial name, the Camellón de San Agustín. Half a block up the street stood the bridge spanning the Río San Agustín. In the next block on the left stood the Palacio de la Carrera, home of Colombia's president. Three blocks farther up Séptima was the city's epicenter, the Plaza de Bolívar. Facing the plaza on the south was the Colombian capitol, the Capitolio, and on its east side stood the cathedral. Next door to the cathedral, across Séptima from the Capitol, was Jesuit-run Colegio San Bartolomé, where Laureano Gómez would later attend school.[34]

Casa San Agustín was Laureano Gómez's home until he left it to begin his own family more than twenty years later. Like most other such houses in downtown Bogotá, it had high wooden doors, shuttered windows, and a balcony affording a view of the city and its outskirts, and of mountains rimming the highland plain some thirty kilometers to the west. The front doors opened to a *zaguán,* or short corridor, leading to the spacious central courtyard. Behind that, through another passageway, was a smaller patio where cooking and laundry were done, and that gave access to the servant quarters. An un-paved open area, the *solar,* lay to the rear of the house. It was filled with chicken coops, clotheslines, a small herb garden, and the miscellany necessary to home maintenance. A parlor, the dining room, José Gómez's home office, and several other rooms opened off the principal courtyard. The family's bed-rooms were on the second floor. All along its left side ran a balcony overlook-ing the courtyard and receiving the afternoon sunshine on those occasional days when skies were clear. That was Dolores de Gómez's favorite spot. She frequently sat on the balcony, occupied with her sewing and chatting with ladies of Bogotá's Ocaña community, who joined her there to drink cups of hot chocolate or *tinto,* demitasses of sweet black coffee.

Life was pleasant in the big house near San Agustín Bridge. Mornings were filled with lessons for the younger children, who in those days were commonly given elementary education at home. Under their mother's tutelage Laureano and his sisters learned reading, writing, basic mathematics, and a smattering of geography and literature. Special care was taken with Laureano's instruction, for as the eldest son he would be the first to earn a high school diploma, the *bachillerato,* a highly regarded achievement that only a small minority of Co-lombians attained. The children spent their afternoons studying or playing in the pleasant central courtyard that was filled with bird cages, flowers, and potted shrubs. Dolores de Gómez and her children stayed close to home, for the street belonged to men and to members of the lower class. Servants nor-mally ventured out to make necessary purchases, and a parade of street ven-dors sold them goods from carts that regularly traveled streets of the residen-tial district. The only regular forays into the outside world came on Sundays, when the family traveled across the street to hear mass. Those occasions were especially important to young Laureano, who after his fifth year assisted with the mass as an acolyte.

Thus passed the days for the family of businessman José Laureano Gómez. Secure in his big two-story house, young Laureano had but to wait until, schoolbooks in hand, he would enter the life of the city. José Gómez was not a member of Colombia's moneyed elite. He neither possessed landed wealth nor was he directly involved in the coffee industry. Still he and his family were members of Colombia's upper class if by no other measure than the house they rented from the early 1890s until 1916. There were only 400 houses of two stories or more in Bogotá at that time, and the rental on a large one in a prime location, such as enjoyed by Casa San Agustín, was on average 200 pesos per month. That was twenty times the average monthly salary of a skilled worker, and equal to the entire monthly salary of the city's alcalde, or mayor.[35]

Bogotá's wealthier citizens were easily distinguishable from the general population in the late nineteenth century. Not only did they live in downtown neighborhoods in imposing houses, but they were generally taller and fairer than their fellow citizens, being either *criollos*—persons of European descent—or, like the Gómez family, *mestizos* of predominately European ancestry. They affected the latest European fashions, clothing purchased at exclusive shops on the Calle de Florián, just north of the Plaza de Bolívar. Foreign visitors to the Colombian capital noted that members of the elite took considerable pains to distance themselves from their fellow citizens. William Curtis, who headed the U.S. trade mission to Colombia in the 1880s, remarked that when dealing with the upper class "it is absolutely necessary to speak French to get along." He also noted that their efforts at self-differentiation extended even to the food they ate—or at least to the food they served foreign visitors: "The streams are full of fish, and the mountains are full of game; but nevertheless the people prefer bacon and codfish to the natural luxuries of their country."[36]

Curtis believed that members of the elite, for whom travel and advanced study in Europe were the norm, preferred France to other countries. Another foreigner, the German Alfred Hettner, who lived in Colombia between 1882 and 1884, agreed that while Bogotá's wealthiest residents might visit England or the United States for commercial reasons, Paris was their preferred destination.[37] That neither José Gómez nor his wife ever visited Europe suggests that they were not of the city's highest social stratum.

Surrounding the exclusive residential neighborhoods of the center city were the homes of Bogotá's middle class. Shopkeepers, tradesmen, and government functionaries, they lived in modest one-story houses smaller in all respects than the balconied dwellings of the wealthy. Monthly rents for tile-roofed single-story houses were between 60 and 120 pesos, which was as much or more than the average monthly salary of a Bogotano holding a white-collar job.[38] That forced many families to take in boarders or relatives who helped pay the rent. Alfred Hettner was impressed by the rents in Bogotá, saying they were higher than those in most German cities. The fact that there were but 3,000 houses of one and two stories in Bogotá at a time when its population approached 100,000 suggests both crowded conditions and upward pressure on rents. Many members of the lower middle class were shopkeepers who lived in the rear of their establishments, which rented for as much as eighty pesos per month.[39] Living conditions there were inhuman by modern standards, for they lacked adequate cooking and sanitary facilities. Household garbage was normally tossed into the street, and night soil deposited in drains running down the center of city streets. As most buildings of the day were built of unfired adobe brick that absorbed moisture, most were cold and damp, unhealthful year round.

Most Bogotanos of the late nineteenth century were members of the lower classes. They lived still farther from downtown in crowded straw-thatched huts. Their diets and lifestyles were simple, as even skilled laborers of that time earned on average fifteen pesos per month, and craftsmen but twenty.[40] Dress distinguished the lower from the middle and upper classes. The latter affected European dress, while the former wore simple woven sandals (*alpargatas*), straw hats, and ruanas. Bogotá's lower class was broad and amorphous. Its elite consisted of craftsmen, many of whom owned their own workshops, and its lower edge was populated by day laborers, the unemployed, and a considerable subclass of beggars and petty thieves.

Foreign visitors remarked on the lack of industry in Bogotá of the 1880s and '90s. French geographer Eliseo Reclús wrote that Colombia, with twice Venezuela's population, had half the industry, and Alfred Hettner was uncertain whether the Bavaria brewery and a few small print shops could even be considered industries. Except for expensive imported luxury goods available in a few stores, domestic goods were shoddy, even primitive. "There are few countries in which the principle of 'cheap and poor' dominate more than in this one," wrote Hettner, explaining that as "a major portion of the population lives from hand to mouth, they're simply unable to incur significant expense."[41] Prices in most Bogotá shops were not fixed, allowing buyers to bargain prices down to acceptable levels.

The commercial spirit dominant in the world's more developed nations had not taken hold in the Bogotá of Laureano Gómez's youth. "The feverish haste so usual in the United States is unknown here," wrote Alfred Hettner. "Everything is done in a leisurely way, and there is always time for a chat, . . . everyone talking for hours, huddling in the middle of the sidewalk oblivious to other pedestrians. Or they enter the shop of some friend with no thought of buying anything or closing a deal, but simply to spend a while chatting." The endless conversation of the city's shopkeepers evidently irritated the German, who added that thanks to their custom of joking with inexperienced foreigners "every transaction requires double, triple—even ten times the time we accord it. Whether for good or ill, the factor of time still hasn't come to be important in the lives of Colombians."[42]

It is hardly surprising that in such a setting citizens related to one another in ways that may be characterized as premodern. Bogotá was tiny by present-day urban standards, and there was little class consciousness in the modern sense of the word. Social distances in late-nineteenth-century Colombia did not, as historian Malcolm Deas observes, foster working-class consciousness: "The distance between Colombian extremes was perhaps modest in comparison with other societies, but in any case the new conflicts were not between such extremes, and they were still conflicts in a society where scale was intimate."[43] Writer Rafael Serrano said as much when he remembered the Bogotá of his youth as a place of placid, monotonous lifestyle, "subject to the same rules that had prevailed from colonial times."[44]

The dynamics of intraclass relations in Colombian cities of those times are suggested in the outbreak of working-class violence that occurred in 1893. Early in January of that year, one José Ignacio Gutiérrez published in the Bogotá weekly *Colombia cristiana* several articles bearing the general title "Mendacity." The writer's theme was the poor of Bogotá, whom he accused of having become dissolute and immoral, addicted to strong drink, once they abandoned the countryside for the city. His indiscriminate condemnation of the poor as a simple undifferentiated class, coupled with his inference that the well-off were inherently superior to the rest, infuriated the city's artisans. Heated meetings ensued and a few took it upon themselves to threaten Gutiérrez. City officials gave the journalist police protection, which further inflamed matters. On the second day of the trouble, January 16, gunfire erupted. Police fired on a mob of artisans, touching off an afternoon and evening of stone throwing. Most of the city's police stations were besieged, and furnishings in the homes of the minister of government, Bogotá's mayor, the governor of Cundinamarca, and several private citizens were destroyed. Rioters also broke into a private house of correction run by José Ignacio Gutiérrez, the Asilo de San José, and liberated all the prisoners there. Meanwhile, acting president Miguel Antonio Caro declared that public order had been disturbed and sent troops into Bogotá. That ended the trouble, but not before one policeman had died, and twenty-one police and thirty-one artisans were injured, by official estimates. Unofficial sources put losses at fifty persons dead.[45]

Bogotá's artisan riot of 1893 was not an overtly class-consciousness movement so much as an outcry of honorable men of the lower class in defense of their honor. In Governor Antonio B. Cuervo's words, it was "not a matter of a political movement nor of any plan comparable to those which socialism and the spirit of anarchism we are accustomed to engendering in society."[46] Still there were in it hints of urban protests yet to come. It has been suggested that some of the rioters were inspired by anarchist ideas, and showed it by waving black banners. Others were heard to shout, "Long live the commune!"[47] Rafael Núñez, remembering public disorders he had observed during his years in Europe, saw in the riots evidence that the "socialist scourge" had invaded Colombia.[48]

Even more indicative that the artisans' riot contained some element of class-based protest against authority was the fact that most of the city's new electric street lights were destroyed by the rioters. It had not been three years since the first of 200 1,800-candlepower arc lights were placed around the downtown area. Three quarters of them were destroyed in the riots of January 14 and 15, 1893. The system was never restored, and it would be seven years before new lights, incandescent street lights, would replace the arc lights.[49]

Most who visited the Colombian capital during the 1880s and 1890s were impressed by the piety and inoffensiveness of the poor, whom they found there in such abundance. In the words of the indefatigable Hettner, the poor were "accustomed to kneel humbly before the crucifix." They were a somber lot. "There does not appear among the masses an attitude of hilarity," as Hettner phrased it, adding that neither were the people given to "reprehensible pushing and shoving at religious ceremonies."[50] Occasionally, however, tragedies occurred in the packed churches of the period, such as the one that touched the family of José Gómez. During one particularly crowded mass at the San Agustín church, young Jesús Gómez was pressed against an altar post by a surging crowd of worshippers. Internal injuries resulted, from which the child died several days later.[51]

Death was no stranger to homes of the city. Mortality rates were high in Bogotá and elsewhere in Colombia during the late nineteenth century. Poor sanitation and contaminated food and drinking water made dysentery, amoebiasis, and gastroenteritis endemic in the population. Leprosy and elephantiasis were common, and from time to time outbreaks of typhus and cholera swept the city. Sewage flowed into the city's two principal rivers, the San Agustín and the San Francisco, whose clouds of flies and evil odors were their most notable features. Prisoners with bamboo poles pushed sewage away from riverbanks where it collected. During cloudbursts, frequent in Bogotá, torrents of water spread refuse to doorsteps even as they flushed river channels. Vultures, of which there were thousands around Bogotá, were said to be the city's chief sanitation officials.

These unpleasant facts of life in preindustrial Bogotá prompted one visitor to pen what stands as the least-flattering description of the city at century's end. North American traveler Francis Nicholas wrote, "The city is a place of vermin and corrupting filth; a place where the common incidents of the streets are not fit to be described; where beggars, displaying revolting sores and rotting limbs, swarm about, even thrusting their filthy bodies where they may touch those who pass by, while they demand, not solicit, alms; where ill-mannered, arrogant, overdressed people make vulgar display of their clothes, as they strut about and crowd for precedence."[52]

Services for social welfare were virtually nonexistent. An orphanage stood across Séptima from the Plaza de Santander. In its wall was a small opening where mothers could abandon sick or unwanted children under cover of darkness. Scenes of casual cruelty passed almost unnoticed in city streets. Nicholas observed one instance of child abuse so appalling that he recalled "how I longed for the Society for the Prevention of Cruelty to Children." But then he remembered that he was a stranger in the city, was unknown to anyone there, and had "found but scant courtesy in ordinary affairs." So he hurried away from Bogotá, a place he remembered whose laws made no provision for its destitute, whose citizens paid the poor no heed, and all of whose streets "were filled with scenes of filth, misery, and degradation."[53]

Bogotá was a cold city, frequently lashed by rains that descended from a range of mountains lying along its eastern edge. The chill, damp weather, and the overcast skies seemed to affect the human population, whose color of preference in dress was black, and whose attitude was sober if not melancholy. Pedestrians frequently bore funereal looks on their faces as they hurried by in the streets, their eyes fixed on the ground. At least that was the impression of Julio Palacio, one of an estimated 10,000 students who studied there in the 1890s. His account of society and politics in the national capital at that time constitutes one of the more insightful descriptions of life in fin de siècle Bogotá. It is particularly valuable because as both a native Colombian and an "outsider" he was able to pen a memoir at once informed and dispassionate. Through Palacio's work one comes to perceive Bogotá of the 1890s as a closed, somewhat forbidding city. Palacio's Bogotá was a place shut away from the outside world, little accessible to those who would become part of its life.

One senses his isolation in the description of a great dress ball at the presidential palace in 1891. It was an exclusive affair to which only the cream of the city's society had been invited. The sixteen-year-old schoolboy was given special permission to watch, from across the street, the arrival of the cachacos[54] and their ladies, who made up Bogotá's elite. Most arrived in closed, horse-drawn landaus, whose iron-clad wheels, he recalled, "made an infernal noise as they rolled over the cobblestone streets." "The only ones we saw arrive on foot," wrote Palacio, "were the elegant single men and bachelors of the era, and a few families who had houses near the Palacio de la Carrera."[55]

José Gómez and his wife were almost certainly not in attendance that night, though their bachelor friend Marco Fidel Suárez surely was. He probably arrived on foot, passing not far from young Julio Palacio. And Laureano Gómez doubtless heard the noise of carriage wheels in the Avenida de la Carrera. Dolores de Gómez may well have stood on the front balcony of her home, holding her firstborn son so he too could watch the exciting scene unfolding up the street, just beyond the Puente San Agustín.

2

Teaching the Generation of the Centenary

The Victorian Mind

Early in 1897, Laureano Gómez, just turned eight, began his formal schooling at the Colegio San Bartolomé, a Jesuit-run institution, located a short two-block walk from his home. Gómez and the other schoolboys who hurried through Bogotá's chilly streets that February morning were to be known as members of the Generation of the Centenary, for they would enter public life at about the time Colombia celebrated its first century of independence in 1910. Among those youngsters who would go on to become Colombia's pre-eminent public men, was nine-year-old Eduardo Santos. Like Gómez he was born in Bogotá to a family recently arrived from the provinces. Another was eleven-year-old Alfonso López, the son of a well-to-do businessman from Honda. At that moment young López was known principally for buckteeth that had earned him the nickname *el muelón* (big-tooth). Trudging in the same direction as López, for they attended the same school, notable for his extraordinary stature and fair complexion, was seventeen-year-old Enrique Olaya, widely referred to as "the blond from Guateque" (*el mono de Guateque*), a town one day's travel north of Bogotá. Each of those young men, plus one other, seven-year-old Mariano Ospina Pérez, who attended school in Medellín, would become president of Colombia, holding office between 1930 and 1953. Those years might justifiably be referred to as the reign of the Centenarians.

Among their peers, all schoolboys in 1897, were Luis López de Mesa, ten; Luis Eduardo Nieto Caballero, nine; and Luis Cano, eight. Roberto Urdaneta, who, like Laureano Gómez, attended San Bartolomé, was seven years old, and Estéban Jaramillo was ten.

An extraordinary professorial corps awaited the young scholars. They were for the most part mature men, whose own generational denomination was Generation of 1870. Sometimes referred to as men of the Classic Generation, they were well versed in Latin and Greek, and in philosophy, most of them having been trained for careers in law and, in a general sense, for the choicest public positions. A few could be classified as professional educators, having spent a goodly portion of their lives as teachers in schools that they themselves had founded. Among them were Jesús Casas, Ignacio Espinoza, Antonio José Iregüi, and Luis A. Robles. Many priests were members of teaching orders. Prominent in that regard were the Augustinians, Jesuits, and Christian Brothers.

Teachers of the Centenarians often spent more of their productive lives outside the classroom than within. That was especially true at the higher levels of education, where doctors, lawyers, and public officials found time to teach a class or two at a favored private school. Most Colombian presidents of the nineteenth and early twentieth centuries had spent years in the classroom either before or after being elevated to that office. Santiago Pérez, Miguel Antonio Caro, José Manuel Marroquín, and Nicolás Esguerra were teachers during the earlier period; Pedro Nel Ospina and Miguel Abadía Méndez taught somewhat later. Abadía, considered by most to have been a better teacher than chief executive, was remarkable in that he continued to teach law at the National University throughout his tenure as president.

Those leaders of Colombian society were well aware that the fate of the nation was in their hands. Highly cultivated as a group, members of an elite class for whom foreign travel and study was not uncommon, they strove to stay abreast of events unfolding in Europe and elsewhere, and to impart their perceptions to their students. Teachers of the Centenarians represented, in short, the best, most worldly professorial corps the nation could offer its future leaders. Their immediate political differences notwithstanding, they shared a vision of the world, a Victorian vision, that transcended Colombia.

The teachers of Laureano Gómez, Alfonso López, and the rest, were confident men, aware that they lived in a time of astonishing change in the world. They were also secure in the knowledge that they stood at the apex of Colombia's social structure. In a country like Colombia, where the masses were as respectful of their betters as they were poor and uneducated, none of them had reason to doubt that they were the ones who would lead the country toward inevitable progress. Even if they occupied a peripheral part of the marvelous Eurocentric world, they were part of it nonetheless, fated to achieve great things in it.

For decades Colombian leaders had waxed eloquent on the approaching changes. At mid-century José Eusebio Caro, a cofounder of the Conservative Party, father of Miguel Antonio Caro, assured his children that by century's end steamships, highways, and telegraphs would invigorate the nation's economy, thereby insuring continued social stability. Miguel Samper, a contemporary of Caro's, envisioned harnessing the nation's rivers, especially Tequendama Falls, whose force, he foresaw, would eventually "transmit light and heat to Bogotá."[1] He very nearly lived to see that dream come true, for his son Miguel Samper Brush did in fact use the Río Bogotá to power the capital's

first electric generator, put into operation in mid-1900. Their contemporary
Salvador Camacho Roldán echoed their faith in the redemptive faith of technology: "To lag behind in the discipline of science," he said in a speech of 1882,
"is to die."[2]

Even the dour Rafael Núñez could not help but be deeply affected by the
physical strides made in the England he knew through years of residence there.
His writings are replete with passages showing that he, too, shared the fundamental optimism of the age. "Societies progress through a movement uniformly accelerated," he wrote. "It is the positivist and utilitarian doctrine of
scientific evolution."[3]

Colombia's leaders were well read in the works of Europe's leading social
theorists, "profits of our idealism," as Armando Solano called them. Like their
contemporaries elsewhere in Latin America, they found hope and comfort in
Herbert Spencer's teaching that human society is analogous to a living organism. Just as organisms evolve, so too does society. Spencer taught that different
societies develop in accord with their own unique characteristics. Thus Colombians could reason that if they but pursued the study of "scientific and practical truth," in Carlos Martínez Silva's words, Colombia could be made to
"meet the requirements of our era of progress and development."[4] That conviction was the rationale for the collaboration between Núñez and Caro during the 1880s and later. They understood that the nation was an entity whose
destiny they themselves could shape, recognizing as their top priority the need
to calm national passions to the end of making possible the progress that had
so far eluded them. Liberals, too, operated on the Spencerian premise that
society was an organic thing. Camacho Roldán told university students in
1882 that they should all think of themselves as gardeners, and of the nation as
a ripening fruit that through careful nurturing could be brought to perfection.
Pedagogue and Radical Liberal Antonio José Iregüi preferred inorganic metaphors. For him "evolutionary history" and "geologic history" were one and
the same. In an 1896 lecture he assured students that the record of human
achievement over time is easily subject to empirical study, like layers of the
earth's crust.[5]

Colombia's Regeneration-era leaders believed that England was the country
they should emulate. England was both the home of the great Herbert Spencer
and a model for less fortunate nations striving to begin their own process of
industrialization. England, Germany, and France had achieved "adulthood,"
Iregüi told his eager listeners. Through such phraseology, members of the
Colombian elite acknowledged their country's inferior position in the global
hierarchy. Still, in their minds there was no reason to feel anger—no more so
than a child should feel anger over not yet being grown. Their time of maturity
was coming, inevitably.

The feeling of backwardness expressed constantly by Colombian leaders during the nineteenth century, standing in curious counterpoint to their deep-seated optimism, was at least in part founded in their country's poverty. That moved them to yearn for help and tutelage from the metropolitan powers. José Eusebio Caro wrote at mid-century, "we can't save ourselves; it will be the hand of England that produces our social salvation." Once Colombians achieve order, he continued, "the English will come with their capital, and the North Americans with their entrepreneurial spirit, opening our doors and windows, giving us light and movement."[6] A half century and numerous civil wars later Carlos Martínez Silva was moved to suggest that Colombia hire an English firm to collect national taxes. "Hasn't Egypt gained immensely under the wise and honorable administration of the English?" he asked.[7]

Europeans living in Colombia reinforced their hosts' perception that if not personally inferior to foreigners, they and their country occupied a distinctly peripheral place in the concert of nations. "These *bogotanos* are superficially read," wrote a British consular official in 1906, adding solicitously, "still they're really quite cultivated given their surroundings." They are, he admitted further, capable of entering into debates around the themes of Darwin and Spencer, "and in some cases on the latest French and English writers."[8]

More often than not foreign visitors tempered their condescension with ridicule, especially when remarking on Bogotá's pretentious nickname, the Athens of South America. "In this Athens of South America they light only seven street lights, this in reverence to the seven wise men of Greece," joked a writer in 1861.[9] Years later a British consular official noted archly that the only thing Bogotá and Athens have in common is that in both countries contract bridge is preferred over Royal Auction bridge. And it can hardly have escaped Colombians that Bogotá was the least-favored posting for British diplomats.

The organic vision of national hierarchies, of superior and inferior nations, that nineteenth-century Colombian leaders learned from their European teachers, jibed perfectly with what they observed at a human level within their country. Their society was exceedingly hierarchical, with vast distances separating social strata. Nine of ten Colombians were illiterate in 1897, when Laureano Gómez entered school in Bogotá. Over 90 percent of the population lived outside the towns and cities, being farmers, or campesinos. Most of them acknowledged their inferiority before the well-to-do and well educated. When the farmer's patron visited from the city, it was common for the campesino of late-nineteenth-century Colombia to greet him on bent knee, hat in hand. The tractability of these Colombians was cause for constant comment throughout the nineteenth century, and well into the twentieth. "None are easier to govern and mold," wrote José María Samper at mid-century: "The police almost do not exist in any part of the country . . . because our masses are essentially submissive."[10] Some sixty years later, in 1906, a British visitor remarked on the high degree of personal safety that foreigners enjoyed throughout Colombia. "There's really no street in Bogotá or anywhere else in the country . . . where a foreigner or a native can't walk at any hour of the day or night."[11]

Colombia's peasants kept this pacific demeanor toward their social superiors well into the twentieth century—at least to the 1920s. Notable in this regard were those living along the country's awakening coffee frontier. Thousands of the humble had taken up land by right of homestead laws passed in the 1870s and '80s, which opened *baldíos*, or unsettled parts of the country. Almost immediately, however, revenues from coffee sales made it clear that the mountainsides were of immense potential value. The homesteaders soon found their lands being encroached upon and even stolen from them by city-dwelling entrepreneurs. The newcomers frequently did so with the help of hired thugs who abused and sometimes killed protesters. Those intrusions of urban-based capitalists frustrated some Colombian politicians who wanted their homestead legislation to stimulate formation of a self-sufficient, economically productive class of yeoman farmers.

Important here is not so much that market forces, the profit motive, and the superior power of well-connected coffee planters worked to the disadvantage of peasant smallholders. What is noteworthy is the way peasants initially responded to the abuse they suffered. They rarely took direct action against planters who harassed them between 1870 and 1920. Instead they went through channels, hiring lawyers to formulate respectfully worded petitions that were forwarded to authorities in the national capital. Far from making demands, they approached metropolitan powers as supplicants. "We implore justice," read a petition, which went on to lament the law "by which the powerful always impose their will upon the weak."[12]

The diffidence and apparent helplessness of the common people buttressed the perception of Colombia's largely creole white elite that the masses were not just socially inferior to them, but were physically inferior too. Superiority of the white race over all others was one of the earliest findings of nineteenth-century social scientists, one that wouldn't be seriously challenged until well into the twentieth century.

Writings of the period are replete with suggestions, sometimes outright assertions, of racist savor. José María Samper published his popular *Ensayo sobre las revoluciones políticas* (Essay on political revolutions) in Paris shortly after the appearance of J. A. Gobineau's disquisition *Essai sur l'inégalité des races humaines* (On the inequality of races).[13] Gobineau's influence seems manifest in Samper's characterization of the Indians of Nariño as "obdurate to civilization, impassive before progress . . . sedentary savages." He hoped that through immigration European blood would invigorate Colombia, causing the nation to develop "a beautiful mixed, though Caucasian-tending race," one combining Hispanic vigor with "the positivism, individualism, enterprise, and tenacity of the Anglo-Saxon, the German, the Dutchman, the Swiss."[14] The popularity of Samper's vision is suggested by immigration laws passed to attract white population in 1845, 1847, 1870, 1871, 1876, and in 1922. That infusion of European blood never came, leading Enrique Cortés, minister of education between 1868 and 1870, to grumble that residents of lowland areas were "an ugly, colorless race which works little and grubs around amidst lush vegetation."[15]

Laureano Gómez, Alfonso López, Enrique Olaya Herrera, Mariano Ospina Pérez, and the rest did not need to be told that they were members of a select group. By one count fewer than 3 of every 100 of their school-age contemporaries received any education at all. And relatively few of them attended the better schools, which tended to be in the larger towns and cities. Gómez was indeed fortunate in being able to attend San Bartolomé, for it was believed by many to be the best school in the country. Only a small minority of those admitted to the Jesuit institution ever graduated. Between 1891 and 1984 nearly 30,000 young men were admitted to San Bartolomé. Only 1,190 graduated.[16] Thus Gómez's class of six in 1904 represented a small fraction of the boys admitted with him eight years earlier.

Texts of the period amply conveyed their authors' conviction that the students who entered these schools were destined for posts of importance in the public sphere. The *Libro de lecturas escogidas,* a reader of the sort Gómez likely used, contains a thirty-seven-page introduction on public speaking drawing liberally from Cicero's admonitions to speakers. Integral to the discussion is a thirteen-page section on appropriate gestures for public speakers drawn from the works of Quintilian. Youngsters having further questions about public speaking are referred to the works of several French and English authorities. There follows a lengthy collection of "ideological readings" that treat themes like respect for family, love of God and country, charity toward the less fortunate, good manners, and the advantages of paying attention.

The epistolary section contains seven of Lord Chesterfield's letters to his son, and a seven-page excerpt from José María Vergara y Vergara's "Advice to a Young Girl." While it is unlikely that many girls studied the *Libro de lecturas escogidas,* certainly not in Bogotá's all-male private schools of the 1890s, its patriarchal message surely wasn't lost on those who did: "Little girl, live happily. If you come to be a wife, be humble and true. Always obey, that you never cease to reign. God, your parents, your husband will be your only masters. Sometimes the world will call them tyrants. Happiness calls them your protectors. Life is not bad, only people are."[17]

Civics books of the period enjoined the well-brought-up to respect authority, exhibit good behavior, and show deference to important people. "Doff your hat to the national president and to the archbishop when you pass them in the street," the text instructed, even if the former "belongs to another political party, or is your adversary," even if the latter "isn't of your religious persuasion." Students were warned against exhibiting bad behavior while observing congressional debates: "Those who abuse freedom of speech by shouting from the visitor galleries have done great harm to the nation."[18]

In these ways, through the texts they studied, from the lectures of their teachers, from what they saw around them and absorbed from the elite culture to which they belonged, schoolboys internalized the social values of Victorian-era Colombia. They learned that it was they who would lead their benighted country in the glorious new century, who would find a way to uplift the backward masses. They learned to intone the stirring final paragraph of Santiago Pérez's homage to the Liberator, Simón Bolívar, first read before the Atheneum of Bogotá in 1884 and reprinted in their literature texts for many years afterward: "Be happy then, Athenians, even when we old ones vainly strain against the rocks to which we're chained! New Promethians are stealing fire from the gods. Each new conquest of science invigorates the spirits of Colombians. Thus will our common fatherland feel the thrust of universal progress, its younger generation mixing in its own accents, peaceful and prophetic, in the infinite hymn of the human word."[19]

Politicized Education in a Historical Context

Sadly, Santiago Pérez's hopes for peace and progress were mocked by three civil wars fought in Colombia during the sixteen years between his speech and his death, in solitary exile, in 1900. Nineteenth-century Colombian teachers may have transmitted Victorian-era values in the classroom, but through their public actions they revealed that much of what they taught was laden with political meaning. That was as much the case in the 1890s as it had been for the half century preceding.

Colombia was hardly a happy place that February of 1897, when Laureano Gómez and his peers walked toward their respective schools. Serious political troubles beset the government. The Regeneration was in its twelfth year, and its maker, the austere Rafael Núñez, more than two years in his grave. Scholarly Miguel Antonio Caro, Núñez's protégé, was now president. Caro was no politician; his heavy-handed and inept leadership of the ruling Nationalist Party was fast alienating even those who had once been the party's ardent supporters. One such person was militant Conservative Carlos Martínez Silva, former cabinet minister under Núñez, journalist, and educator. A year earlier, in February 1896, Martínez Silva and twenty other prominent Conservatives, now referring to themselves as "Historical" Conservatives, broke with Caro, whom they accused of betraying Conservative values.[20]

Eight-year-old Laureano Gómez was too young to understand the frequently byzantine workings of Colombian high politics, though even at that tender age he must have had some feeling for the importance of politics and its practical consequences. He was old enough to remember the civil war that had ended just two years earlier. The dashing Liberal general Rafael Uribe Uribe had been prominent in it, and now the thirty-eight-year-old firebrand was preparing for war against the government that he openly called an "abjectly corrupt tyranny."[21] Strong words appeared early in the political lexicon of Bogotá's schoolboys, many of whom crowded the galleries of the Senate and Chamber of Representatives to hear debates. Alfonso López was one of them. He recalled Uribe Uribe's speeches as "vibrant discourses," delivered with "finely timbered voice, Roman gestures, and irrefutable documentation."[22]

Colombian society was in fact highly politicized in the late nineteenth century, and intensely and bitterly so at the elite level. Parents of the Centenarians knew that family fortunes waxed or waned depending on which party was in power. Many a night their sons fell asleep to the sound of heated discussions of the latest political events.

Under such circumstances it is hardly surprising that schools of the period were themselves politicized. Laureano Gómez's school, San Bartolomé, had been under the direction of the Jesuit order for thirteen years. The Jesuit fathers were put in charge of the state-owned institution as part of Núñez and Caro's plan to bring traditional Catholic values back into the classroom, and at the same time to combat liberal teachings, which they saw as damaging to public morality.

Liberals were furious over Núñez's educational program, especially over the prominent role the Church played in it. They fumed that the Regenerators had turned their country into "a picturesque farm in the tropics owned by priests,"[23] and busied themselves founding private schools where liberal values would be taught and where government inspectors could neither specify the use of texts nor force teachers to sign oaths of fealty to the Church and its doctrines. A host of liberal schools were formed during the 1880s and '90s, among them the Universidad Externado and the Colegio de Araújo, founded by Simón Araújo in the 1880s; the Colegio Académico and the Liceo Mercantil, founded by Manuel Antonio Rueda in 1886 and 1891, respectively; and the Universidad Republicana, whose founders were Luis A. Robles, Antonio José Iregüi, and Eugenio J. Gómez.[24]

Dispute over educational policy was nothing new to Colombia. More than a century earlier, in 1774, Viceroy Manuel Guirior commissioned one of his subalterns, Francisco Antonio Moreno y Escandón, to develop a modern curriculum for use in institutions of higher learning throughout the viceroyalty. Inspired in part by ideas of the European Enlightenment, the changes were aimed at moving New Granada away from the scholastic tradition and toward a mode of instruction encouraging greater empirical analysis. Moreno y Escandón's plan, when submitted, was hardly a revolutionary one. Its greatest departure from the past lay in its stricture that students be allowed to compare the ideas of their several texts in order that conclusions drawn from them be governed by free exercise of reason. In spite of its mildness Moreno y Escandón's plan wasn't fully embraced by the committee assigned to evaluate it, because of fears that if allowed to debate their texts students might fall into dangerous factionalism.

Following independence, leaders like Francisco de Paula Santander gave considerable thought to improving education. New normal schools were founded, curricula revised, and the number of teachers increased. These measures were applauded by educators in the new republic, though another aspect of Santander's plan of 1826 created a furor among the traditional-minded. That involved the inclusion of books by Englishman Jeremy Bentham and liberal French economist Jean Baptiste Say in the common syllabus. Conservatives especially disliked Bentham's identification of pleasure with the good, which they saw as contrary to Christian morality. They prevailed upon Simón Bolívar to banish the offending texts, which he did by a decree of 1827.

During the 1840s political leadership in Colombia, at the time called New Granada, returned to conservative hands. President Mariano Ospina Rodríguez saw to it that offending texts were expunged from official curricula, to be replaced by the writings of neoscholastic philosophers Francisco Suárez and Jaime Balmes. At the university level religious instruction was mandated, along with the study of Roman law. Students were subjected to a strict disciplinary code on the theory that it would improve their morality and personal habits.

Ospina's "counterreform" was brief, soon giving way to an era of liberal experimentation lasting some thirty years and ending with the advent of Núñez and the Regeneration. Those years were turbulent ones marked by civil war and rapid differentiation of the citizenry along party lines. Romantic liberalism was the catalyst bringing about actual party formation. First under President José Hilario López, and later under a succession of Radical presidents, the Liberals implemented a range of reforms aimed at drastically expanding the area of personal freedom enjoyed by the citizenry. The individualist and egalitarian thrust of the reforms is suggested by a law of 1850 eliminating the requirement that university professors possess academic credentials. That, Radical Liberals believed, represented a form of monopoly limiting the individual's freedom to teach.

Radical Liberalism achieved maximum expression in the Constitution of 1863, which among other things decentralized national political power, granted absolute religious freedom, reduced the presidential term of office to two years, and guaranteed freedom of speech and the right to traffic in firearms during peacetime. Not long after the new constitution went into effect, party militant Santiago Pérez published a civics text designed for use in public schools. In it he articulated the Radical Liberals' faith in democracy and individualism. "The individual is the true source of all sovereignty," he wrote, adding that the state's principal purpose lay in guaranteeing individual rights.[25]

The Radical generation's faith in education as a means to progress and civilization took objective form in the Organic Decree of 1870. That law, requiring that elementary education be free and obligatory for children of the republic, also aimed at making schools religiously neutral. Seen by Liberals as ushering in a golden age of Colombian education, the law represented a challenge to Conservatives, who cited it as a chief cause of their uprising against the government in 1876.[26] As schools were being secularized, university curricula also underwent modification in ways highly offensive to Conservatives. During the 1870s government officials mandated the use of specific texts for courses. One of the books most obnoxious to Conservatives was *Ideology* by French philosopher Destutt de Tracy. That work, to be used in philosophy courses, taught that all human ideas spring from objective external sources. Conservatives demanded eclecticism in text selection, meaning that a variety of points of view, including traditional Roman Catholic ones, could be presented in the classroom.

The government reading list touched off what Jaime Jaramillo Uribe has called "the polemic of the textbooks."[27] Conservatives like Miguel Antonio Caro, writing in the party newspaper *El Tradicionalista,* complained that the state was confusing its obligation to educate with the Church's right to indoctrinate. It was clear to Caro and his copartisans that the state, "armed with the sword of the law," was imposing its biases in an unwarranted and capricious way, "invading with scandal and violence the rights of religion and science."[28] Aníbal Galindo answered for the Liberals: "If we've founded a university and if we have a university, it's to teach liberal doctrines in order to form Liberals. None of this eclecticism. Balmes and Bentham can't hold hands in university classrooms. While the Liberal Party remains in power it must teach liberalism. Political honesty requires it. If we in good faith feel that liberalism is good for the country, that's what we are going to teach young people. When the Catholic party comes to power it can follow the example of Philip II and teach Catholicism. It will be its right to do so."[29]

Thus instructed, Conservatives built their own private schools, and planned how they would drive liberalism from school curricula when they should take power. Among their educational institutions were José Vicente Concha's

Colegio Pio IX, founded in 1864, and José Manuel Marroquín's Colegio Yerbabuena and Joaquín Gutiérrez Celis's Colegio La Independencia, established during the 1870s. Others were the Universidad Católica and the Colegio del Espíritu Santo of Carlos Martínez Silva, founded in the 1880s.[30]

Liberal Education or Conservative Education?

Colombia's political and ideological battles of the late nineteenth century were very much part of identical ones occurring elsewhere in the West at that time. Liberals and conservatives in Europe and America alike drew inspiration from philosophical writings favoring their points of view. That was especially true in Colombia, where ideas resonated powerfully in a supercharged political atmosphere. By far the most important supplier of ideological ammunition for Colombian conservatives was the Italian Giovanni Maria Mastai-Ferretti, better known as Pope Pius IX. Seen as a liberal when elected pope in 1846, Pius IX became the world's most vigorous castigator of liberalism following the upsets of 1848 in Europe. Within months of his ordination he began warning his followers that revolutionaries were at war against the Catholic faith. Some years later, in 1864, he published what stand as history's most vigorous indictments of liberalism. In *Quanta cura,* and the *Syllabus of Errors,* released simultaneously with the encyclical, he made it clear that a "terrible conspiracy" was at work against the Catholic Church. "They," who through "criminal schemes" seek to "deprave and delude" the young with their writings, he stated, must be "held as reprobated, denounced, and condemned by all children of the Catholic Church." Pius IX further described enemies of the Church as people of "perversity, of depraved ... evil opinions ... animated by the spirit of Satan." They were "the enemies of the useful sciences, of progress," holders of "monstrous and portentous opinions ... to the very great loss of souls and even to the detriment of civil society."[31]

The Syllabus of Errors made clear just who these dangerous and depraved people were. They were rationalists, latitudinarians (or relativists, such as Protestants, who believed their faith was as much Christian as that of Roman Catholics), socialists, communists, Masons and other members of secret societies, and persons who wanted to separate church and state, or to place the state over the church. Also condemned in the *Syllabus* were proponents of secular education, Kantians (or those who believe that "moral laws do not stand in need of divine sanction"), persons wholly driven by the profit motive, believers in gratification by pleasure, believers in majority rule, civil marriage, and religious freedom. Finally, and for good measure, Pius IX condemned those who believed that the pope "can and ought to reconcile himself and come to terms with progress, liberalism, and modern civilization."[32]

Colombian Conservatives and their allies in the Church used the pope's pronouncements as weapons both on the field of battle and in the classroom. José Vicente Concha is remembered as an educator who prepared "gladiatorial hosts" to fight the "universal apostasy" at large in Colombia. In 1875 Pius IX sent Concha a lengthy letter in which the pontiff praised the Colombian for being steadfast in the fight against erroneous and false doctrines. The pope also said he was pleased that Concha had named his school for him.[33] Not long before, the pope had, in his last encyclical, *Estl multa luctuosa,* again used military metaphor in warning of the "great war" being waged against the church. Masons and others were said to be gathering troops in their "synagogue of Satan," so that they might soon become "masters of the world."[34] When Colombia's Conservative civil war broke out in 1876, it will be recalled that some soldiers carried standards that bore the likenesses of Pius IX. The bishops of Popayán, Pasto, and Antioquia, who justified their actions by citing passages from *Quanta cura,* were subsequently charged as chief instigators of the war and exiled from Colombia for ten years. In Bogotá public high schools closed as their mostly Liberal student bodies rushed to join government armies, and boys too young to fight staged mock wars on Sunday afternoons in the outskirts of the city. Counted among the scores of seven- to twelve-year-olds formed up under blue banners of the Conservative Party were boys from Concha's Colegio Pius IX.[35] Classroom, battlefield, and the Holy See lived in symbiotic balance in Colombia of the 1870s.

Within three years of the conservative uprising, fortune began to smile on the Conservative cause. Rafael Núñez was elected president in 1880, and again in 1884. Following the Liberal uprising of 1885, and subsequent restructuring of national institutions in the Constitution of 1886, Conservatives brought religion back into public education. Núñez and Caro believed that religion would help heal the body politic. Accordingly they placed devout Catholics in key positions and gave them free hand in carrying out the pro-clerical reforms. One of the most vigorous of the religious communities invited to assist in the regeneration of Colombian education was the Society of Jesus. It was placed in charge of the Colegio San Bartolomé, where they taught many of the nation's future leaders, inculcating in them what Laureano Gómez called "a manly concept of life."[36]

Most students who completed the Jesuit's rigorous *ratio studiorum,* featuring study of the classics, Latin and Greek, and religious philosophy, went on to professional study. Those who did usually chose either law or medicine, though by the early twentieth century a good many Bartolinos were, like Laureano Gómez, choosing careers in business or industry.

Laureano Gómez loved San Bartolomé. He was an excellent student remembered both for his outstanding memory and his habit of blushing when called on to recite, a trait that earned him the nickname Electricidad (electricity). He took to the regimen of school life and reveled in its competitiveness, especially in *concertaciones,* public acts in which individual students demonstrated their abilities in academic areas. The only aspect of school life in which the young Gómez didn't excel was athletics, where a slightly clubbed right foot placed him at a disadvantage. Most of all Laureano Gómez loved and respected his austere Jesuit teachers. Their asceticism, intellectualism, and fealty to religious values continually inspired him. The fathers presented him a Christian view of the world buttressed by philosophic teachings that he found coherent, convincing, and satisfying. Gómez claimed never to have forgotten or betrayed the doctrines taught him at San Bartolomé.[37]

Liberals were horrified by the turn of events that seemingly overnight returned confessional education to Colombia's schools. Their unhappiness might have been lessened had the change not been carried out in so draconian a manner. Unfortunately for Colombia, the Roman Catholic Church was entering the most militant phase of its resistance to the complex of ideas and attitudes, founded in Enlightenment rationalism and empiricism, that had come to dominate the Western world. And it was doubly unfortunate that foreign priests, many of them Spaniards fleeing the Carlist Wars—or exiled for excessive militancy—were invited to help return religion to Colombian schools. The Spanish zealots who arrived in increasing numbers during the 1880s and '90s intensified Liberal anger over religious reforms of the Regeneration.

Even as the Liberals were losing their fateful civil war of 1885, Spanish priest Félix Sardá y Salvany was publishing his incendiary and widely read volume *El liberalismo es pecado* (Liberalism is a sin).[38] Monsignor Rafael M. Carrasquilla, inspired both by the Liberal civil war of 1895 and his Spanish colleague's earlier work, published his *Essay on Liberal Doctrine,* which went through three printings in just four years, and which concluded that no Liberal could be a good Catholic.[39] Not to be outdone, Bishop Nicolás Casas of Pasto, writing at the height of the Liberal civil war of 1899–1902, published in quick succession two volumes instructing his followers on the evil political philosophy. Their tenor can be judged from the passage in which the bishop condemned doctrinaire liberalism for its "extreme maliciousness, its horrible impiety and atheistic principles," and for "the enormity of its terrifying monstrosity."[40]

By the Concordat of 1887, diocesan bishops were granted the right to dismiss school teachers whose views they considered religiously unorthodox. In 1888 educator and militant Catholic Jesús Casas, minister of education under acting president Miguel Antonio Caro, equated anti-Catholicism with treason. He criticized public education under Liberal regimes as a chief cause of civic disorder that had to be "cut off at its roots." The anti-Liberal hyperbole of civil and religious leaders took official form in the Oath of Faith for Teachers, which from 1901 required all teachers in public institutions to swear: "I believe in God the Father and in all those principles dealing with faith, dogma, morality, and discipline espoused by the Roman Catholic Church. . . . I utterly condemn and reject, as did the *Syllabus,* various papal encyclicals and the Latin American Council, the basic concepts of liberalism, naturalism, socialism, and rationalism."[41]

Children from better-off Liberal families could escape obnoxious features of Conservative educational policy by attending the schools founded for them. Young Luis Eduardo Nieto Caballero did so, entering the Colegio de Araújo even after people had advised that he study with the Jesuits, as Araújo was a heretic. Nieto found the freethinking Araújo in fact to be a judicious and humane man. Nonetheless the headmaster and his school were Liberal, and Nieto later admitted that during his years there he "became saturated with liberalism without knowing it."[42] That was Alfonso López's reaction to his study at the Liceo Mercantil: "They taught me to read the *Cartilla Liberal* [Liberal Primer], which left an indelible imprint on my spirit. It's a good thing my teachers didn't use the Conservative Primer. Otherwise today I'd be leader of the Conservative Party!"[43]

Education at some Liberal schools was every bit as exclusive as at Conservative ones. Julio Palacio, who studied at the Universidad Republicana during the 1890s, had a professor of constitutional law who did not teach the Constitution of 1886. For him the Rionegro Constitution of 1863 was Colombia's true fundamental charter, and that of 1886 simply "a parenthesis that soon will be closed."[44] Luis María Mora, who studied at the Universidad Externado, recalled that his professors didn't present the ideas of Bentham and Tracy as philosophic concepts, but rather as "axioms to be imposed, with fanatical enthusiasm, battle flags used when annihilating the enemy." Religion class at his school was "the butt of irreverent jokes," and teachers and students alike relished "destroying" the scholastic doctrine that just a few blocks away was so impressing Laureano Gómez.[45]

During 1899 Bogotá's schoolboys were given vivid proof of the close connection between their classrooms and the public world beyond them. The academic year began with a spirited debate over educational policy, carried out in Liberal and Conservative newspapers of the city. Discussion centered on instruction given by the Jesuits at San Bartolomé, which Liberal writers found to be outmoded and entirely inappropriate to the modern age. Emotions ran high on both sides, and at length a riot erupted in the streets outside San Bartolomé. Sixteen- and seventeen-year-olds from Colombia's best educational institutions—the Liberal Universidad Republicana, Liceo Mercantil, and the Colegio de Araújo, and the Conservative San Bartolomé—pummeled one another as shocked adults looked on.[46] It is probable that four future national presidents either observed or took part in the fight. Bartolinos Laureano Gómez and Roberto Urdaneta, then ten and nine years old respectively, likely watched from a safe distance. On the Liberal side, the street-fighting abilities of thirteen-year-old Alfonso López probably weren't needed, as his school, the Liceo Mercantil, was splendidly represented by the blond giant Enrique Olaya Herrera, who cheerfully bloodied the noses of the priest-ridden enemy.

Between semesters of that fateful year, in late June, Rafael Uribe Uribe was imprisoned on the charge of plotting civil war. He was marched away to jail along with other Liberal leaders between two columns of heavily armed soldiers, through Bogotá's busiest streets. By mid-July he was released, and two months after that was headed north toward the department of Santander to help organize the revolution.

Thousands of Liberal Bogotanos followed Uribe in the weeks that followed. The tearful departures at Bogotá train stations so alarmed authorities that a state of siege was declared on October 18 in hopes of slowing the exodus. It did little good. Liberal schools lost teachers and many of their older students to the war, among them Enrique Olaya Herrera, who went to join Liberal forces in western Cundinamarca. Many of the Liberal schools closed, never to reopen. One of them was the Colegio de Araújo, seized by government decree and converted into army barracks. Those events argue for the truth of Mora's remark, "in Colombia's state of continuous revolutions, warfare was in a certain sense the means of completing one's education."[47]

War and Ignominy

Colombia's War of the Thousand Days, wrote Colombian statesman Laureano García Ortiz, began in 1840.[48] He meant of course that the war sprang from the same political exclusiveness, regionalism, and elite factionalism that by Jorge Holguín's count had generated nine major civil wars, fourteen localized conflicts, three military coups, and two international wars over the first century of national history.[49] But if most underlying causes of Colombia's war of 1899–1902 were the same as for earlier conflicts, there were extenuating factors that worked to make this civil war worse than any previous one.

The appearance of coffee as an increasingly vital force in the national economy aggravated existing divisions among Colombian leaders and energized the conflict once it began. Growing exports of the lucrative product both upset old regional balances and encouraged the growth of new local elites, most of whom had connection with the Liberal Party. Liberals tended to be more involved in the coffee trade, for they had been forced into private life just as the boom in coffee began in the 1880s. The Liberals most directly involved in coffee export tended to be young and energetic men like Rafael Uribe Uribe, who during the 1880s and '90s established plantations in mountainous western Cundinamarca, above the Río Magdalena. Planters like Uribe Uribe hated Regeneration-era tariffs, taxes, and inflationary money policies that hampered the coffee trade.

As war approached in the late 1890s, Liberals throughout Colombia, frequently united economically as well as politically, were able to turn commercial networks to use in war planning. Such linkages extended to most corners of the nation, and ran internationally as well. By 1897 much of the commercial correspondence between Liberal coffee growers contained coded information on their party's war preparations. Abroad their collaborators included liberals in Central America, Ecuador, and Venezuela. In the latter nation their most avid supporter was liberal caudillo Cipriano Castro, whose successful seizure of the Venezuelan government in October 1899 Colombian Liberals hoped to emulate.[50]

Elite factionalism was also intensified by the rise of coffee in Colombia. Liberals and Historical Conservatives shared a belief in economic liberalism that made them natural allies. This helps explain their campaign against Nationalist Party leaders like Caro and Marco Fidel Suárez, who were not businessmen and consequently not linked to the export-import economy. Nationalists tended to be men whose economic thought was colored by the mercantilist bias of an earlier era, a fact illustrated in Caro's tax on coffee exports and his extensive use of government monopolies as revenue producers. And as coffee loomed ever larger on the national scene, the cycle of ruinous price declines culminating in 1899 must be entered as another factor contributing to the outbreak of war. Carlos Martínez Silva, leader of the Historicals, described the moneyed classes as suffering "supreme anguish" over the price decline, which, coupled with the government's inflationary monetary policy, had limited exports and driven down Colombian stock issues on European and U.S. exchanges. Increasing numbers of the middle and lower classes found their livelihoods linked to coffee. In 1899, Martínez Silva noted an increase in petty criminality that he traced to the price decline. It had become a common sight to see men in town and countryside arming themselves to protect their possessions. Others whose ruanas had been stolen huddled miserably in Bogotá's chilly streets.[51]

At least as important as the rise of coffee cultivation in unsettling the national scene was the ongoing poverty of the central government. That was in turn rooted in the undeveloped character of the economy. The rise of coffee notwithstanding, Colombia's economy was one of Latin America's least productive in 1899. In per capita exports and foreign investment, to cite but two indicators, Colombia stood last and next-to-last, respectively, among the twenty Latin American nations.[52]

Never was government poverty more apparent than at century's end, when war loomed. The government was forced to dismiss a thousand men from its already understaffed army during June 1899, and to sell two navy cruisers at about the same time—this at a time when most considered war inevitable. Efforts to raise money through foreign loans were fruitless. Falling coffee prices and lingering effects of the civil war of 1895 had caused a default on foreign debt payments that ruined the nation's credit rating. This was doubly embarrassing in that Colombia's public debt, at just five dollars per capita, was one of the smallest of any nation in the world.[53] Six months after the war began, in April 1900, a desperate Colombian government raised five million francs by agreeing to a six-year extension of the new Panama Canal Company concession. This was an ill-advised move, taken under the pressure of war, that would weaken the nation's position in negotiations with the United States over Panama three years later.[54]

In spite of the severe problems from which Colombia suffered in the late 1890s, war still might have been avoided had its top national leader been anyone other than Miguel Antonio Caro. Throughout the decade the Nationalist Party leader had insisted on the sort of tight hold on power that invariably produced grave political strife. In 1896 he attempted a ploy through which he could stand for reelection in 1898, without violating the constitutional ban on reelection. He resigned the presidency in favor of fellow party member Guillermo Quintero Calderón. But when Quintero had the audacity to name a Historical Conservative to his cabinet Caro sacked him and returned to the presidency, remarking that "one can't keep harmony among Catholics by naming Protestant cardinals."[55]

Next Caro hit upon the idea of naming presidential and vice presidential candidates for the 1898–1904 term whom he believed he could control. For president he chose an ailing eighty-four-year-old named Manuel Antonio Sanclemente, a man characterized by writer José María Vargas Vila as "a mummy covered with dust, though venerable."[56] His vice presidential nominee was Manuel Marroquín, a prominent Nationalist whose militant Catholicism had led Liberals to nickname him Torquemada. By Caro's plan, Marroquín would be acting president for the feeble Sanclemente, just has he, Caro, had been for Rafael Núñez.

Caro's plan miscarried soon after his candidates won the election of July 1898—a contest whose fairness can be gauged by the fact that the unpopular Nationalist ticket won overwhelmingly. As soon as Marroquín took over as acting president he began striking out on his own. First he abrogated the unpopular export tax on coffee, and moved toward guaranteeing political representation to Liberals. He then took steps toward abolishing the law depriving civil rights to persons suspected of subversion.[57] Caro moved quickly to rid himself of Marroquín, accomplishing this by forcing Sanclemente to assume his presidency. By November of 1898 the old man was installed in the presidential palace in Bogotá, and was assuring members of his party that he would do nothing to dismantle the edifice of Regeneration legislation. Looking back from a perspective of ten years, Rafael Uribe Uribe recalled that it was events like those—arrogant manipulation of national politics—that "blinded us and drove us to war."[58]

Once President Sanclemente tottered back into office, war preparations moved apace. Soon Sanclemente was gone again in search of a more salubrious climate. He left behind a rubber stamp made up in the likeness of his signature, for use by trusted underlings. All these things were especially disturbing to Historical Conservatives, whose earlier open letters of protest had played heavily on the theme of corruption under the Nationalists. It was widely known, for example, that one of the government's most lucrative monopolies, the salt mine at Zipaquirá, followed no set accounting procedures and in fact kept no books at all. Those abuses and many others would be held up for public ridicule in the novel *Pax,* written after the war by Lorenzo Marroquín, a Nationalist senator and son of the vice president.

Historical Conservatives such as Carlos Martínez Silva were so critical of the government in months just before war, that many Liberals believed the dissidents would join their revolt. A few Historicals did fight beside Liberals early in the conflict, and Historicals in the department of Santander signed an agreement of formal neutrality with Liberals, but most of them quickly fell in line with the government war effort. In November 1899, Peace Liberal Aquileo Parra voiced the feeling of Liberal and Conservative peace seekers when he wrote, "the torrent is dragging us, and it would be neither sensible nor patriotic to insist on opposing it."[59]

Surprisingly, the Liberals won the first engagement of the war, the Battle of Peralonso, fought in mid-December 1899. That victory raised the hopes of all who hoped for an early end to the war. Liberals in general, and Uribe Uribe in particular, hoped that Sanclemente might be willing to enter peace talks through which the Liberals might wring guarantees they had failed to win by peaceful means. When the president, during one of his increasingly rare lucid moments, rejected the overture, many of those interested in ending the war began plotting to overthrow him.

The coup of July 31, 1900, was chiefly the work of Historical Conservatives led by Carlos Martínez Silva, along with a scattering of Peace Liberals and Nationalists. According to their plan, Vice President Marroquín would assume the presidential chair, enter peace talks with the Liberals, and eventually reform the constitution as he had agreed to do late in 1898, when he was acting president. Unfortunately for the plotters, and for Colombia, the illegal change

3. Government soldiers during the War of the Thousand Days, circa 1901. By permission of the Museum of Modern Art, Bogotá.

of government went terribly wrong. Once the new president was in place, the pacific series of events it was supposed to set into motion never occurred. Rather, Marroquín vigorously prosecuted the war, which would continue, with increasing viciousness, for more than two additional years. The explanation of why this should be so is found both in the ideological character of Colombian partisan strife, and in the fact that Marroquín found a lieutenant capable of conducting the war with a single-mindedness that he himself lacked. That man was Aristides Fernández.

Aristides Fernández was a vigorous man of thirty-eight when fate determined that he should play a key role in the coup leading to Sanclemente's fall. At that moment he was director of Bogotá's police force, and it was his timely arrival with a squad of four hundred police, all pledged to support the Historicals, that convinced seventy-three-year-old Marroquín, at the time in hiding at a friend's house, that the coup would work. From that moment until the end of the war two years later, and for nearly a year after the war, Fernández would be Marroquín's alter ego, prosecuting the war with a vigor that made him feared by all Colombians and hated by Liberals.[60] Before his fall Aristides Fernández served the government as governor of Cundinamarca, minister of war, minister of state, and minister of finance. During early 1902 he held two of his ministerial posts simultaneously, one of few Colombians to have done so.

The rise of Fernández and his sudden eclipse in June 1903 tell much about Colombian politics and society at the dawn of the twentieth century. Under

4. Aristides Fernández, circa 1902. By permission of the Museum of Modern Art, Bogotá.

normal circumstances a man of Fernández's obscure origins never would have risen so high in government service. Ministry jobs were reserved for the wealthy and well born, or to those who had extraordinary intellectual ability as well as friends in high places. But the Athens of South America was a city under siege in July 1900, and it was organizational skill and ideological correctness that were most highly prized in government employees. Luckily for Fernández, he shared with Marroquín a loathing for liberalism and all it stood for. They were united in the conviction that public virtue, Christian Colombia, and all things good and pure were at stake in the war. They were one with José Vicente Concha, who early in the conflict had referred to it as a "Holy War," and with Bishop Ezequiel Moreno, who urged government soldiers, "Fight for our religion." Fernández employed that same language of Conservative extremism, saturated with the phraseology of papal encyclicals and given immediate reality and urgency by the Liberal foe. As he kept ferocious pressure on Liberal guerrillas in early 1902, Fernández told enthusiastic supporters in Bogotá that he intended to carry out a "prompt cauterizing of the wound" inflicted on Colombia by Liberalism, an "endemic disease . . . that corrodes and poisons the social organism."[61] Those ideals were acted upon in mid-1902, when Minister of War Fernández ordered government commanders to administer summary justice to Liberal prisoners. When Carlos Martínez Silva protested the executions to President Marroquín, in a letter of September 1902, Fernández did not hesitate to clap him in Bogotá's leprous prison, the Panóptico, along with Liberal Agustín Nieto and two other prominent Historicals.[62]

Marco Fidel Suárez called Fernández "no gentleman," and to Uribe Uribe he was a "national disgrace."[63] But that was precisely why he was so useful to President Marroquín, who by social convention could not have cruelly treated peers like Martínez Silva and Agustín Nieto. But there were no such linkages keeping Fernández from his duty to prosecute the war as he saw fit. Marroquín's merciless pursuer of Liberal revolutionaries was a man of premodern mentality. At a time when he could have become wealthy through war profiteering, as so many were doing around him, by means both legal and illegal, Fernández stole nothing. After the war and his disappearance from public life, he eked out a living selling dolls in a dilapidated shop in downtown Bogotá, eventually dying in utter misery.[64]

Perhaps the greatest tragedy of the war lay not in its immediate impact on Colombia, but in the way it politicized and radicalized the coming generation of national leaders. "The war was what taught me to hate," wrote Luis Eduardo Nieto Caballero, who turned thirteen just as the war entered its bloodiest stage. Nieto and his friends collected and traded cards, slips of paper, and even old banknotes bearing the likenesses of famous Liberal leaders of the past. Later he turned his collection into a mosaic mounted on a piece of cardboard, decorated it with a red ribbon, and put it in a place of honor, "like six or seven saints." During the first year of the war Nieto published a "newspaper," the proceeds from which he donated to the Liberal Party. That stopped suddenly when police came to his house and confiscated the offending documents.[65]

Alfonso López also published a secret Liberal newspaper during the war. He was arrested for it and hauled before Aristides Fernández, who freed him, but not before noting gloomily, "the youngster is already infected."[66]

The partisan loyalties of Laureano Gómez were also shaped by the war. For him Liberal armies were "bands of incendiaries and assassins who bloodied and razed the country."[67] Aristides Fernández had helped convince Gómez that was the case when he displayed three bodies of government soldiers mutilated by Liberal guerrillas across the street from San Bartolomé. On February 25, 1902, less than a week after Laureano Gómez turned thirteen, Fernández wrote a letter to Liberal General Juan MacAlister, in which he swore to begin executing Liberal prisoners held in the Panóptico unless several Conservative officers held by the Liberals were released. Gómez and his schoolmates applauded the action and even sent Fernández a letter congratulating him on his stand. Laureano Gómez greatly admired José Joaquín Casas, the man who replaced Fernández as minister of war shortly after the MacAlister incident. It was Casas who in October 1902 ordered the defeated Uribe Uribe subjected to a summary court martial and then shot "with no afterthought." The order was never carried out.[68] Still, by Gómez's view Casas was an effective minister of war whose energy was matched by his "perspicacity and clear vision."[69]

The War of the Thousand Days ended in the latter months of 1902, with the signing of two major peace treaties. General Uribe Uribe signed the first at a Dutch-owned banana plantation called Neerlandia, near the Atlantic coast. General Benjamín Herrera signed the second aboard the U.S. naval vessel *Wisconsin* anchored off the Panamanian city of Colón. Uribe Uribe had made the sacking of Fernández a central condition of his surrender, which had led Marroquín to temporarily retire his minister of war.[70] No one doubted, however, that it was Fernández whose draconian prosecution of the war drove the Liberals to the bargaining table. As writer Vargas Vila put it, "Fernández ended on the gallows the revolution that his generals had been incapable of ending on the battlefield. He hung it high on the gallows—the cadaver of the war that, through Rafael Uribe Uribe's ineptitude, had already been knifed in the fields of Neerlandia."[71]

Within a month of the war's end Aristides Fernández was back in the government. In a cabinet reorganization of January 1903, he was named minister of finance. Even as he struggled with national finances he joined with Minister of Education Casas in presenting an ultimatum to President Marroquín. The seven-point document represented the ministers' attempt to continue the proscription of Liberals into the postwar period. They backed their demands with the threat of their resignation from the government should it be refused. As both men had become something of a political liability to him, Marroquín accepted their resignations over the vehement protests of their supporters. Ten days later, on the first of June, he issued a decree ending the state of siege and declaring public order restored.[72]

In little more than two months after Marroquín's decree Colombia slipped into a new crisis. On August 10, the Colombian Senate rejected the proposed Hay-Herrán Treaty, under whose terms an interoceanic canal would be constructed across the Isthmus of Panama. Miguel Antonio Caro led senatorial forces opposing the agreement, in part out of the bitter enmity he felt for Marroquín. Events moved rapidly after the vote. Panamanian representatives to Congress returned home and joined others who were plotting secession from Colombia. On the second day of November 1903, Panama declared independence. Three days later the U.S. government, which had encouraged, then supported and assisted the revolution, extended recognition to the new nation. Colombia was able to do little more than protest, as U.S. gunboats effectively protected Panamanian sovereignty.

Bogotá was chaotic after noon on November 3, when telegrams arrived announcing the long-feared loss of Panama. Citizens of all ages and conditions filled the streets in the vain hope that something might be said or done to undo the dismemberment of their country. Many of them, like fourteen-year-old Laureano Gómez, wept with rage and begged to join any military expedition sent to recapture the breakaway department.[73] No such force was organized, as the government remained strangely inactive in the face of what most citizens regarded as a national tragedy.

More than twenty years later Laureano Gómez recounted what General Pedro Nel Ospina told him of his meeting with President Marroquín late that day. Like many others, Ospina went to the presidential palace to offer his services in retaking Panama. When the general arrived the building was dark and deserted. Passing from one room to another he at last came upon the president sitting under one of the incandescent bulbs recently installed in the building, reading a French novel. Marroquín looked up, smiled, and said "Oh, Pedro Nel, every bad thing brings something good. We've lost Panama, but I have the pleasure of seeing you again in this house!"[74] It was clear to Ospina that the president, now in his seventy-seventh year, would do nothing to end the rebellion in Panama.

José Manuel Marroquín left no record of that meeting with Pedro Nel Ospina. But there can be no doubt that his apparent lack of concern over events of the day and his outwardly cheerful demeanor masked unhappiness and resignation, and quite possibly a degree of sardonic satisfaction. His six years in high office had been neither pleasant nor easy. Still he had managed to win the nation's worst, most prolonged civil war, thus preserving Christian Colombia. His tribulations had begun in 1896, when as vice president, Miguel Antonio Caro had tried to make him his puppet. Not happy with Marroquín's attempt to placate the Liberals and thus avoiding war, Caro sacked him in a preemptory and humiliating way. Next came the Historical Conservatives, asking for his help. They too wanted to make him their instrument in ending a war that they themselves, through their scheming with the Liberals, had helped start. And when he, Marroquín, resolved to win the war, the same faction that brought him to power attempted to pull him down by way of yet another coup. Carlos Martínez Silva was the ringleader of both the successful and illegal coup of July 31, 1900, and of the unsuccessful and also illegal coup attempt of August 31, 1901.

In spite of all that, Marroquín had the forbearance and good sense to make Martínez Silva head of the diplomatic mission charged with negotiating a Panama canal treaty with the United States. But again Martínez Silva overstepped his authority, entering negotiations with General Uribe Uribe, who was living in New York City at the time.[75] Was it his fault, then, that he was forced to relieve Martínez Silva of his duties at the most crucial moment in negotiations with Secretary of State Hay, forcing him to send José Vicente Concha to replace him—a man who knew little about what had been transpiring and who didn't even speak English? At the moment of Martínez Silva's indiscretion Liberal guerrillas were staging raids on the outskirts of Bogotá, committing atrocities with their machetes, as Minister of War Fernández so vividly revealed. Wasn't it poetic justice that Carlos Martínez Silva ran afoul of Fernández soon after his return to Colombia? His imprisonment and exile did hasten his death. But even so, that spared Martínez the anguish of seeing the treaty he should have negotiated overwhelmingly defeated in the Senate.[76]

And what of Miguel Antonio Caro's campaign against the treaty? The Hay-Herrán agreement was a bad one, no one doubted that. But no one doubted the might of the United States either, or that Colombia might well lose Panama should Congress reject the agreement. Still that didn't stop Caro from carrying out his vendetta against him, Marroquín. "And finally, General Ospina," Marroquín may have thought, glancing up from his novel, "here you stand before me with eyes that damn me as a doddering old man who allowed the fatherland to be diminished—you who plotted against me in 1901 with Martínez Silva, suffering exile as a result; you who bear as much blame for these recent dreadful events as I. So now Colombia is one province smaller. Am I responsible for that?"

3

Reyes and Republicanism

Aftermath

Immediately after the civil war, Colombia's economy was a shambles, the vast majority of its people were sunk in poverty, disease, and ignorance, and its leaders were full of a complex mix of self-loathing, frustration, anger, and embarrassment. The war's immediate impact was staggering: perhaps as many as a hundred thousand of the nation's young men lay dead, burned out and abandoned buildings filled the countryside, and farmers' fields were invaded by weeds. The loss of Panama, coming just a few months after the war's formal conclusion, compounded national anguish.

Miseries of the postwar period were heightened by the negative image of Colombia abroad. At the London stock exchange Colombia's name figured prominently on the list of countries in default on foreign loans, and at the Paris Exhibition of 1901 a great world map showed Colombia in yellow, signifying that it was the world's most leprous nation.[1] It was an unenviable distinction, owed to the fact that the leprosarium at Agua de Dios had ceased to function, driving thousands of inmates into towns and cities, where they lived in the streets as beggars. Liberal newspaperman Luis Cano spoke for most of his countrymen when he cursed the circumstances that made his country "vile through corruption, and a beggar by ineptitude, waste and impropriety."[2] Conservative Hernando Martínez Santamaría blamed the war for ruining Colombia's image before "the civilized nations of the world."[3]

Over the thousand days of warfare living conditions had deteriorated at every level of society. Formerly affluent families sank into "genteel poverty," while the masses experienced poverty best described as grinding. Food was in short supply everywhere, and a staggering degree of ill health afflicted the general population. Infant mortality in Bogotá was 25 percent, a rate likely equaled elsewhere in the country. Average life expectancy hovered somewhere around thirty years.[4] Along with leprosy, elephantiasis was endemic, and epidemics of waterborne and communicable diseases periodically swept towns and cities. In Bogotá, where the population had grown but little in fifteen years, 675 persons died of typhoid fever in 1905 alone. Physicians estimated that during the great typhoid epidemic of 1908–1909, as many as 2 percent of the city's entire population succumbed to the disease.[5] The better-educated improved their chances of survival by filtering drinking water through pumice stone and then boiling it. The poor often did neither. Compounding the problem of public health in turn-of-the-century Colombia was the fact that most people did not know what made them sick. Antiseptic procedures weren't generally practiced in hospitals, and there was not even a bacteriological laboratory in Colombia until 1905. Indicative of the generalized ignorance of sanitary procedures was the fact that an estimated 70 percent of the young men in Colombia's capital had, in the words of physician José Lombana Barreneche, "experienced the baptism of syphilis."[6] It scarcely need be added that the harsh social conditions insured the availability of prostitutes to administer the carnal rite.

Adding to the miserable aspect of urban Colombia at war's end, and helping explain the disastrous state of public health, was the breakdown of the sanitation service. Residents of Bogotá described the city as "drowning" in uncollected refuse, and "in a state of sanitary collapse."[7] Bogotanos continued to dispose of night soil in open sewers, causing a Cuban visitor to accuse the Colombian capital of smelling like "an unburied cadaver."[8] Come nightfall people locked themselves in their houses, leaving the dark streets virtually deserted. Nor was there much vehicular movement during daylight hours. British visitor Francis Loraine Petre noted that one could walk through Bogotá's streets at any hour with little danger of being run over, "as the President, the Archbishop and a half-dozen others are the only owners of private carriages."[9] Bogotanos of all classes picked their way along muddy streets, the better-off wearing raincoats and carrying umbrellas to defend themselves against water splashed by passing horsemen.

Conditions were no better in the countryside, where most Colombians lived at war's end. Agriculture and cattle raising were significantly disorganized by the years of guerrilla warfare, and many coffee plantations established during the 1890s were bankrupt. Problems in the countryside were compounded by landowners who attempted to reestablish their fortunes at the expense of workers. In the coffee lands of western Cundinamarca employers recruited labor in other departments, especially Boyacá, and then reneged on contracts. By 1906 a magistrate in the coffee zone reported an alarming level of demoralization among contract workers manifested in the stream of complaints issuing from the coffee haciendas.[10]

The disruption of agriculture had produced sharp increases in food costs. In Bogotá there was a sixfold price increase between 1898 and 1901, and another threefold increase by 1904.[11] Deterioration of the nation's transportation network was partly to blame. Between 1895 and 1903 railroads and riverboats increased charges thirty-seven and twenty-seven times, respectively. And all important mule transportation increased in cost fifty-six times. Meanwhile real wages fell by a third, not to regain their pre–civil war level until twelve years afterward.[12] The sad state of Colombia's highways is suggested in an account of travel on the Honda-Bogotá road during 1905. Petre recalled his fright when approaching "a pool of liquid mud" blocking one portion of the trail—which at the time was the Colombian capital's chief link with the outside world. His animal sank to its withers; other riders sank nearly out of sight in similar mud holes.[13]

Problems of transportation effectively blocked national unification well into the 1920s. The rich Río Cauca valley, to cite but the most prominent example, could be reached from the Río Magdalena only after a hellish four-day journey over one of two routes spanning the central cordillera. A surveying team traveled the northernmost pass, the Quindío route, linking Cartago on the western side with Ibagué on the east, in 1910. Its leader, one Dr. Luis Garzón Nieto, described the trail as "a graveyard of men and animals." Over a single four-kilometer stretch he counted nineteen carcasses of animals that had "slipped over enormous slopes, losing themselves and their packs." He concluded that the Quindío trail was "an absurdity for the entire length," recommending that an entirely new road be surveyed and constructed.[14]

Chaos in Colombia's financial markets accompanied deterioration of the country's physical infrastructure. On October 16, 1899, the government decreed the mandatory acceptance of paper currency, and then proceeded to print an immense number of banknotes with which it financed the war effort. By war's end inflation had soared above 20,000 percent. On one occasion the omnivorous government printing presses turned out currency printed on paper intended as candy wrappers.[15] Bad money drove out the good, as it was declared illegal to trade in hard currency. In 1905, Francis Petre claimed not to have seen a single silver or gold coin in use anywhere in the country.[16] Very few businessmen did well during the war. Some of them, like Antioquian entrepreneur José María "Pepe" Sierra, increased their fortunes by assisting the government finance effort. Others, like businessman Pedro A. López, a Liberal, simply fled Colombia. López managed to convert his assets to gold and U.S. dollars early in the conflict. Those forced to remain coped as best they could. Bankers rented strongrooms for storage of the growing stacks of bank notes. Speculation in the wildly inflating currency became the only means of self-defense for many entrepreneurs who by late 1902 borrowed money at high rates of interest on the assumption that inflation would rise from 22,500 percent to 30,000 or even 40,000 percent. Many of them were ruined when rates dropped to 9,500 percent with the declaration of peace in mid-1903.[17]

Speculators bought gold, silver, and even coffee on credit, earning money as the currency inflated, and in Antioquia banks were founded specifically to serve businessmen involved in currency speculation. Deposits were accepted at 5 percent interest per month, and lent at 10 percent. Such was the fragile state of Colombia's economy at war's end that all but one Medellín bank failed in the brief financial crisis of 1904.[18]

Many rural-dwelling Colombians fell back on primitive forms of barter. Salaried urban dwellers frequently made ends meet by selling their future salaries for ready cash. During those years of war-induced austerity, when governments could rarely pay their civil servants on time, it was a common sight in Medellín and other cities to see signs proclaiming "Paychecks Purchased Here," and "Checks Cashed."[19]

Antioquia, a department relatively unscathed by the fighting, and renowned for the energy and entrepreneurial talent of its people, was brought to a standstill during and immediately after the war. Its capital, Medellín, described in 1883 as one of the richest towns in South America in proportion to its population, increased in size but 26 percent over the sixteen years between 1889 and 1905.[20] Two of Colombia's future industrial giants, the Cervecería Antioqueña (Antioquian brewery) and the Compañía Antioqueña de Tejidos (Antioquian textile company) were launched in 1901 and failed three years later, in the financial crisis of 1904. Labor organization was so rudimentary as to be nonexistent. The Artisans' Society of Sonsón, Antioquia, founded in 1903, was one of the first legally recognized labor unions in Colombia. But it hardly perceived its mission as that of fighting for wage increases and improved working conditions. Rather, its stated goals were to lead processionals in honor of Our Lady of the Sacred Heart, to buy medicines for sick members, and to pay for "a first-class funeral for deceased associates."[21] Given the fact that health conditions in Antioquia were no better than those in other parts of the nation, services provided by the Sonsón union were doubtless appropriate to the time and place.

While the period from 1902 to 1903 marked the nadir of Colombia's national existence, there were signs that the nation would surely recover. In December 1902, General Rafael Uribe Uribe pronounced the War of the Thousand Days Colombia's last such conflict, adding that he had learned a bitter lesson from it. That same month, and in charming counterpart to Uribe Uribe's remark, José Joaquín Casas, the man who so recently had ordered the Liberal commander's summary execution, inaugurated Colombia's new Academy of History. Early in 1903 public schools were reopened by presidential decree, and the schools of mathematics, engineering, and medicine at the National University were also reopened. The latter facility had been closed by Aristides Fernández in 1901, because most of its students sympathized with the revolution.[22] Elsewhere the Colombian Geographic Society was founded, and at the Jesuit high school a precocious fifth-year student named Laureano Gómez founded a literary magazine called *El Ateneo de miscelánea* (Atheneum of miscellany). And far away in Medellín, Antioquian millionaire Carlos C. Amador astounded the locals with a marvelous invention imported from France shortly before the war. It was called an automobile, and came complete with a French chauffeur and a French mechanic.[23]

Colombia's position in 1903 was, in short, anomalous. The small number of non-Latin Americans who knew anything about the country regarded it with a mixture of scorn and amusement. A North American engineer, when asked why he had named his new locomotive the *Colombia,* replied that it was for the unprecedented number of revolutions per minute generated by its drive wheels. Colombians viewed themselves as possessing "the weakness of convalescents," and complained that at the dawn of the new century theirs was "the only country in which foreign capital had not penetrated."[24] The perception was accurate. Foreigners had little reason to invest in Colombia as the country promised little return for their money. Figured on a per capita basis, Colombia's exports were among the world's lowest, just 20 percent that of Argentina's, Brazil's, and Peru's, and one-third that of Mexico's.[25]

In spite of their unhappiness over Colombia's dire condition in the aftermath of its recent civil war, Colombian leaders were united in the belief that the country could and would progress if the proper man were placed in charge. The new president must be vigorous, familiar with the economic forces transforming the world at that time, and must be independent of the political cliques responsible for ruining the nation. They found their man in fifty-four-year-old Rafael Reyes, who had made his fortune in business before being drawn into warfare and politics, and who had spent some of the previous ten years representing Colombia in Europe and elsewhere. Once Reyes was elected president and sworn into office, it seemed to most Colombians that the choice had been a good one. To newspaperman Eduardo Santos it appeared that once Reyes took office "the entire nation, with childlike simplicity, surrendered itself to him."[26]

The Quinquenio

Rafael Reyes, whose five years in power are remembered as the Quinquennium (Quinquenio), was inaugurated in Bogotá on August 7, 1904. Reyes was a Conservative, like José Manuel Marroquín, whom he replaced as president, and Miguel Antonio Caro, then leader of the Nationalist Conservative majority in congress. Like them he was from Colombia's interior highlands, born in the town of Santa Rosa de Viterbo, some 200 kilometers north of Bogotá. But there similarities ceased. Whereas Caro and Marroquín were erudite men who moved easily if not happily within the narrow world of Colombian high politics, Reyes was an outsider. His formal education was rudimentary, as he left home at seventeen to join three elder brothers in a family export business. By the time of his inauguration Reyes had made many trips abroad, both in connection with the family business and later as a representative of his government. He had spent years exploring great stretches of Colombia's Amazonian watershed, had commanded troops in the field during two civil wars, and had been active in national government in numerous capacities. He was a family man with grandchildren, and, most important, retained the ebullience and enthusiasm that had characterized all his actions. He was, in short, the antithesis of the dour intellectual whom he succeeded in the presidential chair.

Reyes was hardly the stereotypic native of Boyacá. He was in fact spiritually akin to the Antioquian entrepreneurs who risked capital and personal well-being in the search for opportunities outside their home state. While still in his teens, Reyes joined his brothers Elías, Enrique, and Néstor in gathering quinine from the tropical forests of southern Colombia. When the international quinine market crashed in the early 1880s, he and his brothers extended operations eastward into jungles of the Putumayo and the Amazon, where they challenged Peruvian interests for control of the region's supply of natural rubber. Unluckily the new venture did not flourish. By the mid-1880s, Elías, Enrique, Néstor, and a thousand other company employees had succumbed to the rigors of life in that isolated region, and the business foundered.[27]

Still Reyes had managed to survive and had through his talent for self-promotion even caught the eye of Rafael Núñez. In Reyes the president knew he had just the sort of man who might be able to wrest the state of Panama from Liberal rebels who had seized it during the civil war of 1885. Reyes succeeded against stiff odds, earning praise from Núñez as "the conqueror of the impossible." Subsequently the president dispatched him to the United States and to Europe on political and economic missions, and later called on him to put down the Liberal uprising of 1895, which he did in an exemplary way. Outbreak of the War of the Thousand Days found him in Paris on government business. By then he was a widower, suffering early effects of a malady that would eventually leave his left arm paralyzed. When Secretary of War Guillermo Valencia suggested that he might again be called to active service, Reyes refused, saying, "Tell them that I'm not a pump for putting out fires!"[28] Thus it was that in 1904 Reyes could run for president as a military hero, but one not associated with the terrible conflict just ended.

Members of Colombia's Conservative elite were not happy with the Reyes candidacy. Nationalist leader Caro, who had never liked Reyes, was fond of repeating an admonition reportedly uttered by Rafael Núñez: "Woe to Colombia should Reyes take power." His party's candidate in the 1904 campaign, Joaquín F. Vélez, warned that once in office Reyes would impose a dictatorship similar to the one Porfirio Díaz had by then maintained in Mexico for more than twenty years.[29] Meanwhile Miguel Antonio Caro tried to feed fears of a Reyes dictatorship. "Watch out," he said publicly, "that man is dangerous now that he comes from Mexico. . . ."[30] Historical Conservatives had not trusted Reyes since 1898, when they put him forward as their presidential candidate. Just two days before the election a letter was circulated in which Reyes admitted he was not a Historical. The Historicals and their hastily fielded substitute candidate went on to lose badly to the Sanclemente-Marroquín ticket.

Opposition from both Conservative factions increased subsequent to the election when it was learned that Reyes had defeated Nationalist candidate Vélez thanks only to fraudulent returns in a remote part of the country. Established politicians became frantic when, a month before his inauguration, the president-elect appeared before congress requesting authorization to impose new taxes, raise customs revenues, create a central bank, reorganize the national bureaucracy, and change territorial divisions.[31] The Senate responded by making Joaquín F. Vélez its president. Vélez, still smarting from his defeat, refused to administer the presidential oath, a function normally performed by leader of the Senate.

August 7, 1904 was a doubly gloomy day in Colombian history. The country remained prostrate, and a hostile Congress glared at the new chief executive as Chamber of Deputies president José Vicente Concha administered the oath of office to him. In his preliminary remarks Concha lamented Colombia's history of narrow partisanship whose end result was invariably "to deepen the abyss of general misery."[32] Reyes responded in like terms. "I am certain that we've reached the low point of our calamities," he said, going on to lament Colombia's inability even to defend her national territory, a state of affairs that had led to the perfidious stripping away "of one of the nation's most important departments." Even worse, he continued, "as we were considered people of an inferior civilization . . . the crime was not merely allowed and sanctioned [by other nations], but was considered a transcendent service to universal civilization." The new president concluded by pledging to preserve order and to do his best in carrying forward the work of national reconstruction.[33]

The only levity in an otherwise somber ceremony was provided after the speech by members of the Nationalist caucus. They laughed over the fact that Reyes had not written his inaugural address, entrusting the task to his nephew Clímaco Calderón Reyes. When one congressman expressed his belief that Reyes was half crazy, Miguel Antonio Caro responded, "Then he's improved!"[34]

Congress was determined to block Reyes's ambitious program of national rejuvenation. Its members were further scandalized when the new president included two Liberals in his cabinet, making it one of Colombia's few bipartisan cabinets since that of Manuel María Mallarino, fifty years earlier. Another of Reyes's early acts was to convene a new consultative body that would meet with him regularly to discuss national problems. Liberals were included in that body, which bore the sonorous name Junta of Notables. Reyes's inclusion of Liberals in his government especially infuriated intransigent Conservatives who favored proscribing all members of the enemy party.

Regional economic interests also generated congressional opposition to Reyes and his legislative program. Colombia was very much a nation of loosely united regions in 1904, a fact most clearly revealed in the economic realm. As Reyes attempted to rejuvenate national finances, he found himself in competition with local leaders, such as Antioquian businessman and politician Pedro Nel Ospina, who were equally interested in promoting the development of their home departments. Thus, as Reyes's biographer Eduardo Lemaitre put it, the president's ambitious program to raise moneys for his government, often at the expense of the departments, crystallized the "authentically democratic" and "republican" opposition aimed at blocking his project.[35]

In early October 1904, Reyes appeared before Congress to again request enabling legislation for his reform package. Subsequently he sent written messages to the body urging it to act. On October 19, he again appealed personally to the body. But no congressional action was forthcoming. By early December members of the tiny Liberal minority were berating their Conservative colleagues. Antonio José Restrepo, a prominent Antioquian Liberal, wished good fortune to any national leader who might start "looking toward other horizons." Rafael Uribe Uribe was more explicit. On December 3, 1904, he openly promised to support Reyes should he decide to seize the power needed to implement his reforms.[36] Three days later handbills appeared in the streets of the capital denouncing the "do-nothing" Congress, and five days after that Reyes received two letters. The first was from the president of the Chamber of Representatives, Dionisio Arango, complaining of an ongoing lack of a quorum in his body, and the other was from poet Guillermo Valencia, reminding the president that "since the time of Cromwell governments have rented the houses of hostile parliamentarians." The following day Reyes dissolved Congress and sent telegrams to all parts of the nation requesting support for his action.[37] Five days later, on December 18, another handbill was posted in the streets of Bogotá. It bore the title "A Necessary Explanation," and stated in detail the reasons for congressional opposition to the president, and was signed by twenty-two congressmen, most of them Historical Conservatives. Reyes, buoyed by the outpouring of support for his suspension of Congress, blasted the signatories as "obstructionists and rebellious criminals." Citing one of his own presidential decrees, he threatened any of them who did not publicly denounce the "Necessary Explanation" with exile to the tropical eastern llanos. Half of them refused to do so and soon found themselves on the way to the llanos under military guard.[38] Reyes's acts of late 1904 were illegal under Colombian law, as were many others that he undertook until his ouster in mid-1909. But at the outset most Colombians applauded his taking decisive charge of the nation's recovery. Prominent members of both Conservative factions supported him. Guillermo Valencia, a Historical, was an early supporter, as was Nationalist Marco Fidel Suárez. Liberals were of course enthusiastic supporters of the Conservative president, who, in the colorful phrase of Juan E. Manrique, "placed himself opportunely between the whips of the victors and the backs of the vanquished." General Benjamín Herrera was especially grateful to Reyes for "allowing the Liberals to breathe" for the first time since the Regeneration. He went so far as to call Reyes "the best leader Colombia has had after [Manuel] Murillo Toro."[39]

The groundswell of popular support that Rafael Reyes rode for nearly five years was merely one aspect of a mood dominant throughout the Western world at that time. Since the era of Bismarck nationalists had endorsed benevolent despotism when exercised for the benefit of the fatherland. During the Reyes years in Colombia the example of Germany's late Iron Chancellor continued to instruct the leaders of major European powers. Over both American continents Reyes-like strongmen demonstrated how modernization could be hurried when leaders did not allow themselves to be hobbled by juridic or ethical preconceptions. At the moment Reyes took power in Colombia the Argentines were bidding farewell to their twice president General Julio Roca, "Conqueror of the Desert," so named for opening the pampas to settlement by liquidating the indigenous peoples who had lived there. The Brazilians basked in an era of "order and progress" made possible just a decade earlier when General Floriano Peixoto, "Consolidator of the Republic," overthrew Emperor Pedro II. Porfirio Díaz was at the pinnacle of his prestige in Mexico—Rafael Reyes returned from touring Mexico and meeting personally with Díaz in 1903, full of admiration for his achievements there. But he was less fulsome in his praise of the Mexican dictator than was U.S. Secretary of State Elihu Root, who in 1907 called Díaz "one of the great men to be held up for the hero worship of mankind!" And in the United States Theodore Roosevelt captured the imagination of his own people through his exploits in Cuba, his creation of a first-rate navy for the country, and of course, for his taking of Panama from Colombia.

Reyes, Peixoto, Díaz, and other Latin American leaders of their era were not simply romantic figures who dazzled and intimidated the rest through their charisma and their willingness to deal harshly with anyone who opposed them. Their actions were in fact endorsed and supported by members of their respective intellectual establishments who took the position that their societies required centralized governments headed by strong chief executives if they were to catch up with Europe and the United States. Basing their arguments in the positivism of Auguste Comte and the biological determinism of Herbert Spencer, they reasoned that their peoples had not trod far enough along the evolutionary path to make self-rule work. Intellectuals such as Mexican positivist Emilio Rabasa believed that radical liberals erred when they wrote democratic constitutions that tied their leaders' hands. To Rabasa, their experiments were based in what he called "unworkable, unrealistic sociological law."[40]

Rafael Uribe Uribe was one of those who helped Reyes justify his movement to authoritarian rule. As Reyes was beginning to appreciate that he would never achieve his goals through democratic means, Uribe Uribe made a speech arguing persuasively for strong state intervention in national affairs. Using the analogy of Holland's successful battle to push back the sea, he argued that the central government was the only institution powerful enough to save Colombia from the two forces that thwarted progress, "barbarism and the jungle." Who will defend us from the two? he asked. He answered his own question: "the state, the only true power," he said, would bring progress to benighted Colombia. Uribe Uribe went on to outline a variety of elite-directed programs of national betterment that he referred to as "state socialism."[41]

Once political control was in his hands, Reyes acted quickly. On the first of February he instructed governors of departments, all of whom were his appointees, to name representatives to a new National Assembly. One-third of them were to be Liberals. The body commenced its meetings in Bogotá six weeks later, on March 15, 1905. The puppet body would meet annually from that time until March 1909, when popular pressure forced Reyes's resignation and brought about his subsequent self-imposed exile from Colombia on June 13, 1909.

Between its initial meeting in mid-March 1905, and its adjournment six weeks later, the National Assembly created by Reyes approved a package of constitutional amendments giving the president the power he sought. Among the measures were provisions weakening Colombia's supreme court, allowing the president to convene and dismiss Congress at will, ending restrictions on the president's power to tax, providing for the expropriation of private property in case of public need, removing certain constitutional safeguards of regional interests, and allowing the president to change internal departmental boundaries. One of the last laws was a provision guaranteeing the Liberal Party one-third of the seats in all elected bodies. Shortly before the National Assembly ended its 1905 session on the last day of April, grateful Liberals joined their Conservative colleagues in extending Reyes's term in office an additional four years, to December 31, 1914. The body adjourned after a mere forty-seven days, during which it gave juridic sanction to Colombia's new status as an authoritarian state. "Never in our parliamentary annals has greater harmony existed between the executive and legislative powers," was José Joaquín Guerra's ironic assessment of the Quinquenio period. The same thing must have occurred to Manuel Dávila Flores, Abadía Méndez, and Sotero Peñuela as they straggled back into Bogotá following their brief exile in the eastern llanos.

Early in 1905 Reyes began a frenzy of activity that would not diminish until his fall from power, four years later. As his most pressing needs lay in the area of fiscal affairs he undertook a variety of measures aimed at improving Colombian finances. Tariff duties on agricultural and other exports were raised to 70 percent, paper currency was destroyed until the ratio of paper to gold reached 100 to 1 (down from 10,000 to 1), a bank was founded and given broad powers in the area of revenue raising, and General Jorge Holguín was dispatched to London to inform foreign investors that his nation was putting its financial house in order.

Reyes's fiscal initiatives met with quick and gratifying success. Government revenues first doubled, then tripled. Inflation ended and the nation's foreign debt was paid off during 1907, resulting in Colombia's name being removed from the list of delinquent debtor nations posted at the London Stock Exchange.[42] Colombian bonds, which had earlier sold in London for as little as 14 percent of face value, were selling at 46 percent by 1906. That was owed to the repayment of a substantial portion of the foreign debt earlier that year. By Reyes's fall in 1909 an estimated $3 million worth of foreign capital had been invested in the country.[43] A few foreign companies began operations in Colombia, most notable among them the United Fruit Company of Boston, which responded to Reyes's invitation by opening banana plantations in the northern part of the country.

The government's fiscal program also spurred industrial and agricultural development. Reyes's tariff on imported cloth insured that Medellín's infant textile business would prosper. It is significant that entrepreneurs like future national president Pedro Nel Ospina clearly perceived the benefits both of protection and of government intervention on behalf of the economy at large. Before the Quinquenio ended grateful owners of a successful sugar refinery spontaneously repaid all subsidies that the government had awarded it.[44] The Reyes program set Colombian manufacturing on a course of steady growth that it would maintain for the next two decades.

Export agriculture, especially coffee, benefited under Reyes. Growers had become so prosperous by 1907 that they asked the president to take the one gold peso per hundredweight bounty on coffee previously awarded to them and use it to improve transportation on the Río Magdalena.[45] Aware of the potential profit in coffee, and of its importance to national growth, Reyes awarded ten million hectares of the national domain to domestic capitalists, who agreed to colonize it and bring it into production.[46]

Reyes spent a great deal of the money he raised in improving the nation's ever problematic system of transportation. One of his first acts was to set 4,000 laborers working on the Northern Highway, extending from Bogotá toward Boyacá. Before he left office Reyes had the pleasure of driving his new Cadillac along the 200-kilometer stretch whose terminus was his own home-town of Santa Rosa de Viterbo, more than half the distance to Bucaramanga. He had to thus cut travel time from five days to one. Great money and effort were lavished on the country's rail system. By the end of his regime Reyes had increased railway mileage by 50 percent above what it was when he took office. Most significant, he succeeded in completing the link between the na-tional capital and the Magdalena, something Colombian leaders had been trying to do for more than twenty years. Also important in a country where the overwhelming majority of freight was hauled by animals, Reyes improved many kilometers of existing mule trails and had 780 kilometers of new routes built.

The government spent money on and otherwise encouraged a variety of social and civic improvements. During Reyes's term of office Bogotá and Cartagena witnessed the construction of new water systems. The leper colony at Agua de Dios (Cundinamarca) was put back into operation, and two addi-tional facilities were established in other parts of the country. Two previously neglected groups, women and workers, found their educational needs ad-dressed during the Quinquenio. Reyes brought French nuns of the Sacred Heart of Jesus to open the country's first girls' colegio; he promoted evening vocational courses for workers, and oversaw the founding of a business school as well. Marco Fidel Suárez wrote approvingly of the new parks and streets that the dictator had constructed, as well of the hippodrome he had built for automobile races. Suárez also approved of Reyes's use of public moneys to refurbish the Palacio de San Carlos, as well as for rebuilding the Palacio de la Carrera. Manuel Zamora, author of a city directory published in 1907, noted "a great profusion of carriages circulating through all the streets and, along with automobiles, [taking passengers] to neighboring towns. The city also has a perfectly established street railway system."[47]

Rafael Reyes's administration was especially notable for the extent that new interests became directly involved with the business of government. Within three days of the new president's inauguration, his Liberal treasury minister, Lucas Caballero, called together fifty businessmen and charged them with initiating a national-level Chamber of Commerce. The president himself orga-nized a Society of Coffee Producers, which later became the semiofficial Soci-ety of Colombian Agriculturalists. Hardly one to sit in a solitary office reading

5. Bogotá's Calle Real, circa 1905. (Note streetcar tracks.) By permission of the Museum of Modern Art, Bogotá.

novels, as had his predecessor Marroquín, Reyes filled his workdays with an endless stream of meetings and presidential decrees and directives. Historian Humberto Vélez estimates that during his term of office Reyes granted 11,550 audiences with individuals and groups—some fifteen per day. He met with his cabinet 324 times, formulated 4,742 decrees and 1,316 presidential and fiscal accords, and dispatched 58,750 telegrams.[48]

The president's management style is suggested in an incident said to have taken place in connection with his controversial Central Bank and its equally controversial director Pepe Sierra. When the Bogotá newspaper *El Nuevo Tiempo* attacked Sierra for his handling of the bank, the wealthy *paisa* threatened to resign his directorship. Reyes summoned the paper's editor, Ismael Enrique Arciniegas, to his office, shouted at him and waved his fist under the newspaperman's nose. It was rumored that Reyes also laid hands on Arciniegas and tried to throw him over a balcony and into the patio of the presidential mansion. Meanwhile Pepe Sierra supposedly listened to the exchange in an adjoining room.[49]

However successful Rafael Reyes was in reviving Colombia after its recent war, his tenure in office could never have approached the thirty-five years that

Porfirio Díaz enjoyed in Mexico, or even the eight years that strongman Cipriano Castro had just completed in neighboring Venezuela. Colombians, unlike many other Latin Americans, had a history of not tolerating arbitrary rule for very long. By 1908, Reyes had offended so many of his countrymen that his hold on power had grown tenuous. His attack on departmental prerogatives, especially his nationalization of departmental liquor, tobacco, and other monopolies, infuriated regional elites. The president had struck hard at the regions in 1905 by creating six new departments and a federal district. By 1908 he had created an additional eighteen new departments, bringing the total number to thirty-four—up from the nine that had existed when he entered office.[50] Antioquia alone was metamorphosed from one to five departments. In part because of that, the rich province became the focus of antigovernment opposition. In March 1908, 250 influential paisas, led by businessman Carlos E. Restrepo, founded the Republican Union movement. It quickly became the chief mechanism for aggregating and channeling opposition to the regime in Bogotá. Motivated as well by moral considerations, Republicans also made much of the nepotism and corruption that flourished under Reyes's rule.[51]

For years the enemies of Reyes had tried to get rid of him by illegal means. By 1908 the president had survived two major coup attempts and three plots on his life. Reyes had also confronted a bizarre scheme through which conspirators in Antioquia, Cauca, and Atlantic coast departments plotted to join Panama in forming a new state to be called the Isthmian Republic.[52] The most celebrated attempt to assassinate Reyes came on February 10, 1906. Three men fired on his carriage as it traveled through Bogotá's northern outskirts. Miraculously, they missed both Reyes and his daughter, who accompanied him at the time. When the three men were captured, along with an accomplice, Reyes had them tried and sentenced to death by firing squad. The four executions, illegal under Colombian law—doubly so, as both Reyes and his daughter were uninjured—were conducted publicly as a none-too-subtle exercise in Victorian morality. Official photographers recorded the spectacle, which was carried out at the site of the attack, as a large select audience, prisoners from the nearby Panóptico, looked on with horror.[53]

It was neither assassination, arbitrary executions, nor regional opposition that brought Reyes down. Rather, it was a series of crises centering on Colombia's growing involvement with the United States. First in the chain of events was a financial panic of 1907 affecting New York and London banks—the so-called rich man's crisis. As well as helping drive coffee prices down, the economic downturn caused Jorge Holguín to fail in his attempts to negotiate new loans in London. That moved Reyes, desperate for money to finance his development programs, to take two ill-advised steps. First he sent Laureano García Ortiz to negotiate the leasing of government emerald mines to a foreign consortium, which García Ortiz succeeded in doing just before Christmas 1908.[54] At the same time he urged his foreign minister, Enrique Cortés, to continue negotiations with the Americans to the end of reestablishing good relations with the wealthy nation. Cortés's success in signing a treaty in January 1909, the so-called tripartite agreement, sparked a series of angry public debates. They followed Republican Union member Nicolás Esguerra's angry letter to the National Assembly, in which he argued that the body had no constitutional power to approve treaties. It was soon revealed that in exchange for $2.5 million, to be paid in equal installments over ten years, Colombia would pledge peace and friendship to both the United States and Panama.[55]

In mid-March 1909, student demonstrations erupted in Bogotá, leading Reyes to resign the presidency in favor of his minister of the interior, Jorge Holguín. Angered and disconcerted by continued demonstrations, and a few scattered incidents of stone throwing, Reyes reassumed power almost immediately and quashed the demonstrators. But Reyes knew public opinion ran heavily against him. On June 4, 1909, the president and his family boarded the train for Girardot, en route, so the president said, to a tour of the coastal departments. Pausing briefly in Puerto Wilches to confer with his former vice president Ramón González Valencia, Reyes continued on to Barranquilla, where a gala was scheduled in his honor on June 13. Late on the thirteenth, as the orchestra played and dignitaries glanced nervously at their watches, Rafael Reyes and his family slipped out to sea on a freighter owned by the United Fruit Company. Reyes would never again play a significant role in Colombian politics. The Quinquenio was ended.

Gómez Commences

Colombia's "March Days" of 1909 were doubly significant in the country's political history. They not only hastened the demise of Reyes's Quinquenio, but they also announced that a new political generation had come of age. The college students who successfully challenged the dictator first called themselves Trecemarcistas (March thirteenth-ers), but soon exchanged the cumbersome nickname for the more sonorous Generation of the Centenary. Because their political maturity coincided with the bipartisan Republican Union movement, whose leaders filled the political void left by Reyes, it seemed for a while that the Centenarians might succeed in bridging the ideological chasm that had divided their mentors. As it turned out, the Centenarians could no more unlearn the great truths of Colombian Liberalism and Conservatism so recently instilled in them and underlined in blood during the War of the Thousand Days than could their elders make Republicanism a viable alternative to the violent partisanship that had prevailed for fifty years.

The forces working against bipartisanship in Colombia were not entirely autochthonous ones. In Europe, theorists on both the left and right continued to promote their own mutually antagonistic visions of the social order. Their inspiration would prove invaluable to intransigent Liberals and Conservatives who perceived Republicanism as political relativism, or worse, political apostasy. In the view of Colombia's older generation of Conservative and Liberal ideologues, Republicanism—wedding, as it were, Liberals and Conservatives—was an unnatural, immoral thing to be got rid of as quickly as possible. Hence even as the bipartisan Republican Union movement grew and prospered around the time of Reyes's fall, committed partisans of Liberalism and Conservatism plotted their strategy. They too had welcomed the fall of the dictator Reyes. But unlike the impressionable Centenarians, they watched the political events of March 1909 with a cool and calculating eye.

Throughout the nineteenth and well into the twentieth century, the most dramatic events in Colombian public life frequently took place in the chambers of Congress. During moments of high drama, such as those occurring between February 22 and March 13, 1909, spectators jammed the long semicircular galleries overhanging the scene of debates. Secondary, preparatory school, and college students normally filled a good many of the seats, for Bogotá was then, as it remains today, Colombia's center of higher education. Students from the best families flocked to the capital for advanced formal education. After class they often repaired to the capitol to observe the political goings-on, and, indirectly, to participate in them. They did so by applauding their heroes and registering noisy disapproval of enemy politicians. The student Laureano Gómez, for example, spent many an afternoon observing debates. As a lad of fourteen he had raptly followed Miguel Antonio Caro's successful campaign against the Panama treaty. Now a twenty-year-old university student, he watched the National Assembly attempt to pass Reyes's complicated treaty involving Panama and the United States. On March 9, 1909, he and all the others whistled and jeered a pro-treaty petition from the despised Aristides Fernández, and watched with dismay as yet another distinguished citizen, Adolfo León Gómez, was clapped into the Panóptico for registering vehement opposition to the tripartite pact. A week earlier Reyes had jailed the noted jurist Eduardo Rodríguez Piñeres and General Carlos José Espinosa for opposing them. Rodríguez Piñeres, president of the Colombian Academy of Jurisprudence, had signed his organization's finding that the National Assembly could not legally approve treaties as it was not a legally constituted body.[56]

Demonstrations against Reyes and the tripartite agreement began on

March 10, the day after Aristides Fernández's petition was read before the assembly. They were led by students from the medical school of the National University, the pro-Liberal institution that Fernández had closed during the War of the Thousand Days. Prominent among them were Jorge Martínez Santamaría and Luis López de Mesa. On their way to protest the proposed treaty before the American Consulate, they passed by Simón Araújo's Universidad Republicana, where they enlisted the support of Ramón Rosales, Pedro Juan Navarro, and many others. Soon they were joined by students from the law school of the National University.[57]

The following day, March 11, President Reyes called student leaders and heads of their respective institutions to the presidential palace. Among the latter groups were rectors of the law and medical schools of the National University, as well as Monsignor Rafael M. Carrasquilla of the Colegio del Rosario and Father Vicente Leza of San Bartolomé. Only the rector of the engineering school of the National University and his student representatives failed to attend.

President Reyes had intended to cow his guests, as he had all Colombians for nearly five years. After so doing he planned to mollify them with a luncheon at his residence. But nothing went as he hoped. Only Carrasquilla agreed to keep his students from further protests. Father Leza shocked Reyes and delighted the students by refusing to accept responsibility for what San Bartolomé students did once they left the campus, and several of the students, led by Martínez Santamaría, spoke boldly against approval of the treaties. The student Rafael Abello Salcedo stupefied cabinet members in attendance when he addressed Reyes as Citizen President. Members of the cabinet were required to address the president as "your excellency."

In the end Reyes had clearly lost his composure. The students could see that he was beside himself, his hands trembling, his voice taking on a supplicating tone. Earlier he had torn the tricolored presidential sash from his breast and hurled it to the floor. Students and rectors left the palace, scorning the president's luncheon.[58]

Word of the meeting spread quickly, and in less than two hours a large group of students made its way to the home of Jorge Martínez Santamaría to congratulate him. Notable for their presence were students of the school of engineering of the National University. Their leader, Laureano Gómez, gave an impassioned speech in which he offered the movement his and his companions' support. Not long afterward a detachment of police carrying rifles and fixed bayonets surrounded and arrested the students. Laureano Gómez and Ramón Rosales were among the first taken. As they were marched away to jail, down Calle 12 to the Calle Real, down to and across the Plaza de Bolívar, the students, their faces radiant, sang a spirited rendition of the "Marseillaise."[59]

More demonstrations took place the next day, March 12. On the following day Reyes turned power over to Jorge Holguín, who quickly withdrew the treaties from consideration and released all those jailed during the demonstrations. March 13 also marked the political debut of Enrique Olaya Herrera. Tall, blond, and ten years older than most of his student peers, Olaya captivated the younger men with a Plaza de Bolívar speech notable chiefly for a brilliant improvisation. Glimpsing two of Reyes's daughters passing in a carriage, Olaya pointed to them and thundered, "the diamonds that the daughters of Reyes wear are nothing less than tears of a people who today assume the fullness of their rights and duties."[60]

Olaya's words were premature, for Reyes had resumed the presidency before many more hours passed. But within three months Reyes was gone. In July a popularly elected Congress began its sessions, and by August Ramón González Valencia took office as president, to complete the remaining year of Reyes's original six-year term. As for Enrique Olaya Herrera, he became active in the Republican Union movement, ultimately becoming Colombia's youngest ever minister of foreign affairs—at an astonishing twenty-nine years of age.

Members of the clergy and their ultramontane Conservative allies were distressed by Bogotá's March Days. They saw in the mass schoolboy uprising and in the attending rush toward bipartisanship a dangerous forgetfulness of fundamental social and political values. Liberalism and Conservatism could never be reconciled, they believed. Yet that truth appeared to be forgotten by student leaders Martínez Santamaría and Olaya Herrera, enemies in the recent war. And the sight of young Laureano Gómez braying about "raising the bloody banner" and "marching so that the foul blood may drench our furrows" while happily trotting off to jail alongside Liberal students must have struck them as truly disconcerting. Gómez was, as headmaster Father Vicente Leza and secular activist José Joaquín Casas well knew, the finest product of Jesuit education, a devout Catholic only recently graduated from San Bartolomé at the head of his class. Could it be that he had, while studying at the National University, fallen prey to the disassociative ideas they all feared and about which Aristides Fernández had so eloquently spoken not long before his fall from power?[61]

There was, in the view of Colombia's religious right wing, an equally dangerous element in the recent demonstrations. Immediately after resuming power President Reyes warned that the uprising against him was "fomented and exploited by revolutionary agents."[62] His words were a frightening reaffirmation of Pope Leo XIII's warning in that most famous of modern encyclicals, *De rerum novarum* (1891), that "crafty agitators" were intent on exploiting the differences between rich and poor, in order "to pervert men's judgment and to stir up the people to revolt."[63] Still in the Colombia of 1909 it was clear, as noted above, that socialism was not about to sweep the country. Immediately after the March Days artisans, laborers, and factory workers marched in support of the government crackdown on the students. But that did little to comfort Father Leza, who saw "the tide of Communism incipient today in Colombia," and who warned that "if it is ignored it [can] assume a most disastrous character in the future."[64]

Such remarks were hardly the unique expressions of reactionary conservatives living in one of the Western world's most isolated republics. Rather, they echoed the statements of militant religious activists everywhere in the Roman Catholic world, all of whom were committed to countering a widely perceived threat to Christian morality. That threat was modernism, being defined as everything falling outside the parameters of scholastic learning. Pope Pius X, who had succeeded Leo XIII in 1903, showed the way in encyclicals that were read to all Catholics. In 1907, *Lamentabli sane* and *Pascendi dominici gregis* proscribed the liberal Modernist Movement within the Church, which Pius X had called "the heresy of heresies."[65] Chief among the sins of Modernist theologians was their insistence on an interpretive as opposed to a literal approach to Scripture. Two years earlier, in *Il fermo proposito,* directed to Italian Catholics, the pope urged that they organize politically, "in order to combat anti-Christian civilization by every just and lawful means." While the encyclical was specifically directed to Italian members of the lay organization Catholic Action, Church activists everywhere could not have helped notice the pontiff's injunction for "all Catholics to prepare themselves prudently and seriously for political life in case they should be called to it. . . ."[66] Following the issuing of *Pascendi,* the leading Spanish Conservative politician, Antonio Maura (1853–1925), invigorated his nation's Catholic Action movement by launching a new and even more militant group in 1909, called the Maurista Youth Movement.[67] In France, Charles Maurras and his followers fought the liberal Third Republic, which they called *la gueuse* (the slut), by forming an antiparliamentarian bloc within the French parliament.[68] And in Colombia, José Joaquín Casas, Father Vicente Leza, and their associates, decided to rally Catholic youth by giving them a newspaper.

During the middle months of 1909, Casas and others met privately with a number of young men whom they had identified as both fervent Catholics and as intelligent, articulate, and politically active. Twenty-year-old Laureano Gómez was especially interesting to them, because he, more than any of the others had shown extraordinary qualities of leadership during the recent upset. However, Gómez required special handling, as by that time he was both a "doctor," having just been awarded his college degree, and the head of his family. José Laureano Gómez had died in 1905, shortly after instructing his eldest son that he must become an engineer. Further complicating matters was the fact that Gómez had recently accepted an engineering position with the Antioquia Railroad.

Responsibility for bringing Laureano Gómez into the publishing venture was assigned Father Luis Jáuregui, a Spanish Jesuit who had taught Gómez at San Bartolomé, and whom the young man loved and respected. Jáuregui described the need for a new pro-clerical newspaper dedicated to answering attacks on the Church by its enemies. He described journalism as the noblest of occupations, one whose rewards were many and whose disillusionments few. To Gómez's protests that neither he nor his family was likely to survive on his salary as a journalist, the priest turned to Scripture. "Seek ye first the kingdom of God and His righteousness," he intoned, "and these things shall be given unto you."[69] The Jesuit salesman's pitch was a tour de force. Gómez left Jáuregui's quarters having agreed to join the publishing venture.

During September 1909, an organizational meeting was held to launch the newspaper, which would be called *La Unidad* (Unity). No member of the clergy was present, but fifty-four-year-old José Joaquín Casas was. Casas, who during the war had founded the Colegio Pío X, and who had toyed with the idea of founding a Catholic party in Colombia, along with Aristides Fernández, made clear the pro-clerical intent of the paper. All those in attendance were graduates of San Bartolomé.[70] Like Gómez, most were young, and looked on the famous Dr. Casas with respect verging on veneration. Thanks to Casas and his support, both moral and economic, *La Unidad* published its first edition October 2, 1909. Laureano Gómez was its editor.

Gómez quickly proved to be both a brilliant defender of the religious right and of the notion that Conservatism and the Church were ideologically one and the same—that Catholic values were Conservative values, and vice versa. As he said to José de la Vega on meeting him for the first time, in October 1909, "we must defend the great values of Conservatism."[71] Because he saw Colombia as "an ungovernable country par excellence," the common good required not the liberty advocated by Liberals, but rather "repression of the passions through the exercise of self-control, which in fact constitutes moderate and just use of that same liberty." "That's the true liberty we aspire to," he wrote. "Isn't it more honorable to preach the rigidity and sobriety of Sparta than the dissipation and freedom of Babylonia?"[72] It's hardly surprising that Laureano Gómez supported moderate suppression of press freedom and of other civil liberties.

Gómez believed that as moral ideas are from God and are handed down to man through His church, and thence come to govern human actions through secular law formulated by the state, then church and state must inevitably work together closely. The Conservative Party, then, as political arm of the Church, must control the state if Colombia is to remain a truly Christian nation. That line of thought ran through the *La Unidad* editorial of October 16, 1909, in which Gómez wrote that every political question contains a religious question. Since he also believed that in order to be a Liberal "one must support absolute liberty, which the Church condemns," he was forced to conclude that "the principal and almost exclusive cause of political division among us is the religious question."[73]

Thus the young newspaper editor marked himself as a man of firm convictions from the time of his earliest public statements. In that his view of society was ordered by a set of beliefs that were religious, therefore metaphysical and a matter of personal conviction, they were impervious to attack through rational argument. Laureano Gómez was, in short, an ideological thinker who approached all things with a certainty and intellectual tenacity instilled in him over years of study with the Jesuits. His vision of the world was, at least at the level of morality and social order, one of divinely inspired verities, one of rights and wrongs and of clearly defined hierarchies. As one who saw Colombia's Liberal and Conservative Parties as rooted in diametrically opposed sets of ideas, he resisted any idea that there could be accommodation between them. Heterogeneous elements, he stated bluntly in a *La Unidad* editorial of December 4, 1909, could never form the basis for a lasting political party.

Laureano Gómez could not be other than the avowed enemy of the Republican Union movement, which, as he began his newspaper, held a powerful attraction for moderate Conservatives, who were weary of the old partisan struggle. Gómez thus attacked the coalition party repeatedly as a "hybrid," as "a mix of contradictory ideas." Even worse to the young editor, who believed all human society consisted of a profusion of organic hierarchies in which the best and brightest directed the rest, the Republican Union brought together "men of every class, with no selection whatsoever."[74] He repeatedly attacked the new party, and urged Conservatives to return to their party. Throughout 1912, Gómez supported Marco Fidel Suárez as the man best able to unify Conservatives. He called Suárez "a leader of the first magnitude," and continually urged party members of both factions to join Suárez's orthodox Conservative "Concentration" movement.[75]

Nine months after *La Unidad* began publication, in July 1910, Colombians made ready to celebrate the centenary of their national independence. In Bogotá the normally gloomy nocturnal scene was brightened by strings of incandescent lights hung by the local privately owned electric company, the new Park of the Centenary readied for its inauguration, the old mule-powered tramway, only recently nationalized, was electrified, and numerous pavilions were readied for the inevitable round of speech making. The holiday had special significance for Colombia's Jesuit community, for it marked the twenty-fifth anniversary of their return from Liberal-imposed exile. A celebration marking the event was held at San Bartolomé on July 17, and one of the principal speakers was the 1904 graduate Dr. Laureano Gómez, known by then as editor of the city's most vociferous Catholic newspaper. It was to be his first formal presentation. Appropriately, it honored his Jesuit mentors.

Gómez began the talk by evoking the happy recollections of all who had studied at the school. He praised the Jesuit Fathers for their virtue and wisdom, and expressed profound gratitude for the parental love they showed their charges. He thanked God for allowing him to study with Jesuits, a religious order whose members place "the seal of perfection upon everything that comes under their influence." Gómez ended with a glowing metaphor. San Bartolomé was like a noble oak standing lonely on the secular plain, comforting and giving hope to those who lived there. "Years hence," he concluded, "when old age tires us and when we seek its shelter in search of comfort, a tear of bitterness will cross our withered cheeks: Yet it matters not that impiety, the numbing winter of souls occasionally blights this illustrious institution. Its sap will course again, because it is rooted in Catholic faith. Its venerable trunk will forever be covered with flowers and fruits for the glory of God and Country."[76]

Tears dampened many a cheek, and President González Valencia barely contained himself, rushing to bestow a heartfelt embrace upon the speaker. A visibly moved Father Leza thanked the young orator, and adjourned the ceremony.

"It conferred upon me a relative celebrity," Gómez later said of the president's embrace.[77] That it did, for in less than a year Laureano Gómez won election to Colombia's Chamber of Representatives as Primer Suplente (first deputy) on the "Authentic" Conservative ticket headed by Miguel Abadía Méndez. Thus in mid-1911 he began a parliamentary career that would stretch to more than three decades, and which would be remembered as the most tempestuous in the history of Colombian politics.

Laureano Gómez cut a splendid figure as he took his place, at age twenty-two, in the national legislature. With his three-piece suit, gold-headed cane, and cigarette in hand, he was the very picture of the well-dressed *cachaco*. And he was handsome. Sturdily built, with wavy brown hair and piercing blue-gray eyes, he exuded confidence and vigor. Gómez was a truly charismatic figure who first drew the like-minded to him, and then kept their admiration through personal flair and certainty of purpose. His friend José de la Vega was one of the first to fall under his spell. At about the time Gómez entered Congress, de la Vega dedicated his doctoral thesis in jurisprudence to his parents and to Gómez, whom he described as "a strong and outstanding spirit," possessing "an integral character and privileged talent."[78]

Gómez's spirit of combativeness was an important part of his persona. Fired by religious zeal, he likened himself and his peers to crusaders who gauged their virtue by the numbers of infidels slain. Gómez admitted that time had changed the nature of the contest. "Today," he explained in a speech in 1914, "one must know how to wield the invisible sword of words—words that, if pronounced with sincerity and faith, damage the adversary more than steel."[79]

Colombia's young Conservative activists found a splendid model for their behavior in the Spanish Conservative Party leader Antonio Maura. Gómez and his fellow militants were among Maura's most avid readers, adopting the Spaniard's slogan, "Liberty has become conservative."[80] They admired Maura because he was an ideologist and a staunch foe of anticlericalism, because he was a moralist possessed of a dominating personality, and because he projected an arrogance and self-confidence that prompted some to say, "Maura thinks that *he* made the world." It was also said of Maura that he "cannot speak without wounding. . . . [He] only knows how to convince by falling upon his adversaries and listeners in an unrestrained torrent. . . ." Historian Fredrick Pike wrote that Maura, "seeking a political course of action that would stave off revolution from below, insisted that only those policies that responded to the religious sentiment of the Spanish people were capable of conserving the nation. . . . [He] polarized Spain into bitterly hostile 'Maura, sí' and 'Maura, no' camps."[81] The same would later be said of Colombia's Laureano Gómez.

The earliest public acts of Laureano Gómez were marked by the confrontational style that became his trademark. In August 1911, during his first intervention in a congressional debate of small importance, Gómez ended by charging another representative with knowingly violating the nation's constitution.[82] Several months later he approached the congressional press gallery and exchanged hot words with an opposition newspaper editor. The two then flew at each other, Gómez brandishing his walking stick and the other man a pistol that he pulled from a coat pocket. They were separated before either inflicted physical damage upon the other.[83] During congressional debates the following year his verbal violence so infuriated Gómez's elders, particularly Archbishop Bernardo Herrera Restrepo, that *La Unidad* was forced to suspend publication. At issue was the government's attempt to raise revenue through leasing the Muzo emerald mines in Boyacá to European interests. Gómez was especially critical of Laureano García Ortiz, a distinguished jurist and diplomat whom he accused of profiting personally from the transaction. When Herrera Restrepo threatened to anathematize both *La Unidad* and its editor, Gómez yielded—but not without having the last word. In the editorial in which he announced suspension of his newspaper, Gómez explained his actions as those of one who was simply trying to defend national interests. "But," he stated pointedly, "Muzo has shut us up." "We cease publication with sadness," he concluded, "not for ourselves but for this ill-fated country, where even the highest ecclesiastical officials serve—doubtless in misguided good faith—to whitewash the actions of a frock-coated thief."[84]

Luckily for Gómez, just as he was angering the archbishop he was also pleasing him mightily. In June 1912 the young congressman had joined with Conservative intransigent Sotero Peñuela in sponsoring a law that would ban the Masonic Order from Colombia as a "secret society" and therefore in violation of the national constitution.[85] Then on October 30 he launched a movement from the pages of his newspaper for a national eucharistic congress. The idea caught on among Conservatives and by early 1913 a major effort to organize it was afoot throughout Colombia. All this, plus public statements of contrition by Gómez, brought him and his newspaper back into the good graces of the Church hierarchy. *La Unidad* reappeared in March 1913. Rather than an editorial, that edition contained a letter from Gómez to Archbishop Herrera begging his forgiveness for any trouble he may have caused, and thanking him for having said to Gómez, in an earlier letter, that he wanted nothing more than to see him work in service of the Church "and in accord with directives from the Holy See."[86]

His reconciliation with the archbishop was followed in April by a uniquely self-deprecating letter to *La Unidad* in which Gómez asked his friends not to propose him as a candidate in upcoming congressional elections. As the party is presently weathering stormy times, it must, he wrote, be represented by a candidate "of eminent virtues, great intelligence and illustration. As I possess none of these qualities, I must remove myself as a possible candidate for that post, the suitable fulfilling of which is beyond my modest abilities."[87] His words produced an instant groundswell of support among Conservatives that swept Gómez back into Congress for another term.

As the 1913 session approached, Representative Gómez, Sotero Peñuela, José Joaquín Casas, and other pro-clerical Conservatives hit upon a ploy that they knew would drive members of the Liberal minority to distraction and continue their work of party rejuvenation along Historical lines. They would propose a resolution by which the Colombian Congress would "render homage to Jesus Christ." Liberals, who on principle would not vote for the measure because it mixed religion and politics, would attack its formulators for indulging in cheap political theatrics, which of course they were. But that mattered little to Gómez and the rest, as the Liberals would be forced to go on record as refusing to salute the Redeemer. Additionally, it would neatly unify congressional Historical and Nationalist Conservatives. The measure was debated in the sessions of July 28, 29, and 30.

Representative Ramón Rosales opened for the Liberals, explaining in some detail why he and his colleagues intended to vote against the proposal. It is anti-Liberal, he said, just one more example of how since the 1880s his party had been forced to combat both the Conservative Party and the Church. Thus, Rosales continued, he and other Liberals had good reason to believe that both the matter under debate and the upcoming eucharistic congress would be used against them. Marco Fidel Suárez has already written in *El Nuevo Tiempo* that the congress "would make politics, and politics of the most astute kind," said Rosales. If the priests are openly anti-Liberal during mass, why shouldn't they be so at the congress—why are no Liberals involved in it? Rosales concluded with a rhetorical flourish, asking if it did not seem logical that Liberals should refuse "to weave with their own hands a rope fitted especially to their throats."[88]

Debate continued and at length Liberal Representative Felipe Escobar spoke up, saying that as the proposition was obviously going to pass, Congress should vote to modify it in order that a marble statue of Jesus could be erected on the Palonegro battlefield. The statue should be inscribed with the words "Love one another." To that Representative Gómez interjected, "That is an irony, a sarcasm!" More debate followed, with Liberal Francisco de Paula Borda finally losing patience and accusing Conservatives of raising the issue to delude and distract the masses; the Conservatives were, Borda said, using the Redeemer as a toy. Warming to his theme, the Liberal called the debate a stupid waste of time, a byzantine and unproductive thing to be discussing at a moment when pressing issues of national interest should occupy debate. He called the Regeneration a "mortal wound on the republic" because it made the religious question explode in their midst. He called for the vote, adding that the entire debate did nothing more than illustrate Colombia's lack of culture.[89]

At that point Gómez spoke, saying he'd known all along that he would hear nothing but a series of hapless minority party remarks, the sort of unconstitutional, utilitarian arguments to be expected of Liberals. The only new idea expressed, he said, was the burlesque one about the statue; and Representative Borda had sunk as low as one could, resorting to character assassination. When Borda said, "Who, me?" Gómez elaborated, saying he had heard Borda's anti-Regeneration speech before, adding that the Liberal's accusation that Núñez was poisoned by a Jesuit was a vile lie. Gómez lashed out next at Representative José Manuel Saavedra Galindo for having taken an oath to defend the Church when a high school student on scholarship at the Colegio del Rosario. "Thus, Mr. President," Gómez concluded, addressing the presiding officer of the Cámara, "in voting against this project Representative Saavedra proves himself not merely a hypocrite, but a perjurer as well!"

With those words the Conservatives present burst into "great and prolonged applause," and members of the congressional majority crowded around Gómez to congratulate him and to shake his hand.[90] As the debate had consumed the entire afternoon, the presiding officer adjourned the session.

Saavedra Galindo opened the next day's debate saying, among other things, that Representative Gómez had stooped to character assassination in bringing up his, Saavedra's, humble origins and the free room and board he had been forced to accept when an impoverished student. He professed surprise at hearing someone discussing such mundane subjects in the national congress—subjects properly the domain "of the ill born and of hotel maids." Saavedra's sarcasm had little effect on Gómez. Later in the debate Gómez gave thanks that he had not "squandered the best years of [his] youth in low scenes of hypocrisy, as did a certain student at the Colegio del Rosario."[91]

At last, on July 30, the proposition that the Colombian Chamber of Representatives "render homage to Jesus Christ" was put to the vote. It passed handily, as everyone knew it would. Sixty Conservatives voted for it; thirteen liberals voted against.

These incidents reveal that religion remained a divisive force in early-twentieth-century Colombia, and that young politicians like Laureano Gómez were likely to keep it so into the foreseeable future. At a broader level they are suggestive that as the second decade of the new century wore on, extremists in both major parties had little trouble reviving old patterns of partisan enmity, thus dooming the infant Republican Union movement. That three days of discussions could be devoted to a matter of little practical but of great ideological consequence indicated that Colombia remained a place where the ultramontane right could successfully conduct its war against modernism. Representative Pedro Sicard, who also participated in the debate, was no doubt correct in wailing that the chamber should be debating matters like national defense and public education. But it did not necessarily follow, as his colleague Francisco Borda said, that the Conservatives were simply "throwing dust into the eyes of . . . the unthinking masses, fanaticized by the spirit of party."[92] There were no masses in Colombia in 1913, at least in the sense implied by Borda. Rather, the nation possessed a great majority of pious and unlearned country folk, Liberals and Conservatives, who routinely and sincerely rendered homage to Jesus Christ and attached no greater political significance to it.

The debates went on over an inherently trivial matter because there was no reason for them not to. Politics was in large measure showmanship in the Colombia of that time. The Liberal and Conservative Parties had long since worked out clientelist networks through which the government's limited political largesse was distributed, depending, that is, on whose party held power. The rest was posturing. Not that most Colombians didn't avidly follow the deeds of their leaders in the various national fora. It was nearly as much fun for them to read or hear of Laureano Gómez's followers "deliriously carrying him through the streets" on their shoulders, as Representatives Borda, Sicard, and Saavedra skulked away, "their political reputations ruined" thanks to the young tribune's reasoned attack.[93] Men like Gómez and Saavedra did not represent individual Colombians. Rather, they were the visible representatives of what remained monolithic interest associations—the largest and most inclusive in the nation at that time. Having achieved their exalted status, politicians were expected to represent their constituents with panache, not with substantive programs aimed at the public welfare. In fact such programs had never been realized in Colombia. The evolution of Colombian politics from theatrics to meaningful debate over issues of substance would have to wait until the government commanded more resources and until even hotel maids and the ill-born could exercise direct and meaningful influence on the political process.

Republican Interlude

Colombia's Republican Union became a political party in 1909, and elected its first and only national president, Carlos E. Restrepo, the following year. The party's decline began almost immediately and by 1918 it did not even field a presidential candidate. Still the spirit giving life to Republicanism was broader and more important than its ephemeral political party. If that spirit is understood to have signified elite political partisanship pledged to the cause of national peace and economic progress, then all five men who held office in Colombia between 1906 and 1926 can be considered Republicans. The two decades encompassed by that interval did constitute a time of peace and economic development in the Andean republic. The same can be said for other Latin American nations where caudillo-inspired civil wars had become things of another era, and the social protests that would fill most of the twentieth century still had not begun. Carlos E. Restrepo had his counterparts in Chile's Arturo Alessandri, Argentina's Hipólito Yrigoyen, and to a lesser extent in the Brazilian presidents of the bourgeois Old Republic. All were members of an unchallenged political elite who shared the conviction that their nations must rush to join the industrializing capitalist world whatever the cost.

The leaders who held power during Colombia's Republican interlude not only enjoyed a time of relative peace and prosperity, but they shared a philosophy that enabled them to pursue national development with a remarkable degree of unanimity. That philosophy was positivism, which, as noted earlier, taught that nations inevitably pass through stages, reaching enlightenment through the discovery of rationally deduced scientific truths. Latin American positivists like Restrepo and his peers found Herbert Spencer's "sociological" elaboration of the philosophy especially relevant. The evolutionary process described by Darwin, and applied to human society by Spencer, appeared manifest in Colombia, where the more favored races flourished at the expense of less favored ones.

Restrepo and the others resolved that as members of the select few, it was their duty to help the rest travel the upward-tending path of progress. That would not be easy, for Restrepo knew how long and twisted the path would be. Colombia remained, after all, "a childlike, infant country, of capricious and epileptic impulses, guided by national, political, and religious instincts."[94] That made it imperative for men like him to wean his fellow citizens from puerile attachments to "metaphysical" political beliefs, to help them move up to a truly mature "scientific" approach to public affairs. He repeatedly called for "less politics and more administration," a tenet of scientific politics in the heyday of Latin American positivism. Rafael Reyes said as much when, near the end of his presidency, he called politics "an experimental science." Rafael Uribe Uribe, a political antagonist of Restrepo, shared the latter man's empirical attitude: "let us adopt the experimental and evolutionary method in politics," Uribe Uribe said in a speech of 1911.[95] And like Restrepo, the Liberal caudillo appreciated the vast effort it would require to propel their people to a higher stage of development. "Nearly the entire circumference of Colombia is in the hands of savages," he wrote in 1907, going on to explain his plan for uplifting the Indian population by integrating them into national life.[96]

Men of the Republican interlude were, in short, enthusiastic Victorians steeped in the dominant philosophy of their day. Despite differences of personality and party they shared a scientific spirit and a belief in progress that united them with like-minded leaders across their own continent and elsewhere in the quickening Western world.

Carlos E. Restrepo took office on August 7, 1910, pledged to continue the work of reconciliation begun by his predecessor, Ramón González Valencia. González's term was popularly known as the Christian Year in tongue-in-cheek recognition of the president's extreme piety and desire for peace. Constitutional reform was political Colombia's chief concern during the brief González presidency. The reform was carried out by a constituent assembly dominated by Republican Unionists—who went on to elect Restrepo to the presidency. Hence it bore Restrepo's civilist stamp. The reforms strove to lessen single-party domination principally through limiting the presidential term to four years and specifying that there should be no immediate succession.

President Restrepo was convinced that the two traditional parties were in a state of "decomposition," being rooted in the metaphysical concerns of an age now past. That was the basis of his conviction and his hope that Republicanism was the wave of the future. Through it, Colombians could put behind them their "primitive blood feuds," and enter "the purely social and economic terrain where civilized nations of today are fighting their battles." "When they say to me that metaphysical questions must be discussed along with politics," Restrepo wrote in 1904, "I say to them: let's suspend those questions until some holiday, when we can afford the luxury of metaphysical parties."[97] The remark suggests the great distance separating civilist Conservatives like Restrepo from ultramontane ones like Gómez, Casas, and the others.

It is no coincidence that Antioquians assumed leadership during the two decades of calm between the war and the mid-1920s. They were the most entrepreneurial of all Colombians, and dominated the country's chief coffee-growing region as well. Profits from coffee exports were to help speed Colombian modernization at an accelerating pace throughout the Republican interlude. Carlos E. Restrepo was associated with the more successful business interests in his department. He was president of the Medellín Chamber of Commerce when elected national president in 1910. Pedro Nel Ospina was a member of the chamber at that moment, as was his brother Mariano Ospina Vásquez, another ardent Republican. Yet another brother, Tulio Ospina, cooperated with the government in helping foment economic development. He helped establish what would become the chief organization of Colombia's large landowners, the Society of Colombian Agriculture.[98]

The Republican interlude was accompanied by gratifying economic progress. During Restrepo's administration coffee prices rose by 50 percent and coffee exports doubled, reaching a million sixty-kilo sacks in 1913. Coffee, which represented 42 percent of Colombian exports at the end of Restrepo's first year in office, had risen to 72 percent of exports when Pedro Nel Ospina began his presidency in 1922.[99] Suggestive of the brightening economic picture was the fact that Restrepo was able to pay many public employees in pounds sterling rather than in pesos. The municipality of Bogotá was affluent enough to purchase its trolley system from the private owners in 1910, as it did the privately owned water system the following year. And still there was money left to asphalt the city's main street. Whereas ten years earlier visitors remarked on the lack of traffic in the national capital, by 1912 observers happily described the "animated hubbub of the Calle Florián and the Calle Real . . . the boiling pots of metropolitan life."[100] Other regions shared the newfound prosperity. In 1914 the Antioquia Railroad was completed, linking Medellín with Puerto Berrío, on the Río Magdalena. And Cali, Colombia's third largest city and commercial center of the Río Cauca valley, was joined by rail to the Pacific port city of Buenaventura.

Colombia increased the exploitation of its vast hydroelectric resources during the Republican interlude. Imported generators began to replace the steam engines that had formerly powered workshops and factories. The electric-powered textile plants opening in Antioquia were so much quieter and more efficient than their predecessors that people bought tickets so they could watch the new machines operate.[101] Electricity was the chief power source in Bogotá's new Germania brewery and in the Samper brothers' new flat-glass plant.

Political peace and economic development found dramatic symbolic expression on September 19, 1908, less than a year before Rafael Reyes's fall. On that day the president, in Bogotá, pushed a button inaugurating the Coltejer textile plant in Medellín. Coltejer would soon become one of Colombia's first industrial giants. A reporter captured the event in a newspaper article won- drous as much for its ingenuousness as for its descriptiveness: "The sensational moment has arrived, ladies and gentlemen. Let us draw closer and observe the phenomenon. General Reyes has in his hands the electric button . . . two min- utes pass . . . suddenly an electromagnet activated by the current running from Bogotá through telegraph lines moves a lever which frees a weight that falls, closing a switch, thus permitting electric current to enter, starting dynamos whose axles are connected to machinery suddenly set into dizzying move- ment."[102]

Colombia's need for capital was an ongoing problem during the Republican era. Santiago Pérez Triana, sent by Reyes to find European lessees for the Muzo emerald mines, saw that as his nation's most pressing need. He gave his argu- ment in favor of foreign loans a moral cast by tracing "popular misery [and] the many evils afflicting Colombia" to a lack of personal capital. "Without [money]," he lectured, "moral progress is impossible."[103] Modern studies con- firm Pérez's perception that Colombians had very little disposable capital. In 1917 the currency in circulation was only four pesos per capita, whereas the average in Chile was sixteen pesos and in Argentina forty-six.[104]

The scarcity of investment capital from abroad made it increasingly impor- tant that Colombia improve its relations with the United States. That country's significance in hemispheric finance was manifest in 1906 and 1907, when bank failures in New York dried up European loans. Yet Colombians remained angry over American complicity in the Panama revolt, as evidenced by Foreign Minister Pedro Nel Ospina's refusal to permit a visit by Secretary of State Philander Knox in 1912. At length mutual economic self-interest prevailed, and in mid-1913 the two nations resumed negotiations aimed at settling the Panama matter. The following year both countries signed, in Bogotá, the Urrutia-Thompson Treaty. Among the Colombian signatories were First Des- ignate Marco Fidel Suárez and former president González Valencia. By May the Colombian Congress had ratified the treaty, but not without opposition led by the Historical Conservatives, who at one point stopped Senate deliberations by throwing asafetida on the floor of the chamber.[105] Opponents included Manuel Dávila Flores in the Senate, and Miguel Abadía Méndez, Laureano Gómez, and José de la Vega in the Chamber. The treaty included both a clause stating that United States expressed "sincere regret" for the Panama incident, and another providing for a $25 million indemnity to be paid upon the treaty's ratification by the U.S. Senate. That would not take place for another eight years, however, as Republicans in the U.S. Senate refused to endorse or vote for an agreement that they judged to be an affront to their greatest living leader, Theodore Roosevelt.[106]

As Carlos E. Restrepo's term ended it was clear that his party would not endure. Prominent members of the two traditional parties deserted Republicanism early in his administration. In 1911, José Vicente Concha and Marco Fidel Suárez set aside their mutual dislike and worked to unify Conservatism, which Concha likened to "a chained titan." Uribe Uribe founded his anti-Republican newspaper, *El Liberal,* in 1911, and the following year organized the Liberal Bloc movement. Violence erupted in many parts of the country during elections in March 1913, causing Restrepo to openly lament the widespread Conservative fraud that had helped cause it. Privately he berated Colombia's electoral "rottenness," which proved to him "that we are still an inferior and unworthy nation."[107] In the presidential election of February 1914, Restrepo's candidate, Nicolás Esguerra, lost to Conservative José Vicente Concha by a staggering eight-to-one margin.

Unlike his predecessor, and the two men who followed him as president, José Vicente Concha was not an Antioquian. Nor had he a background in business, as did the paisa industrialists Restrepo and Ospina. Still he shared with the others an abhorrence of partisanship that made him unpopular with extremists in his own party. Many Liberals admired him for his good citizenship and his philosophic commitment to administrative decentralization and laissez-faire policies. To young Juan Lozano y Lozano "Concha was a Liberal, a great Liberal—perhaps the most orthodox Liberal in Colombia. . . . The extreme right always looked at him with a terror that none of the great Liberal leaders—General Uribe Uribe, General Herrera—ever inspired."[108]

Concha got on so well with Rafael Uribe Uribe that the Liberal caudillo backed him in the 1914 election. That shocked many, as it forced him to oppose the highly regarded Republican candidate, Nicolás Esguerra, a fellow Liberal. The new president intended to reward that support by making Uribe Uribe his minister to Great Britain, when the assassination of the Liberal leader removed him from the political stage in late 1914.

World War I coincided precisely with José Vicente Concha's term in office, which meant that economic dislocations condemned his government to an ongoing situation of penury. Sources of foreign credit disappeared, coffee prices fell, customs duties dried up. True to his laissez-faire and hard-money principles, Concha refused to inflate the currency or, save for his imposition of a tax on luxuries that produced little new revenue, to raise taxes. The consequence was that salaries of public servants went unpaid, and government agencies were forced to close. The leprosarium at Agua de Dios once more disgorged its hapless inmates into the towns and cities of central Colombia.

An especially noteworthy consequence of the world conflict was the loss of

Colombia's European markets, and the concomitant expansion of business dealings with the United States. Before the war Colombians sold 40 percent of their exports to Europe and 50 percent to the United States. After the war the corresponding figures were about 15 and 73 percent. The shift in imports was even more striking. Whereas in 1910 Colombia bought approximately two-thirds of its imports in Europe and less than a third from the U.S., after the war the figures were reversed.[109]

In spite of these developments, Colombian-U.S. relations soured over the issue of Colombian neutrality during the war. While the policy was based on long-standing good relations between Colombia and the Central European powers, U.S. officials assumed that the policy indicated a pro-German bias. Consequently they pressured Concha to strike at German interests in his country. Concha remained obdurate, and the Americans could do no more than wring from the Colombian Congress a condemnation of German submarine attacks on neutral shipping.[110]

The placing of Colombian-U.S. relations back on track would become the chief foreign policy goal of Concha's successor, Marco Fidel Suárez. The Conservative Party leader and president of the country between 1918 and 1921 achieved that goal, though it cost him his popularity and ultimately his presidency. His successor, Pedro Nel Ospina, and, ironically, Ospina's anti-U.S. minister of the interior, Laureano Gómez, would reap the immediate rewards of that policy.

By the third decade of the century bipartisan Republicanism as a political movement was dead. It was defeated in a highly unequal contest pitting it against Liberal and Conservative Parties undergirded by vast clientelist networks, given life through emotional attachments generalized in the citizenry and stretching back over many decades, and energized by rising young stars like the Liberal, "El Muelón," Alfonso López, and Bartolino Laureano Gómez. Men of the Republican consensus were by contrast dry-as-dust technocrats whose politically temperate speeches filled spectators of the political process—meaning most Colombians—with ennui. Alfonso López spoke for them when he called Republicanism "apolitical politics." Yet in saying that, he put his finger on the great achievement of Republicanism writ large: through its ideology and agenda modernizing elites found common ground upon which they could start building a modern nation. Their use of the state to foment economic development, their prudent fiscal programs, and their foreign policy aimed at normalizing relations with the United States set precedents for Colombia that would be turned to national advantage in succeeding years.

4

The Bourgeois Republic

Manners and Mentalities

The interval in Colombian history between the War of the Thousand Days and the end of Conservative hegemony in 1930 was pivotal for national economic development. During that period long pent-up forces of economic change were freed, with the result that Colombia made dramatic progress toward closing the gap between itself and other Western nations. The engine driving the process of change was coffee and the revenue it produced. A great many ordinary Colombians worked in the coffee industry, many of them landowning small farmers. The consequences of that fact are many, and go far toward explaining certain unique features of twentieth-century Colombian life. Important to the present discussion is the way coffee-produced revenues found their way into a relatively broad segment of rural society. Moneys earned through the production, processing, transportation, and sale of coffee, and from the manifold other activities connected with the vigorous young industry, revolutionized rural life over a large portion of the nation. Members of Colombia's rural-dwelling majority suddenly began earning cash with which they could purchase the finer things of life, travel, and send their children away to school. They could, in short, aspire to a middle-class lifestyle.

The process described above was hardly a pacific one. Violence and pesos were common currencies on the coffee frontier. Yet the paramount fact remains that in spite of the violence—and often thanks to it—Colombia ended the first quarter of the twentieth century with a sizable rural bourgeoisie that complemented and strengthened its urban counterpart. Colombia had no aristocratic class. Its wealthiest and most accomplished citizens were thoroughly imbued with middle-class values, having themselves only relatively recently risen to social prominence. That is why Colombia in the early twentieth century is appropriately categorized a bourgeois republic. The case of Tulio Ospina serves to illustrate the point.

Tulio Ospina was a notable member of what is arguably one of the most distinguished families of Colombia's national period. Son of national president and Conservative Party cofounder Mariano Ospina Rodríguez (1857–1861), and brother of President Pedro Nel Ospina, he was a prominent and useful citizen in his own right. Sent to specialize in mine engineering at the University of California at Berkeley in 1877, he later became a cofounder and rector of the important National School of Mines in Medellín. A great fomenter of industry in Antioquia, Tulio Ospina also found time to write a treatise on agriculture, to serve in congress, and to publish learned volumes on philology. His considerable accomplishments were, in short, hardly the sort normally associated with the idle rich.

Ospina was in fact descended from smallholders from the Guasca-Gachetá region of northeastern Cundinamarca. Thanks to hard work and prudent marriages, the Ospina family improved its fortunes throughout the eighteenth century. Still, as people of humble origin they could never have advanced in society but for the revolt against Spain in 1810, and the subsequent upward social mobility that national independence occasioned. That made it possible for Santiago Ospina Urbina of Guasca to send his son Mariano to the Colegio de San Bartolomé during the 1820s. Thus Mariano Ospina Rodríguez and his hard-working descendants could go on to play important parts in national affairs. Not far removed from their rural origins, sons of the first President Ospina were hard working and socially conservative. As Roman Catholics and members of the Conservative Party they adhered to the moral and social philosophies of church and party. And as well-traveled and well-educated men they internalized the values and biases of the great bourgeois world whose heartland was circumscribed by London, Paris, and Berlin, and whose principal American salients were Buenos Aires, Rio de Janeiro, and New York.[1]

As men of Victorian and Edwardian temperament, the leaders of Colombia's bourgeoisie did not hesitate to advise their fellow citizens on proper standards of behavior. Their social status allowed them to do so, and their sense of social responsibility required it. Both impulses moved Tulio Ospina to publish in 1919 his *Protocol of Urbanity and Good Manners,* a volume that he knew would be of use to socially aspiring Colombians both at home and abroad. A sense of parental responsibility moved Rafael Reyes, in 1920, to list for his children and grandchildren the precepts they should follow in order to live successful lives. Reyes's principles were temperance, silence, order, resolution, frugality, industry, sincerity, justice, moderation, cleanliness, tranquility, chastity, and humility.[2]

Prominent Colombians strove mightily to live virtuous lives. From childhood they were admonished to do so by their parents and by the priests and nuns charged with religious instruction. Moral idealism had powerful social overtures in Edwardian Colombia, where men of the elite strove to internalize the virtues that they believed must be practiced in society at large, a society whose members respected hierarchy, obeyed the "principle of order," and were deferential to superiors. An excellent statement of personal philosophy penned during the time of Colombia's bourgeois Republican era was that of the young engineer Julián Cock Arango. In 1922, while undertaking advanced study in Paris, he set down what he called his Code of Personal Morality, which included the following personal injunctions: "It is imperative to triumph. You have been very weak; you have been the plaything of your indecision, of your impulsiveness, of your lack of attention. Always flee the terrible corrosive that is emotion, which obscures reality. . . . Be free, absolutely free . . . that neither your friends nor vices enslave you. . . . Eat only what is necessary, and slowly. . . . When necessary, do not reject responsibility, face it, be strong. . . . Be absolutely orderly and methodical. Defeat laziness always and everywhere, even when it is just for the pleasure of doing so. . . . Be reserved in things intimate. Don't make a fool of yourself by talking too much, trying to explain everything. . . . In conclusion, learn to dominate yourself and you will dominate and triumph over others. . . ."[3] Rafael Reyes carefully charted his personal progress toward virtue: "I got a small book in which I devoted a page to each one of the virtues. . . . Thus I was able to note with a black cross each failing that, upon reflection, I decided I had committed during that day."[4]

Men of the bourgeois republic weren't remiss in instructing proper behavior to those farther down the social hierarchy. Women and girls of the middle and upper classes were especially fond of reading Julián Páez's *Cartas a mi sobrina,* first published in 1912. "Do you want to be respected, admired, and loved?" Páez asked in one of his letters. "Wrap yourself in this delicately prestigious cloth, so distant from the vulgar, that's called mystery. . . . To show yourself at your window, to frequent the streets, to attend every dance . . . to talk loudly, elbow your neighbor, be the subject of everyone's conversation—all this, my beloved niece, lessens your prestige and vulgarizes you. It places you within reach of everyone, and breaks the sacred pedestal that woman must forever occupy: mystery."[5] The young bachelor physician and scholar Luis López de Mesa combined scientific fact and romantic, organic metaphor to explain feminine fidelity. Speaking to a largely female audience in 1920, he likened woman's soul to her egg, "that upon receiving the fecund chromatin of the sperm, hardens its ectoplasm with a shield impenetrable to the other elements that seek it." "Thus," López de Mesa concluded, "is woman's soul once it lets enter its great love. It closes its ears to every new flattery."[6]

During the early twentieth century Colombian woman's subordinate place in society was sanctioned and reinforced through two distinct ideological traditions. The first was the Roman Catholic one holding that marriage and homemaking were the proper destiny of most women, and that the married woman should spare no sacrifice for husband and children. The second, exemplified in López de Mesa's pronouncements, offered the same message, but couched in the social Darwinist idiom popular in Colombia of the time.

The Roman Catholic teaching that wives and mothers must sacrifice personal pleasures for their families is called Marianismo. A good statement of the concept can be found toward the end of a pastoral letter issued in 1926 by the archbishop of Medellín, Manuel José Cayzedo. "Queen and lady of the house, the Christian woman manifests there the qualities that God has given her, exercises her virtues, and instills and strengthens them in all those around her. . . . Out of love and virtue she suffers, enjoys, watches, works tirelessly, renouncing personal pleasure with heroic abnegation to the benefit of her family." The archbishop called the carrying out of domestic chores "the supreme destiny of mothers," for whom "there is no labor that tires, no pleasure that seduces, nor sacrifice she won't make to spare her husband and children." Archbishop Cayzedo cited Leo XIII as his authority in restating the age-old teaching, "The male is the head of the household and his wife's superior. She must submit to her husband and obey him, not as a slave but as a companion— that is to say, with decorous and dignified obedience."[7]

In his talk of 1920, López de Mesa presented a secularized version of the same message. In colorful language he evoked the image of prehistoric man, "warrior and wanderer, nervous, vigilant, combative, and strong," who after a wearisome day at the hunt "returned tired, in search of his woman." Meanwhile his mate had busied herself "searching for dry limbs to feed the fire, clearing more space in the cave or in the hollowed out trunk of a tree." Thus from primitive times woman was the homemaker. Citing scientific studies, López de Mesa assured his female listeners that while the feminine intellect may be "in some ways inferior to that of the male," owing to the fact that her brain is smaller, she makes up for it in areas "in keeping with her feminine mission." Among those are "powers of rapid observation, good memory for detail, and others that make her the ideal counselor and companion of the male." His restated version of Archbishop Cayzedo's message reads as follows: "Her will is strong, her character good-natured, generous, and malleable. And the wholeness of her moral structure is so precious and worthy that it enraptures even when viewed through cold psychological analysis."[8]

Colombians not of the elite shared the biases of their social superiors during early decades of the twentieth century. They generally did not do so for any single reason, but rather for a complex of reasons. As has already been suggested, there was great pressure to honor and obey one's social superiors. Traditional Christianity taught that there was a hierarchy of virtue; hence persons of higher social status were blessed not only with more material goods, but were naturally wiser, more intelligent, more virtuous. To put it differently, virtue and justice were thought to be distributive in nature. Even the most highly educated, secular-minded of Colombians, such as the engineers of the Medellín School of Mines, spoke of "the moral ascendance" that they held over their social inferiors, such as the workers whom they were called upon to direct. The engineers were constantly admonished to live "irreproachable private lives" that would serve as examples for their employees.[9] Workers themselves were typically humble, and tended to feel indebted to factory owners for doing them the kindness of hiring them.[10] Early photos of Colombian factories depict what appear to be large family reunions, with men, women, and children posed amid belts, spindles, and other such attributes of modern mechanical culture.

There was widespread belief that in a godly, proper society all citizens obeyed what was commonly called the principle of authority. That was the title of a lengthy series of articles published during the second decade of the century by Laureano Gómez's mentor, Manuel Dávila Flóres. For Marco Fidel Suárez the principle of authority was "the prime instrument used in the long and complicated task of civilizing the human species."[11] Laureano Gómez saw it as undergirding Catholicism: "Doctrine alone, without authority would be a Catholicism that has died."[12]

Country girls around the mountainous bishopric of Santa Rosa de Osos, in Antioquia, obeyed the principle of authority when they walked kilometers over rugged mountain trails, even though common sense suggested they ride the horses or mules readily available to them. But Bishop Miguel Angel Builes had forbidden the practice to women of his diocese, pronouncing the custom of women riding astride "a sin against natural law" for "the disastrous effects that it produces."[13] When General Benjamín Herrera expelled striking workers from his banana plantation early in the century he did so because they had violated the principle of authority. When they demanded an additional peso per bunch harvested, Herrera drove them out by force of arms, reviling them as "disobedient peons."[14]

Further complicating and hardening bourgeois prejudices about the poor of early-twentieth-century Colombia were a set of ideas concerning the supposed inferiority of non-Caucasian peoples, and the "racial decay" of societies where dark-skinned peoples predominated. In a country like Colombia, where a largely Caucasian elite held sway over a mostly swarthy majority, the impact of such belief was necessarily great. The relative quiescence of the Colombian masses in those decades fed race-based prejudices against them. Important too was the fact that the eugenicists, sociologists, and anthropologists who formulated racialist theories made extensive use of empirical data. That could not help but impress positivist-minded Colombian elites. Nor did it hurt that the theories originated in the most advanced centers of Western civilization.

Boyacense physician and Conservative leader Miguel Jiménez López was the leading proponent of the theory that Colombia was suffering the effects of racial decay. During his years as a student he had traveled widely in Europe, where he both heard the theories of Joseph Arthur Gobineau and other racial theorists debated, and studied them himself. During his years of postgraduate study, 1900–1909, three biographies of Gobineau were published in Paris alone, and another appeared in Leipzig. Between 1910 and 1930, while the racial debate raged in Colombia, an additional ten studies of Count Gobineau appeared in France, Germany, and other European countries.[15] No wonder, then, that Jiménez López published a scholarly article in Paris in 1917 in which he concluded that racial decay rendered Colombia's chances of progress nil.[16] Only if his countrymen eventually lightened their skin through European immigration, wrote Jiménez López, could Colombia avoid falling farther behind the more civilized nations.

Jiménez López's ideas were widely discussed in Colombian intellectual circles during the second and third decades of the century. The debate over racial decay reached its height in 1920, during a cycle of conferences on the Problems of Race in Colombia, held in Bogotá's Teatro Colón. Jiménez López, Luis López de Mesa, and other physicians and scientists took part in them. There were of course those who disputed the race decay theory. As the debates took place an *El Tiempo* columnist suggested that another series of debates should be organized around the possibility that the Colombian race was growing stronger.[17]

The fact that many Colombians shared the biases of Jiménez López is evidenced in Rafael Reyes's remark of 1919, that while Colombia should encourage immigration—even Japanese immigration—it should prohibit entry to Chinese and Hindus, "races made degenerate through servility."[18] Three years later, in 1922, members of the national Congress passed a law prohibiting the immigration of Chinese, Hindus, and Turks (Otomanos), but encouraging European immigration. That same year a writer for *El Tiempo* protested Tropical Oil's use of Jamaican guest workers in its Colombian fields, a charge the company "enthusiastically denied." Still, the editorialist concluded, "we hope the government has already taken the means necessary to put an end to an immigration that is absolutely undesirable in every sense, not only because it causes competition for Colombian workers, but because of the grave damage it does to our race."[19]

Casual anti-Semitism also formed part of bourgeois Colombia's racial thought during the early twentieth century. While there were few Jews in Colombia, Jews were frequently mentioned in connection with the Crucifixion, for their alleged control of international banking, and because they were generally perceived as grasping, unattractive individuals, and enemies of Catholicism. Mention of the Hebrew race is frequent in the pastoral letters of Colombian bishops around the turn of the century. Medellín's Archbishop Cayzedo castigated the impious, who, "like the perfidious Jews who rise against Christ," attack Colombia's Christian order. In another of his pastorals he reproved "the enemies of Christ . . . united in their shadowy Masonic societies, who like Jews cry out [against Catholicism]."[20]

An atavistic source of Colombian racial thought is found in preoccupation over "purity of the blood" (*pureza de sangre*). That concern was brought by Spanish conquistadors in the sixteenth century. The Spanish fixation on lineage ran back perhaps as far as the near simultaneous Christianization of the Iberian peninsula and the arrival there of Jews earlier expelled from their land by the Romans. With the persecution of Spanish Jews during the fourteenth and fifteenth centuries, their expulsion from the country in 1492, and their subsequent persecution in both Spain and Spanish America during the succeeding two centuries, it became important to establish that one was not tainted with Moorish, African, and Jewish blood. Not to do so might label one a *converso*, a recent convert to Christianity. And to be a converso, or to be descended from one, raised the possibility that one's family continued to practice Judaism covertly, which invited arrest by the Holy Office and loss of all social position.

Concerns about overt persecution vanished with the independence of Spanish America. While many conversos, or New Christians, as they were also called, may have made their way to New Granada during the colonial period, they appeared to suffer no extraordinary persecution there. Still, through a curious set of circumstances a major segment of Colombia's population, the Antioquians, came to be thought of as descended from Spanish conversos. Exploration of that question is beyond the scope of the present study. But the folk wisdom of paisa Jewishness is important in that it made the Antioquians particularly sensitive both to anti-Semitism and to the greater question of race. Slightly later in Colombian history, during the 1930s and 1940s, when Jewish refugees fled Europe, some Antioquians advocated offering shelter while others argued vociferously against such policy. Earlier, paisa sensitivity toward race made them among Colombia's most vocal proponents of the racial theories and racist attitudes prevalent in the bourgeois republic.

Colombia's most respected scholar, Luis López de Mesa, helped Miguel Jiménez López give currency to racial theories that worked to the disadvantage of their dark-skinned fellow citizens. Like Jiménez, López de Mesa saw Colombians growing lighter in complexion thanks to "a fermentation owing to the fact that the race is cleansing itself of its Negroid sediments."[21] In 1927, López de Mesa authored a commissioned report titled *The Ethnic Factor*. High church officials and government officials received copies of the report, which represented the most advanced thought of the day on the subjects of race, race mixture, and the dire consequences of "population darkening." The following passage suggests the tenor of that report: "The mixture of the Indigenous with the African element, and even with mulattoes deriving from it, would be a fatal error for the spirit and wealth of the nation. Rather than being eliminated, the failings and defects of both races would be augmented. Thus we would have an astute, indolent, ambitious, sensual, hypocritical, and at the same time vain *zambo* (person of mixed indigenous and African ancestry), as well as an ignorant and unhealthy one. This mix of impoverished bloods, from inferior cultures, creates subjects who are unable to adapt, and who are subject to nervous disorders, mental disease, madness, epilepsy, and crime. They come to fill asylums and jails when they enter into contact with civilization."[22]

The literary counterpart of López de Mesa, racial theorist, was paisa essayist Fernando González. His *Los Negroides* (The blacks), 1931, was astonishing for its reviling of Latin America, whose representative figure he called the Great Mulatto. Americans, González wrote, suffer a "complex of illegitimacy" dating from the Spanish conquest, and a "mangled identity" as a consequence. In the volume González heaped scorn on Colombia's leading figures, holding up Enrique Olaya and Laureano Gómez as "homunculi," Abadía Méndez and Miguel Antonio Caro as "sleeping mulattoes whose tongues are moved by European books," Jorge Eliécer Gaitán as "a clownish mestizo."[23]

Fernando González's racism forms a case perhaps more appropriate to psychiatric than historical study. One notes a chilling similarity between his ravings and the racist blasts being heard in European capitals at the same moment. Yet even elitist Colombians, few of whom could be absolutely certain that they possessed purity of the blood 400 years after the conquest, refused to take Fernando González very seriously. A writer for *El Tiempo,* reporting on one of González's public lectures, remarked mildly that the writer's interpretations were a "refreshing change," that watching him perform was like "watching a naked man."[24]

The *El Tiempo* writer's detachment in reporting the eccentricities of Fernando González reflected the aplomb with which educated Colombians observed the human comedy over most of the first quarter of the new century. Most of those in positions of leadership were steeped in a culture variously described as positivist, Victorian, and bourgeois. Only in the late 1920s, when a spirit of combativeness began to invade certain sectors of the non-elite, did prominent Colombians begin to sense that a relatively benign period in their national history was ending. Profound forces were at work in Colombian society that would challenge old assumptions of who Colombians were and what they were about.

Daily Life

Over the first quarter of the twentieth century Colombian society changed in a myriad of ways. Most of those changes were at the level of material culture. At the beginning of the period citizens lived more or less as they always had—

traveling on foot or on the backs of animals. At the end of those twenty-five years they traveled by air, automobile, or electric trolley. Physical improvements also had the effect of demonstrating how far Colombia had yet to go. Rich and poor continued to live in two worlds, and to accept that condition as proper and normal. There was little questioning of the status quo, though incidents sometimes occurred when the poor protested especially egregious affronts, sometimes violently. But even then the protests were brief and had little lasting effect on society.

Social change in Colombia during the time of the bourgeois republic did have revolutionary implications, though only the most discerning eye appreciated that fact. Spokesmen for the Church perceived the changes and protested them loudly, warning of their threat to traditional society. But because the transformations were so incipient, so subtle, conservative clerics were unable to articulate their fears in an especially coherent way. But even if churchmen had been able to do so it would have mattered little, as most Colombians were avid for social change, embracing it warmly when it came. They were delighted that their poor country, long far behind the West's leading nations, at last seemed to be catching up. That spirit moved a wag to say, at the height of Colombia's influenza epidemic of 1918, that his country's citizens were happy to be suffering a disease that was afflicting the world's leading nations at the same moment.

The social and political order was not seriously and overtly threatened until well into the third decade of the century. And at that it was challenged only by a relative few and with unfortunate result. Most people simply marveled at the changes and enjoyed them to the extent they were able. The new wealth could no longer be hid, as it once was, inside foreboding houses that presented only dirty whitewashed walls to the alien eye. Automobiles were to be driven, fashions flaunted, imported liquors drunk. Colombia had a sustained source of money for the first time. And though it was not well distributed, even the poor could afford occasional distractions—wireless transmissions and motion pictures brought a world to them that previously only the wealthy had visited in their travels. Bolivian diplomat Alcides Arguedas was so impressed by the Colombian public's devotion to film that he remarked during his visit there in 1928, "this century has a new religion: it is called Charlie [Chaplin]."[25]

One of the most important changes in Colombian daily life was one of the most gradual and least noticed. That was chlorination of the nation's urban drinking water, which produced astonishing declines in mortality from typhoid fever and other waterborne diseases. Typhoid fever, which in 1905 carried away 672 of Bogotá's citizens, killed just 266 in 1920, and twelve in 1924.[26] A Public Health Committee, formed in 1916, managed to have a law passed requiring the channelization and covering of the San Francisco and San

Agustín rivers, and for the construction of an adequate sewage treatment plant for Bogotá.[27] Those improvements were expensive, however, and there was little discernible progress toward effecting them until the 1920s when moneys became available. By 1926 the projects were well on their way to completion.[28] Costly projects aimed at improving water quality and sanitation were the product of a generally brightening financial situation that had produced a geometric growth of some municipal budgets following the War of the Thousand Days, and that by 1913 brought the first national budget surplus in recent memory. Seen from another perspective, those improvements were but tentative beginnings in improving a generally inferior quality of life for Colombians. Across the nation streets were generally filled with litter and uncollected garbage that, when conditions were dry and windy, became airborne. Bogotá's streets were so filthy that one visitor claimed it gave him the impression of living in a sewer.[29] Only the better-off among the capital's residents bathed regularly, as most possessed nothing resembling the modern bathroom. Pedro Nel Ospina paid weekly visits to the home of his friend Lucas Caballero in order to soak in the latter's cast-iron "American-style" bath tub.[30] Public services were tenuous all over the country. When Bogotá experienced a general strike in 1919, the city narrowly averted a public health catastrophe as its sanitary system collapsed.[31]

Investigative journalists like young José A. Osorio Lizarazo reported that large numbers of Bogotá's residents continued to live in inhuman conditions. In a 1926 piece titled "Mansions of Poverty," he described miserable, sickly squatters living on the yet exposed banks of the Río San Francisco, and in the city's numerous *pasajes*, or twisting alleyways, such as the Pasaje Rivas, where bohemians of an earlier era had written poetry and used heroic drugs.[32] Birth rates remained low through the first three decades, around 20 per 100,000 population, and average life expectancy stood at 34.2 years in 1930.[33] Over the first thirty years of the century total population nearly doubled, rising from about 4 million to 7.5 million in 1930.[34] The striking increase in population was owed to the sharp decrease in deaths of children under five years during the period. At the turn of the century 60 percent of all deaths in Colombia were of infants and young children.[35] Colombia experienced virtually no immigration over the period. One ends with the mixed assessment that the level of Colombian public health conditions was improving rapidly, though they remained appalling.

Through the first two decades of the century, and well into the third, relationships among social groups remained much as they ever had been, as the groups themselves remained relatively undifferentiated because increasing wealth was only at the earliest stage of broadening and complicating social definitions. A corporative ethos continued to prevail by which members of the several social strata continued to regard each other and themselves in terms of categories: *cachacos,* public men, the deserving poor, artisans, and the like. Public men did not spend much time debating the question of poverty, but when they did it was usually in moral, not socioeconomic terms. Nor was the same standard of analysis applied across groups. The debate over the problem of alcoholism serves to illustrate the point. Excessive drinking was acknowledged as serious by leaders, though criticism of it was usually couched in terms of the lower classes. Liberal leader Uribe Uribe hated drinking, calling it "the social cancer that devours us."[36] The Church spoke out continually against it too. Alcohol was commonly referred to as the worst enemy of Colombia, and over most of the period discussed Colombia witnessed an ongoing temperance movement. But as the upper classes campaigned for abstinence among the poor, they themselves drank to excess. "Here they drink like nowhere else in the world," remarked the widely traveled Alcides Arguedas. He described a party he attended in which sixteen friends entertained 200 invited guests. They laid in twenty cases of whiskey, ten of champagne, and another five of assorted other liquors. That was consumed before the party ended and a truck was sent to fetch an emergency supply.[37]

During the time of the bourgeois republic Colombia's poor perceived themselves as making up a valuable, indeed integral part of society, and strove to live in as dignified a manner as possible. One visitor to Bogotá marveled that tiny boys earned money selling penny poems to market women, most of whom could not read them. Yet the women took pleasure in knowing that the poems expressed sentiments of moral uplift, filial devotion, and the pursuit of virtue by humble people such as themselves.[38] In the countryside campesinos bore the abuses of large landowners with remarkable placidity. Aware that in many cases their rights were being violated, they still sought redress of their complaints through legal means, rather than direct action. That would remain the case at least until the mid-1920s, when growing affluence at all levels of society would start changing popular attitudes in the countryside.

The remarkable tranquility of the period also suggests popular adherence to traditional social norms. One searches in vain for meaningful signs of social protest prior to the 1920s. The few outbreaks of popular violence were logical responses to perceived *desafueros* (violations of rights). The riots of 1893, it will be recalled, sprang from a series of defamatory newspaper articles that infuriated Bogotá's artisans. A similar incident occurred in Bogotá seventeen years later, on Colombia's independence day, July 20, 1911. The celebration's high point was to have been a bullfight staged in a new ring then standing on Bogotá's northern edge, near the Bavaria brewery. Unfortunately, the chief attraction, the popular torero Valentín (Antonio Olmedo) performed so miserably as to have insulted the hundreds of aficionados who had flocked to see him that day. Order deteriorated quickly, with the crowd ultimately attacking the bullfighters, pulling boards off the sides of the bullring and making off with the bulls. Police were called in and shortly after their arrival began firing on the crowd. That touched off a major riot that left nine civilians dead, dozens of police injured, and the police station besieged. Only when Minister of War Mariano Ospina Vásquez appeared along with several army officers and a handful of soldiers was order restored.[39]

As in 1893, the independence day riot of 1911 was touched off by ordinary citizens who felt they had been wronged. Their aim was not so much that of destroying property as it was regaining the cost of their ticket. That is why many in the crowd pulled boards off the bullring and carried them away. Their taking of the bulls was more in the spirit of the common good than of common theft, for they drove the animals up to the Panóptico, slaughtered them, and gave the meat to the prisoners. The mob turned on the police not because they represented symbols of authority, but both because they had failed to appreciate what the trouble was about and had fired into the crowd. There would not be another major incident of urban violence in Bogotá for another eight years.

Around the time of the bullring riot of 1911 there were signs that Colombia was at last making real progress in solving its age-old dilemma concerning transportation. First the nation's two major cities were linked to the Río Magdalena by railroad, and shortly thereafter interior Antioquia was linked to the Cauca valley by the Amagá Railroad. Completion of the Amagá Railroad at the end of the century's second decade created palpable excitement among the people of Antioquia and of the Cauca valley. A photo from about 1920 suggests their enthusiasm. It shows ladies in formal gowns and gentlemen in frock coats, seated in chairs arranged along a flatcar being pushed up a grade of the Amagá line by an 1880s-vintage wood-burning locomotive. Those elegantly dressed paisas had laboriously built the railroad, and they clearly intended to have a look at it.[40]

In spite of completion of a few vital rail lines, progress in the area of transportation was frustratingly slow. By 1920, 90 percent of the nation's land routes remained mule trails, and just 1,195 kilometers of railroad track was in service. A very limited amount of highway was passable by truck and automobile. Rafael Uribe Uribe, visiting Chicoral, between Bogotá and Ibagué, near the Río Magdalena, spoke expectantly of the day a traveler could depart Bogotá in the morning, lunch in Ibagué, and retire for the night in Cali. "What an immense change that would be," he mused.[41] Rufino Gutiérrez, a writer on geography, complained of transportation difficulties in the coffee country of southern Antioquia late in the decade, and Ecuadorian visitor Alberto Gutiérrez described the incongruous sight of "rich and powerful persons," who having reached Girardot by train, were then forced to continue their trip northward to Honda on "miserable rented mules" because of low water on the Río Magdalena. The Colombian Gutiérrez, who painted Colombia in glowing terms generally, had to admit that the trip upriver from Barranquilla to Honda was one of unending monotony punctuated by "inhumanly tenacious" mosquitoes and asphyxiating, forgelike heat.[42]

Urban Colombia, too, experienced a lumpen sort of progress in the area of transportation. Early in the second decade the main street of Bogotá and several other important thoroughfares of major cities received new asphalt surfaces. Bogotá's mayor was so enthralled by the smooth surface that he had city workers clean it with kerosene after sweeping it, with the result that Seventh Avenue partially dissolved. While the city's trolleys were electrified in 1910, they moved so slowly as to earn the nickname "comets" (*cometas*) for the infrequence of their appearance. Others laughed at their slowness, claiming that in Bogotá electricity moved more slowly than mules. When Bogotá's first traffic codes were put into effect in 1912, police enforced them on bicycles. Yet in spite of all, those developments portended extraordinary change over the second and third decades of the century. Whereas there were only 100 autos in Bogotá in 1912, by 1920 the number had tripled. By 1930 it had again doubled.[43] In 1921 bus service was inaugurated between Bogotá and Chapinero, and in 1923 the capital registered its first traffic fatality when one Señor Pataquirá was run down by a taxi.

The appearance of an airplane in the skies above Bogotá portended a true transportation revolution for Colombia. The nation's first airplane was brought to Medellín in 1913, and by 1916 enthusiasts in Bogotá had formed an aviation club, though they had no plane. German entrepreneurs in Barranquilla founded a company named the Colombo-German Society of Air Transportation (SCADTA) in 1919, the same year Europe's first commercial route was opened between London and Paris. A year later SCADTA inaugurated Colombia's first commercial service. That made the nation the first in the Western hemisphere to possess a scheduled air line. Twice-weekly mail service linked Barranquilla and Bogotá in 1924, and air service cut the time between Bogotá and Girardot to twenty-two minutes, shortening that journey by a factor of fifty. By the latter part of the decade government officials like Laureano Gómez were flying about the country on business, complaining that the country's railroads were wholly insufficient in comparison to airplanes.[44] Charles Lindbergh praised Colombia's progress in aviation when he visited there in early 1928. The giddy celebration attending his arrival bespoke the joy of a people at last free to soar above their mountains.

Other changes in Colombian daily life rivaled those first air flights in symbolism and significance. New residential patterns became possible thanks both to improvements in the transportation network and to the increase in affluence nationwide. Whereas the wealthy had traditionally lived in two-story colonial-style houses in center city, by the second decade of the century they had begun to move into new residential neighborhoods on the northern outskirts, or even as far as Chapinero. A rapidly expanding middle class began taking up residences in barrios built especially for them. One such was developer Ernesto González's Barrio Santa Anna, located south of the city. It boasted reasonably priced homes, a healthful environment, and location near the streetcar line for easy commuting to work.[45] Meanwhile the poor were left behind in the center city.

The homes built by the wealthy departed radically from the traditional. Decorative eclecticism was the norm in Colombia during the bourgeois decades. Entire barrios were built around themes, such as La Merced in north Bogotá, whose stately row houses followed an English motif. In cities like Cartagena diversity was the rule. Architectural historian Germán Téllez has written of the "fantastic formal transplantation" which took place in that city during the second and third decades of the century. Rich Cartageneros were like "bourgeois kings" in their unique palaces, Téllez writes, their flights of fancy representing what he refers to as the "bourgeoisation" of elegance, the vulgarization of luxury."[46]

Such architectural excess obviously represented conspicuous consumption of the most extreme sort. It was also a peculiarly Victorian way of communicating the owners' social status. But beyond that the new architectural styles gave concrete expression to a growing openness in Colombian society, to a long-standing desire among the country's leaders to emulate the more "highly civilized" nations. Their new English- and French-style housing developments, whose green spaces were moved from the interior patio to the outer, surrounding area, eloquently attested to that significant shift in elite psychology.

The movement of Colombia's elite into their suburbs, and their experimentation with new architectural forms, reflected yet other changes in Colombian society. Throughout all of national history prior to that time, rich and poor had lived in close proximity, the latter deferentially serving the former, who lived downtown. Such a residential pattern, with the elite at the center and non-elites living round about in concentric rings characterized by ever decreasing wealth and status, palpably replicated and reinforced the "hierarchy of virtue" propounded in moral philosophy of the time. When they quit the center city the elite sundered the old residential arrangement that gave real expression to philosophic schemes they continued to endorse. Even as that process occurred, the factors making it possible—technological and attitudinal change, growing affluence, and increasing complexity of the social structure—worked subtle and not-so-subtle changes in attitudes of the non-elite. The implications of those changes, and of the fact that the center city had been abandoned to the urban class, would become clear on the afternoon of April 9, 1948.

For the time being only a few Colombians, most of whom were associated with the religious right, worried about the character of city life. Luis Serrano Blanco, a colleague of Laureano Gómez, warned those attending the Ecumenical Congress of 1913 that urban life threatened orderly society because it eroded faith and awakened an unhealthy materialism in the masses. Whereas the soul of the rustic harbors a pure, angelic faith, said Serrano, the urban setting "muffles" it: "Amidst the book and the newspaper, the club and the committee, the lecture and the hubbub, the soul's clarity is banished." His spirit thus disturbed, the urban dweller fell easy prey to social agitators, to "a torrent of wishes and desires and ambitions without end or measure."[47] Two years later, in 1915, Archbishop Manuel José Cayzedo equated the modern city to ancient Babylonia, a place where evil reigned amid "human vanity and the false splendor of material progress that obscures the true good and perverts the spirit with concupiscent fire." He proclaimed the bankruptcy of faith in national progress, whose poisonous fruit he portrayed as the war at that time raging in Europe.[48]

In the end, members of the religious right found themselves simply talking to one another. Clerics like Archbishop Cayzedo could anathematize urban life, with its "circuses, salons, theaters, motion pictures, clubs, and concerts," all of which he perceived as awakening in the masses "a feverish sensuality [that] invades and corrupts everything."[49] But it was poet Luis Tejada who spoke for and to the average Colombian: "I don't want your cursed peace, the alluring tranquility of your country towns."[50] As the 1920s approached Colombians had seen modernity and decidedly had liked it.

Advances in nonprint media during early decades of the century heightened Colombian sensitivity to the larger world. The appearance first of film, and then of radio, completed the link whose forging began with wire service news reports appearing in their newspapers prior to World War I. Bogotá's first movie house, the Olympia, opened in 1919. That was five years after paisa businessmen had formed a company for the distribution of U.S. films in Medellín. During the 1920s dozens of theaters opened in cities and towns all over the nation, and Colombians of all classes became movie aficionados. In some cities the better-off families rented theater boxes for their weekly movie viewing. Once, when spectators in Bogotá were angered over the poor print quality of a much-anticipated Charlie Chaplin film, they destroyed the interior of the Teatro Olympia. They would have done the same to the new Teatro Faena, where the same movie was showing, were it not for timely arrival of the police.[51] It was Archbishop Cayzedo's nightmare of modern life come to Colombia. Journalist Hernando Téllez echoed the good archbishop's concern some years later when he observed that North American film "hammered and undid" traditional life in old Santa Fe, offering "a new version of love, sport, fashion, comfort—of life in general."[52]

Radio came to Colombia in 1923, when Pedro Nel Ospina hired the Marconi Wireless Company to establish a national telecommunications network. On April 12 of that year, the president inaugurated the service with an effusive greeting to Marconi himself, who was at the time in London. He congratulated the Italian for his invention and expressed hope that radio "might become a tool of moral and material betterment for the Colombian people." Marconi responded in kind, congratulating Colombia on its "drawing closer to . . . the main currents of civilization."[53]

While public men, philosophers, and theologians debated the effect that the new inventions might have on their people, Colombians flung themselves into their long-term love affair with the media. Thanks to the silver screen, the radio, and international wire services, they could at last indulge their avidity for things beyond their mountain fastness. They became fans of foreign film stars, athletes, and celebrities, and emulated them in their own sports clubs and domestic film industry. *El Tiempo* marveled that no political event in recent memory so agitated Bogotanos as did the Dempsey-Tunney bout of 1927. A large crowd of fans stood for three hours in front of the city's telegraph office awaiting periodic announcements of the fight's progress. Many of them no doubt returned home shaken when longtime champ Jack Dempsey lost the famous "fight of the long count."[54]

Urban Colombians thus became close observers of the world scene during years of the bourgeois republic. It was natural that they should become fans and spectators, for in being so they merely continued to fill the role they had played in the political life of their nation. Through the first decades of the century and beyond, most Colombians were political spectators who cheered on their nationally famous leaders, stars of the traditional parties to which they were passionately attached, frequently at the level of personal interest. Politics meant jobs, the control of public policy, and in some cases, personal safety or the lack of it. And beyond that, it made for a decidedly good show. National politics was full of drama, and treated the viewer to an unending series of emotion-laden vignettes that unfolded with the regularity of a modern soap opera. And of course it was free—at least over the short term. One of the most riveting political dramas of early-twentieth-century Colombia took the form of Greek tragedy. Its protagonist was an old man in whom hubris and self-hate jostled for precedence. The old man was pursued by furies who first made him a pariah and then destroyed him. But the old man rose again and lashed out at his tormentors through dreams. It was a wonderful, ultimately satisfying drama. It served too as a kind of coda to a placid yet complex and important era in Colombian history.

The Tribulations of Marco Fidel Suárez

On the afternoon of November 6, 1923, former president Marco Fidel Suárez, then sixty-nine years of age, was knocked down by a freight wagon as he walked down Calle 12 (Twelfth Street) in the center of Bogotá. Luckily he was not badly hurt. Bystanders helped Suárez to his home, which was four blocks away, and he continued work on his newspaper piece "Primer Sueño Internacional" (First international dream), which appeared in the newspaper *El Nuevo Tiempo* a week later. That sort of accident wasn't unusual for him, as throughout his life Marco Fidel Suárez had liked to walk alone in the middle of the street, his head bowed as if oblivious to everything around him. Three years earlier, then president of the nation, he was run over by a cyclist as he walked in the intersection of Calle 10 and Carrera 8 (Tenth Street and Eighth Avenue). He was not seriously hurt that time either, and had the police free the cyclist.[55]

The incidents described above are significant and symbolic, for they shed light both on the character and life of Suárez, and of his country as well. Marco Fidel Suárez was a man of the old Colombia, of the premodern, sleepy republic where save for an occasional mounted rider or slow-moving carriage, the streets were quite safe for pedestrians. Being a man of fixed personal habits, he was not about to change his ways simply because the country was caught up in rapid metamorphosis.

Both accidents took place at low points in his career, the first occurring as he withstood withering criticism for his handling of the nation's highest office, and the second shortly after he was driven from office by a powerful coalition of political enemies. Yet in keeping with his character, Suárez picked himself up and went about his business much as before, sure that he would be vindicated in the end. And to an extent he was vindicated, though in a way typical of Colombian public men of his era. Between his public humiliation in 1921 and his death in 1927, Suárez defended his past actions, expounded on Colombian history, and pilloried his enemies in a series of newspaper articles that ultimately filled twelve volumes bearing the title *Sueños de Luciano Pulgar*. The *Sueños* were constructed as dialogues between Luciano Pulgar (Suárez) and several younger men. Written in measured, elegant style and full of literary allusion as well as learned disquisition on literature, grammar, and vocabulary, the *Sueños* stand as both a classic of Colombian political literature and a monument to the era of Suárez and men like him.

Marco Fidel Suárez was a scholar in the tradition of Miguel Antonio Caro, his mentor and friend. Unfortunately for himself and his party, he was, like Caro, an inept and uncompromising politician who in the end damaged his cause rather than helping it. Above all else, Suárez was a complex personality, a troubled man who never allowed himself or others to forget that fact. The second of three Antioquian presidents during the bourgeois Republican era, Suárez stands as one of the most intriguing personalities of modern Colombian history.

Suárez came into the world burdened by hardships that would have doomed a lesser man to a life of obscurity. He was born in poverty, the illegitimate child of a mixed-blood washerwoman living in the village of Bello. Yet his mother doted on him, and struggled to give him advantages that would in time allow young Marco to enter the priesthood. Rosalía Suárez was known in Bello to be a woman of irreproachable character in spite of her liaison early in life with a young man named José María Barrientos. Barrientos, who later married a woman of his own social class, is believed to have contributed modest financial support to his illegitimate son.[56] Still, the greatest contribution to Suárez's later success came from Suárez himself. From his earliest years he revealed an intellectual brilliance that astonished all who knew him. Shortly after entering the seminary at age fourteen, he so impressed Manuel Uribe Angel, who had lent the youngster an abstruse tome and later had quizzed him on it, that Uribe found himself embracing Suárez and exclaiming "you are the teacher and I your student. You can digest iron, stones, and whatever you'd like!"[57]

Suárez spent seven years in seminary, leaving when the civil war of 1876 forced it to close. That was about the time he decided not to join the priesthood, insisting that his "human smallness" prohibited him from following that sublime vocation. So he became a school teacher. Two years later a friend, Father Baltazar Vélez, convinced Suárez to continue his education in Bogotá, and contributed moneys to that end. That brought the young man into contact with Carlos Martínez Silva and Miguel Antonio Caro, who befriended him, and future public figures like José Vicente Concha and Miguel Abadía Méndez, who were his students. When the Regeneration began in the 1880s, Suárez entered government service, first as Caro's assistant at the National Library, and later as an undersecretary at the Ministry of Foreign Relations. He took up those posts having earned a degree of local celebrity by defeating all challengers in an essay contest on Spanish grammar. Embarrassed when called forward to accept the award for his "Essay sobre la gramática de Andrés Bello," he responded with the outward humility that characterized him: "I receive this award not so much as a prize, but rather as a challenge to make me worthy of it."[58]

The political fortunes of Marco Fidel Suárez waxed and then waned with those of the Nationalist Party, whose cause became his own. Thanks to the party he held high political office at a relatively young age. And thanks to the party he earned money that enabled him to marry the love of his life, Isabel Orrantía, with whom he produced two children before century's end. His service to Nationalism led him from the sublime to the ridiculous. The mid-1890s found him eloquently defending the government in debate against Rafael Uribe Uribe and José Vicente Concha in the Chamber of Representatives, and skittering about the Plaza de Bolívar handing out fireworks to be ignited following a speech by Miguel Antonio Caro.[59]

Suárez's shining moment came on August 1, 1900, when he penned his scathing "Protest" against the overthrow of President Sanclemente. In his letter Suárez called the military coup a barbaric and unpatriotic act that would dishonor Colombia before other nations of the world and would undo public order by weakening the principle of authority. As he saw it, the coup ushered in a phase of barracks revolts and praetorian rule in Colombia that would make public authority "the plaything of public opinion, that is to say, the passions of the mob. . . ."[60] The letter was a statement of principle and moral outrage illuminating Suárez's belief that through manly demonstrations of character one gained wisdom, virtue, and glory. It was also a quixotic act that signaled his withdrawal from politics for an indefinite period. With the letter Suárez charted a path that would lead him into endless misfortune and unhappiness.

Over the next ten years Suárez was in political eclipse. Although he had endorsed Rafael Reyes's suspension of Congress in late 1904, he angered the general a year later by agreeing to defend Conservative Eutimio Sánchez, who along with Suárez's friend Luis Martínez Silva had tried to overthrow Reyes in late 1905. When Reyes fell in 1909, Suárez was put forward by Nationalist Conservatives and Liberals to complete Reyes's presidential term, but lost to Ramón González Valencia by a vote of 47 to 31. The following year Suárez supported the candidacy of Carlos E. Restrepo, an act leading to his political rehabilitation by the Republican Party.[61]

Between 1910 and 1912, Suárez served Restrepo in a number of capacities, most notably as minister of public instruction, the same post he had so spectacularly abandoned on August 1, 1900. But he resigned the position in February 1912, following a disagreement with the president over the power to make appointments. He had held the post only a short time. Within two months of his resignation Suárez broke with Republicanism and began working for Conservative union. That would be his chief political goal for the remaining fifteen years of his life. He sounded his call for peace and reconciliation within the party in a letter of April 23, 1912. Among those receiving copies were José Vicente Concha, Aristides Fernández, Jorge Holguín, José Joaquín Casas, Miguel Abadía Méndez, Alfredo Vásquez Cobo, and Jorge Roa. His initiative bore fruit, and by late 1912 Suárez and Concha headed a rejuvenated Conservative Party directorate. Two weeks before the Eucharistic Congress of September 8–11, 1913, unified Conservatives had settled on Concha as their candidate for the 1914 election. Marco Fidel Suárez had in characteristic fashion sacrificed his own presidential ambitions to the greater cause of Conservative unity.

Suárez no doubt had his own selflessness in mind as he walked the streets of downtown Bogotá in early September, meditating on what would be remembered as one of his finest speeches, his oration titled "Jesus Christ," to be read at the plenary session of the Eucharistic Congress, on September 11. All had seemingly gone smoothly in pulling together fragmented Conservatism. The upcoming congress, he hoped, would serve as a benediction of sorts to the recent work of harmonizing the party representing Catholic Colombia. Still his own sacrifice should not be forgotten, especially three years hence, when it would be time for him to launch his own presidential campaign. Thus it was that Suárez's personal piety combined with his political ambitions and disappointments, to produce one of the more moving passages contained in his speech "Jesus Christ." In it Suárez reflected on the supreme sacrifice of the "God Man": "These virtues of Jesus Christ purify and ennoble human nature. . . . Martyrdom, which is a heroic sacrifice in the service to truth or justice, is fecund with happiness because it produces glory."[62] They were words that Marco Fidel Suárez would have cause to reflect on frequently between that time and his death in 1927. Although he did not suspect it at the time, the process leading to his eventual political martyrdom was already well advanced.

The downfall of Marco Fidel Suárez actually began in January 1896, when his old patron Carlos Martínez Silva, and others, published their "Motives of Dissidence" against the Nationalist Party, thus formalizing the Historical-Nationalist split within Conservatism. Historicals led by José Vicente Concha had refused to seat President Sanclemente in 1898, angering Suárez, who loved and admired the old man. His anger turned to fury in 1900, when Martínez Silva, Concha, and others overthrew Sanclemente, moving Suárez to revile them in his letter of August 1. Suárez exhibited his political ineptness four years later, when he wrote Rafael Reyes praising him for dissolving the national Congress. His letter constituted an indirect criticism of Historical Conservatives, whose congressional opposition had frustrated Reyes's program of national accomplishment, and it was especially imprudent given the fact that prominent Historicals like José Joaquín Casas, Dávila Flores, and Abadía Méndez had either just publicly humiliated themselves before Reyes by retracting their criticism of him, or had suffered exile to Orocué. Suárez struck at José Manuel Marroquín's son, Lorenzo, three years later when the latter published his best-selling anti-Nationalist novel *Pax*. Lorenzo Marroquín was a particularly inviting target because he had counseled Aristides Fernández during the latter's reign of terror. Within months of the appearance of *Pax*, there appeared a slim, luxuriously bound volume titled *Análisis gramatical de*

"Pax" (A grammatical analysis of *Pax*), whose author identified himself simply as "a nephew of González Mogollón" (the fictitious name assigned Miguel Antonio Caro in the novel). Literate Colombians instantly recognized it as Suárez's work, and chuckled over what in essence constituted a 220-page lampoon of Marroquín's careless use of the Spanish language.[63]

Two years after his attack on *Pax,* Suárez again angered Historicals both by running for president against their candidate, González Valencia, and by receiving the vote of their despised enemy Rafael Uribe Uribe. The following year, 1910, he urged his Nationalist followers to support Carlos E. Restrepo in opposition to Historical Conservative candidate Concha. Thus Historical Conservatives had reason to look balefully on Suárez's call for party unity in early 1912, following his break with the Republicans. If ever there was a marriage of convenience, Colombia's Conservative Party unity of 1912–13 exemplified it. All it would take to shatter fragile party harmony was a speech given by young Historical firebrand Laureano Gómez in February 1914, and Suárez's championing of the Urrutia-Thompson Treaty in May of that year.

The old Nationalist and the young Historical Conservative were predisposed to dislike one another. Suárez, and everyone else in Bogotá, knew that Gómez and his newspaper, *La Unidad,* represented Historical and Jesuit interests. Nor was it a secret that Suárez was strongly backed by the secular Church hierarchy, led by Archbishop Herrera Restrepo. Not long after Suárez's call for Conservative union in 1912, Gómez's intemperance toward men prominent in the government of Carlos E. Restrepo had led the archbishop to suspend *La Unidad.* But by early 1913 the newspaper was back in business, and in early 1914 it reported the incidents giving rise to the Gómez-Suárez breach. On February 11, 1914, Gómez delivered a speech before the Academy of Caro, a literary society founded in honor of the Regeneration-era grammarian and politician Miguel Antonio Caro. In it Gómez likened himself and other young Conservative extremists to ideological crusaders who excite the masses with words that wound more terribly than swords.[64] On reading the speech Suárez was reported to have remarked acidly that Gómez advocated "mystic demagoguery." *El Tiempo* and the Liberal establishment seized on Suárez's words as a hopeful sign of Conservative division. A curious event of the previous month hinted that Colombia's Liberals had already found in Gómez someone whom they believed might aid them in their fight against Conservatism. On the twenty-sixth of January, and unbeknownst to Conservatives, Bogotá's Masonic lodge rewarded one Antonio Rincón Gálvis for saving the life of Gómez, who was at the point of drowning in a river near the resort town of Anapoima.[65]

Animosity between Gómez and Suárez became open and acrimonious during April and May 1914, when the latter led a successful campaign to have the Urrutia-Thompson Treaty approved by Congress. Suárez shared the hopes of most Republican Union members that good relations with the United States might be restored. That would bring sorely needed capital to Colombia in the form of cash compensation for the loss of Panama. It was also anticipated that loans from U.S. banks would be forthcoming. Historical Conservatives, on the other hand, under whose regime Panama was lost, harbored a dislike of the northern metropolis that verged on hatred, a view hardly unique among most Colombians. Yet unlike most others they were intransigent in insisting that national honor demanded no reconciliation with the Americans and certainly no acceptance of money from the Yankees. Historicals like Laureano Gómez said such an act would "make vile the concept of patriotism."

Marco Fidel Suárez started working to restore good relations with the United States after March 1913, when President Woodrow Wilson promised, in his inaugural address, to end "Big Stick" diplomacy. Within weeks Suárez had published an *El Nuevo Tiempo* piece arguing for renewed negotiations and referring to the United States as "this great nation."[66] On August 8, Suárez and Nicolás Esguerra were selected to lead an Advisory Commission charged with renewing treaty negotiations with the Americans. All this likely explains Suárez's odd juxtaposition of George Washington and Ecuadorian arch-conservative Gabriel García Moreno in his oration "Jesus Christ," both men given as examples of divine providence acting in history.[67] The Americans were equally anxious to reestablish good relations with Colombia, for in August their consular officer in Bogotá had notified his government that British interests threatened to monopolize oil exploration in the country. Accordingly, the treaty was rushed to completion by early 1914. Signed on April 6, the Urrutia-Thompson Treaty stipulated that Colombia receive a $25 million indemnity for the loss of Panama. It also included a statement of the Americans' "sincere regret" over the events of November 1903.[68]

Congressional debate of the treaty took place during May 1914 and pitted Suárez and members of his committee against Historical Conservatives in both chambers. On May 12 the Senate went into closed session, where Suárez and the Liberal Nicolás Esguerra argued forcefully for the treaty. As he was wont to do in his public statements, Suárez offended his opponents in such a way as to become instantly destructive of his own interests. He insulted young and old Historicals alike. First he assured the Senate that there was nothing to fear from the shouts and threats of the "heroes of mystic demagoguery." Then, after Esguerra concluded his defense of the treaty, Suárez turned to a colleague and said in a loud whisper, "That argument would convince a jackass, save for Dávila Flores." On May 14, Laureano Gómez responded to Suárez in a scathing and sarcastic *La Unidad* editorial titled "Mystic Demagoguery." "It is inconceivable," wrote Gómez, "that a man like Suárez, possessing the sweet wisdom . . . the evangelical gentleness of a good Christian, could ever utter the wretched and vulgar phrases attributed to him." "As Sr. Suárez never has been known as flippant, or biting, or aggressive, or cruel, or angry in his speeches, letters, glosses, and parodies," Gomez continued, "we're certain that he had only words of praise and flattery for Dr. Dávila Flores." Gómez went on to assure his readers that Suárez would never label anyone else a mystic demagogue. "The day we organize a fraternity of mystics, demagogic or traditionalist," Gómez continued, "Sr. Suárez will certainly be our director."

Opponents of the treaty used every conceivable means to obstruct its passage. Their charges were that it impugned national honor and that its negotiators were chiefly interested in the indemnity. One senator suggested that the indemnity be used to purchase a piece of land on which a gallows should be erected and from which members of the treaty commission should hang themselves. The negotiators were likened to Judas Iscariot, and Dávila Flores called Suárez and the rest pharisees more venal than those denounced by the Savior. The Semitic metaphor was extended to the point of finding the treaty an act of repugnant Judaism, something to be expected of a document signed by members of a commission the majority of whose members were Antioquian. They accused Suárez in particular for wanting to place Colombia in orbit around the "Polestar." Suárez admitted the charge, but argued that improved relations with the United States made sound economic sense. He cited Conservative Party cofounder Mariano Ospina Rodríguez, who in 1857 had suggested that Colombia seek annexation by the United States.[69] In the end the treaty was approved by Colombia's Congress, as the Historicals did not have sufficient votes to block it. Still they had the satisfaction of knowing that Henry Cabot Lodge subsequently defeated the treaty in his own Senate, and that they themselves had played a role in his success. At one point during Senate debate, Lodge, a Republican from Massachusetts, had brandished a copy of La Unidad, citing it as proof of Theodore Roosevelt's charge that Colombians were venal, unpatriotic, and thievish, interested only in getting their hands on American dollars.[70]

Having lost their fight against the Urrutia-Thompson Treaty, the Conservative dissidents fell back to regroup. Between June and October 1914, La Unidad suspended publication, during which time the Historicals formed their own party directorate headed by Ramón González Valencia and Manuel Dávila Flores. By early 1915 the battle was joined. Gil Blas editor Benjamín Palacio Uribe called it a "duel to the death." Arrayed on one side were Suárez and the Church hierarchy. On the other were Historical Conservatives and the Jesuits, and their political organ La Unidad, called by some "the Archbishop's nightmare."[71] Early in 1915 wall posters appeared in Bogotá advising Catholics not to read La Unidad, and in August, Suárez circulated a communiqué in which he complained that he could not continue being party leader in the face of the opposition of Gómez and his friends.[72] For his part Gómez was publishing Suárez's letter of December 31, 1904, in which the latter praised Reyes for closing Congress. In his commentary on the letter Gómez warned ominously that "in the not-so-remote future we will see justice done."[73]

The dissidents had picked a fight they could not win. As Gómez denounced his enemies in the Cámara and in the pages of his newspaper, a noose woven of political and ecclesiastical power, and reinforced by popular disapproval of his hot words, began closing about him. In September 1915 wall posters again appeared advising Catholics not to read La Unidad. Even Father Leza, called "the technical director of demagogic mysticism," found himself telling San Bartolomé students not to read the newspaper that he himself had helped found.[74] Leza soon fell victim both to what Palacio Uribe called "the terrible underground battle" raging within Conservatism, and to "the magistral diplomacy" of Marco Fidel Suárez. The Jesuit was removed from his headmastership and not long afterward sent back to Spain. In a Cámara debate of late 1915, the hirsute Conservative Sotero Peñuela became so enraged by Gómez that he lunged at him snarling, "I'll make this swine pay!" Even Liberal editor Benjamín Palacio Uribe, who had once suggested that his party contribute to the support of La Unidad, and who relished the sight of Conservatives tearing at one another, began to criticize Gómez. In an editorial of September 27, 1915, bearing the title "Paragons of Virtue and Garbage Pickers," Palacio opined that prominent citizens like Marco Fidel Suárez merited respect.

During the time of strife Gómez began to receive help from several young followers of Liberal leader Benjamín Herrera. The most important among them was Alfonso López Pumarejo, then thirty years old—three years Gómez's senior. The two formed a working relationship not long after López had absorbed one of Gómez's witty oratorical jabs. López had just concluded his first congressional address when Gómez rose and remarked that everyone had just witnessed the miracle of a man who had spoken for ninety minutes having no discernible subject. Yet June 26, 1916, found the two harassing Marco Fidel Suárez and other Nationalist Conservative ministers who had been called to testify before the Cámara. Gómez spoke first, damning Suárez as nothing more than the "ambitious and suspicious leader of a political party" who, with likeminded men, allowed themselves to be led "like sheep" by the United States. After both Gómez and López spoke, Suárez, who had listened intently, an ironic smile on his face, rose to reply. Standing, head bowed, his arms crossed with hands placed inside his sleeves like a seminary student, he agreed to answer the charges of López. Then he added that he would not answer Gómez's speech, which he had found to be vacuous, contradictory, and generally uninspiring. He went on, praising Gómez for the good memory that enabled him to recite his speeches, memorized over a period of days in the backyard of his house. "The only thing I can't forgive," said Suárez, "is a grammatical sin—the crime he committed in saying sheep, an ill-chosen term that dulls an otherwise brilliant piece. . . . Sr. Gómez . . . has been unable to learn the difference between sheep and lambs. But I'll take this up with him later if God gives me strength, which shall be the case, for the recitations of Sr. Gómez have not yet given me hepatitis."[75]

Suárez's words brought guffaws from representatives and spectators alike. For years afterward Laureano was known by the nickname El Ovejo (the sheep). He was often caricatured as an angry ram draped around the neck of, or otherwise burdening, Marco Fidel Suárez.

Within months of the June 1916 debate, Suárez registered an impressive victory over his young antagonist. He succeeded in ridding himself of *La Unidad* thanks to help from Archbishop Herrera Restrepo and the Vatican. In early August a meeting took place between Gómez and papal internuncio Monseñor Enrique Gasparri. While all of Bogotá's newspapers carried conflicting accounts as to who initiated the meeting, and what was said therein, it seems clear that Gómez was threatened with harsh ecclesiastical sanctions if he continued to publish his newspaper. Gasparri may have suggested that a diplomatic post in Europe might be forthcoming if Gómez made peace with Suárez. An offended Gómez gave his version of the meeting to Liberal journalist Eduardo Santos, who scooped all other newspapers by publishing an article on the affair.[76] Less than a week later Archbishop Herrera Restrepo anathematized *La Unidad*.[77] Six weeks after that Herrera gave the newspaper its coup de grâce by way of a circular, approved by clerics attending an ecclesiastical conference in Bogotá during those weeks. According to the circular, *La Unidad* did not meet the norms handed down by the Holy See and hence was not to be read by Catholics.

Gómez did not close his newspaper quietly. Before *La Unidad* ceased publication at the end of September 1916, its editor had vigorously protested his Catholicism, accused Suárez and his Nationalists of ruining Conservatism, sued *El Nuevo Tiempo* editor Ismael Enrique Arciniegas for libel, and left behind a statement of principles that well may have given Suárez, his followers, and all other Colombians pause for thought: "When all those who resist the vertiginous current of revolution become afraid of it and hide, we will appear. . . . We (emulating a great Spanish tribune) [Antonio Maura] are devoted and intransigent conservatives and Catholics—lifelong conservatives and Catholics, by conviction and conscience, through heartfelt feeling and understanding. We were yesterday, we are today, we will be so tomorrow, and we shall die being so. . . . We obey without hesitation every order of ecclesiastical authority. . . . If we must remain alone, without friends and without followers, we will cry out in our isolation *Suárez no!*"[78]

In the months following Suárez's victory over the Historicals, political Colombia positioned itself for the presidential succession of 1918, even though it was a foregone conclusion that Súarez would be both candidate and victor. No one doubted that he would be borne into office thanks to his control of major power brokers—the Church and regional bosses, who would turn out the vote on election day. Events would soon prove something else that many suspected at the time: the Suárez presidency would be one of the least successful in national history.

Colombia was entering a state of ferment as the second decade of the century drew to a close. With World War I ended, and international trade recovering, the demand for Colombian coffee increased dramatically. The revenues from ever increasing coffee exports would help invigorate the economy. New social ideas were entering the country too, moving growing numbers of ordinary people to perceive the national milieu in new, frequently iconoclastic ways. The period from 1918 to 1922 marked, in short, an important juncture in national history. As such, Colombians should have elected a vigorous, forward-looking leader who might have responded creatively to changing social and economic realities. Instead they placed in office an old man of another era, one who liked to stroll in the streets of Bogotá meditating on his next literary creation, a "fossilized grammarian," in the words of the young Liberal newspaperman Enrique Santos.[79]

Nor was it simply that Suárez was out of touch with the times as he prepared to lead his restive nation in 1918. Throughout his life he was afflicted by a variety of physical and psychological maladies. His health problems had ranged from stomach troubles in his thirties, to intestinal bleeding in his early fifties, to a mild stroke that paralyzed the left side of his face around the time of his presidency. All that heightened the pain he suffered when knocked down periodically while walking in Bogotá streets. His physical ill health complemented Suárez's lifelong feeling of personal inferiority. He viewed himself as a "child of sin" owing to the circumstances of his birth. African ancestry on his mother's side linked him by blood to a people believed at the time to be suffering "racial decay." When Suárez at last, in mid-1917, achieved his goal of winning the Conservative presidential nomination he feigned to reject it, saying, "I can't be president because I lack certain qualifications, and these impede me. . . . It's that . . . I am of illegitimate birth; and there will be no lack of pharisees who, wishing to injure me, will attack me on this point, injuring the party and the country."[80]

Domestic tragedy intensified the physical and psychological disabilities afflicting Marco Fidel Suárez as he took up his presidency in 1918. No sooner than Suárez entered office, he received word that his only son, a lad of nineteen, had succumbed to flu while studying in the United States. All the new president's maladies were aggravated by the ferocious political attack Suárez had suffered from early 1914. By the time he took up his presidential duties Suárez was likely to weep copiously when confronting an emotional situation.

The Suárez candidacy aroused such opposition across Colombia that when asked what he took most pride in during his four years in office, outgoing president Concha replied that it was keeping the army from shooting into crowds protesting the election of February 11, 1918.[81] In spite of Concha's efforts to prevent bloodshed, there was considerable violence across the country as the Conservative political machine made sure that dissident candidate Guillermo Valencia did not win. It was not so much that the holders of political power mistrusted Valencia, a Historical Conservative, as it was they feared the heterogeneous coalition he headed. Formalized in late October 1917, it joined Liberals, Historical Conservatives, and members of the Republican Party in a union that was, as one wag observed, "founded in mutual hatred and mutual fear." Thanks to the Suárez candidacy, Colombians were treated to the incongruous sight of Benjamín Herrera and Alfonso López, representing the Liberals, Valencia and Laureano Gómez, representing the Historicals, and Eduardo Santos and Luis Eduardo Nieto Caballero, representing the Republicans, all stumping the country together. Odd friendships were made during the tempestuous months of late 1917 and early 1918, such as the one that sprang up between young Laureano Gómez and old General Herrera. That the coalition did not work together as smoothly as it might have is suggested in Valencia's complaint that "campaigning with Laureano Gómez [is] like trying to plow with a fighting bull." Still the campaigners generated great excitement on their swing around the countryside, always speaking to large and enthusiastic crowds, and sometimes experiencing violence. It was during those months that Guillermo Valencia characterized Laureano Gómez as "the human storm."

Ugly incidents attended the 1918 campaign. Shots were fired into the homes of Liberals in many parts of the country. Touring coalition members were set upon and beaten by people in the towns of Guasca and Gachetá, north of Bogotá, when a priest there accused them of persecuting the Church and spreading false doctrines. And there was at least one bona fide assassination attempt against Laureano Gómez.[82] In the end machine politics triumphed. Marco Fidel Suárez won handily and was inaugurated August 7, 1918.

The first crisis in Suárez's administration was socioeconomic and had a decided international dimension. It was the shooting of workers in the Plaza de Bolívar on March 16, 1919, an incident that left six dead and eighteen wounded. The trouble originated in the president's decision to purchase foreign-made cloth for army uniforms, which angered the city's artisans. Led by the president of their newly formed Central Workers' Union (Sindicato Central de Obreros), Alberto Manrique Páramo, several hundred of them assembled in the plaza to protest the action. Suárez spoke to the workers, attempting to explain that he had canceled the foreign purchase, deciding instead to have the uniforms produced domestically. But his voice was drowned out and he withdrew to the presidential palace, where he subsequently entered into a shouting match with Manrique Páramo. The labor leader returned to the plaza and egged his followers on. Stones were thrown, and the presidential guard opened fire.[83]

Key to understanding the tragedy is the fact that members of Colombia's social and political establishment interpreted the demonstration as the possible first step in an attempted communist takeover of Colombia. On March 14, Minister of Government Marcelino Arango had alerted governors and prefects around the country of an impending Bolshevik threat. The next day *El Nuevo Tiempo* editor Ismael Enrique Arciniegas used Arango's circular as the basis for an inflammatory editorial titled "Anticipating Bolshevism." And the fact that workers in the Plaza de Bolívar mixed cries of "Long live socialism!" with shouts of "Suárez, no!" heightened the impression that they were dangerous subversives. No matter that organizers of the union made it clear just a month earlier that their movement was non-Marxist, embracing instead what they called a "Christian" approach to progress within a context of class harmony.[84] What men like Suárez, Arciniegas, and others of Colombia's bourgeois republic believed they saw were signs of the same sort of radicalism that so recently had pulled down the czarist regime in Russia. Viewed from that perspective, the firing on unarmed workers in downtown Bogotá was a product of the same impulse that had sent club-wielding, machine-gun-reinforced police into protesting workers in Seattle, Washington, a few weeks before the Plaza de Bolívar shootings. Nor were its dynamics unlike those of the May Day violence that rocked Paris six weeks later.

Problems of both an economic and a diplomatic nature brought the second crisis of Suárez's administration. Early in 1919, matters of mutual economic concern sent Colombia and the United States back to the bargaining table in an effort to resolve their differences over the Panama question and the treaty that would settle it. By August of that year U.S. and Colombian officials had agreed to accept a version of the Urrutia-Thompson Treaty that omitted the "sincere regret" phrase that had long rendered it unacceptable to members of the U.S. Republican Party. Just as it seemed that the treaty and its $25 million indemnity might be forthcoming, the U.S. Senate's Foreign Relations Committee, headed by Henry Cabot Lodge, balked. The North Americans had learned of presidential decree no. 1255B, of June 20, 1919, proclaiming national control of Colombia's subsoil. Suárez responded by announcing that he would suspend the decree if only the Americans would approve the treaty. In his usual ill-timed and clumsy way he followed his decision with a telegram to the Colombian consul in New York instructing him "to explain to interested and influential persons" that his government wanted foreign development capital, and didn't intend to let the matter of petroleum stand in the way of improved Colombian-U.S. relations.[85]

September 16, 1919, found the Plaza de Bolívar once more full of antigovernment demonstrators, all shouting "Suárez, no!" and "Viva" to the anti-Suárez coalition. They had come to hear Eduardo Santos read a resolution in which he mentioned the president's telegram to "interested and influential persons" in the United States, and in which he and his group called for Suárez's resignation. The crowd fell silent when Laureano Gómez climbed into the rented open car that served as the orators' stage, each member of it anticipating the blistering attack that was to come. But a series of explosions cut it short, and Gómez dropped like a stone into the convertible. The crowd scattered, some in it shouting, "They've killed Dr. Gómez!" When the noise died Gómez cautiously lifted his head only to see a member of his erstwhile audience staring back at him wide-eyed, asking lamely, "Dr. Gómez, where is your hat?" "They shot it right off my head," Gómez answered.

Seconds later all understood that they had been victims of a practical joke. A Suárez supporter had tossed a package of firecrackers under the car as Gómez began his speech. Marco Fidel Suárez delighted in the incident, remembered in Colombian history as "the conspiracy of the firecrackers." He retold the vignette lovingly in several of the *Sueños de Luciano Pulgar* that he began publishing soon after resigning the presidency in 1921. His most complete retelling of the event appears in the "Sueño" published July 24, 1923, appropriately titled "The Dream of Gratitude."[86]

During 1920 a variety of problems, most of an economic nature, further eroded support for the Suárez presidency. Colombia had at last entered the era of growth and prosperity that national leaders had anticipated. But as revenues from coffee sales began rolling in, the bonanza created new problems even as it highlighted and intensified old ones. Costs of basic necessities skyrocketed, driven upward both by decreases in food supplies as ever more workers entered the coffee groves, and by the increasing amounts of cash in the pockets of consumers. Urban dwellers were especially hard hit, as food prices in places like Bogotá rose to double and triple the amount paid for comparable items in New York and Paris. Coffee revenues created a flood of imports that clogged ports, illustrating their antiquated condition and the impenetrability of red tape holding those articles in customs. Coffee growers protested ever more loudly the lack of railroads and river boats needed to get their crops to the foreign market, and their pressure for reform intensified. Colombia still had no central bank, and the ongoing imbroglio with the United States sharply limited their access to foreign sources of capital. And owing to the seasonal nature of coffee harvesting, unemployed and vagrant workers periodically appeared in towns and cities. When the twice-yearly harvest took place other crops languished as agricultural workers flocked to earn high wages on coffee *fincas* (farms) large and small. As if all that weren't enough, Colombia and its grammarian president were rocked by strikes and demonstrations that made all the more vivid fervid visions of impending social revolution.

None of these things appeared to concern Suárez as much, however, as did the war raging within his party, and his continuing inability to make progress on the Urrutia-Thompson Treaty. On July 21, 1920, five days after being run down by the cyclist, the president reminded Congress that seventeen years had passed since the loss of Panama, and Colombia had still not received its just reparations from the United States. Furthermore, he pointed out, making reference to a similar remark by U.S. Foreign Affairs Committee member Albert B. Fall, the lack of a treaty harmed the economy and juridic interests of both countries.[87]

From the beginning of his term Suárez had rightly perceived himself as a political pariah, and he constantly spoke of stepping down in favor of a man stronger than he. On September 17, 1920, he had sent a telegraph to the governor of Valle, Ignacio Rengifo, in which he indicated that he was increasingly anxious to resign. That might placate enemies whom, he rightly perceived, had an aversion for him "because they consider me representative of what they call a theocracy."[88] Early in 1921, Suárez made a difficult and rapid journey from Bogotá to Calarcá, Caldas, to personally offer Rengifo the presidency. Rengifo refused the offer for complicated political reasons, though Suárez explained the rejection as resulting from the death of Rengifo's wife.

That the sickly old Colombian president had undertaken a hellish round trip, involving two muleback crossings of the Quindío pass in three days' time, suggests Suárez's desperate state of mind in early 1921. And the fact that a secondary figure like Rengifo had refused the offer, after Pedro Nel Ospina and Carlos Holguín had done the same, hints at the disarray prevailing in Conservatism. All this helps explain how Marco Fidel Suárez came to make the most grievous error of his political career. He welcomed Laureano Gómez back into the party fold.

Two weeks after the president's hurried trip to Caldas, Gómez traveled to the town of Pacho, northwest of Bogotá. Before returning he was feted by local Conservatives. Gómez delivered an emotional impromptu speech there in which he said that he felt no need to renew the seductive newspaper crusades of his younger days, adding that he remained an enthusiastic defender of the Conservative cause, standing ever ready to serve his party if called on to do so.[89] Conservatives around Suárez seized on the remarks as a clear sign that a new, moderate Gómez had emerged. Ismael Enrique Arciniegas passed that

judgment, expressing pleasure that Dr. Gómez, "accidentally retired from po-
litical activities . . . [is] ready to serve the Conservative cause with his energy
and obvious talent."[90] In the succeeding months conversations took place during which Gómez assured party leaders that he was indeed a changed man.
Accordingly his name was added to the Conservative ticket and in elections of
May 1921 he was reelected to the Chamber of Representatives.[91] On June 1,
Gómez was hosted at a banquet at Bogotá's elegant new Hotel Continental.
Photos of the dinner reveal Gómez, arms crossed and a half smile on his face,
looking contentedly at Maestro Arciniegas, seated just to his left.

It was not long before Arciniegas, Suárez, and the rest discovered that they
had made a dreadful mistake. The first sign of that appeared in early July, when
Gómez and his old companions from *La Unidad* broke with Pedro Nel Ospina,
who had been named the official party candidate for the 1922 presidential
election.[92] Then on July 20, when congressional sessions commenced, dissident
Conservatives, most of them Historicals, joined with Liberals to elect Laureano Gómez president of the Chamber of Deputies over the administration's
candidate, Ismael Enrique Arciniegas. Backed by a substantial majority in the
chamber, Gómez was at last ready to confront the government of Marco Fidel
Suárez.

Laureano Gómez used his new congressional office to harass Suárez supporters at every turn. On September 6 his old adversary, the old Conservative
from Boyacá, Sotero Peñuela, could not finish a speech because Gómez allowed hecklers in the visitors' gallery to drown him out. When Gómez lashed
the ministers of Suárez with charges of corruption, onlookers cheered him
heartily. That led Suárez, who had meanwhile attempted to resign once again,
to replace his entire cabinet on September 19, in hopes that it would placate
opponents of the Urrutia-Thompson Treaty. The action bore fruit when, on
October 13, the Senate approved the treaty. Still, acceptance of the document
depended on its passage in the Cámara, many of whose members liked it only
slightly less than they liked their president. As things stood in mid-October
1921, Suárez himself was the chief obstacle to the treaty.

On October 26, Laureano Gómez took the floor of the chamber to debate
Suárez's minister of government, Aristóbulo Archila. He began his speech in a
routine way, as if simply to answer Archila's accusation that he had failed to
specify his charges against the government. Suddenly, about halfway through
the discourse, Gómez shifted the focus of attack from Archila to Suárez, professing to have in his possession at that moment documents proving the president guilty of official wrongdoing so shocking that he, Gómez, was both astonished and tormented. So grievous were the president's sins, continued Gómez,
that the myth of his "piety and mysticism" would be forever laid to rest.
Gómez went on to list in considerable detail charges that Suárez had sinned

6. Laureano Gómez, 1921. By permission of the Museum of Modern Art, Bogotá.

against the nation by selling both his salary and his expense account for ready cash, and by accepting bribes, in the form of loans from interested parties, in exchange for lucrative government contracts. Laureano Gómez concluded his indictment of Suárez by calling for an investigation of the president and for his removal from office.

Gómez's charges created a sensation. Members of Congress formed an investigative committee and called upon the president to appear before them and explain his actions. Then the Chamber of Representatives adjourned and Laureano Gómez was borne away to his nearby residence on the shoulders of friends and admirers. The next day Suárez appeared before the chamber, along with members of his cabinet, to answer Gómez. It was a dejected Marco Fidel Suárez who addressed the body, among whose 112 members he counted only twenty-two supporters. To make matters worse, one of his political enemies, Jesús Perilla, presided over the body that day. Speaking in a hesitant, nearly inaudible voice, Suárez told the representatives that he had indeed sold his salary at a discount and for cash, something not only legal, but something he had done all his life. He only did it, he continued, because he was in urgent need of cash. He also admitted that he had accepted a substantial loan from an American businessman who had sold railroad track to the government, but only because the banker who normally made him short-term loans was low on cash at the moment. None of that, Suárez insisted, impugned his honor or harmed national prestige.

When he turned to leave the podium and exit the chamber a din of hoots and catcalls rose from the packed galleries. Jesús Perilla did nothing to silence them. Mortified and near to swooning, Marco Fidel Suárez had to be helped from the chamber by one of his cabinet members.[93] Within a week a congressional committee cleared Suárez of criminal charges, whereupon he again tendered his resignation. It was accepted, and on November 6, 1921, Jorge Holguín assumed the presidency to complete the last nine months of Suárez's term. In little more than a month the Colombian Chamber of Representatives approved the Urrutia-Thompson Treaty.

Meanwhile Marco Fidel Suárez sat at home planning how he might best salvage his tarnished honor. Before many months had passed he would begin to make public the torment he had suffered for the past eight years at the hands of those he labeled the Eumenides (the Furies). One of his earliest "Sueños" contains the following thinly disguised autobiographical passage: "That whole cloud of enemies came down upon the old man because they said he was a rank fanatic, a diehard sectarian, a hidebound pharisee of falsity having an alarming streak of Machiavellianism. That's the reason they treated him as they did. And if you want to know what was in store for him, learn the verse of the bat: 'they stab you and they slice you, they thrash you, they beat you, they hammer you, they pierce you, they riddle you, they divide you, they cut and cleave you, they dismember you, they split you, they cut your throat, they crack you, they flay you, they crush you, they club you, they batter and bruise you, they destroy you, confound and baffle you.'"[94]

5

Money Comes to Colombia

Pedro Nel Ospina: Businessman President

Colombian leaders had always dreamt of the time their country should become rich. For decades, even centuries, they had repeatedly been told, and had told one another, that their land was a storehouse of untapped wealth, a potential cornucopia. José Celestino Mutis, Spanish-born royal official and savant of the late eighteenth century, had been one of a procession of foreigners who, when gazing upon the country's verdant mountains, flora and fauna, succumbed to their beauty and dedicated major portions of their lives to studying and writing about them. Baron Alexander von Humboldt was similarly impressed by New Granada (Colombia) when he visited and studied it during the lifetime of Mutis. Francisco José Caldas and the great Simón Bolívar, a native and an adopted son, early in Colombia's national period gave their lives seeing to it that the nation's treasures might be enjoyed by their own descendants. Yet all their labors were frustrated by a land that proved to be a cruel though doubtless beautiful mistress. Upward of a century after the passing of Bolívar, Caldas, and other tragic heroes of Colombia's early national era, the people of that country remained, as yet another foreign visitor described them, beggars reposing upon seats of gold.

But at last, in the third decade of the twentieth century, Colombia's long-anticipated bonanza materialized when a tidal wave of dollars rolled into and across the country. The sudden appearance of money in the poor, remote, tradition-bound nation necessarily had profound consequences. And the fact that a great deal of the cash immediately reached the hands of a considerable proportion of the citizenry, especially the rural citizenry, rendered the Colombian case extraordinary. That the major part of the money was generated by coffee, that most coffee was grown by yeoman farmers, and that those farmers were dispersed over a mountain fastness in central Colombia, would have significant consequences for the nation.

Businessman and politician Pedro Nel Ospina presided over the first half of what would prove to be eight years of vertiginous economic growth. Elected in a violence-and-fraud-ridden contest of March 1922, he occupied the presidential chair at the precise instant when his entrepreneurial skills could be of greatest benefit to the country. Ospina belonged to that generation of Colombians imbued with the certainty that progress was inevitable and that they knew exactly how to achieve it. And as a man of sixty-four, he had experienced the full measure of frustration that political turbulence and an intractable physical environment had visited upon Colombia. His earliest memories were of a lengthy foreign exile that he spent with his family, the consequence of political machinations against his father, President Mariano Ospina Rodríguez. In early middle age he fought in the War of the Thousand Days, witnessing the war's baleful effect on the nation. In the course of the war Ospina himself suffered exile by order of President Marroquín, who accused his then minister of war of conspiring against him.

When he became the official candidate of his party in 1921, Ospina began planning how best to improve Colombia's economic position. His concern was not entirely selfless. Over the previous two decades he had dedicated much energy toward personal economic pursuits, frequently seeing those enterprises fail because of Colombia's primitive banking system and its sensitivity to international business cycles. As recently as 1920, he had lost money when Vásquez y Correa, one of the country's largest commission houses, failed in the economic downturn of 1920–1921. Fifteen years before, several of his businesses failed in the crisis of 1904 that brought down most of Medellín's banks. This helps explain why as soon as he was elected, Pedro Nel Ospina traveled to New York to consult with American economists and financiers. The Americans were more than sympathetic to his entreaties for economic assistance, in part because they had learned of potentially rich Colombian oil fields. Within two months of his taking office, in August 1922, Ospina's government had negotiated a $5 million loan from an American bank, a sum equaling almost 20 percent of total government revenues for 1920.[1] Of infinitely greater significance for Colombia's immediate economic future was the arrival soon thereafter of Princeton University economist Edward Kemmerer, employed to help Colombia create a central bank. The bank began to function the following year and instantly produced the anticipated results. Exchange rates stabilized, interest rates fell, and rapidly increasing deposits created significant amounts of new investment capital.[2] As the tempo of business accelerated, national and departmental tax revenues increased steadily. Once the Kemmerer mission concluded its task, Ospina arranged with one of its members, Thomas R. Lill, to reorganize national accounting procedures. Accordingly, Lill left Colombia with a system that one commentator called "something that our greatest industrial concerns might envy."[3]

As Colombian finances strengthened, additional moneys appeared in the form of loans to departmental and municipal governments, most of which proceeded from U.S. banks. Over the decade approximately $200 million was lent. The magnitude of the sum can be appreciated when one considers that those moneys equaled nearly three-quarters of national tax receipts from normal sources collected between 1923 and 1928, the years during which the money was lent.[4] The sum becomes all the more extraordinary when compared to the paltry amount foreigners had invested in Colombia before Pedro Nel Ospina took office. In 1913, Colombia had received but one percent of British and U.S. investment in Latin America. With between $2 million and $4 million in U.S. investment in 1913, Colombia was perhaps the least-favored Latin American nation in that regard.[5]

Twenty-five million dollars from the U.S. indemnity swelled the torrent of money flowing into government coffers during the 1920s. That sum, which became payable the year Ospina took office, was ten times more than all bank reserves in Colombia at that time. Some 25 percent of those moneys were assigned to the new Bank of the Republic and a new sister institution, the Agricultural Mortgage Bank, which began to function in 1926. The rest was distributed among sixteen railroad projects and six additional projects aimed at improving ports and river transportation.[6]

As Pedro Nel Ospina dedicated himself to the welcome task of disbursing the cash choking his treasury, another flood of money entered the private sector of Colombia's economy. That revenue derived from coffee, whose value and quantity had increased steadily after the War of the Thousand Days. Colombia had half a billion trees in production or started as seedlings during the presidency of Pedro Nel Ospina, a man who himself "came from coffee," as one writer put it.[7] Colombians had planted coffee with a vengeance after the war. Influential men like Antonio José Restrepo dedicated themselves to opening coffee lands along a vast frontier south and southeast of Antioquia. Restrepo's experience as a colonizer of the Caldas-Quindío region dated from the 1880s.[8] He and others financed the movement of *colonos* (colonizers) to the coffee frontier. The success of their endeavor is told in statistics showing a 300 percent increase in coffee exports between 1913 and 1929, and a physical expansion of coffee groves that pushed them from 9 percent of the country's cultivated area in 1915, to 15 percent in 1925, to 22 percent in 1937. In 1920, 70 percent of Colombian export earnings derived from coffee, up from 40 percent at the turn of the century.[9] That resounding increase took place in a setting of rising prices marred only by the brief downturn of 1920–1921. Coffee prices rose by 50 percent between 1923 and 1928, and revenue earned from coffee exports doubled.[10]

Revenue earned by coffee, virtually all of which went to private individuals, consistently and substantially exceeded those taken by the government through normal tax revenues. By 1928, the year governmental affluence reached its peak, moneys earned from coffee exports, at 88 million pesos, exceeded all government revenues—including foreign loans—by nearly 12 million pesos. Revenues from petroleum and banana exports brought in an additional 34 million pesos in 1928.[11]

Colombia was, by the mid 1920s, awash with money. This may not have meant that the country or its people were wealthy in absolute terms, but it was the case in a relative sense. In 1928 the combined increase from foreign loans, taxes, and coffee earnings were twelve times what they had been in 1910. And much of that money quickly found its way into private hands, whether through salaries received from work on government-financed public works projects or in the form of moneys earned through some aspect of foreign trade. Colombians characterized it as the time of "the dance of the millions." And it was the paisa industrialist Pedro Nel Ospina who played for the dance. He instituted the reforms that, in the words of Alfonso Patiño Roselli, "represent one of the finest hours of Colombian economic history." Without Ospina's initiatives, writes Patiño Roselli, Colombia "would never have been able to achieve the rate [of growth] that it reached . . . in money, credit, and finance."[12]

The Consequences of Affluence

Money induced Colombians to change lifestyles and aspirations, and it produced changes in social structures as well. The nation went on a spending binge. Wealthier citizens invested in automobiles imported from the United States and Europe. Toward the end of the decade more than 40,000 Pierce-Arrows, Cadillacs, and Stutz-Bearcats traveled Colombian highways, five times the number of just a few years earlier. Nouveau riche coffee growers borrowed money on their land to construct multistory buildings in the cities. The better-off developed expensive tastes. French champagne became de rigueur at upscale celebrations, and middle-class households increasingly boasted new Victrolas bought on credit. The sale of imported musical instruments tripled over the period. During the Abadía Méndez presidency (1926–1930) it became common to repatriate the bodies of prominent Conservatives who had died overseas, and to hold elaborate reinterment ceremonies once they returned home. Pedro Juan Navarro claimed that even middling European and American cities had Colombian consulates during the twenties, only Soviet Russia being spared invasion by affluent Colombians.[13]

Others remarked that while Colombia was a country where most citizens wore *alpargatas* (sandals) and were illiterate, the wealthy routinely squandered great sums of money in highly visible, frequently offensive ways. The flood of imports worked hardship on domestic manufacturers, and as the burden of debt mounted there appeared worrisome budget deficits. When foreign credits dried up in 1928, and Western trading nations entered economic crisis soon thereafter, it became clear that foreign loans and burgeoning coffee exports heightened Colombia's vulnerability to international economic cycles. By early 1928 public figures like Alfonso López were sounding dire warnings of approaching economic contraction owing to the unfavorable balance of trade.

As the 1920s began, Colombian labor suffered the effects of low wages in the face of inflation that would over the decade run between 3 and 8 percent annually.[14] But with just 6 percent of the nation's population living in the three largest cities—Bogotá, Medellín, and Cali—and the nine next largest cities accounting for only another 6 percent, organized labor was not yet the force it would become in succeeding years. Along with their small numbers in the as yet nonurbanized nation, workers experienced the additional liabilities of uncertainty as to the principles under which they should organize, and popular governmental hostility once they did organize. When the Confederation of Social Action was formed in Bogotá following the influenza and typhoid epidemics of 1918, it counted both Laureano Gómez and Marco Fidel Suárez among its members. And when that organization affiliated with the Central Workers' Union early the following year, the umbrella body couched its call for advanced social legislation in terms of the common good and Christian charity on the part of constituted powers.[15] Less than a month later, in March 1919, as described above, union president Manrique Páramo exchanged words with President Suárez, the denouement being the shooting of workers in the Plaza de Bolívar. Soon after the incident Pedro Nel Ospina sent Suárez a telegram congratulating him for decisive action in upholding the principle of authority. The message moved *Gil Blas* editor Benjamín Palacio Uribe to remark that humble workers shot in the back wasn't enough for Ospina. What he would have preferred was a hundred heads of workers preserved in *aguardiente* (raw brandy) and placed at the entrance of the barrio Candelaria as a warning to others thinking of rising against civil authority. Palacio concluded that the telegram warned workers of what they could expect should Ospina ever become president.[16]

The upshot was that while there was growing ferment within Colombian labor during the 1920s, labor became neither a coherent movement nor a significant political force during the period. During the nine years between 1922 and 1930, there were just eighty-three strikes in the entire country—fewer than nine per year.[17] While several of those strikes were historically significant, they were rarely won by the workers.

As public works projects consumed an overwhelming majority of foreign dollars entering Colombia from 1923 to 1930, and as most of the money paid as salaries went to men drawn to railroad and highway projects from rural areas, the *campo* (countryside) was much changed by the new affluence. Some

30,000 campesinos flocked to construction sites where they exchanged their labor for cash. The sums they earned were not great in real terms, but they were lavish in comparison to the pittance they had earned working as day laborers or tenant farmers. Labor on public works in fact paid five times what agricultural work did.[18] It also offered the inestimable inducement of travel and after-work excitement. The noise and activity of railroad work camps, the bright lights of railhead cantinas, and the affordable charms of female camp followers—not to mention the money—proved irresistible lures to adventuresome and underpaid campesinos.

Two sets of interests were threatened by the appearance of money in rural Colombia and the social and economic disruption it produced. Members of the religious establishment quickly grasped the significance of the changes and mounted a campaign against them. Most of the men heading Colombia's Church had rural origins. They were taught in seminary that human society was organic and hierarchical, and that anything not conforming to that ideal was ungodly and to be condemned. Bucolic rural Colombia, as they remembered it from their childhoods, and as they perceived it daily as they exercised pastoral duties, replicated more perfectly than anything else that benign garden where the first man and woman once lived. Modern life and its noisy hubbub, vice, movement, and material lures were corrupting evils that threatened to destroy their sylvan Eden. Thus, in 1922, Antioquian archbishop Cayzedo lamented "depopulation of the campo," and its sad consequences for the nation.[19] His young contemporary, Monsignor Miguel Angel Builes, denounced the "spiritual decadence" that material culture produced. Builes mourned the young people who appeared destined "to lose the innocence preserved in their mountains, to lose it in the highway work camps." "Have you seen that multitude of men who work on the highways?" asked Builes. "Most of them are victims of the atmosphere that those places breathe. . . . Forgetfulness of God, scorn of holy days, dances, games, liquor, abominable gestures, smiles that proclaim licentiousness, frightening voluptuousness, fornication, lubricious thoughts, sinful desires—it is the chariot of Asmodeus, the demon of impurity that pulls down peoples."[20]

As churchmen sounded their warnings, others acted to protect economic interests jeopardized when workers left low-paying jobs for more lucrative ones. The migration to public works projects led both to labor shortages and to upward pressure on wages. In areas such as upland Boyacá, a non-coffee-growing region having a large and impoverished agricultural population, the problem became especially severe during the twice-yearly coffee harvest. So many Boyacenses began leaving traditional pursuits during the 1920s, that the departmental assembly passed a law prohibiting the seasonal migration. The measure, subsequently overturned at the national level, was of course unenforceable. It brought cries of outrage from coffee growers who, through spokesmen like Alejandro López, denounced the law as immoral.[21] Similar protests were lodged when landowners in other departments, most notably El Valle and Tolima, passed "vagrancy laws" carrying prison sentences for migrant workers found loitering in city streets and refusing to accept agricultural employment when offered.[22] All those efforts to coerce labor were unworkable by the 1920s, when the appearance of money in the countryside gave agricultural workers the means to resist the punitive labor practices of earlier eras.

Once Colombians began making money, they started spending it. That had an invigorating effect on national markets, which quickly expanded to supply the products demanded for both personal consumption and investment. Cities like Medellín, Manizales, and Pereira, in the country's principal coffee-growing area, experienced phenomenal growth in their retail and wholesale sectors, and in manufacturing as well. Medellín, especially, witnessed the proliferation of industries satisfying consumer needs: textiles, beer, sugar, cement, and cooking oil. That in turn spurred the construction of new housing and schools, and the expansion of electricity-generating capacity.[23]

Simultaneous economic expansion took place in the campo. Increasing quantities of coffee required greater milling capacity and improved roads and trails for moving the product to market. Ever more pack animals were needed, as were packing materials in the form of locally produced sacks woven from henequen. Foodstuffs had to be produced in ever greater quantity to feed the shoals of new workers entering the expanding frontier. Hard-working *arrieros* (muleteers) and coffee cultivators needed their beef, rice, and cassava (*yuca*), along with copious amounts of chicha, beer, and aguardiente with which to wash it down. Historian José Antonio Ocampo cogently describes the impact of coffee cultivation on Colombia's economy at large: "Coffee at last created the complex of activities that definitively cracked the precapitalist economy inherited from colonial times, which the expansion of exports in the nineteenth century scarcely scratched."[24]

Economist Luis Eduardo Nieto Arteta drew the same conclusion during the 1940s. Coffee, he rightly perceived, had given Colombia a capitalist economy, a development revolutionary in its implications. Thanks to coffee, and revenues derived from it, Nieto Arteta wrote, campesinos "begin contemplating life in terms of economics," and began "to experience those economic realities with intensity."[25]

The truth of Nieto Arteta's remarks is borne out in the story of labor relations on Viotá coffee estates during the 1920s. Comprising some of Colombia's largest and oldest coffee farms, most Viotá plantations belonged to absentee owners, were run by hired managers, and were worked by campesinos living as tenants on small plots of land that they farmed in their spare time. Over the decades the plantation owners of Viotá, which is southwest of Bogotá, had enjoyed a docile workforce thanks both to the campesinos' traditional deference to men of wealth and standing and to the fact that they were kept from making money by growing coffee on the land they occupied. They were allowed to grow foodstuffs for personal consumption only. The landowners' hold over tenants was so complete that they could renege on labor contracts with the certainty that they would suffer little more than complaints from the disgruntled but impotent workers. Viotá's plantation laborers were, in short, among the most exploited, abused workers in Colombian coffee country. At least that was the case before money came to Colombia in the 1920s, until Viotá's workforce began, as Nieto Arteta put it, to contemplate life through economics.

Prohibited from growing coffee, Viotá's tenants tapped into the coffee economy in other ways. They began producing *panela* (unrefined sugar) and chicha, and a variety of other products for local consumption. Sometimes twenty to thirty tenants united to mount small mills that could supply panela to markets embracing two to three thousand persons. Estate managers knew that the cane from which tenants manufactured panela was stolen from plantation lands. So they did their best to skim tenants' profits through tolls, licenses, fees, and other ploys. But they were generally no more successful in taxing the clandestine cottage industries than was the state. Male and female tenants alike became skilled at hiding the products of their toil, selling on the sly, and smuggling them to other regions where they could be more easily sold. Viotá's grassroots capitalism became so pervasive, so persistent during the 1920s, that half of all arrests for tax fraud registered in the region between 1925 and 1928 were of women who manufactured and sold unlicensed chicha. The tenant-entrepreneurs of Viotá were so proficient in not paying taxes that at length estate owners joined forces with them to evade the excisemen who, with their armed escorts, periodically raided the coffee estates searching for tax cheats of any description.[26] Thus began the democratization of law breaking on Colombia's coffee frontier.

The case of Viotá, and of Colombia's entire coffee zone during the affluent twenties, illustrates the truth of economic historian Fernand Braudel's remark that capitalism and the capitalist spirit rest "upon the broad back of material life," which strengthens in proportion to the expansion of markets and money supply.[27] Viotá's tenants had wanted to become prosperous since they first started working the estates in the 1880s. But not until the 1920s did objective conditions start to favor their endeavor. During that decade money arrived in the hands of people who wished to buy whatever Viotá tenants could produce. Meanwhile, improvements in highways were dropping transportation costs in some cases as much as 400 percent.[28] Recent research in an area of subsistence farming well to the west of Colombia's coffee zone has demonstrated that when improvements in transportation are complemented by market economy, capital accumulation becomes possible even on a wage labor basis. When those conditions exist, migrant farmers ultimately become able to purchase their own land.[29] Those conditions were present in Colombia's coffee zone starting in the 1920s. Once they started earning money, campesinos all across the coffee zone could realistically hope that they too might someday own a coffee finca.

There were coffee fincas to be had during the twenties and thereafter. Statistics reveal a tripling of the number of farms in Colombia over the ten years between 1923 and 1932. Production increased by a third over that span of time, from 2 to 3 million sixty-kilo sacks. Over the following twenty-one years—to 1953—total production in Colombia would double again, reaching 6.6 million sacks. And during the twenty-year span between 1932 and 1952, an additional 50,000 coffee fincas would go into production. Save for a severe decline in prices spanning the 1930s, coffee prices enjoyed a steady and striking rise that pushed prices from thirty cents (U.S.) to a high of eighty cents in the mid-1950s.[30]

The most extraordinary aspect of Colombia's coffee boom lay in what is frequently described as its "democratic" character. The tripling of fincas between 1923 and 1932 was owed both to the settling of public lands and, more important, to the breaking up of large holdings either through inheritance or purchase. Finca "La Julia," in Caldas, to cite a prominent example, was described as the department's largest in 1916. It had 200,000 trees in production that year and occupied over 600 hectares of Colombia's best coffee land. Ten years later the finca's original owner, Luis Jaramillo Walker was gone and so too his monster farm. It had been broken into a number of smaller holdings, passing into the hands of heirs and others who bought fractions of it from Jaramillo Walker's kin. By the mid-1920s no finca in Caldas approached the size of Jaramillo Walker's La Julia. And save for the haciendas of land developer Antonio José Restrepo and a dozen other wealthy men, none of the 10,000 coffee farms in the department boasted as many as 100,000 trees on their holdings. In fact most of those many thousand fincas were small ones averaging a few thousand trees each.[31]

Close students of Colombia point out that the coffee frontier was not the democratic place that idealistic students of the settlement process once suggested it was. Many of the best lands, they stress, were bought by the relatively few persons having investment capital during the late nineteenth and early twentieth centuries. And as land values increased rapidly during the twentieth century, landed interests used every means at their disposal, legal and illegal, to maintain their favored position and even to improve it. However, the point to be made here is that in spite of the inequities and strife that attended settlement of Colombia's coffee frontier, the process gave rise to a new social class, a rural middle class empowered by global demand for the mildly addictive brew whose raw material they produced or otherwise helped dispatch to world markets. Colombia had achieved by the second quarter of the twentieth century the dream of nineteenth-century liberals: the nation had created a relatively self-sufficient, relatively affluent yeomanry having a capitalist outlook and convinced of the virtues of free markets. Luis Nieto Arteta perceived this clearly, going so far as to assert that a "new man" had emerged from Colombia's coffee-fueled revolution: "In this century coffee has placed before Colombian sociologists a complex of realities that enrich their subject of study. Without coffee . . . it would never have been possible to study internal conditions leading to the development of Colombian capitalism, the transformation of the Colombian man, of his style of life . . . in sum, the rich set of diverse realities that coffee has created in Colombia."[32]

Nieto Arteta saw coffee as a curative for Colombia's social and political problems. Coffee was for him a medicine capable of reforming the state and producing forgetfulness of partisan ideologies. Unfortunately the hardy farmers who grew coffee were imbued with a complicated set of historically induced cultural values at the time they commenced earning money derived from coffee exports. The tenacity of those beliefs, and Nieto's optimism, led him to mar his otherwise brilliant analysis with a breathtaking misstatement. When he laid down his pen in March 1948, he left the following happy reflection: "The small producers, the landowners who have cultivated the land with their own hands, have triumphed. Peace and tranquility reign in Colombia."[33]

Money and Mentalities

As noted earlier, Colombia had a mostly peasant population before money arrived there in substantial quantity. Most of the poor engaged in subsistence agriculture on land they did not own. They were passive, respectful of authority and hierarchy, their places fixed in a patriarchal order from which they rarely escaped. The average person enjoyed little physical mobility in those times. Such travel as the average poor rural dweller experienced was at another's instruction and direct economic benefit: he worked as an *arriero* or river boatman, or perhaps marched off to defend his *patrón* (patron or master) in one or another of Colombia's frequent civil wars. Except for that, the poor of rural Colombia lived and died near the place they were born, fulfilling the role society had prescribed for them. It was not serfdom, but it wasn't far removed from it.

The lot of the poor was not necessarily unpleasant; nor did they always chafe under conditions of their existence. It was simply all they knew. In areas of old settlement they frequently lived as renters, growing specified crops, working as vaqueros, or performing any other of the designated tasks carried out on archetypical Latin American haciendas. They served their patron, and if one of his sons got the daughter of a peon with child, the girl's father accepted it philosophically: the baby would be the natural child of a wealthy and powerful man; perhaps it would benefit from the connection. At any rate there was little recourse for the poor man living in close proximity to another, and in asymmetrical relationship of power with him. A foreign traveler described the life of hacienda owners and their peasant workforce before money figured in their social equation: "They lived without worry, dining on the cattle that grew in a nearly natural state on the immense plain, and eating fruits of the earth that their renters—a kind of servant of the glebe—produced by the sweat of their brows."[34]

Before Colombians began earning money, developing modern attitudes concerning its use, human relationships in that country tended to be static and organic. The pace of life was slow, noncommercial. Land tended to be poorly utilized and life was in general rustic, primitive. Life's patterns and rhythms accorded perfectly with the organic metaphors so favored by conservative social philosophers of the day, who from their pulpits described godly society as one of hierarchies, closed systems, and absolutes. In those early times social structure harmonized perfectly with the Thomistic metaphysics so loved by enemies of change. That was the vision of static wholeness so idealized in the early twentieth century by clerics like Archbishop Cayzedo in his mountain fastness, by politicians like José Manuel Marroquín on his highland *estancias,* by students like Laureano Gómez at the knees of his Jesuit mentors.

Modern commercial life introduced a host of factors that soon destroyed the system of traditional authority in Colombia and elsewhere. Long before coffee revolutionized the life of the Andean nation, the expansion of markets and growth of international trade changed Europe, giving nations of that continent an urban, capitalist culture. European thinkers pondered the changes and tried to interpret their impact on human society. Karl Marx (1818–1883), who in 1867 published the first volume of *Das Kapital,* offered a positivist vision that looked beyond capitalism to a benign, strife-free world in which the means of production were communally owned. While the Marxian vision would have a certain resonance in twentieth-century Colombia, it was another German thinker, Georg Simmel (1858–1918), who spoke more directly to the Colombian experience. Lecturing in Berlin during the year of Laureano Gómez's birth, Simmel posited money's liberating effect on human society. Rather than an instrument for the enslavement of humankind, he pointed out, money was the Magna Carta of personal freedom for the European peasantry.

Once money became the mechanism for satisfying contractual obligations it freed serfs to pursue a range of remunerative activities by which they could discharge their obligations. Money introduced impersonality in dealings between subordinate and superior. When cash, whether in the form of salaries or payments to satisfy legal obligations between servant and master, became interposed between lord and vassal, it severed the organic link previously uniting them, depersonalizing both parties.[35]

The process of human liberation by money described by Simmel occurred in Europe over centuries, as urban commercial culture supplanted feudal manorial life. In Colombia the transition took place almost overnight. Whereas European modernization occurred by way of measured expansion of commercial networks, capital accumulation, occupational diversification, and evolution of modern business techniques and technologies, Colombia was hurried into the world thanks to a rapid and sustained infusion of cash money and consumer goods. Both those vital elements of modern life appeared suddenly during the 1920s because of the willingness and ability of affluent, industrialized nations to lend Colombia money and to pay high prices for the agricultural product that grew luxuriantly throughout its mountains. For the first time in her history Colombia's mountains helped rather than hindered national development. Colombian peasants had no need to escape into nascent cities to earn money—to "breathe free," as medieval participants in the process phrased it. Some did that, it is true. But most followed the easier route to the coffee frontier, where they could tap the agricultural bonanza.

Money struck the countryside like a bombshell, revolutionizing social structures, lifestyles, and attitudes. It turned topsy-turvy the old lines of authority. Those at the bottom of rural society's social pyramid experienced for the first time the joys of a seller's market. Humble campesinos from highland Boyacá and Cundinamarca were suddenly so prized for their labor that lawmakers in the former department tried futilely to keep them in place. Rural wages rose to unprecedented levels. If landowners refused to pay top dollar, then someone else would. Money, market pressures, and the opportunities they presented worked striking changes in popular attitudes. A new militancy appeared, leading landless tenants to challenge authority for the first time. Examples have been given above of those least favored of Colombia's agriculturalists defying convention by mounting clandestine businesses whose raw materials were often stolen from their patrons' land. Tenants in places like Viotá also stopped speaking to their patrons with the old deference, took to sabotaging hacienda property, killing livestock and carving threatening messages on the carcasses. "Why should we waste our time greeting you?" snapped tenants newly conscious of their personal worth. "Better to greet a tree, which at least waves back." Evidence of the new mentality was all the more striking when the historically submissive Boyacense appeared on the coffee frontier with money for the purchase of his own land. "He arrives all stooped, his eyes lowered, walking at a little half trot, courteously taking off his hat and holding it behind him to greet those he passes," wrote Gonzalo París Lozano of Boyacenses entering the region above Tolima's coffee country. "But wait until he sells his first two crops, buys a riding horse, and puts a machete on his belt," continued París. "When that happens, step aside! The contact with other people and customs lifts from him the weight of ancestral oppression little by little [and] . . . turns him into an aggressive person."[36]

The passage suggests in a colorful, anecdotal way the complicated process through which old linkages between patron and client were rendered tenuous. By joining thousands of others on the coffee frontier, by earning the money that allowed them to achieve higher social status, the campesinos described by París Lozano illustrated what Simmel described as money's "disintegrative effect" on old social institutions as well as its tendency to create new ones. Colombia's new rural middle class was created by coffee earnings. And its members expressed "that inner independence, the feeling of individual self-sufficiency" produced when one comes to possess money.[37]

Coffee thrust Colombia's frontiersmen into a setting dominated both by international markets and by individual competition of nearly Hobbesian dimensions. Personal advancement in that heady setting called into play a range of skills not so necessary when Colombia's economy was based on subsistence. To be successful in the new milieu one needed be industrious, pragmatic, and above all rational—even calculating. Those new habits of mind could not but destroy an authoritarian social order predicated on revealed truths. Self-interested coffee cultivators had progressively less need of the old clientelist networks that once allowed political elites to mobilize campesino armies at will. Thus Professor Anthony McFarlane could write that "coffee exports were to prove a . . . durable and effective vehicle for economic growth and political stabilization, and for the realization of ambitions frustrated during the nineteenth century."[38] A number of social scientists have remarked on the link between market expansion and changes in clientelist networks. Especially important, they find, is the way complex new linkages appear, and then challenge or even replace the simple patron-client bond of premodern times.[39] Nieto Arteta made much of that phenomenon in his essay of 1948. He was especially impressed by the way the National Federation of Coffee Growers (Federación Nacional de Cafeteros), an interest association incorporated in 1927, lessened coffee growers' dependence on the state even as it forced greater pragmatism and rationalism upon them.[40]

As coffee changed attitudes and institutions, it also democratized frontier violence. In earlier times landowners and speculators had their way with pow-

7. Coffee harvesters. By permission of the Museum of Modern Art, Bogotá.

erless and inarticulate peasants. But once money empowered campesinos, turning them into yeoman farmers, they stood able and willing to act, violently if necessary, to promote and protect their interests. By most accounts Colombia's frontier was "a secularized and greedy place" where "money was held up as society's most desirable attribute."[41] That was certainly the message contained in J. A. Osorio Lizarazo's naturalistic novel *La cosecha* (The harvest; 1935). Purporting to describe the coffee frontier of northern Tolima, it portrayed the frontiersmen as grasping, lawless, and much given to machete duels and similar mayhem.[42] That was precisely what saddened and discouraged Antioquia's Archbishop Cayzedo, causing him to cry out, in a pastoral letter in 1927, that "the anxiety to earn money makes us forget law, justice, and honor."[43]

Coffee prosperity did not cause the relative position of rich and poor to change dramatically. But the new material culture purchased with coffee revenues had in itself a liberating, individualizing effect. Stores throughout the coffee zone filled with goods never before seen in the countryside. The poorest campesino could now buy a new machete with decorated leather sheath, a new hat, pistol, or horse. Each new purchase heightened self-esteem and provided tangible evidence that one was getting ahead. Campesinos liked to have formal

8. Formal photograph of an Antioquian campesino, circa 1920. By permission of the Museum of Modern Art, Bogotá.

photographs made of themselves and their new finery. Those photos, framed and hung on the walls of rustic houses scattered through the coffee zone, typically showed the head of household, perhaps with his wife, resplendent in suit, gold watch chain, and leather shoes, showing off new ruanas, and carriels (peasant satchels), posed before backdrops of pastoral scenes like those back home. That was but one way members of Colombia's new yeoman class suggested a heightened sense of self, and evoked the style of life to which they aspired.

Middle-class bourgeois culture was what men and women of the coffee frontier hoped to achieve for themselves and their families. They set their standards by what they had seen in the city, and by what they knew of life in the great metropolitan centers of Europe and the United States. Woe to merchants in better stores of Marinilla and Manizales, of Pereira and Armenia, who could not supply them with fine merchandise. Colombians may have lived in the countryside during the 1920s, '30s, and '40s, but their minds were fixed on urban styles of life. They manifested what a prominent Colombian sociologist found to be "an intense desire to identify with the urban upper classes."[44] Colombia's middle-class coffee farmers used their wealth in ways that allow us to read the direction of their thought. They built two-story houses, the first floor serving as a warehouse where coffee from the finca was stored and where its owner had his office—usually no more than a desk and chair, account books, and sometimes a typewriter. The family lived upstairs in a degree of elegance proportionate to the quantity of coffee passing through the storage area below. Sometimes the home owner advertised his political loyalties by painting shutters and doors red if a Liberal, blue if a Conservative. In those ways they forcefully harmonized a plurality of identities that frequently jostled uncomfortably, even contradicted one another. That was the case with churches of the coffee zone, often built in seeming "blind veneration" of modern architectural style, thereby standing in direct challenge to the pope's encyclical against modernism.[45] Yet pious coffee farmers seemed not to notice the contradiction, worshiping contentedly in them, likely agreeing with Bishop Builes that their daughters should not wear slacks or ride astride as both things were affronts to their honor and sinful as well.

Quindío coffee farmer Luis Jaramillo Walker was one who showed his fellow planters the kind of life they could live when they became rich. Described as a man "of unsullied lineage," first among that "race of titans," the Antioquian coffee entrepreneur, he was among the first to defy convention by mechanizing his farm La Julia. His was the largest finca in Caldas in 1916, one whose waterfalls provided electricity for nearby Pereira, as well as for his own mill, which accommodated 900,000 pounds of coffee per month. Jaramillo Walker built a house on his farm, described by one who had seen it as "a fine residence [where] its owner and guests enjoy at all times all the comforts and luxuries of city life. It may be considered a real pleasure resort, as everything that money can buy is found here." Luis Jaramillo Walker is shown in the finely appointed parlor of his home, in a photograph taken about 1916. An old man at the time, he stares fixedly at the camera, ivory-headed cane in hand, a bowler hat on his head, wearing a three-piece suit surely tailored of the finest British wool.[46] The very image of middle-class respectability, he stood as a model for all to emulate. Luis Jaramillo Walker was Colombia's New Man, a paisa Kubla Khan whose pleasure dome in the mountains of Quindío proclaimed that gentility could indeed come to Colombia's coffee frontier.

Meanwhile urban Colombians scrambled to stay abreast of fad and fashion. As material culture expanded it became increasingly possible for middle-

9. Luis Jaramillo Walker, circa 1916. From *Libro azul de Colombia,* edited by Jorge Posada Callejas (1918).

class Colombians to affect the look of their social superiors even if they could not afford their lifestyles. Dime stores and shops with names like Mundo al Dia (The up-to-date store) sprang up, offering a cornucopia of products at affordable prices. New impersonality entered daily life as the concept of paying fixed prices replaced the time-consuming bargaining of older times. Beauty shops offered patrons a variety of hairstyles—braids, bangs, dips, curls, frizzles, and transformations—all guaranteed to be "Parisian chic." Portrait photographers promised to capture the feminine likeness with such artistry that even the homeliest woman was assured of being depicted "with radiant face, her soul brimming over."[47] All these things were clear indications that the nation was becoming more like the great metropolitan world whose ways had previously been so unattainable. In Colombia, as in Europe and elsewhere, the expansion of physical culture was starting to blur the previously clear distinction between the wealthy and the rest. And the growing availability of money was changing popular mentalities in ways that would soon produce striking changes in national political life.

In the 1920s, Colombia had its flappers and its smart set, whose members roared down city streets in late-model automobiles, guzzling liquor from hip flasks in an open and scandalous manner. The years of the dance of the millions marked a brief moment of camaraderie among the country's young future leaders as they forgot their differences and dedicated themselves to having fun. They lived the good life with esprit and at a level of affluence their parents had never known. When the city's college students launched their 1926 carnival, for example, they did so by way of an elaborate charade that they chronicled in a fifty-page publication complete with photographs and cartoons supplied by Pepe Gómez, the younger brother of Laureano. According to the pamphlet, titled *The Case of Pericles Carnaval y Neira* (*Proceso de Pericles Carnaval y Neira*), on the evening of July 14, seven "dissolute young people," among them Olga Noguera Dávila, Tonny Greiffestein, Germán Arciniegas, and Miguel López Pumarejo, kidnapped the wealthy and fictitious Pericles Carnaval, from whom they planned to extort money for that year's student festival and charity ball.[48] Unfortunately, the victim was injured during the assault, and no amount of brandy liberally applied could keep him from expiring. The malefactors were tried before "Judge" Simón Araújo, and a jury made up of Alberto Lleras Camargo, Helena Ospina, and others. Hernando Uribe Cualla and Julio Holguín Arboleda served as lawyers for the defense. At the end of the mock trial Judge Araújo found the defendants guilty as charged, and sentenced them to raise money for a new "fiesta of flowers," to be held in Independence Park, and to find moneys sufficient for underwriting several other projects relative to the student union and to Hospital San José.

Germán Arciniegas, then twenty-six years old, was the spiritual father of Bogotá's student carnivals. The idea for them had occurred to him four years earlier, in 1922, and when he proposed the idea to his friends it "produced universal enthusiasm" among them.[49] Celebrations, after all, seemed especially appropriate in Colombia of the twenties, when money and champagne flowed, and change was in the air. The beautiful Maruja Vega Jaramillo was elected queen of the students. Costumes were rented, floats constructed, and the festivities scheduled for September 21. On carnival day all went as planned: the student parade tied up traffic in Bogotá streets, and afterward the young people jammed the Teatro Colón for the coronation ball. Maruja I was crowned in a ceremony whose high point was a speech pronounced in her honor by Laureano Gómez, who had been asked to serve as "official orator" for the event. Gómez gave a speech variously described as "lyric," "impressive," and "beautiful"—a discourse entirely appropriate to that memorable night.

Laureano Gómez was at the height of his popularity during the 1920s. A great many Liberals, and increasing numbers of Conservatives, perceived him as precisely the person who should lead the nation. As in the case of his country, money came to Laureano Gómez during the 1920s, and he used it to finance three years of travel and study abroad. When he returned home in 1932, circumstances forced him to alienate many of his old friends, ultimately darkening his historical reputation.

The Most Popular Man in Colombia Discovers Money

Not long before September 29, 1916, when he closed *La Unidad,* Laureano Gómez formed two personal alliances that mitigated his defeat by Marco Fidel Suárez and the Conservative Party establishment. The first came through his marriage to María Hurtado, a few weeks before the demise of his newspaper. The second occurred by way of his political collaboration with Alfonso López Pumarejo, which began in 1915. In both instances Gómez gained an added measure of personal economic security, as the families of his wife and his Liberal friend were among Colombia's wealthiest. Thanks to the influence of María Hurtado and Alfonso López, Gómez learned to appreciate money as something more than a potential corrupter of morals and besmircher of national honor.

María Hurtado was the sixth of eleven children of Simón Hurtado, a humbly born native of Popayán who, by dint of hard work and a modicum of luck, became a well-to-do businessman. In his youth Hurtado had raised a small amount of capital with which he launched a company dedicated principally to the export of quinine. He invested his profits in land, eventually coming into possession of what were described as "magnificent rustic estates" in the districts of Popayán, Puracé, and Silvia. His wealth and reputation for rectitude and honorableness enabled him to marry into a prominent family of the region, and not long afterward fate and quinine brought him into association with Rafael Reyes. Hurtado so impressed the young Boyacense, who was ten years his junior, that Reyes named one of his own daughters after a child of Simón Hurtado. Later, during the Quinquenio, President Reyes made his old friend minister of the interior. By that time the Hurtado family was established in Bogotá, a place Simón Hurtado judged better suited to the furtherance of his business ventures than was Popayán.[50]

When Simón Hurtado and his family made their trip to the savanna of Bogotá sometime before the turn of the century, their party created a sensation. Such numbers of pack animals and quantities of luggage had not been seen on the route from Popayán since Francisco José Caldas had passed that way a century earlier. Upon reaching the highlands, Hurtado left his party for a time in the village of Madrid, on the edge of the savanna, while he sought a suitable residence for them in Bogotá. He raised eyebrows when he purchased an ample house in the northern part of town, on Calle 19 (Nineteenth Avenue), thus inaugurating the move of affluent Bogotanos out of the center city. During the War of the Thousand Days and again after Reyes's fall in 1909, Hurtado removed his family to Europe. With Paris as their headquarters, they all experienced European culture through tours of the continent's principal cities. At the end of each trip they returned home bearing household furnishings and new wardrobes that made them the envy of their peers. Simón Hurtado certainly "knew how to improve his social condition through foreign travel," as one writer put it.[51] Thanks to his wife Isabel Cajiao's friendship with Leonor Córdoba, the wife of José Vicente Concha, August 7, 1914, found Simón and Isabel de Hurtado, and their children, at the new president's inaugural reception.

Laureano Gómez met María Hurtado that August afternoon in the entrance of the newly renovated presidential residence, the Palacio de la Carrera. She was standing quietly beside a large potted palm, away from the noise and excitement going on inside. María Hurtado was by nature a quiet person. Some called her standoffish and aloof; others said she was simply shy and retiring. At any rate it was in keeping with her character that she should be out of the mainstream at Concha's reception, observing the glitter from a certain distance. Not unattractive, but at the time a mature young woman of twenty-six, she was some years beyond the prime marriageable age of young women in society. The recent trip to Europe had taken her away from friends and potential suitors at a crucial moment in her life. As she stood there by the potted plant, watching the other invited guests come and go, she may well have already resigned herself to a life of spinsterhood. One can imagine her surprise when handsome, dashing young congressman and newspaper editor Laureano Gómez, organizer of the recent Eucharistic Congress and bane of both the archbishop and Conservative Party leader Marco Fidel Suárez, approached and engaged her in conversation. She was certainly pleased and astonished that she, so long overlooked, and never the belle of any ball, had attracted the attention of one of the city's most eligible bachelors, who was, moreover, a year younger than she.[52]

Several things drew Gómez to María Hurtado. He knew her and her family, and that she was proper and pious, not given to showing herself unnecessarily in the street. In short she was precisely the sort of woman who would likely keep the quiet, well-ordered house that a public man needed at the end of a fatiguing day in the public eye. Having traveled extensively in Europe, she was much more accomplished than the average Bogotana of good family. And Gómez, who loved Gallic culture only slightly less than that of the Iberian peninsula, must have been charmed and impressed when he learned that María Hurtado spoke excellent French. She would make an excellent companion when he, Laureano Gómez, made his own European tour.

The courtship of María Hurtado and Laureano Gómez lasted for slightly more than two years, and culminated in their marriage on September 9, 1916. Their first child, Cecilia, was born a year later, and was followed in 1919 by a son, Alvaro. Two more sons, Rafael and Enrique, were born in 1922 and 1927 respectively. Meanwhile Gómez scrambled to support his family. The year 1917 found him in partnership with civil engineer Luis Vargas Vásquez. The Vargas and Gómez Engineering Center advertised specializations in home construction and irrigation projects, and promised to develop plans for works of art, remodeling, and interior decoration projects as well. The engineers offered free estimates, and boasted a centrally located office with three telephones.[53] In May 1917, Gómez accepted employment as departmental engineer of Cundinamarca, a post to which the newspaper Gil Blas snidely referred as humble. Nevertheless, it soon gave Laureano Gómez opportunity to inaugurate one of Colombia's major new public buildings, the Savanna Railway Station. He did so on July 20, 1917, in a paean to progress drawing upon Spanish writer Angel Ganivet's notion that railway stations symbolize the degree of a people's cultural level and administrative ability. Gómez's appointment as departmental engineer also coincided with a period of intense seismic activity in central Colombia. Known as "the time of the earthquakes," it necessitated his inspection of damaged buildings across the department. It also caused his bride, his mother, other members of his extended family, and himself to sleep in tents outside their new home in Chapinero until the danger of aftershocks passed.

During his earliest years of marriage, Gómez's friendship with Alfonso López served him in good stead. After quelling his aversion to someone he initially described as a man "of the extreme left," one who dabbled in politics "as if it were a game of polo—for 'sport,'" the two happily worked against Marco Fidel Suárez and the Conservative establishment.[54] In so doing they recreated the Historical-Liberal alliance that first formed during the late 1890s as a vehicle for attacking the Nationalist Party. José Vicente Concha and Rafael Uribe Uribe had led that coalition, and Marco Fidel Suárez had been their chief antagonist in the Chamber of Representatives.

López's business connections were especially welcome to Gómez as the latter struggled to improve his personal fortunes. The year 1918 found López founding his Mercantile Bank of the Americas, and a year later informing his

New York manager, Alfred Meyer, that he had just hired "several young, very important, and highly recommended young men," one of whom was his friend Laureano Gómez.[55] Unfortunately for both López and Gómez, their enthusiasm for politics was greater than for business. Pedro A. López quickly tired of the two closeting themselves in bank offices to smoke cigarettes and "make politics," and he fired them both. That misfortune wasn't especially damaging to Gómez, as in 1919 he won a position with the Tolima Railroad Company.

Toward the end of the century's second decade Laureano Gómez entered the time of his greatest popularity in Colombia. Counted among his friends and supporters were Historical Conservatives like Manuel Dávila Flores and José Joaquín Casas, who had helped him found *La Unidad*, Juan and Guillermo Uribe Cualla, and Guillermo Cote Bautista, who had worked on the newspaper with him. Many of his friends were Liberals. Two of them, future party leaders who lavished fulsome praise on Gómez, were Alfonso López and Eduardo Santos. Nor was their high regard for Gómez entirely self-interested. From 1916, members of the Liberal-Conservative alliance against mainstream Conservatism had combined pleasure with business, honoring one another in an endless stream of celebrations running the gamut from birthday parties, to picnics, to formal dinners, to all-male fetes at the Jockey Club and less exalted watering places around the city. Bipartisan conviviality extended into the home, where friendly visits were exchanged on Sunday afternoons and *tertulias* (social gatherings) took place on week days. Card parties were often given Saturday nights at one or another of the associates' homes. Within such a setting it was logical and natural that Laureano Gómez and Alfonso López should become *compadres* (co-godfathers), as they did during their years of closest collaboration—a fact that seemed incredible to later generations of Colombians. By late 1921, following his exposé of President Marco Fidel Suárez's financial improprieties, Gómez was being lauded by Liberal Armando Solano as Liberalism's best ally in its fight for progress and liberty against "archaic Conservatism." Two years earlier a writer for *El Espectador* had referred to Gómez as "the Lenin of modern Conservatism."[56]

During those halcyon days of coalition attacks on the old regime, Gómez and López approached their work with élan and a spirit of fun. Thus it was that in late May 1922 the two were plotting another campaign in their ongoing war against Marco Fidel Suárez. The fallen Conservative leader had been politically active during the six months following his resignation, among other things composing a lengthy defense of his actions while president. He intended to publish the work under the title "Honores y Deshonra" (Honors and dishonor). Unluckily for him, the manuscript was stolen from the printer and placed in the hands of Laureano Gómez. When Gómez discovered that Suárez had included a colorful blast at him, likening him to a demagogue who, from the heights of Tequendama Falls, heaped abuse on a hapless old man lying battered on the rocks below, Gómez and López conceived a spoof that would yet again subject Suárez to public ridicule even as it absolved them of any complicity in the theft of the manuscript.

Their plan began unfolding on May 29, 1922, when López's newspaper, *El Diario Nacional,* featured a front-page article about a suicide at Tequendama Falls. Accompanying it was a photograph of the victim being hauled from the water beneath the falls. The man, one Aurelio Velandia, had killed himself upon learning that he had contracted elephantiasis and perhaps leprosy following amputation of his left leg. The next day, May 30, *El Diario Nacional* published on its front page a large photo of Laureano Gómez, a letter from Gómez addressed to the newspaper's director, a heavily edited version of "Honores y Deshonra," punctuated by humorous subheadings, and a Ricardo Rendón cartoon showing Suárez seated forlornly on a rock as vultures circled overhead. According to Gómez, a one-legged man had mysteriously delivered the manuscript to his house the previous day. While he had not been home at the time, the man was doubtless Aurelio Velandia, driven to know the place of Suárez's phantasmagoric description in an intimate and final way.

Marco Fidel Suárez was probably correct in calling the account of Velandia's delivery of the manuscript to Gómez a hoax. He subsequently filed suit against Gómez for theft of literary property.

The incident described above suggests something of the Gómez-López relationship at that time, and the vigor with which Marco Fidel Suárez continued his struggle against Laureano Gómez between 1921 and 1927. It was important for two additional reasons. First, it sent Suárez back to his study to devise a safer way of defending his injured honor, through a series of newspaper articles—the "Sueños de Luciano Pulgar." Second, thanks to "Honores y Deshonra" one appreciates what Suárez felt that painful day in the Chamber of Deputies when he attempted to defend himself against the charges of Laureano Gómez. Midway through the rather dry document Suárez inserted a paragraph that Alfonso López termed a "lyric intermezzo," an impressionistic description of Suárez's ordeal before Congress. In it he likened himself to a worthy and wronged old man, a victim of political slander, who had been cast up on one of the great stones at the foot of Tequendama Falls. Suárez painted a Dantesque scene of enormous black rocks alternately exposed to sunlight and blowing spray, a man seated on one of them, "alone and naked, a reprobate of political slander." Above him, on a cliff at the edge of the falls, "gesticulating and shouting," stood Gutenberg Bochica (Littlemouth), who "amidst the stupendous roar of a thousand cannon, blindly and furiously hurled his affronts down upon the eviscerated, wretched Indian." Meanwhile a multitude of spectators, standing on cliffs surrounding the falls listened to and lauded

Gutenberg and rendered him acts of homage: "children, workers, soapbox orators, hangers-on, club men, parliamentarians, and even some magistrates celebrated the unfailing voice of Littlemouth." Suárez concluded by explaining that his downfall was all a function of acoustics, and warning that in spite of all he "bore within his bosom something that didn't allow him to die, something that permitted him to appeal [his case] and to hope. . . ."[57]

At about the same time Gómez and López were roughly handling former president Suárez, Laureano Gómez was becoming a problem for incoming president Pedro Nel Ospina. Gómez had opposed Ospina from mid-1921, when the paisa businessman was selected to succeed Suárez. In early 1922, when the president-elect proposed that Colombia establish a national bank and negotiate foreign development loans, Gómez went on the attack, though not with the same vehemence as against Suárez. During March he argued that the new bank be subject to restrictions lest it give rise to a dangerous "plutocracy of wealth" in the country. He also wanted to restrict Ospina's use of the first $5 million indemnity.[58] He opposed several railroad projects for which indemnity moneys were targeted, but at the same time supported the approval of moneys for the Pacific Railroad whose director was his ally Alfredo Vásquez Cobo. Gómez's initial opposition to Pedro Nel Ospina was rooted in the old and well-documented regional social, economic, and political tension between Antioquians and Colombians living in Cundinamarca, Boyacá, and the Santanders. Laureano Gómez rightly perceived himself as representing constituencies in those interior provinces. Sotero Peñuela accused Gómez of hostility to the Carare Railroad because the commission planning it was dominated by Antioquians.[59] In September, Gómez warned fellow Representatives to carefully scrutinize the contract for a railroad in Antioquia before approving it. He even went so far as to organize a Colombian Society of Engineers and then have it accredited as a certifying body for mining engineers so as to break the monopoly over accreditation exercised by the National School of Mines. October found him arguing against Ospina's proposed $100 million loan on the grounds that such transactions presented a threat to national institutions. By his logic, large sums like that might cause the Chamber of Representatives to become a "punching bag for special interests."[60] By November he had warmed to his task to the extent that he tarred Ospina's minister of the interior, Manuel María Marulanda, for his actions during the Quinquenio, and insisted that Ospina pledge to use the U.S. indemnity payment as collateral for his proposed loan. When the Chamber of Representatives passed the loan proposal on November 30, Gómez and eleven other representatives signed a declaration holding that the measure would harm national institutions.[61]

Meanwhile, Pedro Nel Ospina was conducting an astute courtship of Laureano Gómez, the upshot of which was to turn Gómez into an ardent defender of Ospina and his regime. Ospina had many reasons for doing so; the first and most obvious was to silence Gómez. The strategy would of course alienate Marco Fidel Suárez. But faced with that inevitability, who better to defend his regime against Suárez and his followers than Gómez? Moreover, Gómez would be useful to his administration. He was the most charismatic and popular young politician in the country, after all, an ardent proponent of progress and an experienced engineer, and he was a dedicated Conservative. In other words, Gómez had a great deal in common with Ospina himself. Forgiving Gómez his earlier attacks on his candidacy, Ospina concluded, was an altogether prudent thing to do.

Laureano Gómez had his own well-founded reasons for being receptive to Ospina's overtures. By approaching him the president had indicated his willingness to break with Suárez, a fact that doubtless impressed Gómez. Gómez was ambitious, and having the chief executive's support would do much to further his own political career. Moreover it was highly flattering that a man with the president's power and prestige was willing to offer him the hand of friendship when he had done so little to merit it. Gómez had always responded positively to strong older men, often striving to emulate them. How logical, then, that given the opportunity, he should look up to Ospina, a man who was, among much else, the nation's most famous engineer. Had not the president graciously accepted an honorary membership in Gómez's own Colombian Society of Engineers, praising the organization and its founder for their good works?[62] What a noble gesture, coming from a founding father of the National School of Mines! The new president was obviously no narrow and egotistical paisa, avid to promote his region at the expense of others less fortunate. Finally, and of no small consequence in the eyes of Gómez, Ospina was a Historical Conservative—one who knew what it was to suffer for the sake of political ideals.

Ospina sealed his handling of Gómez by dispatching the obstreperous young politician on a diplomatic mission that would remove him from Colombia's political scene for two years. He appointed Gómez, along with Gómez's old friend Guillermo Valencia, and Liberal Carlos Uribe Echeverri, delegates to the Fifth International Pan American meeting in Santiago, Chile. Following the conference Gómez was to continue on to Buenos Aires, where he would represent Colombia as ambassador. It was his first trip abroad, and as he departed Barranquilla on February 27, 1923, Gómez paused long enough to send a telegram to Benjamín Herrera. "I greet you upon departing the country," it read, "saluting a distinguished citizen whose probity and rectitude have brought great good to the Republic. Your friend, Laureano Gómez."[63] Writing in *El Gráfico*, Luis Eduardo Nieto Caballero mused that the trip would be good for Gómez, whom he judged to be a person "suspicious to the point of illness," who had a way of frustrating the best intentions of colleagues with ironic remarks about hidden motives. Gómez "seduces us with his talent and energy," continued Nieto, who hoped that during his trip Gómez would reflect on the ironies of life "to the extent that he comes to forget the cruelty that takes possession of him in the passion of inspiration, when at the critical moment he injures with his lips. . . ." Cured of that failing, Gómez might return better prepared "to aid in the work of our redemption."[64]

Continuing to Buenos Aires from Santiago by train, Gómez presented his credentials on May 22, 1923. He remained at his post until February 1925. Once installed as minister Gómez carried out his assignment with characteristic enthusiasm. He dedicated schools, hosted a gala reception for the diplomatic community, improved the embassy library, traveled to Paraguay for the inauguration of a new president there, and even found time to share his thoughts on the League of Nations with foreign minister Jorge Vélez. He entertained visiting Colombians, some of them lavishly. When the celebrated novelist and polemicist José María Vargas Vila passed through the city, Gómez gave a banquet in his honor. The writer departed Argentina pleased with his reception, remarking that "in Buenos Aires they paid me the honors usually reserved for prize fighters."[65] The Conservative diplomat and the iconoclastic writer seemingly got on well together. Not long after meeting Gómez, Vargas Vila described him as a paragon of virtue and eloquence, possessing a Danton-like head and "features like those molded by an Indian sculptor charged with carving the Idol of his tribe from the heart of a sacred oak." According to Vargas Vila, Gómez had appeared "like Jesus in the temple of the money lenders, wielding his word like a whip." His words were "the hatchet that decapitates the criminal in full sunlight."[66] Meanwhile, back in Bogotá, Marco Fidel Suárez was informing readers of *El Nuevo Tiempo* that the name Gómez "seems to come from the word 'Goma,' a Gothic surname."[67]

By 1924, Laureano Gómez had begun to appreciate that great endeavors carry a high financial cost. In January of that year he sent Foreign Minister Jorge Vélez a long letter complaining of the high cost of living in Buenos Aires, of the fact that his salary of $1,000 was $200 less than the previous minister earned, of extraordinary medical bills that had caused him to negotiate a short-term loan with his wife's family, and of the $3,000 he had to pay to transport his wife and children to Buenos Aires. He threatened to resign unless sent $1,000 to help cover his expenses. Gómez reminded Vélez that in the event he did resign, the government was required by law to send him $2,000 severance pay. Vélez, who did not like Gómez, instructed subordinates to send the ambassador the thousand dollars he requested and another thousand for his passage home.[68] The money was sent, but Vélez's recall of his ambassador was apparently countermanded, as Gómez remained in Argentina for an additional year. Twelve months later, on February 2, 1925, Gómez again cabled Vélez, saying that economic considerations necessitated his immediate resignation.

News of Gómez's impending return created a flurry of excitement in Colombia, especially when it was learned that he had been offered and had accepted the position of alcalde (mayor) of Bogotá. Residents of the nation's capital had special reason to relish the prospect of having the dynamic, forward-looking engineer and politician as their mayor. Gómez's friend Alfonso López had recently negotiated an immense loan, in the sum of $6 million, from the Dillon Read Company of New York. That money in the hands of one who knew how to use it meant that all the municipal improvements desperately needed and ardently desired for so many years would be soon forthcoming. Alfonso López, caustically described by British diplomats as "a social climber" and "a man who lives beyond his means," thus continued to shape Gómez's appreciation of money, its power, and pleasures.[69] Before his arrival in Colombia, Gómez met in New York with Dillon Read representatives, who showed him all the courtesies normally lavished on a major client.[70]

Following some six weeks in New York, Laureano Gómez and his family returned home. There was a palpable sense of excitement in political circles as rumors flew that he might be put forward as a presidential candidate. In spite of his insistence that his only desire was to work hard at his alcaldeship, and enthusiastic assurances from Bogotá and Cundinamarca to the effect that they appreciated his willingness to do so, many expressed doubts that he would ever take up the post. An *El Tiempo* columnist felt sure that Gómez would reenter politics, and hoped that he would do so much calmed, as Uribe Uribe did following his diplomatic mission to Argentina and Brazil. The writer complemented "the incomparable engineer and parliamentarian" for having completed his formation as a statesman while in Buenos Aires, and for having, "along with his cultured wife, brilliantly represented Colombia" in the Southern Cone.[71]

When asked to comment on national politics, Gómez applauded President Ospina for his progressive attitude and his good will, adding that his character and ability placed him among the first rank of American leaders.[72] Such remarks sent a clear message that Gómez would be receptive to any overture the president cared to make. Meanwhile the ovation continued. Barranquilla's *Diario del Comercio* gushed over Gómez as "the synthetic expression of our collective ideology, representing all in it which is noble and beautiful," referring to him as "this truly new man."[73] Even members of the British diplomatic mission, not given to excessive praise of Colombian politicians, pronounced Gómez "an able and ambitious man who will go far in the public life of the nation; the Presidency, which doubtless is his final objective, will perhaps fall into his hands one day."[74] The only Colombians not pleased to have Gómez back were members of the Conservative old guard. When, on June 17, a member of the Central Social Conservador proposed a greeting to their returned copartisan, a tumult erupted and ten members rose to attack Gómez.[75]

Early in June, Pedro Nel Ospina offered Gómez the Ministry of Public Works. Gómez demurred, observing that the job was demanding and the minister subject to intense public pressure. His indecision did not last long, however, for by June 9, 1925, Gómez had accepted the position.

Gómez took up his duties with the commitment of a man having a job to do and unlimited funds with which to do it. He more than redoubled the efforts of Ospina's two previous ministers, rushing along the twenty-two railroad and other transportation projects for which nearly $20 million of the U.S. indemnity had been designated. The new minister obviously had access to moneys from the Dillon Read loan, and other funds as well, for he hired thousands of workers to undertake projects in and around Bogotá, and in other parts of the country. At the end of his ministry, in mid-1926, Bogotá and its environs had the appearance of an immense work under construction. Among the more notable projects were the narrowing of broad-gauge rails between Bogotá and Facatativá, which made possible uninterrupted railroad travel between the capital and the Río Magdalena, and completion of the long-delayed channelization and covering of the Río San Francisco. In a typically flamboyant gesture Gómez combined the river channelization project with the creation of a new thoroughfare, built on the covered stream, that he named Avenida Jiménez (de Quesada). The broad new boulevard, winding along the river's course, extended through central Bogotá all the way from Third Avenue to the Savanna Railway Station some twenty blocks away. The job required razing many buildings, angering people like Marco Fidel Suárez, who, in his "Sueño de la locura" (madness), blamed Gómez for vaingloriously creating a "Colombian Fifth Avenue" entirely inappropriate to a city of just 150,000 souls.[76]

Ospina's new public works minister also widened and extended Fourteenth Avenue from central city to Chapinero, christening it Avenida Caracas. He completed the capitol building, and remodeled the Plaza de Bolívar, providing it with lighted fountains, parking space for autos, and improved right of way for the trolley. He had the Parque del Centenario remodeled too, filling it with sculpture that included the neoclassical statue *La Rebeca,* by Roberto Henao Buriticá. It was called an exaltation of the human body by some and salacious by others who were offended by its turgid breasts and expanses of unadorned flesh.[77] Public works projects proliferated at such rate under his regime that one wall of the new Palace of Government for Cundinamarca remained unfinished because Gómez had them turned into commemorative plaques for his creations. By May 1926, near the end of his first and only year as minister, Gómez celebrated extension of the Railroad of the North to Chiquinquirá, where he had built a large and ornate neoclassical station to accommodate it. That same month he inaugurated yet another major undertaking, a new highway that would eventually make it possible to travel between Bogotá and Honda by automobile.[78]

In early June 1926, Gómez presented Congress his annual report, which chronicled his accomplishments over the preceding twelve months.[79] It contained numerous photos of railroads, bridges, highways, railroad stations, and monuments. While it did document achievements the likes of which no previous public works minister had ever laid claim to, a good many people complained that poor planning and waste had attended the work. Roberto Urdaneta Arbelaez went so far as to term Gómez's administration of public works "a financial catastrophe."[80] Eugenio J. Gómez aired his charges in a volume that appeared in 1942, the same year José Francisco Socarrás published what stands as the most devastating, detailed, and entertaining account of Gómez's frenzied activities during his year as minister.[81] The charges of poor planning were quite true, as suggested by the fact that Gómez never responded to them. But it should be noted that Colombia had no tradition of public works planning when Laureano Gómez occupied his ministry. Nor would it for another twenty-five years. Significantly, when Colombia finally established its national planning office, it was during the administration of President Laureano Gómez.

The irony of Gómez's position in 1925 and 1926 was lost on no politically aware Colombian. The man who for eight years had cast aspersions on those supporting the lucrative Urrutia-Thompson Treaty was the same one who spent the money provided through it. He not only spent much of the indemnity, but a great deal of the Dillon Read loan of 1925 and the Baker Company loan negotiated early in Ospina's presidency. Even more galling to some was the fact that Gómez was given the assignment of leading Ospina's campaign for congressional authorization of a new $60 million loan. Completing the extraordinary coming together of Laureano Gómez and money during that period in his life was Simón Hurtado's death on June 17, 1925. That made María Hurtado an heiress, and her husband a relatively well-off man for the first time in his life. That circumstance gave rise to a telling incident in the congressional session of October 20, 1925, when Gómez bet Representative Abel Casabianca $1,000 that testimony he had just given was accurate. Casabianca demurred, remarking that not having had a death in his family, he did not possess that kind of money. Gómez rightly lashed out at Casabianca for dragging his family into the debate, but most agreed that Casabianca had won the point.[82]

Pedro Nel Ospina could not have chosen a worse person to cajole Congress into approving the new loan. Gómez and the Suarista majority turned the 1925–26 session into a conflict filled with drama, replete with pathos and bathos. The session was exhilarating, but ended with little meaningful business transacted and Ospina's loan initiative resoundingly defeated. Nevertheless it was great fun, it made for wonderful press, and the session was full of incidents that live on in national political lore. Moments of humor were provided by the Senate president, the perennial Jorge Holguín, who professed to fear that Gómez's eloquence would convince him to vote for the loan even against his will, and who on another occasion feigned disappointment on learning that the cheering which erupted when he rose to speak was in fact for Laureano Gómez, who had just entered the Senate chamber. There were moments of fear and near violence, as when in November 1925, Gómez debated Senators Ignacio Rengifo and Román Gómez. At one point in the debates senators laid hands on one another and there were fears that Gómez might be physically attacked by irate members of the Suarista majority. During the session of November 14, which lasted into the early hours of the fifteenth, the Cámara voted to absolve Marco Fidel Suárez of the charges Laureano Gómez made against him four years earlier. The Senate voted to bar the Minister of Public Works from further sessions. On November 17, *El Tiempo* editorialized that the events signaled a total breakdown of Colombian politics. Nieto Caballero, looking on disapprovingly from the sidelines, called the 1925 Congress a circus, and opined that Laureano Gómez's self-love and rancor would bring about his eventual downfall.[83]

The brouhaha continued when Congress reconvened in mid-1926. Gómez and Ospina had spent the intervening months traveling around the country visiting public works projects, as Marco Fidel Suárez and *El Nuevo Tiempo* maintained their barrage of criticism against Gómez, referring to him variously as "the terror," "a soul in purgatory," and "a hyena with a poisoned soul."[84] Though Gómez had been barred from entering the Senate, he could and did appear before the Chamber of Deputies, always to galleries packed with students, public employees, and others who hung on his every word and cheered his eloquent defenses of himself and of Ospina's government. A memorable moment came in the session of August 2, when Gómez suffered a seeming mental lapse, appearing to confuse Carlos Arango Vélez with his brother, a physician working for an American oil company. When Arango corrected him, saying ingenuously "Sir, you're mistaken, I'm a lawyer," and the crowd applauded, thinking Gómez had blundered, Gómez turned and unleashed a withering attack that began "Ah! So you're not a doctor? Then I declare this debate lacking of all importance," a conclusion he went on to support by pointing out that Arango was a poor lawyer who worked for "a law firm that specialized in losing important cases."[85] His performance brought down the house.

On August 3, Gómez entered the Senate chamber to answer allegations that

10. President Pedro Nel Ospina and Minister of Public Works Laureano Gómez in Bucaramanga, 1926. By permission of the Museum of Modern Art, Bogotá.

Rengifo and Liberal Senator Antonio José Restrepo had made in his absence. The senators reconfirmed their refusal to hear him, and had police escort him from the chamber. Thereupon Gómez made his way to the patio separating the House and Senate wings of the capitol building, made a short speech, and was borne away to his home on the shoulders of supporters. There he addressed them from his balcony. Several hours later Tenth Street was again jammed with people shouting, "Down with Rengifo and Restrepo! Long live Laureano Gómez!" Most of them were students, young Liberals calling themselves Los Nuevos, whose spokesman, Alberto Lleras Camargo, gave a short speech against Rengifo, Restrepo, and national comptroller Alfonso Paláu, who had slashed Gómez's salary some months earlier. After minutes of great commotion, "Vivas," and entreaties that he speak, Gómez appeared on the balcony and gave a blistering peroration centering on Antonio José Restrepo, whom he accused of lacking moral standards, and whom he said was but one of many Liberal leaders who "had dragged his party, like a miserable ragamuffin, through the mud of every corruption and servility."[86] At that point someone shouted, "All of us here are Liberals; be careful with Liberalism," to which Gómez answered that while he recognized the greatness and prestige of their party, it was presently in eclipse thanks to the "corrupt servility" of people like Antonio José Restrepo.[87]

Two days later Carlos Arango Vélez again rose to debate Gómez in the Cámara. His remarks are noteworthy both because they touched on a theme that followed Laureano Gómez to his grave, and beyond, and because they suggest much about the nature of accommodation within Colombia's political elite during the waning years of the Conservative "old republic" as well. First, Arango cited Gómez's reference to Oswald Spengler's *Decline of the West,* which he claimed to be a fascist work. Fascism, charged Arango, who had spent several years studying in Italy, ran through all of Gómez's speeches. Then he added, somewhat incongruously, that Laureano Gómez represented Colombia's "New Politics," whose sources and character were best sought out in movie houses of the city and in the luxurious confines of the Friends Club.[88] The club to which Arango alluded was a short-lived association of Bogotá's social and political leaders notable in its bipartisan aspect. A week before Arango's speech the Friends Club had honored Gómez at a ball among whose invited guests were President Ospina and his wife, Ospina's entire cabinet, Lucas Caballero and his daughter, Enrique Santos, Luis Eduardo Nieto Caballero, Juan and Guillermo Cote Bautista, Juan Uribe Cualla, José and Enrique Gómez Castro, Rafael Parga Cortés, and Jorge Soto del Corral. The guests represented committed Liberals and intransigent Conservatives who shared commitment to material progress, to fighting the old regime, and to political principles ideologically held. For the moment it mattered not that their ideologies were diametrically opposed.

Gómez's place in Colombian politics was anomalous during the late 1920s. Though he never claimed to be other than a doctrinaire Conservative, he was lionized by Liberals and anathematized by members of his own party establishment, which was at the moment controlled by members of the Suárez faction. His own ideas and attitudes had seemingly modernized along with the nation, and in October 1926, he could admit to feeling "temperamentally closer to Santos than to Pulgar."[89] The oddness of his position was especially evident in March 1927, when he attempted to occupy a seat in the Departmental Assembly of Santander, won under suspicious circumstances over a Liberal candidate.

Santander had a long history of electoral fraud, and Liberals there were not pleased to see yet another Conservative deprive them of an assembly seat, even one as noted as Laureano Gómez. But it was the assembly's Suarista Conservative majority that refused to seat Gómez when he arrived there for the opening session. A political deadlock ensued, the assembly was unable to commence its business, and political passions reached a boiling point. Liberals and conservatives fulminated against one another, as did pro- and anti-Gómez factions. Many feared violence, as citizens exhausted stocks of revolvers in area stores.[90] After a stormy week, during which armed guards were posted at the homes of Gómez and other assembly members, the session convened. Gabriel Turbay led anti-Gómez Liberals, who formed a rare united front with the Suaristas. Meanwhile, Gómez protested that he had come to Santander merely to help the department win passage of a loan authorization for public works.[91]

While near chaos reigned in the departmental assembly, Laureano Gómez delivered a lecture in Bucaramanga's principal theater at the invitation of the local chamber of commerce. His subject was loans for public improvements, one not normally thought of as exciting. Yet according to Liberal journalist Milton Puentes, Gómez stunned his audience with an address of such passion and eloquence that he was constantly interrupted by salvos of applause. Drawing on evolutionary theory, and employing colorful metaphor, Gómez argued that when people do not progress "they fall back and die." Colombia, he said, along with geographic "confederates" Venezuela and Ecuador, constitutes "an enormous emporium of immense riches" waiting to be tapped with the help of loans wisely administered. Journalist Puentes left convinced that Laureano Gómez was "one of the most revolutionary spirits the country has produced in recent times, the standard bearer of the enormous transformation that Colombia requires."[92]

A few days later, on April 4, as Gómez continued trying to serve in a legislative body deadlocked by his presence, news of Marco Fidel Suárez's death arrived. Near the end of the session, after the representatives had spent some time drafting a message of condolence, Laureano Gómez asked permission to speak. A witness to the event described Gómez as genuinely moved by the news, his voice barely audible and with the look about him "of one lost in the mystery of the unknown." He spoke slowly, "his voice . . . at the moment weak, trembling and proclaiming intense spiritual distress," going on to deliver an elegant eulogy in which he referred to Suárez as a great citizen, a patriot, and one of the most illustrious sons of the republic. He ended saying that an intense religious sentiment moved him to stammer the same words at that moment being pronounced over Suárez as he reposed on his bier: "Forgive us our debts as we forgive our debtors."[93] The spell was broken when a representative remarked that Gómez had his nerve praising Suárez after having spent years making his life miserable. Gómez shot back recalling words of the French writer Bernard le Bovier de Fontenelle (1657–1757), who had once lamented the lack of a law prohibiting dogs from entering cemeteries.

It was hardly surprising that a storm of criticism followed Gómez's eulogy to Suárez. Alfonso Paláu summed up most people's assessment of it when he accused Gómez of wanting to "turn Sr. Suárez's coffin into a canoe for navigating political waters." There was an element of truth in the remark. A month earlier Gómez had also spoken positively of another old antagonist, Ismael Enrique Arciniegas, but to no avail. The Conservative Party still denied him a Senate seat in congressional elections held during late April.[94]

Shut out of political office by his own party, Laureano Gómez could do little more during late 1927 and early 1928 than meditate on national problems and to criticize President Abadía's handling of national affairs. During that final year before his departure for Europe, Gómez and Alfonso López concentrated on three aspects of politics that they found especially disturbing. The first was the way Antioquian interests seemed to be favored under the new administration. They believed that Antioqueños were receiving more than their share of government assistance, and that paisa industrialists were winning too many government contracts. Second, they charged that Colombia's executive and judicial branches were carelessly and venally giving the nation's oil reserves away to wily international petroleum trusts. Their third complaint was of governmental incompetence. Gómez charged that Abadía, popularly caricatured as sleeping while the nation disintegrated around him, was leading Colombia to ruin.

Gómez shared the traditional jealousy, suspicion, and fearful admiration of paisa economic vigor harbored by Colombians not from that region. His anti-paisa bias was also a function of the growing sophistication with which he viewed money, its uses and influence. It was clear in early 1926, when as minister of public works he chided Antioquian businessmen who complained of his giving public works materials priority in Río Magdalena transport, rather than allowing traffic to proceed in turn as prescribed by law. Why, Gómez asked members of the Medellín Chamber of Commerce, should he allow them to import their cargoes of whiskey, Flemish cheese, and silk clothing, when building materials were needed to help open less fortunate regions.[95]

Alfonso López was Gómez's natural ally in resistance to paisa economic might. In August 1927, López delivered a lecture critical of Antioquian economic exclusiveness and attitude of superiority in things economic.[96] At about that same time López and Gómez were collaborating in an exposé of an Antioquian consortium that they charged with squandering public funds on the Ibagué-Ambalema Railroad. They continued that criticism during late 1927 and into the following year. Early in 1928, El Tiempo published a series of letters from Gómez in which he termed the Antioquian financial group the Leviathan, for its insatiable habit of devouring material resources. The term caught the public imagination, and it quickly became part of the popular idiom. During the student carnival of 1928 a group calling itself the Leviathan won that year's musical competition.[97]

Their concern for propriety and good sense in the handling of national resources moved López and Gómez to jointly oppose a government proposal that a British consortium exploit oil reserves in the Urabá region of western Colombia. Anticipating later developments in Mexico, and in Colombia itself, the two proposed nationalization of oil reserves, and their exploitation by a nationally owned oil company. "We rebel," they wrote, "against the government's idea of putting oil reserves in western Colombia into the hands of those same blue-eyed men who went to India with Warren Hastings and who helped Cecil Rhodes realize his imperialistic dreams in South Africa—this under the pretext of their keeping [Colombian reserves] from falling into the hands of other blond men who are presently lodged in the eastern part of the Republic."[98] When Gómez proposed to speak on the subject of nationalization of oil reserves at the National University law school, the minister of education refused to permit it. Angry students led by Carlos Lleras Restrepo then marched to the Ministry of Education and broke out its windows.[99] Soon thereafter Gómez revealed that many professors at the law school were on retainer from big oil companies, and that one of them had literally wept when Gómez showed unwillingness to drop his opposition to the British Andean National Oil Corporation.[100] Two weeks after the incident Gómez delivered a lecture on the nationalization of oil to 2,000 persons at the Teatro Municipal, the largest audience ever assembled there. Citing sources that included *Izvestia* and *Current History*, he argued that Colombia was incapable of controlling large oil trusts once they gained a foothold in the country. Luis Eduardo Nieto Caballero, who found the talk worthwhile though far from profound, wondered why the government had been so inept as to provoke a conflict with Gómez, "a man of vast prestige," thus giving him a much larger audience than he would have otherwise had.[101] The following month university students led by Germán Arciniegas approved a Manifesto of Anti-imperialist Youth, which endorsed the program of Peru's populist APRA party.[102]

By 1928, Laureano Gómez had entered a period of introspection and study destined to extend through his European sojourn. He had a great deal on which to meditate. He who had begun his career convinced of the rightness of conservatism and the wrongness of liberalism, had come to believe that the nation's two political parties were growing more alike and the thought of their leaders was converging. He who got his political start thanks to the Jesuits had begun to believe that the clergy should not mix in politics. Liberals were no longer the Jacobins of old, feeding on the bodies of priests, he said, for they had learned that priests make a poor breakfast. Conservatives poked fun at such remarks, calling Gómez a "pseudo-Conservative."[103] In truth, most of his friends were Liberals: Lucas Caballero, López de Mesa, Soto y Corral, the Santos brothers, Alfonso López, and many others. Younger Liberals, like Germán Arciniegas and Alberto Lleras Camargo, looked up to him, and still younger ones, like Carlos Lleras Restrepo, grew violent when Gómez's freedom of speech was denied. Liberal Pedro Juan Navarro went so far as to call Gómez the ideal presidential candidate. Meanwhile his immediate political future looked as bleak as that of his Liberal friends. In spite of their constant and withering critique of Abadía's spiritless handling of the public weal, the nation bumbled along in the usual way. Nothing seemed to change. Laureano Gómez grew depressed.

Gómez turned increasingly to books during his struggle to understand his nation's dilemma. The nature of his reading became clear during his political debates and public lectures of 1926 and 1927, when he began citing Spengler, Ratzel, and Ganivet to underline points that were more optimistic than not. By late 1927 and early 1928, he was reading Sigmund Freud and Thomas Carlyle, and finding their analysis of psyche, society, and public men useful in interpreting Colombia's current malaise. In his Teatro Municipal talk of October 1927, he delivered a lengthy analysis of the country based on Freud's study of sleepwalking, which he said was Colombia's situation under Abadía. He cautioned his audience against the use of violence, recommending Freud's approach of "softly calling the patient by name, trying gently to awaken him." Anything more than that might cause the patient to lapse into "a disoriented, maddened state . . . a flailing about that demonstrates loss of control."[104] Early in 1928, Germán Arciniegas asked Gómez to comment on Colombia's current situation. He replied that the nation was sleepwalking. Colombians seemed unable to produce other than mediocre leaders; the art of government had been reduced to nothing more than maintenance of the status quo. Graft and corruption flourished. The nation was in peril.[105]

The Liberal and dissident Conservative campaign against Abadía Méndez was in many ways a continuation of the assault on Conservative hegemony that had been going on since the failure of Republicanism ten years before. By 1928, however, Laureano Gómez's own participation in the movement was increasingly a function of his political ambition, which after all had been effectively thwarted. His criticism of Abadía was also linked to the process of intellectual, psychological, and ideological change he was then undergoing. By 1928, Gómez was at once revising his optimistic view of Colombia and its prospects, struggling to halt his personal ideological drift, and coming to terms with the fact that a political generation was passing and that it would soon be his turn to lead his party—and perhaps the nation. One can chart those developments in three essays that Gómez composed in early and mid-1928.

Gómez published the first essay in Germán Arciniegas's biweekly journal of culture and politics, *Universidad*.[106] Bearing the title "El carácter del general Ospina," it was both a panegyric to Pedro Nel Ospina, who had died the previous July, and a lament over the paucity in Colombian history of great leaders like Ospina. The essay also represented an attempt to define the country's chief political debilities, which Gómez identified as a historic tendency toward political corruption, and the domination of local politics by regional bosses, or caciques. Both those traditions, he argued, had done much to keep the republic from entering the mainstream of progress. Caciquism and corruption, coupled with Colombia's historic lack of exemplary figures, were in Gómez's view the principal causes of the republic's "languidness, and its rachitic character." Throughout most of his essay Gómez argued that Ospina had effectively battled the twin evils of *caciquismo* and corruption, even as he had done an exemplary job of modernizing the nation. In the course of the essay Gómez cited environmental determinist Friedrich Ratzel (1844–1904), whose works he had drawn upon in his Bucaramanga address a year earlier, and he drew upon "great man" and theoretician Thomas Carlyle as well. He also included references to structuralist historian Lucien Febvre (1878–1956), evolutionary theorist Henri Beer (1847–1926), political philosopher and evolutionary psychologist Walter Bagehot (1826–1877), philosopher of "vitalism" Henri-Louis Bergson (1859–1941), and American poet of "transcendentalism" Ralph Waldo Emerson. At a time of kaleidoscopic change in Colombia, Gómez was clearly struggling to understand its implications for his country. Within three months of publishing "El carácter," Laureano Gómez would extend his analysis of Colombia, and would make revealing remarks about his own philosophic position.

Alfonso López provided Gómez a forum for doing so when in April 1928 he organized a series of lectures treating major questions of public concern. Although Gómez was asked to speak on the subject of public works during the Abadía Méndez administration, he chose to present an expanded version of the gloomy piece that he had written four months earlier for Germán Arciniegas. The earlier article had addressed the questions, What are the dominant characteristics of our era in Colombia, how are they explained, and what are their possible consequences? In ignoring the subject of public works Gómez made a wise decision. Had he criticized their administration under Abadía, he would only have repeated the criticisms that so recently had been made of him.

Gómez delivered his first lecture the evening of June 5. First he sketched Colombia's broken and mostly tropical terrain, moving on to deliver a highly negative assessment of the nation's mixed-blood population. Drawing on some of the same sources that his friend López de Mesa had presented a year earlier in his study "El factor étnico" (The ethnic factor), Gómez described Colombia's citizens, most of whom were mestizos, as belonging to a clearly inferior ethnic subgroup. Citing not López de Mesa, but rather an Argentine ethno-determinist named Lucas Ayarragaray, he concluded that climate, geography, and racial mix had suffused Colombians with a vitiating mix of traits that the Argentine, and now Laureano Gómez, labeled "tropicalism." Gómez had embarked on his pessimistic analysis of national failings in order to conclude, as he did at three points in the lecture, that Colombia was "a kind of hothouse culture." Being a place whose social ecology is exceedingly fragile, said Gómez, "we cannot permit ourselves the luxury of ineptitude, or let ourselves follow the road that leads us to economic subjugation and to the loss of sovereignty."[107]

The talk created a sensation among his audience, and in the nation at large. Colombians, and Gómez himself, had generally been optimistic about the country and its prospects during years of the dance of the millions. Thus, in the words of El Tiempo columnist Enrique Santos, the lecture "fell upon a happy and confident town like a gravestone."[108] In spite of some reservations, Liberals tended to accept the harsh diagnosis of national ills, some of them even praising Gómez for his refreshing revisionism. Eduardo Santos labeled Gómez "a superior man," and marveled at the good fortune that seemed inevitably to attend his public acts. A guardian angel, he mused, must watch over Laureano Gómez. Luis Eduardo Nieto Caballero called Gómez "one of the most valuable elements in our democracy," adding, "we applaud the orator with pleasure."[109] Nieto Caballero did poke mild fun at Gómez, noting "the jungle of his oratory," expressing happiness that a hothouse flower like Gómez should appear in a desert like Colombia, sharing his fragrance and intelligence with others less fortunate.

Not all were as charitable. El Espectador's editorial writer opined that most of the theories on which Gómez based his talk had been revised and were no longer discussed in serious academic circles. The editorialist continued, arguing that while Colombia might not figure at the head of racially superior nations, and while it would doubtless be many years before light skin would come to predominate there, a "racially excellent type" was at the moment forming in highland areas of the country. "There as yet remain many zambos, mulattoes, and degenerated Indians in Colombia," he admitted, going on to remind that "other [nations] are populated with even worse."[110]

Geographer J. M. Rosales reacted to the talk by disputing most of Gómez's points in a scholarly work, Colombia, tierra de humanidad (Colombia, land of humanity), that he published two years later. Some members of Congress discussed the possibility of making criticism of the fatherland a punishable offense. And anti-Gómez Conservatives renewed charges that he had ceased being a Conservative.

Gómez answered all this in a second lecture delivered two months later. Whereas most of the second Teatro Municipal talk constituted an answer to criticisms of his first lecture, he touched on two significant new subjects. First he spoke harshly of the selfish individualism that had supplanted Colombia's old "spirit of collective life." He observed that citizens in the new Colombia "are interested exclusively in their businesses and in their individual prosperity," a fact that had reduced politics to little more than an ignoble scramble for tax moneys. "The virtue that triumphs in the country today is hypocrisy," he declared.[111]

Finally, Gómez answered the many members of his own party who accused him of no longer being a Conservative. Particularly painful to him was the charge of an unnamed Jesuit that he had abandoned the values taught him at San Bartolomé. Gómez vigorously disagreed, saying that he had never forgotten the Christian ethical norms instilled in him by the Jesuits. If he had displeased them, he went on, it was only because he had honored their belief that a free man will never bend to iniquitous laws or to tyrannical authority. Alluding to his defeat by Marco Fidel Suárez and the regular clergy in 1916, Gómez recalled how his enemies had reduced him to the status of "an ignorant failure, on whom the light had been turned out." But in spite of all that, the former disciple of the Jesuits had been constantly true to their teachings. "I am where I've always been, said Gómez. It's the others who have changed."[112]

In one of the most interesting portions of his second lecture, Gómez took to task those who would hand national resources over to foreign corporations on the pretext of defending Colombia against communism. It wasn't communism that threatened the nation's independence, he insisted. Rather, it was those who through their own ignorance, incompetence, and lethargy alienated the national patrimony through self-serving business dealings with foreigners.

Laureano Gómez scarcely needed to defend his conservatism in the second Teatro Municipal lecture of 1928. The lectures themselves stand as clear statements of their author's conservatism. The Interrogatories on the Progress of Colombia, as they came to be known, stand as milestones on their author's road back to the orthodoxy of his youth. It is clear in them that Laureano Gómez had begun to perceive the effect that growing affluence and the expansion of material culture were beginning to have on traditional attitudes. What he saw in 1928 was the effect of those changes as manifested in the upper echelons of Colombian society. In coming years he would look on with mounting dismay as those self-serving attitudes invaded all levels of Colombian society.

The year 1928, and the three essays he published then, marked the halfway point in Gómez's return to the outspoken Conservatism of his youth. Between his departure for Europe soon after the Teatro Municipal lectures, and his return home in mid-1932, he would complete the journey. But that lay in the future. In 1928, Laureano Gómez was still perceived as Colombia's New Man, a Conservative of advanced thought whose closest associates were Liberals who felt strong intellectual kinship with him. "Colombian democracy is indebted to Laureano Gómez for his great services," wrote *El Tiempo* columnist Enrique Santos, when Gómez left for Europe on September 3, 1928. Santos wished Gómez Godspeed and a quick return to Colombian soil, "where his prestige grows each day and where he is seen as one of the best hopes for the fatherland." It is "the unanimous wish of his friends," Santos concluded, that Laureano Gómez's stay be brief, "for they consider his presence in the country to be indispensable."

6

Social Change and the Challenge
to Traditional Authority
The Specter of Bolshevism

The 1920s were a time of social ferment in Colombia. As the decade wore on and as the economy modernized, there were increasing demands for corresponding changes in political and social institutions. Reformers confronted a formidable obstacle in the person of president Miguel Abadía Méndez. A sober, uninspiring leader who assumed the presidency in 1926, Abadía was an orthodox Conservative whose service to party began in 1885, when as a seventeen-year-old, he helped defeat the Liberals in the civil war of that year. Abadía and those around him stood fast against a constellation of change makers that included Liberals, labor, university students, and a diverse group of socialists running the gamut from social democrats to self-proclaimed Bolsheviks.

In the end the forces for change prevailed, though not without help from Abadía, who split his party prior to the presidential election of 1930. Liberal Enrique Olaya Herrera won that contest, ending forty-five years of Conservative rule. Olaya's presidency was transitional in the sense that while he addressed several of the most pressing reform issues, especially those involving labor, he governed with considerable Conservative support. Economically conservative, Olaya strove to lessen the effects of global economic contraction by maintaining good relations with the United States, and with private sources of capital in that country. Complicating Olaya's task were outbreaks of violence in many remote towns and villages, where Liberals and Conservatives contested the transfer of political power. Olaya was thus able to answer the most pressing demands for social reform, but was unable to control strife of a political nature. Halfway through Olaya's term Colombia remained tempestuous. It would soon become more so. Laureano Gómez, away from home for nearly four years, returned to occupy his seat in the Senate. Colombians who lived through the heady years preceding the Liberal victory in 1930 remember them as a time of fundamental economic and social change. Reflecting on the Colombia of his youth, Liberal writer Alberto Galindo suggested the excitement he felt during the dance of the millions: "That sudden leap from resigned

poverty to the illusion of opulence, from unconvertible paper money to spar-
kling wealth, from cotton to silk, from mule to touring car, from aguardiente
to champagne, from chronic unemployment to a lack of workers on public
works projects, profoundly jolted the mentality of our people and disjointed
the structure of our pastoral economy so as to pave the way to a new social
consciousness."[1] In that single evocative sentence Galindo captured the essence of the 1920s.

Especially noteworthy is Galindo's use of the phrase "the illusion of opulence," in which he suggests that beneath the sound and fury of Colombia's
economic awakening there lay a substratum of misery that in many ways intensified over the decade. Poverty and inequality tended to increase in the face of
rapid economic change. That in turn invigorated the Colombian labor movement, making it an engine of social reform.

Incipient modernization produced a significant movement of people into
Colombia's larger towns and cities. During the 1920s, Bogotá increased by
nearly 50 percent, to some 224,000 inhabitants by 1929. And there were corresponding increases in Medellín, Cali, and Barranquilla. At the same time
there was little corresponding increase in housing for workers. Housing was
especially tight in Bogotá, where each dwelling sheltered an average of fourteen people.[2] Meanwhile rents rose 350 percent between 1918 and 1928, leading irate tenants in the national capital to protest that half their monthly earnings were consumed by rent payments. During late 1927, Bogotá tenants took
the unprecedented step of declaring a rent strike.

Sanitary conditions in Colombian workers' barrios remained nearly as appalling in the 1920s as they had been a century earlier. Only 5 percent of all
Bogotá homes had running water, which meant that human waste continued to
be disposed of in open sewers. Scarlet fever, diphtheria, and typhus remained
endemic in urban centers, where one of five infants died before its first birthday. In 1929, 42 percent of all deaths in Colombia were from undetermined
causes, owing to lack of an attending physician. Colombia's average life expectancy had risen to but 34.2 years by 1932.[3] In all cases the poor bore a
disproportionate share of the suffering those statistics imply.

Inflation heightened the misery of Colombia's poor. While prices rose at an
annual rate of between 3 and 7.3 percent per year during the 1920s, there were
exceptional price rises during the middle years of the decade. Over the first six
months of 1926, the nation's cost of living index rose from 147 to 219, and by
the end of the decade visitors to Bogotá noted that it was more expensive living
there than in Buenos Aires, Paris, or London.[4]

Racial prejudice complicated Colombia's social problem. Members of the
upper classes looked down on the poor, who generally revealed their indigenous or African ancestry, being swarthy and small in stature. Wealthy Colom-

bians were frequently taller and fairer in complexion, tracing their descent to European forbears. During the 1920s most educated Colombians believed that dark-skinned peoples everywhere were undergoing a process of "racial decay," a conviction that tended to counter the reform impulse. Most affluent Colombians believed that the poor lived in hovels because they deserved to do so, and that if given more money for their labor, they would simply waste it. Shortly before the tragic shooting of banana workers by government troops in late 1928, Minister of Industries José Antonio Montalvo, then in charge of labor relations, opined that if granted a pay raise the workers would throw it away in dissolute pastimes. "The banana worker earns five dollars a day and lives on thirty cents; he wastes the rest," wrote another Conservative.[5]

Poor Colombians also bore the brunt of a national education system geared to the needs of the better-off. The prevailing attitude that the poor simply did not need much education was suggested in 1923, when a German educational mission recommended a plan requiring compulsory primary education for all Colombian children. The proposal created a furor that led to its speedy defeat in Congress, and to the resignation of Education Minister Miguel Arroyo Díez. President Ospina was unable to fill the position until months after the flap. It is hardly surprising that Colombian literacy levels suffered a slight decline during the 1920s.[6]

Colombian artisans and workers were intensely aware of the disdain with which they were held by members of the upper classes, and of the scant concern that the wealthy showed for their plight. They revealed that both in their somber and stoic demeanor before members of the elite, and in the way they warmed to anyone showing a genuine interest in them. They were also capable of acting in defense of their interests when aroused, as they had periodically demonstrated during the preceding century. There was also a tradition of artisanal labor organization in Colombia stretching back through the nineteenth century.

The modern Colombian labor movement was born in early 1919 with the formation of the Sindicato Central Obrero (Central Workers' Union), and its political arm, the Socialist Party. Its baptism came in March of that year, when Marco Fidel Suárez's presidential guard fired on workers in the Plaza de Bolívar. That incident was a metaphor for labor's interaction with the state up to the Conservative loss of power in 1930.

Three things made labor, and issues afflicting the poor, a central issue in Colombian affairs during the 1920s. First was the rise of labor as a political force during the decade. The humble and their spokespersons simply insisted that labor be factored into national life and politics. Second, and a consequence of labor's new assertiveness, was the Liberal Party's embracing the movement, and the "social question" generally, as a means of checking the influence of the newly formed Socialist Party. The third factor of importance was labor's impact on Conservatives. Members of the government party were shocked and frightened by the militancy of a group that for the most part had shown deference to those above them in the social scheme and who had generally been accepting of their social and political leadership. Especially worrisome to Conservatives was working-class admiration for the Russian Revolution of 1917. That, and the fact that most labor leaders and a considerable number of rising young social activists proclaimed their commitment to revolutionary socialism, filled many Conservatives with dread.

Colombia's Liberals had long shown a proprietary interest in Labor. Party leaders were thus not pleased when workers began showing signs of independence during the early twentieth century. Liberal elites did not approve of strikes, which they viewed as threats to private property. And they beheld the new Socialist Party with concern that turned to alarm when the Socialists trounced them in elections held in Medellín during November 1921. Labor successes, coupled with Socialist Party adoption of a platform more socially responsible than any the Liberals had ever formulated, moved them to action. In early 1922, Liberals led by General Benjamín Herrera adopted a party platform that included calls for an eight-hour workday and legal recognition of the right to strike. In this way the Liberals successfully outflanked the Socialists. Labor historian Miguel Urrutia sees these acts as resulting in a "socialization" of the Liberal Party.[7]

Once Colombian workers perceived that the Liberal Party had dropped its historic adherence to laissez-faire principles, they turned away from the Socialist Party. But they continued to hold annual labor congresses, usually in the national capital, during the 1920s. Through such meetings union members could maintain contact, assert a degree of independence from the traditional parties, and remain in the public eye.

Colombian labor's chief characteristic during the 1920s was its diversity. Labor historian Mauricio Archila has found three ideologically distinct though complementary traditions present in the early Colombian labor movement. The oldest and perhaps most dominant was Christian communitarianism, which stressed society's duty to care for the human needs of all its members. Referred to in Roman Catholic social doctrine as the concept of the common good, the principle was powerfully restated in 1891 by Pope Leo XIII in the encyclical *De rerum novarum*. That most famous of modern encyclicals eventually found political expression in Christian Democratic parties which were formed in Europe and in many parts of Latin America beginning in the 1930s. In Colombia it was the workers who attempted, as they put it, to "rescue 'pure' Christianity" from a largely reactionary clergy and the equally hidebound Conservative Party.[8]

The second ideological strain in Colombian labor was founded in classical liberalism, which suffused workers with a rational spirit and a faith that progress would come through scientific culture. Liberalism was the chief source of labor's egalitarian principles—principles through which they sought to combat racial and class-based prejudices arrayed against them. "In this sense," writes Archila, "the nascent working class drank first from founts of the Enlightenment. . . . its members sang the "Marseillaise" before they intoned The International."[9]

Third, Colombian labor embraced the romantic promise of the Russian Revolution. They were taken with the notion that workers like themselves had seized control of a major European nation, and had made equal distribution of property the new state religion. As Mauricio Archila has found, Colombian workers did not know a great deal about the Bolshevik revolution, "but they admired it with true affection." In sum, Colombia's workers, so long scorned and ill treated by society, embraced social teachings that rejected the wisdom that they were members of an inferior, ethnically distinct, and criminally inclined social group doomed to extinction: "They did not shut themselves away from any new idea capable of offering them redemption. While not well read . . . they were attentive to messages of the new social preachers."[10]

One of the most successful proselytizers of new social thinking in Colombia was Russian émigré Silvestre Savitsky, who opened a print shop in Bogotá during the early 1920s. Arriving in Colombia via Siberia and Japan, Savitsky gathered around him some of Bogotá's brightest and most articulate young men, among them Gabriel Turbay, Luis Tejada, Roberto García Peña, and Jorge Eliécer Gaitán. Together they read and discussed Marxist theory and talked of remaking Colombian society. The direction of their revolutionary musings is suggested in the following passage from a letter written by Luis Tejada in 1923: "This morning I spent a long while contemplating the portrait of Lenin that presides over my small communist library. More than ever before I experienced a happy emotion before this clear, sweet, and terrible visage, one profoundly etched by thought, ineffably lighted by invisible flames. Afterward I mused again on what Lenin has done for me, on what I owe to this true man, to this singular savior of the world. I feel too—and this is the most important and useful for me—that to his burning word, his rich and dynamic ideas, I owe my faith and my hope, the intimate grandeur of my being, my acquisition of a pure motive for struggle, my reason for living and working, my strong and optimistic vision of the future, my sincere conviction that the world can be made kind and just, and that mankind can bring to the world an attitude of ennobled human dignity."[11]

Other important foreign socialists who proselytized in Colombia during the 1920s were the Italian Vicente Adamo, and Peruvian Nicolás Gutama, both of whom worked with the labor movement in the Caribbean. In addition, there was Francisco de Heredia, a native-born Marxist who had traveled to Europe to study revolutionary movements on that continent.

Thanks to the steady influx of information concerning proletarian movements in Europe and elsewhere in the world, Colombia's labor movement experienced considerable growth during the mid-1920s. Major labor congresses were held in Bogotá during 1924, 1925, and 1926, and in each of them delegates approved resolutions of solidarity with Soviet workers, voted homage to Lenin, and expressed their adherence to the Communist International. Colombia's Socialists set their meetings on the same dates as the labor congresses. Typically labor met during the day, and the Socialists at night. That way Socialist intellectuals could participate in both sets of meetings. Ramón Manrique, who was on hand for the 1924 congress, wrote of the clash between the "hot-country Socialists" centered in Girardot and the "savanna Socialists" of highland Bogotá. According to Manrique the Bogotá group cited Marx, Engels, and Lenin at every turn, smoked pipes, let their hair grow long, and wore flowery neckties and wide-brimmed hats. Members of the Girardot group were "talkative, boisterous, explosive." They were also, in Manrique's words, "practical, and had a good handle on what represented the bottom line." All of them spoke constantly about "revindication of the proletariat" and of "hands callused by work," and they enthusiastically greeted Gabriel Turbay's resolution that the meeting be called Colombia's first Communist Congress and that its members adhere to the Moscow International.[12]

In 1925 some eighty labor and Socialist newspapers were being published in Colombia, and there were fifteen strikes, nine of them in the transportation industry. That year marked the appearance of a remarkable convert to the Socialist cause, thirty-seven-year-old María Cano, an upper-class librarian and poetess from Medellín. Inspired by revolutionary socialism's message, and by the example of her contemporary Ignacio Torres Giraldo, she became a full-time supporter of the workers' cause, being proclaimed the Flower of Labor in 1925, during Medellín's May Day celebration. The following year María Cano embarked on a series of speaking tours that took her to many parts of Colombia over a period of some two years. Her eloquence on behalf of labor and social revindication earned her the nickname the Red Flower of Labor.

Socialists formed the majority in Colombia's Third Workers' Congress, held late in 1926 in Bogotá. Debate centered on the question of whether delegates should approve the formation of a new workers' party. A minority of them intransigently insisted that labor's cause was best served through collaboration with the Liberal Party. Thereupon the majority walked out and organized the Socialist Revolutionary Party, which placed itself in the vanguard of militant unionism in Colombia.

Colombia's Conservative presidents were vexed by the social ferment attending the nation's economic awakening. They were alerted to the beginning of labor radicalism as early as 1910, when workers in Cartagena founded a newspaper they named *El Comunista*. It proclaimed their intention to combat clericalism, to strive for true democracy, and to seek equality and social equity.[13] The unofficial government newspaper, *El Nuevo Tiempo,* regularly carried articles on foreign revolutionary activity. It likewise gave full attention to the Spartacist uprising in Germany in 1918 and 1919, reporting favorably on the crushing of the revolt. The newspaper also noted with approval the way United States Attorney General A. Mitchell Palmer used police and federal agents against radicals in that country during the "Red Scare" of 1919. Thus it was with foreboding that Colombian Conservatives monitored the steady growth of their domestic socialist movement during the early 1920s. Especially alarming were the constant pledges of solidarity with the Communist International and the calls for radical social reform in Colombia.

Over the early and mid-1920s, Conservative governments addressed the demands of labor with a few mild reforms. In 1922 a social security law was passed, and in 1924 an Office of Labor was established as a dependency of the Minister of Industries. In 1926 it became law that workers could not be required to work on Sundays. But what the government seemed to offer with one hand it more than took back with the other, passing legislation making strikes illegal and allowing for the use of the army and police in breaking strikes. Avid for foreign capital, Colombia's Conservative governments intended to show North American investors that they brooked no threat to foreign investment. Pedro Nel Ospina's handling of the first major strike against the Tropical Oil Company serves as a case in point.

Tropical Oil, a subsidiary of Standard Oil of New Jersey, began production in Colombia in 1922, under a contract negotiated during the administration of Marco Fidel Suárez.[14] Labor trouble began almost immediately as the company installed a pay scale by which Colombian nationals received less than half the salary earned by foreigners doing the same work. Not only did the foreign workers earn three and a half pesos per day, as compared to the one and a half paid to Colombians, but they also received free room and board. Health conditions were appalling at Tropical's plant, near Barrancabermeja, a steamy, malarial site on the Río Magdalena some 200 kilometers north of Honda. Forty percent of the workforce fell ill during 1923, and the following year 1,023 of 2,838 workers contracted diseases which were fatal in five cases.[15] Tropical Oil steadfastly refused to increase pay or to improve working conditions.

In October 1924, Tropical's Barrancabermeja facility was shut down by a strike organized by the charismatic labor activist Raúl Eduardo Mahecha.

Workers demanded a pay increase along with company compliance with a prior agreement to improve sanitary conditions. The company refused to negotiate, saying that Mahecha had no right organizing Tropical workers as he was not one of their employees. The stand-off produced violence, when workers attacked and destroyed company property and paraded in the streets carrying red flags emblazoned with three 8s, signifying their demand for an eight-hour workday, eight hours of rest, and eight hours of education.

The government acted quickly to crush the strike, which it saw as subversive as well as illegal. Mahecha was jailed and Tropical Oil was allowed to fire some 45 percent of its workforce—more than 1,200 men, whom the government obligingly transported out of the region.[16]

Labor's militancy during the 1920s notwithstanding, the fact remained that there was little industrialization in Colombia and consequently no true proletariat. The country was still rural and agricultural, which meant that the men guiding national destinies during the decade, Suárez, Ospina, and Abadía Méndez, were never seriously threatened by organized labor or by social revolutionaries. This in part explains the diffident way Conservative governments persecuted labor activists. There was, it is true, constant harassment of persons connected with the movement, peremptory jailings, and other such violations of constitutional guarantees. But government actions against Torres Giraldo, Eduardo Mahecha, and others like them were, as one person recalled, "lethargic and bloodless."[17]

At the midpoint of the decade Conservatives had no reason to believe that their long dominance of national affairs was near its end. A series of meetings in 1925 resulted in the achieving of Marco Fidel Suárez's dream of a unified party along largely Nationalist lines, and in early 1926 the party was given its candidates for the coming two presidential terms. That was accomplished when Archbishop Bernardo Herrera Restrepo called the two chief contenders for the presidency, Miguel Abadía Méndez and Alfredo Vásquez Cobo, to his private quarters early in 1926. When the two men arrived they were met by the archbishop's coadjutor, Monsignor Ismael Perdomo, who informed them that "superior authorities" had instructed that Abadía should hold office during the 1926–30 term, and that Vásquez Cobo should succeed him in 1930. Thus were Conservative presidential candidates selected during the early decades of the twentieth century. When news of the meeting leaked out Bogotanos remarked wryly that the formidable General Vásquez, whose nickname was the Lion of Valle, was domesticated by the archbishop, who had turned him into a circus lion.

There was more to Vásquez Cobo's failure to win his party's presidential nomination in 1926 than a simple decision made by Colombia's chief ecclesiastic. The fact was that Vásquez Cobo had failed to win congressional endorsement of his nomination, a state of affairs rooted in the machinations of his chief rival, Abadía Méndez. Elections had taken place prior to the 1925 congressional session, and subsequent to that a dispute arose as to whether delegates pledged to Abadía or to Vásquez Cobo would be seated. Abadía, using his power as Pedro Nel Ospina's minister of the interior, challenged the credentials of the Vasquistas, and when they tried to take their seats on the opening day of Congress, had them detained by police. The seclusion of the marshals, as the incident came to be known, represented an abuse of governmental power by Abadía, if not outright illegality on his part.[18] But that was the way the political game was played in Colombia between the War of the Thousand Days and 1930.

When Abadía Méndez took office in August 1926, Colombia's economic boom had neared its apex. Public works projects moved forward in many parts of the country, and while the Panama indemnity money had been exhausted, there were foreign loans to take its place. Consequently Abadía abandoned fiscal restraint and borrowed heavily from abroad, using most of the money to fund public works projects. When food prices skyrocketed once farm hands quit the countryside and flocked to high-paying public works jobs, the new government quickly passed an "emergency law" lowering tariffs on imported foodstuffs. Still inflation cut into workers' paychecks, producing an increase in strike activity. Vásquez Cobo earned the respect of workers on the Pacific Railroad when, in 1926, he agreed to a 20 percent wage increase, thus ending a strike against that company.[19] Popular unhappiness over Abadía's economic policies was an ongoing subject of criticism by antigovernment forces.

In spite of the general disdain with which he was held by those outside official circles, Abadía Méndez had excellent party credentials. He began his political career in the 1880s as a member of the Nationalist Party, writing essays in support of Núñez and of the Regeneration. His talent was such that by 1891, at age twenty-four, he was named editor of Miguel Antonio Caro's newspaper, El Colombiano. When Nationalism declined during the 1890s he joined the dissident Historical Conservative faction, formed by his former teacher Carlos Martínez Silva. During the Marroquín presidency he served variously as minister of education, the interior, and foreign affairs. During the Quinquenio he opposed Rafael Reyes, suffering exile as a result. Following restoration of constitutional government in 1909, Abadía held cabinet posts under presidents González Valencia, Concha, Suárez, and Ospina, and when not serving the chief executive, he held office in the Senate or the Chamber of Deputies. Abadía also served on the nation's Supreme Court and, as noted above, taught law at the National University, an activity he continued through his years as Colombia's president.[20]

Abadía's political success was owed to his extreme religious orthodoxy, a quality that had impressed Herrera Restrepo in 1926. His conservatism was apparent seven years earlier, when, upon accepting the chair Miguel Antonio Caro had once occupied in the Colombian Academy of Language, Abadía cited German romantic writer and linguist Friedrich Schlegel (1772–1829) in blasting what he perceived to be an ongoing process of linguistic corruption that left "the modern Athens of South America [Bogotá] writhing in anguish and shame." He blamed the press for having abandoned its previously high standards, becoming nothing more than "an academy of vulgarity."[21]

The cabinet assembled by Abadía reflected the state of public affairs in Colombia during the mid-1920s. Minister of Industries José Antonio Montalvo was a lawyer who specialized in petroleum legislation, and the wealthy paisa businessman Esteban Jaramillo served as minister of finance. Jaramillo's success in negotiating foreign loans earned him the unofficial title "financier of the regime." The patronage-rich post of public works minister was held consecutively by party wheelhorses Sotero Peñuela and Arturo Hernández. By far the most controversial member of Abadía's cabinet was Minister of War Ignacio Rengifo Borrero. Rengifo believed strongly in prerogatives of the military, and in its constitutional duty to maintain the "principle of authority" before any social force that might challenge it. A man of authoritarian temperament who stood ready to pounce on any leftist who menaced social peace, Ignacio Rengifo, man of action, was the ideal complement to Abadía, scholarly party politician.

Once ensconced in his ministry Rengifo busied himself on several fronts, working to thwart the forces of disorder, whether they be striking workers or avowed revolutionaries like Tomás Uribe Márquez, María Cano, and Ignacio Torres Giraldo. Among his first acts were to beef up the regular army, which he accomplished by March 1927, raising its regular forces from 1,200 to 6,500 men. Little more than a month later Abadía enabled him to crack down on labor and leftists by issuing Decree 707, popularly known as the High Police dictate.[22] Rengifo used troops to break a second strike called against Tropical Oil in January 1927. The strike's chief organizer was again Raúl Eduardo Mahecha, and the principal grievance of Colombian workers was the one-and-a-half-peso pay rate that had been in effect since 1922. Workers rejected the company's offer of a 6 percent increase, holding out for 25 percent, as well as demands for job security, compliance with the new law mandating Sundays off with pay, window screens on company houses, and improvements in working conditions.[23]

The strike dragged on for two weeks, during which time Tropical Oil refused to negotiate. Finally, on January 21, police fired on workers, killing two of them. That touched off fighting between workers and police that moved Abadía to declare a state of siege, after which Mahecha and other strike leaders were arrested. With constitutional guarantees suspended and troops mobilized, the strike collapsed. The government had again sided with foreign management at the expense of labor.[24]

During the middle months of 1927, there was great tumult in Colombia. María Cano and Torres Giraldo continued their tours through towns and cities, where crowds surged to see the "Red Virgin" and to hear her blast the status quo. Meanwhile there was continued ferment on the labor front. Boyacense legislators tried to halt seasonal migrations through legislation, and Bogotá's tailors, desperate for higher wages in the face of soaring food costs, went on strike. Marco Fidel Suárez, in the last of his "Sueños," written a month before his death, fretted that the state of public affairs left him "very preoccupied and uneasy."[25] Minister of War Rengifo was even more exercised. In August he had learned that the Social Revolutionary Party (SRP) intended to launch a nationwide uprising of the proletariat. He warned of "storm clouds" gathering on the nation's horizon. When the party announced its intention to hold a convention in La Dorada, Caldas, during September, he alerted the department's governor and told him to watch the meeting closely. Officials in La Dorada were so zealous in carrying out their orders that they clapped the SRP's leaders in jail just as they began their meeting. Thus members of the party's newly formed Presidium were forced to conduct business furtively, as companions distracted their jailers with noisy card games.[26]

An important consequence of the La Dorada convention was formation of a Social Revolutionary Party subcommittee known as the Concejo Central Conspiritivo (Central Conspiratorial Committee [CCC]). That body was charged with planning an overthrow of the government by means of a coordinated popular uprising. Liberals associated with the party's "militarist" faction, General Leandro Cuberos Niño being chief among them, also participated in the work of the CCC. By early 1928 members of the group were building bombs for use in bringing down the hated Conservative regime. At the same time Conservative Party leaders like Antonio José Uribe and Ignacio Rengifo were calling for new legislation that would give them a free hand in striking at dissidents without regard for constitutional civil rights protections.

Debate over the government plan to pass what came to be known as the Heroic Law filled Colombian newspapers from February through October 1928, when it was finally pushed through Congress. Ignacio Rengifo headed the effort, arguing heatedly that such legislation was needed to stem an imminent communist revolt. Rengifo alleged that communists were at the point of subjecting the nation to a "social conflagration of frightening dimensions."[27] Liberals, and a considerable number of Conservatives, attacked the proposition, calling it high-handed and dictatorial, and warning that if passed the law would produce consequences more dire than those it purported to address.

11. Ignacio Torres Giraldo, María Cano, Raúl Eduardo Mahecha (left to right), and Sofía López (standing). By permission of the Museum of Modern Art, Bogotá.

Conservative representative José Antonio Hoyos warned that "in fleeing from Bolshevism we must not run the risk of falling into an even worse form of fascism."[28]

The Heroic Law passed on October 30, 1928, but not before a Liberal representative raised the issue of the thousands of workers employed by the United Fruit Company, a constant violator of Colombian labor law. What will happen if those workers tire of waiting for the government to come to their aid, wondered one representative: "What if they decide to join a communist movement; what if Sr. Rengifo sends his troops to smash it?"[29] The representative's question would be answered within a very few days.

A week after passage of the Heroic Law, which effectively outlawed organizations like the Social Revolutionary Party, labor trouble erupted in the Caribbean coastal area of Santa Marta, where the United Fruit Company had vast plantations employing some 25,000 workers. Favored by a succession of national and departmental governments anxious for foreign investment, the U.S. company had operated its coastal enclave to optimal advantage. Since 1925, United Fruit had enjoyed a ruling from the Ministry of Industries to the effect that as banana harvesters worked on the basis of individual contracts, they were not technically employees of the company. The ruling was an absurdity in every sense of the word, but it gave United Fruit the right to flout all Colombian labor laws. By 1928 the situation of banana workers had become insupportable, and they resolved to strike unless the company acted to improve working conditions.[30] The company refused to negotiate, and between November 12 and December 6 the banana zone was paralyzed.

Timing for the strike could hardly have been worse. Over the preceding year members of the SRP and the CCC had feverishly stockpiled munitions to be used in the coming revolt. By April 1928 a plan existed by which members of the CCC would launch a general strike and coordinated military actions against the government. The revolutionaries were so full of romantic faith in the inevitability of the proletariat revolt that they talked incessantly and openly of the coming new order. Early in 1928, Leonilde Riaño, the "Red Flower of Cundinamarca," warned Colombian women to prepare to march alongside their men "in the coming global revolution."[31]

Members of the Abadía Méndez government took the threats of revolution seriously. "I am convinced that Colombian communism is ready to explode," said Minister of Industry Montalvo in early 1928. Montalvo went on to note his surprise at seeing "alarming Bolshevik tracts" being read by workers during a recent trip to the Santa Marta banana zone. During April 1928, Minister of War Rengifo worried that Bolsheviks were infiltrating the army. Archbishop Ismael Perdomo, named to replace Bernardo Herrera Restrepo, who died in January of that year, praised the anticommunist stand of the government and urged workers to back the church-supported Unión Colombiana Obrera (Colombian Workers' Union). Defenders of the "principle of order" noted with chagrin the trips of Guillermo Hernández Rodríguez and others to Moscow, and of their tendency to give their newspapers names like *El Moscovita, Ola Roja* (Red wave), and *El Sindicalista.*

There was no coherent force in Colombian public life capable of tempering the coming clash between left and right. The Liberal Party was in disarray, some party members siding with the forces of order, and others supporting the revolutionaries. Highly significant was the fact that most Liberals, and a good many Conservatives as well, dismissed the revolutionaries as innocuous visionaries, and scoffed at the fears of Conservatives like Rengifo. *El Tiempo* cartoonist Ricardo Rendón regularly poked fun at both sides, to the general amusement of Colombians. That seemed only to infuriate and to strengthen the resolve of both extremist factions.

It was in this setting of left- and right-wing extremism that banana workers staged their strike. The day the strike began, November 12, 1928, United Fruit manager Thomas Bradshaw telegraphed Abadía Méndez that "the revolutionary situation here is extremely dangerous."[32] Abadía responded by deploying army units to the Santa Marta region. The strike dragged on for nearly a month, eventually threatening United Fruit with a considerable loss of profits. On December 2, General Cortés Vargas, commander of the government troops, claimed to have intercepted a message from Tomás Uribe Márquez urging strikers to begin sabotaging company property. Then, two days later, it appeared that United Fruit might lose its entire crop as strikers blocked trains taking the fruit to waiting ships.

For an instant it seemed that the strike might succeed. But that fact, coupled with the rumor that the U.S. cruiser *Des Moines* and the battleship *North Dakota* were steaming toward Santa Marta, moved the government to declare a state of siege in the banana zone late on the evening of December 5. Upon receiving that information, and inspired by Ignacio Rengifo's urging that he show no quarter to "the enemy," General Carlos Cortés Vargas decided to disperse workers who had blocked rail shipments through the town of Ciénaga. Arriving at the town's main plaza at 1:30 A.M. on December 6, he deployed 300 heavily armed troops against several thousand strikers camped out next to the railroad station. He ordered the crowd to disperse, giving them three minutes to do so. When the crowd, many members of which had been asleep, refused to move, General Cortés Vargas ordered his troops to fire. Some dozen strikers were killed outright, and scores wounded. In subsequent days, as the army forcefully broke the strike amid sporadic skirmishing and attacks on company property, hundreds of banana workers lost their lives.[33]

The banana zone massacre of late 1928 was a terrible lesson to Colombian workers. It helped convince them that revolutionary redress of their grievances was impossible in the face of the central government's military superiority. Whether they liked it or not, most Colombians had to agree with Liberal activist Heraclio Uribe's assessment that had banana workers continued to strive for change through the Liberal Party, rejecting association with the socialists, the result of the strike would have been far different.[34]

The Fateful Year 1929

Thoughtful Colombians were disconcerted and saddened the first day of 1929. Greeting them in their morning paper was a long state-of-the-nation message from Abadía Méndez in which the president praised the Catholic Church for giving the nation its culture and civilization, and thanked foreign capitalists for having contributed so much to national development. Abadía as much as said that his government would continue to protect United Fruit, Tropical Oil, and other American companies from the demands of their Colombian employees. As the president explained it, public authority would become a mockery unless foreign industry and capital were extended "the most ample protection."[35] He gave special thanks that the forces of truth and justice had triumphed over the spreaders of anarchic and subversive doctrines. Not mincing words, the president called leaders of the recent strike against United Fruit felons and traitors who in their eagerness to triumph did not hesitate to "run their daggers through the loving heart of the motherland."

The progressive-minded did find a bit of grim humor in that gloomy New Year's morning newspaper. Ricardo Rendón's cartoon showed Abadía asleep in bed while all around him alarms sound the danger to the nation from Yankee capitalists, official corruption, and foreign debt. Standing in the shadows is a figure of death, labeled the Banana Zone. Just days earlier a Rendón cartoon titled "Return from the Hunting Trip" had appeared in *El Tiempo*. It shows General Cortés Vargas standing at attention and saluting President Abadía. Behind the general lies a row of human corpses; behind Abadía lies a pile of ducks. "I killed a hundred!" says Cortés. "That's nothing," replies Abadía, "I killed two hundred!"[36]

Economic fears accompanied widespread unhappiness over Abadía's insensitivity to the problems of labor. Early in 1928, U.S. lenders cut off credit following reports that loan monies were being squandered, and as a means of protesting recent Colombian legislation protecting national oil reserves.[37] Cutbacks in public works spending followed, which forced the laying off of thousands of workers. Coffee prices, which stood near thirty cents (U.S.) per pound a year earlier, had begun to slide. By early 1929 they had fallen to twenty-three cents, and by year's end they would reach seventeen cents. With revenues drying up, renters began demanding relief from their obligations. Among the first to do so were the vocal and assertive tenant farmers of the Viotá coffee zone. When campesinos previously employed in public works resumed farming, they found it hard to make money owing to the free import of foodstuffs under Abadía's "Emergency Law" of 1927. Businessmen had begun to suffer as well. Colombian bond prices were falling steadily, losing 20 percent of their value between 1927 and late 1929.[38] A rash of fires in Medellín during February 1929 suggested that overextended builders were resorting to arson to cut their losses.[39] Nearly a year before the stock market crash of October 1929, newspaper editor Eduardo Santos warned that Colombia was in a state of economic crisis.[40]

Early in February national police forces conducted raids in cities around the country and discovered caches of bombs fabricated by members of the Central Conspiratorial Committee. Social Revolutionary Party secretary Tomás Uribe Márquez was arrested, and not long afterward Liberal leader Leandro Cuberos Niño was jailed following the discovery of a pipe bomb in his home. More than a dozen others were arrested in connection with "the conspiracy of the bombs," among them the indefatigable Torres Giraldo and María Cano. Several of the most prominent conspirators were subsequently freed thanks to their skillful defense by attorneys Jorge Eliécer Gaitán and Carlos Lozano. Charges against María Cano were dropped. The Liberal press made light of the

episode, and *El Espectador* accused the president of using the incident to promote the presidential ambitions of Ignacio Rengifo. Cartoonist Rendón characterized the bomb makers as Chaplinesque figures not to be taken seriously,
reflecting a popular attitude that moved a *New York Times* reporter to observe
that the Colombian public didn't attach much importance to the "Red
threat."[41]

By early 1929 it had become clear that the government party had a problem
far more serious than bomb-making revolutionaries, declining economic indicators, or its exceeding unpopularity. Campaigning for the upcoming presidential election had begun and the Conservatives had two presidential candidates. They were Alfredo Vásquez Cobo and Guillermo Valencia, neither of
whom indicated willingness to step aside for the other. That was not supposed
to have been the case, as four years earlier Archbishop Herrera Restrepo had
indicated that Vásquez Cobo should hold the nation's top office from 1930 to
1934. But with Herrera's death, and his succession by the less forceful, less
politically astute Ismael Perdomo, the Church's political voice was weaker
than at any previous time in the twentieth century. Perdomo's political inexpe-
rience might not have mattered had Abadía Méndez not hated Vásquez Cobo
and had not been determined to block the general's path to the presidency. His
antipathy dated at least to 1904, when Abadía suffered a humiliating exile by
order of Rafael Reyes. The troops who hurried Abadía and his colleagues off
to the eastern llanos were commanded by Alfredo Vásquez Cobo, at the time
Reyes's war minister. A man who lived the maxim "Revenge is a dish best eaten
cold," Abadía, the clever machine politician, intended to make General Vásquez Cobo pay for the old affront, regardless of the consequences.

In mid-1929 Abadía and the Conservative establishment experienced still
another crisis, one that heightened its weakness and disunity. On June 5 the
governor of Cundinamarca, Ruperto Melo, fired the mayor of Bogotá, Luis
Augusto Cuervo, who had become obnoxious to the political establishment.
Cuervo's offense was that of firing the director of the lucrative city trolley
company, whom he accused of a host of offenses, not the least of which was
theft. The counterfiring produced a popular outcry because it was widely known
that public monies were being stolen and squandered by members of a gang
(*rosca*) having close ties to the president himself. That, plus the fact that municipal services were being managed incompetently, sent thousands of
Bogotanos, many of them students, into the streets during the sixth and seventh of June. On the seventh the police, commanded by General Cortés Vargas,
shot and killed a student, one Gonzalo Bravo Pérez. The crowd, by then thousands strong, bore the corpse to the presidential residence and demanded action against all those implicated in the affair. Not only did they ask Abadía to
fire his police chief, but public works minister Hernández and war minister

Rengifo as well. Abadía acceded to the demands. With the departure of Rengifo and Arturo Hernández, characterized as backbones of the regime, Abadía's government entered a period of drift from which it never recovered.[42]

July and August were desultory months in Liberal and Conservative Party politics. On the one hand Conservatives floundered toward resolving their problem of settling on a single presidential candidate. Archbishop Perdomo demonstrated political ineptness by first releasing the names of five candidates whom he said would be acceptable as his nominees, and then settled on Vásquez Cobo. "What's most surprising," said the archbishop in a letter of August 20, "is that workers and even communist entities have made it known that they support Vásquez Cobo."[43]

The Liberal Party was at the moment discredited and dispirited, and seemed unlikely to field any presidential candidate. On July 18, Alfonso López had granted a newspaper interview in which he remarked that his party was "absolutely liquidated."[44] At that moment the Liberals were split between their "civilist" and "militarist" factions. The civilists followed Paulo E. Bustamante and, up to his death in Paris in July 1929, Nemesio Camacho. The militarists followed the mercurial General Cuberos Niño, only recently released from prison following his implication in the February bomb scare. Early in June the civilists had held a meeting in Apulio, Cundinamarca, notable chiefly for the fact that no newly elected Liberal congressmen were allowed to attend. They were barred from the convention because they had disobeyed Bustamante's order to abstain from participating in the February election. Late in August, Liberals having Republican Party antecedents had met in Bogotá with former president Carlos E. Restrepo. Among them were Simón Araújo, Eduardo Santos, and Luis Eduardo Nieto Caballero. That group, unofficial representatives of Liberal and Conservative moderates, had hoped they might jointly discover a candidate who would, as Araújo and the others put it, "orient and save the nation."[45] Failing at that, the meeting adjourned and Restrepo returned to Medellín saying he could see nothing but darkness on the political front.

As both traditional parties struggled to resolve their internal problems, the Social Revolutionary Party entered its death throes. By July most of its leaders were imprisoned or in exile. Still, many party members persisted in their dream that the masses would, if given the opportunity, rise as one and abolish capitalism and private property. Following that logic they launched what they hoped would be a nationwide uprising. The effort was abortive. Only in El Líbano, in the coffee zone of northern Tolima, and in two other villages of less consequence, was there a concentrated effort to seize power. Líbano's Bolshevik uprising, led by CCC member Pedro Narváez, was crushed by a hastily assembled bipartisan militia.[46]

July was also the month of Bogotá's student carnival, a weekend of parades, street dances, beauty pageants, and carousing ostensibly aimed at raising money for the Casa de Estudiante and its charitable endeavors. The high point in the 1929 carnival was the contest for student queen, pitting María Teresa Roldán against Josefina Uribe Portocarrero and Elenita Laserna. *El Tiempo* reported "enormous nervousness" in the Colombian capital as supporters of one or the other candidate strove to elect her through the purchase of ballots which sold for twenty cents apiece. During the final hour of balloting there was a frenzy of vote purchasing, with wealthy supporters of the young women paying as much as $7,000 to see their candidate triumph. At length María Teresa Roldán was elected with 170,000 votes. The fund raiser earned the considerable sum of $21,545, making the 1929 carnival one of the decade's most successful. According to Alcides Arguedas, the new queen's coronation took place in the Teatro Colón amid "luxurious dissipation," accompanied by speeches, laughter, and happy students snake-dancing up and down the aisles. Afterward the students turned Calle Real into "a carnival of madmen" in which almost everyone was drunk or feigned being so.[47]

The giddy student carnival of 1929 was the last of its kind. A changed political climate after 1930, accompanied by growing economic austerity, combined to end them. In many ways they were symbolic of the 1920s, when newfound wealth made possible the extravagances that people like Arguedas observed with mixed emotions. But the student celebrations of the twenties were much more than exuberant parties in which children of the privileged scandalized their elders. They were also statements of a student presence that had been signally important in Colombian public life throughout the decade. Colombia's student movement had its formal beginning in 1921, when three young men of twenty-one—Germán Arciniegas, Silvio Villegas, and Augusto Ramírez Moreno—launched the literary journal *Universidad*. Their magazine, and the midyear carnivals that soon followed, had their direct inspiration in events taking place in South America's Southern Cone, especially in the University Reform Movement that began in Córdoba, Argentina, in 1919. In a broader sense they were part of the revolt against bourgeois culture, rigid positivism, and Western imperialism, which had been going on in Europe since the turn of the century. Latin American students found special inspiration in the overthrow of abusive political regimes in Mexico and Russia. And in Colombia the new ideas were all the more energized by the country's economic awakening and overall state of social ferment. Bogotá's student carnivals were thus a showy distillation of general and thoroughgoing intellectual awakening.

The student movement first headed by Arciniegas and the others quickly broadened, and by the middle of the decade counted scores of young people who began referring to themselves as Los Nuevos (the New Ones).[48] In mid-

1925 they launched their own literary magazine, *Los Nuevos,* and used it as a platform from which they expounded their message of literary, political, and social change. Los Nuevos prided themselves on their nationalism, spirituality, and sensitivity to social inequities—especially to the plight of the poor. They wanted to create "a new spirit of human solidarity" by "unleashing a great current entirely ideological in character." Meanwhile they were proud of their ideological diversity, welcoming all those who wished to express themselves freely.

Los Nuevos proclaimed their enmity to the older generation, particularly to their immediate seniors, members of the Generation of the Centenary, which they identified with ideological blandness of the sort seen in the old bipartisan Republican movement. They accused the Centenarians of having a mechanical concept of life and "bastardized appetites" that had robbed the older men of their spirituality. As a group enamored of material culture and wedded to the idea of progress, the Centenarians had thoughtlessly mortgaged the nation to foreign capitalists at the expense of their own people, Los Nuevos argued. They were consequently morally and intellectually bankrupt, sickeningly self-congratulatory, and wholly detrimental to national well-being. "Has the moment arrived to call the previous generation to account, and to assess their role and responsibility in national 'evolution'?" they asked rhetorically. Their answer was a resounding yes.[49] The Centenarians were men of the past, of another era. Their time had come and gone.

The Centenarians did not take kindly to the younger generation's attack. As men still in their thirties, and yet still some years away from shaping national destiny, they scoffed at their premature retirement by a group of precocious, callow twenty-year-olds. A month after *Los Nuevos* began publication, Eduardo Santos denied the charges leveled against his generation.[50] Five months later Alfonso López, himself but thirty-seven, jibed at Los Nuevos, whom he said "with a literary, almost musical criterion, were beginning to intervene in national life." He referred to them as "our radical socialists," accusing them of being members of a privileged group who had learned of human suffering from books. He reminded them that they weren't unique in their reforming zeal, but rather, that they stood squarely in Liberal reform tradition, a tradition that made it unnecessary for them to ape Russian Bolsheviks or European labor organizers.[51]

It was Armando Solano who took greatest umbrage at Los Nuevos' assault. A progressive Liberal who in his youth had militated in the Republican Party, Solano attacked "the irrational, incomprehensible hatred" Los Nuevos had for men such as himself.[52] He characterized the Centenarians as peace-loving men who had sought to remove ideology from national politics. At the same time he viewed Los Nuevos as products of the ideological fragmentation that came in the wake of World War I, a fact that explained their heterodoxy. He found them so caught up in themselves as to be rendered "an almost exclusively literary generation," one that "loves strange emotions and fights with talent to analyze them."[53] He challenged Los Nuevos to cease their explorations of self and to go out and do something that would benefit society as a whole.

Solano's remarks incensed Alberto Lleras, who responded in a polemical open letter. "Where is the labor of the Centenarians to reform this antiquated fragment of colonial times, this grotesque nightmare called the university?" he fumed. He accused men of Solano's generation of having no sense of the contemporary world, and of scandalously, "lasciviously" using their newspapers for endless self-aggrandizement. "We're more in tune with modern humanity than you ever were or are now," he said: "It's not simply an academic matter. We haven't been afraid to break with the past and rally to new ways."[54]

The generational debate resonated in Colombian public life for some forty years after the hot exchanges of the mid-1920s. Over the short term it had precisely the effect that Los Nuevos desired. As in the case of labor's rise during the 1920s, the younger generation's radicalism and outspokenness drove mainstream Liberalism leftward, heightening its sensitivity to social problems. In April 1928, Armando Solano resigned from the Liberal Party, saying that it had lost touch with the people. He explained that he had embraced socialism, which he understood to be a nonviolent movement aimed at the redistribution of private property, not its outright abolition. Less than a week after Solano's letter was published Alfonso López published a scathing letter to Liberal Party leader Nemesio Camacho, telling Camacho to return from the "mental desert" into which he had wandered arm in arm with the Conservatives. We Liberals have never dared protest the misery in which most of our fellow citizens live, he pointed out, and never felt it in our interest "to show them the roads to economic, social, and political independence." Praising the work of Uribe Márquez, Torres Giraldo, and María Cano, López warned that in a time of social and economic revolution, the Liberal Party must remain true to its values or else suffer dire consequences.[55]

When, some fifteen months later, Alfonso López remarked that his party was "liquidated," he meant it as a criticism of the party's current leadership, not as an indication that he had lost faith in the Liberal Party itself. In fact as 1929 wore on, López and other Liberals began to feel that the Conservative deadlock might work to their advantage. In spite of Archbishop Perdomo's declaration of support for Vásquez Cobo, Guillermo Valencia showed no sign that he intended to drop his bid for the presidency. President Abadía continued to aid Valencia behind the scenes, while working to weaken Vásquez Cobo. Public estimation of the Abadía regime sank to new lows during September, as

Congressman Jorge Eliécer Gaitán conducted a sensational exposé of the banana zone massacre. News of the New York stock market crash of October 29, 1929, intensified Colombia's economic problems. Within a month of that event Alfonso López reported the frantic efforts of Medellín businessmen to unload their own stocks.[56] At year's end 80 percent of those employed in public works had been laid off, and salaries of remaining public works employees had been slashed by nearly 50 percent. Property owners were cutting rents by as much as 25 percent, while tenants demanded that their payments be reduced by at least 40 percent.[57]

The Liberal directorate met in mid-November, and party members smiled in disbelief when Alfonso López announced that the Liberal Party should prepare to assume power. Conservatives, for their part, ignored the activities of old antagonists, who as the February 9 elections drew closer had not even fielded a candidate. The Liberals had, however, made sure that party members registered to vote in the election.

As of the November meeting of their directorate (Directorio Liberal Nacional [DLN]), the Liberals believed they had a credible candidate for the upcoming presidential contest: Enrique Olaya Herrera, Colombia's longtime ambassador to the United States. When approached on the matter Olaya had expressed interest in running, but had made it clear that he would not do so on a strictly partisan platform. That disconcerted Liberals like Alfonso López and Gabriel Turbay, who wanted the candidate to demonstrate a more militant liberalism. But it set well with the many Conservatives who liked neither Vásquez Cobo nor Guillermo Valencia. The most important single block of moderate Conservatives were paisas having historic ties to Republicanism, a party neither Valencia nor Vásquez Cobo had countenanced. Another important consideration involved economics. Antioquia was a department likely to suffer economically should either Conservative candidate become president. Vásquez Cobo, from Cali, was certain to favor Cauca valley interests if elected. When director of the Pacific Railroad, the general had dealt the paisas a considerable blow by linking Cali to the port of Buenaventura, taking business away from paisa rail lines linking the lower Río Cauca to the Magdalena. Olaya Herrera, on the other hand, had significant political ties to Antioquia, having been an enthusiastic Republican Party member and Carlos E. Restrepo's foreign minister. Olaya thus had excellent credentials for bipartisanship, and furthermore gave explicit assurances that he would respect Church prerogatives if elected, and that he would form a government in which Conservatives would have an equal voice with Liberals.

All these things made Enrique Olaya Herrera the favored candidate of moderate Antioquian Conservatives and with Liberals who had militated in the old Republican Party. At the end of December even Alfonso López swallowed his anger over Olaya's lukewarm Liberalism, since by that time all Liberals knew that they stood an excellent chance of resuming power after forty-five years in the political desert. Olaya returned to Colombia from Washington, D.C., in mid-January 1930. During January and early February he campaigned before enthusiastic crowds as the Conservatives continued to anguish over their party split.[58]

Conservative political fortunes sank in inverse proportion to those of the Liberals. But at least they had President Abadía's words to console them. In his January 1 message he had encouraged his fellow citizens to be optimistic in the face of adversity. Personal trouble was, he lectured, "a source of undeniable good fortune," for "it steels characters and teaches us to overcome adversity." While Abadía's words referred to the country's economic decline, they were perfectly applicable to his party as well. Thanks to Abadía's machinations, Archbishop Perdomo had been ordered by the Vatican to shift his endorsement from Vásquez Cobo to Guillermo Valencia.[59] The reversal of his position, coming two weeks before election day, sealed the fate of the Conservative Party. Many clerics disliked and mistrusted Valencia, and consequently disobeyed Perdomo's order. They remembered the unholy alliance he had made with the Liberals in 1918, the poet's bohemian past, and the widely known fact that Valencia was a womanizer whose illegitimate children numbered allegedly some 200. They were neither mollified nor convinced by Valencia's shows of piety over the course of his campaign. Consequently a great many clerics ordered their parishioners to continue in support of Vásquez Cobo.

On election day Enrique Olaya Herrera won by a substantial plurality in an election that saw Conservatives neatly split their vote. Olaya's total was 369,934, Valencia's 240,360, and Vásquez Cobo's 213,583. Alberto Castrillón, the Social Revolutionary Party candidate, polled 577 votes. On February 10, the day after the election, stones were thrown at the presidential residence and at Abadía's country home. No one knew whether they were thrown by Liberals or by Conservatives.[60]

Olaya Herrera and the Great Depression

Enrique Olaya Herrera's election in 1930 signaled to many that the Colombian republic had come of age. The peaceful alternation of power there was a happy aberration in Depression-era Latin America, a region where palace coups and military dictatorships were the norm. As he began his four year term, Olaya Herrera enjoyed extraordinarily good relations with the Conservative Party, which allowed him to effectively address economic problems produced by the global economic contraction of the early 1930s. Only outbreaks of political violence clouded an otherwise sunny administrative horizon. But even then Olaya was fortunate. The violence, which was especially severe during his first two years in office, occurred in a distant part of the country, and did not seriously threaten national stability.

It was well that Olaya Herrera enjoyed a high degree of Conservative support between 1930 and 1932, for that was when the Great Depression most severely affected Colombia. The collapse of global trade had an immediate and devastating effect on national finances. Most government revenues came from customs receipts, which fell off sharply after 1929, when they totaled 75 million pesos. Such revenues were down by nearly 30 percent in 1931, to 54 million pesos, and by over 50 percent in 1932, when they produced 35 million pesos. Public works, which had absorbed over half of all government revenues in 1929, shrank to but 15 percent of the minuscule 1931 budget. That signaled the layoff of thousands of workers, who either returned to agricultural pursuits or wandered the countryside in search of employment. Meanwhile agricultural salaries had dropped by 50 to 60 percent. Roving bands of unemployed workers stole food from the better-off and sometimes demanded supplies from frightened landowners.[61]

As the money supply shrank and credit disappeared, renters and property owners fell on hard times. Andrés Samper Gnecco remembers that an "infinity of people" lost their homes in Colombian cities. Unable to pay their mortgages, many of them packed up and returned to ancestral farmsteads.[62] The upper classes suffered setbacks too. Carlos Lleras Restrepo, himself a struggling young lawyer in Bogotá, recalled handling bankruptcy proceedings for the capital's Fiat automobile agency.[63]

The new government moved quickly to address the economic crisis. President-elect Olaya traveled to the United States, where he enlisted the help of a friend, Princeton economist Professor Edwin Kemmerer. Kemmerer and six associates, remunerated to the tune of $100,000 in gold certificates, arrived in Bogotá three days before Olaya's inauguration. They stayed on in Colombia until late November 1930, during which time they framed a financial plan combining fiscal austerity, moderate revenue enhancement, and economic orthodoxy. The Americans urged Olaya to maintain the gold standard and to expand the state's role in fiscal affairs. Especially noteworthy among Kemmerer-inspired taxes was the first-ever duty on bananas exported by the United Fruit Company. And thanks in part to the influence of Kemmerer and his associates, Olaya was able to negotiate a major new loan from private U.S. banks. The money was immensely useful to the government in servicing its $81 million foreign debt.[64]

Edwin Kemmerer's services did not come cheap, but they were worth the price, if for no other reason than the support they garnered for Olaya's economic program. Because they bore the endorsement of the prestigious Dr.

Kemmerer, the president won easy legislative approval for a range of measures that alleviated effects of the economic downturn. Early in 1931, Congress approved a law granting the president broad new powers to intervene in economic matters. Olaya moved quickly to overturn the Emergency Law of 1927, which allowed the duty-free import of certain foodstuffs. Domestic food production increased as a consequence, as did farm prices. Other tariff legislation of 1931 sped import substitution by forbidding the importation of materials that might otherwise be produced internally. Agricultural and other interests benefited from formation of three new credit agencies, the Banco Central Hipotecario (Central Mortgage Bank), the Caja Agraria (Agrarian Bank), and the Caja Colombiano de Ahorros (Colombian Savings Bank). Additionally, Olaya stimulated further expansion of the coffee industry by offering farmers a 10 percent bonus for new production.[65]

Labor benefited from several measures enacted during the first year of Olaya's presidency. By Law 83 of 1931, the right of workers to organize labor unions was protected and union breaking made a civil offense. Subsequent legislation mandated paid vacations and other benefits, as well as a forty-hour work week and Sundays off with pay. Thanks to Olaya's encouragement, the number of labor unions formed between 1930 and 1934 exceeded the total number formed between 1920 and 1930.[66] Not all were pleased with the flurry of pro-labor measures. When members of the Liberal-Conservative coalition attempted to pass legislation providing for unemployment compensation, Conservative Representative Sotero Peñuela opined that most of those out of work were simply loafers. Furthermore, said Sotero, "behind them are agitators, demagogues, and other unsavory types who are corrupting the working class to the point of making them commit crimes and abuses, such as those we are presently seeing attempted in the Chamber of Representatives."[67]

Major strides were made in the area of transportation policy during Olaya's presidency. In May 1931, a law was passed by which national transportation policy shifted from railroad building to the construction of highways and secondary roads and trails. The complex project, denominated Law 88, represented the first step toward national planning in the area of transportation. Under the new law's provisions a national railway commission assumed operation of the fragmented rail system, a master plan was developed for constructing integrated rail and road systems in eastern and western Colombia, and funding for the various projects was removed from the departments and relocated in Bogotá. Critics like Laureano Gómez later found fault with the new transportation bureaucracy, though impartial observers agree that Olaya's initiative was a signally important advance in a vital area of public life.[68]

While the legislative reforms of Olaya's first eighteen months in office held important implications for national recovery and development, problems of an immediate character continued to loom. Hunger marches were common occurrences in Bogotá and other Colombian cities between 1930 and 1932. *El Tiempo*'s editorial writer characterized 1931 as "a terrible year," though he also observed that conditions were worse in other countries.[69] A month later, in January 1932, angry citizens massed in downtown Bogotá, demanding that public works jobs be restored. Olaya Herrera felt sufficiently threatened to jail Guillermo Hernández Rodríguez and Gilberto Viera, communist leaders of the protest. Public pressure gradually forced the government to abandon the economic austerity prescribed by Edwin Kemmerer. Colombia abandoned the gold standard in October 1931, and the government was under continuing pressure to declare a moratorium on foreign debt payments. Olaya grew increasingly unwilling to stand behind the rigorous Kemmerer program. "I have tried to play the Americans' game," he complained. "I have had the oil law they wanted passed, the Barco Contract signed, have tried to protect American interests in [our] tariffs. . . . It breaks my heart to have the Americans let me down in the end."[70]

Olaya's difficulty in extracting new loans from U.S. bankers drove him to expand the money supply through exchange devaluation and other measures. He eventually had to declare a partial moratorium on repayment of the foreign debt, most of which was owed to American banks.[71] Those measures, coupled with increased government spending, insured that Colombia's economic decline would not persist past 1932. In fact even during that dreary year there were signs of recovery. As early as June 1932, Olaya could brag that the nation's banking system was sound, exports running at normal levels, unemployment rates falling, coffee harvests excellent, and new national credit agencies making new loans available. Public works projects in suspension since 1930 were resumed during 1932, leading economic historian Alfonso Patiño to call their resumption "one of the most legitimate motives for pride in Olaya's government."[72] Colombians were in sufficiently good spirits during 1932 to launch a new social institution, the national beauty contest. On May 19, Ana Gutiérrez of Antioquia was crowned Miss Colombia, defeating Margot Manotas of Atlántico and Elvira Rengifo of El Valle del Cauca. Colombia's most beautiful woman was crowned in Bogotá's Teatro Colón amid pageantry reminiscent of that surrounding the city's old student carnivals.

Why Bipartisanship Failed

Olaya Herrera effectively addressed Colombia's economic troubles in large part because of the coalition government he formed on entering office and which served him well for three of his four years as president. Two previous twentieth-century Colombian presidents had governed through bipartisan alliances, though neither enjoyed Olaya's success. Rafael Reyes and Carlos E. Restrepo were Conservatives who had ruled with the help of Liberals. But Reyes spent most of the Quinquenio holding opponents in check with military force, and Restrepo was rendered ineffectual by brittle partisanships that crushed his benign Republicanism "like cotton between glass."[73]

Colombia and its new president were doubly fortunate. Not only did Enrique Olaya Herrera govern during an instant of relative harmony between Liberal and Conservative elites, but he did so as leading western states were rushing toward dictatorship and disaster. Thanks to the Conservative Party imbroglio of 1928–29, Colombia's political elite found itself able to deal with pressing economic problems in an unusually expeditious fashion. Olaya's remarkably effective government of "National Concentration" was thus an accidental one, the product of fortuitous circumstance.

This points up a paradox of the Olaya Herrera presidency. Olaya, suave diplomat, friend of American presidents and tycoons, evenhanded and magnanimous leader, was the creature of Colombia's polarized, elite-directed political system. Born into a modest Liberal family in rural Boyacá, he saw his family ruined by the civil wars of 1885 and 1895. Interparty rivalries and hereditary hatreds led him to bloody the noses of Conservative schoolboys before he was twenty years old, and he had fought in the War of the Thousand Days. But Enrique Olaya Herrera learned to despise partisan militancy. He leapt at the chance to join the paisa-led Republican movement that spearheaded Reyes's overthrow in 1909, and which subsequently made him a career diplomat. Olaya had agreed to run for the presidency in 1930 only when assured that he could do so with significant bipartisan support. Lacking such support, or confronted by a unified Conservative Party, Olaya Herrera would never have become president.

What this reveals is that in 1930 Colombia remained a nation in thrall of its two political parties. In that regard Colombia was no different in 1930 than it had been during the previous eighty years. As chief spokesman of a bipartisan alliance Olaya enjoyed great leeway in addressing economic matters. But old political hatreds and traditions consistently and insidiously eroded his bipartisan support. It was a sad fact of Colombian political life that however much Olaya protested his nonpartisanship, his party was bound to prosper at Conservative expense.

Colombia's political system was a highly centralized one where in addition to members of his own official family, the national president appointed departmental governors who in turn named alcaldes of the more than 800 most important cities and towns in the nation. Those officials staffed their offices and dependencies with political friends and allies, setting in motion a vast bureaucratic reorganization with each change of regime. As in Olaya Herrera's case, when the new regime brought the opposite party to power, few members of the losing collectivity would be asked to continue in their old positions.

It was likewise inevitable that as Liberals took up key governmental positions, the composition of elected bodies would begin to favor them. Parties in power had countless ways of winning elections. Colombia's Liberals had studied the techniques of Conservative election fraud over the previous forty-five years—techniques the followers of Núñez had learned from their predecessors in power, and thus back to the dawn of republicanism in Colombia. The Liberals lost no time in employing every hoary technique of vote rigging to take control of the nation's electoral bodies. By 1933, Liberal majorities existed in more than half the nation's *concejos* and departmental assemblies. When Olaya left office the National Senate and Chamber of Deputies were firmly in Liberal hands.

The inevitable Liberal takeover had filled Conservatives with dread that February in 1930. Rafael Azula Barrera recalled Olaya's election as producing a sense of impending catastrophe among himself and his fellows.[74] Conservatives crowded the nation's churches on February 10, the day after the elections. They prayed for divine intervention, for the death of Olaya Herrera, for anything that would spare the nation and themselves the suffering that approached.[75] Three civil wars had followed their own accession to power in 1880, and in 1930 no one could be sure that party leaders would not go to war to halt their loss of power.

As it turned out no civil war followed Olaya's election. By 1930 the state had grown too powerful to be overthrown by party leaders turned militia generals. However, the state was not yet strong enough to keep bloodshed from marring the harvest of spoils. At the end of Olaya's term in office hundreds of Colombians lay dead, and thousands were driven from their homes.

Colombia's change-of-regime violence raises a number of questions. First, what dynamic sent so many citizens to exile or to death at a time when party leaders in Bogotá counseled moderation? Second, what gave Colombia's Liberal and Conservative Parties their peculiar dynamism at a time when parties bearing those names had vanished over most of Latin America? Finally, why was it not possible for Olaya Herrera to control political strife so bitter as to cause Conservative police to routinely harass Liberal voters prior to 1930, and Liberal police to return the favor after Olaya's installation? It all suggests that there was more at stake than poorly paying government jobs and control of public policymaking.

The peculiar intensity of twentieth-century Colombian politics was rooted in a unique convergence of ecological, cultural, economic, and ideological factors. Colombians were a people who throughout their history had lived isolated by their mountains and in a situation of relative poverty. Their social setting was one of hierarchy and interlocking dependencies of a painfully local and immediate sort. In the early nineteenth century they cut their ties with Spain, and in so doing lost the force that had unified them politically, the monarchy. Once independence was achieved, and revered heroes of the revolution were gone, a process of territorial dissolution set in that by 1840 through 1842, threatened to reduce Colombia, then called New Granada, to a country of warring regions. Political loyalties extended no farther than the local or regional caudillo or cacique, or to one's patron or immediate social superior. The central government in Bogotá was powerless and the nation close to anarchy. Colombians desperately needed some force capable of bridging their regions and enabling them to make their voices heard in Bogotá. They found their unifying force in the Liberal and Conservative Parties.

Latin America's first modern political party, the Liberal Party, was formed by men who wished to carry forward the egalitarian, liberating principles that had given rise to the revolutionary movement itself. They wished to strike at all manner of entrenched privilege and restraints on individual freedom, holding that to do otherwise was both irrational and inconsistent with the democratic spirit of the age. In Colombia and elsewhere liberals approached their task with a zeal that delighted some and horrified others. Members of the latter group tried to counter the liberal reforms by establishing conservative parties.

During the 1840s and 1850s Colombian Liberals worked to make their revolutionary program that of the nation. They struck at human restrictions of every sort and promoted egalitarian social programs, arguing from rational and utilitarian premises that the good society was one affording maximum individual freedom. They crowned their achievement in constitutions framed during 1853 and 1863. Those documents separated church and state and guaranteed religious liberty, decreed universal male suffrage, established a federal system for the nation, abolished the death penalty, and guaranteed full freedom of expression. Other laws passed during the Liberal ascendance abolished slavery, established a system of public education, freed trade, and struck at entrenched social and economic privilege.

Colombian Liberalism, sprung from Enlightenment rationalism, oriented by the vast literature of European and American political writers, and objectified through national law, set into motion a sorting process that quickly polarized the nation. No man of means anywhere in the country could fail to be pleased or angered by the avalanche of reform legislation thrust upon him during the middle decades of the nineteenth century. Members of the elite either cast their lot with the Liberals, or joined forces to oppose them, becoming members of the Conservative Party. And where they went, family members, friends, followers, and all manner of dependents and clients followed.

Colombian Conservatives entered the ranks of their party by numerous routes. Many of the most intransigent members were professed Catholics who found Liberal anticlericalism to be wrongheaded and perverse. Others found their economic interests harmed by the Liberal reforms. And a great many Colombians became Conservatives because someone they loved, respected, or feared did so.

Through their parties Colombians discovered a way of promoting their interests—even shaping government policy when lucky enough to win power. Hence Colombia's two parties played the same role as political parties in Europe and North America. As in those places, the reasons for individual party affiliation in Colombia were diverse, frequently idiosyncratic.

The peculiar durability of Colombia's Liberal and Conservative Parties was in considerable measure a function of the long Conservative dominance stretching to 1930. That in turn was explained in part by the nation's tardy modernization. Because social change was so slow in coming, and the human costs invariably paid through such process slow in becoming manifest, Colombian Conservatives found it relatively easy to keep reformers in check between 1880 and the third decade of the twentieth century. That was the time when Liberalism was coming to the fore over most of Latin America. Their nation's seeming imperviousness to reform was what so frustrated both Los Nuevos and the political activists who tried to launch labor and socialist parties in Colombia. At length, in 1930, the Liberal Party loomed as the logical, indeed the only political conduit to reform in a country whose ingrown political system had ever thwarted easy change.

Colombian scholars have pointed to the combined factors of a weak central state and intense politicization as sources of violence and of the glacial pace of social and political change in their country. Luis López de Mesa counts six historic "frustrations" of national destiny stretching from pre-Columbian times through the Violencia of the 1940s and '50s. He traces his two twentieth-century frustrations, the War of the Thousand Days and the Violencia, to national political elites "who threw the country into the abyss of all imaginable madness."[76] Orlando Fals Borda counts three moments in national history when the utopian dreams of social reformers were dashed by the powerful hold of old patterns of thought and action. The socialist utopia propounded during the 1920s failed before a dominant, elite-directed Liberal-Conservative party system that locked Colombia within a "seignorial bourgeois tradition."[77] Frustration was precisely the sensation Enrique Olaya Herrera felt as political violence weakened the Republican consensus that had served him well during the early years of his presidency.

Violence in the Change of Regimes

Most vexing to Olaya was the extreme difficulty he had in countering violence when it erupted. Incidents of bloodshed usually occurred far from the seat of national power, in the dusty plaza of some remote village lying at the end of a long mule trail. When special peace-keeping forces were dispatched to such places, they usually reached them days after the incident had occurred. The sorting process that had caused Colombians to follow one or the other party had created innumerable points of potential strife across the cruelly broken national terrain. Over the years since the nation's Liberal and Conservative Parties had formed, Colombians had tended to migrate to *municipios* where they could count themselves part of the political majority. By 1930 three-fourths of all municipios, consisting of their *cabeceras* (county seats) and surrounding neighborhoods possessed appreciable Liberal or Conservative majorities. In 159 of them, some 20 percent of the total, 90 percent or more of the residents traditionally voted for either the Liberal or the Conservative Party.[78] Thus when he took office, and began staffing national offices with Liberals, Olaya either directly or indirectly sent fellow party members into places that had not seen Liberal administrators for nearly half a century. Conservatives in such places necessarily viewed the change with alarm. Liberals, on the other hand, frequently saw it as providing them an opportunity for righting old wrongs.

As in the case of municipios, most Colombian departments and regions had either Liberal or Conservative majorities in 1930. The Liberal Party was dominant along the Caribbean coast, in the departments of Atlántico, Bolívar, and Magdalena. El Valle and the sparsely populated territories of the eastern llanos were largely Liberal. Conservatism was dominant among the pious Antioquians and the people of Nariño. Huila, in the upper Magdalena valley was predominantly Conservative whereas Tolima, adjoining it and to the north, tended toward Liberalism. The situation was the reverse in the Santanders, where Santander del Norte was predominantly Conservative and the department of Santander largely Liberal. Rural Cundinamarca was Conservative and Bogotá, Liberal. In fact all of Colombia's larger towns and cities tended toward Liberalism. Boyacenses were among the more pragmatic, perhaps malleable, Colombians, for they tended to vote for whichever party was in power.

Within every department there were regions where one or the other party predominated. For example, Tolima's southern portion was mostly Conservative, save for its mountainous western region, which was Liberal. The reverse was true in the north, where valley towns like Honda, Mariquita, and Armero were notoriously Liberal, and the mountains to the west, settled by paisas, were mostly Conservative. And even within individual departmental regions there were always pockets of opposite-party strength. In northwestern Tolima lay the nonconforming municipio of El Líbano, settled by liberal-minded Antioquian pioneers during the 1860s.[79] Mountainous El Líbano became a Liberal anomaly among her heavily Conservative sister municipalities, Villahermosa, Casabianca, Herveo, and Fresno, to the north, and Santa Isabel and Anzoátegui to the south.

Even municipios such as El Líbano, having well-defined and long-standing partisan allegiance, invariably contained pockets of opposite-party strength. El Líbano again serves to illustrate. Settled by and for Liberals, El Líbano had *veredas* (rural neighborhoods) such as La Yuca, lying along its southern border and adjoining strongly Conservative Santa Isabel. La Yuca had its origin as a colonization project begun by none other than Ismael Perdomo, then bishop of Ibagué. Bishop Perdomo planned the rural neighborhood both as a charitable endeavor in the spirit of the encyclical *De rerum novarum,* and as a convenient way of insinuating confessional Conservatives into El Líbano, a municipio whose founder was a free thinker, and where non-Catholics even had their own cemetery. The nine square kilometers of land that became La Yuca had been owned by Conservative General Manuel Casabianca, governor of Tolima for many years. His heirs sold it to the Church precisely to dilute Liberal strength in El Líbano.[80]

These arcane facts illustrate the truth that each Colombian municipio had its own unique history of settlement and politicization. Liberal El Líbano suffered at Conservative hands between 1885 and 1930. During those years its people saw portions of the municipio annexed to neighboring Villahermosa and Santa Isabel, and they witnessed the assassination of founding father Isidro Parra during the civil war of 1895. When Liberal Libanenses regained power after 1930, they followed the time-honored practice of harassing and occasionally killing Conservatives. One series of election-related outrages during 1933 and 1934 resulted in the deaths of several campesinos from La Yuca, and jailing of the local Conservative leader, José del Carmen Parra.[81]

It was inevitable that every Colombian municipio would experience some degree of political stress after August 7, 1930, when the new administration took office. As the naming of governors, alcaldes, and other officials moved apace, old patterns of patronage were disrupted. Conservatives began losing jobs to Liberals placing stress upon local clientage networks. Local leaders, caciques and *gamonales* (local political bosses), were asked to find ways of alleviating or negating impact of the changes.[82] Ongoing electoral activity during the months after Olaya's possession also heightened tensions. Voters in every municipio were constantly told to steel themselves for three important contests set for 1931. In February there would be elections for departmental assemblies; three months later, in May, voters would send congressmen to the

Cámara de Representantes; and in October they would elect members of municipal *concejos*. During the weeks leading up to the first contest, set for February 5, voting lists were continually revised in many Colombian municipios. Where that occurred entire neighborhoods were set into motion as campesinos trooped into town to reregister, often behind a patron or cacique. They traveled to the *cabecera*, to its central plaza, where offices of the *jurado electoral*, or registrar of voters, was located. That inevitably brought antagonistic groups into confrontation as rival bands mingled on village streets. As every campesino carried a machete, and many bore sidearms, the possibilities for violence were endless.

The violence of 1930 and afterward was most severe in northeastern Colombia across several hundred square kilometers of the rugged eastern cordillera. The area in question embraced most of Santander del Norte below the departmental capital of Cúcuta, and ran down through the contiguous mountains of eastern Santander and Boyacá. An area of old settlement, northeastern Colombia had the reputation of producing strong people of independent spirit. By the 1930s it was both a region in economic decline and overpopulated, its mountainsides deforested and eroded, and many of its most able men and women leaving the region for more promising venues. With onset of the economic decline in 1928 and afterward, northeastern Colombia was especially ill prepared for major political change.

There were signs of impending strife in Santander even before Olaya Herrera entered office. In May 1930 young *santandereano* Rafael Gómez Picón watched the rush of events with mounting concern, observing "absolute demoralization" among all those around him. He wrote that the coming political change had awakened a "brutal exuberance" in the hearts of Liberals as well as Conservatives. Gómez Picón knew that the Liberals of Santander had readied themselves to exact justice for what he called "the frightening cortege of crimes perpetrated under the aegis of a cardboard republic, which [was] in fact the negation of republicanism." He had listened to his fellow Liberals speak guardedly of their attempts to overthrow the Conservative enemy thirty years earlier, of the glorious and terrible battles of Peralonso and Palonegro. "Will the dark swallows return?" Gómez Picón wondered.[83] He did not wait long for an answer.

President Olaya Herrera tried to be evenhanded in his appointment of departmental governors. Seven of the thirteen men he appointed were Conservatives, sent to those departments known to have Conservative majorities. But he sent members of his own party to preside over Liberal El Valle, Tolima, and Santander, and over Boyacá and Cundinamarca as well.[84] Alejandro Gálvis was the best known among the new president's appointees. A staunch party member and a native of Bucaramanga, Gálvis had published the newspaper

Vanguardia Liberal there for more than ten years—a decade during which he had inveighed against the way Conservatives routinely stole elections from the Liberal majority in his department. Those were contests that young Gómez Picón, one of his contributing editors, had characterized as "grotesque and drunken electoral farces, cynical and shameless mockeries of the popular will . . . crude, merciless and brutal persecution of those who don't bend before flattery or threats."[85]

Governor Gálvis set out to assure Liberals of their majority immediately upon taking office. He began by naming Felipe Cordero his secretary of government, his chief administrative lieutenant. Cordero was a native of the embattled Liberal stronghold of García Rovira province, an exceedingly mountainous part of the department whose principal town was Málaga, and whose surrounding communities were Capitanejo, twenty kilometers to the southeast, on the border with Boyacá; Molagavita, ten kilometers to the west; and San Andrés, Guaca, and Cerrito, a day's ride to the north. Fifty kilometers southeast of Málaga, and dominating the landscape, was the Sierra Nevada del Cocuy, whose highest peaks exceeded 5,500 meters. Along its eastern slopes, and just across the departmental border in Boyacá, were villages with names that would become well known during Colombia's later Violencia: Chiscas, Boavita, Güicán, and Chulavita. Over the eighty years since Colombia's parties had taken shape, Boyacá's El Cocuy region became heavily Conservative and García Rovira in Santander, predominantly and militantly Liberal. García Rovira's Liberals had been disfranchised there since 1885, though thanks to Governor Gálvis's efforts the situation was about to change dramatically.

Knowing that the Conservatives would not give up their electoral majority easily, Gálvis named Thousand Day War veteran General Virgilio Amado alcalde of Málaga. The general could guarantee control of the newly hired Liberal police, sent to García Rovira to replace the Conservative ones who had done the bidding of the previous administration. Mayor Amado would also keep watch over a militant group of priests whose spiritual leader was the doughty Bishop Rafael Afanador of Pamplona, and whose firebrand clergy in García Rovira included Father José María Castilla in San Andrés and Father Daniel Jordán in Málaga.[86] Other key Liberal appointees included Liberal alcaldes Ezequiel Herrera in Capitanejo, and Constantino Rueda in Guaca.[87] With men he could trust in place around García Rovira, and with them in turn supported by friendly police, Governor Gálvis knew that voting lists would soon come to reflect the true political makeup of the province.

The first step in reestablishing Liberal political dominance consisted in revising the lists of eligible voters in each of García Rovira's several municipios. And the revision had to be carried out quickly. As Colombian senators were elected by departmental assemblies, the February 1931 assembly elections could conceivably give Liberals a majority in the national body. Every Liberal in García Rovira thus knew that maximum effort would be required in the upcoming contest, which in turn meant helping the new administration insure that Conservative electoral commissions not rig voting lists, as they had since the time of Rafael Núñez.

Conservatives from neighborhoods around García Rovira were prepared for trouble as they trekked down to their corresponding municipal seats that December in 1930. Any time they left the relative safety of their home turf and traveled to town, they entered enemy territory. Their journey over steep mountain trails took them through Liberal veredas and into the cabeceras where members of the opposite party predominated. Now, however, they could not count on friendly police and municipal officials to protect them. All were Liberals now.

"To study and try to solve our social problems, especially that of party violence," wrote Santander native Manuel Serrano Blanco, "one must examine diverse phenomena: economic misery, invincible ignorance, human vengeance, hunger for bureaucratic positions, individual egotism, political ambition, and electoral fraud."[88] All those factors came into play that Monday, December 29, when a group of Conservative campesinos traveled to the village of Capitanejo. They traveled there from the highlands southeast of town, the lower reaches of the Conservative fastness of El Cocuy. Their enemy, the local police detachment, reinforced by numerous Liberal civilians, knew of their approach and waited along one side of the central plaza, not far from offices of the jurado electoral. The Conservatives were led by one Alejandro Herrera, who, according to a later report of the Capitanejo incident published in *El Tiempo,* had bolstered his courage, and that of his followers, with generous applications of aguardiente and cocaine. As the heavily armed group approached the registrar's office words were exchanged, weapons brandished, and the Conservatives withdrew across the plaza with the cry "miserable *godos* [literally, Goths, a pejorative term for Conservatives], we're in charge now!" ringing in their ears.[89] None of them registered to vote that day.

During the night another group of Conservative campesinos joined that of Alejandro Herrera. Meanwhile Liberals under their cacique Joaquín Torres arrived from veredas north of town. All that night and into the next morning members of both groups eyed each other warily in anticipation of the approaching clash.

Gunfire erupted that afternoon, felling more than a score of men in the town plaza. The rest scattered, taking refuge in facing buildings and entering into a pistol and rifle duel lasting many hours. So heavy and sustained was the exchange that many of the wounded bled to death where they lay. There was no way to tend to them until the following day, when the firing subsided. At least a dozen men died in the plaza of Capitanejo and twice as many were wounded.[90] Casualties might have been greater had the Conservatives not cut telephone and telegraph lines, making it impossible for the police to call in reinforcements from Málaga.[91]

García Rovira was but one of numerous places across Colombia experiencing violence during late 1930 and early 1931. On February 1, when the elections for assembly posts were held, over a hundred died in a rash of incidents. In Montería alone twenty-eight persons died when Conservative police fired on Liberal voters, and rioting Conservative civilians burned many Liberals in their homes.[92] Everywhere a host of local factors complicated the inexorable shift from Conservative to Liberal administration.

The Capitanejo incident, and numerous killings in Santander during the assembly elections, moved Alejandro Gálvis to resign his governorship in late February 1931. But he didn't leave the post before entering into an acrimonious debate with Bishop Afanador as to whether Liberal police or Conservative civilians were responsible for the mayhem.[93] As leaders of the respective parties protested their blamelessness, the violence continued. In mid-1931, following a gun battle that left fourteen men dead in Guaca, Father Hernán F. Sanmiguel, the village priest, wrote his superiors: "We find ourselves in a situation worse than war. Only God can contain the political hatred. . . . In Conservative neighborhoods there are many men armed with Gras rifles, the same as in Liberal neighborhoods. . . . The Conservatives of regions around San Andrés— and there are thousands of them—have good Gras rifles . . . all of them are armed and, in their words, simply await the moment when they can overthrow the government."[94]

By early 1931, Olaya Herrera had grown alarmed over the spreading strife. He considered making emergency arms purchases from the United States but dropped the plan, which was sure to be misinterpreted by the opposition. Meanwhile another election approached, that for representatives to the Cámara. Conservative leader Supelio Medina delivered a fiery speech in the departmental assembly of Boyacá, and days later was shot through the head by a hidden assassin as he walked with his wife down a Chiquinquirá street. As the elections drew closer, the Conservative directorate in Chiquinquirá warned party members not to be passive before the "traditional enemy": "If you let yourself be beaten by ballots," the directorate warned ominously, "things will be much different here in the future."[95]

Colombia's Conservatives managed to preserve 50 percent control of the Cámara de Representantes following the May 1931 elections. But they were not so lucky five months later when, in the October 4 elections for municipal concejos, Conservatives won majorities in but 361 of 804 town councils.

By late 1931 and on into 1932, García Rovira and adjoining regions in Boyacá and Santander were sunk in civil war. Eduardo Santos, who had replaced Alejandro Gálvis as governor, summarized the situation in Santander at the time: "The Conservatives . . . feel menaced, persecuted and abandoned, though they exaggerate their plight. Liberals are in a permanent state of crisis. In spite of their overwhelming numerical superiority they believe the slightest incident will cause their ruin. Hence they cause scandals and stage protests [that are] quite reprehensible."[96] Bogotá newspapers regularly published accounts of multiple killings in towns like Molagavita, Flórida, Guaca, and San Antonio. Whole regions were depopulated, as Colombians fled across the border into Venezuela. Manuel Serrano sadly recalled riding through once-flourishing coffee country south of Cúcuta, in Santander del Norte. Houses dotting the hinterland were in ruins, and towns like Arboledas, Ragonvalia, Pamplonita, and Rosario depopulated. Their former residents were either dead or living as refugees.[97] Serrano described the mountains of Santander del Norte as "silent and sad, made desolate by barbarism. . . . The absurd fight had turned it into tragic and cursed ground. Violence made it a no-man's-land."[98]

A particularly ominous aspect of the violence was the formation of militia armies in the most troubled areas. Partisans on both sides felt the need to organize their resistance, and highly placed persons in Bogotá and elsewhere often contributed to the effort. Alejandro Gálvis accused Minister of War Carlos Villamizar of distributing rifles to fellow Conservatives before leaving his post in 1932. That same year Olaya Herrera had to stop Jorge Eliécer Gaitán's organization of Liberal militias. On March 17, 1932, Olaya ordered the disbanding of all "party armies" in Colombia, specifying the Guardia Civil Liberal, Milicias Conservadoras, and Milicias Rojas in his message.[99] Each side blamed the other for helping organize military forces. When the parish priest in San Andrés organized a Conservative militia in mid-1932, Bishop Afanador justified his action saying that as the Liberal police were treating Conservatives like criminals, the Church was right in helping such persons protect themselves. The bishop's attitude led Olaya Herrera to remark that militant priests were responsible for "leading many poor campesinos to the slaughter."[100]

The violence had clearly surpassed Olaya Herrera's ability to control it by mid-1932. Conservative militias had become active in both eastern and western Boyacá, and the stoning of the Conservative directorate in Manizales on June 18 signaled a possible spread of the lawlessness into the central cordillera. But at that moment several things combined to greatly reduce the violence over the succeeding twelve months. First, Laureano Gómez returned from Europe and took charge of the Conservative Party. His attacks on Olaya Herrera, especially regarding the violence, calmed Conservatives living in places such as García Rovira by convincing them that they at last had a strong advocate in Bogotá. Second, the war with Peru, which erupted in September 1932, galvanized Colombians and caused them to rally against the invader. It also removed many young men from the troubled zones, sending them into the army. Finally, the political raison d'être for violence faded with Liberal consolidation of power. The Liberals won a majority of the seats in departmental assemblies and in the national chamber of representatives during 1933. They easily overwhelmed Conservatives in Santander, where army and police closely monitored potential trouble spots and where there was heavy Conservative abstention. The effective consequence was that by 1933 Santander's Conservatives were excluded from the body politic.[101]

One of the more outwardly curious aspects of the Conservative disfranchisement in Santander was that few formal complaints were filed following illegal acts, and witnesses refused to testify in legal proceedings. The fact was that when the aggrieved parties were Conservatives, they had no legal recourse in places like Santander, where civil government was controlled by hostile forces. Between 1930 and 1932, some two thousand Conservative police were fired and replaced by Liberals. In Boyacá, Conservatives charged that departmental police were commanded from Liberal headquarters by Plinio Mendoza Neira, the party leader in the department.[102]

In early 1934, Liberal leader Luis Eduardo Nieto Caballero expressed indignation over the way fellow party members in Santander del Norte connived with a local judge to take valuable coffee farms through the manipulation of land taxes. Nieto Caballero called it "robbery organized in a legal manner, systematic persecution, the reappearance of a cruel sentiment condensed in the phrase 'hatred of the godo.'"[103]

While incidents like the Capitanejo gun battle of 1930 became infrequent after 1933, that did not mean that peace returned to García Rovira or to other troubled areas. Conservatives simply fell back to defensive positions and awaited their chance for revenge. Some acted individually, as in the case of Heraclio Cañón, a campesino from Boyacá: "When in 1930 they began killing Conservatives, police commanded by Sr. Siervo Castro arrived at my house one night; they killed my father and burned the house. I managed to hide myself in a nearby creek, and from there I could see the assassins. All of them have paid for their crimes, because I brought each of them down with this very Gras rifle."[104] Others became refugees in cabeceras in and around the region they had fled. In García Rovira the towns of Capitanejo, Málaga, and Guaca had substantial populations of displaced Conservatives. When elections were held most of them avoided further trouble by refusing to vote.

Highly significant in terms of the Violencia of 1946 through 1953 was the movement of displaced Conservatives out of García Rovira southeast into the El Cocuy region of Boyacá. There they joined compatriots living in veredas like Chulavita, redoubts from which they battled Liberal police and all others to a standstill. Towns like Boavita, Güicán, La Uvita, Guacamayas, and San Mateo remained uniformly Conservative, full of men and women who dreamt of the day when they could strike back at the hated Liberals.

II.

The Dangers of Political Inauthenticity, 1932–1965

7

The Liberal Republic and Its Critics

Waiting for Laureano

Laureano Gómez maintained a significant political presence in Colombia during his nearly four-year European sojourn. Suggestive of that was the newspaper piece titled "How I Interviewed Dr. Laureano Gómez Yesterday," written by columnist Mario Ibero [Fidel Torres González] in June 1930.[1] The article appeared in connection with services commemorating antigovernment demonstrations of June 1929, when students protested corruption in the Abadía Méndez government, losing one of their number to a ricocheting police bullet. Not long afterward Laureano Gómez set forth his analysis of those events in a letter to friend and supporter Hernando Uribe Cualla. Gómez fulminated against Abadía's government—"the sickening normality that the nation endures"—going so far as to suggest direct popular action to topple Abadía.

Colombian politics had changed dramatically between the bloody student demonstrations and publication of Mario Ibero's "interview" with Laureano Gómez. On February 4, 1930, Enrique Olaya Herrera won the presidency, ending the near half-century of Conservative dominance of politics. Gómez followed those events closely from his European vantage point. As a Conservative he was shocked and dismayed by his party's defeat at the polls, but felt vindicated by repudiation of a Conservative Party machine that he himself had attacked as vigorously as had any Liberal. Far from Colombia when the Conservative fall occurred, he bore no direct responsibility for it. That left him positioned to assume party leadership when he returned home.

Colombia was in Laureano Gómez's thoughts during his years abroad, but while he was away, Europe dominated his thinking. The European sojourn constituted for Gómez a never to be repeated time of "quietude and study," not a second of which could be squandered. On departing Bogotá in September 1928, he and his family made straight for Paris, arriving there in mid-October. Once settled in a furnished apartment in the Etoile district, Gómez flung himself at the city's cultural attractions. He attended lectures at the Sorbonne, visited museums, libraries, and bookstores, and sought out those whose writings had influenced his own thought and actions. In Gómez's words, he reached Europe "avid for powerful ideological orientation, disconcerted by the contradictions and uncertainties of the contemporary world."[2] His friend the Francophile José de la Vega, found Gómez "obsessed" with the study of European civilization, and of the way culture was replicated in Europe's American territories.[3] Alfonso López Pumarejo saw Gómez frequently during his time in Europe. "He continues to study," wrote López in March 1929. A month later Gómez complained, "time flies here with disconcerting rapidity. . . . Eight months is too little time to savor Paris."[4]

Appalled by the costliness of Paris, by the way Parisians "place amiable and efficient siphons into the pockets of foreigners," he removed himself and his family to extreme southwestern France in June 1929. There, at St. Jean-de-Luz, a resort area on the Bay of Biscay, it was possible to live more cheaply.[5] Just a few kilometers north of the border with Spain, St. Jean-de-Luz was a tranquil spot for study and meditation, and afforded not-too-difficult access to Madrid and to other places of interest in Spain. St. Jean-de-Luz was also home-in-exile for Spanish philosopher Miguel de Unamuno (1864–1936). Gómez frequently met Unamuno on the beach, where they spoke of Primo de Rivera, who had exiled the philosopher six years earlier. As they conversed Unamuno entertained the Gómez children by making toy castles for them from scrap pieces of paper.[6]

Toward the end of 1929, Laureano Gómez again moved his family, this time north to Brussels, where he enrolled his four children in a private school that offered instruction in both Spanish and French. There was a small group of Colombian expatriates there, one of whom, José María de Guzmán, helped him locate an apartment. Brussels served as the point of departure for the major phase of Gómez's travels, a six-month tour of Italy and Switzerland. During November 1929, not long before his departure for Italy, Gómez attempted to intervene in Colombian politics by convincing José Vicente Concha to offer himself as a compromise Conservative Party candidate for the upcoming presidential contest. The effort was abortive. Concha, at the time Colombia's ambassador to the Vatican, was gravely ill; he died December 9, 1929, two months before the election.

Laureano Gómez undertook the Italian-Swiss phase of his tour with vigor. He was especially taken with Venice, whose people he admired for their ability to wed commercial acumen with brilliant artistic and architectural achievement. María Hurtado, described by her children as "not an agile person," recalled Venice chiefly as a place of personal suffering. She loathed the omnipresent gondolas, which she felt were always on the verge of tumbling her into one of the city's canals.[7] The couple remained long enough in the Swiss capital for Laureano Gómez to consider publishing a volume titled *Babiecas en Ginebra* (Dolts in Geneva). The travelogue was never written and no one knows whether the "dolts" were Gómez and his wife, other tourists, or the people of Geneva.

During his time in Italy, Gómez studied the dictatorial regime that Benito Mussolini had recently established. Just months before he and his wife arrived national elections gave the Fascist Party a huge congressional majority. By early 1930, Mussolini's representatives were completing a series of agreements by which the Vatican would relinquish its claims to the old papal states, in exchange for nearly a billion lira in compensation as well as sovereignty over Vatican City. As an ardent defender of clerical prerogatives, Laureano Gómez was displeased with the Lateran Treaties of February 1930. He scorned both Pius XI, who signed them—"the Pope traded the sovereignty of Rome for a bit of cash," he later said—and Benito Mussolini, who in Gómez's view was a comic-opera dictator.

In May 1930, Gómez and his wife returned to Brussels, collected their children, and repaired to St. Jean-de-Luz, where they recuperated from their travels and studied the political news from home. Colombian newspapers overflowing with election day photographs of exultant Liberals and anguished Conservatives awaited them there. Like all other Conservatives, Laureano Gómez was disoriented by the impending change in government. He resolved to say nothing until his return to Bogotá in September, when the national political scene would be much clearer.[8]

Gómez was spared the necessity of reentering active party politics when word reached him in August 1930 that President-elect Olaya wanted him to accept the post of minister to Germany. Gómez accepted with alacrity. The valises he was readying for shipment home were redirected to Berlin. Olaya and Gómez thus effected a brilliant marriage of convenience that postponed the inevitable clash between them. By bringing Gómez into his government, Olaya insured the silence of his old antagonist while keeping him safely distant. Convincing Gómez to accept the German ministry also brought a tidy savings in transportation costs for the depression-straitened budget of his foreign affairs ministry. The diplomatic posting bought Laureano Gómez time to evolve a strategy for returning the Conservative Party to power under his leadership. Important too, the government posting replenished his personal coffers, sadly depleted by two years' travel on the Continent. Finally, acceptance of the German ministry sent him not merely to a portion of Europe he had not previously visited, but to the continent's most exciting capital.

On September 11, 1930, outgoing minister Pablo Emilio Gurado cabled Bogotá that the German government expressed pleasure in accepting Laureano Gómez as incoming minister. The following day Gómez cabled Bogotá for instructions.[9]

German civilization had reached its most impressive flowering at the moment Laureano Gómez and his family traveled to Berlin in late 1930. Its people were the world's best educated, and its schools and universities the world's finest. Whether the field was architecture, painting, music, drama, or film,

Germany set the standard that others strove to emulate. Just a year earlier, in 1929, the Berlin Music Festival had featured performances by Richard Strauss, Bruno Walter, George Szell, Arturo Toscanini, and Pablo Casals. A year earlier Bertolt Brecht and Kurt Weil's *The Threepenny Opera* was performed throughout Germany and across Europe over 4,000 times, establishing a world record. The Bauhaus attracted visiting artists Paul Klee and Wassily Kandinsky, and composers Béla Bartók, Paul Hindemith, and Igor Stravinsky. Risqué films like Joseph von Sternberg's *The Blue Angel* could be viewed in Berlin but not in Paris, where it was banned, while drama and stage shows touched on themes that were taboo in other European capitals. Germany of the late Weimar period was, in short, the ideal place for Laureano Gómez to complete his European tour.

In spite of its high standing in the arts, Germany was politically troubled in 1930. A month before Gómez arrived, Adolf Hitler's National Socialist Party emerged as a force in national politics, winning 107 seats in the Reichstag. It was Germany's second most popular party after the Socialists, who won 143 seats. The election moved the Nazis ahead of the Communists, who won but 77 seats. Centrist parties lost heavily in the September 14 elections, since global economic decline heightened both popular tension and political extremism.

Battles between the political left and right were at their height during the twenty months that Gómez served in Germany. On more than one occasion members of the Colombian mission watched through windows of the ministry building as Nazi and Communist Party members brawled in the streets below.[10] Twelve-year-old Alvaro Gómez recalled taking refuge in a Berlin subway along with a playmate when one such altercation erupted around them. On another occasion his father took him to the Sports Palace in Berlin to hear one of Hitler's speeches. Neither the elder nor the younger Gómez understood what the Nazi leader said, though both were impressed by his gestures, by the way he pounded the lectern as he spoke, and by the frenzied delight with which the vast audience received his words. The younger Gómez recalled the event in nightmarish terms. His father expressed amazement that so civilized a people as the Germans could be so moved by Hitler's demagoguery.[11]

Laureano Gómez became indirectly caught up in the political tragedy unfolding there. Seven years earlier, when serving as Colombia's public works minister, he had authorized a 4.5 million peso contract with the Julius Berger Consortium, a German engineering firm employed to conduct an exhaustive study of the Río Magdalena and afterward to channelize key stretches of it. Although the technical portion of the study was completed, no dredging was ever undertaken. Laureano Gómez later charged that the company's supervising engineer overbilled for imported equipment, exhausting moneys set aside for the project. While the most serious abuses took place during Abadía's presidency, Gómez remained sensitive to the charge that it was he who signed the Berger contract.[12]

The Berlin posting allowed Laureano Gómez to personally investigate the Berger matter. Such action fell within the scope of his instructions, which directed him to expedite Colombian-German commercial relations. According to one of Gómez's more vocal critics, Liberal Pedro Juan Navarro, Gómez went so far as to hire spies to burglarize Berger Company files in hopes that proof of wrongdoing could be extracted from them.[13] Pursuit of the Berger matter led to at least one exceedingly unpleasant interview between Gómez and Chancellor Paul von Hindenburg.[14] One can but speculate on the heated exchange between the dour German octogenarian and the fiery young South American.

Since the Julius Berger Consortium was a Jewish company and Laureano Gómez was known to rail against "foreign shylocks" who seemed to him ever ready to exploit those less crafty than themselves, the matter came to the attention of Nazi propagandist Joseph Goebbels. Goebbels contacted Gómez to see whether he could publish an expose of the Berger matter in his newspaper, *Der Angriff*. The Colombian minister refused, for reasons of diplomatic etiquette and Gómez's reluctance to air Colombian internal matters beyond national boundaries.[15]

Colombia's chancellery in Berlin constituted a safe haven for Laureano Gómez and his family. Gómez paid regular visits to Berlin's Staatliche Museen, where he was fond of meditating on Rembrandt's *The Man with the Golden Helmet* (ca. 1650). He paid frequent visits to the museums and galleries of Dresden, Leipzig, and Potsdam and even traveled in Poland, where he purchased several paintings.[16] Meanwhile politics grew stormier in Germany, where by early 1932 some six million workers were unemployed, and millions more experienced hunger, uncertainty, and fear. In March, as Laureano Gómez prepared his return to Colombia, a presidential election was held that Hindenburg won handily with eighteen million votes. Still Adolf Hitler garnered eleven million, and his surging popularity led Prime Minister Heinrich Brüning to outlaw the Nazi Storm Troops. Two months later Brüning's government fell, and the new chancellor, Franz von Papen, lifted sanctions against Hitler's private army. Laureano Gómez and his family did not witness the fall of Brüning's government. By June 1932 they were on their way back to Colombia.

When Gómez resigned his diplomatic post in early 1932, his own party was disoriented and divided. Prior even to Olaya Herrera's inauguration the old Nationalist-Historical enmity flared again. On July 20, 1930, when Congress convened, Nationalist Alfredo Vásquez Cobo and Historical Guillermo

Valencia exchanged hot words in the Senate.[17] Olaya Herrera contributed to Conservative division when he revived the old Republican Party by enlisting the support of its only successful presidential candidate, Carlos E. Restrepo. Meanwhile the discredited Suarista–Abadía Méndez faction strove to maintain its integrity, relying heavily on its newspaper, *El Nuevo Tiempo*. As that group's sworn enemy, Laureano Gómez fired epistolary salvos at it from Europe. In his letters Gómez indicted Abadía's group for educating Conservative youth in "seminars of servility and insincerity, and in the minutiae of bureaucratic intrigue." *El Nuevo Tiempo*, he thundered, "should go to the grave!"[18] On the Conservative Party's extreme right wing a group of articulate young men, most of them barely out of their twenties, advocated recasting the Conservative Party along Fascist lines. Calling themselves Los Leopardos, they were led by Silvio Villegas, Augusto Ramírez Moreno, and José Camacho Carreño.

But Olaya Herrera did gravest damage to Conservative Party unity by making it his policy to collaborate with its members. His government of "National Concentration" tempted Conservatives with ministries and department governorships, and strove to forge a bipartisan governing coalition. To that end he cultivated the dissident Conservative from eastern Antioquia, Román Gómez (1879–1954). Román Gómez's chief source of power and influence lay in a vast patronage network that he had constructed during twenty-five years of political and commercial activity in and around the municipality of Maranilla, a coffee-growing region forty kilometers southeast of Medellín. His chief claim to fame was his successful effort to have the national government support construction of a railroad linking Maranilla with the department capital. As well as sealing his reputation as Maranilla's greatest native son, the Tranvía del Oriente served as a bountiful source of employment for the cacique's extensive family and political clientele.[19]

Román Gómez became a key figure in Colombian politics following elections for departmental assemblies in February 1931. Liberals did well in the elections, but failed to win a majority of them. This was crucially important, since departmental assemblies elected the members of Colombia's Senate. Results of the assembly elections left Olaya Herrera without control of Congress, suggesting that his legislative efforts would be stymied unless he could find at least one Conservative willing to vote with the Liberals whenever asked to do so. In Román Gómez the president found his man.

Every aspect of Román Gómez's election to the Senate in 1931 was irregular and productive of discord within his party. During March 1931, the Romanista bloc in the Antioquian assembly allied itself with Liberals to defeat the "conciliation" faction, led by Pedro J. Berrío.[20] Lacking the votes to win a Senate seat in his own department, Román Gómez and the Liberals of Tolima arranged to have the paisa dissident head their senatorial slate. Thus Tolimense Liberals sent an anomalous senatorial delegation to Bogotá in 1931: it consisted of the Conservative Gómez and two Liberal *suplentes* (elected substitutes for a principal candidate).

The discord in Conservative ranks produced by Olaya Herrera's bipartisan polity reached its height in mid-1931. Thanks to the votes of Román Gómez and his supporters, Liberal Pedro Juan Navarro was elected president of the Senate—the first of his party to gain the post in forty-five years. This represented a double affront to the Conservatives, whose directorate had earlier tried to come to terms with their erstwhile colleague. But Román Gómez's position was such that he dismissed their entreaties, saying the "anarchy" within his own party forced him to work with the Liberals.[21] Neither could the Conservative directorate, groping to reestablish party discipline, turn to Laureano Gómez. Not only was Gómez a government employee, but he had gone so far as to congratulate Olaya Herrera following the latter's successful conclusion of negotiations with North American petroleum interests.[22]

In August 1931, congressional Conservatives hosted what was to have been a "unity banquet." But the Romanistas refused to attend, as did General Berrío and Julio Holguín, both of whom had recently resigned from the party directorate. During Manuel Serrano Blanco's plea that Conservatives cease calling for revolution and return to traditional party principles, the Leopardo José Camacho Carreño stalked from the room. *El Tiempo*, which normally reveled in the Conservative opponent's distress, showed compassion, calling the gathering "a banquet of pain."[23]

Three months after the banquet Conservative leaders attempted to resuscitate their dispirited forces by holding a national convention and drafting a party platform—the first in fifty years. The convention was a desultory affair marked by recrudescence of the old Historical-Nationalist strife, personified in bickering between the Valencia and Vásquez Cobo factions. Nearly a quarter of Conservative congressmen declined to attend the event, which was framed against the backdrop of virtual civil war in eastern Santander, Liberal victory in the October 4 concejo elections, and the angry accusation by Pedro J. Berrío that Liberals were trying to "finish off" his party through violence and vote fraud. Berrío warned that his party would go to war if Liberal abuses did not cease.[24]

The convention's only achievement was its drafting of the Program of 1931, a lifeless document whose most notable quality was its heterogeneity. The "program" began with a reaffirmation of traditional party principles and a pledge that conservatism stood behind both the Constitution of 1886 and the Concordat of 1887. Next it proposed two political reforms of a mildly technocratic and corporative character: the first involved creation of a Ministry of

Social Affairs charged with working to harmonize class interests, and the second recommended streamlining the national Congress. Conservative leaders also called for free, compulsory, and confessional public education, for programs aimed at protecting labor, and for laws broadening the state's protection of abandoned women and child workers. By stressing those points, drafters of the 1931 platform reflected sensitivity to Pope Leo XIII's call for social progress within a setting of social order issued forty years earlier in *De rerum novarum,* recently reformulated in Pius XI's *Cuadragesimo anno.*

Portions of the document dealing with economics smacked of nineteenth-century liberalism. Its drafters advocated the democratization of agricultural credit, stimulation of exports, and encouragement of skilled European immigration—all designed to promote growth of an agrarian middle class, "an essential element of social equilibrium and a very important factor in economic and moral progress."[25] Other sections of the document addressed business interests, especially those of agro-industrialists. It called for protection of infant industries, continued low taxes, maintenance of the gold standard, continued improvement of Colombia's transportation infrastructure, and a shift away from "traditional diplomacy" and toward what was termed "economic diplomacy"—clearly a Nationalist plea that Historicals soften their traditional anti-Americanism.

The Conservative Program of 1931 ended with a paean to Colombian democracy, and expression of the hope that the political arena might be kept a "neutral playing field" where political battles might be fought out as "true democratic contests in pursuit of high ideals."[26]

Conventioneers ended their meeting by naming a new three-man directorate consisting of Pedro J. Berrío, Miguel Jiménez López, and Laureano Gómez. A few days later Berrío and Jiménez López cabled Gómez asking him to return home to "help orient" Colombian Conservatism.[27]

By early 1932, Laureano Gómez was prepared to comply with their request. His investigation of the Berger Consortium had reached a definitive if unsatisfactory closure, and an extensive report on his work was in the hands of Ministry of Public Works lawyer Tulio Enrique Tascón.[28] Now he could devote his energies to party leadership. It was obvious that he must do so soon. In February he received a telegram from Manuel Serrano Blanco, Silvio Villegas, and Augusto Ramírez Moreno urging him to resign his ministry and to return home immediately. Three months later Conservative members of the Cundinamarca departmental assembly cabled their "illustrious statesman," begging him to resume party leadership.[29]

The increasingly strident demands for Gómez's return were part of a generalized call for resumption of partisan politics by activists on both sides. Following Manuel Serrano Blanco's speech calling for Conservatives to reaffirm their traditional doctrinal beliefs, *El Tiempo* published several editorials enthusiastically endorsing repolitization along ideological lines. The editorial writer, probably Eduardo Santos, complained that Olaya Herrera's "National Concentration" served only to weaken the traditional parties. "The idea of Liberals and Conservatives doing battle over economic and political principles seduces us," he wrote."[30]

Calls for renewed party competition bore the clear stamp of Alfonso López and Laureano Gómez, both of whom over the years had repeatedly affirmed their steadfastness to party ideals. Gómez and López had often spoken of the need to revitalize partisan politics while in Europe. During one lengthy conversation held in Paris, the two had agreed to fight for electoral reform so as to remove violence from Colombian politics. Allowed to debate program and ideology in a violence-free setting, each was convinced his party would triumph.

Secure in the knowledge that he was universally perceived as conservatism's best hope, Laureano Gómez set out to clarify his party's ideological position in a series of essays that he began writing before departing Europe. An important aspect of that work involved his fixing of conservatism's stance before Marxism-Leninism, fascism, and national socialism, ideologies then at war with "bourgeois" liberal democracy. Gómez decided to couch his critique of Europe's left and right extremisms in brief biographies of their chief proponents: Joseph Stalin, Benito Mussolini, and Adolf Hitler. To balance the study he included an essay on Mahatma Gandhi.

Gómez included Gandhi in his study because the Indian politician was by the 1930s well on his way to achieving through pacific means what Stalin, Hitler, and Mussolini had got through force. And Gandhi's success in leading his followers against the superior might of a political adversary was highly suggestive to Gómez following his own party's loss of power. Laureano Gómez was drawn to the Hindu's self-abnegation, antimaterialism and spiritualism, qualities in harmony with conservative belief in divinely ordered hierarchies and individual acceptance of one's assigned place in them. Gómez found the Mahatma to be "great for his deeds, for his perseverance, and for the steely hardness of his will." "Greater yet is he for his faith," Gómez continued, "which is founded in the power of truth and justice."[31]

Standing in stark contrast to Gandhi were Europe's three dictators. Stalin was described as a "Georgian barbarian" whose governing philosophy violated all Western and Christian values. "Cruel, implacable, active, and cunning . . . no one loves him," Gómez wrote, "Neither does anyone admire or respect him; they simply fear him."[32] Adolf Hitler did not fare any better under Gómez's pen. Gómez described the Nazi leader as a vile assassin who furtively "sinks his dagger into defenseless victims." In Hitler's Germany "there's no code . . . no law . . . nor sacred principles." As early as 1932, Gómez knew that Hitler would fail: "The morality that condemns Hitler will endure when nothing remains of the dictator but the same bitter memory that all tyrants leave behind. His name will be forever linked to his thousands of victims, whose voices will never cease to damn the hand that wrongly injured them."[33]

Gómez saved his most thoroughgoing indictment for fascism, the doctrine most dangerous to orthodox conservatism because of certain common elements in their respective ideologies. Mussolini's doctrine, he began, had brought Italy spurious economic progress, and the "long and total eclipse" of human liberty there. Far from restoring Italy's glory, fascism had devastated the nation's intellectual life, substituting in its stead "bloodshed, arson, and violent persecutions." Whereas Mussolini claimed uniqueness for his ideology, fascism was nothing more than "a company for promoting despotism," being in that regard no different than any other form of dictatorship. "The methods of tyrants are ever the same," wrote Gómez.[34] He ended the essay on Mussolini by warning that Colombian Conservatives must not seek in fascism an antidote to communism: "The moral question is foremost. Power acquired through violence, material victory achieved through bloodshed and institutionalized upon the ruins of human dignity and liberty, cannot yield blessings. The appearance may be lavish, the facade imposing, and the overall impression one of permanence. But universal human experience reveals that [fascism] will last one human lifetime—two at most. Then will come the inevitable fall. We know, well we know, that it is thus."[35]

Through his essays on Stalin, Hitler, and Mussolini, Gómez spelled out what orthodox conservatism was not. It remained for him to explain what conservative beliefs were. That he would do shortly after his return to Colombia. In the meantime there were a few details to be taken care of. First he must pack and return home to occupy his Senate seat. Next he must end the dissidence of Román Gómez. Only then could he orient and lead Conservatism. Three weeks before tendering his resignation Gómez wrote a friend in Bogotá, "I'm going to throw myself into the whirlwind without any illusion; I return perfectly inured against disappointment. . . ."[36]

Vaca Loca

There was excitement in political Colombia during weeks preceding the return of Laureano Gómez. The question in everyone's mind was "what position would the 'fiery tribune' take to confront the current political situation?" Gómez declined to grant interviews, so speculation was rife as to his probable course of action. Members of the Liberal-Romanista alliance feigned indifference to it all, saying that "these times are far from the days when it was easy to triumph with rhetoric."[37] In truth they felt panic as the opening of Congress approached.[38] Some, like Carlos E. Restrepo, did not doubt that Gómez would return "to the violences that have been the chief and only source of his notoriety."[39] Others were not so sure. Gómez watcher Luis Eduardo Nieto Caballero (Lenc) wrote of hearing that the "magnificent tribune" had changed, that he had become "judicious, well-traveled, and tolerant." Still, Lenc mused, it was possible that Gómez would suffer some personal criticism and lose his self-control: "Then, when we least expect it, we'll see a cloud of dust and in it Laureano Gómez in hot pursuit of someone. . . ."[40]

Enrique Santos, who was just beginning his El Tiempo column "Danza de las Horas" (Dance of the Hours), was optimistic: "The era of petty politics, of violence as the only recourse, has passed for Laureano Gómez and for the nation," he wrote on July 4, 1932.

Gómez, his wife, four children, and housekeeper Ana María Camacho reached Bogotá by air on the thirteenth of July, just a week prior to the opening of Congress. Following the party by land were some three dozen trunks, boxes, and suitcases—all the possessions acquired during their years abroad. Gómez continued to refuse interviews, maintaining that he had "resolved to deflate the eternal tropicalism of personalities who arrive making grandiose statements that appear absurd outside Colombia."[41] Meanwhile rumors flew that he intended to purge Román Gómez and others from the Conservative Party. On July 19, the day before Congress convened, the Laureanista newspaper La Unidad of Medellín published a list of eleven paisas who had been singled out for "treason" to the party. Heading the list was Román Gómez, "the most hated of the traitors."

No sooner was Laureano Gómez sworn in as Conservative senator from Cundinamarca than he called for a closed session in which he accused Román Gómez of betraying his party, going on to impugn the Senate at large for crimes against the state.[42] Later, in open session, Román Gómez defended his actions and leveled charges against his antagonist. Over the following month Congress was deadlocked and the nation held spellbound by the drama unfolding in its midst. While the debates—"Gómez vs. Gómez," as Nieto Caballero termed them—went on for nearly six weeks, they reached their climax during the sessions of August 8 and 9. Laureano Gómez began his speech on the eighth brilliantly evoking Toribio Benavente's famous play Los intereses creados (Special interests). "Here is the stage of the old farce!" said the orator, going on to recall Benavente's Crispín, a clownish servant who earned eventual personal salvation by helping his master fulfill his dreams. But, continued Gómez, here we have a modern-day Crispín who is not the subject of an interesting morality tale, but rather stands as the personification of naked self-interest.

On the ninth, Laureano Gómez intensified the attack on Román Gómez in a two-hour peroration remembered as one of the most devastating in Colombian parliamentary history. He concentrated on Román Gómez's business dealings, especially those having to do with the Tranvía del Oriente, called by Gómez "the most extraordinary case of a public company in the history of the nation."[43] At one point he paused to read a long list containing the names of relatives of Román Gómez holding well-paid positions on the railroad, following which someone in the packed spectators' gallery shouted, "Long live the family of Román Gómez!"

As the long speech progressed, spectators warmed to the speaker, "applauding frenetically" whenever Gómez made an especially telling point. When the charge was made that Román Gómez had built and operated an illegal distillery in Marinilla, the cacique screamed, "You miserable liar!" That touched off a frenzied ovation among spectators, who waved white handkerchiefs, shouted, whistled and jeered to such an extent that women seated in a special section reserved for them were "overcome with the anguish of uncertainty." Meanwhile senators rushed to surround both Román and Laureano Gómez, fearing a physical confrontation between them. A furious presiding officer shouted at guards to clear the galleries, evoking "a truly infernal cheer" from spectators that quickly turned into the chant, "Román no! Out with him, out with him!" At length calm was restored and Laureano Gómez continued, interrupted periodically by applause described alternately as "delirious" and "prolonged." Near the end of his speech Laureano Gómez delivered what stands as his most withering denunciation of another public figure:

And you, Crispín, evil man—him of the old farce, violator of the Constitution and the laws. You, Crispín, peddler of influence in support of your own ambitions and those of your relatives, supporters, and servants! You, Crispín, lying trafficker of vile properties, stolen from their afflicted true owners—who today groan in prison cells! You, violator of privileged correspondence to the end of turning that information to your private and political advantage! You, Crispín, who dissimulates clumsily in public offices, as you gather up subsidies from a complacent administration and use them to feed your immense gaggle of uncles, nephews, and other relatives! You, Crispín, who violates the sacrosanct silence of the tomb—which must not be violated—to make slime of the ashes which you then try to fling against me, thinking mistakenly that you will slow me in my path toward truth! You, prosaic slanderer, who cannot back your audacious charges with any but anonymous sources! You, upon whose shoulders weigh through all eternity the horrible tragedy of a life destroyed by your criminal greed, whose ears must forever hear incessant reproaches for a crime that victimized an innocent home! You, Crispín, who stain the Senate by your presence, who darken our surroundings with the shadow of your crimes, you have turned the Republic into an abject thing that we cannot venerate. You lower the Republic and make it vile by your unworthy presence here; it can never again be great as long as you are seated here.[44]

Taken together the seven debates between Laureano Gómez and the Conservative cacique from Marinilla were a resounding triumph for the former and an abject defeat for the latter. After August 1932 the hold of Laureano Gómez on his party was secure, not to be seriously threatened for another twenty years. Román Gómez soon slipped into the political obscurity from whence he had emerged. And as for the "Y tú, Crispín!" of Laureano Gómez, it quickly supplanted José Asuncion Silva's "Nocturno" as the preeminent piece for declamation in *tertulias* around Bogotá and the nation. Luis Eduardo Nieto Caballero penned a splendid description of the Conservative politician as he appeared in the public forum: "Gómez, as orator, is a marvelous spectacle. He gives one the sensation that he is the King of Beasts. . . . He does not know pity. He is never satiated. He rends and tears, then licks his lips, enjoying the contortions of his victim. His competitor shrinks to the size of a rat as he [Gómez] speaks. Then the paw falls and he is disemboweled. All the while his voice is a trumpet, a bell, a Tequendama that spills verbal beauty from his lips. . . . He is a formidable actor who, as such, merits only applause."[45]

As usual Nieto Caballero was squarely on target in fixing upon the entertainment value of Colombian politics. Most Colombians loved the public spectacles that lightened their otherwise humdrum lives. The waving of handkerchiefs in Senate galleries was the gesture of enthusiasm normally seen at sporting events, and the chants of "Out with him!" when Román Gómez lost his composure were not unlike the "Olés!" bestowed on a matador preparing to deliver the killing thrust.

Lenc wondered whether the Senate duel had been in some way damaging to Colombia's body politic. While that well may have been the case, it was useless to pose the question. There was no alternative to such displays of political showmanship. Colombia remained a highly politicized place in 1932, and citizens knew that the relative success or lack thereof among their party leaders impinged upon them in direct and often immediate ways. In addition, the still great distance between the public and private realms in Colombia made celebrities of politicians and turned national politics into a subject of national interest.

In the more than two years following his discrediting of the Man from Marinilla, Laureano Gómez continued to strengthen his hold over the Conservative Party. So catholic was he in lashing out against political enemies and anyone else not perfectly in accord with his view of what the party stood for and how it should proceed, that all Colombians had to come to terms with him in one way or another. Ideological Historical Conservatives assumed a worshipful attitude, lauding his defense of principle and his unwillingness to concede a single point to the proponents of competing ideologies. The Leopardo Silvio Villegas acknowledged that Laureano Gómez "owed all his prestige within the Conservative Party to the extraordinary task fulfilled in the Senate, as leader of the opposition, between 1932 and 1935."[46] Rank-and-file party members in provincial Colombia were inspired by his charisma and his outspoken defense of their interests in the face of political violence. In the eyes of many, the eloquent polemicist was the only person who spoke for them. Their near reverence for him intensified after January 31, 1935, when Gómez was felled by a cerebral hemorrhage. From the 1930s well into the 1960s, it was common to find photos and busts of Laureano Gómez standing next to figures of Christ and the Virgin in the family shrines throughout rural Colombia.

Moderate Conservatives were less enthusiastic about Laureano Gómez and his leadership style. Since the late nineteenth century many of them gave economic development and political transaction precedence over partisanship. Often termed "Nationalist" Conservatives, after the short-lived party of that name founded by Rafael Núñez and Miguel Antonio Caro, they counted many Antioquian entrepreneurs among their number as well as cosmopolitan types such as Roberto Urdaneta Arbeláez. Urdaneta, a personal friend of Laureano Gómez, was the only Conservative of stature who dared serve in President Olaya's cabinet after mid-1932. It was Urdaneta who in the fashion of Conservative moderates rebuked Gómez for his extreme partisanship, in the process giving the volatile politician one of his more humorous nicknames. The occasion was the Senate debate of October 17, 1932, just two months after Gómez's demolition of Román Gómez and one month after Peruvian troops had seized the Amazon River town of Leticia. Gómez was haranguing Olaya Herrera for failing to properly garrison Leticia, an accusation that while undoubtedly true could have been leveled equally at every Colombian president back to and including Simón Bolívar. At one point during his defense of the government, Foreign Minister Urdaneta likened Laureano Gómez to a kind of rocket popular at backcountry fireworks displays. The object in question was the *vaca loca* (crazy cow), which, in Urdaneta's words, "runs everywhere, attacking all it encounters. It explodes against women, against children, against posts and walls. It doesn't respect anything, and nothing stops it; it has no set trajectory. Sometimes it poses a slight danger . . . though when all is said and done, it's harmless." Casting a penetrating glance at Laureano Gómez, Urdaneta concluded that in time of war Colombia could ill afford the antics of its "vaca loca."[47]

Over the months following Gómez's return from Europe, Liberal attitudes toward him changed dramatically. In July 1932 assessments were friendly, though after September they became increasingly hostile. As Gómez's attack on Olaya gained momentum the Liberal attitude became one of loathing. Columnist Enrique Santos took to calling Gómez "our Hitler," while *El Tiempo* writer Antolín Díaz preferred "El Monstruo" (the Monster). In early 1933, Nieto Caballero blasted Gómez as a traitor, and on February 11, 1933, *El Tiempo*'s editorial writer made one of the first references to Gómez as a "fascist."

For his part Laureano Gómez showed no quarter in attacking Olaya and everything the president stood for. The ferocity of those verbal assaults suggests the ingrown, intimate character of Colombian politics. Laureano Gómez had always been physically intimidated by Olaya, who was tall and fair. As a child of ten Gómez had looked on as nineteen-year-old Olaya and his Liberal schoolmates brawled with Conservative students of San Bartolomé. In 1911, when Olaya served as Carlos E. Restrepo's youthful foreign minister, Gómez fumed impotently that his foe was an uncultivated person given to delivering poorly conceived speeches "copied from Iregüi and other rank authors. . . ." Olaya was a friend of the United States, a nation that Gómez detested, and was instrumental in reestablishing good relations with the United States in 1921. Gómez debated Olaya in the Cámara several times during December 1929, at one point sarcastically referring to Olaya as "the foremost orator in the nation, [whom] from this time forward I'll make every effort to try to imitate."[48] Only this long history of personal and political competition with its mix of psychological and partisan factors can explain the depth of Gómez's aversion to Olaya, the mild-mannered Liberal moderate to whom so much had come with seemingly so little personal effort.

Gómez's verbal attacks on Olaya became more strident as the Liberal Party consolidated its hold on power through successive violence-marred elections. By the time Olaya ended his term Gómez openly blamed him for the bloodshed. Olaya's regime was one "running with blood, sunk in the blood of Colombians," he said in July 1934, calling murder "the most effective [Liberal] ploy and the burning of its adversaries' property a habitual phenomenon."[49] Enrique Olaya Herrera was of course not responsible for the violence, which he had condemned from its onset. But neither had he tried hard to stop it through use of the army or police. Indeed Olaya's position relative to the bloodshed was clearly an impossible one. He had intentionally not intervened in the provinces so as not to jeopardize his tenuous Concentración Nacional. He lamented the violence, but denied responsibility for it, attributing it rather to "historical processes."[50]

As the Liberals won majorities in local, departmental, and national governing bodies, some Conservative Party leaders began to talk of electoral abstention. They argued that their followers should be kept away from the polls until guaranteed protection from election-day violence. Calls for abstention became more intense after the Liberals won majorities in the Chamber of Representatives on May 14, 1933. Still some members of the Conservative directorate objected to abstention on the grounds that soon Alfonso López would be president and that Gómez and López had talked extensively of reforming the electoral process so as to eliminate fraud and violence.

Anti-abstention Conservatives were led by Guillermo Valencia and Augusto Ramírez Moreno. Valencia, senior member of the Historical faction, viewed Alfonso López as a moderate Liberal whose anticipated constitutional reform would not threaten Conservative interests provided that Conservatives could oppose it in Congress. Valencia himself professed to be in favor of moderate reform, especially in the area of landownership. His fear was that Conservative abstention would play into the hands of "leftists" who might force López to endorse truly radical measures.[51]

Laureano Gómez led the group favoring abstention because since his return from Europe he had worked against Liberal-Conservative collaboration and for the revival of traditional partisanship. Even before his resignation from Olaya's government in early 1932, Colombia had been rife with rumor that Gómez and López would cooperate to their mutual benefit once the latter became president. Such reasoning was especially popular among those who believed Gómez to be unscrupulous and narrowly self-interested. Thus, if for no other reason than to put these suspicions to rest, Laureano Gómez had no recourse but to pursue a policy of noncooperation with the López government. Anything less would make it impossible for him to maintain party discipline.

Gómez forced his abstention policy on the party in dramatic fashion. On June 9, 1933, he announced his retirement from active politics. For the next several weeks he ostentatiously puttered around the yard of his newly constructed home, Torcoroma, in Fontibón, and spoke of returning to his old profession of engineer. The ploy worked exactly as Gómez knew it would. Conservatives of all descriptions rushed to support him. A party plebiscite was held which revealed an overwhelming desire among party members that Gómez return as their supreme leader. Delegates of young Conservatives trekked to Fontibón during July begging him to rejoin the directorate. Gómez refused, saying in a "Manifesto to His Political Friends" that he could not collaborate with Guillermo Valencia, a man who had helped draft the Rio Protocol, which sanctioned Peru's "act of piracy" against Colombia, and who, furthermore, had never spoken up on behalf of "the thousands of Conservative victims of Liberal violence."[52] Guillermo Valencia understood the message Gómez was sending him. On July 29, 1933, he announced his retirement from politics. Not long afterward he resigned his Senate seat and returned to his family estate outside Popayán.

The Liberal press responded to those events by cartooning Gómez as a Colombian Hitler, complete with swastika armband, imposing dictatorial hold on his party. The questionable appropriateness of the Hitler imagery aside, Laureano Gómez was still not in fact in complete control of his party. Nor was he certain how the emerging policy of noncooperation should proceed. Municipal elections of October 1, 1933, helped bring the issue into sharper focus. Most Colombian Conservatives did not vote in the elections, which allowed the Liberals to win control of a majority of the nation's municipal concejos. That solidified their hold on all levels of Colombian government.

The new electoral defeat helped convince most members of the party directorate that it would do no good to vote in the upcoming presidential election. Only Augusto Ramírez Moreno remained opposed to political abstention. Over the following months Conservatives would pursue the dual policy of refusing to participate in the upcoming election while doing nothing to oppose the candidacy of Alfonso López.

During the consolidation of its abstention policy the Conservative Party directorate sent mixed signals to the nation. On October 15 it held out the possibility of eventual collaboration with López's government "should that become necessary." Four days later Laureano Gómez stated that López would be an "illegitimate" president if elected without Conservative participation. Four days after that Gómez suggested that Conservatives would employ a Gandhian sort of passive resistance to the new regime which would include a refusal to pay taxes, thereby making it impossible for López to govern.[53] At last, on November 14, 1933, the National Conservative Directorate (Directorio Nacional Conservador, DNC) formalized its abstention program, informing that members would neither vote in future elections nor accept posts in the López government.[54]

There was ample reason to question whether Gómez and other Conservative leaders would stand firm in their resolve not to cooperate with the incoming government. Two weeks before his inauguration, López publicly reaffirmed his "profound and deep friendship" for Gómez, and four days before entering office he renewed an earlier offer of cabinet posts to ranking Conservatives.[55] Inauguration day was a love feast in which Gómez, serving as the Senate's presiding officer, administered the oath of office to a man whose friendship had been "a special honor in [his] life."

Yet those who studied the speeches of Gómez and López noted that each man balanced affirmations of personal friendship with frank acknowledgment of their ideological differences. "Sir, you adhere to doctrines that the Conservative mind cannot share with you; you endorse philosophic and political systems that neither excite nor seduce us," said Gómez. López responded that while he eschewed "revolutionary adventurism," he intended to preside over a mass movement that would "jolt the Republic's ideological structure."[56] In this fashion the two friends proclaimed their intention to do political battle on their own terms.

Laureano Gómez had been preparing Conservatives for ideological battle from the moment he returned from Europe two years earlier. One of his first major doctrinal speeches was the one he delivered at a party convention held at Chía, Cundinamarca, in September 1932. In that talk he stressed the Roman Catholic underpinnings of Colombian Conservatism, describing Catholicism as "an ideological and sentimental treasure that constitutes mankind's purest religious belief."[57] All of Gómez's doctrinal statements contained the message that true Conservatives were confessing Roman Catholics guided by natural and divine law. This was the truth Spanish Jesuits had delivered to him at Colegio San Bartolomé thirty-five years earlier. All other ideologies not in conformity with Conservative doctrine were wrong and therefore dangerous to one degree or another. Meanwhile persons for whom ideology was not important—Enrique Olaya Herrera, for example—merited not the respect owed a worthy adversary, but, rather, contempt. This attitude helps explain both the dismissive tone of Gómez's anti-Olaya remarks, and the difficulty Olaya had in understanding the scorn Gómez heaped on him. Gómez explained Olaya's supposed indifference to natural law as functions both of his liberal relativism and to his long residence in Anglo-America: "Olaya . . . isn't a man of deep convictions, or of deep and coherent philosophic thought. . . . His long residence in the United States has been his misfortune, and that of the Nation. Should he have lived elsewhere, he would have been convinced that there are upon the face of the earth values distinct to those peculiar to North America, values that one can love and respect."[58]

Liberals were frequently caught off guard by the philosophical Gómez, as in late 1934, when the Conservative leader rose to engage Minister of Education Luis López de Mesa in erudite debate on the issue of educational reform. The elevated tone of the exchange was all the more surprising since just two weeks earlier Gómez had been at the center of a stormy Senate debate that threatened to deteriorate into physical violence, and which ended with Gómez and his colleagues chanting, "No more outrages!" as they left the chamber en mass.[59]

But when he debated López de Mesa, Gómez adopted a reasoned, scholarly tone in his defense of classical education. Gómez contrasted classical education with what he termed modern "scientistic" education. The latter might cause a man to become educated, he stated, but it could never make him cultivated. Gómez went on to hold up Germany as a nation suffused with the modern, relativistic "Kantian spirit" which made possible Hitlerian slaughters "that would be exotic in a Latin nation whose juridic structure was founded on Roman law." Luis Eduardo Nieto Caballero was charmed by the erudite exchange, praising Laureano Gómez for his subtle, gallant, and ironic remarks that enhanced, rather than diminished, his prestige.[60]

Lenc's praise of Gómez was premature. On December 3, 1934, Alfonso López called Congress into special session to approve the Rio Protocol, which when signed would normalize Colombian-Peruvian relations. Laureano Gómez was violently opposed to the accord, which had been signed prior to López's accession to the presidency. The debates were as tempestuous as any in which Gómez had been involved, with the Conservative leader haranguing all those who had taken part in negotiations leading to the agreements. At one point the normally pacific Luis Cano attempted to strangle Gómez, who had just called him a traitor. Gómez unmercifully berated Eduardo Santos, who had laid Colombia's case against Peru before the League of Nations in February 1933, charging Santos with rank ineptness. He was almost as hard on his fellow party member, Foreign Minister Roberto Urdaneta Arbeláez. In fact Urdaneta bore the brunt of Gómez's ire through a seemingly interminable series of debates described as possessing a "hammerlike" quality.[61]

As January 1935 wore on the strain of his more than two years' party leadership began to tell upon Laureano Gómez. By the latter part of the month Gómez began to ask for rest periods during debates. On January 17 he suffered a fainting spell while at a dinner honoring Conservative congressmen. Nieto Caballero noticed the deterioration in both Gómez's physical condition and his speechmaking. He seemed "fat, flushed, and unkempt, and his gestures those of a madman," said Lenc, going on to describe Gómez's speeches poorly phrased and repetitious, with words like "torpid," "imbecile," "doltish," "docile," and "cretin" tiresomely repeated.[62] A near mob attack on Gómez as he left the Senate session of January 26, and the pummeling of his fifteen-year-old son Alvaro by several youths his own age added to the stress of those days.[63]

But on January 28 and 29, Laureano Gómez debated Urdaneta yet again, delivering what many felt to be his best speech of the session. His declining health notwithstanding, it appeared that thanks to Gómez, Congress would remain deadlocked. Laureano Gómez was single-handedly making good his party's vow to obstruct his friend's grandiose plans for reform.

As that likelihood became clear, a despairing Alfonso López turned to the single person who he felt could challenge and defeat Laureano Gómez on the floor of the Senate: Enrique Olaya Herrera. Olaya was made foreign minister on January 30, and scheduled to debate Gómez the afternoon of the following day.

On the morning of the thirty-first, Laureano Gómez seemed pleased at the prospect of crossing swords with a man at least whose oratorical gifts he respected. "There's no doubt that [Olaya] is a brilliant man and a notable orator," Gómez had said some months earlier, "he has a beautiful voice and his gestures are arrogant; he improvises skillfully and is adroit in his use of oratorical techniques."[64] Before leaving home that morning he had discussed the strategy he intended to employ with son Alvaro. Later that morning his old mentor José Vicente Casas met Gómez leaving the Ministry of Foreign Relations carrying documents and speaking confidently of defeating Olaya on the strength of his superior arguments. Casas noticed that Gómez did not look well and that his face was flushed.[65]

At three that afternoon Gómez arrived for the Senate session complaining that he did not feel well. By 4:30 P.M., Gómez felt decidedly unwell. He beckoned to two of his colleagues for help in leaving the Senate floor. Suddenly the chamber fell silent. Here was a spectacle no one had seen before. As Gómez struggled to stand, helped by Senators Francisco Angulo and Ricardo Tirado Macías, he slumped forward on his desk.

The Senate session was quickly adjourned and spectators were cleared from the hushed galleries. As the chamber emptied one Conservative senator was heard whispering to another, "There goes the brigantine. Man the lifeboats!"[66]

For the next two hours Laureano Gómez lay unconscious on a stretcher in the Capitol as physicians attended him and preparations were made to transport him to a nearby clinic. Meanwhile there was excitement outside. Word had spread quickly through the streets of Bogotá that Laureano Gómez had collapsed, and people ran toward the Plaza de Bolívar. Many of them had been listening to Senate debates over Conservative-owned HJN Radio, the "Voice of Colombia," when they heard the announcer say that Gómez had collapsed after drinking a glass of water. The inference was clearly that he had been poisoned.[67]

Thousands of onlookers crowded the Plaza de Bolívar at 7 P.M., when Laureano Gómez was taken away. He would recover, but not for a full year. During that time Alfonso López and his government would craft the most thoroughgoing set of political reforms Colombia had seen in fifty years. As for the Rio Protocol, it was approved by the unanimous vote of a uniformly Liberal Senate on August 20, 1935.

The Revolution of the 1930s

The first administration of Alfonso López Pumarejo (1934–1938) was by any measure the most successful in twentieth-century Colombian history. López's Revolution on the March was avowedly reformist, aimed at speeding national modernization through the vigorous action of an interventionist state. An admirer of Franklin D. Roosevelt, whom he knew personally,[68] Alfonso López presided over a regime that had much in common with the U.S. chief executive's New Deal. Both reform programs employed Keynesian economic principles; both were expedited by bright younger politicians committed to the vision of their extraordinary chiefs; both the Colombian and the American programs were crowned by rationalization of an agrarian sector fallen into crisis through excessive adherence to laissez-faire economic principles. Perhaps the greatest difference in the Colombian and the North American efforts was that Franklin Roosevelt saw major portions of the New Deal struck down almost immediately after implementation, while Alfonso López suffered no such reversal of his legislation during his term in office.

Three factors explain the success of López's reforms. First and most important was the absence of formal Conservative opposition thanks to that party's boycott of the legislative process during the entirety of López's first term. Second was the happy coincidence that López entered office just as Colombia put the Depression behind it and entered a period of economic growth destined to extend far beyond his administration. Third was López's personal charisma and the inherent dynamism of his program. Unlike the several men who preceded him in office, Alfonso López was an exciting figure who promised to make things happen quickly. "My government wants to stimulate all public and private activity benefiting the general public," he said in his inaugural message of August 7, 1934. In that same speech he addressed the social question, alluding to what he termed "the monstrous injustices" weighing upon Colombian society, many of them supported by laws favoring oligarchic interests. "Equality before the law certainly is not a juridic or moral innovation on my part," said López, adding, "I am certain that concept will produce surprising results when practiced honorably."[69] Colombians heard his words and were convinced by them.

Once in office López acted quickly to address Colombia's most pressing social problem, an agrarian movement of major proportions centered in the coffee-producing mountains south and southwest of the nation's capital. For two years the president cajoled, lectured, and berated the political establishment, at length wringing from it his celebrated agrarian reform embodied in Law 200 of 1936. The reform was encapsulated in the president's phrase "the campesino seeks stability, not revolution; he wants his own farm. . . ."[70] It thus set in motion a process through which greater equity in landownership was introduced to the coffee heartland. Consequently the uncertainty about existing landownership and titles was laid to rest and the last of the nation's coffee haciendas were broken into small and medium holdings.

As the vigorous political response to a demand for greater justice and clarity in the area of land disputes, Law 200 put to rest a serious and potentially disruptive issue. Since the late nineteenth century non-elite Colombians had complained that government and the courts stood idly by, or worse, participated, as the wealthy and well-connected trampled their rights. Such was invariably the case in disputes over landownership as well as those involving the rights of agricultural workers. At length, more than ten years before enactment of Law 200, a series of government actions and court decisions during the administrations of Pedro Nel Ospina and Miguel Abadía Méndez set into motion the agrarian revolt that reached its peak the year Alfonso López was elected president.

The agrarian movement of 1928–1936 marked a historic juncture in the life of the nation. It signaled the transition away from widespread popular acceptance of social hierarchies and notions of distributive justice, toward popular acceptance of individualistic and egalitarian values. Along with the labor movement that slightly preceded it, Colombia's agrarian revolt announced to those astute enough to perceive it that a metamorphosis in popular attitudes had been forged by the social change taking place over the preceding quarter century. Luckily for Colombia that moment of transition occurred when the nation possessed a political regime willing and able to accommodate the popular demand for change.

Colombia's revolution of the 1930s was twofold. First, and most significant, it was a genuinely popular movement. In its earliest phase the uprising was not led by political elites seeking partisan advantage; nor was it led by counterelites driven by ideological visions of radical social change. It was produced by landless campesinos who perceived that their government was at last receptive to their demand for land reform and who acted decisively on that presumption. Thus the agrarian revolt was democratic and populist in character.

Second in importance to its democratic aspect was the unique way political Colombia responded to the agrarian movement. The national government moved quickly and expeditiously, and in a manner satisfactory to the vast majority of those affected. Such response was both unprecedented and unique in the scant history of Colombian popular movements, and it would not be repeated over the remainder of the nation's stormy twentieth century.

The revolution of the 1930s was rooted in economic change following the War of the Thousand Days. Those years were marked by rapid growth driven by progress-intoxicated elites whose desire to earn money quickly became generalized throughout the nation. Rafael Reyes (1904–1909) was the first of several president-entrepreneurs who devoted their energies to modernizing the country. Like his successors Carlos E. Restrepo (1910–1914) and Pedro Nel Ospina (1922–1926), Reyes was a businessman whose fortune was produced through the exploitation of Colombia's vast and largely untapped natural resources. As a youth Reyes had joined family members in extracting quinine and rubber from the tropical forests of the Amazon watershed. Restrepo and

Ospina were Antioquian industrialists who also owed their success to the land. Their enterprises were financed by monies earned through the cultivation and export of coffee. As men whose personal success was owed chiefly to the exploitation of natural resources and agriculture, it was logical that Reyes, Restrepo, and Ospina, and Colombia's other Republican-era presidents, should concentrate their development efforts on the land.

Once Rafael Reyes became president he sponsored a number of government initiatives designed to spur agricultural production, especially in the areas of coffee, banana, and sugar cultivation. To raise capital for his projects he leased government-owned emerald mines and sold expanses of the national domain to individuals and land companies. Between the War of the Thousand Days and 1917, he and the two men who followed him in office awarded 400,000 hectares of public land to anyone who promised to bring it into production.[71]

Transfer of public lands to the private sector through the sale of *baldío* grants was hardly an innovation of Republican-era Colombia. During the nineteenth century over two million hectares of such lands were sold or granted to individuals, the lion's share of them in hopes of stimulating the formation of a self-sufficient and productive yeomanry. That was the avowed goal of the Liberal governments of the 1860s and 1870s, under whose aegis well over a million hectares of land were distributed. Lamentably only a small number of the grants passed directly into the hands of smallholders. One study, embracing the period 1827–1931, found that grants smaller than fifty hectares made up but 3.3 percent of public land sales in coffee-producing regions of Antioquia and Caldas.[72]

Sales of public land in nineteenth- and twentieth-century Colombia may not have fulfilled the democratic aspirations of philosophic liberals, but they did meet the secondary goal of stimulating economic development. Historian Marco Palacios points to a fivefold increase in the price of choice coffee land between 1865 and 1891, a process of valorization that continued after the civil wars of 1895 and 1899–1902.[73] Once peace was reestablished following the War of the Thousand Days, Colombia's coffee boom began in earnest, with production increasing annually at between 4 and 10 percent amid constantly rising prices for the lucrative export.[74]

Students have differed in their views of the process through which rural Colombia became commercialized during the late nineteenth and early twentieth centuries. Geographer Francisco Javier Vergara y Velasco, who witnessed massive privatization of public lands prior to and following the War of the Thousand Days, was appalled by the speculation it produced. He damned the trade in baldío (unpopulated, publicly owned) lands as "the cancer of the territory."[75] Historian Catherine LeGrand has called attention to the "petty speculation [that] ran rampant through *colono* society," finding in it a chief source of strife throughout all of frontier Colombia.[76]

Not all have seen Colombia's frontier experience in a negative light. While historian Charles Bergquist finds that large and small interests in the coffee zone battled it out within the context of their available options, he finds too that it was the small interests that ultimately emerged victorious. By the middle of the twentieth century, writes Bergquist, "property ownership in the coffee economy was widespread . . . and increasing numbers of viable family farms existed." Money earned through coffee cultivation "helped confirm in the minds of individuals of all classes the viability of an economic system based on the tenets of capitalism."[77]

Writing in a similar vein, anthropologist Nola Reinhardt reveals that in Colombia's dynamic rural economy of the early twentieth century not only did small farms compete successfully with large commercial operations, but that through careful budgeting of cash salaries even landless day laborers were eventually able to acquire land. Her study, focusing on the mountainous Dagua region of western Valle, traces the career of one Juan Alvarez (1889–1957), who migrated to the area with his family in 1897. With monies he earned as a *jornalero,* or agricultural day laborer, he first rented land on which he produced a variety of crops for local markets. Eventually, through careful use of his earnings from agricultural sales, he was able to buy several small farms totaling sixty hectares. Thus he entered the ranks of Colombia's middle yeomanry.[78] The story of Juan Alvarez paralleled, though on an infinitely lesser scale, that of Jesús Sarmiento, a somewhat older contemporary who began his career as a peddler of plantains in the Valle del Cauca. Sarmiento was so shrewd a merchant that he went on to become one of the wealthiest men in western Colombia. At the time of his death the phrase "he has nearly as much money as don Jesús Sarmiento" was commonly used in the Valle del Cauca.[79]

Thanks to its coffee-driven prosperity, and to widespread landownership in coffee country, Colombia's rural population in zones of commercial agriculture quickly acquired a capitalist mentality. In that sense the Andean nation occupied a unique place in early-twentieth-century Latin America, a region most of whose rural-dwelling peoples were landless peasants. But Colombians Jesús Sarmiento and Juan Alvarez were neither men of a peasant mentality nor did they live as peasants. They were commercial farmers who while frequently illiterate did not need to be taught the lesson contained in a popular school text of the day: "Profit is just and legitimate for him who owns capital."[80] Hundreds of thousands of campesinos like Sarmiento and Alvarez already knew much of commerce and moneymaking, having transcended the peasant status of their fathers and grandfathers. Thanks to the rapid commercialization of rural central Colombia they had come to exercise absolute ownership of land they exploited commercially. They possessed geographic and social mobility in proportion to the degree of their commercial success, and they presided over nuclear families. They also enjoyed the prospect of almost limitless long-term economic differentiation. None of those were conditions prevailing in true Latin American peasant culture. There extended households, corporative ownership of land, little market rationality, and little social or geographic mobility were the norm.

By the early twentieth century most Colombians of the coffee frontier had ceased being peasants and were men and women of modern mentality, which explains their quick and sometimes violent response to abuses of the sort true peasants traditionally endured stolidly. As the twentieth century progressed, ambitious settlers throughout Colombia registered increasingly strident complaints against the aggressions they suffered from those more powerful than they. A fairly typical example is contained in a petition to Colombia's minister of public works in 1910, demanding that he intercede in a dispute between a colono and one Jorge Walker: "I am a settler living on a piece of land that Sr. Walker wants to grab. I have a little house there which shelters my wife and children, and it would be an injustice to throw us out just to give fourteen more *plazas* [approximately .3 hectares] of land to someone who already owns hundreds." A similar complaint was submitted some years later by campesinos in western Valle: "We do not think it reasonable that simply because our property shares a common boundary with land claimed by the heirs of el señor [Pepe] Sierra, they have the right to call themselves owners of public lands that have never belonged to them."[81] Yet another petition warned that "if the law will not respect our property rights . . . we know which roads we must follow: either the path of crime or that of migration."[82] All were the expressions of ambitious settlers determined not to be denied access to the land from which all national prosperity flowed.

The growing demand for equity on the part of Colombia's emerging yeomanry eventually found echo among that nation's least fortunate campesinos, service tenants (*aparceros*) employed on the coffee estates of southwestern Cundinamarca and eastern Tolima. These agricultural workers lived on holdings acquired by their owners during the boom in baldío grants between 1870 and the War of the Thousand Days. Forbidden to grow coffee on the small plots they rented or were permitted to occupy, or if permitted to cultivate coffee on their plots, forced to sell it to the hacienda at below market prices, they watched as the coffee trees they tended made absentee landowners rich. Service tenants on the coffee estates stood even lower in the rural hierarchy than the peripatetic jornaleros, who exchanged their labor for cash. Jornaleros in coffee-rich Viotá "looked down on the tenants with disdain and sadness," writes a student of that region.[83]

Owners of the coffee estates evolved their labor system during the late nineteenth century, before Colombia began its pell-mell rush toward modernity, propelled by the coffee bonanza. In those early days, when the haciendas of Viotá and Sumapaz were established, few landowners could pay their workers in cash. Consequently most of them took the easy though ill-advised route of securing their workforce through sharecropping, rentals, and other forms of tenancy. By the 1920s, thirty years after they had opted for what was an inherently premodern labor system geared to men of peasant mentality, hacienda owners continued to maintain and defend it, though with increasing difficulty. Continued democratization of landholding in the coffee zone drained the pool of available labor and commercialization of the campo introduced a complex of attitudes that eroded traditional attitudes throughout in the coffee zone. Meanwhile Colombia's burgeoning yeomanry closed in on the coffee haciendas. As the 1930s approached, the large holdings of Viotá and Sumapaz loomed as institutional dinosaurs, ringed by thousands of small farms run by owner-operators. They had become, in the colorful metaphor of one student, "islands in a sea of small and medium holdings of independent peasants."[84]

Service tenants on the estates of Viotá and Sumapaz partook of the coffee-driven prosperity as best they could during the first three decades of the century, producing a variety of foodstuffs on their plots, starting small, usually clandestine businesses, and doing whatever else occurred to them to tap into wealth generated by coffee. Still hacienda owners remained steadfast in denying them direct participation in the coffee boom. This was all the more galling as tenants knew that landowners had illegally established claim to vast stretches of baldío lands far beyond their ability to cultivate. In one of the most flagrant cases, that of 300,000-hectare Hacienda Sumapaz, the putative owners held clear title to just 9,300 hectares.[85] Only a fraction of Hacienda Sumapaz and others like it were given over to coffee production, the vast extent of it lying fallow, unoccupied, and off-limits to settlement.

Adding to the discontent on Colombia's coffee estates was the fact that owners continued to treat their employees with a degree of disrespect suggested by their widespread refusal to grant written service contracts, failure to provide for education of the children of tenants, and unconcern that workers on coffee-covered mountainsides had no protection from the elements. The service tenants of Viotá and Sumapaz were, in short, aware that the estate owners treated and regarded them as peasants.

At length the service tenants of Viotá and Sumapaz received the encouragement they needed to challenge the oppressive conditions under which they labored. That encouragement came from none other than their own national government, which during the 1920s began enacting a series of laws aimed at placating the bellicose young labor movement. Even as they jailed labor leaders and used the army to break strikes, Presidents Súarez, Ospina, and Abadía sponsored laws providing for an eight-hour workday, and improving working conditions and health care for workers. In 1924 a National Labor Bureau (Oficina de Trabajo) was authorized, and within two years it had formulated a National Labor Code.

Most who witnessed the spate of labor legislation clearly perceived that it was defensive in character, designed to counter what a foreign reporter described as "the growing socialist sentiment in Colombia."[86] But few perceived that the laws would provide legal justification for Colombia's agrarian revolt.

Colombians were a conservative, legalistic people, and the service tenants and colonos of Viotá and Sumapaz were no exception. For decades they had waited and watched for some sign that the government might help them rather than forever siding with the influential men for whom they worked. Suddenly, thanks to the labor legislation described above, their patience was rewarded. No sooner than President Ospina's accident and health legislation became law in 1925, service tenants in Viotá and Sumapaz began asking that hacienda owners abide by the new work rules. Most landowners were aghast when unschooled *peones* began making demands of them, and they wasted little time in rejecting the requests out of hand. Only in the municipios of Quipile and Cachipay, embracing a region north of Viotá and west of Bogotá, did hacienda owners comply with the new labor legislation. In 1925 they signed with their tenants the Pact of Quipile, under whose terms employers agreed to shorten both the workday and work week and to improve the workers' food allotment.[87]

At the same time the Pact of Quipile was being negotiated, service tenants on Hacienda El Chocho, in the municipio of Fusagasugá, in northern Sumapaz, were demanding similar concessions from their employers. Unfortunately the brothers Carlos and Manuel Caballero, co-owners of El Chocho, ignored them. The matter stood at an impasse for more than a year. Finally the renters traveled to Bogotá, where they laid their grievances before Minister of Industry José A. Montalvo.

The eleven-point Manifesto of Renters of El Chocho clearly reveals the El Chocho tenants as thoroughly modern in their approach to things economic, and aware of their rights as Colombian citizens. Seven of the articles relate specifically to money, reflecting the renters' understanding of money's power to liberate them from the humiliating and antiquated labor system to which they were subjected. "We demand," they wrote, "the liberty of commerce consecrated in our national constitution. . . . That rent on land . . . be collected solely in cash. . . . That readjustment of rents be conducted only at three-year intervals. . . . That the hacienda pay a just price for improvements [in the event of eviction]. . . . That the hacienda suspend the system of fines. . . . That the hacienda pay the going rate for a workday. . . . That should the Messrs. Caballero not accept these articles, a plan be drawn up by which the renters can purchase their parcels by way of ordinary bank loans." Other articles asked that hacienda owners provide workers written contracts, shelter from inclement weather, the privilege of taking housing materials, notably lumber, from hacienda lands, and that the eight-hour workday, mandated in national law, be respected.[88]

Carlos and Manuel Caballero reacted predictably to their renters' declaration of independence: they tried to expel them from their property—from land that many of the renters had occupied for decades. But the Caballeros' effort was ultimately futile. The time of large, poorly exploited holdings in central Colombia was ending as both landless campesinos and the state rose up against them. Soon even the Caballero brothers recognized that fact. After resisting the demands of their renters for some eight years, until 1933, they sold El Chocho to the government of Cundinamarca, which subdivided and sold it off at modest prices.[89]

The coincidence of popular demand for change in Colombia's land tenure system and willingness of government to respond was owed to the widespread perception that national progress was being hindered by an antiquated agricultural regime, typified by Hacienda El Chocho. Even before labor legislation set the agrarian revolt in motion, thoughtful members of the political elite criticized a political economy that tolerated the ownership of large, poorly exploited tracts of land. Liberal theoretician Alejandro López was one such enemy of what he termed the "feudal" attitudes of his nation's large landowners. By 1931, López was calling for agrarian reform founded in the concept that property ownership entails certain social obligations, a radically new concept in Colombian jurisprudence, though one having antecedents in both liberal and conservative social thought. Through his writings Alejandro López helped popularize the principles later elaborated in Law 200 of 1936. "The Liberal Party is an agrarian party," he wrote in 1931, going on to propose that fellow Liberals endorse radical land redistribution: "We propose to subdivide the land in Colombia through legal, rational, and scientific means, at the expense of the large landholdings. This will be done through fiscal pressure, and in such manner that no land in Colombia fails to fulfill its social function of feeding and maintaining the population. Every family . . . desirous of possessing good land for development through individual effort shall enjoy the protection of the state. Such families shall thus be insured independent and lucrative development."[90] López was so successful a propagandist, and his ideas so attractive to Colombia's rural majority, that by 1931 campesinos justified their invasions of hacienda and baldío lands in terms of the social function of property.

Alejandro López's plan for agrarian reform was rooted in the traditional liberal belief that widespread property ownership in the countryside enhanced stability in democratic societies. "In all civilized nations," he wrote in 1926, "it is the yeoman farmer" who anchors the middle class, which is "the backbone of society, the sinew of stability."[91] By the 1920s, many Conservatives accepted that idea as well. In 1929, Minister of Mines José A. Montalvo called it "imperative" that landownership be widespread, as small, intensively cultivated farms increased land values and thus contributed to the "collective enrichment of society."[92] In 1931 delegates to the Conservative Party convention pledged themselves to "the stimulus of small landownership and to the family farm," through the provision of government-insured loans to aspiring landowners.[93]

In spite of the considerable support for land reform at high levels of government and in the population at large, representatives of landed interests did attempt to preserve the old system. In 1933 right-wing Liberals combined with Conservatives to defeat President Olaya Herrera's proposed agrarian reform. Two years later, in March 1936, large landowners formed their antireform lobbying group, the Asociación Patronal Económica Nacional (APEN). But even had APEN been more than the ineffectual organization it was, spiraling rural unrest and the fears it produced among elites would have negated it by driving its erstwhile supporters into the reform camp. Between 1930 and passage of Law 200, rural unrest increased geometrically. By 1933 the ferment had reached such a state in Sumapaz that *El Tiempo* reported "guerrilla warfare" throughout the region.[94] Well-to-do Colombians feared that their country was on the verge of social revolution.

Prior to the agrarian revolt of the 1930s, service tenants on the large coffee estates had routinely combined to challenge the political system by evading taxes, refusing to answer legal summonses, and smuggling. But once the agrarian revolt began, their opposition became more forthright, as in the case of Hacienda Tolima, in the municipio of Ibagué. In mid-1934 the owners of Hacienda Tolima began legal action to evict one Santos Vergel and his family from a rented parcel that they had occupied for some years. Vergel's fellow tenants joined forces to help him resist the eviction. There ensued an armed confrontation between renters and local police during which two police and thirteen renters died.

The Hacienda Tolima killings, and similar episodes taking place during the early 1930s, heightened public sentiment for the renters and strengthened the hand of pro-reform politicians. On August 15, 1934, the day after the tragedy, both Liberal *El Espectador* and Conservative *El País* defended the tenants' actions and castigated the police of Tolima. That same day fiery young Liberal reformer Jorge Eliécer Gaitán rose in Congress to blast "the moth-eaten laws written to sustain a feudal situation . . . enforced by oppressive and criminal authorities."[95] Within a month of the tragic confrontation newly inaugurated

President Alfonso López Pumarejo pointed to inflamed public opinion in refusing to enforce what he termed "antidemocratic laws favoring landowners."[96]

Gaitán and other left-wing social critics played an important dual role in ensuring success of the agrarian movement. Articulate, charismatic, and usually trained in the law, they offered sorely needed leadership to squatters and service tenants. As members of an avowedly socialist counterelite advocating outright confiscation of large estates, they served the useful additional purpose of driving fearful landowners to support the government's much more moderate reform. Alfonso López pledged that the state would reimburse owners for all private property that his government confiscated and would require that campesinos pay for all such lands received.

At the height of the agrarian movement, 1933–1935, Jorge Eliécer Gaitán and another left-wing lawyer, Erasmo Valencia, organized political parties dedicated to more radical programs of land reform than the one advocated by Alfonso López. But neither Gaitán's Revolutionary Leftist National Union (Unión Nacional Izquierdista Revolucionaria, UNIR) nor Valencia's National Agrarian Party (Partido Agrarista Nacional, PAN) was long lived. UNIR, founded in 1933, was dissolved by its founder in 1935, following a crushing defeat in congressional elections. PAN was even more ephemeral. Organized in 1935, PAN was abandoned by its founder little more than a year later. Still both collectivities, drawing their support principally from squatters and smallholders in Sumapaz, contributed to the multifaceted agrarian reform movement. One noteworthy organizational success of UNIR and PAN involved Hacienda El Chocho. In August 1933, Gaitán and Erasmo Valencia encouraged 3,000 party members to invade the hacienda. Two months later the government of Cundinamarca purchased El Chocho and began subdividing it. UNIR members were also active in organizing the tenants of Hacienda Tolima.

The Colombian Communist Party (Partido Comunista de Colombia, PCC) also played a useful role in the reform effort. Founded in 1930, following the dissolution in late 1928 of its parent body, the Revolutionary Socialist Party, it operated principally in Viotá, where it helped organize peasant leagues, sponsored land invasions, and helped league members defy hacienda owners by planting coffee on their rented plots.

Alfonso López could not have asked for a more propitious setting for his reform initiative of 1935–36. The mushrooming rural unrest gave special weight to the call for land reform standing at the center of his address to Congress of July 20, 1935. A week after the address López borrowed a page from Alejandro López's *Idearium liberal* in asking his party to adopt the following declaration: "The Liberal Party is an agrarian party. It proposes to subdivide the land in Colombia . . . at the expense of large landholdings. It will exercise fiscal pressure to achieve the goal that no lands fail to fulfill their social function. . . . The Liberal Party considers small landholding to be a necessary and indispensable element of economic freedom." López's mostly urban fellow party members rejected the request that they redefine theirs as an agrarian party. They also refused to endorse López's call that their party go on record as favoring tenants and squatters at the expense of large landowners. Supporting the president's populist call, they knew, would further alienate Liberal members of both the antireform lobby, APEN, and the equally conservative Colombian Society of Agriculturalists (Sociedad de Agricultores Colombianos, SAC). Still, a majority of the Liberal conventioneers favored reform, agreeing with their president that latifundia be broken up and made available to the landless. Through the remainder of 1935 and all 1936, pro-reform Liberals, led by Darío Echandía, Carlos Lleras Restrepo, and Francisco José Chaux, combined to push Law 200 through Congress.

As the law moved toward final approval new events combined to further ease its passage. Over the course of 1935, left-wing opposition to López's land reform program ceased abruptly. In March, Jorge Eliécer Gaitán abandoned UNIR following the party's resounding defeat in national elections. He subsequently reintegrated himself into the Liberal Party and shifted the focus of his reform efforts to urban Colombia. Symbolic of Gaitán's change in orientation was his acceptance of the mayoralty of Bogotá fourteen months later. Communist opposition to López and his reform program ceased in November 1935, when party members in Colombia were told by their leaders to join with "progressive bourgeois" elements in the global struggle against fascism. Communist Party members obeyed, becoming supporters of Alfonso López and opponents of all political factions to the right of him.[97]

Erasmo Valencia's Partido Agrarista Nacional suffered a fate similar to that of UNIR, except it was Valencia's party that deserted him rather than vice versa. A year after PAN members sent their leader to the assembly of Cundinamarca, Valencia angered them by opposing departmental parcelization programs. As PAN disintegrated, its members emulated Gaitán by returning to their old parties. Former members wrote to Valencia expressing their disillusionment: "We are naturally confused, as we don't know whether you are a Liberal, a Conservative, a socialist, or a Unirista. And we certainly don't know whether you're affiliated with what they call today the leftists or the rightists."[98]

Law 200 achieved final passage December 14, 1936. Most importantly, it clarified titles throughout the area of land invasions. Landowners who had experienced land invasions prior to 1935, and who failed to prove legal ownership, were made to return such holdings to the nation, which in turn declared the lands baldíos eligible for colonization. Campesinos who had invaded such lands thus gained the status of colonos eligible to hold title to the land they occupied free of charge. All others, including landowners within the coffee zone and elsewhere in the country, could establish legal ownership by producing written evidence of legal ownership extending back at least thirty years before the passage of Law 200. In that regard Law 200 overturned the Supreme Court decision of 1926 that had required all landowners to produce the original title of ownership to a given piece of land.

Law 200 also established special courts for adjudication of disputes over landownership. In legal cases where landowners prevailed over tenants, and then proceeded to evict, owners were required to reimburse their former employees for any improvements made during the time tenants had occupied the land. Should owners be unable to pay squatters for such improvements, tenants had the right to purchase their parcels. Helping them do so was the Caja de Crédito Agrario, Industrial, y Minero (Caja Agraria), established in 1931. At the time of passage of Law 200, more than 133,000 Caja Agraria loans had already been made. Over the following seven years, 1936–1943, an additional 453,618 loans would be approved.[99] Whereas the Caja Agraria loans averaged but 450 to 650 pesos each, such sum was sufficient to purchase a finca of from five to six hectares at the prevailing rate of 70 pesos per hectare in areas of government parcelizations. Thus a Caja Agraria loan bought a farm larger on average than the typical coffee finca in Cundinamarca, Tolima, or Caldas. In summary, a government parcelization program complemented Law 200 and sped the process of land redistribution in central Colombia. By 1940 the government and the Banco Agrícola had purchased 470 large holdings that were subdivided into 20,140 family-sized farms.[100]

The multifaceted government response to agrarian revolt diffused what many viewed as the most serious social problem the nation had faced over the course of its history. Once the archaic coffee haciendas were parcelized and land titles were clarified the agrarian movement collapsed, although neither Law 200 nor the accompanying loan and parcelization programs brought tranquility to rural Colombia. They simply changed the character of rural strife. If anything, agrarian reform heightened strife in rural areas by further individualizing the struggle for land there. Later events would reveal rural Colombia as a place where the competition for land frequently reached Hobbesian dimensions.

A few critics on the left and on the right spoke out against Colombia's agrarian reform, either decrying its bias in favor of private property, its requirement that campesinos pay for lands acquired through parcelization, and its failure to expropriate large holdings legally held, or blasting it as a "communistic" assault on the sacred right to private property. But the words of such critics were lost in the din created by campesinos scrambling to establish their own homesteads. Erasmo Valencia presents perhaps the saddest case of an agrarian leader left behind by the movement to which he had devoted so much effort. Valencia was one of the first among educated, urban-dwelling Colombians to assist the landless campesinos of Viotá and Sumapaz. He began his organizational efforts in 1928, the same year Abadía Méndez inadvertently touched off massive land invasions in western Sumapaz with his Decree 1110, encouraging the colonization of certain baldío lands. Like many of his fellows, Valencia articulated the Marxist philosophy that had been adopted by so many young social critics of his generation. Passionately committed to the cause of the downtrodden renters, service tenants, and colonos, he promoted a strategy of linking the struggle of urban workers with what he perceived to be that of their rural counterparts.

Like many of his fellow activists, Valencia did not fully appreciate the consuming goal of the campesinos he led. They wanted to own a piece of farmland and to set it to producing a cash crop that in turn would allow them to raise the living standard of their families. Erasmo Valencia was an idealist who had dedicated his life to the cause of proletariat revolution. Hence he had opposed the subdivision and privatization and the sale of coffee estates as contradictory to collectivist principles and destructive of the movement which he led. Meanwhile his followers were horrified that Valencia seemed intent on throwing away the very thing they had fought for. In 1937 a group of PAN members from Hacienda El Chocho wrote Valencia: "You helped us file petitions for the Messrs. Caballero and the government ministers, telling them that we did not want to be renters any longer, asking that they either sell us the land or pay us for our improvements to it. . . . Thanks to those petitions the land was placed at our disposal so we could buy it. Then you, as counselor of the rural masses, became an enemy of land purchases, permitting outsiders to come in and buy it . . . often leaving those of us who had fought most for it without anything, and without any honorable way to oppose the newcomers because they too were campesinos."[101]

The service tenants of Hacienda El Chocho, the squatters of Sumapaz, and the thousands of other land-hungry campesinos who benefited from the agrarian reform completed a process of democratization in landholding that had been under way in central Colombia from the beginning of the coffee boom. "The process of parcelization," writes historian José Antonio Ocampo, "did nothing more than fix a tendency that was at base much more profound." Well before the passage of Law 200, more than half of all coffee in Colombia was produced on holdings of under ten hectares. Twenty years after the famous law nearly two-thirds of all coffee exports were produced on medium and small holdings of ten or fewer hectares.[102]

Agrarian reform was fated to take place in Colombia, and the members of all social classes knew it. Even large landowners ultimately accepted Law 200 in much the way one takes bitter medicine to cure a potentially life-threatening illness. "These new land laws of López and the Liberals have just cost me six hundred of my best hectares," complained one of them in 1937, over drinks in Bogotá's Jockey Club: "I've always had the idea that I could shift those Indians if I wanted to. But now I find that I can't. They tell me that they own the land. That's the new rule, they say. Some of them won't even let me go near it. What can I do? Call in the troops to dispossess them? Not likely. This present López government wouldn't back me up. . . . Well, there's lots of land in Colombia. When I ride over my land now, I give those Indians a wide berth."[103]

Colombia's agrarian reform was not revolutionary, based as it was on a process that was largely evolutionary and legislative. A groundswell of popular discontent caused political Colombia first to tremble and then to respond. Colombian history offers no finer example of political accommodation than that provided in Law 200 of 1936. The process producing the law was at once conflict ridden and democratic. Colombia's agrarian revolt would stand as one of the first in a continuing series of popular demands for social reform filling the remainder of Colombia's twentieth century. However, unluckily for the nation and her people, events would not soon conspire to smooth the course of change as they had during the first administration of Alfonso López Pumarejo.

Anatomy of a Trick

In spite of the social transformations that were beginning to take place there, Colombia remained an undeveloped and socially undifferentiated rural nation in the early 1930s. More than a century after independence it continued to confront the paradox of weak national control of outlying regions and political centralization that drew most tax revenues to Bogotá. Consequently regional Colombia had little ability to deal with immediate needs, being rendered economically dependent on a neglectful, sometimes abusive national government. During his four years in office Alfonso López intensified the already strong centralization imposed on Colombia fifty years earlier through the Constitution of 1886. Both efforts drew strength from 300 years of colonial rule geared explicitly to removing political power and tax revenues from the provinces. Meanwhile there was still little social pluralism in Colombia. Industrialization was only beginning, the labor movement was in a formative stage, and there were few important nongovernmental organizations of a socioeconomic character that were removed from gross political manipulation. The two most important among them were the national coffee growers federation, Fedcafé, and the Bank of the Republic, with its bipartisan governing board.

Only the Liberal and Conservative Parties rivaled the national government in their power to influence and to shape the lives of citizens. In some respects the parties surpassed the government in their integrative power. Colombians revered their traditional parties, whereas they tolerated the national government only to the extent that it reflected correct partisan orientation. The exceeding importance of party allegiance lent a somewhat tribal character to political Colombia, a fact explaining why great public attention was lavished on leaders of the Liberal and Conservative Parties. This is why all Colombians were fearful when Conservative leader Laureano Gómez collapsed in the Senate amid rumors that he had been poisoned by the Liberals, why they were reassured when Gómez recovered quickly from what proved to be a mild stroke, and why they reacted with foreboding to Gómez's first public utterance following his recovery: "Alfonso López has tricked me." Their fear was well placed. Gómez's words marked the beginning of an estrangement between himself and Alfonso López that quickly became open enmity. "Alfonso tricked me" was the opening salvo in a contest of wills that soon involved the entire nation. Before the year was out López and Gómez were locked in a contest having dire long-range consequences for Colombia.

Laureano Gómez tried repeatedly to explain how Alfonso López had tricked him in the months and years after May 1935. First he said that the trick—el engaño, as it was called—involved López's failure to control fraud in the issuing of new national identification cards, or *cédulas,* required for voting in future elections, and in his reneging on a promise to effect electoral reform.[104] In September 1935, Gómez referred to López's sponsorship of the Rio Protocol, which the former termed an engaño on the entire nation.[105] Later in 1935, Gómez referred to acts of Liberal violence against Conservatives, especially in Boyacá, as clear indication that a deceitful López spoke of peace while allowing party hacks to persecute his followers with impunity.[106] By March 1936, Gómez was castigating López for having used their friendship as a ploy for gaining the presidency, and in October 1936 he accused López and his supporters of having ceased being true democrats by reason of their corruption by Bolshevism.[107] All the while López stoutly protested that he had never tricked Gómez. El engaño became no clearer over time. Twenty years after the caudillo's death in 1965, Gómez's friend and admirer Arturo Abella told an interviewer, "Laureano never explained to me how he had been tricked."[108]

The difficulty in understanding just what Alfonso López had done to Laureano Gómez, coupled with López's denial of the charge, suggests that el engaño was complicated and multifaceted. At the most obvious level it was a euphemism for the sense of betrayal Gómez felt when his old friend turned to one of their mutual enemies, Enrique Olaya Herrera, to achieve passage of the Rio Protocol over Gómez's heated objections. This action was in turn based in the president's pragmatic desire to get on with his reforms—particularly reform of the national constitution, announced in López's message to Congress of July 20, 1935, when Gómez was recuperating from his stroke. Alfonso López had, in short, put personal considerations aside in order to begin the reforms for which his party clamored.

El engaño was also a function of a certain naiveté to which Laureano Gómez freely admitted. "What I've always been is a simpleton," he said late in his political career, adding that "in more than one political campaign they've taken advantage of my naiveté."[109] On other occasions Gómez protested that he was "not a politician," or was "a bad politician," because he disliked the intrigues common to politics.[110] Alfonso López acknowledged as much when, in 1938, in an obvious reference to Gómez and el engaño, the president praised politicians "for whom politics hold neither surprises nor tricks."[111] Augusto Ramírez Moreno was less oblique in his assessment of Gómez's purported deception at the hands of López: "Laureano Gómez taught us to believe in Alfonso López," wrote Ramírez in 1937, adding, "it is true that López tricked Gómez, and no less exact that Gómez tricked [his own] party."[112] Gómez's naiveté, founded in a tendency to seek the Platonic ideal in all things, was common to Jesuit-taught Conservatives of his generation, especially those of an ideological turn of mind. While perhaps laudable on moral and ethical grounds, the habit of thinking in terms of ideological constructs made for bad practical politics.

Gómez's break with López was also a function of the Colombian tradition dictating that national party leaders could never be bosom companions. As such el engaño was a convenient and necessary construct allowing Gómez to get about the business of opposition leadership that history and tradition demanded he play. Nearly a year earlier López had tried to avoid strife by offering the Conservatives three important ministries in his new government. But the offer was declined under terms of the Conservative abstention policy. Once the Rio Protocol was passed, and López proceeded to implement his reforms, Gómez knew he must go on the attack or run the risk of losing control of his own party.

The growing stridency of Gómez on the twin issues of his supposed betrayal by Alfonso López and that of abstention highlight the inexorable way Colombia's partisan tradition worked to distance Liberals and Conservatives. As late as February 1935, some two years after Conservatives announced their abstention, there was uncertainty as to whether the policy should be extended. Gómez himself doubted its wisdom. When he spoke by radio from his sickbed on March 6, 1935, he urged followers to continue voting, saying that he considered abstention bad for the country. One month later a still ailing Gómez declined to meet with his party directorate because he believed that its members should have a free hand in deciding whether to participate in congressional elections set for May 4. On April 8, 1935, the directorate voted unanimously for abstention.[113] Liberals were delighted with that development, for it meant that their constitutional reform would face no Conservative opposition in Congress. Laureano Gómez went along with the decision, although the unhappy look on his face as he read the declaration of continued abstention suggested that he agreed with *El Tiempo*'s assessment that the policy spelled disaster for the Conservative Party.[114] Over the ensuing months, as a uniformly Liberal Congress moved forward with its reforms, increasing numbers of Conservatives began to feel that the decision to abstain from voting had been a mistake. But by then the die was cast. Party leader Gómez had embraced abstention, enlisting the support of his entire party in attacking López and the Liberals.

In trying to understand el engaño, it is also important to consider the generation to which Gómez and López belonged. Both men were members of the Generation of the Centenary and their earliest memories were of friends, relatives, and personal heroes battling to the death in the War of the Thousand Days. As schoolboys both were steeped in the fiery ideals that drove their loved ones to fight that devastating, fratricidal war. As youngsters Gómez and López embraced the antithetical philosophies that figured prominently in most of Colombia's nineteenth-century civil wars, remaining forever faithful to them. Each recognized their mutual ideological incompatibility even before they became friends. Prior to their first formal meeting Laureano Gómez had criticized Alfonso López in the pages of *La Unidad* as being "of the extreme left," referring to López as "the only Representative of the radical party in parliament."[115] A week later he referred to López as "this brilliant new legislator descended from commission merchants."[116] As for López and his youthful Liberal contemporaries, none doubted that Gómez, "the beloved leader of a combative younger generation," was any the less a Conservative and staunch defender of clerical privilege for being their friend.[117]

Mutual admiration and a common interest in politics first attracted Gómez and López. Those two most flamboyant members of the Generation of the Centenary found common ground first in their enmity toward the Conservative old guard, represented by Marco Fidel Suárez, and later in their opposition to members of their respective parties who had committed the sin of *lèse-parti* by joining the Republican Union coalition during 1909 and 1910. Their mutual dislike of Enrique Olaya Herrera was founded precisely in the fact that the Liberal Olaya had benefited personally by serving the government of Carlos E. Restrepo, Conservative founder of the short-lived Republican Union and its only national president. Until the Conservative fall from power in 1930, and on through Olaya's government of "National Union," Gómez and

López had fought for the reemergence of partisan politics along traditional ideological lines. Finally, in 1935, with open Liberal-Conservative competition reestablished and all of their collaborationist fellow party members vanquished, Gómez and López stood ready to renew the partisan struggle on their own terms. Men of towering egos and dominating personalities, they perceived politics in terms of crusaders battling for the true faith. For reason of personality alone they could hardly have failed to turn on one another in political combat, like fighting cocks placed in close proximity.

Liberal leader López was as much trapped by his upbringing and by Colombia's political idiosyncrasy as was Laureano Gómez. For that reason he was forced to reform the nation's constitution upon entering office. Colombian political tradition demanded reaction against institutional reforms taken by the preceding regime, when it was one of the opposite party. Laws passed by the political enemy were necessarily to be replaced with politically correct ones, beginning with that most fundamental code of laws, the national constitution. At least from the Constitution of Cúcuta of 1821, Liberals and Conservatives had taken turns giving their ideals constitutional form and then attempting to impose them on the nation. The result of that exercise, which was founded in the Roman search for theoretical perfection in legal codes, was that Liberals and Conservatives rewrote or substantially revised their constitution with metronomelike regularity, each succeeding revision in reaction to its predecessor, on the average of once every decade between 1821 and 1936. As the conservative Constitution of 1886 had existed in a largely unrevised form longer than any other, it had been hated by the opposite party for longer than any other in Colombian history. It was thus with good reason that Alfonso López and his party came into power with the burning desire to revise the 1886 document. They obviously had a historical mandate to do so.

The reform impulse may have been rooted in Colombia's partisan tradition, but a good deal of its motive force came from political actors not present in Colombian politics a half-century earlier. Outside the halls of Congress militant workers and land-hungry campesinos employed strikes and land invasions to force changes. Inside Congress Socialists and Communists joined with left Liberals to push through fundamental legal changes highly satisfying to President Alfonso López, who was on record as wishing "in a certain way to disavow the existing social order."[118]

Labor benefited from new Articles 40 and 44, the one declaring work to be a social obligation enjoying special protection by the state, and the other guaranteeing labor the right to strike. Those constitutional innovations were complemented by laws of 1937 and 1938 requiring employers to provide paid Sunday holidays, to offer special protection to pregnant workers, and to limit the number of foreign workers. Article 140 assured state protection and patronage of labor congresses. Under that encouragement the number of Colombian labor unions more than doubled during the four years of López's presidency.

True to his word, López and his fellow reformers struck hard at vested economic interests through constitutional revisions and accompanying legislation having the dual purpose of addressing national social problems and spurring social development. New Article 15 declared that national authorities were to "assure the compliance of social obligations," thus dramatically revising the 1886 constitution's stricture that authorities insure the protection of "natural rights," especially that of property. The notion that property possesses a social function was addressed in new Article 26. Those articles drew inspiration and substance from the French essayist and social thinker Léon Duguit, whose "solidarist" philosophy of socialist savor kindled the imagination of progressive-minded Colombian Liberals.[119]

Another foreign concept, that of scientific management—or the stimulation of industrial production through automatic and assembly line techniques— engendered new Article 28, which declared that the state can intervene in private business and industry to the end of "rationalizing production, distribution, and consumption of natural wealth, and to give the worker the just protection that is his right." That article, along with others enhancing the power of the state in private economic affairs drew inspiration from other foreign sources as well. Among them were the Mexican and Spanish constitutions of 1917 and 1931, the socialist and indigenist APRA movement of Peru, the social democratic and communist initiatives taking place in Europe, and the New Deal of the United States. As a consequence of his reform program Alfonso López was known in some quarters as the Roosevelt of the Andes.

Alfonso López and his lieutenants were very much Keynesians in their insistence that the state tax private wealth, and redistribute the revenues through state programs aimed at stimulating economic growth and promoting public welfare. New laws passed during López's first term more than doubled taxes on incomes, moving them from 8 to 17 percent, and substantially increasing taxes on foreign and domestic corporations. As quickly as the additional revenues were received they were plowed back into programs ranging from social welfare to highway construction. The national education budget nearly quadrupled between 1934 and 1936, thanks to the influx of new tax dollars.[120]

The political reforms of the 1930s embraced the notion that modern liberalism demanded vigorous state action to control the destructive effects of unregulated laissez-faire capitalism. While that represented the rejection of nineteenth-century party principles founded in extreme individualism, it was a position Colombian Liberalism shared with all Western liberal parties at that historic moment. Minister of Government Alberto Lleras Camargo succinctly stated the rationale for state centralization during the first administration of Alfonso López: "The people entrusted to us instruments of action, which were the agencies of the state. But the state that we received was not free; rather, it was chained, diminished, and subject to limitations and mutilations. We have begun to liberate it, and now we can announce that a goodly portion of the weighty task is complete."[121]

The collectivist thrust of Alfonso López and his coterie of zealous young reformers generated powerful centrist opposition. Colombia's political parties had always possessed influential moderate wings sharing the common belief that national economic development took precedence over all other considerations, especially ideological ones. Periodically over the preceding hundred years Liberal and Conservative centrists had collaborated in the interest of national development. Those intervals of bipartisanship had typically followed extended periods during which Liberal and Conservative extremists had subjected the nation to a damaging period of ideologically inspired social experimentation typically ending in civil war. Earlier in the century the moderates found common ground in the Republican Union movement. Thirty years earlier Liberal Rafael Núñez had joined with Miguel Antonio Caro to organize another moderate bipartisan collectivity, the Nationalist Party. However, in both cases the moderates steadily lost ground to their more ideological partisans, who repolarized national politics with unfortunate consequence to the nation. In the earlier period "Peace Liberals" and "Nationalist" Conservatives, representing the moderate wings of their respective parties, failed in their attempt to avoid war. In the latter period members of the old Republican coalition, made up of Liberal and Conservative moderates, were unsuccessful in halting repolitization of the nation along ideological lines, a process presided over by Centenarians Laureano Gómez and Alfonso López.

In spite of their inability to halt López entirely, procapitalist moderates in both parties managed to slow the rush of reforms that in addition to damaging their economic interests frightened many of them into believing that their social peer López, son of a merchant capitalist and banker, was mounting a socialist revolution. Liberal moderates like Ricardo Charria Tobar spoke for many of his cohorts when he wrote that the López revolution "galvanized the nation more through fear than through enthusiasm."[122] Other right Liberals were shriller. The president's own brother, Eduardo López Pumarejo, a mainstay of the antireform lobby, APEN, was one of the administration's harshest critics, as was statesman and senior party member Laureano García Ortiz, who castigated those "who have called, and continued to call themselves Liberals, [but] who are not Liberals but rather are communists."[123] Conservative moderates who fought López were, like the centrist Liberals with whom they made common cause, businessmen and industrialists who in the past had been associated with the Republican Union Party and who were identified with the Nationalist Conservative faction. Prominent among them was Carlos E. Restrepo, Colombia's only Republican Union president. In Restrepo's view the 1886 constitution was being turned into something that was "neither national nor a constitution."[124] Mariano Ospina Pérez, another Nationalist Conservative who, like Restrepo, harbored the paisa's inherent dislike of Bogotá's interference in regional affairs, was especially scathing in accusing the Liberal constitutional reformers of being moved by "bastard political interests." As a member of the National Conservative Directorate, he had helped draft a statement that damned "this revolution on the march," which "is nothing but an attack on private wealth, not to mention capitalism itself."[125]

At length the centrist opposition to López's reforms, seconded by attacks from the ideological right, bore fruit. On January 1, 1937, shortly after final approval of the constitutional revision, López formally announced a "pause" in the area of institutional reform. He said that he wanted to give the nation time to assimilate the new programs and initiatives.[126] Eighteen months later, in the last major address of his first administration, López admitted that the pause had been a mistake, having resulted in the failure of most measures pending at the time he made the announcement. The consequence for Colombia had been, López said, "decomposition, discouragement, and disorder."[127]

The unhappiness that Alfonso López felt at the end of his 1934–1938 term was a function both of the opposition mounted by business interests threatened by his economic reforms, and of the antigovernment campaign directed by the Church and by Conservative defenders of Roman Catholic prerogatives. López and his fellow Liberals had given priority to striking the confessional content from the 1886 constitution, something they did by deleting the four articles which declared Roman Catholicism the state religion and which mandated state control of education (old Articles 38–41). Two new articles replaced them, Articles 13 and 14, which established freedom of conscience and of instruction in Colombia, and charged the state with overseeing public education. While the changes may have seemed innocuous, they set in motion a fateful and tragic chain of events.

Religion had been the chief bone of contention in Colombian politics for a century prior to the López reforms. Since the early nineteenth century, doctrinaire liberals in Colombia and other Latin American nations had worked to weaken the Church, which they viewed as both out of touch with the modern age and the chief supporter of a retrograde status quo. Conservatives, on the other hand, defended the Church as both the formulator and defender of fundamental human rights, and their principal institutional bulwark against immorality and social disorder. Both sets of views formed the ideological bedrock of the Liberal and Conservative Parties in Colombia and elsewhere. For that reason it was inevitable that Liberals should attack the Church when in power, and that the Conservatives should strengthen it when they won the presidency.

Constitutional reform became the order of the day after July 20, 1935, when Alfonso López inaugurated the new all-Liberal Congress with a ringing call for constitutional revision. Anticipating the coming assault on clerical privilege, Laureano Gómez spearheaded organization of an ecumenical congress to be held in Medellín during August, at the moment Darío Echandía presented the government's position on what Liberals termed "the religious problem." In Congress, Minister of Government Echandía echoed his president's pledge to "break the [religious] vertebrae of the Constitution of 1886."[128]

As Liberal congressmen in Bogotá debated how best to secularize the national constitution, several 100,000 Conservatives in Medellín accompanied Colombia's fiery young Archbishop Coadjutor Juan Manuel González Arbeláez in swearing to defend their faith even at the cost of their own lives. During numerous processions and public meetings hecklers supported by Liberal police raised the hackles of more than one speaker. At one point a furious Augusto Ramírez Moreno charged that the "atheistic" reforms of Alfonso López were aimed at turning the sisters of all Colombians into prostitutes. Luis Serrano Blanco reacted similarly to a red banner held aloft by Communist delegates to a workers' congress being held simultaneously in Medellín: "Red rags symbolize bed sheets bloodied during the first nights of marriage," he said, adding "but that red sheet lies because no one in the Popular Front is a virgin—neither the wife, nor the mother, nor the daughter, nor the fiancée."[129] Serrano's words achieved the desired result as the vast crowd hooted at the Communists and their fellow Popular Front members. A fight ensued in which the Communists, Liberals, and Liberal police fought with and injured numerous Conservatives. Shortly thereafter police fired on a Conservative crowd, killing two persons, one of them the son of Conservative Pedro C. Arango. A few hours later Laureano Gómez, who was in Bogotá at the time, received the following telegram: "Police have just murdered my son. This is my contribution in blood. Long live the Conservative Party! Pedro C. Arango."[130]

Debate on the religious question escalated through 1935 and into January 1936. On October 26, the Conservative directorate published a bulletin signed by Ignacio Rengifo, Pedro María Berrío, Laureano Gómez, Mariano Ospina Pérez, Augusto Ramírez Moreno, Pedro María Carreño, and General Amadeo Rodríguez, in which the party leaders declared that Conservatives would not be bound by constitutional reforms they had no part in formulating. They specifically criticized the religious reforms as detrimental to social health and stability.[131] The following month Archbishop Ismael Perdomo sent letters to Alfonso López and to the Colombian Senate lodging his protest against the reforms in general, and singling out the provision guaranteeing religious freedom as having potentially "fatal consequences" for the nation.[132] Meanwhile the Senate committee charged with drafting its version of the reform labored over its task. The position it would take on the church-state issue is suggested by a remark of José Vicente Combariza, who chaired the commission dealing with the religious problem: "The object of the revolution . . . must be to liquidate feudalism, a historic goal of Liberalism not heretofore achieved in this country, which has always been consecrated to theocracy. In that regard it seems to me that the [constitutional] revolution of '86 was eminently antiliberal. It also seems to me that our party must eliminate this theocratic aspect of the state. In principle and in doctrine I favor abolishing the article[s] relating to the Roman Catholic Church."[133]

On January 9, 1936, the Senate unveiled an entirely rewritten constitution so secular in character that even the name of God was deleted from its preamble. Senator Moisés Prieto, a Communist, defended the document in the debate that followed, saying his committee had produced a new fundamental charter, rather than a revision of the 1886 document, as requested by the government, because "the great majority [of Colombians] wish it."[134] The exceedingly secular character of the Senate document was founded in the idea that if Colombians remained wedded to their traditional religion, they would never become good citizens of progressive mentality. Earlier in the debate Senator Manotas Wilches had voiced the sentiment giving rise to that presumption: "across the length and breadth of this nation the illiterate follow the bishop and the priest."[135] Socialist Gerardo Molina elaborated on another aspect of the secularizing intent of fellow senators. Referring to the purging public education of clerical influence, Molina said he and others believed Roman Catholic teachings provided fertile ground for the growth of "fascistoid" corporate doctrines.[136]

There were weeks of heated debate on the proposed new constitution following its presentation on January 9, 1936. Liberal, Communist, and Socialist senators defended the document as in keeping with the anti-individualist tenor of the times, while moderate Liberals and members of the López government argued that it was too radical. At one point Timoleón Moncada defended striking the name of the deity from the preamble as consistent with the principle of public law that public power emanates from the people, not from a metaphysical construct. Leaving God in the preamble, he said, would help perpetuate the theocratic tendency that he and many of his colleagues saw enshrined in the Constitution of 1886.[137]

As the Senate debated whether the reform should be a recodification of the 1886 document, as Alfonso López wanted, or an entirely new charter, as Congress preferred, Conservatives mounted a potent defense against both alterna-

234 | Dangers of Political Inauthenticity, 1932–1965

tives. On February 1, Laureano Gómez and José de la Vega launched *El Siglo*, an avowedly doctrinaire newspaper that soon supplanted the more moderate *El País*. In the first editorial of the new party organ Laureano Gómez answered those who believed the nation's salvation lay in "defanaticizing" the citizenry through forced secularization: "In various ways, on numerous occasions, and almost uninterruptedly, the directors and collaborators of *El Siglo*, have consecrated their activities to the defense of those divinely inspired philosophic principles that bind the individual, with finished logic and the seductive precision of reason, to the luminous system of rights and privileges that fortify, sustain, and nourish the human personality. . . . We pledge not to willfully disparage them, nor to diminish them, nor to abandon them before an absolutism that the modern age necessarily locates in the state, as in ancient times it did in the despot."[138]

Six weeks later, on March 14, the war of words intensified with the inauguration of a series of attacks on the constitutional reform broadcast over the Conservative radio station La Voz de Colombia. Laureano Gómez introduced the series with a short talk that stands as one of the best examples of his scathing oratory: "The nation is being pushed into a whirlpool at whose center is homicidal violence, the arsonist's torch, abject irreligious passion, the rancorous envy of all who have failed at life, civil war, the disintegration of our nationality, and the end of Colombia. . . . The barbarians have tried to destroy God. They have erased His name from the Constitution. Still the Divine Essence should never be evoked on behalf of so malignant a work."[139] The following day public discourse in Colombia deteriorated yet further when an *El Tiempo* columnist attacked Gómez as "the great public sick man," "the illustrious crazy," "a man created for hatred and diatribe," "the hyena orator," and "the creole Hitler." Shortly thereafter the government levied a stiff fine against La Voz de Colombia, and began drawing up legislation to control the content of radio broadcasts. In the meantime Colombia's bishops published an open letter lamenting, among other things, the fact that the new constitution "begins by eliminating the name of God, the source of all authority, from its preamble."[140]

On March 17, amid rumors that former directorate member Amadeo Rodríguez was plotting revolution, Conservative leaders sent Alfonso López a letter warning him that unless he halted the reform, Colombia's democratic equilibrium would be lost, which in turn would "make harmonious and peaceful coexistence of the parties impossible, would provoke social and religious conflict and sow insecurity . . . and multiply the government's problems."[141]

Conservative warnings served only to infuriate Liberals. On April 15, the Senate voted final approval of the reform, in accord with the wishes of Alfonso López. On August 18, 1936, fifty years to the day after the Constitution of

1886 went into effect, the revised charter was presented to the nation as its fundamental law. On that same day Conservatives across Colombia commemorated the fiftieth anniversary of the Constitution of 1886 in celebrations symbolizing their rejection of the Liberal reform.

Not long after the new constitution became law, Alfonso López announced the celebrated "pause" in his revolution. That was just as well, for the momentum for reform had already died in Colombia. During 1937, and into 1938, opposition forces stymied further changes. Centrist and rightist Liberals rallied around their moderate partisan Eduardo Santos, whose forces trounced the president's handpicked successor, Darío Echandía, in the congressional elections of April 1937. A thoroughly dispirited Alfonso López attempted to resign the presidency the following month when it became clear that the new, more conservative Congress would not act on his legislative agenda. All the while doctrinaire Conservatives led by Laureano Gómez castigated the government daily in the pages of *El Siglo*.

Laureano Gómez forced his party to continue its political abstention through the entirety of López's first presidential term, though in the face of increasing opposition from moderates and young turks of the extreme right. Gómez's position as Conservative Party leader grew much more difficult with passage of the constitutional reform. By mid-1936, the party's moderate wing became convinced that abstention had been a terrible mistake and mounted increasing pressure on Gómez to drop the policy. Meanwhile a younger generation of party militants, who had recently formed the fascistic Acción Nacional Derechista (National Rightist Action group), demanded that Conservatives take direct revolutionary action against the López government.[142]

The moderates and the rightists found common cause in their dislike of Gómez's authoritarian party leadership. They mounted such pressure that it produced open revolt during the party convention of July 1937. Laureano Gómez handled the crisis by reading the fascists out of the party, and by "expelling" Fernando Gómez Martínez, director of the Medellín newspaper *El Colombiano* and leader of the paisa anti-Gómez moderates.[143] While it did them little good in the face of Gómez's determination not to abandon abstention, Acción Derechista leaders Silvio Villegas and Gilberto Alzate actively promoted the candidacy of party notable Mariano Ospina Pérez as Conservative presidential candidate for the 1938–1942 term. While Ospina Pérez did not reject the candidacy proffered by Villegas, Alzate, and other rightists, neither did he actively support it.

Following the party split of July 1937, the Conservative dissidents combined to attack Gómez through books, speeches, and newspaper articles. Fascists Silvio Villegas and Daniel Valois Arce published their *No hay enemigos a la derecha* (There are no enemies on the right) and *Itinerario espiritual* (Spiritual itinerary) within months of the turbulent party convention. The first volume, which praised Hitler's violent campaigns against the German left, criticized Gómez for his passivity: "Dr. Gómez, who is impotent for violence, is even more reluctant to engage in civil action. His dogmatic temperament does not permit the slightest contradiction. He feels himself possessed of absolute truth, as much before his friends as before his enemies. Anyone who disagrees with his whims and ideas is [considered] a betrayer, a trafficker, a criminal, a pyromaniac, a son of the night. He never discovers a noble motive in anything anyone else does."[144]

Augusto Ramírez Moreno also broke with Gómez in July 1937. In his volume *La crisis del partido conservador* (The crisis of the Conservative Party), Ramírez argued that Laureano Gómez was an inept politician whose leadership had gravely injured his party.

Gómez weathered the storm within his party in typical fashion: he went on the attack. In the weeks preceding the party convention of July 1937, he published a series of *El Siglo* editorials condemning fascism as "a mistaken tactic" because its penchant for violence and preference for authoritarian government contradicted Conservative principles. In a speech of June 1938, Gómez called fascism "a rightist deviation that implies the destruction and death of liberty," warning that "the fascist dictatorships prevailing in several great nations today offer material well-being in exchange for servitude."[145]

Conservatives opposing abstention argued that the policy was bad for their party because it had given free hand to Alfonso López and "the leftist youngsters" who had helped him carry out his reforms. Those supporting abstention argued that the policy was necessary to reduce Liberal electoral violence against fellow party members, pointing to Boyacá and Santander as places where Conservatives had suffered a great deal of election-related abuse before abstention had relieved them of the obligation to vote. They further pointed out that with the Conservative vote dropping nationwide, a function of the traditional and well-understood electoral chicanery accompanying every change of power at the national level, Liberals could and would have pushed through their reforms whether or not Conservatives were present in Congress.

The political abstention exercised during Alfonso López's first presidency was in fact a brilliant political strategy in the short term, though a painful and frustrating one for Conservatives. With Conservatives outside the formal political process, moderate and right-wing Liberals combined to force the "pause" in the president's progressive reform program soon after it got underway. Meanwhile the policy allowed Gómez and others to launch unmerciful attacks on the administration from outside the formal political system. By the last year of López's administration, Gómez drew freely on examples of atrocities committed against priests during the Spanish Civil War, on the Stalinist purges in the Soviet Union, and on political chaos in France under the Popular Front regime, to warn Colombians of what was in store for them if Alfonso López were not checked. "We swear to form a stout wall against the Muscovite infection . . . that afflicts those who support the stupid government we presently endure," wrote Gómez in *El Siglo,* January 29, 1938. It was but one of dozens of such histrionic indictments leveled at López and his government during 1937 and 1938.

One need look no farther than Alfonso López's message to Congress on July 20, 1938, for proof that political abstention served the interests of the Conservative Party and all others who wished to slow reform. The long, bitter, and bellicose address dwells on the destructive effect of Conservative opposition to his regime. If, however, abstention was a good strategy for stopping the Liberal reforms in their tracks, it was bad for Colombia over the long term. Abstention, and Gómez's attacks on López, turned the two men into enemies and rekindled partisan hatreds that had abated over the preceding thirty years of Republican bipartisanship.

López and Gómez understood their power to rally Colombians through partisan appeals. They also knew that such appeals had produced violence in the past. Laureano Gómez frequently characterized his country as a "hothouse culture," a delicate tropical environment requiring careful management by its leaders. Yet when in middle age he and his Liberal counterpart had the opportunity to exercise national leadership, they were unable to put aside ideology and polemics. They not only failed to moderate their actions and rhetoric, but they scathingly denounced colleagues who wished to revive the old Republican consensus. In his July 1938 address to Congress, Alfonso López repeatedly stressed the doctrinaire character of his regime, boasting that he had been able to mount a "party government" thanks to Conservative abstention. He reviled Republicanism as "a conformist ideology . . . with neither masses nor tradition at the local level." He reveled in the fact that he had succeeded in establishing a "Liberal Republic" in Colombia.[146]

For all their lofty intentions, Alfonso López and Laureano Gómez embittered and lowered the tone of political discourse in Colombia. That ultimately proved disastrous for the rapidly modernizing nation. The anger generated by both political leaders was like a poison weakening civic culture in Colombia.

Laureano Gómez must bear his share of blame for Colombia's slide into political incivility, though as a political "out" and as opposition party leader it was his duty to attack the regime in power. One is forced to ask whether he should be blamed for being born into a culture that rewarded political orthodoxy and skill in polemics. Gómez might have moderated his public statements, it is true. But why should he have done so, believing as he did that ungodly forces were threatening his country? That was hardly a modern view;

yet Gómez made no bones of the fact that his was a metaphysically informed worldview, one that he had sworn to defend at all costs. Given the rules of the political game as understood in early-twentieth-century Colombia, one wonders to what extent Gómez is to be condemned because he played harder and to greater effect than did his opponents.

And what of Alfonso López and his reforms? Could López have been more circumspect in reducing the religious content of the 1886 constitution? Perhaps not. Ideological Liberals could in no way tolerate the pro-clerical document imposed on them fifty years earlier. However, López and his fellow reformers insured the fanatical reaction of doctrinaire Conservatives when they struck at the Church in the name of defanaticizing the nation.

If blame is to be attached for the passionate exchange that sent Colombian politics into decline, then it must be apportioned, with Laureano Gómez receiving the larger share. He moved more easily than any of his peers in the supercharged, polemical, and punitive atmosphere of Colombian party politics. That being the case, one is perhaps best advised to lament the power and pervasiveness of a political tradition that robbed intelligent men of their power to dampen ideological exclusiveness in the interests of the common good.

8

A Society in Flux

Global Depression and World War: Colombia's Economic Boom

Between the early 1930s and mid-1940s, Colombia entered a period of remarkable economic growth that in turn produced equally dramatic social change. Textiles set the pace, leading Colombian industry to a spectacular 10.8 percent annual rate of growth between 1930 and 1945, while gross national product increased at an extraordinary annual rate of 4.7 percent between 1933 and 1939, and at a respectable 3.5 percent between 1939 and 1946.[1] These advances occurred amid shocking disorder in national political life during the late 1930s and the 1940s. Splendid growth in the private sector and increasing chaos in Colombia's public world became constant features of national life over the middle decades of the twentieth century.

Four elements combined to set Colombia on the road to speedy economic modernization during the Depression and World War II. First were the gains of the 1920s, during which an influx of foreign capital allowed local, regional, and national elites to upgrade the country's transportation network. Second was the war with Peru (1932–1933), which forced a burst of government spending that effectively countered deflationary and Depression-induced economic contraction. Third were a host of international events and developments, the Great Depression and World War II principal among them, that brought into play a series of economic measures most of which ultimately worked to Colombia's advantage. Fourth was a bias toward the capitalist model of economic development that was shared by most Colombians and which was especially marked among the national leadership elite.

Prior to the onset of the Depression national leaders made effective use of the monies that poured into their country during Colombia's dance of the millions. They invested the then incredible sum of $280 million — 80 percent of total public investment between 1925 and 1930 — in improving and extending rail, highway, and other transportation links.[2] While the 1,211 kilometers of railroads and 6,000 kilometers of highways resulting from their efforts were not sufficient to produce an integrated transportation network, they vastly facilitated the export of coffee to world markets and opened the nation's heartland to internal trade in local manufactures and foodstuffs. Thus when Colombia approached its industrial boom early in the 1930s, it possessed at least an adequate transportation infrastructure.[3] Over the succeeding fifteen years national administrations more than tripled highway mileage, at the same time expanding railroads by some 25 percent. That in turn led to great expansion in transport services, especially trucking. By 1945, Colombia had 250 trucking companies, whereas in 1930 it could count fewer than twenty.[4] The unlocking of interior Colombia by trucks and buses inevitably heightened popular aspirations. By mid-century, writer Eduardo Caballero Calderón observed that everywhere in the countryside "young campesinos dreamt of becoming the drivers of buses and trucks."[5] Others doubtless harbored the more grandiose desire of someday piloting one of the airplanes that passed overhead with increasing frequency. By 1931 the nation's German-owned SCADTA airline operated 3,410 kilometers of scheduled service, making Colombia the Latin American leader in that regard. In 1931, Medellín became the first Colombian city to put a modern airport into operation, while *El Tiempo* initiated daily air shipment of newspapers to Medellín, Cali, and other major cities.[6]

Colombia's system of roadways, rail lines, river and air communication, without which the remarkable growth of 1930–45 would have been impossible, was the product of infinite sacrifice and effort by a phalanx of national leaders extending back to Bolívar and Santander. Not so the war with Peru. That contest, which began in September 1932, just as Colombia reached the depth of the Depression, produced a burst of patriotic zeal that banished the gloom produced by economic hard times. Unemployment lessened dramatically as thousands of young men rushed to answer the call to arms, and deflation ceased as money was found to repel the perfidious Peruvian. The national government printed new currency issues and sold government defense bonds to pay for the war. Private citizens oversubscribed the bonds and went so far as to contribute their jewelry to the war effort. "Instead of hurting the economy," writes Miguel Urrutia, "the war with Peru pulled the economy from the Great Depression. . . . The war was in reality a Keynesian remedy applied three years before the publication of Keynes's General Theory. It had the perhaps unforeseen but beneficial effect of renewing aggregate demand before that happened in industrialized countries."[7]

Bankers in Colombia had abandoned orthodox economics fully a year before the war with Peru forced them into a Keynesian stance. On September 24, 1931, directors of the Banco de la República abandoned the gold standard. They did so because the similar action of Great Britain three days earlier had touched off a run on Colombian banks by clients demanding gold in exchange for banknotes. As bank manager Julio Caro recalled, at the very moment citizens besieged his offices demanding gold for their paper currency, "foreign bankers, especially those in the United States, cabled us that they had canceled the credits earlier approved for Colombia. It was a full-blown panic."[8]

The actions of the British and Americans worked very much to Colombia's advantage. They allowed President Olaya Herrera to drop the orthodox and monetarist position to which he had sworn his government in September 1930, under urging of the American advisor Edwin Kemmerer. With the gold standard no longer in force the government embarked on a policy of exchange devaluation and monetary expansion that, when coupled with government spending resulting from the war with Peru, effectively lifted Colombia from the Depression. Among the measures that Olaya adopted once he shed economic orthodoxy were the suspension of foreign debt payments, the raising of taxes and tariff duties, the imposition of exchange controls, and the opening of new sources of domestic credit. During 1931 and 1932, three new national banks were founded, the Central Mortgage Bank (Banco Central Hipotecario), the Agrarian Bank (Caja Agraria), and the Colombian Credit Corporation (Caja Colombiana de Ahorros). All three provided sorely needed loans to Depression-straitened businesses and individuals, and became a major source of monetary expansion.[9] Thanks to these measures the nation put the Depression behind it in 1934 and 1935, and resumed the economic growth and development interrupted between 1929 and 1933.

At the broadest level Colombia's turn to extensive state intervention after 1930 was but one example of a revolt against laissez-faire capitalism that was generalized throughout the Western world. European nations like Italy, Spain, and Portugal sought to moderate capitalistic excesses through authoritarian, corporative political reforms. Great Britain and the Scandinavian nations experimented with social democratic solutions to the problems created by earlier capitalist excess. Germans subordinated their economy to the interest of violent national expansion, while the Russians replaced capitalism with state control of the economy in accord with Marxist-Leninist theory.

Western Hemisphere nations were more moderate in their reaction against laissez-faire economics. A common tradition of republicanism and respect for democratic forms, coupled with generalized belief in the efficacy of capitalism, especially among the middle and upper classes, tempered the actions of political leaders. Politicians in Brazil and Argentina experimented with single-party corporate governance during the third and fourth decades of the century, while Mexico's Constitution of 1917, and subsequent evolution of that nation's dominant revolutionary party, provided a unique, enduring example of the wedding of single-party corporativism and capitalist developmentalism. In other countries, Colombia and the United States among them, where the tenets of laissez-faire economics were more deeply rooted in national tradition, political reforms were milder. There they took the form of increasing state intervention in the economic realm, mostly to the end of spurring development. The willingness of Colombia and the United States to pursue developmentalist ends explains why Alfonso López Pumarejo and Franklin D. Roosevelt are often compared. Both were Keynesians who, while sensitive to the plight of the downtrodden in their respective societies, willingly sacrificed the interests of the poor to the cause of economic growth when called upon to do so. The agricultural reforms of López and Roosevelt are cases in point. In each instance the reform was aimed at protecting and encouraging the small property owner, rather than distributing land to the landless. Hence a considerable proportion of the marginal rural population in both Colombia and the United States was forced from the land during the 1930s and afterward. Economic historian Jesús A. Bejarano agrees that during the 1930s and '40s, Colombian leaders were more concerned with development than with public welfare. He points out that over the entire period of the Liberal Republic monies spent on economic development ran from two to three times that expended on public health, education, and welfare. "Far from creating a 'welfare state,'" writes Bejarano, state interventionism in Colombia "was restricted rather to expanding legal control over economic activities and to the encouragement of development."[10]

Another international development working to Colombia's economic advantage from 1930 to 1945 was the rise of the United States to world dominance and its growing commitment to making Colombia a faithful ally. The strengthening of Colombian-U.S. friendship was a development many national leaders had anticipated and toward which they had worked. At least since the mid-nineteenth century prominent Colombians had believed that their nation's economic well-being was linked to that of the United States. Early in the twentieth century development-minded politicians like Marco Fidel Suárez waxed eloquent about the "Polestar," and its significance for Colombia. But not until the third decade of the century did anger over U.S. complicity in the separation of Panama abate sufficiently to permit improved relations between the two states. With the change of government in 1930, Colombian-U.S. relations warmed appreciably. Enrique Olaya Herrera was a longtime friend of America, as was his successor, Alfonso López. And López's successor, Eduardo Santos, embraced Roosevelt's Good Neighbor Policy, seeing to it that Colombia became one of the United States' firmest hemispheric allies.[11] The leaders of both nations knew full well that geopolitics and the doctrine of comparative advantage argued powerfully for Colombian-U.S. friendship. And the fact that both republics were directed by philosophic liberals who embraced democracy, economic freedom, global interdependence, and economic growth and development under capitalist forms made warm relations all the more natural.

The objective bases of Colombo-American friendship became increasingly clear over the late 1930s. In 1936 the two nations signed a trade agreement by which Colombia agreed to freeze tariffs on 161 specified U.S. imports, while the U.S. guaranteed that Colombian coffee would enter its markets duty free.

While the agreement has been damned by economic historian Alfonso Patiño as one of the worst of its kind ever signed by Colombia because of its adverse effect on infant industry, the trade pact reflected the belief of Alfonso López and other national leaders that insuring Colombian coffee free access to the U.S. market warranted ignoring the interests of a nascent industrial sector.[12]

As World War II approached, Colombo-American relations grew warmer, increasingly to Colombia's benefit. By the early 1940s the two nations were cooperating in the exploitation of Colombian strategic materials such as petroleum, gold, platinum, cement, and natural rubber, and the U.S. government was encouraging its own industries to help Colombian counterparts upgrade their technology.[13] In this way Colombian-U.S. interests became ever more closely linked at the economic level over the middle decades of the twentieth century.

World War II, which shut off the supply of most traditional imports to Colombia, had the effect of further stimulating the growth of import-substituting industry. The happy fact was that Colombia was forced into import substitution just as it was eager and able to move in that direction. Since 1931, Colombia had been pursuing what Finance Minister Estéban Jaramillo described as a "rigorously protective" trade policy, complemented by fiscal practices designed to favor domestic industrial growth.[14] A substantial devaluation of the peso between 1930 and 1935, and a 10 to 12 percent annual rate of inflation over the war years, resulted in a 220 percent increase in the money supply by 1941, which made for a favorable investment climate. Revenues from coffee exports, not easily spent on foreign imports during the war, were channeled into import-substituting domestic industries, a practice that followed the tradition, well established during the 1920s, of transferring coffee earnings into industrial investment. Owing to these factors Colombia witnessed a 62.8 percent increase in its number of manufacturing establishments—from 2,805 to 4,462—between 1930 and 1939. Nearly all the new plants were devoted to the elaboration of nondurable goods and foodstuffs which had previously been imported. Accordingly, such products shrank from 30 percent of total imports in 1930 to 9 percent in 1940.[15] Most of the new plants were small and labor intensive, but they nevertheless enjoyed great potential for growth. The Haceb Company, for example, which was founded in a Medellín repair shop by two brothers named Acevedo, grew into one of Colombia's major manufacturers of electric appliances over succeeding decades.

The dynamics of industrial growth were perhaps clearest in Antioquia, where the Depression made paisas more amenable to state intervention in their economic affairs, especially when it was directed by one of their own, the prudent Estéban Jaramillo. After the new national mortgage bank stepped in and saved many foundering businesses, Antioquian entrepreneurs quickly moved to launch a host of new industrial concerns. Among the more notable were Imusa (aluminum); Cementos Samper and Cementos Agros; Cauchoso and Croydon (rubber); and Pepalfa, Indulana, and Paños Santafé (textiles). The Bavaria Brewery of Bogotá was reorganized and fused with the largest beer producers of Antioquia and Caldas.[16] Meanwhile on the Atlantic coast the Santodomingo family began building its industrial empire through the brewing of beer. By the last decade of the century the Santodomingo Group would stand as Colombia's largest and most diversified corporation.[17]

Corporate formation began in Colombia during the burst of import-substituting industrial growth of the 1930s. There was a fivefold increase in corporate holdings (from $20 to $109 million) between 1932 and 1938, and an elevenfold increase (to $1,368 million) by 1941. That encouraged the creation in 1932 of a stock market which enjoyed a tenfold increase in the value of stocks traded (from $4.6 to $55.5 million) between 1932 and 1939.[18]

The growth of incipient industry in Depression-era Colombia produced a ripple effect across the economy. Building trades and construction were invigorated everywhere in urban areas. Data collected in Bogotá reveal that construction between 1933 and 1936 exceeded by 40 percent that of the heady 1926–1929 period.[19] Energy consumption rose steadily between 1930 and 1945, increasing 40 percent by 1935, and growing another 140 percent by 1945.[20]

A final source of Colombia's economic boom during the 1930s and '40s, was the developmental bias shared by most members of the national political elite. Most politicians were also businessmen, a fact explained in part by the necessity of earning money during periods of involuntary exclusion from public office sometimes extending over a lifetime. Prominent Liberals like Rafael Uribe Uribe and Pedro A. López, active during the half-century of Conservative hegemony (ca. 1880 to 1930), dedicated themselves to the coffee industry except during relatively brief intervals when they were either participating in or fleeing civil war. Similarly, after 1930, and over the ensuing sixteen years of the Liberal Republic, Conservatives such as Mariano Ospina Pérez necessarily devoted most of their energies to nonpolitical affairs.

That most Colombian public figures were both businessmen and politicians helps explain the easy osmotic way in which they passed back and forth between the worlds of business and politics. Colombia was replete with businessman-politicians during the years of its industrial boom. The most prominent of them were Alfonso López Pumarejo and his son, corporate lawyer and president-to-be Alfonso López Michelsen; president-to-be and coffee entrepreneur Mariano Ospino Pérez, nephew of Colombia's greatest businessman-president, Pedro Nel Ospina; and corporate lawyer and president-to-be Carlos Lleras Restrepo, nephew of the nation's leading banker, Julio Lleras Acosta.

Carlos Lleras illustrates better than most the public-private dynamic of Colombia's leadership elite. Trained as a lawyer, and in private practice during the early 1930s, Lleras was elected to Congress in 1933 and played a pivotal role in crafting the constitutional reform of 1936. Later he joined the cabinet of Eduardo Santos as minister of finance and public credit. In that capacity, and true to his commitment to the principle of state interventionism, he sponsored creation of the Instituto de Fomento Industrial (IFI; Industrial Development Institute), a government agency charged with promoting the growth of new industry. When Lleras ended his stint as finance minister, he founded and directed the School of Industrial and Commercial Administration at Bogotá's Gimnasio Moderno. Two years later, in 1944, Lleras accepted employment with the newly formed industry group Asociación Nacional de Industrias (ANDI), organized to lobby government agencies, particularly the IFI. Later, with formation of the Frente Nacional in 1958, Lleras reentered government service, going on to become one of Colombia's more successful presidents (1966–1970), especially in the realm of economic management.

The fluid movement of businessmen, politicians, and intellectuals in and out of one another's respective spheres has led most academics to employ Marxian class analysis in trying to explain the phenomenon. Over most of the twentieth century terms such as "dominant class," "oligarchy," and "oligarchic bourgeoisie" have served to describe a powerful few who, in the words of one historian, created a "system of privilege and injustice . . . [that] they have wanted to preserve at all costs."[21] Such interpretation loses much of its persuasive power, however, when considered in terms of the great fluidity of Colombian society during the twentieth century. In fewer than a hundred years the population has progressed from 80 percent illiterate to 90 percent literate. The middle class has expanded from 20 to 50 percent of the population. These data suggest an open and dynamic society, not one dominated by a greedy elite that has deprived the masses of their patrimony.

The liberal-developmentalist philosophy dominant among Colombian leaders from the mid-nineteenth century onward is clearly observed in the handling of national agricultural policy between 1936 and 1944. Alfonso López, a president whose background in private business was extensive prior to 1930, had initially reassured his peers that the agrarian reform embodied in Law 200 of 1936, was aimed at encouraging capitalist transformation of rural Colombia through the freeing of resources immobilized in latifundia. Frightened by the leftist rhetoric accompanying the passage of Law 200, López's peers blocked further reform and proceeded to replace him with the more moderate Eduardo Santos. Subsequent to leaving the presidency in 1938, and as if to demonstrate his moderation on the agrarian question, López agreed to head the landowners' principal interest organization, the Sociedad de

Agricultores de Colombia (SAC; Society of Colombian Agriculturalists) in 1941. Soon thereafter he restated the developmentalist logic that underlay the agrarian reform of 1936 when he told an audience that "the reform was designed merely . . . to protect the rights of property owners, at the same time limiting them . . . [in order to] keep them from impeding national development."[22]

Commercialization and regional specialization moved apace in rural Colombia in the years following the passage of Law 200. By the early 1940s choice agricultural zones of Valle, the llano of Tolima, the highlands of Cundinamarca-Boyacá, and the Caribbean coast were increasingly devoted to the mechanized cultivation of sugarcane, cotton, rice, sesame, and sorghum. In cattle-producing areas technification was increasingly the norm. New breeds of cattle, such as the heat- and pest-resistant Brahmans, began appearing in many places, thanks in part to technical aid missions from abroad.[23] While Colombia's agricultural sector remained unable to supply all products needed for human and industrial consumption, food production consistently outpaced population growth. Agricultural prices increased modestly through the 1940s, and imports of foodstuffs declined from 63.3 percent of imports in the early 1930s, to 37.3 percent by the mid-1940s. On the other hand, Colombia's industrial growth outstripped the nation's ability to satisfy demand for raw materials.[24] Meanwhile marginal populations became urbanized or else moved or were sent into the eastern llanos, where most became involved in cattle raising.[25]

Coffee, Colombia's great income producer, received the ongoing attention of national elites in the years following the passage of the agrarian reform in 1936. Law 200 achieved its principal goal of swelling the coffee yeomanry; but it also caused landowners to fear that their tenants might stake claims to parts of their farms under terms of the law. That led many landowners to expel tenants from their property, producing uncertainty and even violence in many rural areas. The expulsions also produced a sharp fall in private-sector investment in agriculture as well as a decline in the supply of yuca, corn, beans, plantain, and many other foodstuffs previously grown by tenants on their rented plots. By the early 1940s, prominent Colombians were calling for revision of Law 200, citing the "alarming" decrease in locally grown staples. Politicians like Carlos Lleras Restrepo, who had figured prominently in drafting the agrarian reform, charged that a mistaken interpretation of Law 200 "was destroying the juridic notion of land rental in Colombia."[26]

Political Colombia addressed these problems in a series of laws that at once strengthened the hand of landowners against their renters and militated against proletarization of rural labor. Laws 6 and 100 of 1944 clarified and regularized rental procedures, and exempted landowners from the payment of social benefits to their employees. An earlier attempt to guarantee overtime pay and workmen's compensation had failed to receive congressional approval. In that manner political Colombia assured the private sector that investment in rural property would be protected. With the agrarian counter-reform of 1944, private investment capital returned to rural Colombia.[27]

World War II initially hurt Colombia's economy, taking away lucrative European markets—Germany alone consumed 15 percent of the nation's coffee exports by 1939—and drastically reducing the flow of imports. But as was the case in the early thirties, the economy emerged from its travail much strengthened. The war's chief effect was to accelerate industrial growth of import-substituting industry. Rivaling that in importance was the war's effect of drawing Colombia and the United States yet closer. The economic value of U.S. friendship became manifest even before that nation became directly involved in the war. When coffee prices fell by nearly 50 percent in 1939, to a ruinous 7.5 cents per pound, the U.S. stepped in to reverse the decline through sponsorship of the Inter-American Coffee Agreement, negotiated over the course of 1940.[28] That accord, which established import quotas for coffee-producing nations, guaranteed Colombia the sale of 80 percent of its annual production in the American market. Within months of its signing prices rebounded to 35 cents, thus ending the panic among coffee interests. The agreement also produced an important subsidiary effect. After signing the accord, Colombia was faced with the necessity of storing most of the coffee not purchased by the United States. As that country was virtually Colombia's only overseas customer during the war years, 18 percent of the annual harvest had to be warehoused until such time as European markets were restored. The national coffee growers' federation raised funds for construction of the costly storage facilities through creation of the National Coffee Fund (Fondo Nacional del Café), underwritten by taxes and bond issues. As those moneys accrued rapidly, Fedcafé was able not only to construct hundreds of warehouses throughout the coffee zone, but was able to greatly expand its services to producers and processors, all of whom were its affiliates.[29]

Another way the United States helped Colombia withstand war-induced economic reverses was through a series of Export-Import Bank loans granted between 1940 and 1945. Those loans totaled more than $100,000,000 in portfolio investment, and another $100,000,000 in direct investment in mining and petroleum extraction and in the upgrading of public services and highways.[30]

The nation derived additional benefit from the U.S.-directed assault on German companies operating in Colombia when the war began. Under American urging the Colombian government blacklisted all German businesses in the country, replacing their managers with Colombian nationals. In most cases those businesses were eventually purchased by Colombians at a fraction of their book value. The two most important of them were the nation's principal airline, SCADTA, and its second-largest private bank, the Banco Alemán Antioqueño, in Medellín. The former became Colombia's quasi-public air carrier Avianca, and the latter, renamed the Banco Comercial Antioqueño, became a chief underwriter of Antioquian economic growth.[31] The interests of foreign nationals living in countries occupied by Axis powers were placed under fiduciary management of the Banco Central Hipotecario. Most of those, such as the Dutch-owned Handel Maatschappij, a major stockholder in the Bavaria beer group, also quickly passed into Colombian ownership.

Yet another way in which U.S. interests aided Colombian economic growth during the war years was through the mounting of joint ventures with local businesses, principally in the production of strategic materials. Thus Corn Products of America combined with Maizena, Container Corporation of America with Cartón de Colombia, Burlington Mills with Fabricato, and the Grace Company with Coltejer. North American involvement was particularly important to the textile industry, which greatly expanded its manufacturing capacity during the war years. During that period the U.S. government let contracts to Colombian firms for the manufacture of military uniforms and aided in the import of requisite machinery. "There were machines operating under tents while around them buildings were hastily constructed to house them," recalled manufacturer Carlos J. Echavarría.[32] Between 1933 and 1943, Colombian textile plants tripled their capacity to the extent that they were able to produce twelve million square meters of cloth over the course of World War II. One consequence was that the Coltejer Corporation, which had 65,000 shares of stock outstanding in 1937, had more than 3,000,000 shares outstanding by 1945.[33] Its physical plant, valued at $760,000 in 1936, was assessed at $8.7 million at war's end. Thanks to its success Coltejer had entered the fields of banking and insurance by the mid-1940s. So extensive was Coltejer's operation that by 1945, 16 percent of Medellín's population was either employed by the company or were dependents of Coltejer workers.

The Colombian government itself played a significant role in stimulating the growth of import-substituting industry from 1940 to 1945. As early as the 1890s it had been national policy to stimulate business activity through encouraging the formation of chambers of commerce and other such interest groups, and by inviting their participation in government decision-making councils. That corporative approach to national development flowered after 1930, when Liberal regimes embraced state interventionism. Enrique Olaya Herrera's banking reforms and Alfonso López's tax program were expressly designed to insinuate government into the economy to the end of rationalizing capitalist processes. Eduardo Santos continued in that tradition by supporting Carlos Lleras's organization of the Instituto de Fomento Industrial in 1940.

Thanks to grants from the IFI, which a writer termed "one of the finest Liberal achievements,"[34] factories were founded for the manufacture of steel, tires, and chemicals. A shipbuilding industry was launched, and milk-processing plants and similarly complicated food-processing plants were begun.[35]

The knowledge that they could count on government help for risky and costly undertakings buoyed Colombia's business class during the 1940s. Over the first half of the decade its members founded two powerful new interest organizations designed to promote further collaboration between public and private sectors. They were the National Association of Manufacturers (Asociación Nacional de Industrias, ANDI) and the National Federation of Merchants (Federación Nacional de Comerciantes, FENALCO), established in 1944 and 1945. Those associations, having branches in all major cities, joined the chambers of commerce, Fedcafé, the Federation of Wheat Growers, the Sugar Distributors, the National Federation of Land Transportation, and others, in lobbying government for treatment favorable to their respective groups.

An *El Tiempo* article of September 9, 1942, suggests the corporative dynamic at work in the public-private partnership so important in Colombian economic development. Reporting on the initial attempt to organize ANDI, the writer said that the group's steering committee was made up of "some of the most distinguished figures of our industry, by the minister of the economy and the minister of labor, as well as by directors of the Caja Agraria and of the IFI." Among those representing the private sector was Miguel López Pumarejo, younger brother of Alfonso López, at that moment a month into his second presidential term. Carlos Lleras, who had just left the Ministry of Finance, was unanimously elected to head the group. He urged his peers to "recruit the membership of manufacturers in all parts of the nation."[36]

Colombian business had every reason for confidence by 1945. The preceding five years had witnessed a 50 percent growth in industry amid moderate inflation and price rises favorable to domestic investment.[37] Meanwhile a 300 percent increase in the money supply and a 1,000 percent increase in foreign reserves over the preceding ten years, coupled with government sympathy to the cause of industry, suggested that growth would accelerate over the postwar period.[38] Colombian corporate growth had endowed the nation with an aggressive and successful executive class—men like Fernando Mazuera Villegas, who returned from New York early in 1945, bragging of having spent twenty minutes on the telephone there brokering the purchase of rayon for a Medellín textile mill and earning $74,000 for his trouble.[39] Nor did businessmen need to leave Colombia in order to make money. Domestic entrepreneurs experienced their own dance of the millions, as suggested by Carlos Lleras's remark in 1943 that "the lure of earnings received without work awakened in innumerable people who had never invested before the desire to speculate."[40]

Colombia's economic modernization produced the additional benefit of advancing national unification by linking regional elites through their new commercial associations. French sociologist Daniel Pécaut has alluded to the integrative effect of business growth: "Money circulated from one activity to another. . . . It served as a link between the diverse dominant factions."[41] But the economic change linking regions and interests was not limited to members of the elite. The commercial ethic ran deep in Colombian culture, down through all economic strata, taking on the character of a new national ideology. This point is brought home by historian Charles Bergquist, who writes that during the 1940s, "the success of coffee smallholders, and that of industrial capitalists of the manufacturing sector, along with the general growth and development of the Colombian economy, helped consolidate in the minds of individuals of all social classes the fundamental viability of an economic system based in the principles of capitalism."[42]

To say that the coffee smallholder shared in the heady optimism of the period is also to say that a majority of Colombians did so. The coffee industry supported many thousands of persons involved in its harvesting, processing, transportation, sale, and marketing, as well as a host of peripheral activities not directly involved with coffee growing. During the 1940s, coffee held its place as the nation's great producer of national wealth, bringing in between 75 and 80 percent of all foreign exchange.

Coffee prices had held steady after 1940, averaging nearly 20 cents per pound over the first half of the decade. All the while production increased steadily, doubling to nearly six million sixty-kilo sacks harvested in 1945.[43] It augured well, too, that the United States, purchaser of 96 percent of Colombia's coffee exports, had emerged largely unscathed from the war. Furthermore, that nation possessed a large population avid to purchase Colombian coffee at handsome prices. The immediate economic future was indeed bright for the millions of Colombians whose interests were bound up with coffee. Only the worsening national political situation cast shadows over the happy prospect of economic prosperity.

Visions of Social Change

Significant social change took place in Colombia between 1930 and 1945. Society became more diverse, individualistic, and cosmopolitan—in short, more open and democratic. Growing affluence had the effect of swelling the middle class and increasing its political influence. All those developments meant that Colombia was evolving in a manner satisfactory to its national leaders, most of whom had sought such progress for decades.

Still there remained stubborn structural and attitudinal problems that kept a majority of citizens from participating fully in the social transition. Modernization was principally an urban phenomenon. Yet only a third of all Colombians lived in towns and cities by 1945. And the benefits of modernization were unevenly distributed, even in urban areas. Admission to the white-collar occupations, and thence to the middle class, required literacy, and nearly 60 percent of Colombians could neither read nor write. Tension was inevitable in such a setting, where poor, urban-dwelling Colombians saw themselves lagging badly in the scramble for personal advancement, a perception that made them increasingly sensitive to social inequities. Their dissatisfaction was sharpened by dissident politicians who shifted the blame for social inequities and all other social problems to a Liberal Party leadership widely perceived as venal and self-serving. No member of Colombia's counterelite was more effective in tarring the political establishment than Laureano Gómez. Between 1935 and 1945, Gómez elaborated a damning critique of philosophic liberalism and the party that was its institutional manifestation in Colombia. His attacks played a key role in dividing Liberals and paving the way for their loss of power in 1946.

Social indicators improved markedly between 1930 and 1945, thus continuing a trend dating from 1904. Colombia's population shifted from one-fifth to one-third urban over those years, while the total population grew by 40 percent, from 7.5 million to 10.5 million. An internal shift of population occurred simultaneously, as young and ambitious campesinos left eastern and southern parts of the nation and moved into the economically dynamic coffee zone of Antioquia, Caldas, Tolima, and Valle.[44] While 75 percent of the economically active population worked in agricultural and extractive occupations in 1945, only one-third of all new jobs were in those fields. The remaining two-thirds were in the rapidly expanding manufacturing sector.[45] Infant mortality declined over the period, falling from 201 deaths per 1,000 in 1930, to 122 in 1950. Concomitantly, average life expectancy rose from 36.1 years to 48.9 years. Illiteracy in Colombia also declined, from just under 70 percent to slightly less than 60 percent.[46]

The improvement in Colombia's social indicators was closely linked to urbanization. Declining rates of infant mortality, rising educational levels, and all the other signs pointing to an improvement in general living conditions were bound up with accessibility to physicians and hospitals, teachers, and schools—all in short supply in the campo. Likewise in short supply, outside of urban areas, was the sense of excitement present in the city. The campo seemed primitive and unchanging. The city offered movement and economic opportunity along with the possibility of upward social mobility. Furthermore there were those in the city who seemed sincerely interested in helping the poor man and his family, politicians like the Liberal Jorge Eliécer Gaitán, who during a brief term as Bogotá's mayor not only promoted free public education but opened school restaurants, providing free breakfasts for needy children.[47] Such things were miraculous to campesinos, whose patrón's interest in their welfare seemed to manifest itself only around election time.

As the century progressed, Colombia's cities increasingly spearheaded national progress. Dynamic leaders like Bogotá's mayor Gaitán and his successor, Carlos Sanz de Santamaría, responded to their city's rapid growth by extending electric, sewer, and water lines, improving streets and public transportation, and promoting the construction of new residential areas. Under the regime of Sanz (1942–1944), the capital surpassed its traditional northern limit, Calle 26 (Twenty-sixth Street), bordering the Río San Diego. He extended Avenida Caracas, a major north-south route, so as to link Avenida Jiménez (13th Street) with Avenida Chile, fifty-nine blocks farther north, thus speeding the capital's northward expansion.[48]

The direction of urban change in Colombia was manifest in traffic moving along streets of the national capital. Early in the 1930s, buses appeared as an alternative to the popular but slower municipally owned electric streetcars. In 1935, the last of Bogotá's horse-drawn hacks disappeared, replaced by taxis owned by entrepreneur Leonidas Lara. The number of privately owned autos also grew steadily, rising from 1,100 in 1927, to 4,899 by 1940, and 11,884 a decade later.[49] The city's first traffic lights were installed in 1935, and six years later a stringent set of transit regulations was imposed. By 1945, when the city's population stood at half a million, Bogotanos complained that next to the problem of drinking water, transportation was their chief concern. They were especially critical of the publicly owned streetcar line, whose expansion had manifestly not kept pace with the city's growth. By 1945 the lumbering tranvía, increasingly surrounded by swarms of speedier buses and taxis, was, in the words of urban historian Julián Vargas, dangerously close to being "run over in the process of the privatization of public transportation."[50]

The increasing availability of radios quickly democratized that important medium of information and entertainment. Early in the century the "wireless" was enjoyed only by the rich, who shared it with friends. During the 1920s, President Pedro Nel Ospina hosted white-tie socials in order that his guests might hear radio programs broadcast from Europe and the United States.[51] Just two decades later Colombia had fully entered its golden age of radio, with millions of listeners tuning in on the adventures of locally produced comedy and music programs, soap operas, and detective thrillers like *The Adventures of Charlie Chan* (in Colombia, Yon-Fu), adapted from a Cuban program of the same name. The tragic death, in 1936, of tango idol Carlos Gardel, in a fiery Medellín runway collision, gave birth to on-the-spot news reporting. By the 1940s politicians had seized upon radio as an excellent complement to their newspapers for spreading their political messages. During his second administration Alfonso López broadcast a weekly program called *La República Liberal,* and Conservatives answered with their own station, La Voz de Colombia. Meanwhile Liberal maverick Gaitán employed radio personality Rómulo Guzmán to disseminate his message through the program *Ultimas Noticias.* And it was no longer necessary to crowd the Senate galleries to hear the exciting debates of Laureano Gómez, Gaitán, and others. By the 1940s, Colombians could hear every word in the comfort of their living rooms simply by tuning in *The Voice of the Senate.*[52]

As with radio, motion pictures played a growing role in homogenizing Colombian culture. Members of the religious establishment feared movies precisely for the cosmopolitan and nontraditional images they brought to unsophisticated viewers. One Roman Catholic writer warned in 1934, "Cinema is your terrible enemy . . . it robs you of time and money, and it perverts your consciences: flee from it!"[53] But Colombians of all descriptions did just the opposite, flocking to the movies in growing numbers in the thirties. There they thrilled to the mighty ape in *King Kong,* admired Hedy Lamarr's nude figure in *Ecstasy,* and were amazed to hear Greta Garbo's voice in *Hotel,* the first "talkie" shown in Colombia. During the early forties they filled theaters to see Walt Disney's *Fantasia,* to admire Humphrey Bogart in the *Maltese Falcon* and *Casablanca,* and to feast on a steady diet of films starring the Mexican comedian Cantinflas.[54]

The globalizing, individualizing, and democratizing thrust of popular culture was nowhere more evident than in sports. During the early decades of the century, team and individual sports were the purview of the elite, who competed for personal enjoyment in the isolation of their country clubs. But by the thirties sports had escaped those narrow confines and had become popular in a highly symbolic way. Foreign crews from ships transporting coffee and bananas out of the port of Barranquilla commonly passed time at dockside tossing a baseball or kicking a soccer ball, depending on whether they were North Americans or Europeans. The Colombian stevedores with whom they worked soon learned both sports and became proficient in them. Soccer quickly took possession of schoolyards and vacant lots throughout Colombia, while baseball flourished in towns and cities along the Caribbean coast. By the 1940s, Colombian baseball teams were playing international competition in the World Amateur Baseball League, all of whose teams were from the Caribbean region. In 1947, Colombia won the league championship. Soccer was even more successful. Professional teams sprang up in major cities during the thirties and forties, and by the latter decade Colombia was sending teams abroad to compete in the World Cup.[55] Highly significant in the spread of spectator sports is the fact that they were democratic. Members of Colombia's athletic hierarchy earned their fame through individual merit, not through inherited wealth or family connections, as was the case with most other public figures. And Colombia's top professional athletes formed a racially mixed group representative of the nation's mixed-blood population.

The rise in the popularity of sports, whether practiced individually or enjoyed as a spectator, was bound up with the increasing privatization and individualization in Colombian society. Sporting activities distracted Colombians, drew their attention away from the public world and its gladiatorial exchanges in congressional chambers. Spectator sports flourished in reciprocal measure with the expansion of free time, especially after 1934, when a presidential decree granted factory workers paid Sunday holidays. Suddenly it was possible to be a fan, to spend Sunday afternoons at the municipal sports stadium or at home listening to the game by radio.

Radios and other such consumer items took on added importance with the expansion of leisure time. And with the growth of national industries like Haceb and Centrales (producers of consumer electronics), it became increasingly possible to satisfy the growing demand for consumer goods such as radios, record players, refrigerators, and water heaters. Moreover, the end of World War II released a flood of imports from the United States. Magazines and newspapers were suddenly full of ads depicting Hollywood stars touting new products. Starlet Yvonne de Carlo recommended purchase of the luxurious new Musophonic radio-phonograph offered by General Electric. In promoting its new products, RCA advised that "with the advent of peace, many who had been occupied in making instruments of war now work to bring pleasure to the world's free men and women." Colombians read those messages and were convinced. When the merchants Vásquez and Lalinde announced in December 1945 that a planeload of Philco appliances would arrive in time for Christmas, Bogotanos responded by lining the runway at El Techo Airport with buses and autos, whose headlights helped guide the precious cargo to a safe landing.[56]

Urbanization and industrialization, and the occupational diversification they produced, along with the country's rapid expansion of material culture, made possible the most significant social development in Colombia in the twentieth century: the rapid growth of the nation's middle class. The importance of that development has been amply noted by Colombian writers. Scholar and social activist José Gutiérrez writes, "When historians examine events taking place in Colombia during the long period of social agitation beginning in 1942 . . . they will surely find explanatory power in the sudden appearance in national life of the economic middle class."[57] Social historian Carlos Uribe Celis describes "the explosion of the middle class" in Colombia during the 1940s.[58]

Colombia's middle class made known its arrival on the political scene in 1936, when it founded its own political lobby, the Action Committee of the

Colombian Middle Class. Drawing membership from government offices and from the ranks of small merchants, it called for the democratization of credit so that "men of work" might achieve "the realization of their economic independence through personal effort and the help of public entities." The committee's lobbying activities quickly bore fruit. One of its chief objectives was to enlist government support in the form of low-cost loans for the construction of middle-class housing. Their appeals caught the ear of banker Julio Lleras Acosta, who became a leading force in improving middle-class housing. By the late 1930s, a significant portion of loans granted by the Banco Central Hipotecaria, which Lleras Acosta directed, were being earmarked for that purpose. Symbolic too of growing middle-class influence was the example of future president Julio César Turbay—whose father was a petty merchant—forming a part of the committee's leadership. He represented a group calling itself the Union of Nonorganized Middle-Class Associations.[59]

The insurgent middle class found its most aggressive spokesman in former agrarian activist and reform mayor of Bogotá, Jorge Eliécer Gaitán. Gaitán symbolized the able and ambitious individual of modest means who by dint of personal sacrifice has risen from poverty to wealth. Thanks to his and his mother's efforts Gaitán earned a law degree at the National University, going on to take advanced study in Italy under the eminent criminologist Enrico Ferri. Returning home he entered politics, where he quickly gained fame as spokesman for banana workers slain by the army in late 1928. During the early 1930s, he broke with the Liberals to form his UNIR party, which was dedicated to aiding campesinos in their struggle for land. When, in 1935, it became obvious that they were on the verge of achieving that objective thanks to Alfonso López's land reform legislation, Gaitán abandoned UNIR and rejoined the Liberal Party. In recognition of that act López appointed Gaitán alcalde of Bogotá in June 1936.[60]

As a self-made man of the middle class, it is little wonder that Gaitán placed great store in that class and its potential. He correctly judged it to be the most dynamic class to emerge from the modernization process, and he dedicated his life to instilling its values in rank-and-file Colombians.[61] Gaitán viewed society as an entity made up of individuals possessing varying degrees of potential. Acutely aware of prevailing social prejudices and the many inequities rising from them—his own dark skin earned him the nickname El Negro Gaitán—he strove to extend educational opportunity to the neglected popular classes. If afforded equal educational opportunity, he reasoned, the poor could compete with the rich on a more equal footing. Thus the meritorious among them could, as he himself had, improve their social position.

Gaitán believed that private property offered the individual protection, even as property demonstrated one's progress upward through the social hierarchy. That sort of thinking had led the Communists to brand Gaitán a fascist during his UNIR period, and the young left Liberal Germán Arciniegas to damn UNIR as a right-wing movement dedicated to the cause of small land-ownership rather than to the nobler one of communal ownership.[62] But Gaitán was neither a fascist nor a rightist. He was an unabashed proponent of the middle-class lifestyle, who dressed his upper-class wife in furs, drove late-model autos, and installed his family in a fine home in one of Bogotá's tonier neighborhoods. Nor did Gaitán's followers resent the caudillo for it. They merely hoped someday to emulate his example.

It was a foreign visitor who, through his account of Bogotá in 1937, sug-gested the social contradictions that would fire Jorge Eliécer Gaitán's populist movement of 1944–1948. Negley Farson describes the sense of unreality he felt on reaching the Colombian capital after extensive travel through the hin-terland. He was amazed to find the streets full of "purring limousines," trucks, and taxis, and lined by shops "not much inferior to those of Picadilly or the Boulevard des Capucines." In the midst of the glitter he observed "wry Indi-ans" dodging the traffic, "trotting past shops they never went into . . . bandy dwarfs, with a resentful look."[63] Colombian writer Joaquín Tamayo seconds Farson's vision of urban Colombia between 1930 and 1945 as a place of con-trasts: "Never before did Bogotano society enjoy more luxury, nor were its parties more elegant, nor its autos more numerous and costly, nor did the public enjoy more diversions."[64]

The changes at work in Colombian society were felt by the members of all social classes. Poorer citizens increasingly abandoned customs identifying them as members of the "inferior" Indian underclass, and socially concerned members of the middle class worked to support that transition. As alcalde of Bogotá, Jorge Eliécer Gaitán had toured the city's poorer neighborhoods preaching the virtues of oral hygiene and regular bathing, and explaining their relationship to a decorous and dignified lifestyle. In that way he acted on his belief that proper hygiene was "the backbone of the modern state."[65] He de-clared war on traditional modes of dress, especially the ruana, a garment he considered "a disseminator of disease" in his city. He was likewise an enemy of the alpargata, the indigenous hemp-soled sandal worn throughout rural Co-lombia. Gaitán required the suppression of alpargatas in favor of leather shoes which the city purchased and sold to its employees on installments. His avowed goal to achieve "the total civilization of the people" through moral and physical uplift brought his downfall after only eight months on the job. His decree of January 1937, requiring that Bogotá's taxi drivers substitute uniforms for their alpargatas and ruanas, provoked a transportation strike leading Alfonso López to fire him.

Eventually the urban poor were convinced to abandon their traditional dress in favor of modern attire. Merchants like Simón Guberik rejoiced over what he saw as his success in causing ordinary Bogotanos to change their mode of dress: "Finally the triumph was achieved, and say what you will, it improved popular taste."[66] Technological change made it increasingly easy for the upwardly mobile poor to achieve the modern look. Machine-made Everfit suits began appearing in factory outlets in all Colombian cities. And they could be bought on credit, the granting of which signaled that one had achieved middle-class status.

By the 1940s the notion of consumption as an indicator of personal and national advancement was fixed in the minds of Colombians. Arguments were being mounted to the effect that heightened personal sophistication justified increased personal expenditures. Hence consumption was in itself a social good. As political economist Guillermo Torres García put it in a textbook published in 1942, "the necessity of art in a cultured and wealthy person requires abundant expenditure that for another would constitute excessive consumption, and so on down through society. Thus one cannot absolutely condemn [consumption], as it awakens, attracts, and sustains many activities, and from a certain point of view encourages social development."[67] Torres strengthened his argument by pointing out that the world's leading countries, "the Scandinavian and Saxon nations," happened also to be peopled by the world's foremost consumers.

Upper- and middle-class Colombian consumerism found its most dramatic expression in new residential housing built in Bogotá and other cities during the 1930s and '40s. Disdainful of "old-fashioned houses" whose red tile roofs and ample corridors gave them an air of "monotonous uniformity,"[68] they indulged in "a folkloric outburst of eclecticism" that filled suburban neighborhoods with homes of Tudor, Norman, Mediterranean, and California colonial design, as well as with more fanciful structures featuring the modern Art Deco, Moorish, and Egyptian looks. For historian Silvia Arango, the stylistic explosion signified "a sort of architectonic schizophrenia clearly revealing the transitional character of the time."[69] Seen from another perspective the proliferation of styles symbolized the self-indulgence of consumption-driven, upwardly mobile Colombians. Their new houses reflected the narcissism peculiar to the nouveaux riches. That quality is also suggested in the following passage by social historian Patricia Londoño: "The advertisements for makeups and products for personal hygiene were everywhere. Soaps, dusting powders, unguents, and dentifrices promised every woman 'extraordinary beauty,' 'tender lips,' relief from 'periodic pain.' The model of taste was the U.S. lifestyle."[70]

To the extent that Colombia's well-off urban minority hurried toward cosmopolitan eclecticism, it distanced itself from the old communal patterns of national life. Whereas Colombian neighborhoods traditionally looked inward on rectilinear central plazas dominated by symbols of civic authority—church, courts of law, city hall—new neighborhoods like La Merced possessed neither central plaza nor streets constructed in the traditional grid pattern. Those awakening suddenly on one of its curving, tree-shaded streets, and gazing on its close-set and stately Tudor mansions, might think themselves in a posh London suburb where, curiously, everyone spoke Spanish.

Barrios such as La Merced were not built in accord with the abstract communitarian principle conceived in colonial times by an authoritarian and omnipresent Spanish state. Rather they were the product of a rational plan aimed at affording their residents aesthetic pleasure. Their designers strove for "integral self-containment," for the pleasant look of the English "garden city." Through the random placement of green spaces, the construction of curved and transverse streets, they "sought to flee the image of the past, to change their style of life."[71]

Such architectural turning away from the traditional was but one aspect of the ongoing privatization at work in Colombia from the early twentieth century onward. The principle at work was perfectly illustrated in the design of the new homes. Gone were the lofty and spacious corridors that had united the rooms of colonial homes with central patios. Modern home design accentuated "independent spaces," specialized, functional, and discrete from one another, reached by way of connecting hallways. New houses provided secluded bedrooms and studies to which their owners could withdraw whenever they wished. Gone too were the old free-standing wardrobes. They were replaced by built-in closets affording the space required to house expanded quantities of clothing and an accumulation of consumer goods unknown to Colombian households of earlier times. Garages too were de rigueur. Automobiles were required for homeowners in the new neighborhoods, who demanded a fast and private mode of transport.

During the 1930s and '40s, members of Colombia's artistic community interpreted and fed the iconoclastic spirit of their times. In the field of pictorial art there appeared a group of young painters calling themselves Los Bachués (Bachué was a pre-Columbian goddess), dedicated to the exploration of Colombian themes. Led by Antioquian Pedro Nel Gómez, they created murals, sculpture, and canvases dealing with the nation's indigenous past and with the struggle of rural workers. In that sense they paralleled and emulated the work of their Mexican contemporaries Diego Rivera and David Alfaro Siqueiros.[72]

Colombian plastic art received a great boost in the 1940s thanks to the initiative of then Minister of Education Jorge Eliécer Gaitán, who, in mid-1940, organized the first National Salon of Art. Thanks to the salons, which were held annually thereafter, younger artists like Enrique Grau, Alejandro Obregón, and Fernando Botero were able to win public recognition. Controversy marred the second salon after judges rejected as inappropriate for the exhibition Carlos Correa's painting *The Annunciation,* depicting the Virgin as a voluptuous reclining nude. This led many of Colombia's better-known artists to withdraw their works from the competition. Resubmitted and accepted for the third salon under the title *Nude,* Correa's painting was judged the best of the exhibit. Nevertheless, the award, and the work itself, produced an outcry. Members of the Church judged it a "precocious irreverence," and a work of "insensitive perversity [and] blasphemy." Writing in *El Espectador* of October 14, 1942, Emilia Pardo Umaña remarked, "This painting should not be exhibited. . . . One should not so easily forget that Colombia is a Catholic country. . . . The act of changing the title in no way lessens the malign, vitriolic impact of juxtaposing sacred stained-glass windows and a more than disagreeable nude."[73]

No group was more outspoken in its critique of the old ways than Colombia's poets. As members of the generation of Los Nuevos, they celebrated the new freedom, diversity, and eclecticism perceived in contemporary society. Their reaction against their seniors ran from Rafael Maya's restrained criticism of modernists like Guillermo Valencia for their uncritical acceptance of theories and doctrines "that fought against individual sentiments," to León de Greiff's damning of foreign traditionalists as "harlequinesque figures, prodigies of vacuousness, slaves to a precise model."[74] Others, like Luis Vidales and Porfirio Barba Jacob, directed their iconoclasm at society at large. The former frequently worked in an anticlerical mode, proclaiming his goal to be "the negation of the sacred," while the latter, a bohemian who spent most of his life outside Colombia, described his poems as "diabolical" works in "defiance of traditional morality."[75]

The reaction to such departures from poetic and social convention was predictably strong among the traditional-minded. Conservative Laureano Gómez, writing under the pseudonym Jacinto Ventura, responded to León de Greiff's earthy free verse with a series of humorous articles parodying his poetry and suggesting that anyone could learn to emulate it through correspondence courses. Gómez was less gentle with poet Darío Samper, whom he considered a follower of de Greiff. After panning Samper's *Cuaderno del trópico,* Gómez concluded referring to it as a "detestable pamphlet, bad smelling, repellent," one "that cultured persons will hasten to toss into the garbage." Gómez dismissed Barba Jacob's poetry as "worthless." When word came of the poet's death in Mexico, Gómez damned Barba Jacob's oeuvre as "the cry of a criminal or madman, the appropriate place for its recitation the madhouse or the prison." The entirety of his poetic production, wrote Gómez, "should be thrown onto a manure heap."[76]

During the thirties and forties Colombian society and culture clearly teetered between two worlds, one of tradition and the other of change. While

individuals committed to questioning old ways seized the initiative, many others clung to ingrained attitudes and prejudices. Among the notions to which
they clung were a range of racial and sexual stereotypes, chief among them
ideas concerning women.

Women's issues received unprecedented attention following the change to
Liberal government in 1930. During the regime of Olaya Herrera women were
granted both the right to inherit property and to enter into contractual agreements. Thus the traditional concept of woman as a ward of her father, husband, or closest male relative was suppressed. Under the administration of
Alfonso López, discrimination on the basis of sex was declared illegal, and
laws were passed granting women equal access to professional programs. The
National University received its first female student in 1936, and five years
later, the National School of Mines. Following Alfonso López's belief that the
democratization of education would lead to a weakening of "the spirit of
caste" in Colombia, a number of steps were taken to broaden curricula and to
integrate women into publicly supported education programs. High school
degree programs were broadened to allow specialization in the social sciences,
and the Female Pedagogical Institute was made part of the new coeducational
National Superior Normal School.[77] Private efforts at raising the educational
level of women had been going on for some time. Educator Agustín Nieto
Caballero's Gimnasio Femenino graduated its first class in 1932.[78]

Notwithstanding these early efforts to enhance the position of women in
Colombian society, progress toward that end was painfully slow. Few women
took advantage of the enhanced opportunities. At the end of López's first
administration only fourteen of 127 students in the National University's
school of education were female. And by 1954, thirteen years after women
were admitted to the School of Mines in Medellín, only four had graduated.[79]
The hesitance of women to enter the professions was in large part a function of
the near universal male prejudice against women entering the workforce. Even
so, such an otherwise liberal-minded public figure like Germán Arciniegas had
tried to block the admittance of women to the National University, arguing
that "women are not competent to enter certain occupations and professions
that belong and correspond to men."[80] Following the pause in reform after
1936, progress toward equality for women in secondary education slowed,
and was in some cases turned back. Eduardo Santos's minister of education,
Guillermo Nanneti, implemented a special high school program for women
featuring sewing, home economics, interior design, and moral formation.
During the first year of Santos's presidency the state high school in Tunja
ceased admitting females "because the girls did better than the boys, and that
caused problems." Six years later, in 1944, Minister of Education Antonio
Rocha asserted that "unless we force the campesino back to his plot and
women back to the home the integrity of the nation will be in jeopardy."[81]

Progress was more disappointing in the effort to extend women's rights in areas other than education. When, in 1935, Jorge Eliécer Gaitán requested legislation granting women the right to vote, his colleague Armando Solano responded in an article holding that "the interests of democracy would be gravely menaced should women receive the right to vote," because in Colombia "religious sentiments weigh too heavily on the public and private conduct of women."[82]

Germán Arciniegas, Armando Solano, Antonio Rocha, and Guillermo Nanneti were all Liberals whose social thought reflected that of more forward-thinking Colombian males. Others adopted positions as extreme as that of Antioquia's Monsignor Builes, for whom women's riding astride constituted a mortal sin, and who viewed the custom of women dressing in slacks as evidence of a Masonic plot "to rob women of their modesty."[83]

Certain attitudes concerning sex and sexual preferences remained unaltered during the 1930s and '40s. Prostitution flourished as economic prosperity increased during the thirties and afterward. Antioquian women attending the Third Congress of Public Improvement held in Medellín in 1935 were so shocked by the scandalous commerce that they lobbied for strict regulation of the city's red-light district.[84] Homosexuality remained a social taboo not mentioned in public. When on New Year's Eve, 1938, José Camacho Carreño's brother-in-law Rafael Vásquez called Camacho a queer (*marica*) and beat him in public, the Conservative politician armed himself, went to Vásquez's home and shot him dead. Camacho later penned an eloquent defense of his action, stressing the impropriety of Vásquez's public and repeated use of phrases such as "he is a queer, a bugger," "this son-of-a-bitch queer," and "this disgraceful degenerate."[85] In his statement Camacho never denied Vásquez's charge of homosexuality. A sympathetic judge acquitted Camacho of manslaughter and freed him on the grounds that his brother-in-law had threatened to kill him. Less than a year after his release Camacho Carreño drowned while swimming in the sea near Barranquilla.[86]

Racial prejudice, and the underlying belief that racial mixing created inferiority, was another burden that accelerating social change had not lifted from Colombians. Fifteen years and more after European racist theories were first debated in the country, *El Tiempo* writer Alfonso del Corral fretted that "the race mixing produced when Europeans arrived on this continent kept our people from developing a sound psychological makeup." Del Corral was especially hard on his country's nonmestizo population: "Undoubtedly our anthropological and ethnic heritage leaves much to be desired. Still that does not mean we must cease fighting against these ethnic elements. . . . When we observe Indian communities we see that the people there live the almost exclusively vegetative existence characteristic of persons possessing psychologically inferior attitudes. They are almost completely instinctual, showing few signs of having evolved."[87] The persistence of such thinking prompted the founding in 1942 of the Instituto Indigenista, whose chief purpose was to combat the racial decay theory.[88]

Official Colombia reflected the anti-Indian bias of greater society when it renewed the assault on communally held Indian *resguardo* (reservation) lands during the Santos administration. Throughout the nineteenth century it had been an article of liberal faith that turning resguardos into individual land holdings would transform indigenous peoples into socially productive yeoman farmers. In July 1940, Congress signed Acuerdo 1421, a measure designed to speed the breakup of Colombia's remaining resguardos. While Minister of Agriculture Miguel López Pumarejo assured his colleagues that the agreement would "stimulate indigenous workers," its real effect was to speed the transfer of resguardo lands into the hands of non-Indians. By early 1943, the intrepid Indian leader Manuel Quintín Lame complained that he and his people "were being ruined without their lands . . . because [the resguardos] are being auctioned off by the municipal treasurer of Ortega [Tolima]."[89]

Yet another prejudice that stubbornly resisted modification was anti-Semitism. When Hitler's persecutions sent Jews fleeing Germany, Colombia was reluctant to accept them. This was in part the fault of Foreign Minister Luis López de Mesa, who, when consular officials cabled from Berlin asking that Colombia accept an increased flow of refugees, responded that the "five thousand Jews presently established in Colombia constitutes a figure impossible to augment." At that time Colombia's Jewish population stood at 0.05 percent. In official dispatches López de Mesa referred to the asylum seekers as "Jewish elements," the majority of whom were "presumed merchants of doubtful morality," harboring "a parasitic orientation toward life." In 1941, when a Jewish industrialist from the United States offered to build a tinfoil factory in Colombia, López de Mesa responded that "Colombia would be enchanted to receive [the investment] but not the Jewish businessman."[90]

Colombian social change was played out against a backdrop of global war that also shaped the Andean nation between 1939 and 1945. Colombia sided with the Allies during World War II, breaking diplomatic relations first with Japan after that nation attacked the United States in late 1941, and then with Germany after the sinking of the Colombian schooner *Resolute* in June 1942.

Most Colombians endorsed their country's support of the United States and its European allies. A common republican tradition and a shared dislike and fear of the German dictatorship gave Colombia and the United States ample ground for cooperation and collaboration. Cultural and commercial links with France, Belgium, Great Britain, and the other nations suffering Nazi aggression further strengthened Colombia's commitment to the Allied cause. While it is true that Colombia could hardly have done other than support the

Allies, given the dominance of the United States in hemispheric affairs, it is also true that economic considerations alone would have demanded the pro-Allied stance. Axis markets were closed to Colombia after 1939. The United States was not only anxious and able to purchase virtually any raw materials Colombia could produce, but was also willing to supply badly needed economic and technical aid. There was, finally, the fundamental affinity between Colombia and the capitalist democracies at war with Germany and her allies. When the war began, Colombia, the United States, and the nations of western Europe stood united both at the level of economic self-interest and that of their shared faith in liberal free-market capitalism.

Only the more extreme Conservative factions were unhappy with their country's support of the American-led war effort. Those included the traditional-minded Historical wing of the party, whose principal spokesman was Laureano Gómez, and the few belonging to the National Action faction located even further to the right and associated with Gilberto Alzate Avendaño. Their opposition might not have troubled Colombia's Liberal government or its wartime allies but for the fact that chief formulator of the anti-American and neutralist position, Gómez, was also titular head of the party to which nearly half of all Colombians claimed allegiance. It is also significant that Gómez's opposition went beyond simple anti-Americanism and constituted criticism of modern Western civilization as a whole. The passion and skill with which Gómez presented his dissenting vision of social change had the dual effect of inspiring Conservatives and disconcerting Liberals. By the early 1940s, when internal dissension rent the government party, Gómez's message of universal cultural decay owing to pernicious liberalism deepened national demoralization.

Gómez's blasts against Western liberalism were rooted in the doctrine of philosophic conservatism, deriving specific intellectual content from the encyclicals of Pius IX and Leo XIII and from the ideology imparted to him by the Jesuit faculty of San Bartolomé. His earliest public statements reflected an ongoing attempt to explain national and global problems in terms of liberal-inspired subversion of the orderly, hierarchical society depicted in Roman Catholic social philosophy. Gómez's belief in the beneficence of traditional social norms deepened between 1928 and 1932, when he observed firsthand the threat that fascist and communist dictatorships posed to a Europe fatally weakened by two centuries of liberal error. Soon after his return from Europe, Laureano Gómez delivered a series of doctrinal messages in which he explained the Roman Catholic underpinnings of Conservative belief, and vigorously denounced the competing fascist and communist philosophies. In 1938 he began an elaboration of what Colombian Conservatism was not, in a series of speeches whose general theme was that modern society was poisoning the human spirit. Thus he anticipated by a full year Pius XII's encyclical *Summi pontificatus,* in which the pontiff decried the "spiritual emptiness" of the age and lamented that society's "denial and rejection of a universal norm of human morality" had led humankind to the brink of a terrifying abyss.[91]

The critique of Liberalism that Laureano Gómez developed between 1938 and 1942 began with an indictment of the Enlightenment rationalism that had undermined the Western world's belief in divine law. This erosion of faith had produced a confusion in moral standards that made possible the French Revolution and its excesses, a "nightmare for humanity" during which a "diabolical and persistent persecution was carried out aimed at undermining the Catholic and spiritual bases of humanity, forcing mankind toward atheism, Jacobinism, and the cult of the Goddess Reason."[92]

Modern liberalism was, in Gómez's view, the bastard child of French revolutionary anticlericalism, the liberal himself a relativist when not an outright skeptic, and an inveterate persecutor of the Church. As law and justice had their fundamental expression in divine law, the liberal's anticlericalism rendered him an enemy of civilization, in short, a barbarian.[93]

Because Laureano Gómez perceived philosophic liberals as relativists lacking in sound judgment, he believed them to be easy dupes of persons wishing harm to the fatherland. By 1938 he had come to see that the secularism making rapid strides in Colombia obeyed the master plan of subversives anxious to disorient Catholics and lure them away from their Christian traditions. Writing in *El Siglo* of January 19, 1938, he identified Jews, Masons, and Communists as the three chief groups dedicated to bringing Colombia low. Referring to them variously as "the fatal trinity," and "the sinister tripod," he informed readers that Jews, Masons, and Communists were "sustaining the revolutionary activity destined to spread the mantle of desolation and death over the nation." He made specific reference to the government's modernization of curriculum at the public high school in Tunja, which de-emphasized religious instruction and required that the school accept female students. He saw such changes as a "crime against religion" aimed at stripping children of their religion at an early age, thus embittering their spirits. Such a child would inevitably mature into "the man who raises the clenched fist, the cold and cruel incendiary, the cold-blooded murderer, a machine for destroying and killing." He attributed those changes in part to the influence of Jewish refugees recently hired by the Ministry of Education, a "monstrous act, a great treason against the national spirit," for which the name of Alfonso López would be forever execrated.

By 1942, Laureano Gómez had developed a hierarchy of the three evil forces drawing Western peoples away from their Christian beliefs. During a Senate speech of that year he pointed to the "universal phenomenon" of Judaism as having evolved the philosophy of communism, through which it proposed to advance its program of conquest, with the help of the "shadowy social phenomenon" known as Masonry. Jews, he said, were enemies of Christianity and hence dangerous undesirables forever conspiring against the peoples among whom they lived. That is why nations having Jewish populations faced two stark options: "either turn the country over to the Jews, or expel the Jews."[94]

Gómez did not employ conspiracy theory to explain Europe's slide into war. Rather he attributed that debacle to modern man's abandoning moral law in favor of "positive law" based in Kantian rationalism and moral relativism. As early as 1934, in his scathing denunciation of Adolf Hitler's political tactics, Gómez had argued that those excesses were explained by the fact that nineteenth-century Germans had adopted Kantian "scientism," which formed the basis of empirical positive law. Thus they fell away from the Roman law tradition common to Latin and Catholic nations. It was thus liberal, relativistic positive law that made Hitler's excesses juridically possible. Eight years later Gómez was still arguing that point. Writing in *El Siglo* of June 21, 1942, Gómez held that the war was but one consequence of "the fundamental opposition between the Catholic notion of morality and the positivist one." The war, for Gómez, simply stood at the end of a long process beginning in the seventeenth century, when Cartesian rationalism encouraged Westerners to deny natural law. That in turn unleashed a "savage naturalism" upon the earth among whose consequences were the French Revolution and subsequent European wars.

When France fell to Hitler's armies in mid-1940, Gómez held up the event as proof that the liberal Third Republic, shot through with Masonic influence and corruption, persecutor of the Catholic Church for fifty years and more— a "regime of blood and pus"—had been fatally weakened by anti-Christian subversion. He pointed that out in three near exultant *El Siglo* editorials of June 11, 14, and 18, 1940, the last of which was titled "La troisième ha muerto!"

Franco's Spain was for Gómez the great success story of wartime Europe. Spain was the single European nation whose people had been able to halt the process of decay under the Republicans, and, through a terrible civil war, preserved its Roman Catholic underpinnings. General Francisco Franco, leader of the Spanish Nationalists, was for Gómez the "solitary paladin in the battle for Christian culture," a man who had done battle with and defeated the National Front regime that earlier had "bloodied and dishonored Spain." Under the liberal regime that had, in 1933, overthrown the Spanish monarchy, the country had become a "spiritually arid place" where "the people's will [had been] rendered impotent, and their bodies bent beneath the yoke of barbarism." She had been "dominated by a communist revolution, dominated more completely than she had been by the Moors." Gómez made these remarks in a speech that ended as follows: "Praised be God, who allows us to witness this unexpected moment of national transformation! Praised be the events that day by day cause to well from deep inside us the fervent salute: Up with Catholic, imperial Spain!"[95]

The cultural vision that Laureano Gómez presented to his followers was a highly ideological one aimed at convincing them that there was one proper sort of society for Colombia, the harmonious one described in Roman Catholic social philosophy. In such a society the good citizen always placed spiritual concerns above physical ones, directing his actions so as to place the common good over narrow personal considerations. No wonder Laureano Gómez was upset by the yeasty change besetting Colombia during the late thirties and early forties. He could not help but view that process as one orchestrated by non-Catholic enemy cultures that wished his country ill.

Gómez's belief that materialism and spirituality were locked in mortal conflict throughout the world inevitably led him to oppose Colombia's growing economic and diplomatic contact with the United States. For years he had been more strident than those of his country's political left in denouncing the U.S. territorial, commercial, and cultural imperialism that allowed Yankee capitalists to enrich themselves at the expense of Latin America. When, in mid-1940, Foreign Minister López de Mesa asked the Senate to approve a declaration of hemispheric solidarity, Gómez argued against it on grounds that Anglo and Latin America were culturally distinct regions having nothing in common beyond geographic proximity. He further argued that far from constituting "sister republics" and "good neighbors," the relationship between the two regions was a predatory one in which a Moloch-like United States historically revealed an insatiable appetite for Latin American lands from Mexico to Panama and beyond. He asked his colleagues to resist being "influenced by the bad faith and tendentious propaganda of enemy cultures."[96]

As was typical of him, Gómez turned his defense of Colombia into an attack on the predatory Americans, at the same time broadening his argument to embrace the entire Western world. The United States, he said, was a typical "mechanical civilization," forced to colonize weaker peoples in order that its own sons might live in the typical "supercivilized" fashion afforded by modern science. But as that style of life was costly, it was necessary that "a great proportion of humanity . . . be required to live in inferior conditions in order to help pay the cost of those who have achieved it."[97] This was why a minority of the world's peoples, Colombians included, had been reduced to the status of servants by selfish imperialist powers. On the basis of that argument Gómez was able to conclude that "mechanical civilization has failed; it has filled the conscience of man with dreams of a style of life that Mother Earth is incapable of providing."[98]

In the final analysis the argument that Laureano Gómez mounted was antimaterial and metaphysical. Speaking to the party faithful in 1938, he said that the materialist drama was reaching its fatal denouement, having produced "an incomplete human being, a mutilated one . . . [who] has no way of resisting the temptations of the demon." Confronted by the dilemma of having to earn his freedom through suffering or to achieve pleasure at the expense of liberty, modern human beings would inevitably choose the latter. Thus they entrusted to Satan the patrimony received from Christ. That, concluded Gómez, "is the tragedy of modern man."[99]

By the early 1940s, Laureano Gómez had succeeded in painting a frightening picture of a country whose spiritual underpinnings had been eaten away by the disassociative forces of modern life. While his specific analysis of Colombia's ills may not have convinced other than doctrinaire Conservatives like himself, it did nothing to lessen the growing sense of malaise besetting Colombia's public world as the 1940s progressed.

To Make the Republic Unlivable

Not long after the Conservative Party directorate proclaimed its abstention from electoral politics in late 1933, Laureano Gómez put forth the Gandhian principle of civil resistance to state power that would henceforth guide his actions and those of his followers: "Our duty is to make the atmosphere of the Republic almost unlivable," he wrote in an *El País* article of early 1944.[100] Gómez was as good as his word. Over the period of Alfonso López's first presidency the Conservative Party leader steadily increased the stridency of his attacks on the López regime and all things Liberal, until it became clear that he would employ any tactic short of outright violence to hinder López's "Revolution on the March" and further his own party's return to power. "I was born to throw stones," said Gómez, and throw verbal and written stones he did, unmercifully pelting Alfonso López and his successor, Eduardo Santos, between 1935 and 1942. When López won reelection in 1942, Gómez redoubled his assault, in the process making the political nation truly unlivable for López and many other Colombians. At length Gómez's unrelenting obstructionist campaign took its toll, driving López to resign his presidency in July 1945, a full year before his term expired. "I don't think I have sufficient energy to put [new legislation] into effect," López said a month before stepping down, adding, "and even if I did I wouldn't have the will power to put the new laws into effect."[101] Alfonso López left behind a divided and dispirited party.

Laureano Gómez was brilliantly successful in his decade-long campaign of political opposition, though he and Colombia ultimately paid a high price for that success. Gómez earned the hatred of most Liberals. Furthermore, he taught them by example how relatively easy it is to render a complex civil society unlivable. Less than a year after López's resignation Colombia's Liberals would make use of the same divisive strategies they had learned from Laureano Gómez.

After Eduardo Santos assumed office on August 7, 1938, Colombians had reason to think that a return to political normality might be at hand. Conservative leader Gómez, long under pressure from party moderates to drop the policy of political abstention, finally did so. Eduardo Santos had given repeated assurances that should the Conservatives return to active political participation, he would extend them every protection over the months preceding the mid-term congressional elections set for March 1939. Accordingly, Laureano Gómez ended abstention shortly after Santos's inauguration. Shortly thereafter, while campaigning in northeastern Colombia, he paused to telegraph the president: "We have enjoyed all the guarantees promised by your illustrious government while traveling through the Santanders."[102] Tragically that harmonious climate did not last. No Colombian president was able to control the excesses of his copartisans everywhere in the nation, as became clear eight weeks before the election in the mountain village of Gachetá, Cundinamarca. On January 8, 1939, Conservative Party leaders held a political rally there, not knowing that local Liberals had conspired with municipal police, also Liberals, to violently disrupt the event. When the rally began Liberal militants began harassing and beating the Conservatives who stood in the crowd, all of whom had previously been searched and disarmed. When the victims fought back, police opened fire, killing nine outright and wounding numerous others.

The Gachetá massacre produced an angry confrontation between Eduardo Santos and Laureano Gómez, the latter charging the former with betrayal of his pledge to protect Conservatives. Santos expressed his own shock over the incident, promising to investigate it fully and to punish those responsible. But his actions left Gómez and top Conservative leaders of Cundinamarca, several of whom had witnessed the killings, determined to exact revenge for the cowardly attack. In their party convention of January 21, 1939, they pledged themselves to a policy of armed self-defense which Eduardo Santos promptly labeled Intrepid Action. Laureano Gómez heartily endorsed the policy, which he himself termed the Right to Self-Defense of Collectivities. The character of the new policy, and the anger producing it, can be gauged by an *El Siglo* editorial signed by Gómez and published February 14, 1939. Alluding to the legal principle of self-defense, he posited that political collectivities have the same right to defend themselves as do individuals. He termed the parties "transcendental associations," for which generations of Colombians had gladly sacrificed their lives. That being the case party members had a legitimate right to kill persons who threatened their party, for in doing so they were "defending something that [they] value more than life itself."

Next Gómez developed a theory of prophylactic killing that deeply shocked many Colombians. "Experience tells us who the criminals are in each region who massacre our fellow party members," he wrote, adding, "upon these criminals it is necessary to exercise the right of self-defense in a preemptive manner so as to frustrate their plans." Persons who supply them with firearms, he continued "also may be eliminated, if there is no other way of impeding their criminal endeavor." Laureano Gómez concluded his editorial by stating the guidelines which Conservatives were to follow before applying their definitive solution to the problem of Liberal violence: "We must not strike preventive blows against such persons unless we are absolutely sure they are plotting violence. For the violent defense of the collectivity to be licit the following conditions must be met: (1) Public authorities do not wish to, or cannot defend it effectively; (2) There must be solid probability of effective results. . . . ; (3) One must be able to locate with certainty, subject to the approval of directors of the collectivity, the individuals who plot aggression against it in order that defense be exercised upon them."

The implications of the Right of Self-Defense of Collectivities doctrine frightened Colombians. It was certainly not popular with other Conservative Party leaders, who refused to endorse the concept when they met in their national convention during early February 1939. A substantial bloc of them, led by Antioquian Pedro J. Berrío and anti-Gómez dissident Augusto Ramírez Moreno, walked out of the convention in protest. Laureano Gómez must have known that he stood no chance of convincing his colleagues from departments other than Cundinamarca to espouse violent self-defense against Liberals, for he left the country on vacation to Panama and Ecuador in the midst of the meeting. The party platform that emerged from the convention also reflected rejection of Gómez's extreme position. It contained no mention of the policy adopted by Cundinamarca Conservatives and limited itself to deploring Liberal violence, which would, if not ended, produce "catastrophic consequences" for national peace and prosperity.[103]

The March 19, 1939, elections were held in an atmosphere of calm, with the Liberals winning 77 seats in the Chamber of Representatives to the Conservatives' 40, and 142 seats in departmental assemblies to the Conservatives' 94. Many Conservatives believed their showing to be satisfactory, given the fact that they had not voted in any national contest for six years. Clearly Liberal and Conservative moderates had prevailed over their more militant fellows. At least that was the conclusion drawn by Ramírez Moreno, who, while his dissident slate did not win a single Cámara or assembly seat, could write on March 20, "I won the election in that I made Conservatism return to peaceful coexistence [with Liberalism]."[104] Another implication of the March 19 election was that Laureano Gómez would return to the Senate. Senators continued to be elected by departmental assemblies, and the Conservatives' strong showing in departmental contests meant that they would be well represented in the upper chamber through the remainder of Eduardo Santos's presidential term.

Liberals were no less divided than Conservatives when Eduardo Santos took up his presidential duties in 1938. Santos had entered politics at the height of the Republican Union movement (1909–1914), going on to defend Republican bipartisanship in his newspaper *El Tiempo*, which he turned into the nation's most influential journal. Santos's old Republicanism reasserted itself when Olaya constituted his bipartisan government of National Concentration, and the newspaperman went on to serve as the new president's foreign minister. Four years later, when Alfonso López launched his presidential campaign, promising to conduct a "revolutionary" government, Santos found himself in the position of being, after Olaya Herrera, the chief counterweight to López's brand of militant, reform Liberalism. With Olaya's death in 1937, Eduardo Santos inherited the mantle of moderate Liberal leadership. It bore him into the presidency a year later on a platform aimed at placating Liberal centrists.

Thus in 1938 the Liberal Party was divided between Santista moderates drawing heavily from the nation's business classes, and the Lopistas, representing left Liberals, along with a great many rank-and-file party members. The Lopistas made clear their opposition to Santos and his go-slow policies by launching their own newspaper, *El Liberal,* the first day of the new administration. Its editor, Alberto Lleras Camargo, soon emerged as López's heir apparent.

Eduardo Santos demonstrated his willingness to combat the Lopistas by filling his government with anti-Lopistas spanning the political spectrum from the change maker Jorge Eliécer Gaitán, who had never forgiven López for the preemptory way the president had dismissed him as alcalde of Bogotá in 1937, to right-wing Liberal Miguel López Pumarejo, the former president's younger brother. Another exceedingly conservative Liberal briefly included in Santos's government, one of Alfonso López's harshest critics during his first term, was Juan Lozano y Lozano.

During the first year of Eduardo Santos's presidency there emerged a third Liberal faction expressly dedicated to blocking Alfonso López's return to the presidency. It organized an anti-reelection committee in mid-1940 and set about exploring the possibility of promoting an anti-Lopista Liberal candidacy in 1942. Politicians mentioned prominently in that regard were Gabriel

Turbay, Carlos Lozano, and Carlos Arango Vélez. Chief among the concerns of the "anti-reelectionists," as they were called, was whether they could count on Conservative support in blocking a return to the presidency of Alfonso López. And within that question loomed a yet greater one whose answer, if negative, doomed their endeavor. Could their fellow party members muster sufficient enthusiasm to vote for a candidate who was also supported by Laureano Gómez?

It was the same old Gómez, enemy of all things Liberal, who returned to Congress in mid-1939. The Conservative leader threw himself into partisan debate with an élan belying his fifty years, verbally lashing the Santos regime for a range of sins and errors described as only Laureano Gómez knew how. Following adjournment of the congressional session, as the Liberal Party made plans to celebrate the centenary of the death of Francisco de Paula Santander, whom they revered as founder of their party, Gómez began publishing a series of essays holding that Santander was a malevolent figure, not the godlike one of Liberal myth. While the true Santander lay somewhere between either extreme, Eduardo Santos and his fellow party members were sorely vexed by the Conservative leader's gratuitous attack on their hero. In succeeding years more than one Liberal opined that his party could bring itself to forgive Laureano Gómez everything save his unprovoked assault on the reputation of Santander.[105]

Passions had not cooled following the polemic over Santander when the 1940 congressional term began. During the first week of debate Laureano Gómez criticized government activities ranging from its distribution of benefits for veterans of the war with Peru, to its use of additional powers granted the president for dealing with international affairs related to World War II and its forcing the Jesuits from a government-owned building used to house the Colegio San Bartolomé. It was not those issues, however, but rather one that came up in a private conversation between Gómez and three Liberals that became the cause célèbre of the 1940 congressional term.

On September 19, Gómez was chatting in a Senate hallway with Alfonso Romero Aguirre, Alvaro Díaz, and Roberto Durán Durán, members of the newly formed committee working to thwart the reelection of Alfonso López. In the course of their conversation Gómez was heard to say that a López reelection would produce renewed Liberal attacks on Conservatives, which in turn would lead to "civil war and personal attacks." The furor that his words produced forced Laureano Gómez into a rare defensive posture. Later that day when Liberals accused him of threatening civil war and criminal assaults, Gómez attempted to downplay the remark. He said that he had been misunderstood, that the Liberals were wrong in equating "personal assault" with murder and assassination, "because its true technical name is 'self defense,' or 'collective defense,' according to the case." He went on to point out that while he did not advocate violence, he and his followers would fight if made to do so. For good measure he added, "and if we are forced to resort to violence, let us carry it out against the higher-ups, not against the followers." That was a clear reference to Alfonso López. Two days earlier, during debate on September 17, Gómez had cited the writings of Spanish theologians Domingo de Soto (1494–1570), Juan de Mariana (1536–1624), and Francisco Suárez (1548–1617), in justifying the killing of any head of state who permitted violence to exist in his realm: "one whose underlings disregard his orders is a tyrant."[106]

A month before the "personal attack" imbroglio Laureano Gómez delivered his celebrated "Conflict of Two Cultures" speech, in which he compared Anglo-American culture unfavorably with that of Latin America, going on to remind his listeners that the United States had bullied its weaker Hispanic sister republics over the preceding hundred years. He had raised that subject in order to castigate Santos for what in Gómez's view was his kowtowing to U.S. demands at a recent meeting of Western Hemisphere foreign ministers in Havana. There Colombian Foreign Minister Luis López de Mesa had pledged his nation to cooperate with the United States in the event of aggression from any power outside the Americas.[107] Gómez's speech, his threat to launch a civil war should Alfonso López be reelected, and his long history of anti-Americanism earned him the enmity and mistrust of the United States government.

Laureano Gómez's dislike of the Americans was founded in the fury he had felt when, as a lad, he witnessed that nation assist in the separation of Panama. By the time of World War II, when the United States moved to shore up hemispheric defenses, Gómez became Colombia's leading proponent of strict neutrality and a critic of the growing ties with the United States. When in late 1938 Colombia had agreed to accept a U.S. military mission whose goal was to protect the Panama Canal from Axis attacks, Gómez claimed that the Americans opposed fascist dictatorships only when their own interests were at stake. Otherwise they happily supported tyrants like Venezuela's Juan Vicente Gómez as long as such persons were sufficiently pro-U.S.[108] A year later, in December 1939, shortly after Colombia had endorsed a U.S.-sponsored proposal declaring a 300-mile "neutrality zone" around the Panama Canal, Gómez ridiculed the notion. Why, he asked, should his country endorse the U.S. defense of territory the Americans had originally stolen from Colombia.[109]

Prior to the "Conflict of Two Cultures" speech Gómez had lashed Santos for his pro-American stance in El Siglo editorials bearing titles such as "In the Wolf's Gullet," and "Foreign Orders."[110] Through late 1940 and on into early 1941, Gómez and his colleague José de la Vega persisted in their verbal warfare. When in October Gómez learned that Colombia had accepted financial aid in exchange for granting landing rights to U.S. military aircraft, he accused his country's government of prostituting itself. In January 1941 he referred to the United States as a "tearful wolf" bent on deceiving Latin American leaders with "Jewish-inspired propaganda" so that it could continue exploiting the region to the benefit of its greedy "machine culture."[111] Meanwhile José de la Vega published his criticism of Colombo-U.S. foreign policy in *El buen vecino* (The good neighbor).[112]

The United States did not look kindly upon the hostility of Gómez and his followers, especially at a time when many Americans feared that Nazi aggression was imminent in Latin America. Over the course of 1940 the U.S. ambassador to Colombia, Spruille Braden, concluded that the Conservative leader's anti-Americanism was founded in a pro-Nazi attitude. Gómez's statement that his party was prepared to declare civil war should Alfonso López regain the presidency moved Braden to warn U.S. Secretary of State Sumner Wells, "There is good reason to believe [Gómez] has an understanding with the Nazis for them to back him in a possible coup d'état."[113] Colombian Liberals like José Umaña Bernal happily fed the Americans' suspicions and fears. In late 1940, Bernal told U.S. Third Secretary Vernon Fluharty that he was "absolutely certain there will be a Conservative-Nazi attempt to seize power."[114] By year's end U.S. officials were referring to *El Siglo* as "the other Fifth Column" in Colombia, warning their superiors back home that it must be quickly brought to heel.

Suddenly, on March 23, 1941, *El Siglo* readers noted a striking change in the editorial position of their newspaper. Figuring prominently on page one was an article praising a speech on hemispheric solidarity made the previous day by Ambassador Braden. The following day the ambassador received an invitation to dine with Laureano Gómez, his wife, and friends at the Gómez home. One day later Braden arrived for a meeting at the home of diplomat Francisco Urrutia only to discover a smiling Laureano Gómez and José de la Vega awaiting him there.[115] Meanwhile, Gómez had telephoned the editor of stridently anti-U.S. *La Patria* of Manizales, asking him to soften his rhetoric. Laureano Gómez did the same. While he did not abandon his critical attitude toward U.S. interference in Colombian affairs, he turned from attacking to praising the Americans. In Senate debate on September 12, 1941, he said "we are friends of the United States . . . we are absolutely committed to the proposition that in our territory there will never be a conspiracy against their interests."[116] A month later, in an *El Siglo* article taking the U.S. to task for its blacklisting of Colombian companies and disputing Ambassador Braden's insistence that there was a Nazi presence in Colombia, he wrote, "We have said that we are friends of the United States and we stand by that: the capital, power, and talent of the Americans are necessary for our progress. They are welcome here, and we receive them with open arms. But this capital must respect Colombian sovereignty and Colombian laws. It must seek cordiality, not hostility or unjust advantage."[117]

The source of Spruille Braden's success in silencing *El Siglo*'s attacks on his government lay in U.S. economic might and its willingness to wield it to further national goals. In late March 1941, *El Siglo* was on the verge of closing thanks to the loss of advertising from U.S. firms and, still more serious, the cutting off of U.S.-produced newsprint. Faced with the prospect of losing his most powerful political weapon against Colombian Liberalism, Gómez humbled himself before the symbol of U.S. authority, Ambassador Spruille Braden. Once he did so, subsequently making good on his promise to cease his attacks on the United States, *El Siglo*'s paper supply was restored and the advertisements for American cigarettes, beauty aids, and household appliances reappeared in its pages. Spruille Braden's memo to the U.S. Department of State the day after his meeting with Gómez and de la Vega at the home of Francisco Urrutia recommended *El Siglo*'s removal from the American blacklist. Three days later, on March 29, 1941, U.S. embassy Secretary Gerald Keith wrote to Sumner Wells, "I think it would be well for American manufacturers again to advertise in [*El Siglo* and *La Patria*], always providing that they continue their friendly attitude towards us."[118]

The case of Laureano Gómez and his followers, who were tarred as pro-Nazi and forced to support U.S. policy through economic pressure, was a typical example of the overwhelming presence of the United States in Colombian affairs during the war years. Luckily for Colombia its friendliness toward the allied cause saved it from the Americans' wrath. Only at the level of domestic politics did Colombo-American wartime collaboration, and economic consequences thereof, produce certain baleful effects. Toward the end of World War II it became clear that U.S. interference in Colombia's internal affairs bore some responsibility for scandals contributing to the Liberal fall from power in 1946.

One of Ambassador Spruille Braden's first actions on taking up his post in Colombia in 1939 was to ask the nation's cooperation against German business interests deemed dangerous to hemispheric defense. Some of the businesses in question, such as the German-operated airline SCADTA, were genuinely important. Others, like the Trilladora Tolima (Tolima threshing mill), owned by a Nazi military officer, were innocuous. Nevertheless, all of them were blacklisted or otherwise placed under Colombian control, ultimately passing into the hands of Colombian nationals. Should any action of a resident alien be deemed unfriendly to the United States his name and that of his firm soon appeared on the embassy blacklist and that usually signified financial ruin. Colombian nationals weren't immune to blacklisting, as the case of *El Siglo* demonstrated. Because Braden had paid informants scattered throughout the country, no anti-American or enemy of the war effort could be sure when an inadvertent action might bring him low.[119] For example, one such informant wrote that drunken Colombian youths in Barranquilla had destroyed a photograph of Franklin D. Roosevelt, shouting as they did so, "To hell with the democracies! Viva Hitler!" That landed their family's company on the blacklist for the duration of the war.[120]

The American-inspired pressure on firms owned or controlled by Nazi Germany, coupled with the extraordinary economic measures brought through Colombia's close collaboration with the Americans, placed tempting business opportunities before members of the nation's economic elite. That created an exciting though not altogether healthy business environment. Socialist Antonio García remembered it as a time of crisis and uncertainty, of "the anarchic growth of capitalism": "The war produced a . . . proliferation of state-run agencies [that] had the effect of diminishing the state's political effectiveness. . . . Meanwhile those agencies heightened the influence of members of the upper class who were charged with directing them."[121] García describes the unchecked profiteering of "amoral economic upstarts" who gleefully took advantage of "a privileged system of self-enrichment." The acquisition of a government-authorized import license, or permission to engage in currency exchange, wrote García, enriched people more quickly than at any other time in Colombian history.[122] Alfonso López Michelsen, himself a young lawyer caught up in the frenzy, soon to be a chief figure in the scandals that brought down his father, captured the spirit of those days in his novel *Los elegidos* (The chosen), written seven years after the war's end. The younger López wrote of the class he knew best, which he described as "completely divorced from the rest of the nation in education and aspirations," living in exclusive Bogotá neighborhoods "where the only thing that mattered was money."[123] *Los elegidos* is as much an indictment of heavy-handed U.S. interference in Colombian affairs as of the monied class. The novel's protagonist, a German businessman forced to flee his country, eventually runs afoul of the infamous blacklist, is reduced to poverty, and ultimately is imprisoned in a concentration camp near Bogotá built to house German nationals suspected of being Nazi sympathizers.

Novels like López Michelsen's, and academic studies like that of Antonio García, depict a nation driven to excess both by the impersonal forces feeding a turbulent wartime economy and by the demands of its powerful ally. By the end of the war Ambassador Braden and his successor, Arthur Bliss Lane, had forced the Colombian government to violate the rights of resident Germans in a variety of ways, ranging from the preemptory firing of SCADTA employees, to the seizure and forced liquidation of German-owned property, to the physical incarceration of Germans in the concentration camp described by López

Michelsen. They had promoted police surveillance of resident foreign nationals and Colombians with the effect that, by Spruille Braden's own admission, the Colombian government had dramatically improved its ability to monitor the actions of its own citizens. This war-induced social tumult, enlivened by the paranoid atmosphere fed by rumors of Nazi-inspired coup attempts, weighed heavily on Colombian domestic life as the decade of the 1940s progressed.

Alfonso López won easily in the 1942 presidential election. He was opposed in the election by Liberal Carlos Arango Vélez, candidate of anti-reelection Liberals, who was endorsed by Laureano Gómez and Conservatives in February 1942. López's victory confirmed opposition fears that Liberals would refuse to vote for a candidate supported by the Conservatives. By election eve many citizens, President Santos among them, were sure that election day would be marred by violence. Luckily those fears were unfounded. One of the few casualties was Conservative militant Silvio Villegas, who was stabbed in a buttock as he departed the voting booth. Painful though the wound was, it provided Colombians one moment of humor during an otherwise tension-filled day. Not knowing the nature of his injury two of Villegas's admirers sent him a telegram that read, "For all of us your wound will shine like a decoration."[124]

Alfonso López's reelection to the presidency did not negate the fact that he confronted a constellation of forces determined to frustrate any resurgence of his reform program. First there was the emergent business community, wedded to laissez-faire economic principles and dedicated to blocking any return to the interventionist policies of López's first administration. Made up of moderate and right-wing Liberals, and bolstered by Conservatives from the moderate wing of their party, that group gained political coherence and power during López's second administration through their newly organized interest groups ANDI and FENALCO. Two other powerful groups arrayed against López were the ideological Conservatives led by Laureano Gómez and the Colombian army.

The army and the Liberal Party had not been on good terms since 1930, when the Liberals came to power determined to counter Conservative influence in the military. Alfonso López had been especially insistent that he possess an armed force of whose loyalty he was assured. His naming of militant Liberal Plinio Mendoza Neira as minister of war in mid-1936 so intimidated the military that a faction headed by retired General Amadeo Rodríguez considered the possibility of launching a coup.[125] Nothing ever came of it, and tensions between the army and the López government lessened following the decline of the president's reform activity subsequent to 1936. Military-government relations were amicable through the Santos administration, and only with López's return to the presidency did the old antagonisms flare again.[126]

López took up his presidential duties resolved to deal sternly with the army and the Laureanista Conservatives, for he believed the two groups were plotting to overthrow him. One of his first actions upon reentering office was to restate his belief that the army was a parasitic body that would better serve national interests by supervising colonization in frontier regions.[127] Soon thereafter he challenged the military by hinting that he intended to reduce it in order to finance a reorganization of the police.

Early in his second administration Alfonso López also challenged the Conservatives by reviving the church-state issue. As soon as Congress reconvened in 1942, Minister of Government Darío Echandía, recently Colombia's ambassador to the Vatican, presented his government's plan for revision of the Concordat of 1887. The new document permitted an expansion of state power in areas traditionally controlled by the Church.[128]

By introducing religion as a subject of debate, the government insured that the 1942 term would be an especially exciting one. Laureano Gómez led the pro-clerical faction in defending the 1887 document, defying all who wished to reform it, up to and including Pope Pius XII himself.[129] Minister of Government Darío Echandía, who not long before had successfully negotiated with the Vatican revision of the concordat, served as the government's chief spokesman. Debate on the government initiative began in the press in mid-1942 and continued in Congress during October and November of that year, ultimately becoming so heated that it pushed war news to the interior pages of Colombia's newspapers. Laureano Gómez railed that the document's revision was a Masonic plot aimed at eroding national morality, thus speeding the inroads of godless rationalism and "mechanical civilization." On the Liberal side, Alfonso Romero Aguirre defended Masonry as not at all subversive, while Echandía insisted both that he had not been a practicing Mason for years and that Masonry had nothing to do with the concordat's revision in any event.

Ultimately the new document passed in both houses of the Liberal-dominated Congress. Laureano Gómez ended his portion of the debate denouncing Colombia's political system as a tyranny in which minority rights were invariably trampled by the "one-half plus one." Proclaiming majoritarian democracy to be fatally flawed, he vowed never to return to Congress, the scene of his greatest oratorical triumphs for more than thirty years. As for the new concordat, it was not immediately put into effect owing to the supercharged political atmosphere of the moment. Thus even in failure Laureano Gómez had for the time being satisfactorily responded to the government initiative.

The year 1943 began on an uncertain note for Alfonso López, and grew steadily more intolerable for the president, his family, and his government. During January and February rumors of conspiracy gained new intensity,

culminating in March with the arrest of General Eduardo Bonitto, chief spokesman for military officers who were fearful that the army budget was about to
be slashed and angered by public remarks of López to the effect that army
officers were "out of touch with political opinion [and this constituted] an
isolated and useless class."[130] López's harsh words, and harsher charge of treason against Bonitto, came at the end of a long chain of rumors, fed by Nazi-
hunters attached to the U.S. embassy, that the general was plotting with an
outlawed nationalist group, one of whose members was the boxer Francisco A.
Pérez, "Mamatoco." Bonitto and Pérez had been questioned about the alleged
conspiracy in early 1942, and Pérez was held under arrest for several months.
The affair was ridiculed in the Conservative press as the "Mamatoco Conspiracy." The boxer himself made fun of the charges, which were never sub-
stantiated, in a poem reading in part, "On the Senate floor there sounded a
sonorous voice . . . a minister who said, 'And there stands Mamatoco, who has
driven us loco.'"[131] Even Liberals tended to make light of the constant government alarms over an impending coup d'état. Early in 1943, *El Espectador*
writer Darío Bautista had poked fun at Laureano Gómez as "the chief of
conspirators," and at Jorge Eliécer Gaitán as "uneasy and 'revolutionary.'"[132]
Only the government was not amused. For President López, his supporters,
and U.S. embassy personnel, rumors of right-wing revolt were, however unfounded, no laughing matter. And that was just as Laureano Gómez wanted it.
Years earlier he had accepted Alfonso López's challenge to turn back the Revolution on the March if he could and had vowed to make the republic unlivable
until such time as he achieved that goal. The growing despair Gómez observed
in Lopista ranks convinced him that his assaults were weakening the Liberal
edifice.

In August 1943, Alfonso López delivered a lengthy state-of-the-nation address to Congress. While most of the talk dealt with Colombia's economic
health, a considerable portion of it contained the president's analysis of his
country's ongoing political malaise. The speech is especially important in helping interpret the hopes of Lopista reformers and in explaining why they could
never hope to deal with the brand of ideologically inspired opposition practiced by Laureano Gómez.

López used the occasion of his speech to advance the idea that Colombia
had moved beyond ideology, to the point at which "the dividing line between
our two historic collectivities is disappearing," rendered insignificant by economic forces that were rapidly modernizing the nation and wedding it to the
global community. "Let me say it once more," he continued, "it seems to me
that the outstanding aspect of contemporary civil life resides in the fact that we
are moving from the dogmatic ground of religious controversy to that of economic preoccupations . . . to the point that our parties are voluntarily exchang-

ing their old campaign issues [for] new ones." He explained that some of his fellow citizens continued to cling to passé political ideas only because they suffered from an "uncertainty as to concepts," a "lack of mature appreciation of the new terrain of political aspirations."[133]

Thus Alfonso López neatly dismissed ideologically held convictions at variance with his own as the product of "imperfect understanding," a polite way of saying ignorance. By taking the position that ideological traditionalists who peopled the Conservative right were simply unenlightened, he could disparage their concerns as irrelevant to the contemporary nation. This explains the inability of López and others like him to take seriously the religiously founded critique of liberalism, and of modern society generally, that Conservatives like Gómez and his predecessors had been raising for over a hundred years.

Alfonso López's address of August 1943 was delivered at a moment when two great scandals were growing that would at length drive him from the presidency. The first involved the murder on July 14, 1943, of the former boxer and political gadfly Francisco Pérez. The second was a series of financial transactions involving the president's son Alfonso López Michelsen that, while not involving blatant wrongdoing, reeked of private gain through personal favors granted by a constellation of public officials headed by the chief executive himself. Between them, and their merciless exploitation by Laureano Gómez and his followers, the scandals created what one observer catalogued as follows: "an atmosphere of decomposition and insecurity; sensational financial scandals involving personages who enriched themselves unconscionably beneath a sheltering administration; bureaucratic sensualism; a government impotent to set right a critical situation."[134]

Mamatoco was murdered in an exclusive Bogotá neighborhood, and his killers were later identified as minor officials of the national police. The boxer had made enemies among top police officials through his publication of a modest newspaper geared to exposing their misappropriation of funds and other forms of malfeasance. Beyond that, he was a known malcontent who had been implicated in rumored conspiracies against the government. For these and other alleged indiscretions high-ranking police officials determined that Mamatoco should be eliminated. Accordingly they dispatched underlings who stabbed him to death.[135]

Conservative newspapers seized on the murder of Mamatoco with verve, insinuating that it was a crime of state ordered by Alfonso López himself. Those charges were never proved, but in Colombia's political atmosphere of that time rules of evidence did not figure prominently in political discourse. Additionally, the incident was a godsend for Conservatives as it served to support their long-standing charge that the Liberals had politicized the police to serve their own ends.[136] Conservatives in departments such as Boyacá had suffered the heavy hand of Liberal police since the change of government in 1930, and in Cundinamarca the shooting of Conservatives by Gachetá police still rankled in Conservative hearts.[137] The problem of impunity in cases involving Liberal police who had abused Conservatives, and cases in which police did not effectively prosecute Liberal civilians, also angered Conservatives. Those responsible for the Gachetá massacre were never brought to justice. And in the equally celebrated case of Manizales Conservative Clímaco Villegas, who in 1935 was shot in the back and mortally wounded by Liberal cacique Colonel Carlos Barrera Uribe, the justice meted out was slow and paltry. Nearly five years dragged by before Barrera Uribe was jailed. At that he ultimately served but fifteen months of a twenty-month sentence.[138] All these events help explain the merciless way Conservatives exploited the Mamatoco case in Congress and in the press.

The Mamatoco affair served Conservatives as an ideal backdrop against which to highlight the financial scandals tainting the president and his closest family members. Most damaging was a stock speculation scheme in which the president's son used privileged information to help himself and other family members make an extraordinary profit over a short period of time. Alfonso López Michelsen's speculation involved stock of Handel Maatschappij, the Dutch concern that owned a controlling interest in the Bavaria Brewery. As one of Handel's lawyers, López Michelsen became its fiduciary agent after Holland fell to the Nazis. When Handel stock fell on the New York exchange, López family members bought it and later, thanks to government intervention, exchanged it for Bavaria stock valued nearly 100 percent more. Meanwhile the president issued a decree reducing the penalty for such speculation from 100 percent to 15 percent.[139]

Friends of the government were aghast when details of the Handel affair leaked out over the course of 1943. Carlos Lleras Restrepo had warned a year earlier that López Michelsen's involvement with Handel boded ill for the Liberal Party. The then finance minister had told Eduardo Santos that unless the complicated transactions were settled prior to López Pumarejo's inauguration, a scandal might erupt and "the Liberal Party will run the risk of falling."[140] During September and October 1943, the president and his eldest son struggled to combat the scandals. On October 3, Alfonso López Michelsen forwarded a letter to Minister of Government Darío Echandía informing him that he had resigned his vice presidency of the Bavaria Brewery, rented out his coffee mill, and retired from business.[141] Meanwhile the president stoutly maintained that there had been no wrongdoing on his part, or on that of any member of his family. Seven months later he elaborated on his view of wealth and privilege and of the use of public influence to enhance private interests. In his message to Congress on May 15, 1944, much of which was devoted to defending the business dealings of his eldest son, López wrote, "I do not see any valid reason why, as they enter the struggle of life, my sons should not benefit from their family antecedents and from the education and preparation that I have fortunately been able to give them." He continued, "in the liberal capitalist regime people speculate on the basis of government rulings, whenever they are believed to be possible, whenever they are said to be probable."[142] Some months later Darío Echandía found himself defending the López family's financial dealings in a celebrated debate with Enrique Caballero Escobar that came to be known as The Clean Hands Debate. During that exchange Echandía made the point that thanks to the actions of López Michelsen lucrative property previously owned by foreigners passed into Colombian hands. In Echandía's words, "the wealth was [thus] socialized."[143]

On November 16, 1943, Alfonso López Pumarejo requested and was granted permission to abandon the presidency in order to take his ailing wife to the United States for medical treatment. Alfonso López Michelsen traveled with his parents as he had been invited by the United States government to undertake a college lecture tour.[144] The presidential party left behind an administration under heavy attack by enemies ranging from Laureano Gómez to Jorge Eliécer Gaitán. Administration supporters like Carlos Lleras Restrepo, who again occupied the post of minister of finance, now under acting president Darío Echandía, admitted that his constant testimony before a hostile Congress had become hateful to him. Lleras recalled in his memoirs that he too had come to sense the atmosphere of political and social decomposition that grew heavier as the year progressed.[145]

Of those who have tried to explore the implications of the Handel affair, historian Rafael Serrano Camargo comes closest to suggesting how it was perceived by the average citizen: "Once Congress ended its investigation the man in the street kept asking himself what Handel had been all about, because neither he nor a majority of citizens could get clear in their minds what was or was not crooked in such complicated intrigues."[146] Serrano also calls attention to the fact that of all who had been involved in the Handel matter, ten had occupied, or were destined to occupy, the presidency: Liberals Eduardo Santos, Alfonso López Pumarejo, Alfonso López Michelsen, Darío Echandía, Carlos Lleras Restrepo, Julio César Turbay Ayala, and Alberto Lleras Camargo defended the transactions. Conservatives Laureano Gómez, Mariano Ospina Pérez, and Guillermo León Valencia attacked them. While the average citizen may not have understood the intricacies of Handel, all knew that one way or another it linked their most prestigious leaders to financial dealings of a questionable nature.

Once ensconced in the United States Alfonso López let it be known that he was not anxious to return to Colombia. Word reaching him from home did

little to convince him otherwise. Laureano Gómez, sensing that his long campaign against the Liberals was bearing fruit, had heightened his invective. On
January 9, 1944, he published an *El Siglo* editorial stating, "We believe there
is sufficient reason to declare civil war, but given that we are physically unable
to do so, we merely hold up this regime for the condemnation of history, this
regime that has made robbery, murder, and theft a system of government." A
month later, when Minister of Government Alberto Lleras filed libel charges
against Gómez, the wily Conservative allowed himself to be jailed so he could
pronounce histrionically from his cell, "When assassins, thieves, and liars are
in the government, the only place in the country for me is prison. From there
I shall speak until the end!" Seeing that its jailing of Laureano Gómez had
infuriated even Conservative moderates, the government quickly freed him.[147]

When frantic Lopistas at last prevailed on their chief to return home, López
arrived in a fighting mood, though not so much that he was ready to resume his
presidential duties. In a series of speeches replete with hints that he would
never return to the presidency, he gave the Conservatives a taste of their own
intemperate rhetoric. Speaking in Barranquilla the day of his return, López
said: "In 1942 the Conservative Party not only opposed the government . . .
but it tried to block the election of the Liberal candidate, to combat my name
with a series of threats. The same Intrepid Action that had been ordered
against the government of Santos, the same civil war that had been declared in
the Santanders against Olaya, was augmented by a new form of violence:
personal attacks to impede the person elected."[148] He followed with similar
indictments of the Laureanista opposition in addresses delivered later in
Medellín and Bogotá.

Political Colombia remained chaotic through early 1944. Alfonso López
refused to resume the presidency, Laureanistas continued their assault on
"morally bankrupt" Liberalism, and organized labor and followers of the increasingly vocal Jorge Eliécer Gaitán loudly and sometimes violently promoted
their respective agendas. At last, on May 15, Alfonso López presented Congress a formal request that he be allowed to resign the presidency. As he did so
on the eve of a general strike called on his behalf by the nation's workers, who
were his most fervent supporters, it was obvious that he knew his request
would be refused. That proved to be the case. Accordingly López resumed the
presidency, to the relief of his Liberal followers and to the joy of labor and the
political left.

The nation continued to drift over the two months following López's return
as chief executive. Congress was ill disposed to implement any new reforms; its
members were divided, their attention focused on the 1946 presidential contest. Laureano Gómez and his followers vociferated that López's party had
committed suicide, and that the president had fallen prisoner to the commu-

nists—meaning to labor and the left.[149] Severe discontent continued to run through the ranks of the military. Ironically it was the army that indirectly helped Alfonso López salvage the third year of his second presidency. On July 10, 1944, while traveling in the department of Pasto in southern Colombia, López was arrested by soldiers who presented him with a sheet of paper containing a statement of his resignation in favor of one Colonel Diógenes Gil. López angrily refused to sign the document. Because in legalistic Colombia no transaction was possible unless accompanied by a sheet of official legal paper, which Gil had not used, the president's military kidnappers became disoriented and their coup attempt collapsed. Diógenes Gil later explained that his action was a spur-of-the-moment impulse born of frustration over the sad state of the Colombian army. Except for isolated incidents in Ibagué and Bucaramanga, the military remained loyal to López and hostile to Gil and his supporters.[150]

The Pasto incident gave new life to López and his administration. Organized labor staged demonstrations in Bogotá and elsewhere celebrating López's return to the presidential palace on July 12. In the meantime a state of siege was declared under whose terms it was possible for López to push through the last two major reforms of his presidency. In September 1944 he issued Decree 2350, which served as the model for Law 6 of 1945, on comprehensive labor. And in early 1945, López pushed through a constitutional revision notable in its effect of increasing political democratization and further strengthening the state at the expense of the departments.

Both the labor legislation of 1944 and 1945 and the constitutional reform reflected ongoing progressive Liberal commitment to the advancement of democracy and social welfare through the guiding hand of the state. The most notable feature of the constitutional revision was its removal from departmental assemblies of the right to elect senators; this privilege was now made subject to popular vote. At the same time departmental assemblies lost other powers, and the state was granted new ones to intervene in business and industry through the creation of new consultative and regulative bodies. Meanwhile labor was granted the right to written contracts, severance and retirement pay, sickness and accident insurance, as well as to protection from unfair practices on the part of management. The new legislation also restricted labor by declaring strikes in transportation and public services illegal, by prescribing the procedures to be followed in collective bargaining, and by prohibiting parallel unionism.[151]

The year 1945 dawned with Alfonso López returning to his theme that party differences—"unreasonable hatreds . . . fiefs mystically rooted in ancient soil"—were rapidly becoming a thing of the past in Colombia. Political parties, he said, are transactional institutions based on the pragmatic, immediate concerns of their members, their programs arrived at through rational interest aggregation rather than "by acts of faith."[152] But each time López assured the nation that Liberals and Conservatives were forgetting their old differences, Laureano Gómez responded that ideological Conservatism was alive and well, ever disposed to combat the "unabashed Liberal concept of materialistic politics" responsible for the "spiritual decline of our people."[153]

Laureano Gómez was far from alone in opposing the Lopista vision of a Colombia moving rapidly toward political consensus. Liberal members of the informal anti-López coalition continued their harassment of his administration. On February 6, 1945, Laureanista Guillermo León Valencia read an open letter from former police officer and Liberal Carlos Gálvis Gómez on the Senate floor. The letter accused high administration officials of complicity in the Mamatoco killing. Lopistas called the charges "as vile as they were inept." Yet the exchange signaled that politics were again descending toward the level of a year earlier.[154]

Succeeding months were marked by a series of incidents that Santista congressman Atilio Velásquez remembered as creating "a sensation of tumult, of latent menace and of dangerous instability."[155] The March 1945 congressional elections were accompanied by new rumors of conspiracy that soared to new heights when a cache of explosive devices was discovered hidden in Bogotá's cathedral. Liberals were at one another's throats over the presidential succession, both for the 1946–50 term and the last year of Alfonso López's term. The president had again resolved to retire from public life, spurred by the incessant criticism of his commingling the public and private spheres, and fearful of another coup attempt by the military.

It was a tired and discouraged Alfonso López who addressed a special session of Congress on June 26, 1945, which he had called to announce that public order had been restored and to describe his government's actions following the Pasto incident. While the president lauded the constitutional revision and the new measures concerning labor, López bitterly condemned all who had opposed them. He complained that the labor initiative had touched off an anticommunist crusade among its opponents that had the effect of "reigniting the torch of class warfare" in Colombia.[156]

Near the end of his address Alfonso López again voiced his desire to quit the presidency, expressing the hope that Congress might find someone to replace him "whose life was not forever being threatened on the floor of the Senate in terms founded in doctrines of Spanish theologians bent on justifying the assassination of peninsular tyrants."[157] That was an explicit reference to the speeches Laureano Gómez had made nearly five years earlier, concerning the likelihood of renewed attacks on Conservatives in the event Alfonso López were reelected in 1942. Gómez had insisted that such violence would justify assassination of the diabolical López Pumarejo. Those words had played a major role in making the republic unlivable for Alfonso López and the rest of the nation. In his resignation message forwarded to and accepted by Congress three weeks later, on July 20, 1945, López referred to the "systematic effort to foment discomfort and tumult" in Colombia that had produced a "deformation of political spirit" throughout the nation.[158] It was his admission that a dedicated political opposition had been able to bring his democratically constituted regime to its knees.

In that manner Laureano Gómez triumphed over his former friend Alfonso López Pumarejo, maker of the despised Liberal revolution. But Gómez was not yet done castigating the Liberals. Soon his campaign would achieve its long-intended end of pulling the Liberal Party from power. With that it would be the Conservatives' turn to experience the misery of attempting to lead a society half of which was dedicated to frustrating and impeding the governmental process. Following their fall in less than a year's time, Colombia's Liberals would demonstrate that they had learned well the obstructionist tactics taught them by Laureano Gómez over a period of sixteen years. They would also demonstrate their ability to perfect new strategies for making Colombia unlivable.

9

Orchestrating the War of Seven Thousand Days
Introduction: The Early Violencia

When Alfonso López resigned his presidency in 1945, Colombia's political elite embarked on a self-destructive course that within five years had subjected the nation to civil war and the suspension of democratic government. The inability of leading public figures to work together, and their willingness to enlist the citizenry in their partisan and personal struggles, spread violence and death over extensive portions of the nation. The armed struggle, first noted in sporadic incidents taking place in 1946, intensified over succeeding years, ultimately causing the suspension of civil liberties and the imposition of authoritarian rule in late 1949. The social upset that commenced in the mid-1940s, known to Colombian history as La Violencia, was destined to plague Colombia for nearly two decades—seven times longer than the civil war of 1899–1902, called the War of the Thousand Days. The Violencia eventually consumed some 200,000 lives and considerable national treasure. A complex phenomenon, it could not be effectively addressed until its traditional partisan aspect was neutralized in 1958, through the Liberal-Conservative power-sharing agreement called the Frente Nacional. Colombia's civil turmoil of the 1940s and succeeding decades has proved difficult to assess, in part because it occurred against a backdrop of burgeoning economic prosperity and social modernization. Thus, as politicians argued and campesinos died, Colombian social change moved apace.

The coexistence of violence and rapid economic progress is not necessarily contradictory. That was manifestly the case in Colombia. One important reason that the Violencia and social progress could occur simultaneously was that the bloodshed was peripatetic and rural, and thus only rarely prejudicial to economic modernization. As an eminently rural phenomenon, restricted to the most inaccessible parts of departments where it existed, the Violencia never directly affected more than a minority of Colombians even in hard-hit departments such as Tolima. And as a phenomenon extending over two decades during which Colombia urbanized and industrialized, the atrocious and destructive Violencia clearly played a peripheral role in national life. When examined on a year-by-year basis, the Violencia is seen to have produced the deaths of only a tiny percentage of the Colombian population. No wonder, then, that as the Violencia progressed, the great majority of Colombians both managed to keep their distance from it and to remain ignorant of its severity.

This seeming paradox has made Colombia's recent history difficult to comprehend, a condition aggravated by the tendency of analysts to focus almost exclusively on the Violencia, and later manifestations of social nonconformity, along with the political system that produced them. Meanwhile the greater nation has been little studied, its dramatic social and economic changes either ignored or accepted unreflectively.

The Gaitán Phenomenon

Only occasionally have perceptive Colombians drawn attention to the unfortunate ascendance of Colombia's public realm over its private one and tried to bridge the gap between them to the benefit of both. Jorge Eliécer Gaitán was one of the first to speak of the dichotomy between the "political nation" (*país político*), as he called it, and the "popular nation" (*país nacional*, literally "national nation"). He made much of the fact that the few members of society who dominated politics abused their power at the expense of the vast majority of Colombians, citizens of the "popular nation." During the 1940s Gaitán built a political movement dedicated to the proposition that most of Colombia's public figures were machine politicians having no vision of the commonwealth. Members of the political establishment, said Gaitán, were members of a plutocracy who viewed public offices "as a cash cow" rather than as "a place of work for contributing to national greatness."[1] Gaitán's pledge was to rescue Colombia's public world and to insure that the average citizen received social justice. He damned most national figures, Alfonso López included, as members of the "political nation," men ever willing to move the levers of public power to their own advantage and to that of family and friends.

Gaitán's message that greater Colombia must free itself from the domination of its political establishment resonated powerfully throughout the nation, especially in urban areas, where the striving for personal advancement worked to blur traditional partisan hatreds. But those hatreds remained strong in the countryside, where a majority of Colombians continued to live during the 1940s and where the Violencia began. Ultimately not even Gaitán could escape the fact that he was a Liberal as well as a populist. Once he gained control of the Liberal Party in 1947, he found it impossible to reconcile his liberalism with his populism. As Liberals began dying in the countryside, Gaitán increasingly turned to the partisan rhetoric of traditional political discourse. He thus ended sounding much like members of the "political nation" whom he had earlier castigated.

When Gaitán was assassinated in early 1948, his followers in the Gaitanista heartland of Bogotá struck out against those whom they accused of murdering their leader. The spontaneous Gaitanista riot of April 9, 1948, the Bogotazo, as it came to be known, failed in its immediate objective of overthrowing the Conservative government in power at the time. When after two hours that failure became apparent, the rioters quickly shifted their attention to the pursuit of personal ends through an orgy of looting that extended up to the moment public order was restored four to five hours later. As the riot and looting ran their course, political counterelites tried to channel popular anger and energy along partisan channels. The rioters ignored those appeals, pursuing immediate personal goals as public order lay prostrate before them.

Gaitán's murder convinced many Colombians that their public world was not worth saving. While the assassination had the effect of intensifying partisan violence in outlying regions, the death of Gaitán led urban Colombians to adopt a position of indifference to public affairs. Students of Colombian history point to Gaitán's assassination and to the violent reaction it produced as hurrying the nation toward political breakdown and civil war. Yet even more significant was the way it advanced the affective chasm dividing ordinary Colombians from their public leaders and causing a significant proportion of citizens to exchange traditional partisanship for political indifference. Those Colombians who on April 9, 1948, ignored calls to turn their anger to political ends were among the first to turn their backs on an ineffectual and self-destructive political world that did not serve their interests.

The frustration that progressively alienated Colombians from their political establishment became apparent around the time Alfonso López resigned the presidency in 1945. López was brought down by two intractable problems. First, the economic progress he and his fellow Liberals had done so much to bring about had a negative by-product—inflation. Inflation running at about 12 percent per year hurt the common people in their struggle to survive.[2] Second, there was the widespread belief that the government was rife with corruption, a belief López himself did much to foment in his 1944 remarks in defense of the economic advantages enjoyed by himself and his family. In a liberal democracy such as Colombia, he said, citizens compete equally for individual advantage, with those who were better off logically becoming more prosperous than the rest.[3]

The popular dissatisfaction with those two problems served the interests of populism and López's bitterest enemy within the Liberal Party, Jorge Eliécer Gaitán. As López and his supporters struggled to answer the charges of official corruption being hurled at them during 1943 and 1944, Gaitán skillfully turned popular anger against the political status quo to his advantage.

Gaitán was ideal as leader of the campaign against Colombia's political establishment. Risen from humble origins, he had cut a brilliant figure in congressional debates during the late 1920s, attacking the Conservative regime in power at the time. But his aggressiveness and high opinion of his own abilities, both characteristics of the generation that entered politics during the 1920s, sorely tried his elders within the Liberal Party, chief among them Alfonso López. By the late 1930s and early '40s, Gaitán had established his reputation as a Liberal maverick who stood ready to battle his party's leaders at every turn. When Liberal leaders threatened to exclude him from the party directorate during their 1939 convention, a rowdy group of Gaitán's followers entered the hall and threatened violence if their chief were slighted.[4] During the party convention of 1941, when Alfonso López was put forth as Liberal candidate for the 1942–46 term, Gaitán led a walk-out protesting the "dictatorial" manner in which the López candidacy had been won.[5] López's subsequent reelection to the presidency so angered Gaitán that he again contemplated bolting the Liberal Party as he had a decade earlier. Late in 1942 he warmly greeted the proposal of a bipartisan group which proposed that he head a national crusade aimed at replacing Colombia's constitution with a corporative one of technocratic cast, thus replacing Colombia's "parliament of politicians" with a "moral" apolitical one.[6] But Gaitán was too astute a politician to embrace corporatism at a moment more propitious to mass movements of a populist savor.

Three things combined during 1943 to set Jorge Eliécer Gaitán on the path that led him to sole leadership of the Liberal Party. First was the sudden rise and shocking fall of Francisco A. Pérez, "Mamatoco." Pérez, who like Gaitán had been tarred as a fascist, and who was mocked for vainglorious statements such as, "I am one who is predestined, who intends to redeem [the people] from the oligarchy of money," and, "I promise to stand with the people [*pueblo*] and to fight its battles," had begun to make political waves in Bogotá, when he was struck down by assassins.[7] The fiery populism of Pérez impressed Gaitán, as it did other enemies of Alfonso López and his clique. Simultaneous with the Mamatoco assassination, and second among factors leading Gaitán to launch his final assault on the Liberal old guard, was the rash of financial scandals tainting the administration during 1943 and lending added weight to the question, Who killed Mamatoco? The Handel, Trilladora Tolima, and other incidents, seized upon by the Conservative opposition, convinced Gaitán that the administration was vulnerable to attack on ethical as well as moral grounds. The third and final political development helping Gaitán define his subsequent strategy for winning the presidency was the furious quasi-populist assault on López and his government by Conservative congressmen in late 1943. During the congressional session of that year, while serving as president of the Senate, Gaitán watched as Silvio Villegas attacked top administration

officials as venal and corrupt oligarchs, noting the way delighted Villegas supporters in the visitors' gallery cheered the Laureanista senator with cries of "A
la carga!" (Charge!).

Gaitán unofficially announced his intention to challenge the Liberal leadership yet again when in August 1943 he criticized López for operating on the
basis of simple "machine politics" rather than transcendent social ideals.[8]
Early the following year Gaitán formally launched his presidential campaign
with the formation of Gaitanista committees in major cities and the establishment of his headquarters in Bogotá. Liberal Party regulars tried to ignore
Gaitán's challenge, not an easy thing to do as fanatical Gaitanistas, known as
the Jega (an acronym drawn from the initial letters of Gaitán's name), disrupted party meetings in which their caudillo was slighted, and they stoned
establishment newspapers that failed to give Gaitán coverage.[9] Such incidents
were possible because the police of Bogotá, sympathetic to Gaitán's populist
message, stood idly by when the Jega struck, enjoying the discomfort of
Bogotá's political "oligarchy." One early victim of Gaitanista violence was
Carlos Lleras Restrepo, who announced his candidacy for the presidency in a
Teatro Municipal conference held March 24, 1944. The Jega packed the hall
and disrupted Lleras's speech. When Lleras and his supporters left the audito-
rium they were threatened by a Gaitanista mob that followed them to Lleras's
home, which they then stoned. Lleras renounced his candidacy a week later
and soon left the country to represent Colombia at the Bretton Woods Conference.

Late in 1944, as Darío Echandía gamely defended the administration
against charges concerning the Handel transaction in his Clean Hands Debate
with Enrique Caballero Escobar, Gaitán launched what he christened his Pro-
Democracy and Moral Restoration Movement. In congressional elections of
March 1945, Gaitanistas demonstrated their growing strength by winning as
many seats as Lopista and Santista Liberals. On the eve of the Liberal convention of June 22, dominated by Gaitán's enemies and consequently boycotted
by him, Gaitán blasted the Liberal Party as "a closed oligarchy" bent on
thwarting popular aspirations.[10] Meanwhile conventioneers had their revenge
by failing to mention Gaitán's name during their proceedings, nominating
Gabriel Turbay as the official Liberal Party presidential candidate for 1946,
and designating Alberto Lleras Camargo their choice to serve out the last year
of Alfonso López's presidential term.

Two months later, in September 1945, Gaitán answered party regulars by
organizing his own nominating convention in Bogotá. Billed as the first truly
open and democratic party convention in Colombian history, the event demonstrated Gaitanista power through impressive torchlight parades, marches,
and demonstrations that paralyzed traffic in downtown Bogotá for the better

part of a week. In his acceptance speech Gaitán lauded those who achieved social and economic mobility through hard work and personal merit, while damning members of the "political nation" for corrupting public morals through their cronyism and venality. "An inadmissible marriage prevails between business and politics," he said, adding that "the corruption within our parties has risen to disconcerting levels. The selection process of candidates through assemblies, conventions, and committees is becoming a black market of every vice."[11] As thousands of Gaitanistas filed out of the open-air bullring where Gaitán had delivered his speech they chanted, "En el Círculo de Santamaría murió la oligarcía!" (In the Bullring of Santamaría the oligarchy has died!).[12]

Political Colombia had never seen anything like the Gaitanista convention of September 1945. The mass demonstrations, torchlight parades, and harangues against the nation's sociopolitical establishment "at last opened the eyes of the Liberal press," wrote *El Tiempo* columnist Enrique Santos on September 24, 1945. But what was it that Liberal leaders and the spokesmen of other political groups saw in Gaitán? To Liberal moderates of the Santista persuasion Gaitán was "more dangerous to Colombia than Laureano Gómez," being a man who would lead the nation down the path of "personalist ambition, antidemocracy and totalitarianism."[13] Conservative moderates appreciated Gaitán's anticommunism and his promise to restore morality to public administration, but like their Liberal counterparts they feared his followers, whom one of them characterized as "Negroes, Indians, mulattoes, and mestizos; rancorous, vengeful men of knives and clubs; frustrated and ambitious tricksters."[14]

Lopista Liberals, who resented Gaitán's attacks on their leader, refused to name him in the pages of their newspaper *El Liberal*. Those on the left were at least as hostile to Gaitán, who had consistently been more successful than they in mobilizing the masses and who made anticommunism a key element in his political platform. Their typical response was to denounce the populist leader as a fascist. Those on the extreme right, Laureano Gómez and his followers, appreciated the way Gaitán helped them split the Liberal Party. But beyond that they found things to praise in Gaitán's program. Gómez liked the "Maurras-like" way Gaitán lashed the government with the term *país político* and the organic conception of society implicit in the term *país nacional*.[15] Gómez also approved of Gaitán's call for moral restoration. A decade earlier the two men had been political allies in a battle against political corruption in their home department of Cundinamarca. During that campaign they had praised one another fulsomely.[16]

The material appeal of Gaitán's program lay in its promise of upward mobility within a setting of social democracy. Through mechanisms such as state

12. Jorge Eliécer Gaitán, 1946. By permission of Lunga.

intervention to benefit labor and the middle class and state regulation of economic activity, Gaitán proposed to level the economic playing field. His movement is thus subject to class analysis, though not in a way acceptable to Marxists. Historian Herbert Braun points out that Gaitán's principal clientele were members of a rising petit bourgeois class, as was the caudillo himself, and that he accepted his and his nation's subordinate place in the international capitalist order. Because it was predicated on helping the disadvantaged achieve upward social and economic mobility in a country entering a period of vigorous capitalist growth, Gaitán's open-ended, populist movement bore the seeds of its own destruction. Once his followers joined the middle class they left their militancy behind, as they began to identify their interests with those of the status quo. Leftist Gaitanistas, who took control of Gaitán's movement following the caudillo's assassination, complained bitterly of the constant desertions of those who had most benefited by it. Writing in 1949, one such Gaitanista lamented that "when a young man of the economically deprived classes demonstrates outstanding ability, his success signifies his acceptance of all the ideas of the oppressors of the people, when he does not actually place himself at the service of oligarchic interests."[17]

There was a mystique in Gaitanismo that members of Colombia's hard-pressed urban lower and lower middle class found hard to resist. Gaitán established a personal link between himself and his followers, drinking beer and playing *tejo*[18] with them, and employing organic metaphors when he spoke in ways strikingly similar to the familiar terminology of Roman Catholic social discourse. During those speeches Gaitán punctuated his phrases with dramatic gestures, brandishing a raised fist, sweating through his clothing. Critics said Gaitán merely aped the speaking style of Benito Mussolini, and they made fun of the way he lightly oiled his hair in order that "it not present resistance to the force of his eloquence."[19] While such criticisms were certainly true, they made little difference to loyal Gaitanistas, who fully identified with their hero.

Gaitán even resembled his followers. Stocky and dark-skinned, the young Gaitán had impressed schoolmates with remarks such as, "I owe my success with women not to my great intellectual aptitudes, but rather to my gypsy eyes and my dark beauty."[20] The sight of Gaitán haranguing a multitude of wildly enthusiastic and equally swarthy followers was intimidating to the staid members of Colombia's país político. Even Gaitán's teeth intimidated his political enemies. Large and slightly protuberant, they were seen by some as metaphors for the menacing movement he led.[21]

The 1946 Presidential Election

Race and skin color played a significant role in Colombia's 1946 presidential election. As the May 5 voting day drew near, members of the largely white upper class worried that they might suffer physical harm if "el negro Gaitán" and his "*chusma*" (rabble) won the contest.[22] Gaitán and his followers countered by pointing with pride to their dark skin and Spanish surnames as constituting irrefutable proof that they were one-hundred-percent Colombians and therefore more deserving of public trust than was Gabriel Turbay, to whom they referred disparagingly as the Turk.

The race issue made the 1946 presidential campaign especially unpleasant for Gabriel Turbay, a son of Syrian immigrants. It was in fact Turbay's chief supporter, Eduardo Santos, who first made an issue of his candidate's "foreignness" in an imprudent remark of September 25, 1945. "If only he had been named Juan Ramírez," said Santos. Turbay's enemies turned those words into a weapon, charging that he was not worthy of governing the country as "not a drop of Colombian blood" flowed in his veins. They accused Turbay of not having been born on Colombian soil; he therefore was barred from occupying the nation's highest office on constitutional grounds. Their charge was unprovable.[23] Baptized in Bucaramanga and reared a Roman Catholic, Turbay's citizenship was in fact unimpeachable.

Laureanista Conservatives were especially vehement in exploiting the race issue against Gabriel Turbay. There had been bad blood between Gómez and Turbay since they had exchanged words in the Santander assembly during 1927. The two debated each other seven years later in the Senate, when Turbay represented the Olaya government as minister of government. "You merit only my profound disdain," said Laureano Gómez, irate over Turbay's insistence that Conservatives killed in political violence deserved their fate because they had rebelled against Liberal authorities.[24] Six years after that, when Turbay served as ambassador to the United States, Laureanistas published a humorous though barbed spoof about a leftist Middle Eastern immigrant named Bengalí, who spent his life trying to save an unnamed Western nation from its backward ways.[25] The novel's humorous and ineffectual protagonist wore a fez and looked strikingly like Gabriel Turbay.

As the presidential contest grew heated in 1946, Conservatives went so far as to employ anti-Muslim rhetoric in their attacks on the Turbay candidacy, professing to see "the Koran and bloody scimitars" lurking behind it. Let us unleash "a new crusade against the Turk," a "new battle of Lepanto," fulminated Guillermo León Valencia.[26] On other occasions Conservatives made fun of the Arabic surnames of Turbay's mother, Avinader Cafure. Nor were Gaitanistas above using Turbay's foreign ancestry against him. Hecklers constantly interrupted Turbay's speeches with shouts of "Turco no!" and campaign workers insisted that while their own candidate was viscerally Colombian, Turbay was Colombian only "by the skin of his teeth." Once Gaitanistas went so far as to charge that the Turbay candidacy was an affront "to the wombs of Colombian mothers."[27]

There were abundant political and personal grounds for the vehement assault on Turbay's candidacy. The Santander Liberal was a proud and arrogant man, as well as a consummate machine politician who, it was said, managed his party "like a theater of marionettes."[28] It was precisely that tight hold over party machinery that led Gaitán to boycott the Liberal convention in 1945, the gathering which unanimously named Turbay its candidate for the 1946–50 term. At that meeting Turbay had also engineered the naming of Alberto Lleras first *designado,* to serve out the remainder of Alfonso López's presidency.[29]

Part of a complex maneuver to block a Lopista-Conservative effort to elect an anti-Turbay designado, the gambit backfired when Lleras did nothing to promote Turbay's candidacy, and in fact hurt it by forbidding Liberal office holders to participate actively in the campaign of either Gaitán or Turbay. Thus Turbay later complained that Lleras had surrounded him "with a barbed-wire fence of guarantees."[30]

While Gabriel Turbay may have perceived Alberto Lleras as harming his candidacy through the exercise of excessive impartiality, Conservatives were pleased with the way Lleras worked to dampen political passions prior to the October 7, 1945, election for municipal concejos and with his effort to combat the plague of vote fraud.[31] Late in 1945 Laureano Gómez announced that his party would collaborate with Lleras's government, while it praised the president's evenhandedness. The Conservatives could afford to be magnanimous in the face of the Liberal Party's self-destruction.

Early in 1946, Alfonso López deepened and complicated the Liberal division by announcing from retirement that while he could support neither Gaitán nor Turbay, he would endorse a Liberal presidential candidate acceptable to both moderate Liberals and Conservatives. That candidate, to be selected by Conservatives from a list of six prominent Liberals, would subsequently form a "national front" government in which Conservatives were guaranteed a third of all appointive posts.[32] López's suggestion was a political bombshell. Eduardo Santos said that the National Front scheme represented hara-kiri for the Liberal Party, and Juan Lozano said it would "revive treason upon the ashes of [Rafael] Núñez."[33] And Gabriel Turbay attacked Alfonso López and Alberto Lleras as "Nazi-fascists" bent on wrecking his candidacy along with their party.[34] Even the Conservatives scoffed at López's idea. Writing in El Siglo of February 23, 1946, Laureano Gómez opined that his party would be stupid to enter into such an agreement.

The Conservatives were in fact growing increasingly confident that it was they, not the Liberals, who would win the upcoming contest. They had not fielded a presidential candidate for sixteen years and, through the early months of 1946, steadfastly insisted that they had no intention of breaking that tradition. Still from time to time Conservative leaders let slip hints that the approaching election would produce surprises, as when at a social gathering Laureano Gómez wagered Liberal Abelardo Forero that Gabriel Turbay "would cry real tears" on election day.[35] The remark raised a few eyebrows but touched off no panic in Liberal ranks, since Gómez had for months insisted that he intended to vote for Jorge Eliécer Gaitán.

Up to the eve of their March 23, 1946, party convention, Conservatives lulled Liberals into thinking that they would not put forth a candidate. On March 4, Laureano Gómez wrote in El Siglo that "the National Front tempts us more than the idea of fielding our own candidate," and on March 15, he feigned surprise over *El Tiempo* columnist Enrique Santos's suggestion that he might not have all his political cards on the table, a remark Gómez termed neither patriotic nor high-minded.[36]

On March 24, 1946, Conservatives meeting in convention produced their own political bombshell. They selected Mariano Ospina Pérez, nephew and grandson of presidents, to be their candidate for the May 5 contest. Their selection of Ospina was a brilliant one. A wealthy Antioquian businessman and industrialist representing the moderate Nationalist wing of his party, Ospina did not present an image of Conservative sectarianism. In fact Ospina was far more acceptable to moderate and right-wing Liberals than either of their own candidates. Turbay, for example, had proclaimed his Marxist sympathies in his youth and was now supported by the Communist Party, while Gaitán had angered and frightened moderate Liberals with his talk of popular revindication at their expense. To further assuage Liberal fears that a Conservative return to power might result in violence and persecution, Ospina announced that if elected, he would govern in accord with a power-sharing formula more generous than the one proposed by Alfonso López. It would be one of "National Union," in which the Liberals would enjoy equal representation with Conservatives.

During March and April 1946, Liberal Party leaders redoubled their efforts to convince Gaitán to renounce his candidacy in favor of Turbay. They seemed to be on the verge of success thanks to lengthy meetings held between the two candidates during early April. But Turbay's arrogance — "I am more qualified than you to be president of the republic," he told his rival at one point in their discussions — and Gaitán's knowledge that by stepping aside, even with assurances of his party's presidential nomination in 1950, he would alienate many of his followers, doomed the talks.[37] Consequently Gaitán renewed his attack on the país político and its lackeys at the Teatro Municipal two days after the talks failed. "Here there can no longer be any conversations," he said in a speech that historian Braun describes as "breathless, confused, and directionless." Characterizing Turbay and other party regulars as "cold people" and "calculating chess players" who had attempted to toy with him, Gaitán concluded the harangue by swearing to his followers that "in the moment of danger, when the call to battle has been proclaimed . . . I will be present in the streets leading you!"[38]

The last weeks of the 1946 presidential campaign were difficult ones for Liberalism. Alfonso López restated his resolve to support neither candidate, while Gaitán and Turbay redoubled their attacks on one another. Ironically some of Colombia's earliest Violencia involved the stoning of Turbay by Gaitanistas in Barranquilla, an incident to which the candidate responded by

13. Laureano Gómez at home, mid-1940s. By permission of Lunga.

brandishing a revolver, and the injury of Gaitán's wife by a stone-throwing
Turbay supporter in Medellín. Meanwhile Gaitanistas attacked Liberal headquarters and the *El Tiempo* building in Bogotá in the course of a riot that had
to be broken up with tear gas.[39] All the while Conservative candidate Ospina
Pérez projected a presidential image, traveling about the country delivering
addresses on national economic problems.

Election day found Gabriel Turbay confident of victory. He had invited
friends and top supporters to monitor election returns with him at home the
afternoon of May 5 and planned to fete them with an elegant victory banquet
that evening. But Turbay's ebullience vanished when returns from urban centers showed voters giving Gaitán comfortable leads over him. Then later in the

day results from outlying regions showed Ospina Pérez establishing an unbeatable lead over both Liberal candidates. At length it became clear that the victory belonged to Mariano Ospina Pérez. Turbay's gloom became depression, and one by one his friends expressed their condolences and disappeared into the night. The banquet was canceled, and the servants dismissed. Gabriel Turbay ended the evening seated alone before his fireplace, weeping as he burned his personal archive containing the record of twenty five years' service to party and nation.[40]

Ospina's victory caused "stupor and surprise" among Liberals, many of whom attributed it to vote fraud.[41] Meanwhile Conservative leader Laureano Gómez interpreted the vote as clear evidence that the "traditionalist masses" in fact constituted a national majority, his logic being that many of the Liberal votes were fraudulent.[42] In spite of those conflicting claims it is likely that the 1946 presidential vote was a fairly accurate reflection of Liberal and Conservative voting strength—Albert Lleras had, after all, done what he could to insure that the election was honest. Ospina Pérez won 41 percent, Turbay 32 percent, and Gaitán 27 percent. In succeeding elections not marred by vote fraud or abstention the Conservatives would win in the neighborhood of 40 percent of the vote and the Liberals around 60 percent.

Liberal division continued over the months following the election. Alfonso López retired from politics, and a year later his chief lieutenant, Alberto Lleras Camargo, left the country to head the Organization of American States in Washington, D.C. A deeply embittered Gabriel Turbay renounced politics, turning his back on Colombia as well. He left for France soon after the election, taking up residence in Paris. There he died in early 1947, at the age of forty-six, from complications arising from chronic asthma. Only Eduardo Santos and ranking Santista Carlos Lleras Restrepo remained behind to represent moderate Liberalism in the struggle for party leadership with Jorge Eliécer Gaitán.

Both Liberal factions, the Santistas and Gaitanistas, looked to the March 1947 congressional elections to decide which of them would orient Liberal opposition to Ospina Pérez's government. Meanwhile Gaitán made it known that he did not favor Liberal collaboration with the Conservative regime to take power on August 7, 1946. Accordingly Ospina did not invite Gaitán or any of his followers to join his first cabinet. Through his actions Gaitán showed fellow party members that he would not rest until Liberal Party control rested in his hands. Five months after Ospina took office, in January 1947, Gaitán held a second national Gaitanista convention. During the convention he hammered out a program which required that any Liberal who won elective office or accepted a position in the government of Ospina Pérez must abide by the Gaitanista document. Far from revolutionary, the 1947 Gaitanista program restated the traditional left-Liberal goals of increasing state intervention in national life, of extending economic protections and benefits to the lower and middle classes, and of maintaining good relations with the United States and reformist governments throughout the hemisphere. The moderation of Gaitán's 1947 party platform in fact represented a sop thrown to non-Gaitanista Liberals, who were expected to accept it in the event that Gaitán triumphed in the March congressional elections.

Gaitán's followers went on to defeat their Santista rivals in those elections, thus insuring their control of Congress over the next two years and Gaitán's control of the Liberal Party. The magnitude of Gaitán's triumph was suggested in the caudillo's trouncing of Carlos Lleras Restrepo in the Cundinamarca senatorial race, 32,780 votes to 9,761.[43]

Eduardo Santos announced his retirement from politics shortly after the 1947 congressional elections, and Carlos Lleras returned to his law practice. Gaitán had at last achieved his goal of dominating the Liberal Party. The only question that remained to be answered was whether he could reconcile his role as populist caudillo with that of leader of a multiclass party in which considerably more than half of all Colombians claimed membership.

To Make the Republic Unlivable, Reprise

Changes in political regime were never easy for Colombia during its first century and a half of national existence. Transfer of power at the national level always produced strife. First came a presidential election that the party in power managed to lose in spite of its control of the machinery of government nationwide. Upon taking office the new president replaced all departmental governors, who in turn sent alcaldes of their choosing to each of Colombia's many hundred municipalities. All the new appointees soon hired friends, relatives, and political supporters to staff state and municipal offices, sending all those appointed by the previous regime to join the ranks of the unemployed. Meanwhile in Bogotá the new regime commenced formulating a set of reforms usually culminating in drastic modification of the national constitution. The new legislation was justified on grounds that it corrected errors of the previous regime springing from its wrongheaded, pernicious political ideology. Since all those bureaucratic and juridic initiatives required the approval of elective representative bodies at national, state, and local levels, it became imperative to win working majorities in each of them. This was never difficult thanks to vote fraud and to the often violent intimidation of individual voters by zealous new political appointees. Elections were constantly being held in Colombia. The election of city councils and the Chamber of Deputies came at two-year intervals; departmental assembly and Senate elections were held every four years.

All these contests, along with the quadrennial presidential elections, were held independently of one another.

During the nineteenth century the political renovation just described normally resulted in the losing party's eventual declaration of war against a government that it rightly claimed had become hegemonic. Leaders of the losing party donned military uniforms and became the commanders of armies that rarely toppled the government but invariably desolated wide expanses of the country.

After the turn of the century Colombia became more prosperous and its government more powerful. Its army became better equipped and thus too formidable for citizen-soldiers to challenge as they had during the preceding century. As the twentieth century progressed all that leaders of a losing party could do was look on as the winners moved inexorably to fix their hold on the nation. After the Liberal victory in 1930, Conservative leader Laureano Gómez had responded as best he could to the Liberal bureaucratic housecleaning and attendant violence, mounting a kind of civil resistance aimed at making the republic unlivable for members of the governing party. Sixteen years later, when the Conservatives returned to power, Liberal leaders returned the favor.

The political change of 1930 had produced violence in extensive portions of the eastern cordillera north of Bogotá, a densely settled and highly politicized region. Several thousand citizens, most of them Conservatives, died in fighting that was mercifully cut short in 1932 by the brief war with Peru, which rallied citizens to the flag and sent many young men off to fight Peruvians rather than one another. Colombians were not so lucky in 1946. In addition to having no foreign aggressor to distract them from the painful political transition, four additional factors combined to make change-of-regime turmoil much worse than under Olaya Herrera. First, Liberals viewed Ospina as a nonentity whose victory was accidental; hence they could regard his regime as not fully legitimate. Second, Colombia experienced unprecedented economic growth and heightened affluence throughout the entire Violencia period. That gave a decidedly pecuniary cast to much of the Violencia, particularly in its latter phases. Third, since the Violencia coincided with the onset of the Cold War, many Conservatives came to believe that international communist conspiracy underlay it, and this fear made their response to it especially vigorous.

Fourth, and by far the most important factor feeding change-of-regime violence, was the revolutionary atmosphere at large in Colombia at the time of the Conservative takeover. Militants representing a wide range of counterelites made their chief goal that of driving Ospina from power. One day after the election militant Gaitanistas begged their caudillo to lead a coup d'état, while the small but strident Social Democratic (Communist) Party charged that a "fascist criminal" like Ospina Pérez had no right to be president.[44] The labor movement did its best to force Ospina's resignation by mounting hundreds of work stoppages and calling two general strikes within the first two years of his presidency. All such opposition was carried out against a backdrop of mostly anti-Liberal provincial violence, further convincing political counterelites that Ospina and the Conservatives must be deprived of national leadership.

During Ospina's first months in office opposition groups found little to contradict their belief that the new president was a weak leader and thus easy to unseat. Ospina appeared anxious to avoid antagonizing any social group, an attitude he took into meetings of his bipartisan cabinet, over which he presided without attempting to dominate.[45] On October 28, 1946, ex-president Alberto Lleras confirmed suspicions of the new chief executive's weakness when he wrote in the first edition of his new weekly news magazine *Semana*, "[When] Mr. Ospina makes a decision he is indecisive; he turns his back at moments requiring resolve."

Three days after Lleras's harsh analysis of Ospina, and as if to test its validity, a series of strikes and riots broke out in Cali and Bogotá, quickly spreading to the oil-producing center of Barrancabermeja. Labor leader Gilberto Zapata Izasa described the actions as part of the plan of radical unions "to create conflicts in order to hobble the government, and, if possible, to bring about the resignation of a president who represented a national minority."[46]

The Bogotá rioting of October 31 to November 1 was especially frightening. Gaitanista police looked on as union members, street people and petty criminals—"an amorphous delinquent mass," as Zapata Izasa described them—broke shop windows, looted stores, and burned a number of autos.[47] As the riot gathered momentum in streets outside the presidential mansion, a tense scene was enacted inside. Director of Police General Carlos Vanegas, a Liberal, declined to obey Ospina's order to halt the rioting, explaining that he was "a good friend of those boys [the rioters]" and assuring the president that they would soon tire of their rowdiness.[48] Faced with Vanegas's refusal to take action in the face of an upset that unnerved his superiors, Ospina replaced him soon afterward with a police commander he could trust, General Delfín Torres Durán, a Conservative. It also produced a remark by Laureano Gómez that foreshadowed the coming transformation of Colombia's largely Liberal police force into a body uniformly Conservative: "We've inherited a police force that is an enemy of the new regime, that believes itself to be at the service of the Liberal Party and not of the government. To transform that body is not the work of a single day. . . . But we must begin the process."[49]

Ospina Pérez's reaction to labor unrest was to impose a state of siege in Valle, which in turn produced a cabinet crisis. Luckily the labor troubles soon subsided, the state of siege was lifted, and Ospina was able to reconstitute his bipartisan cabinet during December 1946.

Ospina's next test came during the congressional elections of March 1947.

That contest was more turbulent than normal, as it marked the first time senators were to be elected by popular vote. Two nights before the voting, Ospina invited Liberal Party leaders Eduardo Santos and Jorge Eliécer Gaitán, and Conservative spokesman Laureano Gómez, to address the nation by radio from the presidential palace. The three men did so, asking their followers to act with restraint. In spite of the plea twenty Colombians died on election day, one of them a priest.[50]

The 1947 congressional contest strengthened extremists on both the left and right and made Ospina's bipartisan consensus increasingly difficult to maintain. Conservative anticollaborationists like Gilberto Alzate Avendaño, Silvio Villegas, and Guillermo León Valencia were heartened by returns showing their party winning majorities in Boyacá, Norte de Santander, and Nariño—nearly doing so in Santander—and substantially reducing Liberal majorities in both houses of Congress.[51] Meanwhile, Liberal moderates lost badly to their Gaitanista foes. The moderates were little comforted when Gaitán crowed that Liberalism had clearly voted with "a leftist criterion."[52]

Once the March 1947 elections confirmed him party chief, Gaitán seemed uncertain whether to continue his populist attacks on oligarchs of the país político or to assume leadership of a party in which such persons were well represented. The vacillation harmed both his party and his reputation. After the election Ospina invited three Gaitanista ministers into his cabinet; Gaitán refused to support them. When the labor movement attempted to overthrow Ospina by means of a general strike in May 1947, Gaitán remained silent until it was clear the strike had failed, only then denouncing it. That produced a flurry of criticism in the non-Gaitanista Liberal press. "You clammed up like a fish during the strike, waiting to see what would happen," accused Juan Lozano in his newspaper, *La Razón,* holding up Gaitán's action as an example of the party chief's *malicia indígena.*[53] Meanwhile rural violence rising from change-of-regime violence hardened Liberal and Conservative attitudes resulting in legislative paralysis.

In late August 1947, Gaitán briefly joined hands with the Conservatives in an attempt to slow the spiraling rural violence, on August 29, he and Laureano Gómez issued a complicated proposal aimed at reducing violence through vigorous government intervention. Sadly neither party chief was capable of maintaining his equanimity as levels of violence grew, nourished by preparations for a new round of elections in early October. On September 7, Gaitán denounced Ospina's National Union Government as encouraging regional caciques to assassinate workers.[54] Six days later he attacked Ospina for importing tear gas, which he claimed would be used by the government to establish dictatorial rule. Meanwhile Conservative Party chief Gómez rebutted the Liberals by insisting that "the political violence is engendered by fraud" perpetrated by Liberals through their stockpile of more than a million fake voting cards.[55]

Colombian politics became even more chaotic toward the end of 1947. The October 5 elections, like the March elections, further strengthened extremist factions in both parties. While they did not win a majority of municipal concejo seats, Conservatives closed the gap in the number of city councils they controlled, while Gaitanista Liberals replaced most of their more moderate colleagues in Colombia's 779 municipal city councils.[56] In Congress the followers of Gaitán continued using their majorities to harry Ospina's government. Late in 1946 Congress had pushed through a revision of the electoral law that benefited Liberals, and in September 1947 it launched an investigation of Ospina in conjunction with the tear gas purchase. That produced yet another cabinet change whereby the urbane Minister of Government Roberto Urdaneta was replaced by the hot-tempered José Antonio Montalvo.

Following the October city council elections, congressional Liberals responded to the problem of rural violence by proposing legislation that would move the national police from executive to congressional jurisdiction. Liberals believed that the violence was chiefly the work of sectarian Conservative police acting on order of Conservative Party officials.[57] Ospina and all other Conservatives were outraged by the proposal and the assumption that underlay it. Thus he sent his new minister of government to answer the congressional challenge. On November 6, José Antonio Montalvo uttered the phrase that ever after would be held up by Liberals as confirmation that the Conservatives intended to destroy them. "If the police are charged with maintaining public order," said Montalvo, and "if the police are the government's and the president's best instrument for achieving these constitutional ends," then "the government must defend with blood and fire democratic institutions, the authority of the president, and of the police, all essential elements of order and stability of the state." Montalvo's ill-chosen words created such an outcry among Liberal leaders, and struck such fear into the hearts of the rank and file, that the government distributed the text of his speech in an effort to demonstrate that he had not in fact said that the government intended to exterminate Liberals with blood and fire.[58]

When José Antonio Montalvo delivered his heated speech in late 1947, political violence had already poisoned Colombian public life. From early in the year reports that Liberals and Conservatives were dying at each other's hands in the countryside set party leaders at one another's throats in a series of highly publicized exchanges that only served to heighten tensions. By the end of 1947, some 14,000 Colombians had died, making that year the fourth worst in what soon became universally known as the Violencia.[59]

Colombia's fraternal slaughter began even before the inauguration of Mariano Ospina Pérez set in motion the familiar action-reaction process traditionally accompanying regime changes. As soon as they learned of their loss in the May 5, 1946, presidential contest, shocked, outraged, and frightened Liberals in departments that had suffered serious violence between 1930 and 1933 struck out in anticipation of the persecution they knew was sure to follow. In Bucaramanga a riot broke out on May 6; rioters burned the Conservative newspapers *El Deber* and *El Frente* and looted shops, homes, and offices belonging to prominent Conservatives.[60] Army patrols kept postelection rioting to a minimum in Cúcuta, the capital of Norte de Santander. Nevertheless, only a week after Conservatives there gave thanks for their victories during a Te Deum in the cathedral, the building was badly damaged by a fire of suspicious origin.[61]

Following their first panic-inspired reaction, Liberals in the Santanders, Boyacá, and elsewhere turned to civil resistance as a means of heading off approaching loss of power. Even before Ospina's inauguration members of the Liberal majority in the departmental assembly of Norte de Santander taunted members of the minority by voting to honor Santander writer José María Vargas Vila by having his anticlerical books placed in school libraries across the department. Conservatives reacted as expected, denouncing Vargas Vila as a "pornographic writer" and claiming that the Liberal action showed the people of Santander to be "kaffirs, ignorant mulattoes, and people lacking civilized principles."[62]

Following Ospina's inauguration, Liberal civil resistance increased. When the president named a Conservative to the governorship of Santander, the departmental assembly voted to reduce the police force from 500 to sixty men, to reduce the salaries of gubernatorial appointees from pesos to centavos, to raffle off official vehicles, and to abolish several official posts under the governor's jurisdiction.[63] Late in 1947, Gaitanistas in the national Congress began discussing strategies for impeaching Ospina, a ploy *El Siglo* denounced as "revolutionary fascism."[64]

Colombia's Violencia had an air of inevitability about it and government efforts to slow it had little effect. One such effort involved placing neutral military alcaldes in towns where political violence threatened. As soon as he took office, in August 1945, Alberto Lleras Camargo began dispatching military alcaldes to known trouble spots, and by the end of his brief term more than 100 had been so designated. Not long before the 1946 presidential election Lleras bitterly denounced the local dynamics of violence, pointing to "the sectarian obligation" imposed on ordinary citizens by all manner of local leaders.[65]

Ospina Pérez followed Lleras's example: he doubled the number of military alcaldes to 200 during his first term in office, hoping thereby to reduce sectarian strife. For a while vigorous young officers like twenty-two-year-old Lieutenant José Matallana, who presided over San Vicente de Chucurí, Santander, maintained peace by confiscating and destroying the weapons of Liberal and

Conservative militants.[66] But at length such measures were insufficient to counter the constellation of forces bent on quickly Conservatizing the bureaucracy. Those forces ran from Conservative militancy represented by Boyacá's new governor Alfonso Rivera Valderrama, who bragged that after the March 1947 elections, "Conservatism would begin to rule," and Gilberto Alzate, who gloated that his party would "exhume the remains of the Liberal Republic" slain in the previous year's presidential election, to Conservative revenge for past offenses, as in the case of impoverished campesinos of Valle who began killing Liberals who had taken their land during the previous Liberal regime.[67]

Some of the worst early violence was in the department of Boyacá, whose overwhelmingly rural population had the reputation of being *"gobernista,"* or willing to vote for whichever party happened to be in power at the moment. The gobernista stereotype had led the department's Liberal Party chief, Plinio Mendoza Neira, to spare no effort in quickly Liberalizing the department during the early 1930s. Fifteen years later Mendoza's counterpart, Boyacá Conservative Party leader José María Villarreal, returned the favor. Both men assumed that Boyacá possessed "natural majorities" favoring their respective parties, but that owing to their docile natures voters in the department had been forced to vote against their true inclination by unscrupulous politicians of the opposite party. During the 1930s, Mendoza Neira had not hesitated to bring forth Boyacá's "natural" Liberal majority through force and intimidation. Thus, writes one student of the department, "official violence exercised by the Liberal government [of Olaya Herrera] planted a thirst for violence that flowered years later with the Conservative return to power in 1946."[68] José María ("Chepe") Villarreal helped Boyacense Conservatives slake their thirst for revenge during 1947 and early 1948 when he used his power as governor to organize a sectarian police corps known as the Chulavitas.

As soon as he was appointed governor in early 1947, succeeding fellow Conservative Alfredo Rivera, Villarreal quickly moved forward with his plan to neutralize Liberal influence within the police and elsewhere. His express intent was to insure that Conservative Boyacenses could freely exercise their right to vote in the two general elections of 1947. To find the men he needed the governor turned to his *patria chica* (hometown, province) of El Cocuy, in highland northeastern Boyacá, where he knew he could find "rough and humble young men not easily intimidated" by Liberals.[69] The men from heavily Conservative municipios along the slopes of El Cocuy had shown their valor fifteen years earlier when they, along with refugees from war-torn García Rovira in neighboring Santander, had declared the region off-limits to Liberals. Any Liberal policeman who dared to enter a town like uniformly Conservative Boavita—especially its vereda of Chúluva—during the violence of the early 1930s was unlikely to leave there alive. One of Villarreal's men acknowledged that heritage when, in early 1948, he described himself and his fellows: "We're old-time Chulavitas . . . those from 1930, those who went to Chúluva and waited for the fall of the damned Reds, those who went with Governor Chepe Villarreal and did what he told us to do, those who [would] let them kill us before being humiliated by a Liberal. . . . They persecuted us after they got power and almost wiped us from the face of the earth. . . . [But] we're in charge now."[70]

Given their background, it was not hard to convince the men of northeastern Boyacá that their duty was to punish the Liberal enemy. One Chulavita recruit described the sort of training he received at police headquarters in Tunja: "They said 'You've got to go out and harass and kill because remember what they did to us in 1933.' In the police they said to us, 'How many here had their grandfathers or other family members killed?' The recruits answered, 'I did, Captain! I did, Lieutenant!' Well, the moment finally came! To arms! Then they sent us out, some to this place, others to another. That was the assignment. When they sent policemen to do whatever, first they filled them with aguardiente or beer. That was like unleashing wild animals, as you can imagine. They were people who could not even sign their own names—and drunk!"[71]

Boyacá and the Santanders were hotbeds of Colombia's Violencia during 1947. On January 4, *Semana* magazine, which just a week before had editorialized that the nation had escaped serious violence during 1946, featured Boyacá as the most highly politicized and violence prone of all Colombia's departments.[72] One week later, on January 11, 1947, an *El Siglo* writer complained that Boyacá's bureaucracy, still overwhelmingly controlled by Liberals, was persecuting members of the Conservative minority in thirty of its 128 municipios. Over succeeding weeks Boyacense violence increased markedly as Conservatives bent on vindication and revenge battled Liberal police and officeholders intent on protecting their persons and their jobs. And through it all ran the theme of personal economic self-interest that would emerge as an increasingly prominent feature of Colombia's political upset as the Violencia dragged on. Even as Boyacá's Conservatives planned their return to power, members of their party directorate sold rifles and ammunition to the highest bidder, even to Liberals, who in all probability would turn them against Conservatives.[73]

Political leaders at all levels fanned the flames that consumed the lives of their followers in outlying areas. The year 1947 was marred by the threat of gunplay in several departmental legislatures as well as in the national Congress itself. On May 17, Conservatives and Gaitanista representatives in the departmental assembly of Valle trained pistols on one another during an especially tense vote. During the August 24 session of the national Chamber of Representatives, Gaitanista César Ordóñez Quintero, a representative from Santander, became so incensed that he hurled a trash basket at a Conservative colleague and then made as if to draw a pistol.[74] That created pandemonium, leading radio listeners to conclude that a slaughter was about to take place. An even more serious incident involving Ordóñez Quintero occurred during Cámara debates of December 13, 1947, when he first challenged Minister of War Roberto Urdaneta to a machete duel and later placed a pistol on his lectern as he leveled charges against Conservatives Augusto Ramírez Moreno and Pablo A. Toro. Toro drew his own revolver and pointed it at Ordóñez as representatives flung themselves to the floor to escape the bullets they feared were about to fly. Photographs of the revolver-wielding Toro subsequently appeared in most of Colombia's newspapers. As in the incident of the previous August, thousands of Colombians listened to the scandalous and frightening exchanges over their radios.

The year 1948, the second most deadly year of Colombia's Violencia, dawned with Liberals and Conservatives at war with one another over the entire southern third of Norte de Santander, and in other parts of the country as well. In the Santander fighting thousands of Liberal refugees fled to nearby Venezuela in tragic repetition of the strife that sixteen years earlier had displaced thousands of Conservatives. A sympathetic Venezuela fed the conflict in 1948 by providing substantial quantities of military supplies to the Liberals.[75] So too did the Colombian Communists, who formed bands of antigovernment guerrillas, dubbed Popular Committees against the Reactionary Violence, and sent them into the combat zone.[76] President Ospina placed the department under military rule on January 17, 1948, and the army was at length able to position its units between the combatants, thus halting the worst of the fighting.[77]

During those stormy months party leaders Gaitán and Gómez showed no sign of moderating either their rhetoric or the mutual animosity that played such an important role in nourishing the passion of their followers. One day after Norte de Santander was placed under military rule, *El Siglo* blamed the trouble on Gaitanista violence.[78] Ten days later Gaitán and other Liberal leaders presented President Ospina a "Memorial of Grievances" that detailed in graphic fashion hundreds of Liberal deaths attributed to administration henchmen.

Political Colombia became increasingly turbulent during February and March of 1948. As Ospina and his government attempted to cope with the Violencia, they were also busy preparing to host the Ninth Inter-American Conference, set to open on March 30. It was generally known that the meeting's chief activity would be the drafting of an anticommunist resolution to be sponsored by the United States and put forth by General George C.

14. Laureano Gómez and Mariano Ospina Pérez shortly before April 9, 1948. By permission of Lunga.

Marshall, that nation's chief delegate to the meeting. For months Jorge Eliécer Gaitán had criticized Marshall's initiative, suggesting that while the Americans gave Europe the lucrative Marshall Plan, all Latin America could expect was American opposition to the movement for popular vindication. Thus the upcoming Inter-American Conference became yet another point of contention in the struggle between Gaitán's Liberal-populist movement and the national government that it tarred as reactionary and oligarchic.

Ospina Pérez did not ask Jorge Eliécer Gaitán to serve as a delegate to the meeting, but rather nominated moderate and right-wing Liberals led by Darío Echandía, Luis López de Mesa, and Carlos Lleras Restrepo, to join Laureano Gómez and Roberto Urdaneta Arbeláez in representing Colombia at the meeting. Ospina's refusal to ask Gaitán to join the group was a tactical error on his part, an understandable one, however, in that not long before the meeting, on February 7, Gaitán had staged a massive torchlight rally in Bogotá during which he implied that the president could halt the Violencia if he wished to do so. On March 1, Gaitán responded to his exclusion from the Inter-American Conference and the worsening political violence by ordering Liberals to cease all collaboration with Ospina's government. The loss of Liberal delegates to the conference embarrassed Ospina. And the resignation of Liberal officehold-ers following Gaitán's call for noncollaboration further heightened political turmoil.

As the Ninth Inter-American Conference approached, life in Bogotá and many other parts of Colombia became insupportable. Organized labor added to the confusion by staging strikes aimed at disrupting the national transporta-tion system. There were riots and student demonstrations in Bogotá in mid-March, serious violence in the countryside, and a steady arrival in the Colom-bian capital of leftists from sister republics whose goal was to protest the anticommunist resolution. On the eve of George Marshall's arrival in Bogotá signs appeared on the walls of buildings reading, The People Must React against the Jackals of Yankee Imperialism. Ordinary Bogotanos were angry because lavish preparations for the meeting had driven up costs in the city; and meeting organizer Laureano Gómez's edict banishing all street people from the center city angered many as a slap at the Gaitanista pueblo.

Thus it was not a happy Colombia that greeted delegates to the Ninth Inter-American Conference of 1948. As the meeting commenced a somber atmo-sphere pervaded Bogotá and greater Colombia, making it seem that nothing could worsen that strife-filled and unhappy nation.

Assassination, Self-Interest, Civil War

It was just after 1 P.M. on April 9, 1948, when Jorge Eliécer Gaitán, accompa-nied by Plinio Mendoza Neira and three other associates, left his law office at the corner of Carrera Séptima and Avenida Jiménez, the capital's busiest inter-section. No sooner had the group emerged from the building than an obscure drifter named Juan Roa Sierra stepped up behind Gaitán and fired two .38 caliber bullets into his back and another into his skull. Gaitán was rushed to a nearby clinic where he was pronounced dead at 1:55 P.M. Meanwhile a crowd seized Roa Sierra and kicked him to death.

The Gaitán assassination touched off a riot of proportions previously un-known in Colombia. By the time it ran its course some 2,500 people lay dead in the streets, many thousands were injured, and nearly 200 private businesses, government buildings, parochial schools, and churches lay in smoldering ruin.[79] While the riot, or Bogotazo, as it soon became known, did not bring about any change in the social or political status quo, it did speed Colombia on its way to the political collapse and civil war that awaited it nineteen months later. The Nueve de Abril tragedy also widened and deepened the breech be-tween Colombia's país político and its país nacional.

Gaitán's shooting threw his followers into a frenzy. Even before the caudillo's death was announced, the cry "They've killed Gaitán!" flew through city streets that quickly became jammed with thousands of people. Bogotanos who experienced those first anger-filled hours recalled that in the confusion close friends passed unrecognized in the street, their faces transformed by grief and rage.[80]

The initial assumption of the rioters was that the Conservative government had ordered Gaitán's murder. In symbolic expression of that conviction they dragged Roa Sierra's lifeless body five blocks down Carrera Séptima, leaving it on the doorstep of the presidential palace. The Liberal-versus-Conservative cast of the riot was captured by the lone figure who stood sobbing on a street corner, crying to no one in particular, "Come on, you cowards, kill me! I defy you. I'm a Liberal. Kill me!"[81]

A dual impulse laid hold of the Bogotá rioters. One was the desire to arm themselves; the other was to exact justice for the crime. Accordingly one of the crowd's first acts was to break into hardware and gun shops in search of pistols, shotguns, machetes, and anything else that might be of use in striking out against the government and its minions. It was the sense of many in the crowd that a political revolt was under way, its inevitable result to be establishment by force of the Liberal, Gaitanista regime that the slain leader had failed to achieve through democratic means. Hence the cries of "Long live Colombia!" and "Down with the Conservatives!" Most of the city's police were caught up in the frenzy, supporting the uprising and turning their weapons over to apparent leaders of the mob. By mid-afternoon the entire ninth precinct station, located at the edge of the heavily Gaitanista working-class neighborhood of La Perseverancia went over to the revolt, inviting a "revolutionary junta" to establish itself there. Rifles and munitions were distributed with instructions that they were to be used "to kill *godos.*"[82]

The rioters were drawn irresistibly to the presidential palace, just down Bogotá's main street from the assassination site. A group of some hundred Gaitanistas walked in that direction as soon as their leader's death was confirmed, moved by the desire both to ask President Ospina's explanation for the murder and to demand his resignation. As the leaders of the crowd, Gaitanista lieutenants Gabriel Muñoz and Jorge Uribe Márquez, reached the presidential palace, someone snatched a rifle from a soldier and was promptly shot dead by another member of the Presidential Guard. Not long after that the crowd swelled and surged toward the two dozen troops positioned in Carrera Séptima just a block north of the presidential residence. The soldiers opened fire, killing and wounding many in the crowd. Those deaths occurred less than an hour after Gaitán's death was announced.[83]

Within minutes of the shooting, Gaitán's followers, militant Liberals, Socialists, and Communists seized radio stations and began a series of impassioned broadcasts informing Colombians of the caudillo's death and the attendant uprising. They spoke in the most incendiary of tones, creating fanciful scenarios in which the bodies of Laureano Gómez, Guillermo León Valencia, and José Antonio Montalvo were swinging from lampposts, and Ospina Pérez driven from power, replaced by a Liberal revolutionary junta. All of Bogotá, they said, was in flames.

Those radio broadcasts were enormously damaging to Colombian public life, sparking many localized revolts against the government and considerable violence against Conservatives. The broadcasts had the effect of transmitting the Violencia to hundreds of places not previously affected. One Conservative succinctly stated the connection between the radio broadcasts emanating from Bogotá and the violence he suffered at Liberal hands on Nueve de Abril: "The radio invited everyone to the slaughter. They wanted to make their comrades participants."[84]

Radio broadcasts had the effect of intensifying the Bogotazo itself. The public assertion that prominent Conservatives had ordered Gaitán's assassination led to much destruction of Conservative property in and around the city. Less than half an hour after Roa Sierra's fateful shots, a large crowd gathered in the street outside *El Siglo,* the quasi-official government newspaper owned by Laureano Gómez. One man wept hysterically as he tore at the building's brick wall with his fingernails.[85] The mob battered down the door, set fire to the building, and subsequently dynamited it. In the village of Viotá, Gaitanista mayor Joaquín Tiberio Gálvez gathered several men and made straight for Gómez's home in Fontibón, which they burned.[86] Others did the same to the posh restaurant El Venado de Oro, which Gómez had constructed for the purpose of feting delegates to the Inter-American Conference. Still others broke into and sacked the Palacio de San Carlos, recently refurbished by Gómez, headquarters of the conference. Its elegant furnishings were tossed from the windows, piled in the streets below, and burned. As that took place a passerby salvaged a cushion from the fire and tried to carry it away. The cushion was taken from him and tossed back into the heap with the explanation, "We have come here to destroy . . . to end everything, not to steal!"[87]

Other government buildings singled out for attack were the national capitol—where delegates to the Inter-American Conference narrowly escaped being trapped by the mob—the Gobernación of Cundinamarca, the attorney general's office, and the ministries of education, government, and justice. The latter building housed prisoners who were freed in the course of the riot. Before fleeing, the escapees were careful to destroy all record of the judicial proceedings being conducted against them.

Churches and other religious structures also constituted popular targets of the mob. The Church was traditionally associated with the Conservative Party; thus when snipers began firing on passersby from church towers, many concluded that priests were doing the shooting. In the course of the Bogotazo, La Salle High School was burned; the Jesuit school San Bartolomé barely escaped the same fate thanks to the timely arrival of the military. The archbishop's palace, church offices, Bogotá's cathedral, and numerous other religious structures were burned. West of Bogotá, in the village of Apulio, eighty-four priests and nuns were imprisoned, and farther west, in Armero, Tolima, priest Pedro María Ramírez was lynched.[88]

Foreign-owned businesses were yet another target of Gaitanista anger. Popularly referred to as "Turks," or "Polacks," the Syrian, Lebanese, Jewish, Turkish, and European merchants whose small shops lined Carrera Séptima south of the assassination site saw their businesses not merely looted and burned, but dynamited as well. Herbert Braun, whose German immigrant father lost his hardware store in the rioting, explains that the xenophobic outburst was justified by the foreign merchants' high markups and unsympathetic policies.[89] Historian Gonzalo Sánchez takes a similar position, finding the singling out of foreign businesses both functions of social protest against the foreigners' speculation and the high cost of living.[90] Psychiatrist José Gutiérrez sees in the attacks on foreign property evidence of the racism to which populist movements are prone, and which, in the case of Gaitanismo, was the expression of "atavistic resentment engendered by social and racial discrimination."[91]

After two hours of rioting the first, ostensibly political, phase of the Bogotazo ended when army trucks and tanks arrived to reinforce the beleaguered Presidential Guard, which had repulsed three attacks by the rioters since Gaitán's assassination. It was 4 P.M. when the last of the column of three tanks stopped at the Plaza de Bolívar and turned its guns on the rioters. At that instant all hopes for a successful Liberal Gaitanista rebellion died. The rioters withdrew from the increasingly militarized area around the government buildings, which at the time of the tanks' arrival was littered with corpses, and turned to looting undefended shops and stores north of the Plaza de Bolívar.

Most Colombian politicians have misinterpreted the second phase of the Bogotazo, during which citizens of all classes helped themselves to merchandise in stores left vulnerable when the city's police joined the riot. Communist Party secretary Gilberto Viera viewed the looting as akin to a premature victory celebration staged by persons who thought the revolution had succeeded.[92] His party's Central Committee took the position that the "orgy of pillaging" which "robbed the rebellion of its true nature" was the fault of the several thousand prisoners unleashed on the city when rioters opened prison doors.[93] Most Conservatives agreed with Laureano Gómez's assessment that "the horrible events were produced according to infamous [Communist] plan" and "carried out by the Liberal masses." The Liberals had, in short, "placed themselves at the service of 'the beast.'"[94]

Both those visions ignored the fact that Gaitán's followers were not revolutionaries but rather members of Bogotá's upwardly mobile poor and petit bourgeois classes. They had heard Gaitán's promise to represent their political interests in a government headed by himself and had believed he could do so. Gaitán had, in the words of Herbert Braun, "taken his followers from a life in which they were excluded from the decisions that affected them to another in which they felt they were participating in those decisions."[95] In that sense he discovered a populist route to reconciling the país nacional and the país político.

The Bogotazo's symbolic importance is found not so much in the Gaitanista riot occurring between 2 and 4 P.M. on that April day, but rather in the looting of Bogotá's business district that followed. When rioters moved away from the Plaza de Bolívar, Colombia's political epicenter, and fanned out into the business district to take what they could, they served notice that from that time forward the pursuit of individual goals would dominate the thinking of a citizenry increasingly alienated from its public world. That was the real sense in which the Bogotazo symbolically ended one phase of Colombia's national history and introduced another. Perceiving its only political option to be closed, the Gaitanista mob figuratively shrugged its shoulders and set about attending to its own immediate physical needs. That moment marked the end of Gaitanista populism.[96]

Witnesses marveled at the alacrity with which Bogotanos of all classes turned to looting. Newsreel footage reveals men and women snatching stolen items from each other. A young girl watching from the relative safety of her parents' rooftop saw a drunken rioter, his arm covered with looted wristwatches, set upon by a fellow rioter who hacked at his arm with a machete.[97]

As word spread through Bogotá that goods could be had for the taking, Bogotanos flooded the business district. U.S. Ambassador Willard Beaulac, whose embassy was at the edge of that neighborhood, recalled the heavy traffic flowing toward the shops and stores from midafternoon of Nueve de Abril, reversing hours later as looters returned home lugging their booty. "Amidst the sickening tragedy we were witnessing," wrote Beaulac, "we could not help but be amused at the businesslike manner in which those people were carrying on their new trade, and at some of the objects they had selected to 'liberate' from downtown shops. . . . Barefoot women trudged by, their arms loaded with fur coats or fancy lingerie. One ragged individual carried an electric stove on his back. Bathroom fixtures, floor lamps, sofas, calculating machines, all found their way into hands of the looters."[98] Put in the language of social philosophy, the looters took advantage of a prostrate public world to enhance their private ones. One photograph taken that day illustrates the social dynamics of the looting. It shows three women, two of them tall, fair-skinned, and well-dressed, obviously of the upper class, chatting as they carry away fur coats and an elegant floor lamp. Three paces behind, bent under the weight of a burlap bag, is a third woman, short and swarthy, wearing a hat and ruana. The contents of the bag aren't visible, but it obviously does not contain fur coats and floor lamps. It likely contains more mundane items that she carried away to a home probably not wired for electricity.

A great many photos taken in downtown Bogotá during the rioting of April 9, 1948, show the burning or charred wreckage of the city's municipally owned trolleys. Those slow-moving and idiosyncratic electric vehicles had served the city for thirty-eight years and were regarded affectionately by Bogotanos as symbols of the quaint old city of premodern times. Destruction of the trolleys was initially thought to be a function of mob vengeance on the symbols of public authority. However, recent scholarship maintains that the fiery demise of Bogotá's street railway was a calculated act of economic opportunism. Half of all the trolleys destroyed that day were burned by employees of Bogotá's privately owned bus companies who used the upheaval of April 9 as a convenient cover for eliminating their chief source of competition. Immediately after Nueve de Abril, bus fares doubled. The bus companies were also given permission to import new buses for their fleets.[99]

If Gaitán's assassination hastened the alienation of ordinary citizens from politics, it had a no less detrimental impact on national politics itself. Members of Colombia's balkanized political elite rushed to capitalize on the caudillo's death in ways highly destructive to civic and political culture. Liberal centrists, Gaitán's enemies in life, used the murder as an excuse to demand Ospina Pérez's resignation, going so far as to wire Eduardo Santos asking him to assume the presidency when it fell vacant. Right-wing Conservatives became even more intransigent after Nueve de Abril, holding up the assassination and reaction to it as proof of the need for stepped-up repression of those who opposed the government. Laureano Gómez, from his refuge in the Ministry of Defense, phoned Ospina Pérez with the demand that he relinquish power to a military junta. Even foreigners turned Colombia's Nueve de Abril to their own purposes. United States policymakers cited events of that day as proof that communist subversion was rife throughout the hemisphere and used the supposed threat to justify stepped-up covert activities. Gaitán's assassination was thus an indirect stimulus for formation of the Central Intelligence Agency, which became active in Latin America shortly after 1950.[100]

Left Liberals, Socialists, and Communists, most of whom were enemies of Jorge Eliécer Gaitán, also made use of the caudillo's murder in a way injurious to the social order. When they seized Bogotá's radio stations and proceeded to tailor news broadcasts to fit their political agendas they incited regional politicians to form "revolutionary juntas" in scores of places around the country. Many of their listeners later paid stiff penalties for believing the radio broad-

15. Looters in Bogotá, April 9, 1948. By permission of Focine.

casts emanating from Bogotá. In Tolima, Governor Gonzalo París Lozano, an Ospina appointee, joined the revolt and thereby ruined his political career. The leader of Cali's Revolutionary Junta, Humberto Jordán, had no sooner telegraphed fellow Liberals around the department of Valle, urging them to "confront with courage and resolve the bandit assassins who have sacrificed the caudillo of the pueblo" than he and a thousand others were placed under arrest and packed off to military prison in Pasto. The revolutionary optimism of Jordán and others was entirely a function of radio broadcasts made during the brief interval prior to the retaking of the Bogotá stations by army units. The Cali junta's actions ignored the fact that outside the government building, which they had seized, soldiers under the command of Colonel Gustavo Rojas Pinilla were easily restoring order to the city.[101]

Misled by the inflammatory radio broadcasts, Liberal rebels in Medellín made elaborate plans to liberate the entire department of Antioquia from government control, plans that even included destruction of bridges leading into the department. Unbeknownst to them, Liberal Party leader Darío Echandía was at that moment reconstituting the bipartisan National Union government that had broken down just ten days earlier. When, on the evening of April 10, Echandía addressed the nation by radio from the presidential palace to ask all Liberals to support the reconstituted bipartisan accord, erstwhile rebels across

Colombia shuddered. "We knew from that moment forward," wrote one of them, "that nothing short of the most . . . tremendous persecution would befall us."[102]

Political Colombia was a grim place in the months following Gaitán's assassination. While Darío Echandía, who replaced Laureano Gómez as minister of government, worked with Ospina to restrain the militants in both their parties, their labors were largely in vain. Before departing Colombia for voluntary exile in Spain some weeks after Gaitán's assassination, Gómez warned Ospina that he must cease his attempts to collaborate with the Liberals and must instead build an entirely Conservative government. His logic was that the Liberals had shown themselves to be anything but trustworthy on Nueve de Abril. Congressional Liberals, who made up a substantial majority of that body, did little to contradict that judgment over the ensuing months. On July 20, 1948, they remained seated when Ospina inaugurated the session. Their first official act was to send greetings to "political prisoners of Nueve de Abril," among them Cali's Humberto Jordán and Medellín's Gilberto Zapata, who were still under arrest.

In spite of the intransigence prevailing in both their parties, Ospina and Echandía labored through the 1948 congressional term to effect reforms that they believed would lessen political violence. Key among them were the nationalization of Colombia's police forces, promotion of bipartisan administration at every level of government (termed "crossed" administrations), and passage of an electoral law whose chief purpose was to reduce vote fraud.

Another of Ospina's actions designed to reduce political tension was the postponement of congressional elections from October 1948 to June 1949. Unfortunately that only extended the period of time over which militants in both parties could taunt and bait each other. Thus 1948 ended with the nation's political class seemingly having learned nothing from the bloody events of April 9. Seasoned politicians warned that unless passions cooled, the nation faced even more turmoil. On December 4, Antioquian Conservative Fernando Gómez Martínez sounded a cautionary note to the citizens of his department. "In Colombia we live the act of governing with too much passion," he said; he went on to ask parents to teach their children "that politics is not hatred, that parties aren't corps of gladiators, that the exercise of government is not a function of reprisal . . . that to vote is not a manner of expressing rancor until the moment to kill arrives."[103]

Sadly his words were heard but not acted on. Young turks in both parties began girding their loins for the June 1949 elections. "The Liberal Party is armed, and if it does not triumph in the elections it will declare civil war," trumpeted Liberal senator Gilberto Moreno, while his Conservative counterpart, Gilberto Alzate, warned his copartisans, "We must gain victory, because if not, Conservatives, you will be wiped from the face of the earth!"[104] Those were challenges disturbingly reminiscent of the ones exchanged immediately before the War of the Thousand Days.

Colombia rushed toward civil war over the course of 1949. Except for brief lapses, as when Carlos Lleras and Guillermo León Valencia signed a bipartisan peace accord on March 17, the leaders of both parties maintained postures of intransigence and mutual antipathy whose consequence could be nothing less than the suspension of democratic government. The Liberal strategy was based on their belief that, as theirs was the nation's majority party, they had the right to direct the government. In May they indicated the course they would follow by withdrawing a fourth and final time from Ospina's government in protest against his inability to control the Violencia in several departments. They reconfirmed their majority status in the June congressional elections, which they won handily, and when Congress convened on July 20, 1949, Liberal leaders set out to use their legislative power to control Ospina Pérez, whom they continued to regard as a weak and accidental president.

The Liberal strategy was in fact severely flawed. It rested on two assumptions—that Colombia's political institutions were solid enough to withstand ongoing warfare between the legislative and executive branches of government, and that, as Liberal Party leader Carlos Lleras believed, in true republics minorities must never dominate majorities. What that strategy failed to consider were the formidable powers vested in the presidency, among them the power to suspend Congress when, in the president's opinion, public order was disturbed. As it turned out the Liberal directorate had committed itself to a course of action during 1949 that produced the party's total exclusion from the formal exercise of political power once Ospina Pérez imposed a state of siege on November 9, 1949. After that date, the Liberal leadership believed it had no other recourse than to arm guerrillas, especially in the llanos. The Conservative government and the Liberal opposition thus found themselves in a state of open civil war. In consequence Colombia experienced its worst Violencia during 1950, when 50,000 citizens fell in fighting between government troops and the largely Liberal guerrillas.

If the prologue to Colombia's political tragedy was the Liberal withdrawal from Ospina's government in May 1949, its first chapter began with the inauguration of Congress on July 20. For the first time since 1823, Liberal congressmen refused to rise when the president and his ministers entered the chamber. The traditional welcome message to the president was at first delayed by a shouting match between members of opposite parties, and then was not read at all. Following the briefest presidential address ever delivered to Congress, there was an attempt to banish Ospina Pérez from all further congressional proceedings. When that failed, Alfonso Romero Aguirre rose and said to Ospina, "Mister President, you have tricked the party that is the great majority in Colombia. When this party extended its hand and offered the collaboration of its leaders . . . you responded ignobly, allowing your subalterns to assassinate its members."[105]

Following that inauspicious opening session congressional Liberals proposed a package of laws whose effect would be to strip the president of his power by removing the police and military from his control, requiring prior approval of his cabinet appointments, and eliminating his power to name governors and other department officials. Congressional Liberals also advanced the coming presidential election from June 1950 to November 27, 1949, explaining that they did so in order that government employees, "little better than emissaries of death," as one of them said, would have less opportunity to steal the election through fraud.[106] Two days later, in the session of July 22, Liberals proposed the formation of an investigatory commission to look into the violation of civil rights, managing to do so with such aggressiveness that Conservative members physically attacked President of the Cámara Francisco Eladio Ramírez. Later in the session Representative Manuel José Gaitán, brother of the slain caudillo, rose and said that he had evidence proving the complicity of Representative Enrique Gómez Hurtado, son of the Conservative Party leader, in the caudillo's assassination. The following day, when Enrique Gómez rose to defend himself against the charges, he was denied the right to speak.[107] When Congress next convened, members of the Conservative minority, led by Alvaro Gómez, oldest son of Laureano Gómez, disrupted business by blowing a police whistle. That led to the hurling of ashtrays, one of which badly lacerated the scalp of Conservative Representative Eusebio Cabrales.[108]

Colombians who wondered to what depths their national Congress would fall received their answer on September 8, when a gun battle erupted in the Cámara. The deadly exchange, which was transmitted live to the nation via radio, was a product of the supercharged political atmosphere of the moment and two decades of animosity sprung from past acts of political violence. Principals in the shoot-out were representatives from the martyred department of Boyacá. Conservative representative Carlos del Castillo touched off the exchange when he rose to defend himself against an earlier attack by Liberal Julio Salazar Ferro. Salazar had charged that Boyacá Conservative caciques (like del Castillo) were responsible for girls as young as eleven and twelve being raped in the presence of their parents.[109] Del Castillo answered by attacking Salazar as an assassin for having helped plan the Gachetá massacre of 1939. At that, presiding officer Julio César Turbay Ayala called a recess. His hope was that tempers would be calmer when the session resumed. Sadly that was not to be the case, as most representatives spent the break at the congressional bar fortifying themselves for the coming debate.

No sooner had del Castillo resumed his tirade against Salazar than Gaitanista Gustavo Jiménez, who had drunk heavily during the break, rose and accused the Conservative of being nothing more than the son of common campesinos. "I am the son of humble campesinos," replied Castillo, "but I am not a natural son, as are you, sir. React, react!" At that both men reached for their weapons and a five-minute gun battle ensued during which most representatives emptied their weapons wildly in the direction of their political opposition while hidden behind their respective desks. One who did not hide as he fired was General Amadeo Rodríguez, who stood, took aim, and shot Gustavo Jiménez dead. For years afterward a popular toast among Conservatives was, "Long live Amadeo's pistol!" The tragic toll of that day was one killed outright, another mortally wounded, and two others with flesh wounds.[110]

The Cold War descended on Colombia with full fury in 1949, further complicating the disastrous political situation. Slightly more than a month before the Chamber of Representatives incident Laureano Gómez returned from Spain after an absence of thirteen months, bearing the warning that communist subversion was rife in his country. In typically flamboyant fashion Gómez electrified Colombians with the message that the Liberal Party had fallen under the influence of communists bent on turning Christian Colombia into a Marxist-Leninist dictatorship. Gómez held up Gaitán's assassination as unquestionably the work of communist agents provocateurs, and the Liberal uprising it provoked as proof that Colombia's minuscule Communist Party had learned how to make the Liberals do their bidding. He evoked the basilisk, a mythical reptile with a gross and terrifying body and a tiny obscene head. "Nueve de Abril was a typically communist phenomenon," said Gómez, "and it was carried out by the basilisk. . . . The tiny, nearly invisible head planned it, and the body carried it out, to the shame of the nation."[111]

Gómez's insistence that Colombia had been subverted by international communism infuriated Liberals, many of whom were as ardent in their anticommunism as was Gómez himself. At the moment Gómez raised the issue, Liberal leader Carlos Lleras Restrepo was rooting communists out of the nation's largest labor union in compliance with wishes of the United States.[112] In the weeks following what came to be known as the Basilisk Address, Liberals attacked Gómez and his thesis, along with Ospina Pérez, for making Colombia the first nation in Latin America to accept U.S. "Point Four" moneys for the purpose of combating Soviet-inspired communism.[113] Their fear was that money and equipment received through the program would be used to persecute Liberals, who, thanks to Gómez's offensive, were being tarred as communist fellow travelers.

From the moment Laureano Gómez set foot on Colombian soil in June 1949, fear gripped Liberal hearts. It was clear to them that their old adversary intended to take control of the nation by winning the upcoming presidential contest. Moderate Conservatives, chief among them Mariano Ospina Pérez, also feared that a Gómez victory on November 27 would worsen the already atrocious Violencia. These considerations set moderates in both parties scrambling to reduce bloodshed in the countryside and to frustrate Gómez's presidential bid. In early August a bipartisan peace commission was formed, among whose members were Liberals Luis López de Mesa and Antonio Rocha, and whose Conservative representatives were Eduardo Zuleta Angel and Francisco de Paula Pérez. Two months later Ospina Pérez launched a major initiative to calm passions by reviving Alfonso López's idea of a bipartisan power-sharing scheme that if put into effect would have postponed the election for four years and entrusted the nation to the direction of a plural executive whose two Liberals and two Conservatives would alternate in office at one-year intervals.[114] Unfortunately the peace initiatives came to nothing as extremists on both sides continued to attack one another both in public fora and in thousands of private venues across the country.

Laureano Gómez phrased his endorsement of peace in terms seemingly designed to anger Liberals: "When Conservative lips proclaim peace, they do so with sincerity; our hearts are not poisoned with hateful desires to destroy the Christian order and replace it with Communist tyranny."[115] Liberals like Gaitanista César Ordóñez Quintero responded that Gómez alone was responsible for the Violencia, calling him a "deflowerer of virgins and a destroyer of cities." Shortly after Laureano Gómez accepted his party's presidential nomination, Carlos Lleras characterized the Conservative leader as a man whose destiny was to transform hateful invective into "incendiary flames [and] tremendous massacres."[116]

Lleras made his intemperate remarks in an epochal speech of October 28, 1949, in which he ordered Liberals to sever all ties with Conservatives, even at the personal level. This was in part a reaction to the ghastly slaughter of Liberals by Conservative gunmen at the site of a party rally in Cali six days earlier. The "Casa Liberal" massacre negated efforts to save the country's bipartisan democracy. Nothing more was said of bipartisan power sharing until early 1956, when Alfonso López Pumarejo revived the notion as a way of ending the onerous military rule of General Gustavo Rojas Pinilla. The simple fact was that in October 1949, even experienced politicians like Alfonso López, whose commitment to power-sharing arrangements was amply demonstrated in 1946, were incapable of compromising with the political enemy. When Ospina Pérez announced his plan for a plural executive, López brushed it aside as an invitation to a "dictatorship through compact."[117]

The next step in Colombia's dismal journey toward civil war came in early November, when Liberal leaders proclaimed abstention from the November 27 election and began planning the impeachment of Ospina Pérez for permitting "political assassinations carried out by mayors and by police in the most savage orgy of blood recorded in national history."[118] However, the plan failed when, on November 9, Ospina Pérez closed Congress and placed the nation under a state of siege. Carlos Lleras, Darío Echandía, César Ordóñez Quintero, and other Liberal leaders were rapidly exhausting the means through which they could legally oppose the regime on which they placed sole blame for the Violencia.

Writing during the late 1950s, leftist historian Enrique Cuéllar Vargas refers to the period from late 1949 to early 1950 as "the second *patria boba* in Colombia."[119] It is difficult to fault his judgment. In their desperation to topple Ospina as a way of ending the Violencia, Liberal leaders evolved a two-part plan that only served to worsen it. First, they worked to arm their followers in anticipation of an uprising set for November 25, two days before the election; second they called a general strike for the same day. Both parts of the scheme failed. Rather than thwarting the election of Laureano Gómez, the attempted Liberal revolution merely produced a new harvest of dead, among them Darío Echandía's brother.

The action-reaction dynamic inherent in Colombia's Violencia was appallingly clear in November 1949. In the Santanders, the llanos, Tolima, Antioquia, and elsewhere, Liberals and Conservatives answered their leaders' calls to arms with an alacrity that pushed the Violencia to its highest level in the nearly two-decades-long conflict. Incidents of November 16, in El Carmen, Norte de Santander, and of November 27, in San Vicente de Chucurí, Santander, illustrate the point.

In late October 1949, Minister of Government José Antonio Andrade notified Governor Lucio Pabón Núñez that Liberals were stockpiling weapons and harassing Conservative police throughout the region of El Carmen, 100 kilometers northwest of Cúcuta. Pabón, who like Andrade was a militant and sectarian Laureanista, dispatched police and detectives to seized the munitions stored in El Carmen. But the police were unable to do so in the face of guerrilla resistance. Pabón then sent a detachment of 117 police, who entered and secured the town during November 16 and 17 following a day-long battle during which two police and at least two dozen Liberals died.[120]

As in Cali's Casa Liberal massacre a month earlier, Liberals across Colombia condemned the El Carmen killings as the product of unconscionable Chulavita excesses. While most of them expressed their outrage verbally or in writing, guerrilla leader Rafael Rangel answered the affront in a more direct way. Ten days after Pabón Núñez sent his police into El Carmen, Rangel assaulted the plaza of San Vicente de Chucrí, killing more than 100 citizens of all ages, most of them Conservatives who were there to cast their vote for Laureano Gómez.[121]

The year 1950 began on a surreal note. A confident president-elect Laureano Gómez delivered a new year's greeting to the nation in tones of a loving father whose children could anticipate a bright future if only they followed time-tested truths. "Our immense difficulties will disappear," he said, "when it is possible to instill in each citizen the conviction that he must do unto others as he would have others do unto him."[122] The speech was full of Gómez's optimism that 1950 would be a splendid year for the nation if everyone worked together in a spirit of patriotic harmony.

The president-elect's optimism was sadly misplaced. Rather than a year marked by Colombia's sons "working for the well-being and greatness of the country," their warfare with one another produced 50,000 deaths, a quarter of all those killed over the course of the Violencia. Over much of the national territory a thoroughly Conservatized police force conducted a reign of terror, beating, raping, and killing Liberals at the slightest provocation, or on no pretext whatever. "How they killed, burned, insulted, stole, raped, and did so many things because we were Liberals!" said Tolimense Teófilo Rojas of the Chulavita police who arrived in his village during late 1949.[123]

Thoughtful Conservatives, even those who had experienced the Liberal harassment of sixteen years earlier, were unable to explain the ferocious persecution of Liberals during 1949 and 1950. "I was perplexed before the outpouring of sadism unleashed by Conservative vandals, protected by official weapons, who staged midnight attacks on their political adversaries trapped inside their homes," wrote Antioquian Conservative Miguel Zapata Restrepo. In his eyes, "the persecution against Liberals was turned into a kind of holy war."[124]

Liberals could hardly accept such persecution without fighting back. Party leaders like Carlos Lleras Restrepo traveled to the United States in search of support for the guerrillas; other leaders sought armaments closer to home, in neighboring Ecuador, Venezuela, and Panama. Meanwhile other party leaders worked at forming alliances with any group whose members were willing to take up arms against the government. In December 1949, Plinio Mendoza Neira approached Communist Party leaders for help in manning guerrilla units.[125] As a consequence of those efforts the Liberals were able to establish guerrilla units in Antioquia, Caldas, Tolima, Huila, Cundinamarca, Boyacá, the Santanders, and the llanos. By mid-1950 the llanos force stood at some 2,500 men operating under a central command. Elsewhere guerrilla units totaled roughly 2,000 men operating independently of one another in the several departments of central Colombia.[126] Hence as Ospina Pérez's presidency drew to a close there were at least 4,500 Liberal guerrillas battling Chulavita police throughout Colombia.

From the onset Colombia's Liberals made it clear that they would not recognize as legitimate any government constituted on the basis of the November 27, 1949, election. Their directorate stated their position in a message of November 9, 1949, which read, "Liberalism declares that the electoral farce of

November 27 will give no one the right to exercise power without valid title, nor will it require the obedience or compliance of a free people."[127] Liberal activists maintained that attitude over the first half of 1950, concentrating their efforts on building a fighting force capable of resisting government police. Even the mildest suggestion that the party might consider negotiating with the government was dismissed out of hand. That was something Alfonso López Pumarejo learned to his dismay when, during the Liberal convention of April 1950, younger party members jeered and hooted when he remarked that his colleagues should not fear renewal of their collaboration with the Conservatives. A shaken and ashen-faced López went on to say that he did not demand agreement from his fellow party members, merely courtesy. His statement was answered by renewed jeering.[128]

The intransigence of Liberal Party leaders before the election of Laureano Gómez was in part a function of the old Generational Quarrel (Pleito de las Generaciones) that had bedeviled Colombian politics for more than a quarter century. Party leader Lleras and his contemporaries were members of the group known as Los Nuevos, that during the 1920s had battled the Conservative government of Abadía Méndez, as well as the "elders" of their own party, men at the time in their thirties and forties. But Los Nuevos had been consistently frustrated by members of the political generation that preceded them, most notably by Alfonso López and Laureano Gómez, leaders of the Generation of the Centenary. That López, Laureano Gómez's former bosom companion, should suggest collaboration with the administration that would assume power on August 7, 1950, amid a fearful persecution of Liberals, was more than Los Nuevos could endure.

Party leader Carlos Lleras also turned a deaf ear to the advice of his political mentor, Eduardo Santos, who, along with his influential brother Enrique, espoused the political middle ground rather than intransigence. Eduardo Santos warned his copartisans not to follow those who were "determined to create disorder with the purpose of compromising the Liberals in a blind venture that would become the pretext for reprisals."[129] Not only did party activists ignore the advice, but they persisted in challenging the government. Two months after Santos's call for moderation, Liberal leaders sent "warm greetings" from the convention to Eliseo Velásquez, guerrilla leader of the llanos, lauding him as "an illustrious fighter for the Liberal cause [who is] an example to the Liberal Party."[130]

Liberal bellicosity achieved little beyond heightening Conservative intransigence. Asked early in 1950 what Colombia most needed, Minister of Government Luis Ignacio Andrade snapped, "What this country needs is the discipline of the rifle butt."[131] When Liberals sent Ospina Pérez a letter accusing him of having turned Colombia into a dictatorship, the president replied that "to ignore the parliament's responsibility in the renewal of sectarian hatreds . . . is to willfully deform the reality of the events."[132]

To say that by August 7, 1950, Colombia was in a state of political collapse born of civil war is to belabor the obvious. Even Laureano Gómez knew it. Chatting with Abel Naranjo Villegas before the Palacio de San Carlos the day of his inauguration, the soon-to-be president asked Naranjo how he viewed the political situation. The younger man replied, "terrible." "I agree," said Gómez, adding, "if I weren't in the middle of it, I would be in opposition."[133]

Most Liberals boycotted the inauguration of Laureano Gómez. Those who did attend were subsequently expelled from the party. Liberals took the unprecedented step of mentioning neither Gómez's name nor word of his inauguration in their newspapers, an eloquent response to Gómez's presidential address, which was replete with references to the common good and calls for Colombians to attain national greatness by working together in a spirit of Christian solidarity.[134]

Yet it was not the Liberals but rather a Conservative who had the last word in rejecting the new president. Like most members of her family, María Antonia Suárez never forgave Laureano Gómez for spearheading the movement that drove her father from the presidency twenty-seven years earlier. On several occasions she remarked that she could not bear living in a Colombia governed by Laureano Gómez. True to her word, María Antonia Suárez died of what were described as natural causes hours before Gómez recited his oath of office.

10

Economic Progress and Social Change:
From Ospina Pérez to the National Front

The False Paradox of Economic Progress amid Violence

Colombia enjoyed unparalleled economic growth over the fifteen years following World War II. The boom extended into the first administration of the Liberal-Conservative power-sharing accord, the Frente Nacional (National Front, 1958–1962). It was financed by extraordinary earnings from coffee exports and given continuity by prudent macroeconomic management by development-minded political and economic elites. Those elites worked together harmoniously to ensure national economic progress and were aided by international agencies, the most notable being the World Bank.

For Colombia the period from 1945 to 1960 was a golden age of corporate growth and the expansion of import-substituting industry. It was also a time of ongoing democratization of landholding throughout the zone where the nation's fine mild coffee was produced. Organized labor was relatively peaceful during the period. Unions were tightly controlled during the postwar years and real wages low, but so too was unemployment, with unskilled migrants from the campo easily finding work in the burgeoning import-substituting sector.

Economic growth in postwar Colombia was accompanied by social change of such magnitude that demographers describe it as one of "the most dramatic known in contemporary history."[1] Birth rates ran at better than thirty per 1,000 population during the 1950s, while corresponding improvements in public health caused Colombia's population to double over the twenty-six years between 1938 and 1964—and to double once more over the succeeding two and a half decades.[2] Thus a population that stood at 8,701,800 in 1938 rose to 17,584,500 in 1964, and to some 35,000,000 by the final decade of the century. This spectacular population growth was founded in a steady increase in life expectancy, caused by rapidly falling levels of infant mortality. Average life expectancy which stood at 40.2 years in 1940 jumped to 48.9 years in 1950, and to 58.2 years in 1960. Infant mortality fell from 175 per 1,000 live births in 1940, to 122 per 1,000 in 1950, to 78.2 per 1,000 in the early 1960s.[3]

Meanwhile Colombia experienced a dynamic process of urbanization that transformed its population from 75 percent rural in 1930 to 75 percent urban half a century later. More than half of its population was urban by the 1960s, and the urbanization process quickened thereafter.[4]

Amid these changes Colombia became ever more integrated into greater Western culture. The appearance of television, bouffant hair styles, and hula hoops over the course of the 1950s eloquently testified to that fact. Traditional Colombia protested the rush to modernity, as when in 1951 the nation's bishops condemned newspapers for publishing photos of beauty pageant participants clad only in bathing suits. "These painful occurrences oblige us to cry out with the Divine Master: Woe to the world because of such offenses, woe to the man by whom the offense comes!"[5] But social change in postwar Colombia was neither checked nor slowed. And that change provided Colombians a degree of freedom and self-absorption unknown to earlier generations. The ultimate expression of this trend occurred during the late 1950s with the appearance of bohemian poets who called themselves Nadaístas (from *nada*, nothing), Colombia's counterparts to the North American beatniks. "We offer delinquent violence against morality, against established values," wrote Nadaísta Eduardo Escobar, who fondly recalled orgies at plush suburban villas, like the one at El Pedrezal in Medellín, "a nocturnal gathering of madmen and beggars, of vagrants and wanderers, of renegade hermits, wealthy dowagers, temporary widows, nymphomaniacs who would do anything, perfumed playboys and their dark-skinned beauties, knife-wielding whores, old maids avid for a fling, menopausal coquettes, insidious crazies, aged intellectuals, repentant Conservatives, socialist voyeurs, light-fingered guests who picked pockets, unscrupulous virtuosos — all of whom accidentally or because God willed it, copulated in the gardens, attempted suicide, threw one another from windows, drugged themselves, raped servants, trampled a drunk, wounded one another in jealous brawls, and drowned in the swimming pool."[6]

The paradox of booming economic growth and pell-mell social change in a country suffering widespread rural violence was more apparent than real. Colombia's economic growth in the twentieth century has in fact been guided by political moderates who unobtrusively steered the economy through channels of capitalist development even as newspaper headlines trumpeted the doings of their militant counterparts. In much the same fashion rank-and-file citizens looked to their own interests as an unfortunate minority was caught up in traditional political battles involving issues that grew less meaningful over time. What in fact occurred in Colombia during the 1940s and 1950s was that most citizens managed either to avoid the politically inspired Violencia or to turn it to their advantage. And all the while the focus of national life was increasingly urban. The mountains, jungles, and sparsely populated llanos, where most of the Violencia occurred and where a minority of the nation's population resided, gradually receded from the experience of the average Colombian.

During the late twentieth century Colombian scholarship has paid disproportionate attention to the Violencia and to the nation's stormy political history. Consequently the socioeconomic changes which affected vastly more Colombians and which took place concurrently with political violence have been examined relatively little. Luis López de Mesa was one of the first to steer scholarly analysis in the direction of Violencia studies when he asserted that his nation had suffered an institutional "heart attack" in November 1949.[7] López de Mesa referred to the suspension of Congress by President Ospina Pérez and the formation by militant Liberals of antigovernment guerrilla forces subsequent to that time. According to his logic Colombia hovered near death, in a state of institutional cardiac arrest throughout the 1950s, until the nation's lifeblood began flowing again in August 1958, when the bipartisan Frente Nacional government began functioning.

The notion that Colombia suffered near fatal institutional collapse in 1949 has led students to focus on politics and violence and to ignore socioeconomic developments taking place during the 1940s and 1950s that were in fact more momentous for the nation. It has kept them from perceiving that save for the Liberal and Conservative Parties and the formal political structure which they defined, most Colombian institutions grew significantly stronger during the years of Violencia.

Interest associations of all sorts enjoyed rapid growth during the years of Colombia's Violencia. Labor historian Miguel Urrutia points out that industry and commercial lobbying organizations known as *gremios* enjoyed a "golden age of power and influence" during the years of the Violencia.[8] So effective had such institutions become by 1957 that they were able to coordinate the bloodless coup against the Rojas Pinilla dictatorship in May of that year. Organized labor underwent a major tactical reorientation during the late 1940s and 1950s, turning from the confrontational tactics of earlier decades to pursue bread and butter issues. Thus by the time of the Frente Nacional, labor stood ready to begin an exponential growth that would carry through the 1960s. Government agencies and institutions also proliferated and flourished during the Violencia years as Colombian society grew more complex. A similar evolution occurred within the quasi-public Federación Nacional de Cafeteros (Fedcafé), considered by many to be a "state within the Colombian state." Fedcafé made wise use of vast revenues flowing into its coffers during the 1950s, using them to launch the important Banco Cafetero, purchase numerous new vessels for its shipping company, and support scores of development projects throughout the coffee zone, including many aimed at restoring prosperity to coffee-growing areas hard hit by the Violencia.

All these developments reflected a growth and strengthening of institutions in Colombia between 1945 and 1960. Thus, while the nation's political heart skipped several beats during those turbulent years, other organs vital to the body politic more than ensured that society escaped a fatal decline.

Colombia's Economic Golden Age

From the mid-1940s to the end of the 1950s, Colombia experienced a rate of economic growth exceeding even that of the preceding fifteen years. Termed both "smooth" and "constant" by economic historians, its economic progress was all the more notable in that it was accompanied by low national budget deficits and comparatively low levels of state investment in economic infrastructure.[9] Gross domestic product increased at an annual rate of 6 percent between 1945 and 1953, and at slightly under 5 percent annually for the entire period (1945–1959).[10]

Those exceptional levels of growth were fueled initially by Colombia's large foreign currency reserves at the end of World War II, and by government monetary policies aimed at spurring the purchase of capital equipment by the private sector. A burgeoning coffee sector lent continuity and dynamism to domestic industrial growth. Coffee prices rose steadily at war's end, from between 15 to 20 cents per pound between 1941 and 1945, to better than 50 cents per pound by 1950. During the 1950s Colombia entered a time of bonanza as prices rose to a historic high of 86.3 cents in 1954, entering a decline only toward the end of the decade.[11] As well as generating monies for industrial development, the coffee bonanza benefited those millions of Colombians involved in the coffee industry. The democratization of earnings moved apace over the extensive area of coffee cultivation, through marked increases in the number of coffee farms, in the number of hectares exploited, and the amount of coffee produced. Between 1932 and 1955, the number of coffee farms, nearly 80 percent of which were managed by owner-operators, grew in number from 149,300 to 234,700, and the area covered by those fincas more than doubled. Production increased correspondingly, rising from 3.5 million sixty-kilo sacks in 1932, to 7 million sacks by 1960. High coffee prices and increasing population produced the breakup of the last of Colombia's large coffee haciendas during the 1950s. By the end of the decade the average size of a coffee finca was but 20.1 hectares, just 3.3 hectares of which was planted in coffee.[12]

Illustrative of the ongoing economic boom itself was the fact of coffee's decline from 1950 onward in terms of its share in the nation's gross domestic product. From generating better than 10 percent of the nation's GDP in 1950–1954, coffee dropped to 8.2 percent in 1960–1964, and to 4 percent in 1970–1975. In terms of percentage of GDP in agriculture, coffee dropped from 28 percent in 1950–1954, to 26 percent in 1960–1964, and to 17 percent in 1970–1975.[13]

It was Colombia's good fortune that its coffee bonanza coincided with and went far toward financing its spurt of import substitution. The industrialization process had been under way for twenty years prior to the coffee bonanza of the 1950s. Between 1930 and 1950 the proportion of nondurable goods as a percent of total imports fell from 30 percent to 3 percent, owing to the growth of import-substituting industry. However, the process became yet more meaningful following World War II, when the country greatly accelerated domestic production of intermediate and capital goods. Between 1950 and 1960, Colombian industry grew by 89.5 percent, with the production of consumer goods continuing to make up the lion's share of manufacturing, but with the manufacture of intermediate and capital goods moving apace. By 1960 those more highly elaborated manufactures totaled 40 percent of all industrial production.[14]

The growth of import-substituting industry in post–World War II Colombia produced two effects beyond easing the country's dependence on foreign manufactured goods. First, the new factories absorbed a large proportion of migrants who reached the nation's cities in growing numbers during the 1950s. In 1955, for example, migrants found a record 18,000 new factory jobs awaiting them in Colombian cities.[15] Second, the growth taking place in import-substituting industry during the 1950s occurred outside the traditional strongholds of manufacturing, Medellín and Bogotá. A great many of the new industries were located in the Cauca Valley, in and around the city of Cali. Others sprang up in Bucaramanga, Pereira, Armenia, and other secondary cities. The effect was a reduction in the relative significance of the Antioquian business community in national economic affairs and the ascendance of Colombia as Latin America's leading nation in terms of geo-industrial balance.[16]

As was the case fifteen years earlier, international developments worked to Colombia's advantage in the economic sphere. Following World War II, the United States and other industrialized nations adopted the policy of promoting free trade through tariff reduction. While that strategy invigorated global commerce, it worked to the disadvantage of countries like Colombia, in the early stages of industrialization and struggling to protect infant industry. Luckily for development-minded Colombians, their nation had been a staunch ally of the United States during the war and hence stood in a position to resist that nation's tariff-lowering initiatives. In fact Colombia, with U.S. blessings, was able to sharply increase tariffs to protect infant import-substituting industry. During 1950 and 1951, and later, in 1958, Colombia negotiated new agreements with the Americans through which it was able to protect its industry from foreign competition. The Americans demanded in exchange a promise that Colombia would not expropriate U.S. businesses and would facilitate the remission of profits by foreign investors.[17] Such conditions imposed no burden on Colombian leaders, since they were eager for foreign investment.

That Colombian leaders were committed to both economic development and capitalism insured them a favorable hearing by international lending agencies. Nor did it harm Colombia's prospects that all presidents holding office from 1945 through the 1950s were outspoken anticommunists who clearly matched the political profile required of those receiving aid from the World Bank and the International Bank for Reconstruction and Development during the early Cold War era. Thus when Colombia applied for a $78 million World Bank development loan shortly after Gaitán's assassination in 1948, the recently formed lending agency quickly took the proposal under study and sent prominent economist Lauchlin Currie to explore the feasibility of large-scale economic assistance for Colombia. Currie's report, submitted in mid-1950, recommended a broad-based, integrated approach to economic development featuring road construction as well as fiscal and land reform. The Currie report, the first of its kind commissioned by the World Bank, produced controversy in Colombia and raised eyebrows in the United States. "We can't go messing around with education and health . . . we're a bank!" exclaimed World Bank vice president Robert Gardner upon studying the plan.[18] "Look, Dr. Currie," said Manuel Mejía, president of powerful Fedcafé, "from the technical point of view what you're suggesting is feasible. But I tell you it will never work in Colombia."[19] Others were more outspoken. Landowners, whom Currie proposed forcing to commercialize their holdings through punitive taxes, damned the scheme as "markedly socialist in orientation" and its author as a malignant reincarnation of Henry George.[20] Marxist critic Rafael Baquero called Currie's reforms "a plan of imperialist colonization" for its proposed integration of national highways toward the end of allowing the developed world easier access to Colombian exports, and socialist Antonio García rejected the report out of hand.[21]

Nevertheless, Laureano Gómez and members of his government embraced the Currie plan. Gómez and his advisors saw it as helping legitimize their own economic program, which stressed fiscal austerity, the improvement of highways and other aspects of the nation's infrastructure, and the encouragement of business and industry. Members of the Gómez administration agreed with World Bank officials that social reforms should be subordinated to those strictly fiscal and administrative. Hence Currie's land reform was quietly shelved in favor of a heterogeneous series of measures that penalized the holders of only the most fertile unused lands.[22] On the other hand, great attention was paid to expediting portions of the plan involving highway construction, irrigation and hydroelectric projects, and the like. This harmony of interests between Colombian and World Bank officials made the Andean nation one of the bank's favored clients in succeeding years. By 1963, Colombia had received more World Bank support for highway construction than any other nation.[23]

The most immediate and far-reaching consequence of World Bank involvement in Colombian affairs lay in the area of banking and monetary policy. During the 1940s and through 1950, Colombia was prone to economic instability sprung from the speculative frenzy set into motion by wartime conditions. Following the war foreign exchange continued to pour into public and private hands, with much of it quickly entering the economy to prevent speculative investment. Inflation was consequently an ongoing problem during those years, hitting the poor and persons on fixed incomes especially hard. Ospina Pérez struggled to slow speculative lending early in his administration, though his commitment to national industrialization caused him to retreat from that position when members of the business community criticized his action.[24] Rapid increases in the cost of living thus became a constant feature of national life during the late forties and were one of the factors aggravating both the rioting of April 9, 1948, and Colombia's subsequent Violencia.[25]

Their ongoing and unsuccessful struggle to control inflation made Colombia's economic elites especially receptive to World Bank recommendations aimed at insuring greater monetary stability. When Currie and his colleagues advised giving the Bank of the Republic central bank features, Colombian leaders rushed to comply. Through Decree 756 of 1951, Laureano Gómez and his finance minister, Antonio Alvarez Restrepo, granted the Bank of the Republic broad new authority over monetary and credit policy nationwide. Especially important in terms of national industrialization were regulations allowing the bank to both mandate and encourage the financing of key basic industries.[26]

Thanks to their enhanced control over the banking system Gómez and Restrepo reduced inflation to acceptable levels during 1951, even as they dropped exchange restrictions and sharply devalued the currency toward the end of increasing exports—both recommendations of the Currie commission. On August 28, 1951, *El Siglo*, at the time Colombia's semiofficial newspaper, praised the government's economic measures as having brought real benefits to average Colombians by cutting their cost of living. Even socialist Antonio García, never one to praise Laureano Gómez or his party, was impressed by the sharp fall in inflation during 1951.[27]

As Colombia's national bank moved away from the orthodoxy imposed on it a quarter century earlier by Edwin Kemmerer and began aggressively encouraging national development, three new semiofficial banks were created. In

1950 the municipality of Bogotá was authorized to establish what became the Banco Popular, whose mission was to serve the needs of the lower and middle classes. Three years later the Banco Cafetero was established to serve Colombia's coffee growers. Its assets were provided and controlled by Fedcafé, and its first president was Antonio Alvarez Restrepo, who had been in involuntary retirement since the coup of Gustavo Rojas Pinilla. In 1955, Rojas Pinilla created the Banco Ganadero to support the cattle industry. Some years earlier, in 1949, Colombia's merchants, acting through their interest association, FENALCO, organized the Banco de Comercio. Its initial task was to redeem government bonds issued to merchants who had suffered losses at the hands of rioters on Nueve de Abril.[28]

Such was Colombia's economic dynamism during the late 1940s and 50s that it could ignore Lauchlin Currie's insistence that the government not undertake ambitious and expensive state-funded development programs. Two major state corporations were authorized between 1948 and 1951—the first a steel mill to be located at Paz del Río, in Boyacá, and the second a national petroleum company, the Empresa Colombiana de Petróleo (ECOPETROL). A third costly undertaking, a shipping company called the Flota Mercante Grancolombiana, financed by the semipublic Federación Nacional de Cafeteros, was organized in July 1946.

All three enterprises were to a certain extent products of the economic nationalism prevalent in developing nations during the mid-twentieth century. Numerous such nations in Latin America, Africa, and Asia attempted to become economically self-sufficient through the construction of costly, publicly financed industrial projects. While such projects frequently were not cost effective and ended as drains on public coffers, Colombia's experiments in shipping, steel making, and oil production were reasonably successful. Of the three, ECOPETROL was least so, as it quickly became politicized. Still the oil monopoly did give Colombia its first effective control over its petroleum reserves, something anti-imperialists had demanded for thirty years. The Flota Mercante Grancolombiana was considerably more successful. Initially formed with the collaboration of Ecuador and Venezuela, it had become largely Colombian by the mid-1950s, comprising a fleet of twenty-one ships, most of whose freight consisted of coffee bound for North American and European ports.[29] Unlike ECOPETROL, the Flota avoided politicization since its ships were purchased and controlled by the affluent and apolitical Fedcafé.

Paz del Río was perhaps the most successful of Colombia's three mid-century experiments in large-scale publicly financed industrial projects. Although not an especially large steel mill, it entered production just as the nation's import-substituting industry began demanding substantial quantities of steel for manifold purposes. Hence in spite of serious startup problems, featherbedding, and an abominable record of plant safety and maintenance, Paz del Río played a significant role in Colombia's industrial development. It also rejuvenated the economy of the highland region where it was located. After the plant began production in 1954, it made possible the appearance of "a countless number of small- and medium-sized factories producing metal furniture, agricultural tools, and domestic articles."[30] Paz del Río also generated a range of subsidiary chemical industries, most notably Carboquímica in Bogotá, which began operation in 1956, producing benzol, xylene, naphtha, and other chemicals derived from coke produced at the Boyacá plant. Suggestive of its success was the fact that two years after it went into operation, financially strapped Gustavo Rojas Pinilla privatized the plant, selling most of its stock to the public.[31]

Thanks in part to the opening of Paz del Río, Colombia experienced a satisfactory evolution in its manufacturing profile. Between 1950 and 1958 capital goods increased from 5 to 10 percent of the nation's total industrial output, while intermediate manufacturing increased to more than 25 percent of all goods produced. The nation's industrial base increased steadily over the 1940s and 1950s, expanding at an annual rate of 10 percent between 1945 and 1950, and 7.4 percent between 1950 and 1958.[32]

As industry expanded Colombian agriculture entered a phase of remarkable transition. When Lauchlin Currie published his famous report in 1950, he called attention to the severe underuse of productive land, which, when considered alongside considerable imports of agricultural goods to satisfy human and industrial needs, spelled trouble for the national economy. But what Currie failed to perceive — a failure for which he was criticized fifteen years later by fellow economist Albert Hirschman — was that Colombia had already begun the process that in fifteen years would bring its best lands into production and thereby end the age-old problem of leaving such lands fallow or devoted to noncommercial prestige uses such as cattle grazing.[33]

From the time Colombia began building its industrial base economists and political leaders had been aware of the costs of importing agricultural commodities that the country should rightly produce itself. During the 1940s they started taking steps to encourage increased agricultural production, steps which had only begun to yield results when Lauchlin Currie first reached the country in 1949. In 1945 the national Congress approved a five-year plan which featured the encouragement of export agriculture through an integrated program of protection and investment credit administered by the Caja Agraria and given additional support by the newly founded Instituto Nacional de Abastecimientos (INA). Five years later, in 1950, commercial banks were authorized to grant special five-year loans earmarked for agricultural development, and a year later the Bank of the Republic was authorized to force commercial banks to invest in agriculture through the purchase of agricultural bonds.[34]

Mariano Ospina Pérez, himself an industrialist with long experience in agriculture, entered office determined to restrain speculative investment in industry and to channel more capital into agriculture, which during the mid-1940s received but 5 percent of the nation's investment dollar. He was especially determined to encourage the production of cotton, which represented a substantial percentage of national imports and was of vital importance to the Antioquian textile industry. Accordingly, and in the face of grumbling from textile magnates that it was "utopian" to think Colombia could ever become self-sufficient in cotton, Ospina adopted a policy of "integral protection," which forced the textile industry to supplement its imports with locally grown cotton.[35] In July 1948, Ospina decreed the formation of the Instituto de Fomento Algodonero, an agency charged with encouraging and overseeing Colombia's nascent cotton industry. Meanwhile he stressed the importance of investing export earnings equally in the nation's agriculture, transportation, and industrial sectors.

During the 1950s, Colombia's efforts to modernize its agricultural sector began to bear fruit. Agricultural production increased by more than 40 percent between 1945 and 1958—and at a steady 3.7 percent annual rate over the twenty-five years following 1950.[36] The industrial sector played its role in this growth, contributing an increasingly sophisticated array of farm implements and machinery. The use of fertilizers increased sixfold between 1949 and 1961, thanks in part to their production at the Paz del Río steel facility. In spite of the pessimistic pronouncements of paisa textile manufacturers, Colombia not only became self-sufficient in cotton but, thanks to a 105 percent increase in cotton production by 1960, began exporting that commodity.[37] Meanwhile middle- and upper-income investors had responded to financial incentives by gaining access to unexploited land through purchase or rental agreements. All across the nation, from Valle del Cauca and the llanos of Tolima, to highland Cundinamarca and Boyacá, and north through the tropical Caribbean lowlands, commercially grown cotton, rice, sorghum, sugarcane, and sesame appeared where none had grown before.

These developments in Colombian agriculture had a dramatic impact on the nation's rural population. Between 1938 and 1951 alone an estimated 850,000 campesinos, approximately 10 percent of the total, quit the land and moved to urban areas.[38] That migration represented only the beginning of a process of rapid urbanization some of whose consequences will be discussed in greater detail below.

By the latter 1950s, Colombia's economy was so fundamentally healthy that even the mismanagement of President Gustavo Rojas Pinilla failed to produce any lasting detrimental effect. Within a year of the "coup by public opinion" that toppled Rojas, and under the steady hand of Antonio Alvarez Restrepo, reinstated as finance minister by the military junta that presided over the country, budgets were balanced, inflation fell to acceptable levels, and so did cost of living indices. When Alberto Lleras Camargo took office in August 1958, he was able to resume the prudent developmentalism that had characterized his brief presidency (1945–1946), and those of his successors Mariano Ospina Pérez and Laureano Gómez.

Labor, Interest Associations, Social Programs, and the Economic Boom

Labor and management alike strove to turn economic growth to their advantage during the 1940s and '50s. Meanwhile the governments in power between 1946 and 1958 took advantage of the boom to launch a variety of programs aimed at improving living conditions of the middle and lower classes. Ospina, Gómez, and Rojas Pinilla promoted social welfare in hopes that their initiatives would lessen the chances that the masses would choose the Marxist-Leninist path to social change.

The economic growth taking place in Colombia between 1925 and 1950 doubled workers' salaries in real terms and produced improvements in the standard of living, as reflected in a range of basic indicators. Colombia's gross domestic product increased an average of 27 percent in each of the five decades following 1925. Worker productivity increased 500 percent over that fifty-year span. But Colombian labor did not perceive itself as having benefited from those advances, an impression not entirely misplaced. By 1951, Colombia had reached its nadir in equity of income distribution, with the wealthiest 5 percent of the population receiving between 40 and 45 percent of national income, and the poorest 20 percent but 2 to 3 percent. Meanwhile a more than 100 percent increase in living costs between 1945 and 1951, a time during which wages increased by less than 50 percent, produced anger and frustration among urban workers.[39] As mentioned above, the rioting and looting that followed the assassination of Jorge Eliécer Gaitán in early 1948 was in no small part attributable to these unpleasant economic realities.

In spite of the nation's rapid urbanization and industrialization during the 1940s and '50s, Colombian labor did not enter a period of sustained growth until the launching of the National Front government in 1958. The explanation for that retarded evolution lay both in the fragmentation that plagued labor during the 1940s and the intensification of that fragmentation over the following decade by Communist gains in the labor movement. The forties dawned with Colombia's most powerful union, the Confederación de Trabajadores Colombianos (CTC), weakened from within by conflict between its

Liberal and Communist members, and attacked from without by Gaitanista labor and a national government highly critical of "political unionism." As early as 1938, Minister of Labor Alberto Lleras Camargo had suggested the coming confrontation between unions and the government when he told delegates attending a labor congress in Cali that "unionism having political goals is corrupting," and pointed out that Colombian labor had its best friend in the Liberal Party.[40] The meaning of his words became clear in 1945, when the national government, at the time headed by Lleras Camargo himself, approved a sweeping new labor law and shortly thereafter crushed a powerful union whose members refused to abide by it. Law 6 of September 1945 marked a turning point for labor because it sanctioned the use of strikes only in the event of the failure of prescribed arbitration procedures. Three months after the legislation went into effect, and as if to test it, the Communist-dominated union FEDENAL paralyzed traffic on the Río Magdalena through the declaration of an illegal strike. Announcing that "Colombia cannot have two governments, one in Bogotá and another on the Magdalena," Lleras militarized river transportation and revoked legal recognition of FEDENAL, effectively ending its existence.

Labor did not learn from the FEDENAL incident. No sooner did Conservative president Mauriano Ospina take office in mid-1948 than the CTC joined Liberal militants in attempting to overthrow him by launching a seemingly endless series of strikes. Results of the unequal struggle between the anarchized CTC and the Colombian government were predictable. Following the failed general strike of May 1947, Ospina Pérez emulated his predecessor, Lleras Camargo, by removing legal recognition of the CTC, which had coordinated the strike, thereby dealing it a crippling blow.[41]

Militant, political unionism declined precipitously following decertification of the CTC in 1947. After the two failed general strikes of April 1948 and November 1949, many Liberal and Communist labor leaders joined the guerrilla forces opposing the regimes of Ospina Pérez and Laureano Gómez. This left Liberal and Communist union leaders, who opposed the government through peaceful means, open to harassment, torture, and even murder by official and paramilitary forces during the early 1950s. Chief among the labor leaders killed by police were Aurelio Rodríguez, Angel María Cano, and Julio Rincón.[42]

Working men and women across Colombia were hardly oblivious to the repeated setbacks of the militantly political CTC and affiliated federations such as the FEDENAL. Most of them understood that their minuscule urban labor corps (only 5 percent of Colombian labor was unionized in the 1950s) was uselessly expending energy and resources through confrontational tactics, a fact workers made clear by turning their backs on the CTC and joining unaffiliated "base unions" organized within individual plants and factories under provisions contained in Law 6 of 1945. Between 1943 and 1947, 342 such independent unions were created, while the number of locals affiliated with federations dropped, from 642 to 324. The success of Colombia's base unions, a direct consequence of the protection contained in the 1945 comprehensive labor law, stimulated the rapid unionization of factories in Medellín and Bogotá. Once the organization of those industries was complete, in the mid-1950s, real salaries began to rise rapidly and union membership increased markedly, from 165,000 in 1947 to 250,000 in 1959.[43]

Urban workers also responded favorably to a new labor confederation, the Unión de Trabajadores Colombianos (UTC), organized in mid-1946. Formed by the Roman Catholic Church and strongly encouraged by the government, the UTC endorsed the notion of harmonious unionism spelled out more than a half-century earlier in the encyclical *De rerum novarum* of Leo XIII. Antiliberal and strongly anticommunist, the UTC eschewed political confrontation and its leaders concentrated instead on bread-and-butter unionism at the local level. Termed a "confessional union" by its critics, all UTC affiliates possessed chaplains and "moral assessors" who preached a paternalistic approach to relations between labor and management. UTC clerical advisors, all of whom were priests, frequently said mass on company premises, led workers on spiritual retreats, and sometimes heard the confession of union members alongside the machines they were charged with tending.[44]

The UTC was hardly as nonpolitical as it claimed to be, for a majority of its members were also members of the Conservative Party. Yet, as it was pledged to principles of collective bargaining spelled out in Law 6 of 1945, and as the union was principally committed to improving wages, benefits and working conditions through nonconfrontational means, many workers not affiliated with the Conservative Party joined and supported the UTC. Yet another factor benefiting the UTC was its anticommunist stance. Many Colombian workers were openly critical of the way "the Comrades infiltrated the labor movement" prior to the appearance of the UTC.[45] A final and highly significant factor contributing to the success of the UTC model of labor federation was that its growth coincided with Colombia's economic boom of the 1950s. In spite of the widespread perception among radical workers that management was benefiting at their expense, labor in fact enjoyed better physical conditions during the 1950s than at any previous time in Colombian history. Jobs were plentiful, salaries on the rise, and the Violencia far from factories and workshops. Hence labor historian Mauricio Archila has characterized the workers active in base unions during the 1950s as generally positive about their union experience.[46]

During the mid-1950s, President Gustavo Rojas Pinilla emulated his predecessors by creating a labor federation made in his own political image. Copying Juan Perón, whose success was owed to the support of workers in

Argentina's cities, Rojas created the Confederación Nacional de Trabajo (CNT), having links with the international Peronist labor group ATLAS. Like its chief rival, the UTC, the CNT was anticommunist. However it lacked the confessional character of its Church-backed rival. For that reason Rojas's union was actively opposed by the Church, never enjoyed much success, and disappeared shortly after the dictator's fall from power.[47]

Colombian labor was poised to enter its time of most vigorous growth as Alberto Lleras Camargo, first president under the Frente Nacional, took office in 1958. Real salaries were in the process of rising 30 percent between 1950 and 1965, and income distribution was beginning to improve as a result of more effective government tax collection and stepped-up government programs of a redistributive nature.[48]

Labor hardly constituted a major force in Colombian society at the end of the 1950s. Its history had been too much one of rank-and-file union members being used to advance the cause of one or another political cause. Yet labor was not impotent. Early in the term of Alberto Lleras bank employees in all of Colombia's major cities went out on strike. Urged on by the influential industry lobby, the Asociación Nacional de Industrias (ANDI), Lleras attempted to break the strike by declaring bank work a public service. But the tellers and other bank employees held firm under the leadership of their UTC-affiliated union, the Asociación de Empleados Bancarios. The banks remained closed. At length Lleras was forced to arbitrate an agreement that resulted in the awarding of a pay raise and enhanced benefits for bank workers.[49]

Colombia's employer associations such as ANDI, known collectively as gremios, played an important role in promoting social and economic stability during the politically turbulent 1940s and 1950s. Unlike the country's labor unions, which tended to pursue confrontational tactics, the gremios lobbied government officials for legislation benefiting their respective constituencies. The gremios owed much of their success to their corporative character, meaning that they served the interests of all those working in a given industry or profession. Of course the gremios were headed by the wealthiest, most influential members of the nation's several occupational groups. In that respect they were twentieth-century incarnations of corporative organizations that exercised great political influence both in medieval Spain and colonial Latin America. Most of Colombia's gremios, however, had mid-twentieth-century origins.

Economist Miguel Urrutia points to four functions of the gremios as insurers of Colombian democracy at a time when irresponsible party leaders had rendered the formal political system dysfunctional.[50] First, by their independent existence they insured that all major economic interests would have a voice in the shaping of government policies affecting the fortunes of that group's members. Powerful national interest groups competed for influence, thus suffusing their sector of Colombian politics with a healthy pluralism. Even during the era of economic protection aimed at encouraging the growth of import-substituting industry, Colombian merchants waged an ongoing campaign, through their gremio, FENALCO, in favor of free markets in accord with principles established in the international General Agreement on Tariffs and Trade (GATT), implemented in 1949. While they made little headway with their arguments through the 1960s, the members of FENALCO served as a salutary counterweight to the preponderant influence of the industrialists.[51] Eventually FENALCO's free trade position came to prevail in Colombia, and the protectionism advocated by FENALCO's chief antagonist, the manufacturer's gremio, ANDI, gave way to less protectionist policies.

A second key function of the gremios lay in their ability to serve as a conduit for the articulation of regional interests. The principal gremios had chapters in every department, thus insuring that local elites could make their feelings known at the seat of national power. This was especially important from 1949 to 1958, when normal channels of political discourse were closed under terms of the state of siege.

The third political function of the gremios lay in the way they provided Colombian leaders a setting within which they could eschew the partisan hatreds that so divided them in public life. Colombian elites clearly found refuge from politics within their gremios, and acted to insulate those business associations from destructive partisanship. In November 1951, during one of the most intense phases of the Violencia, Conservative Eugenio Gómez declined nomination as president of SAC, throwing his support to Liberal Luis Castillo de la Parra on the grounds that "we must seek to alternate the presidency."[52] Three years later Liberal and Conservative cattlemen, acting through their gremio, the Unión Nacional de Ganaderos, joined hands in opposing policies of President Rojas Pinilla that ran counter to their interests.[53] These examples illustrate both how gremios provided nonpartisan mechanisms of political action at a time when Colombia's Liberal and Conservative Parties were in suspension and how they pointed the way toward bipartisan power sharing in the political realm.

A fourth important function of the gremios lay in their helping insulate Colombia from the sort of populist excesses that troubled the postwar economies and politics of Argentina, Peru, and other Latin American nations. By giving power and voice to a wide range of constituent groups representing millions of Colombians, the gremios lessened chances that national politics would fall prey to populist caudillismo. Through the effective representation of constituencies in all parts of the nation gremios were able to moderate the demands of citizens concentrated in Bogotá and other metropolitan areas.[54]

The National Federation of Coffee Growers (Fedcafé) was the gremio most responsible for moderating populist demands. One of the nation's oldest interest associations, and by far the largest and most affluent, Fedcafé was more than a gremio, having much in common with the "peak associations"—broad interest associations having organic links with government—of modern European states. Such was Fedcafé's power that it has been called a "parallel state" in Colombia. Fedcafé's president was sufficiently influential to enjoy instant and direct access to the national president, a perquisite no member of the chief executive's own cabinet could claim.[55] While five of the eleven members of Fedcafé's governing board were indirectly named by the national government, the organization retained control of its own operations. For that reason it was able to resist Rojas Pinilla's efforts to loot the Fondo Cafetero during the mid-1950s. Fedcafé also played a significant role in overthrowing the dictator in 1957.

Fedcafé's governing board was traditionally dominated by the nation's more important coffee growers, processors, and exporters. Yet the organization was structured democratically, with elected committees functioning in half of Colombia's nearly 1,000 municipios. Thanks to its considerable liquid assets, contained in the Fondo Cafetero, Fedcafé offered varied services to coffee growers. These monies underwrote loan programs and financial services, educational and agricultural extension programs, and the construction of highways and electric power networks. These services were offered in addition to the basic one of supporting coffee prices through warehousing and merchandising activities.

Through these activities the coffee growers' federation, Colombia's foremost gremio, served as the voice and institutional anchor of the nation's most significant rural group, the coffee-producing yeoman farmer. Fedcafé, along with ANDI, FENALCO, SAC, and scores of lesser such groups subjected Colombia to what political scientist Robert Dix called "a kind of anarchy of direct action" and to which economists Edgar Revez and María José Pérez referred as the "gremialization" of the Colombian state.[56] But in spite of their exclusive character, Colombia's competing interest associations served that nation as vigorous representative institutions during a trying period when its formal organs of political representation, the Liberal and Conservative Parties, had ceased to function.

In spite of Colombia's grave political problems during the emergence of the gremios, a number of important government social programs were launched during the Violencia years. The rioting attending Gaitán's assassination, which demonstrated the revolutionary potential of the masses, forced Conservatives and Liberals alike to address the needs of the nation's poorest citizens. In months following the Bogotazo, Ospina Pérez ordered the establishment of a new program of land colonization and parcelization and a system of technical education funded by private industry. While the former was abortive, the latter eventually evolved into the highly successful Servicio Nacional de Aprendizaje (SENA). Another law, sparked by public health concerns and by the drunken excesses of April 9, 1948, was the outlawing of chicha, that unhygienically prepared, mildly alcoholic drink made from fermented corn.[57]

Two major pieces of social legislation decreed late in the Ospina Pérez administration were Colombia's social security law of 1949 and its first labor code. Among the provisions of the code were measures mandating severance pay, housing subsidies, paid vacations, and private recreational clubs for employees. Laureano Gómez went on to implement those measures during his brief period as chief executive. During 1950 and 1951, Gómez called into existence the Colombian Social Security Institute (Instituto Colombiano de Seguros Sociales) and also approved special funding for technical education, a program called the Colombian Institute for Technical Education Abroad (Instituto Colombiano para Educación Técnica en el Exterior, ICETEX).

Government-sponsored social programs expanded further under Rojas Pinilla and during the fifteen-month caretaker military regime that followed Rojas's overthrow. The most ambitious of Rojas Pinilla's programs was a multipurpose state welfare agency known as SENDAS. Another of Rojas's initiatives was a system of large quasi-public shopping centers known as Colsubsidio. Rojas also revived the land colonization program initiated under Ospina Pérez. The military junta that ruled between May 1957 and August 1958 expanded the system of quasi-public shopping centers through the founding of CAFAM (Cajas de Cooperación Familiar), and by putting into operation the apprenticeship and technical education program SENA, authorized during the Ospina Pérez administration.

Social Change, 1946–1960

Social change quickened in Colombia following World War II. By 1960 half of all citizens in the once overwhelmingly rural nation lived in cities. Urbanization was rapid and continuous in Colombia from mid-century onward. Population also increased rapidly owing to high birth rates and the decline in infant mortality. Meanwhile political attitudes underwent transformation. Activists grew ever more disillusioned with the old Liberal and Conservative Parties, whose internecine struggles had produced the atrocious Violencia. Colombians who were not activists—and a vast majority fell into that category—found it increasingly easy to distance themselves from both politics and the Violencia thanks to rising income levels and growing social complexity, as well as to the urbanization process that removed them from Violencia-ridden areas.

The social ferment that Colombia experienced from the mid-twentieth century onward had underpinnings in a process of explosive population increase and urbanization that demographers have described as both "uncontrollable," and as "one of the most dramatic demographic transformations of contemporary history."[58] By the 1950s population growth had swelled to an annual rate of thirty-two per 100,000, a rate it would maintain until the early 1960s, when nearly half of all Colombians were under fifteen years of age. By 1960, Colombia's population would double in a mere twenty-two years.[59]

Colombia experienced astonishing growth in the area of education between 1946 and 1958. Those years witnessed a 111 percent increase in public primary education and a 537 percent increase in private primary schools. Secondary education grew by 209 percent, with well over half of that expansion occurring in private colegios.[60] During the 1940s and 1950s Colombians rushed to meet the burgeoning demand for university education. The most notable growth occurred in private institutions, which, while more expensive than public colleges, were rarely disrupted by revolutionary student violence. Colombia's top private universities were founded over a ten-year span beginning in 1948, the more notable among them the universities of Los Andes (1948), Medellín (1950), Gran Colombia (1951), America (1952), Jorge Tadeo Lozano (1954), INCCA (1955), Indesco (1958), and Santiago de Cali (1958). Enrollment in Colombia's private universities increased by 309 percent between 1946 and 1958.[61] Meanwhile the national government opened public universities in several departmental capitals—Ibagué, Bucaramanga, Pereira, and Barranquilla among them—in the process more than doubling the network of state-supported institutions.

By the late 1950s, Colombians were flocking to these institutions, and were sending their children to the new primary and secondary schools at an unprecedented rate. Whereas in 1951 slightly more than half of all school age children were in class, by 1964 that figure stood at 86 percent. Accordingly illiteracy began to decline, falling below 50 percent early in the 1950s, to 27 percent during the 1960s, and reaching 15 percent by the 1980s.[62]

This avidity for education, like the urbanization process itself, bore a direct and immediate relationship to income level and desire for social mobility. Poor Colombians knew that their standard of living was far more likely to improve in the city than in the campo and that their children would experience social ascent to the extent that they became educated. Such understanding, generalized throughout fervid, burgeoning Colombia of the postwar period, could not but produce change at every level of society. However, change did not necessarily mean affluence, except in a relative sense. Colombia was one of Latin America's poorest nations as the twentieth century began, with 80 percent illiteracy and fewer than 20 percent of the citizenry living in urban areas. The fact that fewer than 50 percent of the population was illiterate and rural fifty years later indicates a notable social evolution in a scant five decades. Fully a quarter of the population was reasonably well-off by the decade of the 1960s. Another quarter of the population fell somewhere in the middle class. Historian Jesús A. Bejarano captures the somewhat ambiguous position of a poor yet improving Colombia around 1960. He finds that while on average Colombians were far from well-off, "they were better off than [they had been] fifteen years earlier."[63]

Rapid urbanization, population growth, and new demands on the education system were just three aspects of the social transformation bringing rank-and-file Colombians into the mainstream of national history. Those changes also sped the attack on traditional custom and convention. Women were major beneficiaries of social change in the sense that as they removed themselves to the nation's cities, they became freer than ever before to control their personal destinies. Increasing numbers of women began defying convention by entering into free unions or by marrying civilly, thereby bypassing the conventional Catholic church wedding. Whereas only 10 percent of all urban women married outside the Church or lived in free relationships in 1912, 30 percent did so in 1950, and 60 percent did so at the end of the 1960s.[64] Their increased access to medical care made it possible for Colombian women to explore modern family-planning techniques for the first time in their history. As a consequence the nation that had experienced one of the continent's highest rates of natural increase during the 1950s saw that trend slow to one of Latin America's lowest near century's end.[65] Yet another gain for Colombian women was their right to vote, granted in 1954 by President Gustavo Rojas Pinilla.

As Colombians moved to the city and as society broadened and became more complex, popular culture also started to reflect growing diversity. Colombians bought radios in such numbers that by 1950 there were half a million in the nation—one for every twenty people—and those radios were tuned to receive an increasingly diverse range of programs. The more humble classes preferred melodramas and music, especially Caribbean rhythms, *vallenatos* from Colombia's Caribbean coast, and Mexican *rancheras*. Middle-class teenagers scandalized their parents by listening to North American rock and roll, which members of the older generation regarded as "jungle rhythms." Locally produced comedy and news programs were popular, as were dramas bearing titles like *The Right to Life, Hotel Hubbub,* and *Angel of the Street*. Liberals and Conservatives extended their competition to the airwaves, the former launching the nation's first radio network, Caracol, in 1948, and the latter following suit with their channel, RCN, early the following year. In 1949 the Catholic Church entered the competition for listeners too, founding Radio Sutatenza in Boyacá, and gearing it to the interests of rural listeners. Colombian television made its appearance on June 13, 1954, the anniversary of Rojas Pinilla's ascension to power. It was appropriate that Rojas should initiate his nation's television era, as he was one of the first Colombians to have seen its invention, demonstrated in conjunction with a German military exhibition held in 1936.[66]

Long frustrated by cultural, economic, and environmental barriers that isolated them from the greater world, Colombians embraced modernity in the years following World War II. Consumption increased at an annual rate of 6.2 percent between 1945 and 1953, with variety store chains like Ley and Tía providing low-cost mass-produced goods to the lower and middle classes.[67] Fast food emporia and drive-in restaurants catered to the more affluent classes, whose children came to be known as Cocacolos for the avidity with which they consumed that beverage. Old habits of mind and social conventions of every sort were denounced everywhere as symbols of an antediluvian past.

The nation's architects and builders were among the most iconoclastic of all Colombians. As cities like Bogotá grew sixteenfold in the half-century following 1935, architects embraced modernism as their guiding creed. Minimalist, rectilinear glass-and-steel skyscrapers were to them pristine expressions of the modern age. "Urbanism," one of them wrote effusively, "is happiness, it is to live with gusto, it is light, it is hygiene."[68]

When the high priest of modernism, Le Corbusier (1887–1965), visited Bogotá in 1947, the Frenchman's followers gave themselves over to him with what has been described as "adolescent totality." Adopting Corbusian slogans such as "The house is a machine for living," they rallied against Karl Brunner's "feudal urbanism" of the late 1930s and early '40s, which had given Bogotá neighborhoods like Bosque Izquierdo and La Merced, featuring curving tree-lined boulevards and streets that intersected at other than right angles.[69] Anything constructed earlier was beneath contempt, suitable only for the wrecking ball. Consequently the late 1940s and 1950s featured wholesale destruction of buildings dating from the Republican era, considered reprehensible by modern standards.

Young modernists loathed the informal neighborhoods that were springing up pell-mell around urban centers. They stressed instead order and rationality in residential planning. They gave substance to their ideas by designing housing developments like Centro Antonio Nariño and Ciudad Kennedy, featuring moderately priced multifamily apartment buildings. The former, inaugurated during the early 1950s, was for members of the middle class. The latter, opened for occupancy ten years later, and featuring multistory structures simple in design and bereft of decoration, provided housing for the popular classes.

Colombia's idealistic young modernists did their best to bring order and rationality to an increasingly frenetic urban scene. They echoed Le Corbusier's remark that "Bogotá's chaotic urbanism reminds me of the young woman who, at seventeen, decides to leave home and embark upon life's adventure with no supervision whatsoever."[70] A later generation of Colombian architects criticized the movement as ahistorical "paper urbanism, slavishly imitative of foreign models," and driven by "an uncontrollable mania for physical trans-formation" born of an uncritical acceptance of foreign, largely North Ameri-can, trends.[71] While that was undoubtedly the case, the infatuation with mod-ernism affecting Colombia's architectural community during the postwar years was simply one more symptom of the nation's growing cosmopolitanism.

The ongoing effort of Colombians to put tradition behind them after the war, and the growth of individualism in society at large, are clearly revealed in the field of pictorial art. Members of the artistic community were in full revolt against classical canons during the late 1940s. By 1949 critic Fernando Guillén Martínez could proclaim the battle against formalism won, exulting that Co-lombian art had "broken nearly every link with an academic past." After view-ing works exhibited in the 1949 salon held in Bogotá, Guillén wrote that "spiritual merit" had at last triumphed over banal naturalism.[72] Guillén's words were prophetic in the sense that over the course of the following decade surreal and abstract works dominated the Colombian art world. Writing of the 1957 national exhibition, Luis Alberto Acuña referred to the "homogeneous spirit of tendentious modernism that unifies the salon."[73]

A year later, in the National Salon of 1958, young artist Fernando Botero emerged as one of his nation's premier artists with his acclaimed *La camera degli sposi*. Neither abstract nor surreal, the painting was filled with the obese figures that would become his hallmark. Marta Traba, on her way to becoming her nation's foremost critic, praised the piece as exceptionally original. She found it "as antibaroque as it was anticlassical, as antiexpressionist as it was antiabstract."[74] Thus, with Botero, Colombian artists moved toward authen-tic, indeed autochthonous, modes of expression. Still more important for the present analysis, Botero's 1958 canvas captured the quality of individualism that was increasingly coming to dominate Colombian life. Critic Walter Engel suggested that facet of the disconcerting *La camera* in a commentary that might equally serve as an apostrophe directed to Colombia and its people in the latter twentieth century: "It is a difficult and disconcerting work at first contact. It does not make concessions. It does not approach the viewer, it does not aid in the receptive process, it does not try to please. It keeps itself at a majestic distance, in ironlike immobility, in distant, autonomous, and arrogant self-existence."[75]

Colombian literature revealed an intense politicization during the postwar years. The country's top novelists—Jorge Zalamea, Eduardo Caballero Cal-derón, and Gabriel García Márquez—were all men with strong left and Liberal Party ties. Therefore during the period of Conservative ascendance they focused their efforts on exposing the failings of the regime in power. Laureano Gómez served as a model for Zalamea's two best works, *La metamórfosis de su excelencia* (1949) and *El Gran Burundún Burundá ha muerto* (1952). Eduardo Caballero Calderón dealt with the Violencia in his best-known work, *Cristo de espaldas* (1952). As well as serving as notable examples of writing on Colombia's Violencia, the works cited here served the political end of portraying Liberals and their party as hapless victims of Conservative rule.

Less encumbered by political baggage than the writers of prose, Colombia's poets cast their critique of postwar society more broadly. They expressed anguish over what they perceived as the dehumanization of contemporary society by consumerism and the expansion of material culture, decrying "a world increasingly given over to utilitarian values and to the machine." They sought some impulse that might counter "the alien forces in society that are progressively stripping the world's peoples of their humanity." Failing to find any such antidote to modernism many younger poets adopted the apolitical rejectionism of the Nadaístas, only to be denounced by critics as "pseudo hippies," and as "not having serious theoretical bases . . . being a mix of anarchism and clichéd existentialism." Many Nadaístas took refuge from the world in alcohol and drugs.[76] Thus, like the movement's founder, paisa Gonzalo Arango (1931–1976), they lived brief lives, bequeathing their countrymen a body of poetry evenhanded in its rejection of both capitalist and Marxist visions of Colombian society. Gonzalo Arango's poem "La Universidad" illustrates this poetic perspective: "The bourgeoisie can produce only black market values—values of class privilege and sectarianism . . . Rotary Club and garden club ideals, culture subordinated to the interest of power and money. The politicized university offers no more: it is dogmatic and demagogic, utopian and passionate. It idolizes dogma; its victim is freedom of conscience, its Bible is *Das Kapital.*"[77]

Looking back on Colombia's postwar period, social historian Patricia Londoño Vega reflects that the latter 1940s and the 1950s were a time of fragmentation of national life. During those years "things lost value in and of themselves and were converted into symbols." Colombians renounced their traditional "interior style of life," the simple virtues and pleasures of premodern times were lost.[78] Carlos Niño echoes those words, pointing to the "impoverishment of the quality of life" in Colombia from the mid-1940s onward, attributing it to the combined impact of "consumption and massification."[79] Foreigners who spent time in Colombia during the 1950s tended to agree with those assessments. French priest Louis Lebret, commissioned by Rojas Pinilla in 1955 to assess Colombian social needs, was appalled by the near absence of cooperative organizations in the country and was shocked when he discovered that 70 percent of all students who accepted government scholarships to study in state normal schools used their high school for social advancement, turning their backs on teaching in favor of higher-paying jobs. Lebret denounced that trend as selfish and dishonorable.[80] Another French visitor, Yvon Le Bot, wrote sourly of Colombia's privately funded, state-sponsored apprenticeship programs such as ICETEX and SENA, which he found to be accomplishing no more than moving the nation's workforce "from primitive capitalism to organized capitalism."[81]

These observations suggest that the process of privatization and turning away from collective public concerns had indeed gained momentum in Colombia after World War II. Idealists of varied political persuasion protested these developments. Right-wing zealots like doughty Monsignor Builes fulminated against the growing "dechristianization and paganization" of Colombians. Many on the left castigated their like-minded elders for having failed to instill in the citizenry "compassion, communitarian solidarity, respect for others, and an appreciation for the public sphere."[82] Marxists rejected bourgeois culture as hopelessly individualistic and partisan democracy as practiced in Colombia as an anarchizing social force.

As political elites debated the proper form of social organization, frequently shedding blood in the process of attempting to impose their respective ideological visions on each other, Colombians increasingly rejected those solutions as out of step with national life. Between 1950 and 1957 two men attempted to impose unrealistic political arrangements on the nation. First, Laureano Gómez tried to restructure national institutions along corporative lines; next Gustavo Rojas Pinilla moved to impose populist authoritarianism on the people. As those two political experiments were conducted, the nation entered the second decade of the Violencia, testifying to the self-destructive character of traditional political partisanship.

I I

Politics and Violence under Gómez and Rojas

Laureano Gómez and the Quest for Harmony

No Colombian president took office amid greater adversity than did Laureano Gómez. When Gómez accepted his nation's top political post from Mariano Ospina Pérez on August 7, 1950, he faced intransigent opposition from the majority Liberal Party. While Liberal leaders agreed that their preeminent goal was to remove Gómez from power, they were seriously at odds as to how that should be done. Moderates like Darío Echandía endorsed strict noncooperation with the government and electoral abstention, while militants such as Carlos Lleras promoted continuation of the armed resistance that had placed 10,000 Liberal guerrillas in the field during the eight months following Gómez's election in late 1949. The new president's own party was seriously split between his own ideological faction and that of moderates headed by Mariano Ospina Pérez. Conservative factionalism was complicated by the dissidence of Gilberto Alzate Avendaño, leader of a younger generation of politicians whose ambitions had for decades been frustrated by the implacable Gómez. Thus, Laureano Gómez took office as the leader of a factionalized minority party whose task it was to preside over a nation torn by civil war. Compounding his problems was the fact that Gómez was a sick man when he took up his presidential duties. Decades of cigarette smoking had taken its toll on the caudillo, then in his sixty-first year, afflicting him with heart disease, arteriosclerosis, and high blood pressure. Given his physical and political disabilities, it is remarkable that Laureano Gómez remained titular head of Colombia until his overthrow in the military coup of June 1953.

Gómez was filled with the best of intentions when he took office. From the time of his election he had given his public pronouncements a statesmanlike tone, promising to be "president of all Colombians" and vowing that "the primordial preoccupation of my government will be to guarantee the right to life of all citizens."[1] In his inaugural address he professed to be tired of "politics as usual" (*politiquería*), promising the nation a "new style of politics."[2] Following Liberal rejection of his offer to include them in his government, Gómez put together a cabinet that roused the ire of Laureanistas like Antonio

Escobar Camargo, who judged it to be full of "lukewarm, 'liberal-tending' Conservatives." Escobar also found Gómez to be "obsessed" with giving Colombia a national, nonsectarian administration. "I don't know what the Liberals want," said Gómez, "but we must listen to what they're saying. . . . We must sacrifice all to the pacification of the nation."[3] A few months into his administration one of Gómez's bitterest political enemies, *El Tiempo* columnist Enrique Santos, wrote the president complaining that one of his appointees, Carlos Arturo Torres Poveda, governor of Boyacá, had publicly slandered him. When Gómez verified that was indeed the case, he sacked Torres.[4]

Gómez's effort to placate the Liberals was too little too late. It was impossible for Liberals to forgive or forget the previous twenty years during which the Conservative leader had fought the Liberal Republic, returning his party to power in 1946. Furthermore the Liberal Party was hopelessly fragmented in 1950. Its largest and most vocal faction was that headed by Eduardo Santos and Carlos Lleras Restrepo, itself divided by Santos's disavowal of the guerrillas and Lleras's support of them. Opposing both Santos and Lleras was Alfonso López Pumarejo, who emerged from retirement to oppose the rejectionists. López's goal was to discover a mechanism through which Liberals might enter into a peace pact with the Gómez government. His lot was especially thankless, as a majority of his fellow party members could not tolerate the thought of dealing with the hated Gómez. Delegates to the 1951 Liberal convention rejected López's call for negotiation in favor of a platform summarized as "abstention all along the line, civil opposition all along the line." López later remarked laconically that his colleagues had "left me standing there alone." Following yet another year of fruitless effort aimed at leading his party into peace negotiations, Alfonso López resigned from the Liberal directorate and announced his retirement from politics.[5]

Yet another division in Liberal ranks, one presaging the serious party split of a decade later, was represented by resurgent Gaitanista dissidence. In late 1950 a new group, the Popular Liberal Junta (Junta Popular Liberal, JPL), was organized. Its announced goal was to wrest party control from "rightist oligarchs" like Carlos Lleras, and to end the Violencia by supporting Gómez's government. JPL leaders said they would do so "if it is true that [Gómez] is inexorably against crime and impunity, if he dedicates himself to the task of healing the wounds of Colombians, and if he genuinely believes that the greatest need of the nation is peace."[6]

Colombia's political deadlock of the early 1950s was rooted in the Violencia and in the mutually exclusive views of it held by Liberals and Conservatives. Liberals saw guerrilla warfare as a necessary response to what they considered Conservative tyranny. For Liberals the guerrilla fighter was a heroic figure who braved daunting odds in order to defend himself and his family from the depredations of murderous Chulavita police. Conservatives viewed the civil war as another face of Liberal rebellion against the legal, democratically elected regimes of Ospina Pérez and Laureano Gómez. They saw the guerrillas as a mix of Liberals, Communists, and bandits. Convinced that simple criminals predominated among the *violentos,* the governments of Ospina and Gómez were committed to attacking them with all the armed force at their command. One of Roberto Urdaneta Arbeláez's first acts as minister of war was to warn that all adult Colombians living in the llanos who opposed the army or police would be considered bandits, subject to summary execution.[7]

The Cold War further complicated Colombia's Violencia, as the two phenomena shared the same historical moment. Winston Churchill delivered his famous "Iron Curtain" speech in Fulton, Missouri, two months before the election of Ospina Pérez to the Colombian presidency. Joseph McCarthy launched his anticommunist crusade in Wheeling, West Virginia, in February 1950, two months after Laureano Gómez was elected president and seven months before Gómez, Colombia's most vehement anticommunist, entered office. Never mind that Carlos Lleras and most of the Liberal leadership were also anticommunists. The fact that they accepted help from their nation's minuscule Communist Party was sufficient to tar them as accomplices in what cold warriors viewed as the Soviet-backed assault on the Christian, capitalist West. For staunch anticommunists like Minister of Government Roberto Urdaneta the Liberal-Communist tie lent credence to Laureano Gómez's charge of July 1949, that the Liberals were pawns in a game directed from Moscow, whose goal was the nation's "communization." Hence in mid-1951, Urdaneta announced that Liberal support of the guerrillas possessed an "undeniably communist style and savor," and that it followed a plan whose object was "to destroy the national economy and to hurl Colombia into chaos."[8] Some years later Urdaneta explained the Violencia itself as part of a global communist conspiracy. Beginning with the historically inadmissible premise that guerrilla fighters were "exotic among us" and thus could not have emerged spontaneously on Colombian soil, he reasoned that the Violencia necessarily was "the fruit of a preconceived plan skillfully executed by persons outside our bipartisan political tradition."[9]

His own anticommunism, coupled with his desire to support the hemisphere's leading anticommunist power, the United States, were among the reasons that caused Laureano Gómez to eagerly support the American-backed UN police action in Korea. During his inaugural address he had promised that Colombia would join the United States in its effort to defend the sovereignty of nations and of "the liberty and dignity of men, that communist tyranny destroys." Earlier in the talk and in allusion to Nueve de Abril, Gómez had praised the Army for preserving Colombia's traditional culture and insuring that the nation did not fall to "the communist tyranny."[10] Accordingly, within three months of taking office Gómez had dispatched the frigate *Almirante Padilla* to join U.S. forces. Early the following year a battalion of Colombian infantry joined the allied war effort in Korea, the only Latin American forces so committed.[11]

Five weeks before the *Almirante Padilla* set sail for eventual service off the coast of Korea, Laureano Gómez suffered a life-threatening attack of hypertension while touring military bases in southern Colombia. Quick surgical intervention lowered the president's blood pressure, and within two days Gómez was back at work.[12] The attack shocked and frightened Conservatives because at that moment the next in line for the presidency was none other than Liberal Eduardo Santos, whom Congress had elected designado prior to its dissolution the year before. Gómez acted quickly to decree the post of designado vacant under the state of siege that had been in effect for nearly a year, and to establish a new order of presidential succession through the cabinet. The minister of government would henceforth serve as first designate, followed by the foreign and war ministers. Gómez justified his action as vital to the common good and necessitated by the ongoing hostility between Liberals and Conservatives.[13]

One day after announcing Santos's replacement by Minister of Government Domingo Sarasty, Santos forwarded an open letter of protest to Sarasty and his fellow cabinet members. That letter and the response to it stand as two of the most intemperate in Colombian political literature. As such they illustrate both the depth of bitterness between political elites and the impossibility of political accommodation as long as Laureano Gómez remained president. Santos accused the government of exercising dictatorial rule over the nation, while Sarasty defended the legality of his government's action. Santos charged that Conservative violence in 1949 had resulted in "elections every bit as totalitarian as those held in Moscow, Madrid, and Ciudad Trujillo." Sarasty countered with a concise statement of his party's view of Liberal responsibility for the ongoing political turmoil: "You defend neither law, nor justice, nor liberty, nor the separation of public powers, nor the sanctity of the Constitution, but rather a personal and political hope that today stands frustrated. . . . Your intent is clear. You think you can use a national misfortune to gain for your party what you could not get through the failed coup attempts of 1948 and 1949, as well as to reclaim for yourself a canceled designacy. In doing so you may second the questionable work of your party, but you do not pursue any point of law."[14]

After resolving the question of presidential succession to his liking, Laureano Gómez turned to implementing his political and economic agendas.

But his efforts were limited by ill health. Only through following a severely reduced work schedule was Gómez able to remain in office through 1950 and most of 1951. But even that proved too much. On October 28, 1951, he suffered a life-threatening heart attack that left him an invalid. Three days later Congress granted his request to temporarily retire from the presidency.

Laureano Gómez may have left the presidency, but he made certain he controlled the government from his sickbed. He did so in three ways. First, he left behind a corps of lieutenants whom he could trust to carry out his programs. Key among them were Roberto Urdaneta, confirmed acting president in early November, Luis Ignacio Andrade, a longtime Laureanista who was named minister of government, Jorge Leyva, a Gómez protégé who retained his post as minister of public works, and his son Alvaro Gómez Hurtado, who led the Laureanistas in the Senate. Second, Gómez maintained control over the Conservative Party by turning back the attempt of Gilberto Alzate Avendaño to gain control of the party directorate. Not long after his defeat Alzate grumbled, "I hate the government, I detest its representatives, I despise the president and his ministers, I repudiate their actions, [and] I combat their errors."[15] He would later play a leading role in overthrowing Gómez.

Finally Gómez attempted to maintain his influence by reforming the national constitution. His plan was to vastly strengthen the executive branch of government at the expense of Congress, which would be given a corporative and technocratic character. Regional and local autonomy would be sharply curtailed, and the heads of families granted a double vote in local elections on the theory that married men were more prudent than single ones. The reform, which was to take effect in mid-1953, was aimed at promoting the common good by curtailing the disassociative and anarchizing effects of majoritarian democracy.

Laureano Gómez was not the first president to try to impose his legal and social ideology on the nation through fundamental constitutional reform. Alfonso López, Miguel Antonio Caro, and other chief executives had also undertaken sweeping constitutional changes. The expectation that political leaders could and should impose their views on the nation was rooted in Latin America's legalistic and administrative tradition and was augmented by the elitist presumption that highly educated men knew what was best for their fellow citizens and therefore were obligated to lead them along the path to greater virtue. Laureano Gómez demonstrated such inclination shortly after taking office. Convinced that Liberalism had corrupted the nation's youth, he launched a program of "re-Christianizing" the nation's educational establishment by injecting heavy doses of religion into the curriculum and firing teachers who were not confessing Catholics.[16] His reform of the constitution, begun a year after his education decrees, was viewed by Gómez and his followers as yet another step toward social harmony and the common good through striking at pernicious liberalism.

Laureano Gómez outlined his plan of constitutional reform in a message to Congress on October 30, 1951. That document, sent from his sick bed, called for the transformation of the national Congress into a partially corporative body whose upper chamber would be drawn from employer and professional associations, labor organizations, the Church, and other such groups. Memories of the disastrous 1949 session, in which Congress tried to impeach Ospina Pérez and consequently was suspended by him, were still fresh in the minds of Colombian Conservatives. Laureano Gómez and the others found in corporatism what they believed to be a suitable way of moderating the effects of majoritarian democracy by strengthening presidential control over Congress.

Corporative political schemes were nothing new to Colombia. As early as the nineteenth century Conservative politicians like Sergio Arboleda and Miguel Antonio Caro had endorsed corporatism as compatible with their organic social vision and a useful antidote to the majoritarian democracy they viewed as inevitably subversive of social order. Liberals Rafael Uribe Uribe and Jorge Eliécer Gaitán had on occasion endorsed the idea of reorganizing the national Senate along corporative lines, turning it into a "working chamber," as Uribe Uribe had put it. Writing in 1930, young industrialist and politician Mariano Ospina Pérez had also called for a more technical organization of Congress.

In the late 1930s and early 1940s, Conservative intellectuals had published a spate of works advocating corporative political arrangements as a means of immunizing the nation from radical political experiments sponsored by an ever more mass-based electorate.[17] Laureano Gómez had reflected the growing Conservative fear of majoritarian democracy when he announced his "disenchantment" with Congress and his decision to give up his Senate seat at the end of 1942. At that time he began advocating a "mixed" democratic system with corporative overtones and defending corporatism as not synonymous with Nazism, fascism, or falangism.[18]

Gómez's interest in corporative political organization increased sharply following Nueve de Abril. Interviewed in Spain in October 1948, he opined that while Colombia possessed a "pure and unsullied democracy," popular rule had become ineffective and political leaders "incapable of halting or subduing the Communist revolution." He admitted to searching for a political system that was neither totalitarian nor predicated on universal suffrage, adding that he had found the corporative regime implanted in Spain by Generalissimo Francisco Franco to be worthy of study.[19] Six months before his inauguration as president, Gómez stated that when national legislation is formulated by

persons sent to Congress by distinct occupational groups — labor unions, farmers, industrialists — the quality of representative government is improved.[20]

The ill-fated attempt to recast the national constitution along corporative
lines occupied Laureanista politicians over the entirety of 1952. Liberals boycotted the Constituent Assembly convened by acting president Urdaneta in
midyear, as did anti-Laureanistas, who were rapidly coalescing around the
leadership of Gilberto Alzate Avendaño and Mariano Ospina Pérez. Those
who did choose to attend the sessions of the body, known by its acronym
ANAC (Asamblea Nacional Constituyente), labored diligently at their assigned task, at length producing a document conveying its writers' intent to
create an authoritarian system of government headed by an all-powerful president. To that end they proposed reducing the length of the congressional session (Article 68), increasing the length of the president's term to six years
(Article 114), and removing from Congress the right to elect members of the
Supreme Court (Article 145), to impeach the chief executive (Article 131), and
to perform numerous other functions traditionally required of that body.[21]

Members of ANAC took pains to reverse the secularizing trend seen in the
1936 constitutional reform. They renewed church-state ties that the Liberals
had severed, again granting Roman Catholicism the special protection of the
state. Proselytizing by other religions was restricted (New Title III), public
education was to be carried out in accord with Catholic religious doctrine
(New Title III), and the sovereignty of the Church within its own sphere was
guaranteed (Article 53).

Overtly corporative aspects of the constitutional revision were those dividing the national Senate equally between members directly elected by the citizenry and those drawn from professional and occupational groups. The family, referred to as the "principal and fundamental unit of society," was
accorded special protection by the state (New Title IV, par. 7). Conservative
belief that the family, rather than the individual, was the nuclear unit of society
led to one of the more curious provisions, by which married persons had a
double vote in concejo elections (New Title XX, par. 11). The Conservative
conviction that the state is ordained by natural law, and that its citizens possess
certain God-given rights and obligations, accounted for the moralistic tone of
the "Reform of 1953." Throughout the document citizens were enjoined to
comport themselves in a moral and harmonious fashion. Class conflict was
expressly prohibited (New Title IV, par. 1) and members of Congress were
required to be ever mindful of the common good during their deliberations
(Article 105). Public officials were charged with maintaining a high level of
social responsibility, and failing that were stripped of their right to vote (Articles 143, 180).

Laureano Gómez was well pleased with the handiwork of his constitution
writers. In late 1952 he published an essay, "Effects of the Reform of 1953,"

in which he described the salutary effects he believed the revised constitution would have on national life. Among them were the salvation of the nation from leftists bent on communizing Colombia in accord with a master plan drawn up in Moscow and Belgrade. By allowing the president to deal firmly with subversives, the new constitution would lead to a quick resolution of the Violencia, which Gómez described dismissively as an "upset" inspired by communists who goaded police into overreacting in order to discredit the government. Through the document's corporatism Colombians would free themselves from the "myth of universal suffrage," which had caused so many other peoples to fall under rule of the one-half plus one. The new document would respond to the "Encyclopedist sophistry" of universal suffrage, continued Gómez, through its organicism and its reliance on moral law quarried from "the inexhaustible mine of the perennial philosophy." Having set its fundamental governing institutions right, the Conservative caudillo concluded, Colombia would soon be hailed by all other countries as a nation that "knew how to liberate itself from the anguish and uncertainty presently afflicting the world."[22]

Gómez's panglossian reading of his country's immediate prospects underlined the troubling, even surreal image that Colombia presented at the end of 1952. On the one hand, the country was making great economic strides. Business was booming, coffee prices were rising as never before, and social modernization was transforming the nation. Yet relations between leaders of the Liberal and Conservative Parties stood at an all-time low, and the Violencia grew worse with each passing day. More than 13,000 citizens perished in the Violencia in 1952.[23] Not only had the civil war shown no sign of abating in areas where the Liberal guerrillas and government police and army confronted one another in the field, but the fighting was rapidly expanding into the rugged Sumapaz region south of Bogotá.

Colombians were initially hopeful that 1952 might bring resolution of the Violencia. New acting president Roberto Urdaneta initiated conversations with guerrilla leaders operating in the llanos, sending senior Liberal leaders to meet with Eduardo Franco Isaza on December 21, 1951.[24] Earlier that year Urdaneta, then minister of war, had dispatched Conservative José Gnecco Mozo to discuss peace prospects with the llano guerrillas. At about the time of Gnecco's visit the leader of Liberal forces in southwest Antioquia, Juan de Jesús Franco, wrote his peers in the llanos asking that they not attack Army units but concentrate instead on the Chulavita police. Meanwhile the Army reciprocated by avoiding combat with the llano guerrillas whenever possible.[25]

Unfortunately the Violencia was too far entrenched by 1952 to allow for its quick resolution. Roberto Urdaneta was Laureano Gómez's man after all, and the guerrilla had sworn to remain in the field until the hated Gómez was driven from power. Even had it been possible to reach a modus vivendi between the government and the 10,000 guerrillas fighting under Franco Isaza, Guadalupe Salcedo, Tulio Bautista, and the other llanos chieftains, there were simply too many other armed groups operating over too much of the national territory for any regional truce to be binding. At the moment Alfonso López and Eduardo Franco Isaza toasted their peace conversations with imported Scotch whiskey in late 1951, there were at least 10,000 guerrillas operating outside the llanos in the central and eastern cordillera. By one estimate Juan de Jesús Franco Yepes commanded several thousand troops fighting on twenty-two fronts in southeastern Antioquia.[26] The fact that Liberals and Conservatives were far from unified in their approach to peacemaking also made it impossible for Urdaneta and López to halt the Violencia. Even as the acting president promoted dialogue between the guerrillas and the government, Urdaneta's minister of government, the intransigent Luis Ignacio Andrade, instructed department governors to use all means at their disposal to halt the Liberal subversion. Meanwhile *El Siglo* continued its diatribe against "Liberal banditry."[27] Liberal militants led by Carlos Lleras continued their strident support of the guerrillas, whom they described as "nothing more than the natural fruit of the situation that Conservative authorities created in the nation."[28]

An illustration of the intractable character of the Violencia in 1952 came on April 6, when a group of Liberals and Conservatives, among whom was a son of Urdaneta Arbeláez, were ambushed by Liberal guerrillas while returning from a visit to the Violencia-plagued mountain town of El Líbano, Tolima. The president's son and other dignitaries escaped unharmed, but an accompanying army escort was trapped and massacred. Government response was quick and brutal. The area was cordoned off and army units then moved through it killing anyone suspected of being a guerrilla. Some 1,500 persons died during the operation, a majority of them civilians not involved in the ambush. Those who had staged the initial attack had long since fled, leaving those living in the heavily populated coffee-growing region to bear the brunt of the military's fury.[29]

Public order continued to deteriorate as the year progressed. Incidents such as the one in El Líbano produced an outcry that aborted the "Crusade for Peace," a program launched by acting president Urdaneta and Archbishop Luque in May 1952.[30] The renewed violence merely strengthened the resolve of combatants on either side. By mid-1952 the partial truce between army and guerrillas in the llanos had collapsed. The progressive integration of members of the national police into army units had diminished the army's image as an honest broker in the llano fighting.[31] That fact was underscored on July 12, when Guadalupe Salcedo and Alberto Hoyos ambushed and wiped out a ninety-six-man rifle company near Puerto López, an action signaling sharply renewed conflict throughout the region. The massacre of soldiers reintensified debate over the role of Liberal leaders in encouraging armed resistance in the llanos. Government supporters began repeating a favorite aphorism of Monsignor Builes: "The snake does not kill from its tail but from its head." Even nominally benign Conservatives like newspaper editor Fernando Gómez Martínez began openly attacking Liberal leaders. "You Liberals . . . are playing war," Gómez Martínez fumed in an open letter of August 21, 1952, to newspaper editor Eduardo Uribe Escobar: "You do not make war directly, but neither do you condemn it . . . when members of the armed forces lose their lives in battle."[32]

Shortly after the ambush in the llanos, prominent Liberals in Bogotá began receiving death threats. In late August a bomb was thrown at the home of Liberal Party director José Joaquín Castro Martínez. Government officials condemned the act, yet Liberals correctly saw it as a warning that the Violencia would soon touch themselves directly.[33] One month after the bombing of Castro Martínez's home, Conservative mobs rampaged in Bogotá, destroying the offices of El Tiempo and El Espectador as well as the homes of Carlos Lleras Restrepo and Alfonso López Pumarejo. President Urdaneta was out of town when the events of September 6, 1952, took place, but had he been on hand it is not likely that he could have halted them. Much as had been the case on Nueve de Abril, partisan police looked on approvingly as their fellow Conservatives destroyed property belonging to Liberals.[34]

Alfonso López was trebly devastated by the events of September 6. As well as producing financial losses and the destruction of irreplaceable personal possessions, the Bogotá rioting caused López's exile from Colombia and underlined his inability to mediate the Liberal-Conservative violence. López had resigned from the Liberal directorate on August 22, citing discouragement over his inability to bring about peace between his party and the government. When López and Lleras departed Bogotá for foreign exile on October 1, they left behind them a shattered, dispirited, and leaderless Liberal Party.

All the while the Violencia flourished and spread. In eastern Tolima and Sumapaz, where twenty years earlier Juan de la Cruz Varela had led massive land invasions, he now organized campesinos to fight the army and Chulavita police.[35] Meanwhile farther west an even more ominous development had taken place. In northern Valle the armed forces and Conservative leaders had begun employing private assassins to help them dominate a terrified Liberal community. Thus were born the infamous "pájaros," peripatetic killers, the most celebrated of whom was one León María Lozano, "El Cóndor."

The exile of López and Lleras reconfirmed what Rafael Uribe Uribe and Benjamín Herrera had learned a half-century earlier: irregular forces in the field could not overcome the superior power of a central government possessing the confidence and support of the nation's armed forces. Still the Liberal leaders would have departed Colombia with lighter hearts had they known that Gilberto Alzate Avendaño and other leading Conservatives were well advanced in their plot to topple the weak regime of Roberto Urdaneta and Laureano Gómez.

Gilberto Alzate had sound reasons for leading the antigovernment campaign, aside from wanting to be elected Colombia's president in 1958. A man of authoritarian tendencies who during the 1930s had launched a short-lived nationalist party, Alzate had been anathematized by Gómez as a fascistoid schismatic. Only in the mid-1940s did Gómez readmit Alzate to Conservatism's inner circle. Alzate was of paisa stock, born in the Antioquian hinterland of Caldas. He thus had an affinity for Conservatives like Ospina Pérez, though that attraction was based in traditional Antioquian resistance to domination from Bogotá rather than any shared "Nationalist" Conservative tendency toward political moderation. Generationally Alzate could not but oppose Gómez. The Manizales native had entered politics with the group known as Los Nuevos, young activists who made their appearance during the 1920s, only to have their ambitions frustrated by men of the Centenarian Generation who refused to yield power to them. Finally, Alzate was a successful and charismatic politician in his own right. In May 1952 he challenged the official party by holding a convention of Alzatista Conservatives. By year's end he was universally recognized as one of the titular president's most dangerous enemies. "We have been adversaries and victims of Señor Laureano Gómez," wrote Alzate of his ailing opponent. "I have never been attracted by his methods, his temperament, his style, his obsessive ideas, his false virtue as he spews his excessive passion . . . his patented morality, his spurious use of spiritual values, or of his incongruencies and contradictions."[36]

Colombia was a political wasteland as 1953 dawned. On the first day of that year Liberal guerrillas staged a daring raid on Palanquero Air Force Base near Bogotá, causing the death of six airmen. The ongoing Violencia in the llanos was accompanied by an extension of the bloodshed into eastern Tolima and Sumapaz, with intensification of the fighting in both places over the month of February. Elections were held in mid-March amid Liberal refusal to participate and massive public apathy and by near universal criticism of the recently published constitutional reform. When supporters of Mariano Ospina Pérez announced that they would commemorate his heroism of April 9, 1948, with a rally at Bogotá's Plaza de Bolívar, the government prohibited it as constituting an unfriendly act.[37] Angry Ospinistas rescheduled the event as a private fund-raising dinner to be held at Bogotá's Temel Restaurant, saying that they would announce Ospina's candidacy for the 1954 election at the event.

Tickets for the April 11 launching of Ospina Pérez's candidacy were much sought after during the days preceding the event, as many suspected that the former president would use the occasion to formulate serious criticisms of the government. The public was not disappointed. Ospina blistered Laureano Gómez with an indirect but nonetheless severe criticism of his handling of the presidency since taking office, going on to compare his own presidency favorably with that of Gómez. Ospina had the temerity to suggest that he had won the presidency in 1946 without much help from Laureano Gómez, and that four years later he had transmitted a calm and orderly nation to Gómez.[38]

Those remarks delighted Ospina's supporters and were received by members of the foreign diplomatic corps "with an amazement bordering on shock."[39] They infuriated Laureano Gómez, who one week later responded with a nationally broadcast radio address in which he ridiculed Ospina's claim to have entered the presidency "almost alone" in 1946, recounting his struggles to return Conservatism to power between 1930 and 1946, years during which Ospina "enjoyed the well-deserved privilege of dedicating his time to private business affairs."[40] Ospina was subsequently denied air time to answer Gómez, and censorship was tightened on administration critics. In order to circumvent the censor, who did not read English, Medellín's *El Colombiano* began running classified ads in English, advertisements such as the following one for a business chief executive officer: "Wanted: a free and prosperous enterprise urgently needs all the freedom to say what it believes should be said and whatever free enterprise of its kind in the world is allowed to say."[41]

Colombian politics took on new life with the Ospina-Gómez exchange of mid-April 1953. "The present political moment is like a chess game," Laureano Gómez had said the evening of his speech against Ospina. He went on to deliver one of the finest doctrinal addresses of his political career. The talk was delivered in the style that Colombians knew well, punishing the person against whom it was directed, attacking philosophic liberalism as a pernicious doctrine that had led the nation to ruin, and praising ideological conservatism as the only doctrine capable of saving the republic from its enemies.[42] Over the weeks following his polemic against Ospina Pérez, Gómez restated his arguments in favor of order and hierarchy in a series of writings defending his new semicorporative constitution. Those articles, published in *El Siglo* during May and early June 1953, were among the most heated of his career. On May 10, for example, in a piece titled "The Mother of All Calamities," he chronicled the nation's decline from the Constitution of Cúcuta of 1830, which he said marked the beginning of Liberal subversion of Christian Colombia.

Laureano Gómez's reemergence surprised and disconcerted his political enemies, most of whom expected him not to recover from the illness that had nearly killed him eighteen months earlier. Yet there he was again, playing political chess as he always had, sure of victory and ever on the attack. Perhaps that caused them to pursue a gambit sharply at variance with the way the political game had been played in Colombia since 1900, when another ailing and unpopular president was overthrown: they enlisted the help of the armed forces. In the case of the overthrow of Laureano Gómez, it was Gilberto Alzate Avendaño who masterminded the plot.

"I was involved in the conspiracy to the marrow of my bones," Alzate said not long after the coup of June 13, 1953.[43] Alzate had leaned toward a military solution to Colombia's problems for some time, lavishly praising the army and its commander, General Gustavo Rojas Pinilla, in the columns of his newspaper, *Diario Nacional*. He had called Rojas a "patriot," drawing attention to Rojas's Conservative background, to his expeditious handling of Nueve de Abril rioting in Cali.[44] In April 1953, when Laureano Gómez began showing signs of reassuming the presidency, Alzate and his followers intensified their plotting. On May 30, 1953, two weeks before the coup was effected, Alzate could say, "Everything is ready, all roads are closed. If he tries to resume power, the armed forces will stop him."[45] Alzate's faith rested in army commander Gustavo Rojas Pinilla.

Rojas Pinilla had prospered following the Conservative return to power after 1946. An affable man popular with subordinates, he had represented Colombia abroad in numerous capacities, served a brief stint in the cabinet of Mariano Ospina Pérez as minister of public works, and by September 1952 had returned to active duty as commander of the nation's armed forces. Laureano Gómez recognized the threat posed by Rojas. Thus he kept Urdaneta from making Rojas his war minister and had the general sent abroad on several foreign missions. As talk of a military coup began circulating during April 1953, Gómez again saw to it that Rojas was ordered abroad. It was his intent to replace Rojas with Laureanista general Régulo Gaitán during the former's absence in Europe. But by then the plot to overthrow Gómez was well underway. Subordinates kept Rojas from leaving the country, at which point Alzate Avendaño gloated, "Now we've got Gómez where we want him."[46] Only a pretext was needed to execute the coup d'état. That came in early June with the military's arrest of one Felipe Echavarría, an Antioquian industrialist and friend of the government. Echavarría was imprisoned on the charge of plotting to assassinate Rojas, Alzate, and other anti-Laureanistas. He was taken to Bogotá, beaten by his captors, and forced to sit on a block of ice as a means of extracting a confession from him. At length word of the case reached Gómez, moving him to set into motion the events of June 13.[47]

At ten o'clock on the morning of June 13, Laureano Gómez summoned the members of Urdaneta's cabinet to a meeting at the presidential palace. Urdaneta's minister of government, Antonio Escobar Camargo, recalled that he and his fellow ministers were surprised by the call, for Gómez and his family had been in seclusion following the death of the caudillo's youngest son, Rafael, in an airplane accident only a few days earlier. Gómez greeted the cabinet with a short lecture on the character of the state and the ideals of the Conservative Party. Then he turned to the matter of Echavarría and his torture by the military, concluding with the surprising announcement that he had reassumed the presidency following Urdaneta's refusal to sack Gustavo Rojas Pinilla, on whom Gómez placed direct blame for the scandal. Gómez further explained that he was resolved to remove Rojas as army commander, instructing Minister of War Lucio Pabón Núñez to so instruct the military. Pabón, who had previously been told by Urdaneta that Gómez had resumed the presidency and why, then read a prepared statement that concluded, "Laureano Gómez has been a father to me. I owe my unconditional support to no man save Laureano Gómez. But in this case I must accept the same fate as Dr. Urdaneta." Gómez responded, "In my house Lucio is not a friend, but rather another of my sons. That is how I have treated him throughout his life. Thus I judge his solidarity with [Urdaneta] to be baseless, and I beg him not to refuse the issuing of this order."[48] But Pabón again refused to comply with the order framed as a supplication. At that instant Laureano Gómez doubtless knew that he had lost the political chess match. With his most trusted confidants defying him, the Gómez presidency was as good as ended.

No sooner did Gómez appear at the presidential palace than the plot to unseat him moved forward. The conspirators had told servants in the palace to alert them should Gómez appear there. Accordingly, when the caudillo met with Urdaneta's cabinet, telephone calls were made alerting interested parties to that fact. One such call was to Berta Hernández de Ospina, wife of the former president, who began making calls of her own, the first to General Gustavo Berrío. "The president is in the palace," she said to Berrío, adding, "get a move on and tell General Rojas. Look lively!"[49] Acting on such warnings Berrío and his fellow officers contacted their commander, who at the time was vacationing in Melgar, Tolima. By early afternoon Rojas and other members of his family were aboard a military aircraft en route to Bogotá. Meanwhile, General Berrío personally informed Ospina that the army was moving against the government.[50] All this transpired as Gómez sat in closed session with Pabón Núñez and the others.

The cabinet meeting ended at about 1:30 P.M., with a reshuffle that moved Public Works Minister Jorge Leyva into the war ministry, replacing Pabón, who stalked from the meeting in high dudgeon. The new cabinet was formalized in one of three decrees, the other two of which removed Rojas Pinilla as army commander, replacing him with Régulo Gaitán. When Gómez adjourned the meeting he returned to his home, leaving Jorge Leyva the thankless and at that point dangerous task of informing the army that its commandant had been sacked.[51]

Word of the government's impending fall spread rapidly through Colombian official circles. Troops at bases around the federal district had been previously confined to their barracks. Around 3 P.M. base commanders ordered the majors and captains in charge of the troops to tell them what was taking place. Thus soldiers at the Military Institute (Instituto Militar) in Bogotá heard young Captain Alvaro Valencia Tovar explain to them that "in light of the chaos prevailing in the nation caused by the partisan struggle, and lacking any political alternative, military action [is taking place] as the only way of resolving . . . [the] civil war."[52] At about that same moment Alfredo Vásquez Carrizosa, secretary of Colombia's foreign ministry, was delivering the following telephone message to his brother: "Come here quickly because I need help removing private files from my office. A coup d'état is under way."[53]

Late on the afternoon of June 13, Jorge Leyva and Generals Régulo Gaitán and Mariano Ospina Rodríguez drove to Battalion Caldas to inform army commander Alfredo Duarte Blum that Rojas Pinilla had been dismissed by presidential order. When they arrived, they were arrested by soldiers carrying rifles with fixed bayonets. They were taken before an angry Rojas Pinilla, just arrived in Bogotá, who at one point called Gaitán and Ospina traitors. One of the officers present drew his pistol to shoot Gaitán, but Rojas's wife, who had flown to Bogotá with her husband, interceded.[54] Shortly thereafter Rojas ordered troops to surround the home of Laureano Gómez. Next he phoned Roberto Urdaneta, asking the former acting chief executive to meet with him at the presidential palace in two hours.

Minister of Justice Antonio Escobar Camargo and two members of the Conservative directorate arrived at the home of Laureano Gómez at 4:30 P.M. They were told by Alvaro Gómez that Generals Régulo Gaitán and Mariano Ospina Rodríguez had met there briefly with the president an hour earlier and were on their way to relieve Rojas Pinilla of his command. For the next ninety minutes Escobar and his companions waited in vain to see Gómez, as a telephone rang incessantly in the background. Apparently one of the callers informed them that troops were approaching, for shortly after 5:30 P.M. Gómez and other members of his family slipped away to take refuge at the home of a friend. Meanwhile military vehicles were converging on the presidential palace.[55]

With the coup against Laureano Gómez a fait accompli, all that remained was for those who had carried it out to decide precisely how the new government would be run. Pandemonium reigned at the palace as leading politicians arrived there during the early evening. Soldiers guarding the doors admitted only those whose names appeared on a list headed by Mariano Ospina Pérez and Gilberto Alzate Avendaño, and their closest collaborators.[56] Rojas Pinilla conferred first with Urdaneta Arbeláez and then with Ospina Pérez, asking each in turn to accept the presidency. But Urdaneta insisted that having been dismissed by Laureano Gómez he could not legally resume the post. Ospina flatly refused the office. That left Rojas Pinilla no recourse but to take the presidency. On the excuse that Laureano Gómez was nowhere to be found, and, as he stated ingenuously, "the nation cannot be without a government," Lt. General Gustavo Rojas Pinilla became Colombia's president with the words, "I assume power."[57] Shortly thereafter, at 10 P.M., state radio informed Colombians of the change of government. Two hours later Gustavo Rojas Pinilla addressed the nation, asking citizens to rally around him for the common good. In the course of his brief address he uttered three sentences that his followers subsequently seized upon as the platform for the general's four-year regime: "No more blood, no more depredations in the name of any political party, no more rancor between sons of the same immortal Colombia. Peace, law, and justice for all, without distinction, but with special consideration for those less favored by fortune—for the workers, for the poor. The Motherland cannot live in peace while its children are hungry and naked."[58]

Gustavo Rojas Pinilla: Quasi-Populist, Anticommunist

Rojas Pinilla's takeover was greeted by Colombians with relief. Some have even suggested that Laureano Gómez, aware that he had no other alternative, simply stepped aside and allowed the coup to run its course.[59] Gilberto Alzate wrote on June 15 that Colombians accepted the change of government "with jubilation," though that phrase was more descriptive of Alzate's personal feeling about the change of government that he had engineered.[60] As so often in the past, Darío Echandía provided the truest characterization of the military takeover. He termed it a "coup by public opinion," sprung from the generalized understanding that there could be no end to the Violencia while Laureano Gómez remained in office. In keeping with that truth guerrilla forces prepared to demobilize when Rojas installed himself in the presidential palace, and Liberals everywhere recited the stanza from Colombia's national anthem, "the horrible night has ended." Other Colombians reflected on the old saw: "Colombia es un país de cosas singulares: dan guerra los civiles y paz los militares" (Colombia is a singular nation: civilians make war and the military brings peace).

The military takeover of June 13, 1953, was in many respects an ideal solution to Colombia's political impasse. Except for the super-gremio Fedcafé, the army was the only major social institution not hopelessly politicized.

Therefore, it was uniquely qualified to deal with guerrillas who at that moment were in their fourth year of war against the government. As a military man Gustavo Rojas Pinilla provided an attractive political alternative to Colombians sickened by the fratricidal turn that traditional politics had taken. Many of them hoped he might lead them beyond sterile Liberal and Conservative partisanship, toward a broad and socially conscious polity that all Colombians could embrace. In that regard Rojas inherited the popular yearning for change that had once suffused Gaitanismo. Hoping their new president might fill the void left by Gaitán, political counterelites rallied around him.

Rojas made his political philosophy known during a round of political speeches delivered during the months following June 13. Damning the traditional parties for having led the nation to ruin, he promised that his "Government of the Armed Forces" would unite Colombians through the application of Christian and "Bolivarian" principles. He founded a new government agency, the Directorate of Information and State Propaganda (Dirección de Información y Propaganda del Estado) to help him publicize his ideas. The agency's first major effort was a lavishly illustrated volume titled *Seis meses de gobierno,* containing speeches delivered by Rojas subsequent to his takeover, messages of support from home and abroad, and reports on successful government initiatives, most notably its Office for Aid and Rehabilitation, which provided money to victims of the Violencia.

The anonymous editors of *Seis meses de gobierno* introduced the volume with a statement presaging Rojas Pinilla's abortive attempt to launch a populist third party slightly more than a year later. It was a pithy indictment of the traditional parties and their leaders as bearing responsibility for the Violencia and all other social problems: "The growing economic difficulty of the poor, the clamor of dark-skinned dwellers of our mountain fastness, the vocal protests and veiled murmuring of political corruption, the apparent or outright profiteering of private persons at public expense, and the shadowy murders all remained heaped up in a suspicious penumbra. The scant interest shown by the dominant group in clarifying doubts surrounding these matters reveals to the people their leaders' scant concern over these crimes. That is what bore the nation into social chaos and political anarchy." In Rojas Pinilla, "custodian of the most authentic wishes of Bolívar," those staffing the new government propaganda ministry, and many others as well, believed they had found the man who would mend a shattered Colombia.[61]

Sadly, those who helped Rojas launch his populist movement ended by repeating the error of earlier political leaders who tried to address national problems from a position of strength. They filled the government with personal and ideological friends of the president, thus turning it into something of a closed corporation. For that reason it did not take long for the members of

16. Alfonso López Pumarejo (left) and Mariano Ospina Pérez (right), with President Gustavo Rojas Pinilla, May 1953. By permission of Lunga.

groups excluded from power to join in seeking a way to drive Rojas from office. Rojismo was further weakened by its lack of ideological coherence. While it claimed superiority over competing ideologies, it was in fact a heterogeneous collection of ideas cobbled together from liberalism, conservatism, and socialism, and strongly seasoned with nationalism and caudillismo.

And there was the problem of Rojas's personal history. In spite of his followers' efforts to portray him as a leader standing above party, the new president was Conservative by family connection and personal inclination if not by formal party affiliation. In historian César Ayala's cogent phrase, "Rojas was a creature of the Conservative Party."[62] Many of the general's contemporaries appreciated that fact. When young Liberal José Consuegra arrived in Bogotá to offer his services to Rojas, referring to the general as a national hero, *El Tiempo* editor Daniel García Peña brought Consuegra down to earth, saying, "He's no national hero or anything of the sort. This Rojas Pinilla is just a godo like the others, and democrats and lovers of liberty can't expect anything from him!"[63] The new president was also a committed cold warrior who believed that Colombia might fall victim to communist subversion at any moment. He spoke of the need for vigilance against communist infiltration during a banquet honoring Nicaragua's General Anastasio Somoza given in October 1953. In an interview granted to novelist Camilo José Cela two weeks after driving Laureano Gómez from power, he praised Francoist Spain as "a bulwark against international communism" and "a model for all Latin America."[64] Rojas was in short a military man with all the biases common to soldiers in the anticommunist West in the early 1950s. While indispensable qualities in a Cold War–era leader having close ties with the United States, they were poor qualifications for governing a modernizing nation that had historically demonstrated little tolerance for military rule.

What Colombia's yeasty society required in 1953 was a government offering political space both to emerging power contenders and to old entrenched interests. What it got was a leader of limited ability who instead of offering the nation plural and democratic rule became more authoritarian as time passed. Rojas quickly became attached to the presidency and its perquisites. He accepted gifts of blooded cattle for his finca in Melgar, which magically grew in size, achieving the status of hacienda by the end of his rule. The patrimony of his family members and close associates also increased rapidly. As his feet of clay became more evident, so too did opposition to Rojas. At first he was opposed by no more than discredited Laureanistas and numerically insignificant communists. But opposition to the government increased steadily as Rojas Pinilla stumbled from mistake to mistake. At length, in early 1957, most major social groups combined to force him from power and into exile.

In retrospect the presidency of Gustavo Rojas Pinilla was yet another political opportunity lost for Colombia, another episode in which political elites failed to provide the open democratic form of government increasingly demanded by its citizens. President Rojas Pinilla could not escape a 400-year political tradition demanding autocratic, prescriptive administration for his country. Still, no one could know in mid-1953 that Rojas would overstay his welcome. At that moment he was acclaimed as the ideal man to stop the Violencia and to set the nation right.

Four days after his accession to power was legalized by the Constituent Assembly, Rojas issued a general amnesty to all those involved in the Violencia, whether Liberal guerrillas or members of Conservative paramilitary groups. Air force planes had already begun leafleting guerrilla strongholds in the llanos, Antioquia, and Tolima, advising men under arms there that Laureano Gómez had fallen and that the government extended guarantees to all who wished to lay down their weapons.

Guerrilla leaders rushed to accept the amnesty. Following preliminary discussions during which the terms of surrender were set, there took place a flurry of gratifying and well-publicized meetings between army and guerrillas during which ex-combatants stacked arms and returned to their abandoned farms.[65]

17. A guerrilla father greets his soldier son during the surrenders in Tolima, September 1953. By permission of *El Espectador*.

Between July and September 1953, over 10,000 guerrillas accepted the government's terms, and at year's end resettlement workers had helped nearly 5,000 persons displaced by the Violencia return to their homes and had aided more than 30,000 others who had fled to Bogotá and other towns and cities.[66] The human side of that extraordinary demobilization of irregular forces by the Colombian army was captured in a photograph published in *El Espectador* following the surrender of Liberal guerrillas in Rovira, Tolima, on August 3, 1953. It showed a young soldier embracing his guerrilla father during the demobilization carried out that day.

Few Colombian presidents enjoyed a more satisfying honeymoon period than did Gustavo Rojas Pinilla. Liberal leaders supported the new president, and some like Abelardo Forero Benavides collaborated with him. The Church also endorsed the new government. In a letter of August 18, 1953, Cardinal Cristiano Luque informed Laureano Gómez that the Constituent Assembly, the public, and Luque himself endorsed the legality of Rojas's coup.[67] Even nature smiled on the new regime. At the precise moment of Rojas's takeover a frost decimated Brazil's coffee crop, sending the world price of Colombian coffee into volcanic ascent. By early 1954, Rojas could impose a tax on excess profits from coffee sales that sent a flood of dollars into his treasury. Meanwhile the Violencia dropped to exceptionally low levels amid cries of "Hallelujah!" from the general's admirers.[68]

Rojas Pinilla lashed out at his political enemies several times in late 1953 and early 1954, but did so in such a way that it little diminished his popularity. In September 1953 he closed *El Siglo* for defying government censors. The newspaper had published letters written by Laureano Gómez in which the choleric old caudillo blasted the military government as illegitimate. Rojas took similar action in March 1954, when he suspended the infant Laureanista journal *La Unidad,* founded by the young paisa Conservative Belisario Betancur. Again the charge was publishing letters from Gómez, who was at the time living in Barcelona. Some months earlier, in November 1953, Rojas had rebuked circuit court Judge Rafael Rocha for overturning the conviction of Felipe Echavarría, the man charged with conspiring to murder Rojas before the June 13 coup, and several other men said to have conspired along with Echavarría. The president went on to criticize members of the judiciary as partisan and corrupt, strong words that caused all members of Colombia's Supreme Court to resign. The incident blew over when Rojas named eight Liberals to the court, thereby granting them parity in the body for the first time in four years.[69]

Rojas's stern actions against the judiciary and the Laureanistas paled before an incident of early June 1954 that set Colombians wondering whether their new military government was as benign as they had previously believed. On June 8 police and soldiers clashed with unarmed university students returning from a ceremony honoring Gonzalo Bravo, the student killed by a police bullet during the administration of Miguel Abadía Méndez. Shots were fired, killing National University student Uriel Gutiérrez. The following day thousands of students marched down Carrera Séptima to protest Gutiérrez's killing. Several blocks before reaching the Plaza de Bolívar they found their path blocked by several dozen hastily assembled soldiers and police. Hot words were exchanged, and the armed guard panicked and fired into the densely packed crowd. Eight students died and an additional forty were wounded. Government officials subsequently arrested 200 Communist and socialist leaders, among them Gilberto Viera, Gerardo Molina, and Antonio García, explaining to an incredulous nation that Communist and Laureanista agents provocateurs had infiltrated the crowd, and had egged the soldiers into firing.[70]

The tragic events of June 8 and 9, 1954, shocked Colombians but did not seriously erode their support of the government. Rojas assured his fellow citizens that he abhorred the killings and he promised to have them fully investigated. Twenty-seven soldiers and eighteen police were subsequently disciplined for firing their weapons without sufficient provocation.

Meanwhile a flurry of political activity coupled with good economic news kept citizens from dwelling too long on the slaughter. Rojas Pinilla had kept the constituent assembly, which had originally been charged with constitutional reform under Laureano Gómez, in session following his coup. By packing it with his own supporters, Rojas turned ANAC into his puppet. In July the assembly elected Rojas as its national president for the 1954–1958 term. Previously it had selected Mariano Ospina Pérez as its presiding officer. The presence of Ospina, as well as that of many prominent Liberals in ANAC, lent the body a certain air of legitimacy during its first year of activity following Rojas Pinilla's takeover. As it was finally constituted, ANAC contained fifty-nine Conservatives and thirty-three Liberals. That makeup guaranteed the president that the body's eight obstreperous Laureanista members could not influence its decisions.[71]

In September, Rojas founded a major new social agency called the National Secretariat of Social Assistance (Secretariado Nacional de Asistencia Social, SENDAS), thereby demonstrating to Colombians and foreigners alike that he was sincere in helping the poor. SENDAS invested moneys from the coffee bonanza in an array of social programs ranging from hospitals and housing projects to direct aid for victims of the Violencia. Rojas placed his twenty-one-year-old daughter María Eugenia in charge of the ambitious umbrella agency.[72] One month later the president further enhanced his popularity when he inaugurated the Paz del Río steel mill in Boyacá. The dream of becoming self-sufficient in steel manufacture had been a dream of Colombia's economic and political elites for generations. Paz del Río thus provided objective proof that in spite of its manifold social and political problems the nation was making excellent economic progress.

The year 1954 ended on a highly satisfactory note, with the return from Korea of Colombia's thousand-man army battalion. That seemed an appropriate end to a twelve-month span marked by certain low points but on balance highly favorable in terms of the military government's performance.

Gustavo Rojas Pinilla enjoyed much success over the eighteen months following his assumption of power in June 1953, though a number of debilities together doomed his presidency. First was Rojas's lack of formal affiliation with either of Colombia's two principal political parties. While it is true that the Liberal-Conservative conflict had always produced violence in Colombia, the parties had also played a vital integrative role for the nation, knitting the regionally diverse regions together in twin affective and functionally useful structures. The parties were like two trees having roots deep in the nation's tropical soil, ever battling one another for light and sustenance. Rojas made no secret of his enmity toward the two collectivities and their supporters. He was particularly critical of the Antioquian businessmen who traditionally had peopled the Nationalist faction of the Conservative Party.

The second limitation which Rojas suffered and which inevitably led to his downfall was his passionate anticommunism. Rojas was much like Laureano

Gómez in his reverence for Colombia's Hispanic and Christian heritage and in his abhorrence of the way modern secular society had eroded traditional society. And like Gómez, Rojas blamed many of Colombia's social problems, notably the Violencia, on persons who followed "disassociative" philosophies and who were bent on overturning the old ways. But Rojas was more extreme in those views than was Gómez, for he held them in a more visceral and less sophisticated way. Gómez learned to embrace traditionalism and reject modernism at the knee of Jesuit pedagogues who taught the Perennial Philosophy rooted in Church doctrine running back through the writings of early Church fathers. Rojas learned his anticommunism in the barracks, where soldiers were charged with defending Christian civilization against dark and divisive forces. His dislike of leftist ideology was heightened through years spent in the United States, years during which men like Joseph McCarthy and General Douglas MacArthur preached that a Moscow-directed conspiracy was at the point of producing an atheistic communist holocaust throughout the Christian world.

Thus Rojas's own credibility and martial simplicity led him to interpret Colombia's Violencia paradigmatically, through communist conspiracy theory. In 1949, Rojas watchers in the United States embassy had jibed that the rising army officer "sees a red behind every coffee bush," and that he "cannot tell a communist from a Liberal."[73] But three years later, when U.S. embassy officials had themselves become convinced that the communist threat was real, they fretted that Rojas and his military colleagues were not equipped to combat the communist element within the guerrilla movement. Hence they encouraged the U.S. government to materially assist him in his struggle against the irregular forces.[74]

Once in power Rojas gave vent to his anticommunism with tragic consequences for thousands of campesinos living in eastern Tolima and the contiguous Sumapaz region of Cundinamarca. An army raid carried out near Villarrica, Tolima, in late 1954 resulted in the deaths of several campesinos said to be communists, as well as the arrest of Isauro Yosa ("Lister"), who had fought with Charro Negro's Communist forces in southern Tolima prior to the overthrow of Laureano Gómez. The reasons for Villarrica's involvement in the Violencia were complex. A rugged, heavily Liberal region of recent settlement and a history of agrarian conflict, Villarrica had witnessed constant strife between larger, better-established landowners and less affluent campesinos, many of whom had fought with Liberal guerrillas prior to the guerrilla demobilization of 1953. Many of those returning to claim homesteads abandoned during the fighting discovered that others had laid claim to their land and were supported by the army.[75] A complicating factor for the peasants of the region was the fact that they counted socialists, Marxists, and Communist revolutionaries among their number. One of them, socialist Juan de la Cruz Varela, had been active in the agrarian movement of the 1930s. He had urged followers not to surrender their rifles when the guerrillas were demobilized, on the grounds that the government could not be trusted.[76] Others, like Communist Manuel Marulanda Vélez ("Tiro Fijo") made his dislike of Rojas more than explicit, calling Rojas in June 1953, "the vilest delinquent in the nation, in power as a result of murder and massacre," and warning, "Don't believe the false promises of propaganda thrown from airplanes of the dictatorship."[77]

Thus it was that both the citizens of eastern Tolima and the army regarded each other with hostility and fear from late 1952 onward. The army, which had been formally combined with the national police shortly after Rojas's takeover, began patrolling the region after the arrest of Isauro Yosa. The situation's potential for tragedy was realized in late March 1955, when a large group of armed men fell upon an infantry company patrolling in the area, killing nearly all its members. A furious Rojas Pinilla declared eastern Tolima a Zone of Military Operations on April 4, 1955, and made ready to pound the rebellious campesinos into submission.

The history of the "Villarrica War" has been told in greater detail elsewhere.[78] Suffice it to say that the Colombian army grossly overreacted against a lightly armed citizenry among whom the presence of communists was wildly exaggerated. Inhabitants of entire veredas were displaced in the course of the military encirclement, many of them fleeing into the inhospitable mountains of Sumapaz to the east, far from sources of food and medicine. "The army killed many of us," wrote one woman who participated in the exodus. "And we had to kill many of them in order to defend ourselves. . . . The troops burned everything; they cut down coffee groves with machetes, they destroyed crops of yuca and anything else that was edible. . . . Of my seven children all but three died."[79] Stories like hers found their way back to urban Colombia over the course of 1955, doing much to harden attitudes against Rojas Pinilla and his government.

As the Violencia swelled in Colombia, Rojas became politically active in ways that turned Liberal and Conservative leaders increasingly against him. Liberal leaders had begun plotting anti-Rojas strategy soon after the general came to power. Alfonso López Pumarejo was one who from the first had argued that members of his party should refuse to collaborate with the military regime.[80] Support for the noncollaborationist position increased among Conservatives as well as Liberals following Rojas Pinilla's 1955 New Year's message in which he said that he did not intend to lift the state of siege. Immediately thereafter Rojas had announced the formation of his own political party, the National Action Movement (Movimiento de Acción National, MAN), in which a number of prominent Liberals and Conservatives agreed to participate. MAN did not flourish over the months following its formation. Liberal and Conservative leaders combined with members of the Church hierarchy, who viewed MAN as "Peronist and anti-Catholic," to condemn the new party.

The tightening of government censorship also worked to lessen Rojas's popularity. Like Laureano Gómez, Rojas had not wanted the press to report his failure to contain the Violencia. But Rojas curbed the press much more than did Gómez, in part because he believed it responsible for exacerbating traditional political hatreds. During 1955 he increased censorship and established his own propaganda organ, *Diario Oficial*. The tightening grip of government censors produced the temporary closing of *El Tiempo* in August 1955, and the suspension of Bogotá's principal Liberal dailies the following year.[81]

Battles involving press censorship were merely one facet of the quickening struggle between leaders of the traditional parties and the government. However, more important than the parties' opposition to Rojas was the elaborate Liberal-Conservative courtship that began in earnest during 1955, culminating in mid-1956 with an epochal meeting in Spain between Laureano Gómez and Alberto Lleras Camargo. The route to that meeting was circuitous, and it led through Antioquia.

Alfonso López Pumarejo was chief instigator of the movement to unite Liberals and Conservatives toward the end of loosening Rojas's grip on power. The Liberal leader gained a valuable ally when Alberto Lleras returned to Colombia in mid-1955, having completed a ten-year stint as president of the Organization of American States. Lleras, of conciliatory temperament, was quickly won over to his old political mentor's collaborationist thesis. By year's end he had joined López in calling for creation of a bipartisan Civic Front aimed at restoring peace and constitutional rule to the nation. Still there were three serious problems to overcome before anything like a bipartisan agreement could be achieved. First, the Santos faction of the party must be cajoled into dealing with Laureano Gómez and his followers, whom Santos and his supporters thoroughly despised. Second, Ospinista Conservative moderates, a majority of whom were paisas, must be distanced from the military government, which had amply rewarded their support. Finally, Laureano Gómez, who historically had disparaged bipartisanship as a betrayal of party principles, must be convinced to endorse the accord.

Colombia's military president effectively—though inadvertently—aided his political enemies over the course of 1956. Rojas Pinilla's popularity suffered severe blows in February and again in August when his underlings committed errors of judgment that cost the lives of well over 1,000 citizens, which in turn caused the average person to lose faith in the government. The incident took place in Bogotá on Sunday, February 5, in the course of that afternoon's bullfight. Unbeknownst to Rojas hundreds of his supporters had packed the Plaza de Santamaría in order to exact vengeance for an incident of the previous week, when members of the crowd had shouted insults at members of the president's family. At a predetermined moment the Rojistas raised cheers for the president, carefully noting those who failed to join them, or who answered their "Vivas" with boos and catcalls. The Rojistas then beat them with such brutality that eight persons died and another 112 were injured. Six months later, on August 6, 1956, an army officer leading a convoy of munitions to Bogotá from the port of Buenaventura foolishly ordered the dangerous cargo parked in downtown Cali. Early on the morning of August 7 the munitions exploded, leveling entire blocks and killing more than 1,000 people. It was soon known that casualties were much higher than they might have been, because the convoy had been moved into a densely populated center city barrio so as not to endanger the exclusive neighborhood where the trucks were initially parked.[82] Rojas labeled the accident an act of sabotage perpetrated by Liberal and Conservative leaders, who at that moment were uniting to drive him from power. The president's far-fetched attempt to blame political opponents for a tragedy caused by military incompetence produced shock and outrage among Colombians. Rojas was forced to grudgingly retract his preposterous and unfounded charge that Alfonso López, Eduardo Santos, and others of their ilk had blown up a significant portion of the nation's third largest city.[83]

Rojas Pinilla accused Liberal and Conservative leaders of complicity in the Cali tragedy because at the moment it occurred he felt a political noose tightening around his neck. It was a noose of bipartisanship that had been some months in the making.

In early March 1956, Alfonso López had written to Antioquian Liberals advising them that should a bipartisan accord be reached they must stand ready to cast their votes for a Conservative presidential candidate.[84] López's words shocked paisa Liberals. But his letter was sufficiently convincing to party leaders that they authorized Alberto Lleras Camargo to initiate contact with Conservative leaders. Lleras first approached Mariano Ospina Pérez, asking if he and others of his faction would join the Civic Front against Rojas Pinilla. Ospina, who had been a nominal supporter of Rojas up to that time, refused on the grounds that if he did so the two-party accord would surely fail. By Ospina's reasoning, Laureano Gómez and his followers would never agree to join a Liberal-Ospinista coalition. Hence the Civic Front would inevitably fail.[85]

In July 1956, Alberto Lleras Camargo flew to Spain, where he hoped to enlist Laureano Gómez's support in the bipartisan agreement. The old caudillo received Lleras warmly, indicating that he was pleased to join his former political enemies to restore civil government to Colombia. On July 24 he and Lleras signed the Pact of Benidorm, which joined Liberals and Laureanistas in a "campaign for retaking the fatherland."[86] The pact affirmed that as it would not be sensible for Liberals and Conservatives to renew their struggle for power immediately following the restoration of civil government, both sides should explore routes toward equable power sharing.

Many Liberals were irate when they learned that after years of internecine strife the two parties could so easily decide to cooperate, even to the extent of dealing with the "Monster," Laureano Gómez. The weekly newspaper *Sábado* expressed these sentiments in its edition of August 4, which asked rhetorically, "And now we're expected to deal with Dr. Laureano, with Dr. Andrade, with Dr. Mantalvo? Holy Mother of God!" Two weeks later, on August 18, *Sábado* answered its earlier question in an editorial bearing the following heading: "We Shall Never Negotiate With Laureano Gómez!"

Yet while *Sábado* and *Semana* spoke for rank-and-file Liberals, they did not reflect the reality of Liberal Party politics. On August 4, none other than Carlos Lleras Restrepo wired Lleras Camargo in Spain, expressing his enthusiastic support for bipartisan cooperation.[87] By late 1956 only Conservatism's Ospinista wing and those party members closely associated with the military government had failed to endorse the Benidorm agreement.

As 1956 drew to a close it became increasingly obvious to Colombians that Gustavo Rojas Pinilla's Government of the Armed Forces had failed to bring either peace or prosperity to the nation. The Violencia claimed more than 11,000 new victims in 1956, making that year the sixth worst in the bloody history of the conflict. Tolima was especially affected. Refugees continued to stream from the war zone around Villarrica into lowland towns and villages, and in southern Tolima, Liberal guerrillas begged for government assistance in their war with communist groups operating in the same area. According to Tolima's leading newspaper, *Tribuna*, there were between seven and ten thousand guerrillas operating in the department's mountainous northern, southern, and eastern regions during December 1956.[88] Confronted with the government's inability to drive the communist guerrillas from the department, some army officers advocated government support of "campesino self-defense leagues."[89] Such groups did in fact exist and had been in operation from the moment it became known that the Communists had refused the government's amnesty offer in 1953. But the Liberal guerrillas were tired of fighting. Having given up hope that Rojas Pinilla possessed any solution to their problem, one of the larger irregular forces, the Liberal National Revolutionary Movement of Southern Tolima, led by Leopoldo García ("General Peligro," General Danger), had turned to civilian political leaders for help in bringing peace to their devastated region.[90]

An especially dismaying aspect of resurgent Violencia under Rojas Pinilla was the proliferation of Conservative paramilitary organizations known as *pájaros azules* (blue birds), or simply *pájaros*. These groups were composed of civilian gunmen who could be called upon to act singly or in groups to help the army and police enforce their rule. But it was a terrible sort of order. Victims of the pájaros never knew when they had been marked for assassination, and as the pájaros were highly peripatetic, frequently strangers to areas where they were sent, they represented a particularly frightening aspect of the Violencia. "To do things like a bird, on the fly . . . that's how it worked," was one Liberal's description of the pájaros.[91]

The pájaros had their origin in the department of Valle. Rojas Pinilla had in fact helped create them when he turned to civilians for assistance in pacifying Cali during the Liberal uprising of April 9–10, 1948. Then commander of Colombia's Third Brigade, Rojas made use of pájaros in years following Nueve de Abril, later explaining that by maintaining contact with men like León María Lozano, "El Cóndor," he was able to control indirectly the Violencia in Valle. He defended his association with Lozano by stating that after popular outcry forced him to expel the pájaro from Valle in 1955, "rather than ending, the Violencia increased because a great many people lacked anyone to control [the Violencia], because he [Lozano] controlled it."[92]

Further complicating the Violencia during Rojas Pinilla's administration were members of the government's new secret police, the Servicio de Inteligencia Colombiana (SIC), who frequently made use of pájaros to help them control persons whom the government considered undesirable. In turn SIC agents often helped protect pájaros against other members of the armed forces bent on eliminating them. Hence on September 6, 1955, Tolima's military governor, César Cuéllar, complained to his superior, Colonel Luis Ordóñez, that his attempts to arrest pájaros were being frustrated by SIC agents who told the gunmen when and where the raids were to take place.[93]

Thus did the Violencia return to Colombia over the course of Rojas Pinilla's administration. And in the case of the pájaros, the president was at least indirectly responsible for the resurgence. That frustrated and embittered increasing numbers of Colombians and helped pave the way for Rojas's overthrow in early 1957.

Rojas Pinilla did no better in handling Colombia's economy than he did in finding a lasting solution to the Violencia. The robust economy he inherited on June 13, 1953, soon weakened and stagnated thanks to the new regime's profligacy and mismanagement. Abundant revenues and the desire to curry favor with voters led the president and his advisors to spend lavishly on public works projects. Often money earmarked for such expenditures was mismanaged and even stolen. The naming of the president's daughter, 21-year-old María Eugenia Rojas, to head Colombia's new welfare agency SENDAS symbolized the administration's casual and personalist approach to the handling of public moneys.

Coffee prices began falling in late 1954, aggravating and accelerating problems brought on by poor fiscal management. Although the slide continued over the remainder of Rojas's term, the president did not alter his spending practices. During 1956 the foreign debt increased at an alarming rate and international lending agencies took steps to cut off credit. Meanwhile, Rojas placed orders for new air force jets and a destroyer for the navy and moved ahead on the construction of plush new facilities at the nation's principal army bases. The president's only effort to resolve the mounting fiscal crisis was to replace Finance Minister Carlos Villaveces with fiscally conservative Luis Morales Gómez. While Morales made progress in calming the nation's foreign creditors by stepping up payments to them and imposing austerity measures, those actions came too late to help Rojas Pinilla preserve his hold on power.[94]

The end came quickly for Rojas Pinilla's administration. In late January 1957 the president's chief supporter within the military, Minister of War Gabriel París, made it known that Rojas intended to extend his rule through 1962. This news disconcerted ranking military officials, especially army commander Rafael Navas Pardo, who, though a friend and supporter of Rojas, was alarmed at the tenfold increase in the Violencia since 1955.

Rojas's decision to prolong his presidency galvanized political Colombia, moving the leaders of all major Liberal and Conservative factions to formalize their opposition to the dictatorship.[95] They did so via a joint declaration, the "March Pact," expressing their intention "to fight tirelessly to reestablish constitutional rule in Colombia." Alberto Lleras Camargo and Guillermo León Valencia, presidents of the Liberal and Conservative directorates, signed for their parties. Following their signatures were the 105 other leading Liberal and Conservative politicians.[96]

As the joint manifesto was being circulated, the Constituent Assembly, ANAC, now headed by Rojas Pinilla's chief collaborator, Lucio Pabón Núñez, was taking steps to insure the president's continuation in office. Pabón's manipulation of that body drove all non-Rojistas to resign their seats on March 23.[97] Two weeks later, on April 8, 1957, the bipartisan Civic Front proclaimed Guillermo León Valencia its candidate for the 1958–1962 presidential term. Colombia's political battle had been joined once again.

Rojas Pinilla sped his fall by attempting to answer the bipartisan political challenge with force. One day after the Valencia candidacy was announced, SIC agents arrested and jailed Belisario Betancur and other Conservative politicians as they left a political meeting at the Colegio del Rosario.[98] The president's secret police increased surveillance on opposition leaders, placing Guillermo León Valencia under house arrest in Popayán. Those clumsy uses of armed force merely served to inflame public opinion against the dictatorship. On May 2, 1957, one day after troops had surrounded the home of Valencia, police and students clashed in Bogotá, as the latter distributed handbills reading, "Drop dead Rojas!"[99]

During the period from the joint Liberal-Conservative manifesto of March 20 to the sporadic clashes between students and armed forces on May 2, two powerful new interest groups aligned themselves against the government. In late April, Archbishop Cristiano Luque blasted the regime as "illegal" in the eyes of the Church and its followers. Just a week earlier the president of Colombia's association of industrialists, ANDI, had written Rojas asking that he return the nation to constitutional rule. But the president remained obdurate. He answered by saying that ongoing disorder made it impossible for him to lift the state of siege.[100] His response to the Church was less diplomatic. On the first Sunday following Luque's condemnation of Rojas, administration officials stationed troops outside churches as a warning to clerics not to fan the flames of dissidence. When SIC agents informed troops outside the Porciúncula, a large church in northern Bogotá, that Father Severo Velásquez had delivered a fiery anti-Rojas homily, soldiers doused departing parishioners with water from fire hoses, pelted them with red dye, and fired tear gas canisters into their midst. The next day an irate Cristiano Luque wrote an open letter of protest to Rojas, attacking the police actions carried out in Bogotá, Cali, and elsewhere as "inhuman," "anti-Christian," and guaranteed to "produce bitter fruit and still greater evils."[101]

Over the days preceding Luque's May 6 letter, Civic Front leaders had organized a general strike aimed at paralyzing the country and forcing Rojas Pinilla from power. Unlike earlier unsuccessful attempts to topple governments through use of the general strike, the work stoppage of May 6–10, 1957, enlisted most major social groups rather than a select few. Strike leaders Alberto Lleras Camargo and Guillermo León Valencia assured the military in advance that their movement was in opposition to Rojas Pinilla only and not directed against the armed forces.[102] This assurance effectively neutralized the last major interest group supporting the Rojas dictatorship.

Meanwhile the strike tightened its hold on the nation. Banks failed to open on Monday, May 6. When the government sent managers to operate the banks on an emergency basis they were told that tellers had disappeared with the keys to all the cash drawers. In Antioquia factories ceased operation. Their owners, whose support had been enlisted by none other than Alfonso López Pumarejo, promised their workers full pay while the strike was in effect, which was the case too for white collar employees across the nation. Their employers, many of whom were affiliated with the trade association FENALCO, had ordered them to take paid vacations.[103]

In Cali the movement against Rojas was at once broad based, passionate, and bloody. Caleños had not ceased to blame Rojas for the explosion of munitions that killed 1,000 citizens eight months earlier. Cali was the Colombian city most afflicted by the paramilitary pájaros, and as the civic strike made its effects felt in Cali, army officers used the assassins as strikebreakers. "Phantom autos" full of pájaros attacked protesters in the streets, and on May 9 pájaros lay in wait for Caleños as they made their way home from a giant rally held at the city's central plaza.

The killing of innocent and unarmed civilians by thugs enjoying the protection of the military incensed the nation and turned it against the armed forces. That, in turn, hastened Rojas's fall. The army had traditionally been respected by Colombians, and reports emanating from Cali to the effect that Caleños were subjecting soldiers to "verbal attacks" produced great concern in General Navas and his fellow officers.[104] Within hours of the May 9 shootings in Cali, Navas would oversee the resignation of Rojas Pinilla.

Gustavo Rojas Pinilla was slow to grasp that his final moment in the presidency had arrived. On Wednesday, May 8, in the midst of a near total paralysis of national institutions, he welcomed his "reelection" as president by the puppet Constituent Assembly. In remarks celebrating that spurious election, delivered to the nation by radio later that day, Rojas lashed his tormentors with populist and socialist rhetoric: "I do not want class warfare to break out . . . but the oligarchs, who always have money enough to live elegantly, must understand that their money cannot be used to sacrifice Colombia. Rather, it should be used to dignify the working masses."[105] The words rang hollow. Colombians listened to the diatribe, but what they heard was a discredited leader who had lost most of his original supporters.

Failing to whip up a popular enthusiasm for continuation of his presidency, Rojas attempted one last gambit that if successful would have kept him in power at least until August 7, 1958. He embraced the Conservative Party, hoping to enlist top Ospinista and Alzatista leaders in propping up his regime. He did that by offering them most of the top positions in his government. On the afternoon of May 9, Rojas huddled with his cabinet and Antonio Alvarez Restrepo, former minister of finance under Laureano Gómez and until his resignation four days earlier, director of the Banco Cafetero. At the end of the conference Alvarez had the temerity to ask the president, "Why don't you simply restore freedom?" Rojas ignored the question and asked the banker to organize a meeting of "leading Conservatives" to help him resolve the crisis.[106]

Alvarez Restrepo left the presidential palace and convened a meeting of leading Conservatives at his home. During the evening of May 9, and into the early hours of May 10, the group debated how Colombia should be governed once Rojas stepped down. Anxious to learn whether they had accepted his offer to constitute a hegemonic military-Conservative regime, one over which he might remain as titular head, Rojas dispatched General Navas Pardo to

Alvarez's home. Navas arrived there at approximately 10 P.M.; six hours later he left to inform Rojas that the nation's immediate political future had been decided.

The scene played out at the home of Alvarez Restrepo was both dramatic and uniquely Colombian. Prior to Navas's arrival the Conservatives decided both that Rojas must step down and that the government replacing him was to be a bipartisan one. Navas, representing the military, accepted the civilians' condition that Rojas relinquish power, but insisted that he and his fellow officers should preside over the nation until Rojas Pinilla's initial presidential term ended — that is, until August 7, 1958, at which time civilian government would resume. Over the course of the evening Civic Front leaders Lleras Camargo and León Valencia were assured by telephone that the Liberal-Conservative "Civic Front" idea, formalized a year earlier through the Benidorm pact, would be honored. Gilberto Alzate Avendaño and Carlos Villaveces arrived uninvited at the deliberations only to be "brusquely turned away" by those present, most of whom blamed Alzate for having brought Rojas to power.[107] The shape of Colombian politics in the post-Rojas period was becoming clear.

Amid the hubbub and coming and going of that evening, there were those who made sure that interested parties not present were kept fully apprised of what took place as Navas Pardo met with the Conservative notables. Thus happy Bogotanos were already in the streets "jubilantly heralding the fall of Rojas" as Navas Pardo went to tell the president that he must resign immediately. Those taking to the streets, many of them blowing car horns, one man playing a saxophone, were Liberals ecstatic that their party could reenter the civil political process that it had forsworn more than seven years earlier.

It was a none too happy Gustavo Rojas Pinilla who greeted army commander Navas Pardo early on the morning of May 10. When told that his proposed plan for a joint military-Conservative government headed by himself had been rejected, Rojas asked simply, "What do they propose, then?" Navas explained that the civilians demanded his immediate resignation but agreed to accept transitional rule by the military. "Navas, it seems to me that this formula is acceptable," responded Rojas, who would be allowed to select members of the junta as a face-saving gesture.[108] With that, he withdrew to his private quarters, where he composed his message of resignation and packed his personal effects. Later that morning Rojas read his message of resignation over national radio. The din of more than 100,000 cheering Colombians massed around government buildings could be heard in the background. Later that day, May 10, 1957, he departed by air, ultimately reaching Spain, the same nation that sheltered the man he had driven into exile nearly four years earlier.

A Time of Transition, 1957–1965

The National Front

Over the months following Rojas Pinilla's fall, Liberal and Conservative leaders worked out details of the power-sharing arrangement called the National Front (Frente Nacional). By its provisions, spelled out in a plebiscite of December 1957, and in subsequent legislation, the two parties would govern jointly for twelve years. Later they extended the period to sixteen years. The presidency would be alternated at four-year intervals, cabinet posts divided between the two parties, and all other elective and appointive posts shared equally. Politicians who were not affiliated with either the Liberal or Conservative Party were barred from holding elective positions over the agreed-upon period.

Students of politics classify such legally constituted power-sharing regimes as "consociational," in which political elites calm chaotic democratic systems by striking bargains on behalf of their constituents. The chief drawback of consociational arrangements lies in the restrictions they place on democratic processes. And Colombia's National Front accord was an exceptionally narrow form of consociationalism that limited access to the electoral process to members of the nation's traditional parties. Yet when the National Front was conceived, and during its early years, most Colombians saw it as an ideal mechanism for restoring democratic rule and ending the Violencia.[1] In addition it enabled the government to effect a series of social reforms that found favor with most citizens. Foremost among them were the notable expansion of public education and the launching of a heralded land reform program. Thanks to the accord Colombia was able to continue the economic and social modernization that had altered it so profoundly over the twentieth century.

Popular enthusiasm for the National Front was accompanied by criticism from several quarters. Some Liberals opposed the requirement that the minority Conservatives should be guaranteed political posts that they could never have won under normal conditions, and politicians who were neither Liberal nor Conservative, Communists and socialists for example, protested an agreement that shut them out of the political process for sixteen years. Among the enemies of the National Front figured a radical fringe that chose to express its anger in the time-honored Colombian fashion of taking up arms against the government.

Anger on the part of persons legally barred from politics under terms of the National Front increased as time passed. Ordinary citizens, too, quickly tired of the arrangement. In that sense the accord succeeded too well. It depoliticized Colombian society at a time when growing social diversity and sophistication worked to the detriment of traditional beliefs of all kinds. Politics became less interesting to Colombians as its impact on their daily lives lessened, and as the National Front swelled the size of government, vastly invigorating cronyism, clientelism, waste, and corruption, it had the additional effect of alienating Colombians from politics generally. Still, popular dissatisfaction with the quasi-democratic National Front increased slowly at first. Over the accord's initial years there was a honeymoon during which average Colombians thanked their traditional leaders for having restored democratic rule.

Immediately following the overthrow of Rojas Pinilla, on May 10, 1957, Colombians were riveted by the sight of their traditional political leaders forging their unique pact. Alfonso López Pumarejo won honors as the man who more than any other espoused bipartisanship as a way of transcending Liberal-Conservative strife. Years earlier, in 1946, he had made the improbable suggestion that Conservative Party leaders choose their presidential candidate for that year's election from a list submitted by the Liberal directorate. Conservatives rejected the offer as a ludicrous ploy aimed at unifying Liberals toward the end of defeating their candidate, Mariano Ospina Pérez. López revived the idea of Liberal-Conservative collaboration a decade later as the nation reeled from the combined effect of the Violencia and Rojas Pinilla's increasing authoritarianism. In March 1956 he proposed bipartisan cooperation in the form of power sharing in elective bodies and a promise that Liberals would vote a Conservative into office following Rojas Pinilla's fall. Rank-and-file Liberals were aghast at the idea of casting their votes for a Conservative—perhaps even the hated Laureano Gómez—as the price for restoring civil rule. But López's audacious proposal set them to considering some form of joint action with their erstwhile enemy. The coalition building continued when, months later, Liberal Party director Alberto Lleras Camargo traveled to Benidorm, Spain, to win Laureano Gómez's consent to the plan.

Over his career Laureano Gómez had opposed such accords as a betrayal of Conservative principles. But three years of exile had given him the opportunity to reconsider his position. He embraced both Lleras and the power-sharing idea, going so far as to draft the final version of the Benidorm Agreement himself. While a major portion of the text damned Rojas and his regime, it also contained Gómez's express approval of the creation of "a broad coalition government, or a series of such governments embracing both parties."[2]

The next step toward effecting Colombia's National Front came eight months later, in March 1957, less than two months before Rojas's fall. The so-called March Pact repeated the call for power sharing and alternation of the presidency. It was signed by leading Liberals and Conservatives. The same group of political leaders, calling themselves the Civic Front, next planned and executed Rojas's overthrow. It also settled on Guillermo León Valencia as the Conservative who would stand for election as the first coalition president.

In the days immediately following Rojas Pinilla's fall most Colombians, politicians and nonpoliticians alike, assumed that Valencia would indeed become president in 1958. But Valencia's candidacy quickly foundered on the shoals of Conservative Party division. Valencia was unacceptable to Laureano Gómez and his followers, ostensibly because the Cauca politician's chief supporters were Conservatives who had overthrown Gómez in 1953. On a more subtle level Valencia fell victim to a division that was at once regional and philosophic, and which had ever set Conservatives against one another. Moderate Conservatives—the "Nationalists" of earlier times—whose bastion was Antioquia and its hinterlands, had always resisted the blandishments of their more ideological counterparts, whose geographic source of strength ran from Cundinamarca northward through Boyacá and Santander.

Ten days after Rojas Pinilla departed Colombia, Laureano Gómez gave notice that he must be reckoned with. "I don't support Guillermo León's candidacy," he told aide Camilo Vázquez. Gómez added disingenuously, "The party abandoned me, and now I'm not obliged to tell it what it must do."[3]

When Valencia learned of Gómez's opposition he tried to placate the old caudillo through a series of public pronouncements. But Valencia was a politician whose speeches, while witty, were full of "misstatements and imprudencies so clumsy that while at once making supporters laugh they also filled them with dread."[4] He soon demonstrated his oratorical ineptitude. Speaking in Medellín on June 24, 1957, before a banquet hosted by leading Antioquian Conservatives, Valencia said, "The return of Rojas Pinilla will be that of an escaped criminal; but when Laureano Gómez returns to Colombia, the nation will regain its heart." His words fell like ice water on his audience. It was not simply that Valencia had lavished praise on the man whom Ospinistas most detested, and whom they happily conspired to overthrow in 1953, but that he did so before his own chief supporters.[5]

Alberto Lleras Camargo was also in attendance that evening. As Pedronel Giraldo recalled it, when Valencia reviled Rojas and praised Gómez, "Lleras lifted his eyes as if gazing at a distant horizon." Then he addressed the gathering "with calibrated and nuanced words, with great restraint, and with the timbered voice of a radio announcer." Liberal Party members in attendance applauded his speech enthusiastically, leaving Conservatives with the premo-

18. Laureano Gómez and Alberto Lleras Camargo in Sitges, Spain, July 1957. By permission of Alvaro Gómez Hurtado.

nition that it was Alberto Lleras, not Guillermo León Valencia, who would be the nation's next president.[6]

Liberal leaders wasted no time in placating Laureano Gómez at Valencia's and the Ospinistas' expense. Less than a month after the Medellín banquet, Alberto Lleras traveled to Spain a second time. There he and Laureano Gómez drew up a document specifically endorsing parity in elective and appointive bodies and a three-term alternating presidency, whose first designate would be a Conservative. While the Pact of Sitges was drafted by Lleras, it clearly put forth the Laureanista thesis that Rojas Pinilla was a tyrant and that his Ospinista-dominated constituent assembly was a spurious body "whose invalidity was amply demonstrated when the entire country rose in revolt against its acts."[7]

Conservative discord intensified as Laureano Gómez prepared to return home. Even before the Sitges pact the exiled leader's strategy of attacking Rojas Pinilla's Ospinista collaborators had become clear. On July 4, 1957, *El Siglo* editorialized that Ospina Pérez, Gilberto Alzate, and others who had planned the June 13, 1953, coup should not be allowed to help reconstitute civil government.

Gómez returned to Colombia on October 5, 1957, timing his arrival to coincide with a convention of Ospinista Conservatives being held in Bogotá. He traveled straight to Cali, where his followers had organized a rump party convention. On his arrival Gómez drafted an open letter to Luis Navarro

Ospina, chairman of the Bogotá meeting. It was one of the most polemical ever penned by Gómez, and it revived the old charge that paisas—especially the Ospinistas—placed economic concerns above all others: "The gang that collaborated with the tyrant in the ruin of the republic, that was blind to waste and administrative immorality, complains today of the grave economic situation they helped create while enriching themselves. Today they want the public to forgive them and to let them maintain the dominant position that they usurped. If the Conservative division is a great evil, and if the country is ruined, you alone are the ones responsible."[8]

Gómez was not to be denied in his campaign to punish the Ospinistas. On October 19, 1957, he delivered the last of his major doctrinal messages, an address titled "Gold and Dross." The speech struck the same note as did his first editorials published nearly half a century earlier in *La Unidad*. With a first aid team standing by to revive him if necessary, Gómez praised his own brand of "doctrinaire" Conservatism as the party's one true faith. While calling for party unity, he deplored the idea of joining hands with "delinquents," as he called all those who had either actively supported or passively accepted Rojas Pinilla.[9] In the course of their meeting Laureanistas repeatedly denounced Mariano Ospina Pérez, Roberto Urdaneta Arbeláez, Lucio Pabón Núñez, Gilberto Alzate Avendaño, and others who had dealt with Rojas between June 13, 1953, and May 10, 1957. They also formally rejected the candidacy of Guillermo León Valencia.

Following adjournment of the Cali convention, Gómez once more stood ready to bend national politics to his will. During their deliberations the Laureanistas had decided that they could negate Valencia's presidential bid by insisting that Conservatives sitting in the national Congress democratically select their own candidate for the presidency. As Laureanista candidates stood to win a majority of Conservative seats in the upcoming contest, Gómez and his followers would be in position to name the first National Front president. However, one serious problem loomed. As of late 1957 the presidential and congressional contests were set to be held on the same day, with Guillermo León Valencia the only announced candidate for the top post. Gómez's task, then, was to force acceptance of congressional elections in advance of the presidential vote. He addressed it through the simple expedient of demanding, in a speech read over national radio, that the congressional elections be held in advance of the presidential contest.

The speech had precisely the effect intended. Members of the military junta hurriedly gathered the nation's leading politicians and asked them to resolve the impasse. After several days of negotiations Laureano Gómez got what he wanted. It was agreed that congressional elections would precede the presidential contest, and that following the vote Conservatives and Liberals would either ratify Valencia's candidacy or find someone else acceptable to both parties. In exchange Gómez agreed to let the plebiscite proceed as scheduled, on December 1, 1957.

Colombians overwhelmingly endorsed the National Front through the plebiscite. Over four million ballots were cast in favor, as opposed to just 200,000 against. That represented by far the largest turnout in national history, in part explained by the fact that women were allowed to vote for the first time. The plebiscite also stipulated that 10 percent of the national budget would henceforth be devoted to education.

Hard campaigning for the upcoming congressional elections occupied the early months of 1958. *El Siglo* ran a succession of front-page photos showing prominent Ospinistas feting Rojas Pinilla during the early days of the general's regime. Meanwhile enemies of Gómez depicted their antagonist as a man who had established his own dictatorial regime. On March 16 the elections bore out Gómez's prediction that his candidates would triumph. Nearly 60 percent of all Conservatives voted Laureanista. Most of the rest voted for Ospinista candidates. Once the ballots were counted it was clear that Valencia's candidacy was dead; it would be Laureano Gómez and the Liberals, whose candidates won more than 60 percent of the vote, who would select the next president.

Colombian political history holds few moments more fraught with strangeness and paradox than the period between the March congressional election and the presidential contest held in early May. The nation's leaders had over the previous year crafted a remarkable agreement aimed at depoliticizing a system whose collapse was most complete during the truncated presidency of Laureano Gómez. Gómez was the man most Colombians blamed for the Violencia, which by that time had claimed upward of 200 lives. He was hated by many of his countrymen. Yet all looked to him during March and April 1958. Nor did the oddness of the moment stop there. Called upon to play kingmaker yet another time, Laureano Gómez, the man who had sacrificed everything to defend Conservatism, chose a Liberal to be the first National Front president. In late March 1958 he wrote Alberto Lleras Camargo suggesting Lleras as his candidate for the May election![10]

The history of the turbulent six weeks between the election of Lleras and the congressional contest preceding it is told in greater detail elsewhere. Suffice it to say that Conservatives were shocked, many of them outraged, that Gómez had chosen a Liberal. They condemned him as a traitor to his party, and many of them deserted his ranks. Yet Alberto Lleras was unquestionably the most popular man in Colombia at that moment, the leader of the nation's largest political party and a Liberal whom Gómez liked and trusted. By selecting Lleras, Gómez administered the coup de grâce to Guillermo León Valencia's candidacy and dealt a stinging defeat to his Ospinista foes. More significant, by sponsoring the Lleras candidacy, Gómez in fact served the interests of his party. When they accepted Lleras the Liberals committed themselves to support a Conservative for the 1962–1966 term. Subsequently they agreed to support a Conservative for the 1970–1974 term, thus extending the National Front to sixteen years. In that way Gómez, the leader of one faction of a party not to command a national majority for many years, guaranteed himself not one but two presidencies.

Alberto Lleras delayed accepting the candidacy until a week before the election. During those hectic days he and Laureano Gómez enthusiastically promoted the arrangement under whose terms Colombia would end the Violencia. On April 27, Gómez closed the campaign with a statement of his faith in the National Front: "We are at the dawn of a new life that aspires to peace, to well-being and reconciliation. I believe in it, and for that reason I have dedicated all my energies to it. Let us move forward, then, along the broad paths that open before us, with the serene confidence of those who have known how to fulfill their duty."[11] Alberto Lleras was no less eloquent. Speaking in Medellín on April 21, he promised that the National Front would help educate Colombians in democratic procedures. "And how will that singular process of education in democracy be achieved?" he asked. "It will be done by taking away all incentives to a sectarianism that feeds not only on tradition, cruel memories and unadulterated passion, but that feeds on improper use of public moneys, on the distribution of jobs to those who are inept, on the awarding of services and the covering up of delinquency."[12]

A few were unwilling to accept the tutelage that Lleras and Gómez offered. A number of Rojas Pinilla's most ardent supporters tried to sabotage the election by organizing a military putsch. In Bogotá troops following army official Hernando Forero briefly kidnapped Lleras Camargo. Rojas crossed the Venezuelan border and was prepared to march triumphantly into Bogotá. Gilberto Alzate Avendaño went so far as to draft a proclamation on behalf of the constituent assembly dissolved a year earlier, announcing resumption of the general's rule. But the coup attempt fizzled. Loyal troops freed Lleras and arrested his kidnappers. Rojas returned to Venezuela and Alzate tore up his proclamation. The election was held on May 4, 1958, with Lleras winning nearly 2.5 million votes. A last-minute Conservative protest candidate, Jorge Leyva, won 600,000 votes.[13]

A spirit of bipartisan harmony hovered over Colombia in the weeks after Lleras's election. On July 20, Congress met for the first time in nearly nine years. Members of the Liberal-Laureanista majority rose and applauded when Laureano Gómez, who had won a Senate seat on March 16, entered the chamber. Senators went on to elect Gómez Senate president, just as they had done twenty-four years before, when Alfonso López Pumarejo was Colombia's president-elect. Gómez thanked the body, and reiterated his support for the National Front. When a fellow Conservative started to criticize the military junta that had governed the nation since Rojas's fall, Gómez silenced him, saying, "We came here to work for the reconstruction of the fatherland. . . . We did not come here to ruin the climate of peace."[14]

On August 7, 1958, Laureano Gómez found himself yet again at the center of national attention when, as Senate president, he administered the oath of office to Alberto Lleras. Noting that he had occupied that spot twice before, in 1934 and in 1950, when he himself assumed the presidency, Gómez expressed hope for Colombia's future as well as a measure of contrition for his old militancy: "When we can kill the sectarianism within us we will be close to achieving harmony and peace. . . . How gratifying it is when words of friendship and fraternity, of collaboration and sympathy leave our lips, and not bitter words destined to ignite rancor and sterile discord! We have all made mistakes. But the harsh hand that oppressed us made us understand our error and caused us to turn our backs quickly and decidedly on the old methods of combat and to give ourselves over to this generous and fecund labor, which is destined to fundamentally correct the public life of our nation."[15]

Alberto Lleras devoted most of his acceptance speech to discussion of the Violencia. He had done the same a year earlier at Sitges, producing a document replete with references to the bloodshed whose intensity and persistence shocked Colombians and tarnished their nation's image before the world. Lleras termed suppression of the Violencia "this supreme labor," affirming that the bloodshed filled the country's public figures "with a spirit of contrition." The Violencia had instilled in them the resolve "to amend our errors," to be "humbly repentant that any of our words or acts might have contributed to the overflowing of the madness."[16] For Lleras the Violencia was a disease that found an ideal medium in Colombia's underclass. As he put it: "We have understood, and late, but still in time, that our civilization and culture were deceptively skin deep, and that our controversial and intransigent words were transformed as they fell upon the lower strata of a primitive society, becoming the sectarian cudgel, the murderous gunshot, the abuse and cruelty unleashed by nothing more than justification from on high." It was an analysis couched in the elitist idiom of traditional Colombian politics. Yet it conveyed Alberto Lleras's intention to end the Violencia quickly so he could devote full attention to promoting national economic development, which he believed would lift Colombia from its "precarious colonial situation."[17]

The First National Front Presidency

The Violencia, then in its eleventh year, continued to punish wide expanses of central Colombia as Alberto Lleras took office in mid-1958. Much reduced from the peaks it reached in 1948 and 1950, years when forty to fifty thousand Colombians died in the sectarian fighting, the conflict still claimed several thousand lives each year.[18] Over the first six months of 1958 alone, more than

2,300 citizens died of Violencia-related causes in Tolima, Valle, and Caldas.[19] Tolima, the smallest of the three departments, was worst affected, with more than a thousand. In late May 1958, Tolimense leaders cried out in their local press that the upset was ruining their department. Bandit gangs led by men like "Sangrenegra" (Black Blood), "Chispas" (Sparks), and "Desquite" (Revenge) roamed the coffee-growing uplands, murdering people at will. The difficulties inherent in eliminating the gangs is suggested by the fact that halfway through Lleras's term nearly 800 violentos operated in seventeen gangs scattered over Tolima, while another fifteen such groups were periodically active.[20]

The military junta that ruled from May 1957 to August 1958, when Alberto Lleras became president, had offered amnesty to the men under arms immediately upon taking charge. Many accepted, with the result that Violencia-related deaths over the course of 1957 dropped to 2,877, down from 11,136 in 1956. Alberto Lleras extended the amnesty into mid-1959, and in addition pursued a variety of anti-Violencia strategies. Even before taking office the military junta had allowed him to appoint a seven-man commission to study and report on the phenomenon. Immediately upon taking office he created a second committee charged with effecting rehabilitation of Violencia victims.[21] As a result, public moneys were applied to a range of resettlement activities, the most important of which were in the Ariari region of Meta, in the eastern llanos. Lleras also sent distinguished citizens to govern the most troubled departments. Foremost among them was Darío Echandía, sent to administer his native Tolima.

Lleras's efforts to reduce the Violencia were only partially successful. During 1959, Violencia-related deaths were down by a third over the previous year, but more than 2,500 Colombians still lost their lives. The phenomenon had not simply ended with the advent of bipartisanship. While the president's minister of war announced in May 1959 that the end of the conflict was in sight, the following month found Lleras placating a group of Tolimense women who perceived no decline in the bloodletting.[22]

The difficulties inherent in stopping the Violencia were suggested by two incidents in Tolima during 1959. Early that year the young violento Teófilo Rojas Varón ("Chispas") wrote to Father Germán Guzmán, who had formerly served as parish priest in the Violencia-lashed municipio of Líbano. Guzmán knew Chispas from the commission's work in southern Tolima. The young man, at the time just twenty-three years old, had tried to take advantage of the government's amnesty program, settling on a farmstead in the municipio of Rovira. But too many of his neighbors were interested in settling old scores, and this made it impossible for him to resume the life of a simple campesino. "Tell these people not to persecute me," he implored Father Guzmán.[23] But the priest was powerless to protect him. A short time later Chispas reconstituted his gang and resumed operations in western Tolima and southeastern Caldas.

A second incident that took place in northern Tolima illustrates in awful detail the problem of periodically active outlaw gangs. On October 18, 1959, a gang of fifteen armed men hacked to death twelve people—infants and small children among them—as they breakfasted at their home in upland Alto el Oso, in the municipio of El Líbano. Both political and economic motives were present in the atrocity. Its perpetrators were poor men who stole everything of value after committing the murders. The victims were all Liberals and the perpetrators all Conservatives. Those singled out for slaughter died because a day earlier, and in the same area, Liberal bandits had murdered twelve members of a Conservative family.[24]

The Alto el Oso massacre was investigated and its perpetrators soon arrested and brought to justice. But sadly that was the exception rather than the rule during Colombia's late Violencia. During the latter 1950s and on into the early 1960s, rural-dwelling Colombians in the nation's central cordillera continued to die at the hands of dozens of notorious violentos and their gangs.

Colombia's stubborn rural violence was merely one facet of a turbulent rural scene. As Alberto Lleras Camargo grappled with the problem of the Violencia, his country reached and passed the midpoint in its rapid shift from rural to urban. The movement of Colombians from country to city was intimately bound to the mechanization of agriculture, a process having both positive and negative effects. The commercialization of agriculture heightened inequalities in farm earnings, leaving 5 percent of farmers with 43 percent of total domestic income and 70 percent of them with less than 26 percent of income by 1960. Small landholdings of twenty or fewer hectares made up 86 percent of all farms. Most of those small holdings produced coffee and basic foodstuffs for local markets, and they tended to be less mechanized than the larger operations.[25] Rapid population growth during the 1950s placed increasing pressure on those landholdings. Additionally, there was a large group of landless agricultural workers who lived in penury and economic uncertainty. Thus Colombia's agricultural sector presented the mixed picture of a modernized commercial sector coexisting with impoverished smallholder and landless sectors.

The social and economic disparities existing in rural Colombia resulted in part from government policies aimed at promoting industrial growth. From the late 1930s national leaders had worked to modernize the campo in such a way that it would feed raw materials to import substituting industries. Alberto Lleras Camargo, who entered politics as Colombia's developmentalist economic strategy took shape, stood squarely in the tradition of Colombian modernizing elites. In his inaugural address on August 7, 1958, he reminded listeners of the great effort that the nation had expended to promote industrialization and asked for their support in helping Colombia consolidate its industrial base. Four months later, in his New Year's message, he stressed the need to increase economic prosperity at all social levels. Failure to do so, he warned, might subjugate Colombia to foreign powers "and thus cause us to cease being an independent republic."[26] That language illustrated Colombia's sense of vulnerability before a developed world that sold it expensive manufactured goods in exchange for cheap raw materials and placed Lleras in the "dependency school" of economic analysis embraced by most Latin American leaders of his generation. Spelled out chiefly in the writings of Argentine Raul Prebisch, head of the Economic Commission for Latin America (ECLA), the school called for protection aimed at increasing import substitution, freeing developing economies from having to purchase expensive foreign-made goods. By the late 1950s, with import substitution nearly complete in the more developed Latin American economies, leaders like Lleras were exploring the idea of forming regional trade blocks capable of excluding cheap products from outside Latin America and providing a supranational market for the manufactured products of individual nations.

Alberto Lleras recognized that many of rural Colombia's problems rose from the government's long-term pursuit of development economics. The year 1958 had been marked by land invasions in Viotá and Sumapaz, the same regions where landless campesinos had occupied haciendas twenty-five years before. Lleras addressed the crisis looming in the countryside by harking back to his party's agrarian reform tradition, specifically to that inculcated in Law 200 of 1936. Thus his New Year's address of December 31, 1958, not only called for a lessening of Colombia's economic dependence through increased industrialization, but also contained the president's promise of land reform. Lleras's struggle to make good on the promise to redistribute land and colonize wilderness areas constituted the chief activity of his presidency.

Lleras made clear at the outset that his idea of land reform conformed to classical liberal theory concerning man's relationship to the land. Nineteenth-century liberals viewed the yeoman as one of capitalist society's anchors, placing high priority on protecting and encouraging him. Lleras expressed his liberal view of reform in terms of the burning issue of the moment, the Cold War: "In Russia, in China, in Poland, in Hungary, and, generally, in all nations subjected to communist dictatorship, the great obstacle to communism has been the heroic or passive resistance of the campesino to collectivization of the land and to destruction of the concept of private property. This single consideration leads us to suggest that the creation of more smallholders will be the most effective way of affirming and preserving the political system that Colombia's traditional parties have consistently endorsed."[27] Lleras went on to order invaders occupying privately held lands to withdraw or face expulsion by the army.

Lleras's agrarian reform proposal soon was given impetus by events unfolding in Cuba. The evening of his New Year's message, guerrilla forces under the command of Fidel Castro occupied Havana, ending the dictatorship of Fulgencio Batista. Castro immediately launched a thoroughgoing program of land redistribution. By late 1959 he had seized and broken up most large privately held properties, turning them over to peasant operators in a series of highly publicized ceremonies. That alarmed officials in the United States, causing Assistant Secretary of State Chester Bowles to view sweeping changes in land tenure throughout Latin America as inevitable. "Only one question remains," said Bowles in November 1959, "How will these changes come? Through bloody revolution, or through long-range democratic planning?"[28] Colombians in both major parties echoed Bowles's concern. "If the next congress fails to produce an agrarian reform," said Conservative Diego Tovar Concha in July 1960, "revolution will be inevitable."[29] Two months later, in an address titled "Amid Nationwide Uncertainty," Carlos Lleras Restrepo reported that with the success of the Cuban Revolution communism could no longer be seen "as a remote and strange thing [that] could never come to have consequences in nations such as ours."[30]

During 1960 Lleras Restrepo became the chief spokesman for Lleras Camargo's agrarian reform initiative. Ongoing unrest in the countryside coupled with the appearance of the Castroite Movimiento Obrero-Estudiantil-Campesino (MOEC) helped produce strong support for the legislative package. The reform was drafted chiefly by Carlos Lleras Restrepo. Law 135 of December 13, 1961, provided for an agrarian reform institute known as INCORA (Instituto Colombiano de Reforma Agraria). Soon after the law's passage, the government launched a program of land redistribution and colonization, and the construction of rural penetration roads. Credit was made available for those programs, which continued the thrust toward agricultural modernization and the rationalization of large holdings.[31]

The United States supported Colombia's agrarian reform. Responding to Alberto Lleras's lightly veiled threat that unless substantial U.S. aid were forthcoming there would be a "revolution of poverty" throughout the region, the Americans stepped forward with substantial assistance under the Alliance for Progress program launched by President John F. Kennedy in 1961. Kennedy and his wife were on hand in Bogotá the week Law 135 was signed. Before then the United States attempted to make Colombia the showpiece of the Alliance for Progress in Latin America. Over the life of the program the United States and international lending agencies lent Colombia more than $1,000,000,000 — 11 percent of total alliance funding — much of which helped underwrite INCORA initiatives.[32] A variety of peripheral assistance, such as the dispatching of more than 1,000 U.S. Peace Corps volunteers to work in development projects during the 1960s, also formed part of the U.S. contribution.

Agrarian reform was welcomed in Colombia and abroad. U.S. economist Albert O. Hirschman, who served as a consultant during conceptualization of the reform, wrote that with the passage of Law 135 Colombia was "living what is surely its finest hours."[33] Subsequent to its passage the reform failed to live up to expectations. Still, its achievements were not insignificant. Not only did INCORA eventually provide grants of land to some 250,000 families, most of those grants from the public domain, but it also helped solidify the position of smallholders in Colombia's agrarian sector.[34]

The debate surrounding land reform produced a resurgence of Mariano Ospina Pérez's Conservative Party faction. In like measure it sent Laureanismo into eclipse. As a founder of the National Front and a supporter of its Liberal first president, Laureano Gómez found himself forced to support the reform initiative when Lleras Camargo first announced it. While he did so tepidly, calling for prior compensation for any property taken, Gómez's action allowed Ospina Pérez to take command of antireform forces. Ospina went on to head the group of agro-industrialists, large and small landowners who opposed any modification of prevailing land legislation. Ospinista candidates were especially effective in attacking a proposed new tax on large landholdings. That strategy paid off when Ospinista congressional candidates prevailed over Laureanistas in midterm elections held in March 1960. Finding his faction suddenly in the minority, Gómez broke with the government, soon becoming one of land reform's harshest critics. At the end of 1960 he was castigating the reform as "a badly drafted, confused, and abstract document that sins against the hermeneutics of all law while hiding its deficiencies and outright damage in excessive length."[35] Meanwhile Alberto Lleras and his chief lieutenant in the reform struggle, Carlos Lleras, negotiated the bill's finer points with Mariano Ospina Pérez, whose followers had replaced those of Gómez as Conservatism's leading faction.[36]

Laureanismo's decline, and the advance of Ospinismo, continued over the remainder of Alberto Lleras's presidency. In 1962, Laureano Gómez supported Belisario Betancur for the 1962–1966 presidential term. The caudillo's followers, however, lost badly to Ospinista candidates in the March 1962 congressional contest, thus enabling Ospina's followers to nominate Guillermo León Valencia for the presidency. The loss was a bitter one for Gómez, who tried to put the best possible face on it. "I'm like new," he told Arturo Abella not long afterward. "I feel as though they've lifted a load of bricks from my shoulders. I can't 'make' presidential candidates any longer. Now I'm tranquil and have already selected my favorite box for the spectacle we are about to witness."[37]

Colombia's 1962 congressional and presidential contests were notable because two groups of candidates ran strongly against the National Front. Alfonso López Michelsen, son of López Pumarejo, presented himself as an authentic Liberal alternative to those pledged to hand the presidency over to the minority Conservatives at four-year intervals. The second group was headed by none other than Gustavo Rojas Pinilla. Rojas had returned to Colombia in October 1958 following his brief Spanish exile. The Rojistas attacked the National Front in all its particulars and presented themselves as a democratic alternative to the deal struck by men who had given Colombia, among other things, the Violencia.

Alfonso López Michelsen launched his Movement for Liberal Recuperation in 1959, the year of his father's death. Soon renamed Movimiento Revolucionario Liberal (MRL), it strove to recreate the enthusiasm of the elder López's "Revolution on the March."[38] The younger López hoped to emulate his father's successes of 1934, when, following on the heels of Enrique Olaya Herrera's power-sharing regime (1930–1934), the elder López was able to win the 1934 presidential election on a reform platform.

The MRL appealed to Liberal activists who valued militant defense of principle and scorned compromise. It gave voice to Liberal ideologues, much as Laureanismo did to Conservative intransigents. This ideological approach to politics explained the old friendship of Alfonso López Pumarejo and Laureano Gómez. The two men, political opposites in most respects, were sufficiently close during their youth to name one another godfathers of their firstborn sons, Alfonso and Alvaro, who kept alive their fathers' doctrinaire styles.

López Michelsen's splinter party reached the height of its popularity during the 1962 elections, when it won 35 percent of the Liberal congressional vote—nearly 20 percent of the total. López had hoped to challenge Guillermo León Valencia in the presidential contest, but was kept from doing so by outgoing president Lleras Camargo. Lleras was forced into the embarrassing position of prohibiting López's name from being printed on presidential ballots.

The MRL gave political voice to left-wing political militants. It skillfully evoked Fidel Castro's success with slogans like, "Will all passengers for the revolution please board." López Michelsen allied his movement with the Communist Party and claimed solidarity with all other groups excluded from political participation by the "McCarthyite tactics of the National Front."[39] In his "January Plan" of 1960 López and his followers endorsed thoroughgoing nationalization of natural resources and agrarian reform not hobbled by political deal making. The platform featured a special salute to Fidel Castro as the "great captain of the Cuban Revolution."[40] During the 1960 congressional campaign López called for "a revolution for all," denouncing a ruling class that "funnels its private wealth into the acquisition of luxury cars, furs, jewels, and other kinds of sumptuous spending."[41]

After reaching the height of its success in 1962, the MRL entered an inevitable decline—inevitable because López Michelsen's understanding of the word *revolution* was seriously at odds with that of his more radical colleagues. At most López was a social democrat committed to reducing social inequities. He had no intention of challenging the capitalist system to which his family owed its rise from relative obscurity in a hundred years' time. As early as

March 1961 the MRL's radical wing had proclaimed that the party could not simultaneously represent "the interests of the country's capitalist and large landowning classes."[42] A year later MRL hard-liners sent Communist and agrarian activist Juan de la Cruz Varela to Congress. López Michelsen protested, and refused to share party leadership with the leftist from Sumapaz. The division produced by his action underscored the fact that the MRL was, in the words of the movement's historian, Mauricio Botero, "a halfway house between the Liberal Party and the guerrillas."[43] It was a transitory one at that. By the late 1960s López Michelsen had returned to the Liberal Party, while MRL hard-liners continued to support genuine revolutionary change.

Colombia's National Front not only heightened factionalism within the traditional political parties, but it also stimulated the formation of third parties. The most significant of them was the one headed by Gustavo Rojas Pinilla. Rojas's movement was in some respects the counterpart of that headed by López Michelsen. Its candidates in the 1962 congressional race presented themselves as members of Conservatism's Rojista wing. As such they elected two senators and six representatives, gaining 3.4 percent of the popular vote.[44] The general had first called his party the National Popular Catholic Alliance, but eventually settled on National Popular Alliance (Alianza Nacional Popular), or ANAPO. In its early years ANAPO gave voice to Conservatives who simply could not tolerate coalition government.

ANAPO's early leadership came chiefly from persons who had worked closely with Rojas Pinilla during his presidency. An important moment in its early history came in late 1960, when Gilberto Alzate Avendaño died suddenly of complications arising from gluttony. Up to that moment the Caldense politician had led his own Conservative faction, known as Alzatismo. Alzate was of course the man chiefly responsible for bringing Rojas Pinilla to power in 1953. Hence upon his death many of his followers enlisted in the ranks of Rojismo.

Where ANAPO differed significantly from López Michelsen's MRL was in its populism. Rojas Pinilla spoke what he himself termed the "panela dialectic," meaning that when the price of staples like panela (raw sugar) rose, placing new burdens on the poor, support for his party increased. His First Anapista Platform, unveiled in late 1961, promised changes highly attractive to poor Colombians: jobs with good pay, free primary and secondary education, economical medical service and free medicines, urban reform, and affordable housing for the lower and middle classes. Stressing its coalition aspect, that of an "alliance" uniting the poor regardless of traditional party affiliation, ANAPO evolved into what historian César Ayala has termed a "National Front of the underclasses," providing a political alternative to broad social sectors lacking political space and unhappy with the new power structure established at the end of the 1950s.[45]

At first the Anapistas thought they could win power by means of a military coup. Rojas Pinilla had after all been catapulted into power via a coup. His followers within the army tried to move against the ruling junta in November 1957 and again in May 1958. The Rojistas attempted to overthrow Lleras Camargo twice following his inauguration, the first time in December 1958, and again in January 1962. There would be yet another failed coup, against Guillermo León Valencia, in early 1963.

Those repeated uprisings were born of the Rojista belief that the government was persecuting their leader. When Rojas returned to Colombia in October 1958, he was placed under house arrest and tried for malfeasance in office three months later. Found guilty by the Colombian Senate, he was stripped of his military pension and honors, along with his right to vote and to hold public office. He was subsequently held under modified house arrest until mid-1960.

Government attempts to make an example of Rojas Pinilla miscarried badly. The general's supporters used the trial as a forum for attacking the National Front and its creators. They were especially critical of Laureano Gómez, whom they tarred as author of the Violencia.[46] Gómez, for his part, did not mince words when speaking of the Rojistas. In a radio speech of December 1958 he described one of their coup attempts as "monstrous, horrible, and revealing of sick and criminal minds lacking any concept of humanity, knowing nothing of virtue and distant from and alien to the most elemental principles of social morality." Those behind the plot possessed "minds impregnated with crime, festering with pestilential juices and evil and perverse viruses, fed with the terrible rot of hatred, of intransigence, and stupidity."[47]

Anapismo soon abandoned the military coup as a route to power, instead making its voice heard through democratic channels. The 1962 congressional elections marked the beginning of ANAPO's success. Rojas Pinilla's movement would grow in popularity over the 1960s, at length nearly toppling the National Front.

Still neither Rojas Pinilla's ANAPO movement nor López Michelsen's MRL seriously challenged the National Front in 1962. Guillermo León Valencia was elected president on May 6 of that year. His subsequent inauguration stood as a major achievement of Colombia's unique power-sharing arrangement.

The Violencia Ends, Armed Struggle Continues

Colombia's Violencia existed in its final and most perverse phase during early years of the National Front. When Valencia took office in mid-1962, bandit gangs continued to murder hapless campesinos and ambushed army and police patrols at will. Most of the armed groups were small—ten or twelve strong—nearly all claiming allegiance to one or the other traditional party. Most members were young, illiterate campesinos drawn to bandit life by its excitement and easy profits.

Several things fed the diffuse late Violencia. During the time he presided over the national government Alberto Lleras did not use the army to pursue bandit gangs with vigor. His fear was that such an approach would simply worsen the fighting. Instead he was content to strengthen military posts in regions of ongoing Violencia while pursuing peaceful approaches to the crisis. An unintended consequence of his policy was to convince some that the army actually operated in complicity with the bandits. It was an easy inference to make when killers like "Sangrenegra" taunted the military with notes sent to their posts from nearby mountains. One of them read "*Carbineros* of Murillo: Greetings from your friend Sangrenegra, who invites you to . . . bring about 150 of your friends to see if we can have a little talk. . . . I'll be waiting to test your courage, to see how brave you really are."[48] During the late 1950s and early '60s residents of Tolima and Caldas begged the government to strike hard against the bandit gangs, but to little avail. Thus an Ibagué newspaper could publish what it titled "A Realistic Picture of Tolima" during mid-1959. It showed two men staring into an open grave.[49]

A complex of local factors stimulated Colombia's late Violencia. Simple fear was a powerful motive force. When Conservative bandits robbed and murdered civilians, they invariably targeted Liberals. Liberal bandits likewise operated almost exclusively against Conservatives. As rural neighborhoods, and sometimes entire municipios, tended to be predominantly Liberal or Conservative, the people living there frequently aided the outlaws with whom they shared partisan affiliation. In areas of heavy Violencia local residents often played an active role in encouraging irregular forces that they viewed as their protectors. That dynamic was perfectly clear when, following the massacre of twelve Conservative campesinos in upland Tolima on October 17, 1959, Conservatives living in the nearby village of Santa Isabel dispatched the bandit "Cabo Yate" to take the lives of twelve Liberals at nearby Alto el Oso. This moved civic leaders in Liberal El Líbano to ask for protection from the notorious Liberal violentos Roberto González ("Pedro Brincos") and William Arangueren ("Desquite").[50]

Simple greed and a willingness to profit at another's expense were other important sources of Colombia's late Violencia. Individuals throughout the region affected by the late Violencia, which embraced a great portion of the coffee zone, received coffee and other stolen property from violentos. The Violencia typically swept the region during the semiannual coffee harvest, when the crop was frequently stolen from farms whose owners were too frightened to guard them.[51] Local merchants and other petty capitalists purchased such farms at bargain prices, frequently from the widows of Violencia victims.

Thus an entire class of nouveaux riches entered the social structure in places like Quindío during the years of the late Violencia. Carlos Miguel Ortiz writes that while those who were rich prior to the Violencia usually remained so afterward, many having humble origins gained social prominence during the Violencia years.[52]

An especially vexing aspect of the late Violencia was the claim of violentos that they were fighting on behalf of the Liberal Party, at a time when Liberal supporters of the National Front struggled to combat the bloodshed. Para-doxically most Liberal bandits of the late Violencia claimed allegiance both to the splinter MRL and to local politicians having MRL ties. Gonzalo Sánchez and Donny Meertens, authors of the best work on bandits and their political allies, wrote that in Tolima "Pedro Brincos," "Desquite," and others "acted . . . under the aegis of the MRL, which occupied the space left by traditional *gamonales;* at the local and regional levels that made possible highly diverse interpretations of [the MRL's] revolutionary slogans."[53] Carlos Miguel Ortiz finds that in Quindío allegiance to the MRL served both bandits and local political elites, especially in municipios where "old scores had not yet been settled" when the National Front began.[54] For their part the bandits used MRL allegiance as a convenient cover. In that way opportunistic violentos like "Sangrenegra" could battle the national army all the while crowing, "Long live . . . the MRL and its campaigns!"[55]

Ecological factors played a crucial role in allowing the late Violencia to flourish in the central cordillera. Rugged and heavily forested, with wilderness areas in its highest reaches, most of the region below 3,000 meters was heavily populated with villages and farms. Outlaw gangs thus had ready access to shelter and supplies, as well as the ability to lose themselves in the mountain fastness when pursued by army or police. The central cordillera had the added advantage of overlooking the rich and heavily populated Magdalena Valley to the east and the Cauca Valley to the west, offering easy access to both. Coupled with the near absence of highways and the state's scant presence in the region, the central cordillera was a haven for bandits during the late Violencia.

The complex logic of Colombia's late Violencia can be appreciated through the stories of the violentos themselves, of men like William Aranguren, "Desquite." Born into a family of small landowners in Rovira, Tolima, in 1936, Aranguren saw a Conservative murder his father during the Violencia that swept Rovira after 1948. Several years later the young man left his mother's farm to follow the coffee harvest around Sevilla, in northern Valle. There he fell in with companions who taught him to smoke marijuana and to enjoy the attractions available to footloose young men with money to spend. As Aranguren's sister recalled, the young man became a ne'er-do-well who when at home slept until noon, smoked marijuana with his cousins, and never listened to anyone's advice. For the latter reason family members nicknamed him "El Orejón" (The Big Ear).[56]

Aranguren became obsessed with finding and killing his father's murderer, one Ovidio Hinojosa. At length he discovered the man's whereabouts. Armed with pistol and machete, and accompanied by his cousins, El Orejón went to Hinojosa's house, called him outside, and murdered him. In the heat of the moment Aranguren and his relatives also killed the man's wife and children. "Today I've screwed up," Aranguren said later to his cousins, "from now on my destiny is in the mountains."[57]

The young violento fled to Valle, where for a time he helped an outlaw gang stage depredations in the northern part of that department. Soon the group made its way back to Tolima, where it specialized in hijacking motor vehicles. In April 1957, Aranguren and eight others were arrested after killing the driver of a Colombian Tobacco Company truck and stealing a payroll. He was tried, convicted, and sent to Bogotá's La Picota prison.[58] There Aranguren was read passages from Eduardo Franco Isaza's Las guerrillas del llano, and speeches by Jorge Eliécer Gaitán. Thus was his political consciousness raised. A short time later, on May 10, 1957, he escaped from La Picota during an uprising of prisoners. He returned to Tolima, where he joined the gang of "Chispas." But a disagreement sent him northward to the municipio of El Líbano, where "Sangrenegra," "Pedro Brincos," and "Tarzán" (Noel Lombana Osorio) were already ensconced. By that time Aranguren had acquired his nom de guerre, "Desquite" (Revenge). He installed himself near the vereda of Santa Teresa where he set up housekeeping with Rosalba Velásquez, whose father owned a coffee farm.[59]

"Desquite" moved to Líbano just as that municipio entered its worst period of Violencia. On average a dozen people died there each month between 1957 and 1964, many of them in multiple homicides, such as the one committed at Alto el Oso. Local leaders met sporadically to discuss ways of reducing the bloodshed. One such meeting held during early 1961 included the violento "Pedro Brincos," a confidant of "Desquite."[60]

By late 1961 "Desquite" was the most famous of Líbano's bandits. His gang numbered sixty-five men, and received cash support from Liberal landowners, who considered him their insurance against Conservative bandits. His growing success led the violento, along with "Pedro Brincos" and "Sangrenegra," to stage one of their most audacious undertakings. On April 12, 1962, they ambushed and annihilated a fourteen-man army patrol traveling along the road between El Líbano and Santa Teresa. The El Taburete incident, as it came to be known, constituted vivid proof both of bandit strength in northern Tolima and of the National Front's failure to end the Violencia. Early in 1963 citizens of Líbano wrote President Guillermo León Valencia threatening to place "Desquite" in charge of pacifying the municipio unless the army battalion stationed there quickly did so.[61]

The letter of January 8, 1963, was a harsh indictment of the government's inability to police its territory. But it was written at the moment an ambitious plan for ending the Violencia was starting to unfold. Broadly known as Plan Lazo (lasso), the scheme was evolved chiefly by the military. And it had the department of Tolima—specifically, northern Tolima—as its focal point.

Plan Lazo possessed both political and military dimensions. First, it aimed at enlisting the support of northern Tolima's most prominent Liberal politician, Alfonso Jaramillo Salazar. Thus it won favor with most of the region's Liberal population, as Jaramillo fell into line with the government's anti-Violencia plan. In mid-1962 Jaramillo accepted Tolima's governorship. Local violentos accordingly lost a major portion of their regional support. Second, Valencia's minister of war, Alberto Ruiz Novoa, put Plan Lazo's military component in operation. Over the first half of 1963 the army began an aggressive campaign against the bandits throughout the central cordillera. By midyear specially trained units were in hot pursuit of "Desquite," "Sangrenegra," and the rest. The army established a special base in the uplands of Venadillo, a municipio whose western edge abutted El Líbano, where "Desquite" had lived for five years. Flushed from his familiar haunts, the violento fled northward into the highlands between Tolima and Caldas. He paused on August 15 to block the road between the villages of La Italia and Marquetalia, Caldas. There he slaughtered thirty-nine hapless Conservatives and then proceeded eastward toward the Río Magdalena, holing up in a rocky no-man's-land south of Falan, Tolima. Thinking it had him cornered the army called for air support in the form of a helicopter recently received from the United States. However "Desquite" escaped his pursuers, later complaining that it wasn't proper for President Kennedy "to send aircraft to kill people instead of money for the poor."[62]

But time had clearly run out for "Desquite." He was cut off from local support, hotly pursued by the military, and damned for his excesses by Liberals and Conservatives alike. He hid out in the mountains near Venadillo in early 1964. On March 18 of that year a young campesino happened on him at a deserted hut. "Desquite" asked him to bring batteries for his transistor radio; the campesino instead told the military. In less than an hour "Desquite" was surrounded by an army unit and shot to death. His body was then taken by helicopter to Líbano, Santa Teresa, and other villages of northern Tolima, where it was placed for a time in town plazas for all to see. The army wanted there to be no mistaking either the fact or the circumstance of his death.

Most of Colombia's notorious violentos fell to the army between 1963 and 1965, owing to the soundness of the military's antibandit program and to the effectiveness of its execution. Plan Lazo, for example, consisted of four phases. First came its initial conceptualization, carried out both in domestic and inter-American settings. Fidel Castro's success in late 1958 vastly heightened interest in counterinsurgency techniques throughout Latin America. Thus when General Ruiz Novoa unveiled his pacification plan in 1962, he did so not in Colombia but at a meeting of U.S. and Latin American military leaders held at Fort Gulick in the Panama Canal Zone. Over the preceding two years Colombia and the United States had held joint military maneuvers and had met jointly on numerous occasions through an organization called the Conference of American Armies.[63]

The second phase of Plan Lazo involved a variety of covert and psychological activities. Studies of leading violentos and their followers were conducted, undercover agents sent to infiltrate their gangs, and soldiers disguised as violentos to sow confusion among bandits and civilians alike. Meanwhile members of the military circulated among the civilian population, convincing them that the army's only goal was to bring peace to Violencia-ravaged zones. The military also offered rewards for information leading to the apprehension of violentos. Symbolism, too, had its place in Plan Lazo. As the famous bandits fell, their bodies were lashed to struts beneath army helicopters and taken from one village to another for public viewing. To some persons on the ground the helicopters suggested birds of prey clutching hapless creatures in their talons.[64]

Phase three of Plan Lazo involved the mounting of special base camps such as the one in northern Tolima, from which "Desquite" was successfully pursued. These served as bases for training and dispatching anti-insurgent units that systematically killed most of the notorious bandits of the late Violencia, between 1963 and 1965. In some cases the violentos were ambushed while arriving to pick up money extorted from campesinos. In others they were ambushed as they traveled unsuspectingly down mountain roads and trails. It was a brutal and effective campaign carried out against an enemy not known for its own quality of mercy.[65]

The fourth and final stage in Plan Lazo involved an extended period of social work and reconstruction in former Violencia zones. The army program, called Civic-Military Action, ran the gamut from road construction, to policing, to the teaching of literacy. Other branches of government contributed to the effort. INCORA launched land redistribution and resettlement efforts in hard-hit regions, and the Caja Agraria provided loans to farmers living there. A community self-help program known as Acción Comunal (Community Action), launched during the Lleras Camargo presidency, was heavily promoted as a mechanism for helping campesinos work together for the common good even as it reinforced the presence of the state in the countryside.[66] Military and nonmilitary foreign assistance was provided, much of it under auspices of the

U.S. Alliance for Progress. Significant additional aid was funneled into rural Colombia during the 1960s through Catholic charities and the international program known as CARE.[67]

Plan Lazo received great motive force from the Cold War. Relations between Colombia and Cuba had cooled rapidly as Fidel Castro moved leftward after 1959 and turned hostile in late 1961, as Alberto Lleras Camargo prepared to receive a state visit from U.S. President John F. Kennedy and his wife. Two weeks before the Kennedys' December 17 visit, Castro proclaimed his allegiance to Marxism-Leninism. A week later, on December 9, 1961, Colombia broke diplomatic relations with Cuba. Lleras Camargo explained his action as produced by Castro's attempts to subvert Colombia's government.[68]

There were solid grounds for Lleras's fears. During his first years in power Castro had welcomed Colombian visitors, most of whom were vocal, even violent critics of the National Front. Among them were leaders of López Michelsen's MRL, and Antonio Larrota, a founder of the revolutionary MOEC. Larrota, whose organization had been denounced by the Colombian Communist Party as extremist and anarchistic, had lived in Cuba from mid-1959 to mid-1961. Upon his return home he traveled to Cauca, where he joined the Liberal bandit Adán de Jesús Aguirre ("El Aguila"), who soon murdered him to collect a government reward for Larrota's capture.[69]

MOEC members had slightly better luck in the llanos. There in 1961, Ramón Larrota, brother of Antonio, anarchist physician Tulio Bayer, and former Liberal guerrilla Rosendo Colmenares launched a revolutionary movement at the remote village of Santa Rita, on the banks of the Río Vichada. The army easily put down the uprising in October 1961 and arrested Bayer and Colmenares. The two were handed over to civil authorities who sentenced them to short prison terms. Ramón Larrota escaped. On December 7, 1961, two days before Lleras Camargo severed relations with Cuba, Larrota wrote Che Guevara to ask for military assistance. Three days after that Larrota again wrote to Cuba, informing Fidel Castro that "compelled to fight for a Colombia free from Yankee imperialism and the Colombian oligarchy this Command has resolved . . . to take up with you matters related to our Revolution."[70]

Tulio Bayer's revolutionary movement produced a flurry of excitement in Colombia, giving the government's Conservative opponents an issue to use against it.[71] Thus it was that on November 29, Alvaro Gómez Hurtado rose to address the Senate on the issue of communist revolutionary movements that he viewed as endemic in Colombia. Gómez argued that the government was standing idly by as communists established footholds throughout the nation. No one had seemed to notice, he said sarcastically, that "in this country there is a group of independent republics that do not recognize the sovereignty of the Colombian state, where the Colombian army cannot enter, where people say the army's presence is a frightening abomination. . . . There is the independent republic of Sumapaz . . . of Planadas . . . of Río Chiquito . . . and now we have the newborn independent republic of Vichada. National sovereignty is collapsing like a handkerchief."[72]

Alvaro Gómez's speech was timely in that it came two days before Castro openly embraced Marxism-Leninism, ten days before Colombia broke relations with Cuba, and two weeks before John F. Kennedy's visit. An embarrassed national government soon mounted an offensive against the "independent republic of Planadas," a small communist enclave in southern Tolima. Although the operation was canceled without comment early in 1962, the excitement that Alvaro Gómez's words produced in anticommunist circles struck home.

Colombian authorities had known for years that small communist-controlled enclaves existed in remote parts of national territory. Originating as self-defense zones established during the civil warfare of 1949–1953, they had continued to exist as self-governing agrarian communes throughout the Rojas Pinilla years. During the demobilization of guerrilla forces following Rojas's fall, the communists of southern Tolima had declined to give up their weapons. They and their leader, "Charro Negro" (Jacobo Prías Alape), knew that they would soon need them for self-defense against the anticommunists who encircled them.

"Charro Negro's" enclave lay south of Planadas, Tolima, in a region of narrow valleys and steep, heavily forested mountains that he and his followers called Marquetalia. Occupying the extreme southern tip of the department, Marquetalia lay some two days' march from the larger enclave of Río Chiquito. Ciro Trujillo Castaño ("Mayor Ciro") commanded Río Chiquito, a broken, well-watered zone covering a portion of northeastern Cauca. The two areas maintained contact along a formidable hidden trail constructed during the late 1950s and early '60s. The route was the one taken by the communists of Marquetalia when the army expelled them in May 1964.

When Alvaro Gómez coined the phrase "independent republics," two schools of thought existed concerning the degree of danger that they posed. According to the first, the enclaves presented little or no threat to national sovereignty and therefore should be left alone. The second held that each of the "republics" harbored dangerous revolutionaries capable of overthrowing Colombia's capitalist regime. According to historian Alvaro Valencia Tovar, who as an army lieutenant colonel helped design and execute Plan Lazo, most Colombians endorsed the first view. Marquetalia and the other enclaves, they believed, would evolve as had Viotá, in Cundinamarca, where the inhabitants had become smallholders and had over time "integrated themselves in the [capitalist] national community."[73]

The second perspective was in line with contemporary Cold War thought holding that communism was like a contagious disease that unless vigorously combated would spread through society. Lieutenant Colonel José Joaquín Matallana, a contemporary of Valencia Tovar, subscribed to that traditional Cold War perspective. He stated in 1963 that "entire regions in southern Tolima [were] being won over to communist, or to procommunist, philosophy."[74]

Whether communal Marquetalia would have followed Viotá into bourgeois respectability will never be known, since the army eventually invaded and destroyed it. This was especially unfortunate given the error of Colonel Matallana's perception that communism was on the march in southern Tolima. The few dozen families making up the "independent republic" of Marquetalia were in fact barely holding their own in an internecine battle with Liberal guerrillas as the Colombian army readied its attack.

The Liberal and communist guerrillas operating in southern Tolima had acted jointly for a time during the early 1950s. But their ideological differences were unbridgeable and within a few years they were at war with one another. When the army staged its attack on Marquetalia in May 1964, the enclave had been reduced to a small region west of the village of Gaitania.

Southern Tolima's Liberal guerrillas had always shared the values of most Colombians. They jealously guarded individual freedom and pursued individual interests in a mountain fastness where the Colombian state never fully established its presence. In that sense they lived in a setting that accorded well with classical liberal theory. The communists of "Charro Negro" embraced values diametrically opposed to those of the Liberals. They valued communalism of the sort described in the writings of Karl Marx and other utopian socialists.

The ideological gulf separating southern Tolima's Liberal guerrillas, or *limpios,* and the communists, or *comunes,* had been noted and commented on since early in the Violencia. The communists saw the Liberals as undisciplined and self-centered. They complained of the Liberals' "unhealthy sense of private property, their sickening individualism, their tendency toward banditry." The communists belittled the Liberals "for not accepting that the war isn't for enriching oneself but rather for pursuing noble and advanced objectives."[75]

The Liberals despised what the communists glorified. Writing to Gerardo Loayza, limpio leader of southern Tolima, members of the Liberal directorate in Ibagué instructed: "You are limpio Liberals and the others are comunes, or communists, and we cannot unite with them because they are our deadly enemies: the communists are against the private property that we Liberals defend; the communists are enemies of God, and we are Roman Catholic believers. Therefore you cannot, you must not continue your alliance with them. You must break with them immediately. We are going to take the government, and when we do, we will get rid of the communists."[76] The Liberal directorate went on to charge the communists with "breaking the unity and hierarchy of the family" when they gave women and children weapons and uniforms and asked them to fight alongside the men. That, wrote the Liberals, "distanced [women] from their accustomed tasks in the home."[77]

The disagreement between the Liberals and communists in southern Tolima set off a chain of events that helped ensure the success of Plan Lazo. In 1959, when the Violencia was building all over the department, the two groups came together briefly for a joint operation against police in the zone to which they referred as El Davis. Afterward one of the Liberal combatants, either unaware of or not accepting the communist rule requiring the redistribution of weapons taken in battle, returned home with a rifle he had liberated. Months later a communist patrol happened on the man, whose nom de guerre was El Diablo, and, acting on Charro Negro's instruction, confiscated the rifle. That infuriated Gerardo Loayza, who vowed to avenge the crime against that form of private property most valued by the guerrillero. Some weeks later, on January 11, 1960, three of Loayza's men appeared at communist headquarters asking to speak with Charro Negro. When he appeared, they shot him to death and fled.[78] Charro Negro's assassination signaled a mobilization of Liberal and communist forces. In the warfare that followed some fifty Liberals, among them Gerardo Loayza and twenty-five communists, were killed. That made way for new leadership on both sides. The new Liberal chief was a former Protestant minister named Jesús María Oviedo ("Mariachi"). Pedro Antonio Marín ("Tiro Fijo," alias Manuel Marulanda Vélez) assumed leadership of the communists.

Tolima's intraguerrilla civil war of the early 1960s represented but one aspect of the amorphous Violencia existing there at the time. As Liberals and communists slaughtered each other in the south, and as bandits massacred entire families in the north, the army methodically implemented Plan Lazo. The plan's military phase, operationalized during 1963, had achieved such success against Tolima's bandit population by early 1964 that the army could address the perceived problem of communist southern Tolima. Thus it formulated a surprise attack on Marquetalia, under the code name Operation Sovereignty. The plan's three goals were to capture Tiro Fijo, to liquidate the Marquetalia commune, and to establish a permanent military presence in the region.

Three battalions, totaling some 2,000 men, were committed to the Marquetalia operation. Elaborate preparations were made for the attack that began on May 27. Aircraft strafed the guerrilla villages as artillery shelled them. On June 14, Lieutenant Colonel Matallana led 250 soldiers in a helicopter assault against the few score defenders who had remained behind to defend their headquarters. Women and children had been evacuated earlier over the hidden trail leading to Río Chiquito.[79] The communists stood off Matallana and his troops all that day, then withdrew toward Río Chiquito before dawn on June 15. They set fire to their huts as they departed. While the army's victory over a few dozen poorly armed campesinos was hardly a glorious one, and while it failed in its aim of capturing Tiro Fijo, Operation Sovereignty achieved its goal of removing the communist presence from southern Tolima and placing it under control of the Colombian state.

Tiro Fijo and his followers spent the succeeding year with his colleague "Mayor Ciro" in Río Chiquito, but that enclave was invaded and occupied by the army in September 1965. Meanwhile the other "independent republics" were attacked and reduced by the military. Denied the possibility of defending any single region, communist leaders retreated from the central cordillera, crossing the Magdalena Valley into trackless forests and mountains of the eastern cordillera and thence into the virtually uninhabited jungles of Caquetá and Meta.[80] Thus reduced to a peripatetic existence, Tiro Fijo and his colleagues reconstituted their movement as that of a mobile guerrilla force.[81]

The destruction of the "independent republics" and the near simultaneous stamping out of rural banditry closed the book on Colombia's Violencia, the conflict that began in 1947 as a Liberal-Conservative power struggle. Over its eighteen years it claimed nearly 200,000 lives. Yet with the escape of Tiro Fijo, Mayor Ciro, and their followers, and the communists' subsequent formation of mobile revolutionary units, Colombia was guaranteed continued political violence of a sort distinct from the traditional partisan strife that produced the Violencia.

Frustrations of the State of Siege Generation

Popular unhappiness was widespread in Colombia during the early 1960s. Low coffee prices and a slowdown in import-substituting industrial growth, complicated by unacceptable levels of public debt, hurt ordinary citizens in a variety of ways. Inflation and unemployment increased steadily. Wage increases, which were constant during the 1950s, slowed during the early 1960s and were in decline by mid-decade.

These signs of economic stagnation fed the popular perception that powerful and wealthy men having links to interest associations like SAC, ANDI, and FENALCO manipulated the system to their benefit. Worsening income distribution during the 1960s seemed to bear out the charge. Economists Albert Berry and Miguel Urrutia concluded that as of 1965 Colombia suffered unequal income distribution, second only to Brazil among major Latin American nations. Fully half the Colombian population existed at what they termed "extremely low standards of living."[82]

In spite of promises that social welfare programs would receive top priority under the National Front, public welfare spending had not increased markedly. Colombian tax revenues were simply too low to fund significant new programs. Nor could the government offer much help to the unemployed. At a time when most Latin American nations were committed to statist economic policies featuring make-work programs and extensive government investment in the public sector, the Colombian state played a relatively small role in the economy.

Whether fairly or not, a great many Colombians blamed the government for their social and economic problems. They increasingly showed their displeasure by turning away from politics. Growing indifference to politics was seen most graphically in a sharp decline in voting over the early years of the National Front. Electoral participation plummeted following 1957, when a record 72 percent of those eligible voted. By the second National Front presidency slightly more than a third of those eligible exercised the franchise.[83]

Guillermo León Valencia was in part responsible for the falling acceptance of the National Front. A Conservative, he never would have been elected had the predominately Liberal population been given the chance to vote for a Liberal candidate. Valencia was a poor president in his own right. He had little understanding of or interest in economics—this at a time when the country was sliding into a serious recession. Most of his time seemed to be spent in divvying up political posts under terms of National Front power-sharing canons, hosting drunken state banquets, and enjoying duck-hunting trips on his Cauca estate.

Another of Valencia's problems as national leader lay in his anachronistic image. He seemed to have stepped from the era when Liberals were not allowed to win elections and Conservatives could do so only when bearing the archbishop's imprimatur. The Cauca politician heightened that impression by affecting the foppish look of his more talented father, the poet Guillermo Valencia.

While most Colombians demonstrated their unhappiness with politics through growing indifference to or rejection of the public world, two minorities challenged the system. The first was labor, and the second consisted of an intellectual and political counterelite described as the State of Siege Generation.

Organized labor doubled its proportion of the workforce between 1958 and 1965, from 5.5 percent of the total to 13.4 percent.[84] That rapid expansion, and the fact that most of its growth took place in public-sector unions, gave labor a considerable voice in public affairs.

Along with the rise of public-sector unionism came changes in the UTC and the CTC. The former, the country's largest labor federation by the early 1960s, shed its confessional character and developed a newfound militancy, while the Liberal-dominated CTC expelled its communist members in 1962. Two years later communist workers formed their own federation, the Confederación Sindical de Trabajadores de Colombia (CSTC).

Colombian labor achieved the remarkable feat of awakening President Valencia and moving him to action in early 1965. It did so by threatening a general strike, the culmination of continuous strike activity during the early sixties. Valencia responded with labor law reforms offering increased protection to workers. Strikes declined sharply thereafter.[85] One unique feature of the 1965 labor crisis was its mediation through the intervention of ANDI, FENALCO, and other employer associations. The fact that the gremios, rather than the political parties, played that role further evidenced the enduring strength of corporative entities within Colombia's increasingly pluralistic society.

In May 1965, four months after the general strike was canceled, Valencia placed the nation under a state of siege. Student protests had swept the country over preceding weeks as young Colombians demonstrated against the army's liquidation of the "independent republics," U.S. military intervention in the Dominican Republic, the nation's economic woes, and Valencia's despised government.

The generation that came of age during the 1950s and '60s referred to itself variously as the State of Siege Generation, the Nueve de Abril Generation, and the Rebellious Generation. Its members had never known an extended period during which Colombia was at peace, a fact causing them to be uniformly scornful of their country's political leadership. They agreed with Jorge Gaitán Durán that the National Front was "a vacuous project."[86] It was seen as narrowing political opportunities as to be undemocratic, elitist, and anachronistic—a system foisted on the country by men whose ideas were outdated.[87] They agreed with one of their generation's senior members, Eduardo Caballero Calderón, that to be truly valid political institutions "must emanate from below like the distillation of popular needs, preoccupations, and realities."[88] Young Colombians choked on Lleras Camargo's phrase attributing the Violencia to "a reserve of barbarism in our people that defied entire centuries of Christian teaching."[89] Psychiatrist José Gutiérrez cited such remarks as proof that Colombia was a "pseudo-aristocracy" where "we don't play with ideas, but rather with formulae."[90]

Their sense that they lived under a profoundly antipopular regime led several intellectuals to conclude that Colombia's story was one of unending frustration of popular aspirations. Caballero Calderón concluded his exploration of that theme by expressing uncertainty as to whether "our history can be considered altogether as one frustration, or whether it is preferable to see it as a successive series of frustrations."[91] Scholar Luis López de Mesa, good positivist that he was, had earlier listed six historical moments when Colombia's national destiny had been frustrated. The last of them began during the 1940s, when willful and shortsighted leaders "threw the nation into the abyss of all imaginable madness, robbing it of the moral quality with which a virtuous generation had honored it over forty years of equanimity, probity, and justice."[92]

Sociologist Orlando Fals Borda, a leading member of the State of Siege Generation, published an extended analysis of frustration in Colombian history in his 1967 monograph *La subversión en Colombia*. There he examined a series of cases in which utopian socialists had tried to change Colombian society for the better, only to find their hopes dashed by the ruling class. The Violencia, Fals determined, stood as "the greatest and most dramatic monument to the frustration of socialist subversion of the seignorial-bourgeois tradition." Fals ended his monograph on a hopeful note. He pointed out that by the mid-1960s a vigorous new utopian movement flourished in Colombia. Peopled by "neosocialist counterelites and egalitarian-minded university students and teachers," along with progressive-minded Liberals and the leaders of various popular movements—all of whom were "encouraged by the example of contemporary Latin American revolutions"—they stood ready to attack "the incongruencies, injustices, and contradictions of the prevailing order."[93]

La subversión en Colombia formed part of a wide-ranging reevaluation of national culture and history by members of the State of Siege Generation. Broadly Marxist in outlook, many of these works were based on what Orlando Fals Borda termed "action research," an engagé form of social science writing that eschewed objectivity to "take sides openly on real political issues . . . to accelerate the process of structural and revolutionary change."[94] Fals Borda urged his colleagues to step beyond the Newtonian era and use their knowledge on behalf of those who had been victims of development politics, "to identify class enemies" toward the end of forging a successful revolutionary party.[95]

Nationalism and anti-imperialism occupied an important place in the thinking of the State of Siege Generation. Running from Jorge Gaitán Durán's mild call for Colombia's bourgeoisie to become the "lance point against imperialism" and the fount of national modernization, to Mauricio Torres's shrill, "North American imperialists are and shall be . . . those most hated by our people," their messages provided a certain continuity in Colombia's generational critique.[96] Jorge Child's denunciation of the National Front for allowing reformist ideas of the Alliance for Progress "to circulate without resistance through all strata of national life" is not unlike Laureano Gómez's warning three decades earlier that economic development must not come at the expense of giving away national resources, mortgaging the nation, and corrupting the political system.[97] Laureano Gómez's concern expressed in 1915, that concessions to the United Fruit Company placed national sovereignty at risk, paralleled Mario Arrubla's assertion fifty years later that Colombia's neocolonial economic status laid it open to "imperialist blackmail" by the great powers.[98]

The conviction that Colombia stood in a "neocolonial" relationship to the developed world made the government's economic policy entirely unacceptable to the counterelites. While government leaders founded their modernization schemes in capitalist development and integration into the Western trading system, antigovernment elites believed, with Lenin, that imperialism was the highest, most exploitative stage of capitalism. They therefore rejected in its entirety the economic developmentalism promoted by the National Front. Colombia could not become modern, they argued, as long as its economy was bound to and dependent on trade with the more developed world. Cheap coffee benefited the United States, as did America's sale to Colombia of its ever more expensive capital goods.[99]

Members of the State of Siege Generation embraced dependency analysis to guide their economic critique. They called for replacing the oligarchic National Front with a genuinely popular and interventionist government, minimizing trade relationships with Western imperialist nations, and pursuing national industrialization through import substitution supported by high tariffs. Socialist Antonio García, writing in the late 1960s, urged progressive thinkers to pursue dependency analysis as "the most transcendental analytic category of social science analysis in Latin America."[100] Earlier Mario Arrubla had written that scholars hoping to understand Colombia from any other than a *dependentista* stance "are either buffoons or villains."[101]

Colombian higher education was transformed by the State of Siege Generation. The geometric growth of colleges and universities during the 1950s and '60s, coupled with the belief among academicians that national problems could be solved with the help of social science, had the effect of creating a corps of activist intellectuals seemingly overnight. Increasing numbers of graduate students traveled abroad, taking advanced degrees in the finest schools of Europe and North America, not to mention at institutions in the Soviet bloc. Soon they were back home instructing students of their own in the most advanced theoretical and methodological concepts. In so doing they revolutionized the conceptualization and subject matter of scholarly writing in Colombia. That process was especially clear in the area of history.

Prior to the National Front most historians were prominent citizens, a majority of them lawyers by profession, grouped around the Colombian Academy of History. Members of the academy avoided writing about subjects that were either controversial or recent, preferring instead to treat themes from either the independence or colonial periods. They did so in large part because as militants in either the Liberal or Conservative Party they feared the political consequences of dealing with sensitive topics. Thus their history tended to be chronologically distant from their readers, heavy on biography and political history. Through the 1950s Colombian historical writing merited its reputation as "a kind of distilled extract exclusively dedicated to torturing the memory and simultaneously deadening the critical sense and imagination of students."[102]

The Colombian Academy of History, its erudite members, and their fusty brand of scholarship were scorned by the new professional historians headquartered in the nation's universities. The more outspoken among them damned the academy as an academic counterpart of the National Front, full of complacent and smug men bent on monopolizing their craft and perpetuating the status quo. "In Colombia until very recently," wrote Mario Arrubla, "the only [serious] writers were members of the dominant classes [who] wrote to confirm their privileged status." Arrubla continued, "It's not merely that they're reactionaries, empiricists, and apologists; they are all those things, with the addition that they write from a base of intellectual poverty."[103] Like his contemporary Orlando Fals Borda, Arrubla called for an aggressive, ideological scholarship capable of illuminating the path toward reform of a society "governed by a group of capitalists who dedicate their lives and minds to their speculative games."[104]

Activist scholarship achieved its highest expression in the School of Sociology of Colombia's National University. Founded in late 1960 by Orlando Fals Borda and Father Camilo Torres Restrepo, with the help of a Ford Foundation grant, teachers and students alike sought to combine social activism and academic pursuits to achieve social transformation. The school's leading lights became so intent on fomenting revolutionary change that for a time employers were afraid to hire sociology graduates. Camilo Torres's militancy ultimately drove him to rebellion against his country's bourgeois, capitalist government, and thence to an untimely death. In that sense Camilo Torres, more than any other, inculcated both the high hopes and the bitter frustrations of his generation.[105]

Born to a well-to-do Antioquian family, Torres seemed destined to rise high in Colombia's religious establishment. He was physically imposing, personable, intelligent, and, above all, energetic. Following his ordination in 1954, the twenty-five-year-old priest traveled to the United States and Belgium, where he undertook graduate study in sociology at the University of Louvain. Returning home in 1959, he was named chaplain of the National University.

Almost immediately he became embroiled in controversy. During his first year he won student sympathies by stating his desire "to substitute the bourgeois spirit prevailing in Colombia's universities with a revolutionary, social, and Christian one."[106] He backed his words with deeds, taking an activist ministry into Bogotá's poorest neighborhoods. He drew student militants, like MOEC founder Antonio Larrota, into a collaboration that led to his founding, with Fals Borda, of the university's sociology and social work departments.

A sermon of mid-1962 ended Camilo Torres's chaplaincy. His suggestion that revolutionary students go to heaven when killed fighting for their beliefs angered his erstwhile patron, Cardinal Luis Concha, who summarily relieved him of the post. Afterward Torres pursued his social ministry while working for the state-supported Advanced School of Public Administration (ESAP) between 1962 and 1965. During those years he worked with the new land reform institute, INCORA, promoting an elaborate rural development program in the llanos.[107] Meanwhile he continued his university lecturing and research into Colombian social problems and traveled to sociological congresses with friend and colleague Fals Borda. At one of them he presented a paper in which he argued that the Violencia had generated class consciousness among Colombian peasants, disposing them to support revolutionary movements. The essay, which became celebrated in Marxist circles, illustrated both the priest's growing radicalization and his anger over the slow pace of change under the National Front.[108] In it he constantly referred to the frustration felt by rural-dwelling Colombians, thus revealing his own feeling of impotence before a national government that had slowed the pace of agrarian reform. In late 1963 the government, then headed by Conservative Guillermo León Valencia, vetoed Camilo Torres's llanos project, an action coinciding with the government's military campaigns against the several communist enclaves.

In early 1964, as the army prepared for the definitive assault on Marquetalia, Camilo Torres, Fals Borda, and others lobbied unsuccessfully against the operation. Afterward Torres lashed out against a ruling class that rather than communicating with Colombia's poor, which he put at 85 percent of the population, spent millions of pesos on "the massacre of patriotic guerrillas."[109] His remarks infuriated Cardinal Concha, who reprimanded him and demanded that the priest temper his public utterances.

In early 1965 an event took place that thrilled Colombian Marxist-Leninists and set Camilo Torres on an overtly revolutionary path. On January 7 former university student Fabio Vásquez Castaño and seventeen companions seized the village of Simacota, Santander, in the name of a new revolutionary organization, the Ejército de Liberación Nacional (ELN). They soon withdrew, leaving behind a manifesto reading, in part, "Long live the unity of campesinos, workers, students, professionals and honorable people who want to make Colombia a nation worthy of honest citizens! Liberation or death!" One guerrilla died in the attack and two others deserted. Three policemen were killed and the Caja Agraria robbed of 54,000 pesos.[110]

Camilo Torres made contact with ELN members following the Simacota raid. Events moved swiftly thereafter. The Colombian left was in a state of high excitement from late 1964 into the early months of the following year. The hated Ruiz Novoa, who had sent troops into Marquetalia seven months earlier, was replaced as army commander by Gabriel Revéiz Pizarro. Army troops then moved into Sumapaz and attacked the "El Pato" commune, during March 1965. Settlers calling themselves the Guayabero Guerrilla Command wrote Camilo Torres, imploring, "What can we do Father Camilo? Stand here with our arms folded? . . . Faced with government violence, we have organized: now we are guerrilleros. . . ." Father Torres replied, "Receive with this letter our support for your new ministry. With men like you, with the support of the combatants of Marquetalia, El Pato, Río Chiquito, Simacota, along with help from the cities—from students, workers, and the people in general, we will at last bring about the change that we need so badly."[111]

As the Colombian army moved through Sumapaz in mid-1965, an action that coincided with U.S. invasion of the Dominican Republic, Camilo Torres entered into regular communication with the ELN. In July he visited the mountains of Santander where he met with the group's leaders. By then defrocked, he threw himself into revolutionary activity. His assignment was to unite the left in a movement capable of overthrowing the government.[112] He did so immediately upon leaving the mountains of Santander, calling his organization the Frente Unido (United Front).

August and September 1965 were frenetic months for Torres and his entourage. In the brief span of eight weeks he founded a newspaper, *Frente Unido,* stumped the nation making scores of speeches aimed at uniting the left against National Front oligarchs and Yankee imperialists, and penned a series of messages to Colombians in which he explained his revolutionary goals.[113] But by October 1965 he was forced to suspend all those activities, for the authorities in Santander had captured documents implicating him as an ELN member. It became too dangerous for the United Front leader to remain in civil society while his guerrilla colleagues waged war against the government. He slipped away to join them on October 18, 1965. Camilo Torres left behind a worshipful body of followers, many of whom believed that revolution was on the horizon.[114] But most Colombians were not convinced by his rhetoric. The average citizen viewed Camilo Torres much as did one middle-class coffee farmer who, some years after hearing Torres speak during his whirlwind tour of Colombia, reflected, "He was a formidable man, but his ideas weren't very sound."[115]

Colombia in 1965

The young radicals of Camilo Torres's Frente Unido could be excused for believing the decisive revolutionary moment was at hand. Colombia was in fact in the midst of pell-mell, revolutionary social change when the fiery ex-priest joined the guerrillas in late 1965.[116] But it was a revolution hardly conducive to group solidarity and class consciousness. Colombia's social transformation in fact fragmented society in ways destructive of communal and civic spirit.

Only a few Colombians were pleased with modernization's effect on the country. Economist Miguel Urrutia was unique among leading academic writers in portraying the process in positive terms. "There is no doubt that the benefits of economic development in Colombia have been very superior to its costs," he wrote in an assessment of national progress after 1950. Urrutia went on to point out that modernization "not only radically improved the way of life of the great mass of the people, but it also radically bettered their lives."[117]

For most others the modernizing Colombia of 1965 was a glass half empty. By their view modernization had not noticeably improved the lot of most citizens. At the midpoint of the 1960s, 45 percent of Colombians were considered poor, only half the rural population had access to clean drinking water, and infant mortality stood at eight times that of the world's most advanced nations.[118] The list of social problems afflicting the lower half of society was endless. Meanwhile, Colombia was found to be sorely wanting in terms of civic culture. In 1965 naturalized citizen Lauchlin Currie wrote that his fellow Colombians lacked patriotism, had little respect for law, and were wanting in a sense of shared purpose.[119]

Sober analysts of the national scene blamed the National Front for corrupting politics. Alvaro Gómez Hurtado charged that the consociational arrangement made it impossible to deal with issues on their merits. It caused national politics to turn on a clientelist pivot, robbed the traditional parties of their ideological foundations, and reduced politics to nothing more than "a technique for gratifying [the people]."[120] Historian Alvaro Tirado Mejía pointed to the National Front's cloying effect on all political institutions. He found that at a critical juncture in Colombian life, when the state might have met the needs of its people in innovative ways, the power-sharing arrangement worked to disillusion and alienate Colombians. That in turn drove them increasingly to address social problems in other than political ways, through reliance on narrow interest associations, through individual action, and sometimes through antisocial violence. The sense of shared purpose was lost in the struggle of all against all. Under the National Front the state became nothing more than a "negotiator of individual interests." Thus, writes Tirado, "we reached a situation in which the social contract disappeared as shared, globalizing elements were erased."[121]

Mass culture and consumerism, rooted in the modernization process, were also tarred for weakening social unity. Social historian Alberto Mayor found that by the mid-1960s average Colombians were giving themselves over to an array of distractions never available to them before: "Television, sports, poor-quality serialized novels, print and film pornography, mass-circulation yellow journals occupied an ever larger proportion of free time of the population."[122] Marxist critics of Colombia's developmental approach to modernization found popular culture playing a sinister role in national life. Television, omnipresent in urban Colombia by 1965, presented a vision of egalitarian liberal society that critics believed to be at odds with actual social conditions. Advertisements depicting the well-off at play suggested that upward social mobility and the good life pertaining thereto were available to all who could purchase it. That in turn reinforced popular acceptance of market capitalism and further diluted progressive appeals to class consciousness.[123]

Traditional social institutions weakened under the onslaught of modernization. Women left the home in growing numbers, freed by new educational and employment opportunities, as well as by the adoption of modern contraceptive methods. Colombian women embraced the birth control pill in what social historian Carlos Uribe Celis termed "world record time."[124] By the mid-1960s the tastes of young Colombians were not much different from those of their peers in Europe and North America. They listened to the same music, wore the same blue jeans, and reveled in the counterculture at whose center were sexual freedom, denunciation of bourgeois society and its values, and an incipient drug culture.[125]

Colombia in 1965 was, in short, a complex and intriguing place rushing into a future that would be anything but placid. Jet aircraft roared away from Bogotá's new international airport over a city thirty-five times larger than the one into which Laureano Gómez had been born eight decades before, over city streets that were dusty and unpaved when Dolores de Gómez and her yet unborn son rode through them in 1888.

How can one suggest what Colombia had become over the span of a single lifetime? One way is to seize on a symbol: the apartment complex rising on Bogotá's western edge the year Laureano Gómez lay dying is appropriate for this purpose. Capitalized by the national mortgage bank, it was designed to house middle-class Colombians having the wherewithal to escape the city's congested center. The construction project, known simply as the Carrera Thirty complex, owed much to the revolutionary atmosphere pervading the National University and its School of Architecture during the early 1960s. In those years students of architecture participated in radical colloquia during

19. The Carrera Thirty complex. By permission of *El Espectador*.

which the architect's political role was discussed. Criticism of the dominant Modernist school as "formalistic and elitist," and the act of design itself as "reactionary," paralyzed creative activity for some time. But the overall effect was beneficial. Colombia's architectural community was forced to rethink its subject matter, to amplify the universe of thought concerning architectural production, and to elevate the level of complexity in design.[126]

The Carrera Thirty complex, designed by architects Luis Esguerra and Ernesto Herrera, was a product of that movement, a work of studied individualism. It was also a metaphor for the Colombia of 1965. Built by and for members of the nation's emerging middle class, it rose soberly over a city filled with sober and industrious people. The apartments owed their uniqueness to a radical critique of architectural design that was organically linked to the frequently violent criticism of all national institutions. Angular and unyielding, not so much beautiful as notable, the building projected to the discerning eye what architectural historian Silvia Arango describes as "an interesting play of light and shadow."[127] That, then, was Colombia in 1965: a place of contrasts, of light and shadow, whose ensemble—whose formidable history—while often disconcerting was invariably illuminating, ever redefining itself in sobering and sometimes uplifting ways.

Epilogue: The Passing of the Centenarians

The Legacy of the Centenarians

Laureano Gómez died in the afternoon of July 13, 1965. His counterpart, Alfonso López Pumarejo, had preceded him to the grave by more than five years, and others of their generation had preceded them both: Liberals Luis Eduardo Nieto Caballero and Enrique Olaya Herrera, Conservatives José de la Vega and Aquilino Villegas. They were all members of the Generation of the Centenary, men who dominated Colombian society and politics between 1930 and 1966.

Colombia had experienced profound changes over the decades of Centenarian dominance. A population that was respectful of social distinctions and accepting of the vast gaps separating it from its betters at the moment Laureano Gómez and Alfonso López entered public life progressively rejected such differentiation as social modernization moved apace. Growing affluence, rising educational levels, and expanded social mobility enabled young Colombians to critically judge leaders whom their parents had revered. Such changing perceptions, born of a revolution in attitudes and values in Colombia and elsewhere in the world, have made it difficult to assess the Centenarians and their legacy. Attempts to do so are also colored by the social and political violence that attended Centenarian rule. All this has combined to cast a shadow over the Centenarians and their contribution to Colombian history, a perception shared by many Centenarians themselves. Near the end of his life Luis López de Mesa wrote that his generation had been "touched by madness."[1] Laureano Gómez opined that "the vestiges left behind by the Generation of the Centenary are neither scant nor fortunate."[2]

Yet to judge the Centenarians in terms of their political excesses is shortsighted and ultimately misleading. To do so is to overlook the exceedingly significant contribution of that generation's moderate members, men who insured that the nation's extraordinary economic development continued uninterrupted over the entirety of their dominance. In spite of ongoing political violence moderate Centenarians in both parties constantly sought and found ways to thwart their extremist colleagues. In that sense they formed a bipartisan and largely apolitical superparty committed to moving the nation forward in a direction satisfying to themselves and to the citizenry at large. The constancy of Colombia's economic growth over the time of Centenarian dominance was unequaled elsewhere in Latin America. Such growth provided the foundation for the transformation that in a few decades turned Colombia from a woefully undeveloped place into a rapidly modernizing one. This was the chief legacy of the Generation of the Centenary and the millions of Colombians who supported it. Moderate Centenarians eschewed ideology and concentrated instead on the creation of wealth. Only when that aspect of Centenarian thought and action is examined will the generation's legacy be fully understood.

The Place of Laureano Gómez in Colombian History and Historiography

Laureano Gómez was peerless among his generation's political militants. He seldom backed away from a fight, and he won most of his political battles. A master at bending Colombia's elite-led democracy to his will, he so thoroughly frustrated the Liberal Party during the 1940s that at the end of the decade Liberal extremists took up arms against the Conservative-dominated government.

Late in his career Gómez seemed to moderate his militancy, dropping his lifelong abhorrence of compromise and frankly endorsing bipartisanship. By then he and his Liberal counterparts understood and repented of their intemperance of earlier days, recognizing that their heated exchanges had somehow produced the Violencia. Gómez's Saul-like conversion gratified Colombians. They read his fulsome praise of the National Front as evidence that he had shed his narrow partisanship. Further assurance came through the old caudillo's actions during the early years of the National Front. He spent as much time breaking bread with Liberals then as he had thirty years earlier, when he had worked closely with Liberals like Alfonso López to drive the Conservative old guard from power. One such moment of apparent bipartisan harmony came in May 1959, when Gómez attended a ceremony honoring López Pumarejo. It was held at the National University and involved the awarding of a doctorate *honoris causa* to the Liberal leader.

The setting that day was extraordinary. University Rector Mario Laserna presided, and most of the nation's leading public figures were in attendance. President Alberto Lleras Camargo, Carlos Holguín, and Mariano Ospina Pérez sat at the head table, to the right of the honoree. Laserna sat to his left, flanked by Laureano Gómez and Darío Echandía. Outside crowds surged, hoping to catch a last glimpse of López before his departure to become Colombia's ambassador to Great Britain. There were rumors that the old politician was ill, and some guessed correctly that the speech would be López's last major address.

20. Laureano Gómez (third from left) congratulates Alfonso López Pumarejo upon the latter's receipt of a doctorate *honoris causa,* May 1962. By permission of Alvaro Gómez Hurtado.

López began his remarks with a series of reminiscences of his childhood and early career. He nostalgically reflected on his father and on other personages long since dead. When he turned to his first presidency, he grew animated. He evoked the stirring years of the Liberal Republic and the Revolution on the March, of his reformist first administration and his unrivaled leadership of the Liberal Party. Warming to his subject, he seized upon the opportunity to publicly castigate Laureano Gómez for his heated opposition to the López reforms. "At that time they practiced a barbaric and ferocious sort of opposition that I pray has disappeared forever from our annals," said López, standing with his back toward Gómez. He continued even more bitingly: "Those who frown at any sort of dissent today once preached that the republic must be made unlivable. They ordered the use of any means necessary, of assaults on individuals, of intrepid action. In short they advocated the sort of violence that later left its vile mark on our political life, penetrating the lowest levels of society. That violence was initiated at the highest political levels. We say with reason that the Violencia did not originate among the people, but that in philosophy and practice it came from on high."[3] Alfonso López's words were a concise summary of the Liberal charge that Laureano Gómez was chiefly responsible for the previous twenty years of violence and attending political turmoil.

López ended his talk and remained standing, his back still to Gómez, acknowledging applause ranging from hearty to merely polite. Suddenly Laureano Gómez rose, reached out and pulled López around to face him. It was a dramatic moment. Would there be a confrontation? But the tableau passed in an instant. Gómez smiled, shook López's hand, and returned to his seat. The old Conservative's genteel gesture was at once startling and gratifying to those present. Rector Laserna breathed a sigh of relief and the historic event moved to adjournment.[4]

Those who believed Laureano Gómez was transformed that day in 1959 were sadly mistaken. His shaking of López's hand was in fact the act of a victor congratulating an opponent whom he has bested. The handshake may in fact have marked Laureano Gómez's most satisfying moment in Colombian politics. Alfonso López was but six months from the grave when Gómez attended the ceremony honoring him. Colombia was governed by a Liberal president named by and beholden to Laureano Gómez. The Conservative leader had maneuvered the majority Liberals into guaranteeing his party two presidencies and an equal sharing of political spoils over an extended period of time. He had humiliated and defeated his own Conservative enemies: the Ospinistas, the Alzatistas, and the Rojistas. It was his eldest son, and not the son of López Pumarejo, who sat close to the source of presidential power, speaking for Conservatism in Congress and brokering political appointments under terms of the National Front compact. Laureano Gómez could afford that statesmanlike gesture, the smile he bestowed upon an old adversary who had just attacked him personally. At that moment he was largely satisfied with the way history had unfolded.

To the end Laureano Gómez played the political game as he had been taught it: without quarter. He was an extraordinary product of his political milieu. Not loved except by those closest to him, he was universally respected, even by those who feared and disliked him. Colombians called Gómez "El Monstruo," the Monster. Standing at the caudillo's graveside in 1965, historian Malcolm Deas reflected on that nickname: "It is a half-admiring name, given to prodigies and indestructibles, which in France is given to actresses past criticism, and which in Colombia was given to him with something of the same awe."[5]

What of Gómez's role in the Violencia? It is beyond doubt that Colombia's political militants, Gómez foremost among them, touched off the tragic civil conflict which existed in one degree or another from early in the administration of Enrique Olaya Herrera, and which intensified during the presidency of Mario Ospina Pérez. When the National Front was crafted, Gómez and the rest admitted and apologized for the oratorical excesses that were taken as signaling their approval of physical excesses on the part of their followers. Still, Laureano Gómez was not the only Colombian politician who allowed intemperate words to escape his lips. Extremist language was the coinage of a great many politicians of the Centenarian generation. Laureano Gómez simply possessed a greater store of it, and used his words more effectively, with greater eloquence, than did any of his contemporaries.

Colombia's great twentieth-century Conservative caudillo has received a drubbing at the hands of historians. Much of what has been written about Gómez was produced by his bitterest political enemies: Ospinistas and other Conservative moderates, followers of Gustavo Rojas Pinilla and Gilberto Alzate Avendaño. Virtually no Liberal writer has treated the historical Gómez with equanimity. And the left unanimously condemns Laureano Gómez as the most malevolent of all Colombia's modern public figures.

This historical vision of Laureano Gómez is largely the product of a politicized tradition of discourse having deep roots in Colombian life. Gómez understood and accepted this, no doubt comforted by the fact that when it came to inflicting verbal punishment, he was the master. Still it is unfortunate that the historical Laureano Gómez has been dealt with largely in terms of polemic. That clouds a greater national history that is wondrous in its complexity and its ability to instruct.

Appendix 1. Distribution of Violencia-Related Deaths by Department

	1946–1957	1958–1966
Norte de Santander	20,885	negligible
Santander	19,424	649
Boyacá	5,363	142
Meta	5,842	166
Cundinamarca	4,033	334
Antioquia	26,115	2,127
Valle	13,106	5,016
Huila	4,111	733
Tolima	30,912	5,257
Antiguo Caldas	44,255	2,606
Totals:	174,046	17,030

Source: Paul Oquist, *Violencia, conflicto,* 16, 19.

Appendix 2. Violencia-Related Deaths by Year, 1947–1966

Year	Population*	Violencia-Related Deaths**	Violencia-Related Deaths per 100,000
1947	10,462,000 (est.)	13,968	133.5
1948	10,723,600 (est.)	43,557	406.2
1949	10,991,700 (est.)	18,519	168.5
1950	11,266,500 (est.)	50,253	446.0
1951	11,548,200 (est.)	10,319	89.4
1952	11,912,800 (est.)	13,250	111.2
1953	12,286,900 (est.)	8,650	70.4
1954	12,704,700 (est.)	900	7.1
1955	13,136,700 (est.)	1,013	7.7
1956	13,583,400 (est.)	11,136	82.0
1957	14,045,200 (est.)	2,877	20.5
1958	14,522,700 (est.)	3,796	26.1
1959	15,016,500 (est.)	2,550	17.0
1960	15,527,100 (est.)	2,557	16.5
1961	16,055,000 (est.)	3,173	19.8
1962	16,600,800 (est.)	2,370	14.3
1963	17,085,600 (est.)	1,711	10.0
1964	17,584,500	972	5.5
1965	18,097,900	950	5.2
1966	18,626,300	496	2.7
Total Violencia-Related Deaths		193,017	
Average Violencia-Related Deaths per 100,000, 1947–1966			83.0

*Estimated population figures are based on total population of 1951 and 1964 and annual birth rates per 1,000. These figures are from José Rueda Plata, "Historia de la población de Colombia, 1880–2000," 383.
**Violencia-related deaths are from Paul Oquist, *Violencia conflictiva,* 18, 20, 59.

Appendix 3. Violencia-Related Deaths per 100,000 Population as a Percentage of 1960 and 1966 Intentional Deaths in Colombia; Intentional Deaths in Colombia Compared with Those in Other Countries

Colombia

	Total Violencia-Related	Per 100,000	Total Intentional	Per 100,000
1960	2,557	16.5	c 5,300	34.4
1966	496	2.7	c 3,900	21.3

Colombia and Other Countries

Country	Intentional Deaths per 100,000 Population	
Colombia	34.4 (1960)	21.3 (1966)
Mexico	31.1 (1958)	18.7 (1966)
Nicaragua	22.8 (1959)	29.3 (1965)
South Africa	21.2 (1959)	
Burma	10.8 (1959)	
Aden	9.9 (1956)	
Guatemala	9.8 (1960)	10.2 (1965)
Turkey	6.1 (1959)	
Panama	5.9 (1969)	4.8 (1966)

Sources: Paul Oquist, *Violencia conflictiva*, 11, 63.
José Rueda Plata, "Historia de la Población de Colombia, 1880–2000," 383.

Notes

Introduction

1. Santamaría S. and Silva Luján, *Proceso político en Colombia,* 29.
2. Colombia, DANE, *Colombia,* 1:7; Dix, *Colombia,* 32; Colombia, Banco de la República, *Cuentas nacionales;* Hartlyn, "Colombia," 311.

1. Fin de Siècle Colombia

1. In the colonial era and through much of the nineteenth century, Colombia was called New Granada.
2. Rostow, *World Economy,* 70–71.
3. Woodruff, *International Economy,* 7.
4. Delpar, *Red against Blue,* 70.
5. This information, which is in the nature of Gómez family lore, has been gathered through conversations with children of Laureano Gómez, Alvaro and Enrique Gómez Hurtado, and Gómez de Mazuera. Their recollections are based on stories told to them by Laureano Gómez. Alvaro Gómez accorded me lengthy interviews from April 15 to 18, 1984.
6. Mollien, "Recorriendo," 1:18.
7. Ibid., 1:31.
8. Vargas and Zambrano, "Santa Fe y Bogotá," 19.
9. García Ortiz, *Conversando,* 313. The ruana is a square of wool cloth with a slit in the middle.
10. Vargas and Zambrano, "Santa Fe y Bogotá," 38.
11. McGreevey, *Economic History of Colombia,* 256.
12. Hettner, *Viajes por los andes colombianos,* 106–7.
13. McGreevey, *Economic History,* 245.
14. Curtis, *Capitals of Spanish America,* 242–48.
15. McGreevey, *Economic History,* 245–46.
16. Curtis, *Capitals,* 241.
17. Briceño, *Revolución,* 212–322, passim.
18. Wilde, "Conversations among Gentlemen," 28–81.
19. Núñez, *Reforma política,* 1:87.
20. Núñez, *Reforma política,* xi–xii.
21. Hale, "Political and Social Ideas," 382–414.
22. Cited in Delpar, *Red against Blue,* 31.
23. Liévano Aguirre, *Rafael Núñez,* 319.

24. Núñez, *Reforma política*, 1:357.

25. Ibid., 1:387, 393–94.

26. Ospina Vásquez, *Industria y protección*, 277, 280–81.

27. Palacio, *Mi vida*, 178–82.

28. Liévano Aguirre, *Rafael Núñez*, 372.

29. Ibid., 360.

30. Palacio, *Mi vida*, 176.

31. Ibid., 176–77.

32. Reclus, *Colombia*, 193.

33. The children were, in order of birth, Ana Josefa, Anatonia, Laureano, José (Pepe), Jesús, Dolores.

34. Gómez Hurtado, interview by author, April 15–18, 1984.

35. Hettner, *Viajes*, 83–84; Urrutia and Arrubla, *Compendio*, 47, 55–56.

36. Curtis, *Capitals*, 248, 252.

37. Hettner, *Viajes*, 91.

38. Urrutia and Arrubla, *Compendio*, 59.

39. Hettner, *Viajes*, 83.

40. Urrutia and Arrubla, *Compendio*, 147.

41. Hettner, *Viajes*, 116.

42. Ibid., 85, 117.

43. Deas, "Colombia," 660, 661.

44. Serrano Camargo, *En aquella ciudad*, 24.

45. Palacio, *Mi vida*, 186–92; Delpar, *Red against Blue*, 156; Sowell, "Latin American Labor Movement," 108.

46. Delpar, *Red against Blue*, 156.

47. Archila, "Clase obrera, 1886–1930," 3:220.

48. Delpar, *Red against Blue*, 156.

49. Vargas and Zambrano, "Santa Fe y Bogotá," 58.

50. Hettner, *Viajes*, 74, 128.

51. Alvaro Gómez interview, April 15–18, 1984.

52. Nicholas, *Across Panama*, 345.

53. Ibid., 347.

54. *Cachaco* (dandy, dude) was a synonym for the stylishly dressed Bogotano.

55. Palacio, *Mi vida*, 33, 154.

2. Teaching the Generation of the Centenary

1. Miguel Samper, *Escritos*, 2:161.

2. Camacho Roldán, *Artículos escogidos*, 71.

3. Estrada Monsalve, *Núñez*, 132.

4. Martínez Delgado, *A propósito*, 209.

5. Iregüi, *Tercera conferencia*, 65.

6. Jaramillo Uribe, *Pensamiento*, 203–4.

7. Martínez Silva, *Capítulos*, 1:142.

8. Palacios, *Estado y clases*, 30.

9. Vargas and Zambrano, "Santa Fe y Bogotá," 56.

10. José María Samper, *Ensayo*, 267–68, 269, 276–78.

11. Palacios, *Estado y clases*, 26.

12. LeGrand, *Frontier Expansion,* 64–65, 83.

13. Gobineau, *Essai sur l'inequalité des races humaines.*

14. José María Samper, *Ensayo,* 80, 86.

15. Palacios, *Coffee in Colombia,* 72.

16. Farrell, "Catholic Church," 65.

17. Bernal, *Lecturas escogidas,* 7–34, 163.

18. Posada and Cortazar, *Instrucción civica,* 59.

19. Bernal, *Lecturas escogidas,* 329.

20. For the famous "Manifesto of the 21," see Martínez Delgado, *A propósito,* 209–31.

21. Santa, *Rafael Uribe,* 100.

22. Latorre Cabral, *Mi novela,* 241.

23. Ibid., 37.

24. Hoenigsberg, *Fronteras,* 126; Palacio, *Mi vida,* 76; Nieto Caballero, *Escritos escogidos,* 2:29–30.

25. Santiago Pérez, *Manual del ciudadano,* 64–65.

26. Farrell, "Catholic Church," 7; Loy, "Modernization," 203–7; Jaramillo Uribe, "El proceso," 3:264–65.

27. Jaramillo Uribe discusses the debate in "Proceso," 314–22.

28. Ibid., 316–17.

29. Ibid., 317.

30. Mora, *Croniquillas,* 58; Joaquín Ospina, *Diccionario,* 2:154–55.

31. Fremantle, *Papal Encyclicals,* 130–42.

32. Ibid., 143–52.

33. Joaquin Ospina, *Diccionario,* 1:568. The pope's letter can be found in Cordovez Moure, *Reminiscencias,* 46–48.

34. Fremantle, *Papal Encyclicals,* 153.

35. Mora, *Croniquillas,* 39–41.

36. *La Unidad,* August 16, 1911.

37. *El Siglo,* November 17, 1953.

38. Sardá y Salvany, *El liberalismo es pecado.*

39. Carrasquilla, *Ensayo.*

40. Casas, *Enseñanzas,* 53.

41. Farrell, "Catholic Church," 305–6, 308.

42. Nieto Caballero, *Escritos escogidos,* 2:29.

43. Gustavo Rodríguez, *Olaya Herrera,* 10.

44. Palacio, *Mi vida,* 26.

45. Mora, *Croniquillas,* 74.

46. Nieto Caballero, *Escritos escogidos,* 2:28–30.

47. Mora, *Croniquillas,* 133–34.

48. García Ortiz, *Estudios históricos,* 209.

49. Lemaitre, *Rafael Reyes,* 237–38.

50. Carlos Jaramillo, "Antecedentes," 1:68, 72, 76–77.

51. Martínez Silva, *Capítulos,* 3:269–72.

52. Ocampo, *Colombia,* 53; Kalmanovitz, *Economía y nación,* 169–77.

53. Bergquist, *Coffee and Conflict,* 117–18; Carlos Jaramillo, "Antecedentes," 75.

54. Bergquist, *Coffee and Conflict,* 148–49.

55. Carlos Jaramillo, "Antecedentes," 70.

56. Vargas Vila, *Vargas Vila,* 160.

57. The antisubversion measure provided legal basis for Santiago Pérez's deportation in 1892. It originated in a law of 1888, the infamous "Law of the Horses." For more detail on this most unpopular law of the Regeneration, see Delpar, *Red against Blue,* 144ff.; Bergquist, *Coffee and Conflict,* 37ff.

58. Santa, *Rafael Uribe Uribe,* 304.

59. Delpar, *Red against Blue,* 182.

60. One of the best sketches of Aristides Fernández is that contained in Bergquist, *Coffee and Conflict,* 176–78.

61. Ibid., 182.

62. Martínez Delgado, *A propósito,* 469–77.

63. Bergquist, *Coffee and Conflict,* 186.

64. Nieto Caballero, *Escritos escogidos,* 2:31.

65. Ibid., 2:31–41.

66. Latorre Cabral, *Mi novela,* 290–91.

67. Laureano Gómez, *Obras completas,* 3:13.

68. Carlos Jaramillo, "Guerra de los Mil Días," 1:107.

69. Laureano Gómez, *Obras completas,* 3:13.

70. Bergquist, *Coffee and Conflict,* 186.

71. Vargas Vila, *Vargas Vila,* 117.

72. Bergquist, *Coffee and Conflict,* 204–10.

73. *El Siglo,* December 5, 1939.

74. Laureano Gómez, *Obras completas,* 3:41.

75. Martínez Delgado, *A propósito,* 378–416.

76. Valderrama, *Discursos.*

3. Reyes and Republicanism

1. Vélez, "Rafael Reyes," 203.

2. *El Espectador,* June 27, 1904.

3. Felipe Pérez, ed., *Periodistas liberales,* 257.

4. Osterling, *Democracy in Colombia,* 9.

5. Miranda, "Medicina colombiana," 4:266–67.

6. Ibid., 4:37, 266.

7. Vargas and Zambrano, "Santa Fe y Bogotá," 43.

8. Lemaitre, *Rafael Reyes,* 236.

9. Petre, *Republic of Colombia,* 125.

10. Gilhodes, "Cuestión agraria," 307–88.

11. Christie, *Colombia,* 91.

12. Bergquist, *Coffee and Conflict,* 203; Christie, *Colombia,* 91.

13. Petre, *Republic of Colombia,* 189.

14. Veatch, *Quito to Bogotá,* 202–3.

15. Bergquist, *Coffee and Conflict,* 200.

16. Petre, *Republic of Colombia,* 301.

17. Ibid., 303.

18. Christie, *Colombia,* 91; Bergquist, *Coffee and Conflict,* 201–2.

19. Lemaitre, *Rafael Reyes,* 240.

20. Between 1905 and 1908 it would increase in size by 131 percent! Constanza Toro, "Medellín," 300.

21. Restrepo Yusti, "Historia de la industria," 270; Osorio O., "Sindicalismo antioqueño," 280.

22. Poveda Ramos, "Cien años de ciencia colombiana," 164.

23. Londoño Vega and Londoño Vélez, "Vida diaria en las ciudades colombianas," 320–21.

24. Reyes, *Escritos varios,* 218.

25. Ocampo, *Colombia y la economía mundial,* 25.

26. Vélez, "Rafael Reyes," 192.

27. Lemaitre, *Rafael Reyes,* 53–103; Correa, *Diccionario,* 273–74.

28. Lemaitre, *Rafael Reyes,* 102, 180.

29. Felipe Pérez, *Periodistas liberales,* 174.

30. Lemaitre, *Rafael Reyes,* 267.

31. Lael, *Arrogant Diplomacy,* 65.

32. Vásquez Carrizosa, *Poder presidencial,* 242.

33. Colombia, Presidencia, *Diez de febrero,* vii, viii.

34. Lemaitre, *Rafael Reyes,* 267.

35. Ibid., 275.

36. Guerra, *Estudios históricos,* 244.

37. Lemaitre, *Rafael Reyes,* 279.

38. Serrano Camargo, *En aquella ciudad,* 32; Lemaitre, *Rafael Reyes,* 280–81; Guerra, *Estudios históricos,* 341–42.

39. Mesa, "Vida política," 3:104; Infante, *Dios y patria,* 2:177; Nieto Caballero, *Escritos escogidos,* 2:55.

40. Hale, "Political and Social Ideas," 412.

41. Uribe Uribe, *Obras selectas,* 1:29–47.

42. Holguín, *Desde cerca,* 115; Kalmanovitz, *Economía y nación,* 222; Bergquist, *Coffee and Conflict,* 204, 232.

43. Petre, *Republic of Colombia,* 2:301ff.; Bergquist, *Coffee and Conflict,* 234.

44. Bergquist, *Coffee and Conflict,* 238.

45. Ibid., 238–39.

46. Myriam Jimeno, "Procesos," 3:375.

47. Suárez, *Obras,* 3:778; Lemaitre, *Rafael Reyes,* 323, 332; Martínez, ed., *Bogotá reseñada,* 130.

48. Vélez, "Rafael Reyes," 186, 196.

49. *La Unidad,* February 21, 1916.

50. García Samudio, "División departamental," 1–14.

51. Infante, *Dios y patria,* 2:159–62.

52. Serrano Camargo, *General Uribe,* 254.

53. Colombia, *Diez de febrero.*

54. Marco Fidel Suárez, *Obras,* 2:1053–54; Nieto Caballero, *Obras selectas,* 5:495.

55. Lemaitre, *Rafael Reyes,* 350; Bergquist, *Coffee and Conflict,* 243–44; Lael, *Arrogant Diplomacy,* 53–83.

56. Díaz, *Páginas de historia,* 83–100.

57. Ibid., 88–89.

58. Ibid., 91–92.

59. Ibid., 92.

60. Ibid., 95.

61. Fernández's remarks are described in Bergquist, *Coffee and Conflict*, 182.

62. Medina, *Protesta urbana*, 29.

63. Fremantle, *Papal Encyclicals*, 167.

64. Abel, "Conservative Party," 230.

65. Kurtz, *Politics of Heresy*, 50.

66. Fremantle, *Papal Encyclicals*, 212–13.

67. Pike, *Hispanismo*, 100.

68. Magraw, *France*, 362–63.

69. *El Siglo*, July 14, 1965.

70. Felipe Molina, *Laureano Gómez*, 168.

71. *El Siglo*, February 3, 1941.

72. *La Unidad*, October 14, 1905; October 5, 1909; October 21, 1911.

73. *La Unidad*, October 16, December 9, 1909.

74. *La Unidad*, December 4, 1909.

75. *La Unidad*, December 19, 1911; April 23, 1912.

76. Laureano Gómez, "Bodas de Plata," 162.

77. *El Siglo*, July 14, 1965.

78. José de la Vega, *La federación en Colombia, 1810–1912*, xi.

79. *La Unidad*, February 14, 1914.

80. *El Siglo*, July 6, 1937.

81. Pike, *Hispanismo*, 99, 100.

82. Colombia, Cámara de Representantes, October 2, 1911, 411.

83. Arizmendi Posada, *Gobernantes colombianos*, 285.

84. *La Unidad*, November 30, 1912.

85. Colombia, Cámara, *Anales*, August 9, 1912, 62.

86. *La Unidad*, March 8–10, 1913.

87. *La Unidad*, April 11, 1913.

88. Colombia, Cámara, *Anales*, September 9, 1913, 234.

89. Ibid., September 9, 1913, 242.

90. Ibid., September 9, 1913, 247.

91. Ibid., September 11, 1913, 261, 255.

92. Ibid., September 9, 1913, 241.

93. *La Unidad*, July 29, 1913.

94. Carlos Restrepo, *Orientación republicana*, 1:409.

95. *El Liberal*, April 17, 1911.

96. Jimeno, "Procesos," 373.

97. Carlos Restrepo, *Orientación republicana*, 1:32, 334–35.

98. Gilhodes, "Cuestión agraria," 310.

99. Bergquist, *Coffee and Conflict*, 254–55; Gilhodes, "Cuestión agraria," 309.

100. Londoño Vega and Londoño Vélez, "Vida diaria en las ciudades," 327; Martínez, *Bogotá reseñada*, 135.

101. Mayor, "Historia de la industria," 5:319–20.

102. Ibid., 318.

103. Pérez Triana, *Eslabones sueltos*, xxxii, xlvii.

104. Kalmanovitz, *Economía y nación*, 259.

105. *El Tiempo*, May 23, 1914.

106. Lael, *Arrogant Diplomacy*, 85–106, has a full account of these negotiations.

107. Carlos Restrepo, *Orientación republicana*, 2:81, 84, 85–92.

108. Lozano, *Ensayos críticos*, 360.

109. Tovar Zambrano, "Economía colombiana," 5:46–47.

110. Vega, *Federación*, 121–29.

4. The Bourgeois Republic

1. Helguera, "Ospinas"; Restrepo Posada, "Estudios Genealogicos."

2. Reyes, *Escritos varios*, 590–91.

3. Mayor, *Etica, trabajo y productividad*, 101–2.

4. Reyes, *Escritos varios*, 592.

5. Páez, *Cartas a mi sobrina*, 130.

6. López de Mesa, *Obras selectas*, 161.

7. Cayzedo, *Combate*, 165, 166.

8. López de Mesa, *Obras selectas*, 163, 165.

9. Mayor, *Etica*, 106–7.

10. Archila, "Memoria histórica," 6, 7.

11. Suárez, *Sueños*, 5:130.

12. Laureano Gómez, *Obras selectas*, 718.

13. Zapata Restrepo, *Mitra azul*, 94.

14. Kalmanovitz, *Economía y nación*, 225.

15. Biddiss, *Father of Racist Ideology*, 305–6.

16. Rosselli, *Historia de la psiquiatría*, 2:290.

17. *El Tiempo*, March 30, 1920.

18. Reyes, *Escritos varios*, 159.

19. *El Tiempo*, October 3, 1922.

20. Cayzedo, *Combate*, 51, 232.

21. Restrepo Arango, "El pensamiento social," 380.

22. Ibid., 379–80.

23. Fernando González, *Los Negroides*, 97–98.

24. *El Tiempo*, July 25, 1931.

25. Arguedas, *Danza*, 827.

26. Vargas and Zambrano, "Santa Fe y Bogotá," 47.

27. Jorge Posada Callejas, ed., *Libro azul de Colombia*, 353.

28. Carlos Uribe Celis, *Los años veinte en Colombia*, 131.

29. Arguedas, *Danza*, 825–26.

30. Eduardo Caballero Calderón, *Memorias infantiles*, 44.

31. Vargas and Zambrano, "Santa Fe y Bogotá," 44.

32. Osorio Lizarazo, *Novelas y crónicas*, 302–8.

33. Jimeno, "Procesos," 375; Osterling, *Democracy in Colombia*, 9.

34. Tovar Zambrano, "Economía colombiana," 17, gives the figure for 1905 as 4.1 million, and in 1928 as 7.2 million.

35. Rueda Plata, "Historia de la Población," 5:364.

36. Uribe Uribe, *Obras selectas*, 1:236.

37. Arguedas, *Danza*, 763.

38. Niles, *Colombia*, 289.

39. Pardo Umaña, *Toros en Bogotá*, 37–39; Sowell, "Worker's Labor Movement," 20.

40. The photo can be seen in Londoño Vega and Londoño Vélez, "Vida diaria," 325.

41. Uribe Uribe, *Obras selectas*, vol. 2, 460.

42. Rufino Gutiérrez, *Monografías*, 1:330.

43. Vargas and Zambrano, "Santa Fe y Bogotá," 76, 78–79.

44. *El Espectador,* April 12, 1927.

45. Posada Callejas, *Libro azul*, 407.

46. Germán Téllez, "Arquitectura . . . republicana," 2:499, 503, 509.

47. Congreso Eucaristico Nacional, *Primer Congreso Eucarístico*, 123.

48. Cayzedo, *Combate*, 47.

49. Ibid., 61.

50. Cited in Londoño Vega, "Vida diaria," 327.

51. Arguedas, *Danza*, 828–29.

52. Hernando Téllez B., *Textos no recogidos en libro*, 1:243.

53. Hernando Téllez B., *Cincuenta años de radiofusión*, 9, 19–26.

54. *El Tiempo*, September 24, 1927.

55. Ortega Torres, *Suárez*, 534, 542.

56. Gálvis Salazar, *Don Marco Fidel Suárez*, 25–36.

57. Díaz, *Páginas de historia*, 135.

58. Ortega Torres, *Suárez*, 505.

59. Gálvis Salazar, *Don Marco*, 117–19.

60. Martínez Delgado, *A propósito*, 264–67.

61. Gustavo Rodríguez, *Benjamín Herrera*, 215–16; Díaz, *Páginas de historia*, 136; Sánchez Camacho, *General Ospina*, 133ff.

62. Congreso Eucaristico Nacional, *Primer Congreso Eucarístico*, 364.

63. Suárez, *Análisis gramatical*.

64. *La Unidad,* February 14, 1914.

65. Carnicelli, *Masonería*, 394–95.

66. Suárez, *Doctrinas internacionales*, 148.

67. Congreso Eucarístico Nacional, *Primer Congreso Eucarístico*, 369.

68. Lael, *Arrogant Diplomacy*, 85–106.

69. Suárez, *Doctrinas internacionales*, 164.

70. The incident is described by Luis Eduardo Nieto Caballero in *El Tiempo,* January 14, 1935; Suárez, *Sueños*, 10:71.

71. *Gil Blas*, May 19, 1914.

72. *El Nuevo Tiempo*, August 8, 1915.

73. *La Unidad,* May 8, July 8, 1915.

74. *Gil Blas*, September 24, November 10, 1915; March 7, 13, 1916.

75. *Gil Blas*, August 11, 1916.

76. *El Tiempo*, August 5, 1927.

77. *Gil Blas*, August 9, 11, 1916; *El Nuevo Tiempo*, August 6, 1916; *La Unidad*, August 7, 1916.

78. *La Unidad,* August 17, 1916.

79. Villegas and Yunis, *Sucesos colombianos*, 317.

80. Díaz, *Páginas de historia*, 148.

81. Lozano, *Ensayos críticos*, 368.

82. *Gil Blas*, February 4, 7, 1918; *El Tiempo*, February 17, 1918; *El Nuevo Tiempo*, February 7, 1918; F. A. Molina, *Laureano Gómez*, 206.

83. *El Tiempo*, March 17, 1919; Urrutia, *Historia del sindicalismo*, 91–94; Sowell, "Worker's Labor Movement," 44–47.

84. Urrutia, *Historia del sindicalismo*, 91–92.

85. Lael, *Arrogant Diplomacy*, 144–54; Gálvis Gálvis, *Memorias*, 1:53.

86. Suárez, *Obras*, 2:814–57; *El Espectador*, September 17, 1919.

87. Villegas and Yunis, *Sucesos colombianos*, 366.

88. Navia, *Caudillo y gobernante*, 97–98.

89. *El Tiempo*, February 23, 1921.

90. *El Nuevo Tiempo*, February 22, 1921; *Cromos*, June 4, 1921; *El Tiempo*, June 3, 1921; *La Crónica*, June 2, 1921; *La Nación*, June 2, 1921.

91. *El Nuevo Tiempo*, May 3, 8, 1921.

92. *La Nación*, June 30, 1921.

93. *El Espectador*, October 27, 28, 1921; *El Tiempo*, October 27, 28, 1921; Gálvis Salazar, *Don Marco*, 274–80; F. A. Molina, *Laureano Gómez*, 209–13; Navarro, *Parlamento*, 32–35; Sánchez Camacho, *General Ospina*, 159–60; Martínez Delgado, *Jorge Holguín*, 211–18.

94. Suárez, *Obras*, 2:89–90.

5. Money Comes to Colombia

1. Rippy, *Capitalists and Colombia*, 199–207.

2. Patiño, *Prosperidad*, 27–35; Tovar Zambrano, *Intervención económica*, 137–48.

3. Sánchez Camacho, *General Ospina*, 172.

4. Rippy, *Capitalists*, 154–61; LeGrand, *Frontier Expansion*, 92; Germán Colmenares, *Ricardo Rendón*, 222; Tovar Zambrano, "Economía colombiana," 32; Urrutia, *Historia del sindicalismo*, 117.

5. Palacios, *Estado y clases*, 154; Rippy, *Capitalists*, 152.

6. Sánchez Camacho, *General Ospina*, 176.

7. Nieto Arteta, *Café*, 56; Monsalve, *Colombia cafetera*, 203.

8. Joaquín Ospina, *Diccionario*, 3:427–29.

9. Bejarano Avila, "Economía," 26, 31.

10. Patiño, *Prosperidad*, 40–41.

11. Ibid.; Tovar Zambrano, *Intervención económica*, 92.

12. Patiño, *Prosperidad*, 36.

13. Navarro, *Parlamento*, 199–200; Londoño Vega and Londoño Vélez, "Vida diaria," 320.

14. Patiño, *Prosperidad*, 88.

15. Urrutia, *Historia del sindicalismo*, 90–92; Sowell, "Worker's Labor Movement," 97.

16. *Gil Blas*, April 26, 1919.

17. Archila, "Revolución social," 93–102.

18. Jorge Melo, "República Conservadora," 94; Bejarano Avila, "Economía colombiana entre 1922 y 1929," 55–59.

19. Cayzedo, *Combate*, 170.

20. Zapata Restrepo, *Mitra azul*, 171, 275.

21. López, *Obras selectas,* 290.

22. Villegas and Yunis, *Sucesos colombianos,* 279–80.

23. Mayor, "Historia de la industria," 328–31.

24. Ocampo, "Orígenes," 5:232.

25. Nieto Arteta, *Café,* 79, 87.

26. Jiménez, "Class, Gender, and Peasant Resistance," 127–28.

27. Braudel, *Afterthoughts,* 63.

28. Parsons, *Antioqueño colonization,* 213.

29. Reinhardt, *Our Daily Bread,* 17–37.

30. Ocampo, "Orígenes," 223, 237, 240; Bergquist, *Coffee and Conflict,* 230; Palacios, *Coffee in Colombia,* 232; *Colombia Today,* 25:4 (1990):2.

31. Posada Callejas, *Libro azul,* 335; Monsalve, *Colombia cafetera,* 331–58.

32. LeGrand, *Frontier Expansion,* 167ff.; Nieto Arteta, *Café,* 81–82.

33. Nieto Arteta, *Café,* 45.

34. Pereira Gamba, *Vida en los Andes,* 146.

35. Simmel, *Philosophy of Money,* 1904.

36. Jiménez, "Class, Gender," 130; París, *Geografía económica,* 82–83.

37. Simmel, *Philosophy of Money,* 343–47, 298.

38. McFarlane, "Transition," 120–21.

39. See, for example, Powell, "Peasant Society"; Archer, "Transition."

40. Nieto Arteta, *El café,* 79–82.

41. Palacios, *Estado y clases,* 195.

42. Osorio Lizarazo, *Cosecha.*

43. Cayzedo, *Combate,* 275.

44. Fals Borda, *Teoría y la realidad,* 24.

45. Palacios, *Estado y clases,* 200.

46. Posada Callejas, *Libro azul,* 335.

47. Ibid., 370–71.

48. Arciniegas et al., *Proceso de Pericles Carnaval y Neira.*

49. Cacua Prada, *Si viviera Laureano,* 33.

50. Arboleda, *Diccionario,* 215–16; Alvaro Gómez interview.

51. Arboleda, *Diccionario,* 215–16; Alvaro Gómez interview.

52. Alvaro Gómez interview.

53. *El Conservador,* April 15, May 15, 1917.

54. *La Unidad,* August 22, 1915.

55. Zuleta Angel, *Presidente López,* 19.

56. *El Espectador,* December 10, 1921; September 11, 1919.

57. Suárez, *Sueños,* 1:34.

58. *El Tiempo,* March 31, 1922.

59. *El Tiempo,* April 24, 1922.

60. *El Tiempo,* September 28, 1922.

61. The debate is contained in *Obras completas,* vol. 4, pt. 1, 286–96. It is reported in *El Tiempo,* November 6, 25, 27, 1922; December 1, 1922.

62. *El Tiempo,* October 15, 1922.

63. Text of the telegram is contained in *El Tiempo,* February 27, 1923.

64. *El Gráfico,* February 24, 1923.

65. Vargas Vila, *Vargas Vila,* 297.

66. Bedoya Cardona, *De desterrado,* 73, 78.

67. Suárez, *Obras,* 2:1921.

68. Colombia, Ministerio de Relaciones Exteriores, *Legajo de Argentina,* 1923–31.

69. Palacios, *Estado y clases,* 72.

70. *El Tiempo,* November 16, 1925.

71. *El Tiempo,* "Cosas del Día," April 8, 1925. See also *El Espectador,* March 4, 1925; *El Gráfico,* March 7, 21, 1925.

72. *El Tiempo,* May 24, 1925.

73. Cited in *El Tiempo,* May 25, 1925.

74. Palacios, *Estado y clases,* 70–71.

75. *El Tiempo,* June 19, 1925.

76. Suárez, *Sueños,* 3rd ed. (1940), 10:358.

77. Uribe Celis, *Años veinte,* 123, 128.

78. *El Tiempo,* October 22, 1926; May 13, 26, 1929.

79. Colombia, Ministerio de Obras Publicas, *Memoria,* 1926.

80. Urdaneta, *Escritos y discursos,* 37–44.

81. Eugenio Gómez, *Problemas colombianos,* 329–410; Socarrás, *Laureano Gómez,* 16–24, 341–74.

82. Laureano Gómez, *Obras selectas,* 1:398–403; *El Tiempo,* October 20, 1925.

83. *El Gráfico,* November 21, 1925.

84. *El Nuevo Tiempo,* March 17–24, 1926; Suárez, "El Sueño del Purgatorio," *Sueños,* 4th ed. (1952), 12:51.

85. *El Tiempo,* August 3, 1926; Laureano Gómez, *Obras completas,* vol. 4, pt. 1, 349–63.

86. Laureano Gómez, *Obras completas,* vol. 4, pt. 1, 370.

87. Navia, *Caudillo y gobernante,* 83–88; Navarro, *Parlamento,* 161–63.

88. *El Tiempo,* August 6, 1926.

89. *El Nuevo Tiempo,* October 10, 1926.

90. *El Nuevo Tiempo,* March 8, 1927.

91. *El Diario Nacional,* March 21, 23, 25, 1927; *El Nuevo Tiempo,* March 23, 1927; *Vanguardia Liberal,* March 30, 31, 1927.

92. *Vanguardia Liberal,* March 26, 1927.

93. *Vanguardia Liberal,* April 4, 1927; Laureano Gómez, *Obras completas,* vol. 4, pt. 1, 372–73.

94. *El Nuevo Tiempo,* March 6, April 5, 1927; *El Tiempo,* March 7, April 26, 1927.

95. *El Espectador,* February 3, 1926.

96. *El Tiempo,* August 19, 1927.

97. Kalmanovitz, *Economía y política,* 288–89; Patiño, *Prosperidad,* 112.

98. *El Tiempo,* September 27, 1927.

99. *El Tiempo,* October 1, 4, 1927.

100. *El Tiempo,* October 30, 1927.

101. *El Tiempo,* October 14, 19, 1927.

102. *Universidad,* November 26, 1927, 526. APRA, the Alianza Popular Revolucionaria Americana, was founded in 1924 by Víctor Raúl Haya de la Torre. Strongly anti-imperialistic, APRA's declared goal was to unite oppressed peoples and classes across Latin America.

103. *El Nuevo Tiempo,* October 10, 1926.

104. *El Tiempo,* October 15, 1927.
105. *Universidad,* February 18, 1928, 119, 139.
106. *Universidad,* February 11, 25; March 10, 31, 1928.
107. Laureano Gómez, *Interrogantes,* 63.
108. *El Tiempo,* June 5, 1928.
109. *El Tiempo,* June 7, August 4, 1928; *El Gráfico,* June 9, 1928.
110. *El Espectador,* June 6, 1928.
111. Laureano Gómez, *Interrogantes,* 141–43.
112. Laureano Gómez, *Interrogantes,* 148.

6. Social Change and the Challenge to Traditional Authority

1. Galindo, "República Liberal," 64.
2. Vargas and Zambrano, "Santa Fe y Bogotá," 25.
3. Ibid., 40; Osterling, *Democracy in Colombia,* 9.
4. Patiño, *Prosperidad,* 88; Colmenares, "Ospina y Abadía," 256; Arguedas, *Danza,* 866.
5. Navia, *Caudillo y gobernante,* 150.
6. Fernán González, *Educación y estado,* 71–75; Silva, "Educación en Colombia," 85; McGreevey, *Economic History,* 234.
7. Urrutia, *Development,* 73–76.
8. Archila, "Clase obrera, 1886–1930," 224–31.
9. Ibid., 225.
10. Ibid., 226.
11. Rodríguez Garavito, *Gabriel Turbay,* 64.
12. Manrique, *Signo de la hoz,* 196–97.
13. Medófilo Medina, *Historia del Partido,* 33–40; Medófilo Medina, "Terceros partidos."
14. Jorge Villegas, *Petróleo colombiano,* 37–38.
15. Urrutia, *Development,* 93–94.
16. Ibid., 94–96.
17. Zapata Isaza, *¿Patricios o asesinos?* 50; Zapata Restrepo, *Mitra azul,* 117.
18. Navarro, *Parlamento,* 188–89; Serrano, *En aquella ciudad,* 161–62.
19. Torres Giraldo, *Inconformes,* 3:829–36.
20. López de Mesa, *Historia de la Cancillería,* 330–33; Joaquín Ospina, *Diccionario,* 1:16–17; Perry, *Quién es Quién,* 7.
21. Abadía Méndez, *Discurso,* 34.
22. Decree 707 enabled police forces to jail anyone suspected of being a subversive.
23. Urrutia, *Development,* 96–98, discusses the strike.
24. Torres Giraldo, *Inconformes,* 4:849–66; Gutiérrez Navarro, *Luz de una vida,* 202–44.
25. Suárez, *Sueños,* 12:386.
26. Torres Giraldo, *Inconformes,* 4:886–91.
27. Colmenares, *Ricardo Rendón,* 263.
28. Jorge Melo, *Historia y política,* 146.
29. Ibid., 151.
30. LeGrand, "Conflicto de las bananeras," 183–218.
31. *Diario Nacional,* February 23, 1928.

32. LeGrand, "Conflicto de las bananeras," 206.

33. Navia, *Caudillo y gobernante*, 316–17.

34. Horgan, "Liberals Come to Power," 42.

35. *El Tiempo*, January 1, 1929.

36. Colmenares, *Ricardo Rendón*, 260.

37. Ibid., 206.

38. Carlos Posada Posada, "Gran crisis," 4:81.

39. Horgan, "Liberals," 22.

40. *El Tiempo*, January 15, 1919.

41. *El Espectador*, February 7, 1929; Colmenares, *Ricardo Rendón*, 261–63; Horgan, "Liberals," 46–50.

42. Medófilo Medina, *Protesta urbana*, 38–44; Serrano Camargo, *En aquella ciudad*, 59–63; Navia, *Caudillo y gobernante*, 161–88.

43. *El Espectador*, August 21, 1929; Restrepo Posada, *Iglesia*, 61.

44. *La Prensa*, July 18, 1929.

45. Carlos Restrepo, *Orientación republicana*, 2:505.

46. Torres Giraldo, *Inconformes*, 4:990; Partido Comunista, *Treinta años de lucha*, 11; Gonzalo Sánchez, "*Bolcheviques del Líbano*"; Henderson, *When Colombia Bled*, 68–72.

47. Arguedas, *Danza*, 746.

48. They included Alberto Lleras Camargo, Jorge Eliécer Gaitán, and Jorge Zalamea.

49. Zalamea, *Literatura*, 595.

50. He did so in an *El Tiempo* editorial of July 19, 1925.

51. López Pumarejo, *Obras Selectas*, 1:49–53.

52. Solano, *Paipa, mi pueblo*, 132–33.

53. Solano, *Glosas y ensayos*, 329.

54. Rodríguez Garavito, *Gabriel Turbay*, 176.

55. López Pumarejo, *Obras selectas*, 1:55–61.

56. López Michelsen, *Últimos días de López*, 95–96.

57. Patiño, *Prosperidad*, 248–49.

58. Rumazo G., *Enrique Olaya Herrera*, 109–44; Gustavo Rodríguez, *Olaya Herrera*, 145–53; Carlos Restrepo, *Orientación republicana*, 2:510–613; Horgan, "Liberals," 121–59.

59. Restrepo Posada, *Iglesia*, 68–79.

60. Nieto Caballero, *Escritos escogidos*, 1:265.

61. Antonio García, *Gaitán y el problema*, 261; Pollock, "Evaluating Regime Performance," 14–15; LeGrand, *Frontier Expansion*, 106–8.

62. Samper Gnecco, *Cuando Bogotá no tuvo tranvía*, 78–79.

63. Lleras Restrepo, *Crónica de mi propia vida*, 1:30–31.

64. Drake, *Money Doctor*, 56, 68–72.

65. Patiño, *Prosperidad*, 372–75; Torres Giraldo, *Inconformes*, 4:1039–42.

66. Urrutia, *Development*, 53, 117–18.

67. Patiño, *Prosperidad*, 375.

68. Barnhart, "Colombian Transport"; Hartwig, *Roads to Reason*, 105–11.

69. *El Tiempo*, December 24, 1931.

70. Drake, *Money Doctor*, 66.

71. Ibid., 74; Patiño, *Prosperidad,* 572.
72. Patiño, *Prosperidad,* 458–59.
73. A phrase coined by *El Tiempo* editor Eduardo Santos.
74. Azula, *De la revolución,* 23.
75. Latorre Rueda, "1930–1934: Olaya Herrera," 1:283.
76. López de Mesa, *Escrutinio,* 72.
77. Fals Borda, *Subversión en Colombia,* 185.
78. Oquist, "Elecciones presidenciales."
79. Santa, *Arrieros y fundadores;* Henderson, *When Colombia Bled,* 153–80.
80. Henderson, *When Colombia Bled,* 67–68, 157–58.
81. Ibid., 166–67.
82. Horgan, "Liberals"; Deas, "Algunas notas," 29–44.
83. Gómez Picón, *Estampillas de timbre parroquial,* 172, 173, 179.
84. Horgan, "Liberals," 216–24.
85. Gómez Picón, *Estampillas,* 18.
86. Abel, "Conservative Party," 218–20.
87. Gálvis Gálvis, *Memorias,* 1:231–34; Horgan, "Liberals," 245–46.
88. Serrano Blanco, *Viñas del odio,* 16.
89. *El Tiempo,* December 31, 1930; Guzmán, *Violencia: Parte descriptiva,* 1:23.
90. *El Espectador,* December 29, 1930, reported 16 killed and 50 wounded.
91. Gálvis Gálvis, *Memorias,* 1:244–96; Horgan, "Liberals," 245ff.; Guzmán, *Violencia: Parte descriptiva,* 2 vols., 1:23; Latorre Rueda, "Olaya Herrera," 288; Oquist, *Violencia conflicto,* 197–98; *El Espectador,* December 29–30, 1930; *El Tiempo,* December 31, 1930; January 29, 1931.
92. The complex events leading up to the Montería tragedy are discussed in Horgan, "Liberals," 252–53.
93. Gálvis Gálvis, *Memorias,* 1:287–88.
94. Guzmán, *Violencia: Parte descriptiva,* 1:20–21.
95. Betancourt, "Pájaros," 2.
96. Horgan, "Liberals," 250.
97. *El Espectador,* June 30, 1931; March 29, May 17, July 1, 1932. See also *El Tiempo,* December 10, 1931.
98. Serrano Blanco, *Viñas del odio,* 44, 46.
99. Gálvis Gálvis, *Memorias,* 1:382; Torres Giraldo, *Inconformes,* 4:1069.
100. Horgan, "Liberals," 550, 560.
101. Ibid., 565–66, 599.
102. Ibid., 560, 588–89.
103. *El Gráfico,* January 20, 1934, 478–79.
104. Hilarión, *Balas de la ley,* 129.

7. The Liberal Republic and Its Critics

1. *El Tiempo,* June 10, 1930.
2. Laureano Gómez, "Decadencia y grandeza de España," 257.
3. José de la Vega, in Laureano Gómez, *Cuadrilátero,* xxv–xxvi.
4. F. A. Molina, *Laureano Gómez,* 237.
5. Ibid., 237–38.
6. Alvaro Gómez interview.

7. Ibid.

8. Ibid.; *El Tiempo*, June 10, 1930.

9. Colombia, Ministerio de Relaciones Exteriores, *Legajo de Alemania*, 1929–36.

10. Dangond Uribe, *Hacia una nueva política*, 62–74.

11. Alvaro Gómez interview.

12. Barnhart, "Colombian Transport," 7; Patiño, *Prosperidad*, 66–67; *El País*, September 6, 1932; Alfonso Gómez interview.

13. Navarro, *Parlamento*, 136.

14. Alvaro Gómez interview.

15. Ibid.

16. Ibid.

17. *El Tiempo*, July 21, 1930.

18. *El Tiempo*, April 28, 1931; *La Unidad*, June 15, 1932.

19. Giraldo, *Don Fernando*, 93–96.

20. *El Tiempo*, March 13, 1931.

21. *El Tiempo*, March 18, 1931.

22. *El Tiempo*, July 16, 1931.

23. *El Tiempo*, August 23, 1932; Paxton, *Penthouse in Bogotá*, 286–87.

24. Berrío's speech is reported in *El Tiempo*, November 17, 1931.

25. Conservative Party of Colombia, *Programas*, 114.

26. Ibid., 115.

27. *El Tiempo*, December 2, 1931.

28. *El Tiempo*, January 13, 1932.

29. Serrano Blanco, *Vida es así*, 202–3; *El País*, May 10, 1932.

30. *El Tiempo*, May 17, 19, 1932.

31. Laureano Gómez, *Cuadrilátero*, 297.

32. Ibid., 202.

33. Ibid., 146.

34. Ibid., 72–74, 75.

35. Ibid., 78–79.

36. F. A. Molina, *Laureano Gómez*, 243.

37. *El Espectador*, July 15, 1932.

38. Enrique Santos, writing in *El Tiempo*, July 26, 1932.

39. Horgan, "Liberals," 544, note 7.

40. *El Gráfico*, May 7, 1932, 1367–68.

41. *El Espectador*, July 4, 1932.

42. *El País*, July 22, 1932.

43. Laureano Gómez, *Obras Completas*, vol. 4, pt. 2, 30.

44. Ibid.

45. *El Gráfico*, August 13, 1932, 2013–15.

46. Silvio Villegas, *No hay enemigos*, 208.

47. Urdaneta, *Escritos y discursos*, 101–2.

48. Laureano Gómez, *Obras completas*, vol. 4, pt. 1, 252–70.

49. *El País*, July 27, 1934; *El Espectador*, July 24, 1934.

50. *El Tiempo*, February 6, 1935.

51. *El Tiempo*, June 12, 1933.

52. *El País*, July 22, 1933.

53. *El Tiempo*, October 16, 19, 23, 1933.

54. *El País*, November 15, 1933.

55. López Pumarejo, *Alfonso López*, 33–37.

56. Laureano Gómez, *Obras completas*, vol. 4, pt. 2, 33–40; López Pumarejo, *Alfonso López*, 39, 47.

57. Laureano Gómez, *Obras selectas*, 1:789–94.

58. Laureano Gómez, *Comentarios a un régimen*, 227.

59. *El País*, October 20, 1934; *El Tiempo*, October 20, 1934.

60. *El País* and *El Tiempo*, November 3–4, 1934; *El Gráfico*, November 10, 1934.

61. Urdaneta, *Escritos y discursos*, 163–233; Laureano Gómez, *Obras completas*, vol. 4, pt. 2, 304–81.

62. *El Gráfico*, January 26, 1935; *El Tiempo*, January 27, 1935.

63. *El Tiempo*, January 27, 1935.

64. Laureano Gómez, *Comentarios*, 226.

65. Laureano Gómez, *Obras completas*, vol. 4, pt. 2, 381.

66. Attributed to Julio H. Palacio. Francisco Plata Bermúdez, interview by author, Bogotá, May 14, 1989.

67. Alvaro Gómez interview; Eddy Torres, interview by author, Bogotá, May 30, 1982.

68. Tirado Mejía, "Pensamiento."

69. Ibid., 46.

70. López Pumarejo, *Política oficial*, 3:85.

71. LeGrand, *Frontier Expansion*, 185–204. A hectare is equivalent to 2.47 acres.

72. Ibid., 185–204; Palacios, *Estado y clases*, 160–61.

73. Palacios, *Coffee in Colombia*, 37.

74. Drake, *Money Doctor*, 31; Monsalve, *Colombia cafetera*, 628; Bergquist, *Coffee and Conflict*, 247; Posada Posada, "Gran crisis," 78.

75. Jimeno, "Procesos," 377.

76. LeGrand, *Frontier Expansion*, 36.

77. Bergquist, *Coffee and Conflict*, 98–99; Bergquist et al., *Violence in Colombia*, 61, 17.

78. Reinhardt, *Our Daily Bread*, 60–69.

79. Rojas Garrido, *Empresarios y tecnología*, 82–87.

80. Posada and Cortazar, *Instrucción cívica*, 207.

81. Betancourt and García, *Matones y cuadrilleros*, 48–49.

82. LeGrand, *Frontier Expansion*, 65.

83. Jiménez, "Class, Gender," 126.

84. Palacios, *Coffee in Colombia*, 103.

85. LeGrand, *Frontier Expansion*, 113.

86. *New York Times*, March 4, 1928.

87. Bejarano Avila, *Régimen agrario*, 262–64.

88. Tovar, *Movimiento campesino*, 78–80.

89. Marulanda Alvarez, *Colonización y conflicto*, 103–19; Tovar, *Movimiento campesino*, 76–88; Bejarano Avila, *Régimen agrario*, 264–66.

90. Alejandro López, *Obras selectas*, 412.

91. Ibid., 22.

92. LeGrand, *Frontier Expansion*, 97.

93. Conservative Party, *Programas*, 110–11.

94. *El Tiempo*, September 3, 1933.

95. Gaitán, *Mejores discursos de Gaitán*, 61.

96. López Pumarejo, *Política oficial*, 3:69–70.

97. What is described as that "change of direction" in party strategy is treated in Medófilo Medina, *Historia del Partido*, 263–69.

98. Marulanda Alvarez, *Colonización y conflicto*, 111.

99. Lleras Restrepo, "Obra económica," 2:15.

100. Ibid., 15; LeGrand, *Frontier Expansion*, 139–40; Pécaut, *Orden y violencia*, 1:69; Fajardo, *Haciendas*, 57.

101. Marulanda Alvarez, *Colonización y conflicto*, 111.

102. Ocampo, "Consolidación," 5:239, 260.

103. Farson, *Transgressor*, 175.

104. *Revista Colombiana*, May 1, 1935, 65–69.

105. *El País*, September 21, 1935.

106. Velasco A., *Ecco Homo*, 139.

107. *El Siglo*, March 27, 1936.

108. *El Tiempo*, October 27, 1985.

109. Remark made to Arturo Abella, *El Tiempo*, October 27, 1985.

110. *El Siglo*, September 17, 1940; *La Unidad*, February 11, 1954.

111. López Pumarejo, *Obras selectas*, 2:184.

112. Ramírez Moreno, *La crisis del partido conservador*, 92, 93.

113. *El País*, April 7, 9, 1935.

114. *El País*, April 17, 1935.

115. *La Unidad*, August 22, 1915.

116. *La Unidad*, August 27, 1915.

117. Nieto Caballero, *Colombia joven*, 44.

118. Tirado Mejía, *Aspectos políticos*, 11.

119. Tirado Mejía, "López Pumarejo," 1:322–23; Victor Mosquera Chaux, *El Tiempo*, November 1, 1992; Carbonell, *Quincena politica*, 4:75–178.

120. Helg, *Civiliser le peuple*, 128.

121. Lleras Camargo, "Pasado y Presente del Liberalismo," 3:83.

122. Charria Tobar, *República de Santos*, 123.

123. *La Razón*, November 23, 1936.

124. Carbonell, *Quincena politica*, 5:347.

125. Echandía, *Obras selectas*, 1:103–4.

126. López Pumarejo, *Obras selectas*, 2:233.

127. Ibid.

128. Tirado Mejía and Velásquez, *Reforma constitucional*, 220.

129. Jorge Melo, *Historia de Antioquia*, 158.

130. Carbonell, *Quincena politica*, 5:77.

131. *El País*, October 26, 1935.

132. Tirado Mejía and Velásquez, *Reforma constitucional*, 225–33.

133. Ibid., 118.

134. Ibid., 301.

135. Ibid., 224.

136. González, *Educación y estado*, 101.

137. Tirado Mejía and Velásquez, *Reforma constitucional,* 308–9.

138. Laureano Gómez, *Obras selectas,* 2:13.

139. Laureano Gómez et al., *Constitución de 1886,* 13, 15.

140. Cadavid, *Fueros de la Iglesia,* 78.

141. Laureano Gómez et al., *Constitución,* 389.

142. Medófilo Medina, "Terceros partidos," 289–90.

143. Giraldo, *Don Fernando,* 121–23.

144. Silvio Villegas, *No hay enemigos,* 216; Valois, *Itinerario espiritual.*

145. *El Siglo,* June 16, 1938.

146. Tirado Mejía and Velásquez, *Reforma constitucional,* 223.

8. A Society in Flux

1. Bejarano, "Economía entre 1930 y 1945," 116–19; Arrubla, *Estudios sobre el subdesarrollo colombiano,* 181.

2. Thorp and Londoño, "Effect of the Great Depression," 90.

3. Barnhardt, "Colombian Transport," 12.

4. Hartwig, *Roads to Reason,* 107–8.

5. Eduardo Caballero Calderón, *Obras,* 2:202.

6. Abel, "Conservative Party," 588; Jorge Melo, *Historia de Antioquia,* 297; *El Tiempo,* August 29, 1931.

7. Urrutia, *Cincuenta años de desarrollo,* 181.

8. Sánchez Torres, "Aspectos monetarios de la gran depresión," 208; Oscar Rodríguez, *Efectos de la gran depresión.*

9. José Antonio Ocampo, "Colombian Economy," 131–32.

10. Bejarano, "Economía entre 1930 y 1945."

11. See Bushnell, *Eduardo Santos and the Good Neighbor.*

12. Patiño, *Prosperidad,* 643.

13. Lleras Restrepo, *Memoria de hacienda,* 2:7–46; Oscar Rodríguez, *Efectos,* 120ff.; Mayor, "Historia de la industria, 1930–1963," 339–40.

14. Estéban Jaramillo, *Memoria,* 112.

15. Abel and Palacios, "Colombia, 1930–1958," 590.

16. Vallejo, *Cien años de Bavaria,* 43–45; Echavarría Uribe, "Bancos y finanzas," 258–59; Melo, "*Historia de Antioquia,*" 276–77.

17. Bejarano, "Economía entre 1930 y 1945," 334–38; *El Tiempo,* December 3, 1992.

18. Bejarano, "Economía entre 1930 y 1945," 121–22.

19. Patiño, *Prosperidad,* 717.

20. René de la Pedraja, *Historia de la energía,* 212.

21. Sáenz, *Ofensiva empresarial,* 218.

22. Gilhodes, "Cuestión agraria," 333.

23. Jimeno, "Procesos," 383; Estrada, *Sucesos colombianos,* 622.

24. Fajardo, *Haciendas,* 75–85.

25. Molano, *Selva adentro,* 37.

26. Gilhodes, "Cuestión agraria," 333, 335.

27. Bejarano, "Economía entre 1930 y 1945," 130.

28. Ibid., 124; Abel and Palacios, "Colombia, 1930–1958," 607; Restrepo Yusti, "Historia de la industria," 278.

29. Ocampo, "Consolidación," 255–59.
30. Randall, *Diplomacy*, 211–13.
31. Ibid., 146–16; Echavarría Uribe, "Bancos y finanzas," 261.
32. Jorge Melo, *Historia de Antioqueña*, 278.
33. Mayor, "Historia de la industria," 339; Restrepo Yusti, "Historia de la industria," 278.
34. Angel, "Industrias," 221.
35. Lleras Restrepo, *Memoria*, 1:xix–xx, 87–89 (1940); *Memoria*, 2:122–31.
36. Pécaut, *Orden y violencia*, 1:194.
37. Thorp, *Economic Management*, 17.
38. Banco de la República, *El Banco de la República*, 364.
39. Mayor, "Historia de la industria," 339.
40. Pécaut, *Orden y violencia*, 1:297.
41. Ibid.
42. Bergquist, "Luchas del campesinado," 308.
43. Bejarano, "Economía entre 1930 y 1945," 237, 234.
44. Rueda Plata, "Historia de la población," 367.
45. Bejarano, "Economía entre 1930 y 1945," 118.
46. Rueda Plata, "Historia de la población," 364; Londoño Vega, "La vida diaria," 346.
47. Sharpless, *Gaitán*, 90–93.
48. Vargas and Zambrano, "Santa Fe y Bogotá," 11–91; Hernando Téllez, *Cincuenta años*, 41.
49. Vargas and Zambrano, "Santa Fe y Bogotá," 79. See also Uribe Celis, *Mentalidad del colombiano*, 70.
50. Vargas and Zambrano, "Santa Fe y Bogotá," 83.
51. Alvaro Gómez interview.
52. Uribe Celis, *Mentalidad del colombiano*, 82–83.
53. Londoño Vega and Londoño Vélez, "Vida diaria," 366.
54. Uribe Celis, *Mentalidad del colombiano*, 69.
55. Londoño Vega and Londoño Vélez, "Vida diaria," 368.
56. Ibid., 383, 339.
57. José Gutiérrez, *Rebeldía colombiana*, 22.
58. Uribe Celis, *Mentalidad del colombiano*, 51.
59. Quintana Pereyra, *Redención de la clase media*, 158.
60. Sharpless, *Gaitán*, 29–94.
61. Braun, *Assassination of Gaitán*, 51–76.
62. Ibid., 53.
63. Farson, *Transgressor*, 148–51, 152.
64. Londoño Vega and Londoño Vélez, "Vida diaria," 338.
65. Braun, *Assassination*, 70.
66. Guberik, *Yo vi crecer un país*, 44.
67. Torres García, *Nociones de economía política*, 177.
68. Londoño Vega and Londoño Vélez, "Vida diaria," 383, citing a 1945 edition of *Cromos*.
69. Arango, *Historia de la arquitectura en Colombia*, 181–83.
70. Londoño Vega and Londoño Vélez, "Vida diaria," 338.
71. Niño Murcia, *Arquitectura y estado*, 104.

72. Editorial Salvat, *Historia del arte colombiano*; Rubiano, "Artes plásticas en el siglo veinte," 417–22.

73. Calderón Schrader, *Cincuenta años: Salón Nacional de Artistas*, x, 25, 27.

74. Maya, *Obra crítica*, 2:120; Gutiérrez Girardot, "Literatura colombiana," 491.

75. Gutiérrez Girardot, "Literatura colombiana," 494, 499; Uribe Celis, *Mentalidad*, 46.

76. Laureano Gómez, *Obras completas*, 1:16–20, 36–44, 52–61, 67, 106.

77. Herrera, "Escuela Normal Superior."

78. Jaramillo Uribe, "Proceso," 87–110.

79. Murry, "Feminizing the Fraternity," 4–5.

80. Velásquez Toro, "Condición jurídica y social," 28.

81. Jaramillo Uribe, "Proceso," 105–6.

82. Lleras Restrepo, *Borradores*, 415–16.

83. Londoño Vega and Londoño Vélez, "Vida diaria," 338–39.

84. Ibid., 334.

85. Camacho Carreño, *Leopardo mártir*, 52, 61, 74.

86. Camacho Carreño, *Último leopardo*.

87. *El Tiempo*, June 27, 1935.

88. Herrera, "Escuela," 66.

89. *El Tiempo*, January 18, 1943; Lamé, *Luchas del indio*; Castrillón Arboleda, *Indio Quintín Lamé*.

90. Gálvis and Donadio, *Colombia nazi*, 239–40, 249.

91. Fremantle, *Papal Encyclicals*, 263–64, 269.

92. Laureano Gómez, "Opresión del mundo moderno."

93. *El Siglo*, March 14, 1936.

94. Laureano Gómez, *Obras selectas*, 1:677–94.

95. *Revista colombiana*, 9:105 (February 1, 1938): 160–62.

96. Laureano Gómez, *Obras selectas*, 1:547.

97. Ibid., 535.

98. Ibid., 535.

99. Ibid., 807.

100. Lleras Restrepo, *Borradores*, 339.

101. López Pumarejo, *Obras selectas*, 2:632.

102. Santos, *Obras selectas*, 2:156.

103. Conservative Party, *Programas*, 121.

104. Lleras Restrepo, *Crónica*, 2:152.

105. Laureano Gómez, *Mito de Santander*.

106. Laureano Gómez, *Obras completas*, vol. 4, pt. 3, 170–71, 199, 206, 208.

107. Bushnell, *Eduardo Santos*, 34, 51, 64.

108. *El Siglo*, November 24, 1938, "El peligro fascista."

109. Laureano Gómez, *Obras selectas*, 2:30–67.

110. *El Siglo*, June 25, July 7, 1940.

111. *El Siglo*, January 23, 26, 1941.

112. José de la Vega, *Buen vecino*.

113. United States, Department of State, Braden to Secretary of State, December 9, 1940.

114. Ibid., December 19, 1940.

115. Ibid., March 26, 1941.

116. Laureano Gómez, *Obras selectas*, 1:621.

117. *El Siglo*, October 10, 1941.

118. United States, Department of State, Gerald Keith to Secretary of State, March 26, 1941.

119. Kesler, "Spruille Braden," 107; Gálvis and Donadio, *Colombia nazi*, 48–53, 120–21.

120. Gálvis and Donadio, *Colombia nazi*, 101–40; Kesler, "Spruille Braden," 109.

121. Antonio García, *Gaitán*, 286–87.

122. Antonio García, *Gaitán*, 287.

123. López Michelsen, *Elegidos*, 37.

124. Lleras Restrepo, *Crónica*, 4:269.

125. Amadeo Rodríguez, *Caminos de guerra*; Iriarte, *Episodios bogotanos*, 77; Tirado Mejía, *Aspectos políticos*, 290–91.

126. Abel, *Política, Iglesia, y partidos*, 231–39.

127. Valencia Tovar, *Testimonio*, 58–59.

128. Fernán González, "Iglesia católica," 377–81.

129. *El Tiempo*, October 27, 1985.

130. Abel, *Política, Iglesia*, 239–40.

131. Rueda Uribe, *Proceso Mamatoco*, 8.

132. Darío Bautista, *Personaje y los hechos*, 18–20.

133. Alfonso López, *Obras selectas*, 2:242, 243–44.

134. Montaña Cuellar, *Colombia*, 166.

135. Rueda Uribe, *Proceso Mamatoco*.

136. Abel, *Política, Iglesia*, 231–44; Gálvis Gómez, *Porqué cayó López*.

137. Guerrero, *Años del olvido*, 192–226.

138. Christie, *Oligarcas*, 155–86.

139. Giraldo, *Don Fernando*; Burnett, "Recent Colombian Party System," 88–89; Eduardo Caballero Calderón, *Rabo de paja*.

140. Lleras Restrepo, *Crónica*, 4:371.

141. Estrada, *Sucesos*, 676.

142. Echandía, *Obras selectas*, 2:543, 545.

143. Ibid., 4:234.

144. Gálvis and Donadio, *Colombia nazi*, 98–99.

145. Lleras Restrepo, *Crónica*, 5:158, 335, 352–54.

146. Serrano Camargo, *En aquella ciudad*, 277.

147. *El Siglo*, February 10, 1944.

148. López Pumarejo, *Documentos*, 40.

149. *El Siglo*, May 21, June 1, 1944.

150. The best study of the 1944 coup attempt is Quintero, *Consacá*.

151. Archila, "La clase obrera, 1930–1945," and *Cultura e identidad*, 316–17; Bergquist, *Violence in Colombia*, 69–70; Urrutia, *Development*, 200–202; Pécaut, *Orden y violencia*, 303–4, 411–15, 435.

152. López Pumarejo, *Obras selectas*, 2:610. Address to Congress of January 22, 1945.

153. *El Siglo*, March 29, 1945.

154. Gálvis Gómez, *Porqué cayó López*, 21–41; López Pumarejo, *Documentos*, 283.

155. Atilio Velásquez, *El padre*, 213.

156. Ibid., 213.

157. López Pumarejo, *Obras selectas* 2:627, 628.

158. Ibid., 2:632.

9. Orchestrating the War of Seven Thousand Days

1. Gaitán, *Mejores discursos*, 429.

2. Thorp, *Economic Management*, 17.

3. López Pumarejo, *Obras selectas*, 2:543, 545.

4. José Francisco Ocampo, *Memorias inconclusas*, 278–79.

5. Lleras Restrepo, *Crónica*, 4:296; *El Siglo*, September 24, 1941.

6. Braun, *Assassination*, 81.

7. Bautista, *Personaje*, 27, 31.

8. Lleras Restrepo, *Crónica*, 5:219.

9. Both *El Tiempo* and *El Espectador* were stoned on March 11, 1944.

10. Lleras Restrepo, *Crónica*, 7:36–37.

11. Gaitán, *Mejores discursos*, 397.

12. Braun, *Assassination*, 91–99.

13. Ibid., 91–99.

14. Giraldo, *Don Fernando*, 217.

15. Gómez writing in *El Siglo*, March 29, 1946.

16. For detail see *El País*, March 10, 1934.

17. Ortiz Sarmiento, *Estado y subversión*, 96.

18. *Tejo* is a game indigenous to the Cundi-Boyacense region, akin to horseshoes.

19. Bautista, *Personaje*, 74; Osorio Lizarazo, *Gaitán*, 117–18.

20. Lucas Caballero Calderón, *Figuras políticas de Colombia*, 52.

21. Braun, *Assassination*, 82–86, 117.

22. Azula, *De la revolución*, 193.

23. *El Siglo*, April 26, 1946.

24. *El País*, October 19, 1933.

25. Bedel, *Bengalí*.

26. Giraldo, *Don Fernando*, 235.

27. Pécaut, *Orden y violencia*, 2:390.

28. Buenahora, *Biografía de una voluntad*, 141–42.

29. *The designado* occupies the presidency when that office falls vacant.

30. Navia, *Yo ví cerrar el Congreso*, 50–53.

31. Lleras Camargo, *Año de gobierno*, 89ff.; *El Siglo*, December 8, 1945.

32. Latorre Cabral, *Dos reportajes*.

33. Ibid., 31; Giraldo, *Don Fernando*, 23.

34. Estrada, *Sucesos*, 733.

35. *El Siglo*, February 12, 1946.

36. *El Siglo*, March 15, 1946.

37. Alape, *Bogotazo*, 36.

38. Braun, *Assassination*, 108.

39. Lleras Restrepo, *Crónica*, 7:461.

40. Buenahora, *Biografía*, 147; Azula, *De la revolución*, 194.

41. Velásquez, *Padre*, 257.

42. *El Siglo*, May 7, 1946.

43. Catalina Reyes, "Gobierno de Mauriano Ospina Pérez," 6.
44. Osorio Lizarazo, *Gaitán*, 281–82.
45. Abel, *Política*, 147.
46. Zapata Isaza, *¿Patricios o asesinos?* 160.
47. Ibid., 162–63.
48. Azula, *De la revolución*, 224.
49. Ibid., 225.
50. Guzmán, *Violencia: Parte descriptiva*, 25.
51. Pécaut, *Orden y violencia*, 2:468.
52. Gaitán, *Mejores discursos*, 480–81.
53. *Malicia indígena* means literally "Indian perverseness."
54. *El Tiempo*, September 7, 1947.
55. "El fraude y la violencia," *El Siglo*, September 2, 1947.
56. *Semana*, October 6, 1947, 3.
57. It will be shown below that much of the Violencia was indeed generated in such fashion.
58. Montalvo, *Exposición*.
59. Oquist, *Violencia, conflicto y política*, 17, 18, 20, 59.
60. Harker, *Quinientos años de lágrimas*, 37.
61. Solano Benítez, *Cincuenta años de vida nortesantandereana*, 4:382ff.
62. Ibid., 4:385.
63. *Semana*, May 17, 1947, 7; Harker, *Quinientos años*, 38.
64. Paul Oquist, *Violencia conflictiva*, 264; *El Siglo*, January 6, 1948.
65. Lleras Camargo, *Año de gobierno*, 233–34.
66. Vargas Velásquez, *Colonización y conflicto armado*, 101–2.
67. Zapata Izasa, *¿Patricios o asesinos?* 179; Giraldo, *Don Fernando*, 244–45; Betancourt and García, *Matones y cuadrillas*, 44.
68. Uribe, *Limpiar la tierra*, 78.
69. José María Villarreal, interview by author, Bogotá, July 9, 1971.
70. *El Espectador*, January 23, 1948.
71. Rojas de Segura, "Violencia en Boyacá," 302.
72. *Semana*, January 4, 1947, 3–5; December 30, 1946, 3.
73. Ramsey, "Modern Violence in Colombia," 197.
74. *Semana*, August 30, 1947, 3.
75. Ramsey, "*Bogotazo*," 10.
76. Medófilo Medina, *Historia del Partido*, 557.
77. Solano Benítez, *Cincuenta años*, 529–54.
78. *El Siglo*, January 18, 1948.
79. Oquist, *Violencia conflictiva*, 235.
80. Braun, *Assassination*, 157–58.
81. Ibid., 159.
82. Aprile, *Impacto del nueve de abril*, 90.
83. Braun, *Assassination*, 146–47.
84. Harker, *Otros autores santandereanos*, 376.
85. Braun, *Assassination*, 155.
86. Michael Jiménez, interview by author, New York, December 30, 1989.
87. Braun, *Assassination*, 160.
88. Rodolfo de Roux, "Iglesia y sociedad," 126–35; Henderson, *Cuando Colombia*

se desangró, 151–54.

89. Braun, *Assassination,* 164.

90. Gonzalo Sánchez, "Violencia, guerrillas, y estructuras agrarias," 132.

91. José Gutiérrez, *Rebeldía,* 52, 71.

92. Pécaut, *Orden y violencia,* 2:477–78.

93. Communist Party, *Treinta años de lucha,* 83.

94. Velasco, *Ecce homo,* 249.

95. Braun, *Assassination,* 203.

96. This point is also made by Pécaut, *Orden y violencia,* 2:481.

97. Lucía Torres de Restrepo, interview by author, Bogotá, April 20, 1993.

98. Beaulac, *Career Ambassador,* 249.

99. Aprile, *Impacto,* 83–103.

100. Palacios, *Delgada corteza de nuestra civilización,* 95.

101. Gálvis and Donadio, *Jefe supremo,* 38–90.

102. Zapata Izasa, *¿Patricios o asesinos?* 218.

103. Giraldo, *Don Fernando,* 292.

104. Ibid., 292.

105. Colombia, Senado, *Anales del Senado,* 1949, 264.

106. Colombia, Cámara, *Anales,* 1949, 219.

107. *El Siglo,* July 24, 1949.

108. Zapata Izasa, *¿Patricios o asesinos?* 258.

109. Villaveces, *Derrota,* 26–27.

110. Forero, *Grandes fechas,* 153–57; Fonnegra, *Parlamento colombiano,* 233–38; *Semana,* September 12, 1949; *El Siglo,* Sept. 8, 10, 1949; Rincón, *Biográfia de Gustavo Jiménez.*

111. Laureano Gómez, *Obras selectas,* 2:413–17.

112. Sáenz, "Documentos," 309–12.

113. *Hispanic World Report,* August 1949.

114. Fonnegra, *Parlamento colombiano,* 245; Guzmán, *Violencia: Parte descriptiva,* 1:241–42; Jaramillo Ocampo, *1946–1950,* 326–32; Cuellar, *Trece años de Violencia,* 96–99.

115. *Time,* October 24, 1949, 43.

116. Lleras Restrepo, *De la República a la dictadura,* 211.

117. Jaramillo Ocampo, *1946–1950,* 331.

118. Fonnegra, *Parlamento colombiano,* 257.

119. Cuéllar Vargas, *Trece años,* 90.

120. Solano Benítez, *Cincuenta años,* 4:710–62.

121. Ramsey, "Modern Violence," 223–24.

122. *El Siglo,* January 2, 1950.

123. Guzmán, *Violencia: Parte descriptiva,* 303.

124. Zapata Restrepo, *Mitra azul,* 448, 453.

125. Pizarro, *FARC,* 41.

126. Ramsey, "Modern Violence," 233.

127. Guzmán, *Violencia: Parte descriptiva,* 78.

128. Martz, *Colombia,* 103.

129. Ibid., 102, citing *Newsweek* of April 3, 1950.

130. Ramsey, "Modern Violence," 243.

131. Rivera, *Latin America,* 243.

132. Colombia, Presidencia, *Oposición y el gobierno,* 45.

133. Abel Naranjo Villegas, interview by author, Bogotá, June 18, 1986.

134. Laureano Gómez, *Obras completas,* 2:595–611.

10. Economic Progress and Social Change

1. Rueda Plata, "Historia de la población," 382.

2. Ibid.

3. Londoño Botero, "Crisis y recomposición," 346; Rueda Plata, "Historia de la población," 364, 383.

4. Bejarano, "Economía entre 1945–1958," 158; Rueda Plata, "Historia de la población," 376.

5. Editorial Selesiana, *Conferencias episcopales,* vol. 1, *1908–1953,* 497–98.

6. Escobar, *Gonzalo Arango,* 21–22.

7. López de Mesa, *Escrutinio,* 209.

8. Urrutia, *Gremios.*

9. Kalmanovitz, "Colombia," 71; Thorp, *Economic Management,* 17–18.

10. Bejarano, "La economía entre 1946 y 1958," 150; Colombia, Concejo Nacional, *Colombia: Plan general;* Dix, *Colombia,* 32.

11. Ocampo, "Consolidación," 237.

12. Bergquist, "Luchas del campesinado," 303–4; Junguito and Pizano, eds., *Producción de café,* 12, 36–37, 51, 55; Machado, *Café,* 258.

13. Junguito and Pizano, *Producción,* 43.

14. Thorp, *Economic Management,* 49.

15. Hartlyn, *Politics,* 49.

16. Thorp, *Economic Management,* 57; Medhurst, *Church and Labour,* 96.

17. Sáenz, *Ofensiva,* 212.

18. Hartwig, *Roads to Reason,* 120.

19. Morales, *Historias económicas,* 77.

20. Bejarano, *Economía y poder,* 283.

21. Baquero, "Plan de colonización imperialista," 110.

22. Bejarano, *Economía y poder,* 283.

23. Hartwig, *Roads to Reason,* 116–17.

24. Zapata Izasa, *¿Patricios o asesinos?* 156; Jaramillo Ocampo, *1946–1950,* 59ff.

25. Meisel, "De la inflación," 406.

26. Alvarez Restrepo, *Testimonio,* 156.

27. García, *Gaitán,* 334.

28. Caballero Argaez, *Cincuenta años de economía,* 78–80; José Francisco Ocampo, *Memorias inconclusas,* 486.

29. Morales and Pizano, *Don Manuel,* 2:272–77.

30. Mayor, "Historia de la industria," 348.

31. Kalmanovitz, *Economía y nación,* 405–6.

32. Bejarano, "Economía entre 1946 y 1958," 155, 157.

33. Sandilands, *Life of Currie,* 162–63; Hirschman, *Journeys toward Progress,* 162.

34. Robles Bohórquez, *Agricultura,* 27; Bejarano, *Economía y poder,* 3, 76.

35. Jaramillo Ocampo, *1946–1950,* 59; Thorp, *Economic Management,* 18; Reyes, "Mariano Ospina Pérez," 5.

36. Bejarano, "Economía entre 1946 y 1958," 158; Bejarano, *Economía y poder,* 243.

37. Hirschman, *Journeys toward Progress,* 177; Bejarano, "Economía entre 1946 y 1958," 162.

38. Rueda Plata, "Historia de la población," 376.

39. Urrutia, "Desarrollo," 186–87; Hartlyn, *Politics;* Meisel, "Banco de la República," 417.

40. Estrada, *Sucesos,* 557.

41. Medófilo Medina, *Historia del Partido,* 527; *El Siglo,* May 13, 1947; Saénz, *Ofensiva,* 80–81.

42. Jorge Regueros Peralta, interview by author, Bogotá, June 15, 26, 1993; Pizarro, *FARC,* 63; Londoño Botero, "Crisis y recomposición," 281.

43. Medhurst, *Church,* 184; Urrutia, "Desarrollo," 239–40; Londoño Botero, "Crisis y recomposición," 277.

44. Urrutia, *Development,* 201–27; Londoño Botero, "Crisis y recomposición," 276–83; Medhurst, *Church,* 37, 65–92, 99–146, 151–75; Silvia Arango, *Historia,* 153–74.

45. Archila, "Obreros colombianos," 17.

46. Ibid., 17.

47. Londoño Botero, "Crisis y recomposición," 281–82.

48. Urrutia, "Desarrollo," 198.

49. Martz, *Colombia,* 289–90.

50. He does so in his monograph *Gremios, política económica, y democrácia.*

51. José Francisco Ocampo, *Memorias inconclusas,* 482–97.

52. Bejarano, *Economía y poder,* 24.

53. Echeverri, *Elites y proceso político,* 34–35.

54. Urrutia, "On the Absence of Economic Populism."

55. Urrutia, *Gremios,* 115–23.

56. Dix, *Colombia,* 322; Revez Roldán and Pérez Piñeros, "Algunas hipótesis," 44.

57. Abel, "Themes in the History of Public Health."

58. Flórez, *Transición demográfica,* 24; Rueda Plata, "Historia de la población," 382.

59. Rueda Plata, "Historia de la población," 377, 383.

60. Helg, "La educación en Colombia," 118.

61. Fernán González, *Educación y estado,* 110–11; Helg, "Educación," 118.

62. Thorp, *Economic Management,* 60.

63. Bejarano, "Economía entre 1946 y 1958," 166.

64. Zamudio and Rubiano, *Nupcialidad,* 39.

65. Rueda Restrepo, "Población," 382.

66. Téllez B., *Cincuenta años,* 93–161.

67. Bejarano, "Economía entre 1946 y 1958," 150.

68. Silvia Arango, *Historia,* 212.

69. Germán Téllez, "Arquitectura," 373–74; Silvia Arango, *Historia,* 212.

70. Vargas and Zambrano, "Santa Fe y Bogotá," 80.

71. Silvia Arango, *Historia,* 211.

72. Calderón, *Cincuenta años,* 49.

73. Ibid., 49.

74. Ibid., 86.

75. Ibid., 84.

76. Restrepo, "Literatura y pensamiento," 525, 536.

77. Gonzalo Arango, *Fuego en el altar,* 33.
78. Londoño Vega and Londoño Vélez, "Vida diaria," 341.
79. Niño, *Arquitectura,* 240.
80. Lebret, *Estudio,* 83.
81. Le Bot, *Educación e ideología,* 46.
82. Niño, *Arquitectura,* 323.

11. Politics and Violence under Gómez and Rojas

1. *El Siglo,* June 18, 20, 1951.
2. Laureano Gómez, *Obras selectas,* 2:597–611.
3. Escobar Camargo, *En el Salón de los Virreyes,* 134.
4. Rodrigo Noguera Laborde, interview by author, Bogotá, November 18, 1992.
5. Tirado, *Alfonso López Pumarejo,* 186–228; Giraldo, *Don Fernando,* 321; *Hispanic American Report,* January and September 1951.
6. Martz, *Colombia,* 119.
7. Ibid., 116.
8. Colombia, Presidencia, *Año de gobierno,* 1:181.
9. Urdaneta, *Materialismo contra la dignidad del hombre,* 341.
10. Laureano Gómez, *Obras selectas,* 2:610–11, 607.
11. Ramsey, "The Colombian Battalion," 9; Walthour, "Laureano Gómez."
12. Julio Tobón Páramo, interview by author, Bogotá, January 17, 1982.
13. Laureano Gómez, *Obras selectas,* 2:615–16.
14. Colombia, Presidencia, *Dos cartas.*
15. Alape, *La paz, la violencia,* 106.
16. Hoenigsberg, *Fronteras,* 199–242.
17. Chief among them are Felix Restrepo, *Corporatismo,* and *Colombia en la encrucijada;* Rafael Bernal Jiménez, *Cuestión social,* and *Hacia una democracía orgánica;* Ignacio de Guzmán, *Hombre frente al estado;* Victor Dugand, *Entre Conservadores;* Alfredo García Cadena, *Unas ideas elementales;* José Camacho Carreño, *Último leopardo.*
18. *El Siglo,* July 1, 1943, reprint of an interview that first appeared in *El Liberal.*
19. *El Siglo,* October 14, 1948.
20. *El Siglo,* January 30, 1950.
21. Colombia, Ministerio de Gobierno, *Estudios constitucionales.*
22. Laureano Gómez, *Efectos de la Reforma de 1953.*
23. See appendix 2.
24. Franco Isaza, *Guerrillas del llano,* 266–67.
25. Guzmán, *Violencia: Parte descriptiva,* 1:203–5.
26. Londoño Vega and Londoño Vélez, "Vida diaria," 334.
27. *El Siglo,* March 10, 1952.
28. Lleras Restrepo, *De la república a la dictadura,* 351.
29. Henderson, *When Colombia Bled,* 177–80.
30. The crusade is featured in *Semana,* May 17, 1952.
31. Valencia Tovar, *Testimonio,* 186–89.
32. Giraldo, *Don Fernando,* 356.
33. *Semana,* August 2, 1952, 9.
34. Lleras Restrepo, *Crónica,* 11, 417–36.
35. Marulanda Alvarez, *Colonización y conflicto,* 249–51.

36. Henao Ospina, *Gilberto Alzate Avendaño*, 152–53.
37. Martz, *Colombia*, 159.
38. Giraldo, *Don Fernando*, 384–85.
39. United States, Lankenau.
40. Laureano Gómez, *Obras selectas*, 2:473.
41. Giraldo, *Don Fernando*, 389.
42. Laureano Gómez, *Obras completas*, 2:471–83.
43. Ortiz Sarmiento, *Estado y subversión*, 173.
44. Ayala, "Discurso de la conciliación," 208.
45. Forero, *Grandes fechas*, 231.
46. Ibid., 231.
47. Echavarría Olózaga, *Historia*; Forero, *Grandes fechas*, 217; Rojas Pinilla, *Rojas Pinilla ante el Senado*, 490–91.
48. Escobar Camargo, *En el Salón*, 25–26.
49. Navia, *Yo ví*, 222.
50. Jaramillo Ocampo, *Momentos estelares*, 75.
51. Escobar Camargo, *En el Salón*, 31.
52. Valencia, *Testimonio*, 198.
53. Vásquez Carrizosa, *Poder presidencial*, 295. Vásquez criticizes the coup of June 13, 1953, as unconstitutional and therefore damaging to Colombian national institutions.
54. Escobar Camargo, *En el Salón*, 68–70.
55. Ibid., 57–58.
56. Ibid., 73.
57. Rojas Pinilla, *Rojas Pinilla ante el Senado*, 601.
58. Rojas Pinilla, *Seis meses de gobierno*, 11.
59. Abel Naranjo interview.
60. Alzate Avendaño, *Obras selectas*, 345.
61. Colombia, Presidencia, *Seis meses de gobierno*, 8, 9.
62. Ayala, "Discurso," 207.
63. Sánchez Juliao, *Hombre a través de la anécdota*, 105.
64. Colombia, *Seis meses de gobierno*, 181, 311.
65. Gonzalo Sánchez, *Ensayos*, 223–58.
66. Alape, *Paz*, 130; Guzmán, *Violencia: Parte descriptiva*, 1:137–57.
67. Laureano Gómez, *Desde el exilio*, 235–36.
68. Oquist, *Violencia conflictivo*, 63.
69. Martz, *Colombia*, 180–81.
70. Fernández de Soto, *¿Quien llamó la policía?*; Navia, *Yo ví*, 296–300; Martz, *Colombia*, 186–88; Gálvis and Donadio, *Jefe supremo*, 350–69.
71. Martz, *Colombia*, 184–85.
72. Fluharty, *Dance of the Millions*, 249–52.
73. United States, Gerberich to Mills.
74. Randall, *Colombia*, 210.
75. Gonzalo Sánchez, "Violencia: De Rojas al Frente Nacional," 166.
76. Marulanda Alvarez, *Colonización y conflicto*, 250–62.
77. Marulanda Vélez, *Cuadernos de campaña*, 52.
78. Henderson, *When Colombia Bled*, 191–98; Ramsey, *Guerrilleros y soldados*, 240–43.

79. Guzmán, *Violencia: Parte descriptiva*, 178, 179.

80. Gartner, *Mis memorias*, 319–20.

81. Agudelo and Montoya, *Guerrilleros intelectuales;* Gómez Martínez, *Mordaza.*

82. Medófilo Medina, *Protesta urbana*, 112.

83. Silvia Gálvis, *Jefe supremo*, 465–76, 507–13; Dix, *Colombia*, 217–20, 224–25.

84. López Pumarejo, *Alfonso López Pumarejo*, 253–54.

85. Abel Naranjo interview.

86. Vásquez Cobo Carrizosa, *Frente Nacional*, 145–65.

87. Ibid., 196–97.

88. *Tribuna*, December 1, 1956.

89. *Tribuna*, December 6, 1956.

90. Henderson, *When Colombia Bled*, 181–202; Ortiz Sarmiento, *Estado y subversión*, 211–34.

91. Molano, *Años de tropel*, 13–172.

92. Colombia, Senado, *Proceso*, 2:726; Silvia Gálvis, *Jefe supremo*, 207–44.

93. Guzmán, *Violencia: Parte descriptiva*, 64.

94. Martz, *Colombia*, 231–33.

95. José Francisco Ocampo, *Memorias inconclusas*, 462–63.

96. José Bernardo García, *Explosión de mayo*, 24–35.

97. Martz, *Colombia*, 228–31, 233–36.

98. Belisario Betancur Cuartas, interview by author, Bogotá, July 2, 1985.

99. Medófilo Medina, *Protesta urbana;* José García, *Explosión*, 55–61.

100. Navia, *Yo ví*, 378–79.

101. José García, *Explosión*, 82–83.

102. Medófilo Medina, *Protesta urbana*, 109.

103. José Francisco Ocampo, *Memorias inconclusas*, 464–66; Medófilo Medina, *Protesta urbana*, 101–8.

104. *El Tiempo*, May 10, 1959.

105. Navia, *Yo ví*, 431.

106. Alvarez Restrepo, *Testimonio*, 201–6.

107. Ibid., 202–12; José Francisco Ocampo, *Memorias inconclusas*, 462–74; Jaramillo Ocampo, *Momentos estelares*, 119–52; *El Tiempo*, May 10, 1959; Navia, *Yo ví*, 441–501.

108. Escobar Camargo, *En el Salón*, 240; Daniel, *Rural Violence*, 100.

12. A Time of Transition, 1957–1965

1. By the 1960s, Colombians were calling the bloodshed of 1947–1965 La Violencia. Thus they distinguished it from other instances of civil violence that came before and after it.

2. Vázquez Cobo, *Frente Nacional*, 164. For discussion of Lleras's trip, see 147–65.

3. Vázquez Cobo, *Frente Nacional*, 261.

4. Ibid., 269.

5. Giraldo, *Don Fernando*, 472–73.

6. Ibid., 473.

7. The document is contained in Vázquez Cobo, *Frente Nacional*, 277–83.

8. *El Siglo*, October 13, 1957.

9. Conservative Party of Colombia, *Oro y escoria.*

10. Laureano Gómez, *Obras selectas*, 2:797–99.

11. Ibid., 2:805.

12. Lleras Camargo, *Sus mejores páginas,* 193.

13. *El Espectador,* September 20, 1992; Valencia Tovar, *Testamento,* 335–47; Hartlyn, *Politics,* 66–68; Premo, "Alianza Nacional Popular," 71.

14. *El Siglo,* July 21, 1958.

15. Laureano Gómez, *Obras Selectas,* 2:810.

16. Lleras Camargo, *Primer gobierno del Frente Nacional,* 1:60.

17. Ibid., 1:60, 69.

18. Year-by-year figures for Violencia-related mortality are contained in appendix 2.

19. Sánchez and Meertens, *Bandoleros,* 193.

20. Guzmán, *Violencia: Parte descriptiva,* 397–98; Henderson, *When Colombia Bled,* 207.

21. Gonzalo Sánchez, "Rehabilitación y violencia," 21.

22. Lleras Camargo, *Primer gobierno,* 1:391–94.

23. Guzmán, *Violencia: Parte descriptiva,* 1:192.

24. Henderson, *When Colombia Bled,* 208–11.

25. Gilhodes, "Cuestión agraria en Colombia, 1958–1985," 341–43; Bejarano, "Técnicas agropecuarias," 301–10.

26. Bejarano, "Técnicas agropecuarias," 225.

27. Lleras Camargo, *Primer gobierno,* 1:221–36, 249.

28. *New York Times,* November 22, 1959.

29. Hirschman, *Journeys toward Progress,* 193.

30. Lleras Restrepo, *Hacia la restauración democrática,* 2:280.

31. Bagley, "Political Power"; Duff, *Agrarian Reform;* Hirschman, *Journeys toward Progress,* 131–213; Bejarano, "Técnicas agropecuarias," 301–10; Gilhodes, "Cuestión agraria, 1958–1985," 341–54.

32. Randall, *Colombia and the United States,* 231–35.

33. Hirschman, *Journeys toward Progress,* 213.

34. Bushnell, *Colombia,* 233–35.

35. *El Siglo,* November 29, 1960.

36. Bagley, "Political Power," 169–71.

37. *El Tiempo,* October 27, 1985.

38. Botero, *MRL,* 246.

39. Ibid., 225.

40. Gallón, *Entre movimientos y caudillos,* 73–74.

41. López Michelsen, *Colombia en la hora cero,* 284.

42. Gallón, *Entre movimientos,* 74.

43. Botero, *MRL,* 188.

44. Ayala, "Orígenes del anapismo," 38.

45. Ibid., 32.

46. See, for example, Valois Arce, *Enjuiciamiento de Laureano Gómez.*

47. *El Siglo,* December 4, 1958.

48. Guzmán, *Violencia: Parte descriptiva,* 409.

49. *Tribuna,* September 3, 1959.

50. Sánchez and Meertens, *Bandoleros;* Henderson, *When Colombia Bled,* 263–64.

51. Rafael Parga Cortés, interview by author, Ibagué, March 24, 1971.

52. Ortiz Sarmiento, "'Business of the Violence,'" 151.

53. Sánchez and Meertens, *Bandoleros,* 130.
54. Ortiz Sarmiento, "Guerrillas liberales," 142, n77.
55. Guzmán, *Violencia: Parte descriptiva,* 409.
56. Pedro Téllez, *Crónicas de la vida bandolera,* 156.
57. Ibid., 158.
58. The account of the crime, the arrest, and the subsequent trial is in *Tribuna,* April 14, 22, 1957.
59. Pedro Téllez, *Crónicas,* 159–68.
60. Sánchez and Meertens, *Bandoleros,* 126.
61. Ibid., 126, 143.
62. Fajardo, *Violencia y desarrollo,* 202.
63. Valencia Tovar, *Testimonio,* 409–20, 421–47; Bermúdez Rossi, *Poder militar,* 123–25; Daniel, *Rural Violence,* 129; Ramsey, "Internal Defense," 356–62.
64. Alberto Gómez Botero, interview by author, El Líbano, Tolima, March 4, 1971.
65. Valencia Tovar, *Testimonio,* 413; Ramsey, "Modern Violence," 430–31; Alba, *Vida, confesión, y muerte,* 112–19; Pedro Téllèz, *Crónicas,* 112–19.
66. Triana, *Acción comunal.*
67. Cepeda and Pardo, "Política exterior colombiana, 1964–1974"; Leal Buitrago, "Surgimiento, auge, y crisis," 6–34.
68. Lleras Camargo, *Primer gobierno,* 4:89–98.
69. Pizarro, "Revolutionary Guerrilla Groups," 176.
70. Moncada, *Aspecto de la Violencia,* 407–8.
71. Valencia Tovar, *Testimonio,* 370–96; Moncada, *Aspecto,* 391–430; Bayer, *Carretera al mar.*
72. Alape, *Paz,* 245.
73. Valencia Tovar, *Testimonio,* 452.
74. Arango Z., ed., *FARC,* 210.
75. Ibid., 187, 188; Gonzalo Sánchez, *Ensayos de historia social,* 264–71.
76. "Comandante Olimpio" in Arango Z., *FARC,* 188.
77. Gonzalo Sánchez, *Ensayos,* 266.
78. Arango Z., *FARC,* 188–91; Henderson, *When Colombia Bled,* 219–20.
79. Arenas, *Cese el fuego,* 205–29; Marulanda Vélez, *Cuadernos,* 79–80; Alape, *Diario de un guerrillero,* 71–74; Arango Z., *FARC,* 125, 155–60; Arenas, *Diario de la resistencia.*
80. Pizarro, *FARC,* 190; González, *Estigma.*
81. Pizarro, *FARC.*
82. Berry and Urrutia, *Income Distribution,* 31, 40.
83. Dix, *Colombia,* 162.
84. Hartlyn, *Politics,* 183–84; Londoño Botero, "Crisis y recomposición," 283.
85. Caicedo, *Conflictos sociales,* 298–300; Bagley, "Political Power," 119f.; Urrutia, *Development,* 248–49.
86. Gaitán Durán, *Revolución invisible,* 26.
87. Leal Buitrago, "Frustración política," 297–326.
88. Caballero Calderón, *Obras,* 2:333.
89. Lleras Camargo, *Primer gobierno,* 1:59.
90. José Gutiérrez, *De la pseudo-aristocracia a la autenticidad,* 156.
91. Caballero Calderón, *Obras,* 2:365 (357–65).

92. Luis López de Mesa, *Crónica de los tres comentadores.*

93. Fals Borda, *Subversión,* 185, 251.

94. Fals Borda, "Negation of Sociology," 165.

95. Anisur Rahman and Fals Borda, "Romper el monopolio," 46.

96. Gaitán Durán, *Revolución,* 80; Mauricio Torres, *Naturaleza de la revolución,* 142.

97. Child, *López y el pensamiento liberal,* 27; Laureano Gómez, *Interrogantes,* 62–63.

98. Arrubla, *Estudios,* 222.

99. Héctor Melo and López, *Imperio clandestino del cafe,* 149.

100. Antonio García, *Hacia una teoría latinoamericana,* 34.

101. Arrubla, *Estudios,* 33.

102. Jaramillo Agudelo, *Nueva Historia de Colombia,* 8.

103. Arrubla, *Colombia hoy,* 8, 9.

104. Ibid., 11.

105. Rueda Enciso, "Antigua Facultad de Sociología de la Universidad Nacional."

106. *Reforma Universitaria,* 1:1 (April 1960), 1.

107. Broderick, *Camilo Torres,* 165–72.

108. Torres Restrepo, "Social Change and Rural Violence in Colombia."

109. Broderick, *Camilo Torres,* 206.

110. Arenas, *Guerrilla por dentro,* 48.

111. Guzmán, *Violencia: Parte descriptiva,* 445, 446.

112. Broderick, *Camilo Torres,* 260–70.

113. Alvarez García, *Camilo Torres.*

114. Alape, *Paz,* 233, 234.

115. Alberto Gómez Botero, interview by author, March 4, 1971.

116. Torres died in a skirmish with an army patrol on February 15, 1966.

117. Urrutia, *Cuarenta años de desarrollo,* 12, 14.

118. Thorp, *Economic Management,* 224.

119. Currie, *Accelerating Development,* 152.

120. Emiliani, *Laureano el grande,* xx–xxi.

121. Tirado Mejía, "Del Frente Nacional," 406.

122. Mayor, "Historia de la industria," 362.

123. Bonilla, "Sexos y la publicidad," 75–91.

124. Uribe Celis, *Mentalidad,* 101–2.

125. Salazar and Jaramillo, *Medellín,* 12–15.

126. Silvia Arango, *Historia,* 237.

127. Ibid., 238.

Epilogue: The Passing of the Centenarians

1. López de Mesa, *Crónica,* 157.

2. *El Siglo,* December 27, 1957.

3. Noguera Mendoza, *Aproximación a Alfonso López,* 460.

4. Mario Laserna, interview by author, Bogotá, April 17, 1994.

5. Deas, "Laureano Gómez."

Bibliography

Abadía Méndez, Miguel. *Discurso del doctor don Miguel Abadía al recibirse como individuo de número en la sesión solemne del 6 de agosto de 1919*. Bogotá: Imprenta La Luz, 1919.

Abel, Christopher. "The Conservative Party in Colombia." Ph.D. thesis, Oxford University, 1974.

———. *Política, iglesia, y partidos en Colombia: 1886–1953*. Bogotá: FAES, Universidad Nacional de Colombia, 1987.

———. "Themes in the History of Public Health, Colombia since the 1940s." American Historical Association meeting, New York, December 28, 1991. Typescript.

Abel, Christopher, and Marco Palacios. "Colombia, 1930–1958." In *The Cambridge History of Latin America*. Vol. 8., *Latin America since 1930: Spanish South America,* ed. Leslie Bethell, 132–92. New York: Cambridge University Press, 1991.

Abella, Arturo. "Como se frustran las memorias de Laureano Gómez." *El Tiempo,* October 27, 1985.

Agudelo Ramírez, Luis E., and Rafael Montoya y Montoya. *Los guerrilleros intelectuales, cartas, documentos, e informaciones que prohibió la censura*. Medellín: Editorial Bedout, 1957.

Alape, Arturo. *Diario de un guerrillero*. 3d ed. Bogotá: Ecoe Editor, 1978.

———. *El bogotazo: Memorias del olvido*. 3d ed. Bogotá: Editorial Pluma, 1984.

———, ed. *La paz, la violencia: Testigos de excepción*. 3d ed. Bogotá: Editorial Planeta, 1987.

Alba, J. Tito. *Vida, confesión, y muerte de Efraín González*. 2d ed. Bogotá: Tipografía Bermúdez, 1971.

Alvarez García, John, ed. *Camilo Torres: Biografía, plataforma, mensajes*. Medellín: Ediciones Carpell-Antorcha, 1966.

Alvarez Restrepo, Antonio. *Testimonio de un hijo del siglo*. Bogotá: Ediciones Fundo Cultural Cafetero, 1992.

Alzate Avendaño, Gilberto. *Obras selectas*. Bogotá: Imprenta Nacional, 1979.

Angel Echeverri, Heliodoro. "Las industrias." In *El liberalismo en el poder,* 3 vols., ed. Plinio Mendoza Neira, 2:195–230. Bogotá: Editorial Minerva, 1946.

Anisur Rahman, Mohammed, and Orlando Fals Borda. "Romper el monopolio del conocimiento: Situación actual y perspectivas de la Investigación-Acción Participativa en el Mundo." *Análisis político* (Universidad Nacional de Colombia, Bogotá) 5 (September 1988): 44–55.

Aprile Gniset, Jacques. *El impacto del nueve de abril sobre el centro de Bogotá*. Bogotá: Centro Cultural Jorge Eliécer Gaitán, 1983.

Arango, Gonzalo. *Fuego en el altar.* Barcelona: Plaza y Janes, 1974.

Arango, Silvia. *Historia de la arquitectura en Colombia.* Bogotá: Universidad Nacional de Colombia, 1989.

Arango Z., Carlos, ed. *FARC, veinte años: De Marquetalia a la Uribe.* Bogotá: Ediciones Aurora, 1984.

Arboleda, Gustavo. *Diccionario biográfico y genealógico del antiguo departamento del Cauca.* 2d ed. Bogotá: Librería Horizontes, 1962.

Archer, Ronald P. "The Transition from Traditional to Broker Clientelism in Colombia: Political Stability and Social Unrest." Paper presented at the annual meeting of the Latin American Studies Association, Miami, 1989.

Archila, Mauricio. "La clase obrera colombiana, 1886–1930." In *Nueva Historia de Colombia,* 6 vols., ed. Alvaro Tirado Mejía, 3:219–44. Bogotá: Editorial Planeta, 1989.

———. "La clase obrera colombiana, 1930–1945." In *Nueva Historia de Colombia.* 6 vols., ed. Alvaro Tirado Mejía, 3:245–70. Bogotá: Editorial Planeta, 1989.

———. *Cultura e identidad obrera: Colombia 1910–1945.* Bogotá: Ediciones Antropos, 1991.

———. "¿De la revolución social a la conciliación? Algunas hipótesis sobre la transformación de la clase obrera colombiana, 1919–1935." *Anuario colombiano de historia social y de la cultura* (Bogotá) 12 (1984): 51–102.

———. "*La Humanidad,* el periódico obrero de los años veinte." *Boletín cultural y bibliográfico* (Banco de la República, Bogotá) 12:3 (1985): 19–33.

———. "La memoria histórica de los trabajadores de Medellín y Bogotá, Colombia, 1910–1945." Paper presented at the annual meeting of the Latin American Studies Association, Miami, 1989.

———. "Los obreros colombianos y la violencia, 1946–1958: ¿Infierno o paraíso?" Department of History, Universidad Nacional de Colombia, 1992. Typescript.

Arciniegas, Germán. *Proceso de Pericles Carnaval y Neira.* Bogotá: Editorial "Patria," 1926.

Arenas, Jacobo. *Cese el fuego: Una historia política de las FARC.* Bogotá: Editorial Oveja Negra, 1985.

———. *Diario de la resistencia de Marquetalia.* 2d ed. Bogotá: Ediciones Abejón, 1972.

Arenas, Jaime. *La guerrilla por dentro: Análisis del ELN colombiano.* Bogotá: Tercer Mundo, 1971.

Arguedas, Alcides. *La danza de las sombras.* In *Obras selectas,* ed. Luis Alberto Sánchez. 2 vols. Mexico City: Aguilar, 1959.

Arizmendi Posada, Ignacio. *Gobernantes colombianos, 1819–1980.* Medellín: Editorial Albón, 1980.

———. *Presidentes de Colombia, 1810–1990.* Bogotá: Editorial Planeta, 1989.

Arrubla, Mario. *Estudios sobre el subdesarrollo colombiano.* 7th ed. Medellín: Editorial la Carreta, 1974.

Arrubla, Mario, Jesús Antonio Bejarano, J. G. Cobo Borda, Jaime Jaramillo Uribe, Salomón Kalmanovitz, Jorge Orlando Melo, Alvaro Tirado Mejía, eds. *Colombia hoy.* 6th ed. Bogotá: Siglo Veintiuno, 1980.

Ayala Diago, César Augusto. "El discurso de la conciliación: Análisis cuantitativo de las intervenciones de Gustavo Rojas Pinilla entre 1952 y 1959." *Anuario colombiano de historia social y de la cultura* (Universidad Nacional de Colombia, Bogotá) 18–19 (1990–91): 205–44.

———. "Los orígines del anapismo como variante colombiana del populismo, 1959–1965." In *Ensayos sobre cultura política colombiana,* comp. Fabio López de la Roche. Bogotá: CINEP, 1990.

Azula Barrera, Rafael. *De la revolución al orden nuevo.* Bogotá: Editorial Kelly, 1956.

Bagley, Bruce M. "Political Power, Public Policy, and the State in Colombia." Ph.D. thesis, University of California, Los Angeles, 1979.

Banco de la República. *El Banco de la República: Antecedentes, evolución, y estructura.* Bogotá: Banco de la República, 1990.

Baquero, Rafael. "Un plan de colonización imperialista." In *Colombia, estructura política y agraria,* ed. Gonzalo Cataño, 110–35. Bogotá: Oveja Negra, 1976.

Barnhart, Donald S. "Colombian Transport and the Reforms of 1931: An Evaluation." *Hispanic American Historical Review* (Duke University Press, Durham) 38:2 (1958): 1–24.

Bautista Olaya, Darío. *El personaje y los hechos: Testimonio de un reportero.* Bogotá: Editorial Andes, 1984.

Bayer, Tulio. *Carretera al mar.* Bogotá: Editorial Iqueima, 1960.

Beaulac, Willard L. *Career Ambassador.* New York: Macmillan, 1951.

Becera, Alvaro Salom. *Un ocasio en el cenit: Gilberto Alzate Avendaño.* Bogotá: Tercer Mundo, 1985.

Bedel, Mauricio [pseud.]. *Bengalí.* Bogotá: Editorial Santafé, 1939.

Bedoya Cardona, Ernesto. *De desterrado a presidente.* Medellín: Gráficos Estilo, 1950.

Bejarano Avila, Jesús Antonio. *Economía y poder: La SAC y el desarrollo agropecuario colombiano, 1871–1984.* Bogotá: Fondo Editorial CEREC, 1985.

———. *El régimen agrario de la economía exportadora a la economía industrial.* Bogotá: La Carreta, 1979.

———. "La economía." In *Manual de historia de Colombia,* 3 vols., ed. Jaime Jaramillo Uribe, 3:17–79. Bogotá: Instituto Colombiano de Cultura, 1980.

———. "La economía colombiana entre 1922 y 1929." In *Nueva Historia de Colombia.* 6 vols., ed. Alvaro Tirado Mejía, 5:51–114. Bogotá: Editorial Planeta, 1989.

———. "La economía entre 1930 y 1945." In *Nueva Historia de Colombia.* 6 vols., ed. Alvaro Tirado Mejía, 5:115–48. Bogotá: Editorial Planeta, 1989.

———. "La economía entre 1946 y 1958." In *Nueva Historia de Colombia.* 6 vols., ed. Alvaro Tirado Mejía, 5:149–66. Bogotá: Editorial Planeta, 1989.

———. "Las técnicas agropecuarias en el siglo veinte." In *Nueva Historia de Colombia,* 6 vols., ed. Alvaro Tirado Mejía, 4:285–314. Bogotá: Editorial Planeta, 1989.

Berger, Peter, Brigitte Berger, and Hansfried Kellner. *The Homeless Mind. Modernization and Consciousness.* New York: Vintage, 1974.

Bergquist, Charles W. *Coffee and Conflict in Colombia, 1886–1910.* Durham: Duke University Press, 1978.

———. "Luchas del campesinado cafetero, 1930–1946." In *Nueva Historia de Colombia,* 6 vols., ed. Alvaro Tirado Mejía, 5:115–48. Bogotá: Editorial Planeta, 1989.

Bergquist, Charles, Gonzalo Sánchez, and Ricardo Peñaranda, eds. *Violence in Colombia: The Contemporary Crisis in Historical Perspective.* Wilmington, Del.: Scholarly Resources, 1991.

Berlin, Isaiah. "The Counter Enlightenment." In *Against the Current, Essays in the History of Ideas,* ed. Henry Hardy, 1–24. New York: Viking, 1980.

Bermúdez, Alberto. *El buen gobierno: Administración Laureano Gómez.* Bogotá: Editorial Italgraf, 1974.

————. *Historia de un pueblo rebelde: El Quindío de la conquista al departamento.* Armenia: Universidad del Quindío, 1992.

————. Interview by author. Bogotá, June 10, 1985.

Bermúdez Rossi, Gonzalo. *El poder militar en Colombia: De la colonia al Frente Nacional.* Bogotá: Editorial Americana Latina, 1982.

Bernal, Rodolfo D. *Libro de lecturas escogidas.* Bogotá: Imprenta Nacional, 1897.

Bernal Jiménez, Rafael. *La cuestion social y la lucha de clases.* Bogotá: Editorial Centro, 1940.

————. *Hacia una democracía orgánica.* Madrid: Afrodisio Aguado, 1951.

Berry, Albert, and Miguel Urrutia. *Income Distribution in Colombia.* New Haven: Yale University Press, 1976.

Betancourt E., Darío. "De los 'pájaros' a las cuadrillas liberales del norte del Valle." Paper presented at the Quinto Congreso de Historia de Colombia, Armenia, 1985.

Betancourt E., Darío, and Martha L. García. *Matones y cuadrilleros: Origen y evolución de la violencia en el occidente colombiano, 1946–1965.* Bogotá: Tercer Mundo, 1990.

Betancur Cuartas, Belisario. Interview by author. Bogotá, July 2, 1985.

Biddiss, Michael D. *Father of Racist Ideology: The Social and Political Thought of Count Gobineau.* London: Weidenfeld and Nicolson, 1970.

Blandón Berrío, Fidel [Ernesto León Herrera]. *Lo que el cielo no perdona: Novela histórica.* 2d ed. Bogotá: Editorial ARGRA, 1954.

Bonilla de Ramos, Elssy. "Los sexos y la publicidad: El caso de la televisión colombiana." *Desarrollo y sociedad* (CEDE, Universidad de los Andes) 11 (May 1983): 75–91.

Botero Gómez, Fabio. "Las vías de comunicación y el transporte." In *Historia de Antioquia,* ed. Jorge Orlando Melo, 286–98. Medellín: Editorial Presencia, 1988.

Botero Montoya, Mauricio. *El MRL.* Bogotá: Universidad Central, 1990.

Braudel, Fernand. *Afterthoughts on Material Civilization and Capitalism.* Baltimore: Johns Hopkins University Press, 1977.

Braun, Herbert. *The Assassination of Gaitán: Public Life and Urban Violence in Colombia.* Madison: University of Wisconsin Press, 1985.

Briceño, Manuel. *La revolución, 1876–1877: Recuerdos para la historia.* 2d ed. Biblioteca de Historia Nacional, no. 77. Bogotá: Imprenta Nacional, 1947.

Broderick, Walter J. *Camilo Torres: A Biography of the Priest-Guerrillero.* New York: Doubleday, 1975.

Buenahora, Gonzalo. *Biografía de una voluntad.* Bogotá: Editorial ABC, 1948.

Burnett, Ben G. "The Recent Colombian Party System: Its Organization and Procedure." Ph.D. dissertation, University of California, Los Angeles, 1955.

Bushnell, David. *Colombia: A Nation in Spite of Itself.* Berkeley: University of California Press, 1993.

————. *Eduardo Santos and the Good Neighbor, 1938–1942.* Gainesville: University of Florida Press, 1967.

Caballero Argaez, Carlos. *Cincuenta años de economía: De la crísis del Treinta a la del Ochenta.* Bogotá: Editorial Presencia, 1987.

Caballero Calderón, Eduardo. *El cristo de espaldas.* Vol. 3 of *Obras.* Medellín: Editorial Bedout, 1964.

————. *Memorias infantiles, 1916–1924.* Medellín: Editorial Bedout, 1964.

————. *Obras.* 3 vols. Medellín: Editorial Bedout, 1964.

Caballero Calderón, Eduardo, Enrique Caballero Escovar, and Lucas Caballero. *Rabo de paja: Por el liberalismo y contra Castro.* 2d ed. Bogotá: Editorial Iqueima, 1962.

Caballero Calderón, Lucas. *Figuras Políticas de Colombia.* Bogotá: Editorial Kelly, 1945.

Caballero Escovar, Enrique. *El Mesías de Handel.* Medellín: Ediciones Hombre Nuevo, 1982.

Cacua Prada, Antonio. *Si viviera Laureano.* Bogotá: Editorial Kelly, 1989.

Cadavid G., J. Iván. *Los fueros de la Iglesia ante el liberalismo y el conservatismo en Colombia.* Medellín: Editorial Bedout, 1955.

Caicedo, Edgar. *Conflictos sociales del siglo veinte en Colombia.* Bogotá: Editores Colombia, 1976.

Calderón Schrader, Camilo, ed. *Cinquenta años: Salón Nacional de Artistas.* Bogotá: Colcultura, 1990.

Camacho Carreño, José. *El leopardo mártir: Memoria de una tragedia nacional inconmensurable.* Bogotá: Editorial Romero, n.d.

———. *El ultimo leopardo: Capitulos de la República Liberal que no se le olvidaron a un conservador.* Bogotá: Mundo al Dia, 1935.

Camacho Roldán, Salvador. *Artículos escogidos.* Bogotá: Librería Colombiana, n.d.

Canal Ramírez, Gonzalo. *Estampas y testimonios de violencia.* Bogotá: Canal Ramírez, 1966.

———. *Nueve de abril, 1948.* Bogotá: Litografía y Editorial Cahur, 1948.

Carbonell, Abel. *La quincena politica.* 6 vols. Bogotá: Imprenta Nacional, 1952.

Carnicelli, Américo. *La Masonería en la independencia de América.* 2 vols. Bogotá: Artes Gráficas, 1970.

Caro, Miguel Antonio. *Discursos y otras intervenciones en el Senado de la República, 1903–1904.* Edited by Carlos Valderrama Andrade. Bogotá: Instituto Caro y Cuervo, 1979.

Carrasquilla, Rafael M. *Ensayo sobre la doctrina liberal.* 3d ed. Bogotá: Imprenta de Luis M. Holguín, 1899.

Casas, Nicolás. *Enseñanzas de la iglesia sobre el liberalismo.* Bogotá: Tipografía Salesiana, 1901.

———. *Instrucciones del ilustrísimo señor obispo de Pasto al clero de su diócesis, sobre la conducta que ha de observar con los liberales en el púlpito y en algunas cuestiones de confesionario.* Pasto, 1902.

Castillo, José Vicente. *De Colombia a Berlín.* Bogotá: Camacho Roldán, 1983.

Castrillón, Alberto. *Ciento veinte días bajo el terror militar.* Bogotá: Editorial Tupac-Amaru, 1974.

Castrillón Arboleda, Diego. *El indio Quintín Lame.* Bogotá: Tercer Mundo, 1973.

Cayzedo, Manuel José. *El combate por la Fe y por la Iglesia.* Medellín: Tipografía Bedout, 1931.

Cepeda Ulloa, Fernando, and Rodrigo Pardo García-Peña. "La política exterior colombiana, 1946–1974." In *Nueva Historia de Colombia,* 6 vols., ed. Alvaro Tirado Mejía, 3:29–54. Bogotá: Editorial Planeta, 1989.

Charria Tobar, Ricardo. *La República de Santos.* Bogotá: Editorial Santafé, 1939.

Charry Lara, Alberto. *Desarrollo histórico de la estadística nacional en Colombia.* Bogotá: Imprenta Nacional, 1954.

Child, Jorge. *López y el pensamiento liberal.* Bogotá: Tercer Mundo, 1974.

Christie, Keith H. *Colombia.* Hong Kong: Continental Printing, 1975.

————. *Oligarcas, campesinos, y política en Colombia: Aspectos de la historia socio-política de la frontera antioqueña.* Bogotá: Universidad Nacional de Colombia, 1986.

Chu, David S. "The Great Depression and Industrialization in Colombia." Santa Monica, Calif.: Rand Corporation, 1977.

Colmenares, Germán. "Ospina y Abadía: La política en el decenio de los veinte." In *Nueva Historia de Colombia,* 6 vols., ed. Alvaro Tirado Mejía, 1:243–68.

————. *Partidos políticos y clases sociales en Colombia.* Bogotá: Universidad de los Andes, 1964.

————. *Ricardo Rendón, una fuente para la historia de la opinión pública.* Bogotá: Fondo Cultural Cafetero, 1984.

Colombia. Banco de la República. *Cuentas nacionales.* Bogotá: Banco de la República, 1961–64.

————. Cámara de Representantes. *Anales de la Cámara de Representantes.* Bogotá, 1913.

————. Cámara de Representantes. *Por qué y cómo se forjó el Frente Nacional.* Bogotá: Imprenta Nacional, 1959.

————. Concejo Nacional de Política Económica y Planeación y Servicios Técnicos. *Colombia. Plan general de desarrollo económico y social.* 2 vols. Bogotá: Departamento Administrativo de Planeación, 1961–62.

————. Congreso. *Constitución política de la República de Colombia.* Bogotá: Imprenta Nacional, 1945.

————. DANE. *Colombia: Plan general de desarrollo económico y social.* 2 vols. Bogotá: Departamento Administrativo Nacional de Estadística, 1961–62.

————. Departamento Administrativo Nacional de Estadística. *Boletín* 1 (October 25, 1951).

————. Ministerio de Gobierno. *Estudios constitucionales.* 2 vols. Bogotá: Imprenta Nacional, 1952.

————. Ministerio de Obras Públicas. *Memoria.* Bogotá, 1926.

————. Ministerio de Relaciones Exteriores. *Legajo de Argentina.* Bogotá, 1923–31.

————. Ministerio de Relaciones Exteriores. *Legajo de Alemania.* Bogotá, 1929–36.

————. Presidencia. *Un año de gobierno.* 2 vols. Bogotá: Imprenta Nacional, 1951.

————. Presidencia. *El Diez de febrero.* New York: Imprenta Hispano-Americana, 1908(?).

————. Presidencia. *Dos cartas.* Bogotá: Imprenta Nacional, 1950.

————. Presidencia. *La oposición y el gobierno: Del 9 de abril 1948 al 9 de abril 1950.* Bogotá: Imprenta Nacional, 1950.

————. Senado. *El proceso contra Gustavo Rojas Pinilla ante el Congreso de Colombia.* Bogotá: Imprenta Nacional, 1960.

Communist Party of Colombia. *Treinta años de lucha del Partido comunista de Colombia.* Bogotá: Ediciones Paz y Socialismo, 1960.

Congrains Martín, Enrique, ed. *Las maravillas de Colombia: Sorprendentes y poco conocidas.* 4 vols. Bogotá: Editorial Forja, 1979.

Congreso Eucarístico Nacional de Colombia. *Primer Congreso Eucarístico Nacional de Colombia.* Bogotá: Escuela Tipográfica Salesiana, 1914.

Conservative Party of Colombia. *Los programas del conservatismo.* Bogotá: Directora Nacional Conservador, 1967.

————. Directorio Conservador de Cundinamarca. *Oro y escoria.* Bogotá: Ediciones LV, 1958.

Correa, Ramón C., ed. *Diccionario de boyacenses ilustres.* Tunja: Academia Boyacense de Historia, 1957.

Cruz Santos, Abel. "La administración de Reyes." *Boletín Cultural y Bibliográfico* (Banco de la República, Bogotá) 7:10, 1778–98.

Cuellar Vargas, Enrique. *Trece años de Violencia: Asesinos intelectuales de Gaitán, dictaduras, militarismo, alternación.* Bogotá: Ediciones Cultura Social Colombiana, 1960.

Currie, Lauchlin. *Accelerating Development: The Necessity and the Means.* New York: McGraw-Hill, 1966.

Curtis, William Elroy. *The Capitals of Spanish America.* New York: Harper and Brothers, 1888.

Dangond Uribe, Alberto. *Hacia una nueva política: Memorias de un iluso.* Bogotá: Plaza and Janes, 1977.

Daniel, James M. *Rural Violence in Colombia since 1946.* Princeton, N.J.: Princeton University Press, 1965.

Davis, Roger P. *Bogotá and the Athens of the Americas: Coincident Cultures in Nineteenth Century Colombia.* Tempe, Arizona: Center for Latin American Studies, 1977.

Deas, Malcolm. "Algunas notas sobre la historia del caciquismo en Colombia." *Revista de Historia* (Bogotá) 2:1 (May 1974): 29–44.

————. "Colombia, Ecuador, and Venezuela." In *The Cambridge History of Latin America,* vol. 5, ed. Leslie Bethell, 641–84. New York: Cambridge University Press, 1986.

————. "Laureano Gómez." Typescript, Bogotá, July 30, 1965.

————, ed. *Latin America in Perspective.* Boston: Houghton Mifflin, 1991.

de Guzmán, Ignacio. *El Hombre frente al estado.* Bogotá: Editorial Antena, 1940.

de la Pedraja Toman, René. *Historia de la energía en Colombia, 1537–1930.* Bogotá: El Ancora Editores, 1985.

de la Vega, José. *El buen vecino.* Bogotá: Libreria Voluntad, 1941.

Delpar, Helen. *Red against Blue: The Liberal Party in Colombian Politics, 1863–1899.* University: University of Alabama Press, 1981.

Díaz, Carlos Arturo. *Páginas de historia colombiana.* Bucaramanga: Imprenta del Departamento, 1967.

Dix, Robert H. *Colombia: The Political Dimensions of Change.* New Haven: Yale University Press, 1967.

Dixon, Roger, and Stefan Muthesius. *Victorian Architecture.* New York: Oxford University Press, 1978.

Drake, Paul. *The Money Doctor in the Andes: The Kemmerer Missions, 1923–1933.* Durham, N.C.: Duke University Press, 1989.

Duff, Ernest A. *Agrarian Reform in Colombia.* New York: Praeger, 1968.

Dugand, Victor. *Entre Conservadores.* Barranquilla: Editorial America Española, 1941.

Echandía, Darío. *Obras selectas.* 5 vols. Bogotá: Banco de la República, 1981.

Echavarría Olózaga, Felipe, ed. *Historia de una monstruosa farsa: Selección de documentos y escritos tomados de "el proceso del gobierno del 13 de junio contra F. Echavarría."* Madrid: Blas Tipográfica, 1964.

Echavarría Uribe, Juan Fernando. "Bancos y finanzas en el siglo veinte." In *Historia de Antioquia,* ed. Jorge Orlando Melo, 257–66. Medellín: Editorial Presencia, 1988.

Echeverri Uruburu, Alvaro. *Elites y proceso político en Colombia, 1950–1978.* Bogotá: Fundación Universitaria Autónoma de Colombia, 1987.

Editorial Salvat. *Historia del arte colombiano.* Bogotá: Editorial Salvat, 1975.

Editorial Selesiana. *Conferencias episcopales,* 2 vols. Bogotá: Editorial Selesiana, 1953.

Emiliani Román, Raimundo. *Laureano el grande.* Bogotá: Italgraf, 1989.

Escobar, Eduardo, ed. *Gonzalo Arango: Correspondencia violada.* Bogotá: Colcultura, 1980.

Escobar Camargo, Antonio. *En el Salón de los virreyes: Testimonio civil de un golpe militar.* Bogotá: Editorial Kelly, 1957.

Escobar Sierra, Hugo. Interview by author. Bogotá, June 24, July 26, 1986.

Espinosa Valderrama, Augusto. *Escritos políticos y económicos.* Bogotá: Contraloría General de la República, 1986.

Estrada, Efraín. *Sucesos colombianos, 1925–1950.* Medellín: Universidad de Antioquia, 1990.

Estrada Monsalve, Joaquín. *Núñez: El político y el hombre.* Bogotá: Siglo Veinte, 1946.

Fajardo M., Darío. *Haciendas, campesinos, y políticas agrarias en Colombia, 1920–1980.* Bogotá: Oveja Negra, 1983.

———. *Violencia y desarrollo, transformaciones sociales en tres regiones cafetaleras del Tolima, 1936–1970.* Bogotá: Fondo Editorial Suramericana, 1979.

Fals Borda, Orlando. *La subversión en Colombia: Visión del cambio social en la historia.* Bogotá: Tercer Mundo, 1967.

———. *La teoría y la realidad del cambio sociocultural en Colombia.* Bogotá: Universidad Nacional de Colombia, n.d.

———. "The Negation of Sociology and Its Promise: Perspectives of Social Science in Latin America Today." *Latin American Research Review* 15:1 (1980): 161–66.

Farrell, Robert Vincent. "The Catholic Church and Colombian Education, 1886–1930: In Search of a Tradition." Ph.D. dissertation, Columbia University, 1974.

Farson, Negley. *Transgressor in the Tropics.* New York: Harcourt, Brace, 1938.

Fernández de Soto, Abraham. *¿Quién llamó la policía?* Bogotá: Editorial Minerva, 1954.

Fernández de Soto, Mario. *Ideología política.* Paris: Editorial Excelsior, 1926.

Ferrero, Guglielmo. *El genio latino y el mundo moderno.* Santiago, Chile: Editorial Mundo Nuevo, 1937.

Flórez, Carmen Elisa. *La transición demográfica en Colombia.* Bogotá: Tercer Mundo, 1990.

Fluharty, Vernon Lee. *Dance of the Millions. Military Rule and the Social Revolution in Colombia, 1930–1956.* Pittsburgh: University of Pittsburgh Press, 1957.

Fonnegra Sierra, Guillermo. *El parlamento colombiano.* Bogotá: Gráficos Centauro, 1953.

Forero Benavides, Abelardo. *Grandes fechas.* Bogotá: DANE, 1979.

Franco Isaza, Eduardo. *Las guerrillas del llano.* Bogotá: Librería Mundial, 1959.

Fremantle, Ann. *The Papal Encyclicals in Their Historical Context.* New York: Putnam, 1956.

Gaitán, Jorge Eliécer. *Los mejores discursos de Gaitán.* 2d ed. Bogotá: Editorial Jorvi, 1968.

Bibliography | 467

Gaitán Durán, Jorge. *La revolución invisible: Apuntes sobre la crisis y el desarrollo de Colombia.* Bogotá: Antares, 1959.

Galindo, Alberto. "La República Liberal." In *El Liberalismo en el gobierno,* 3 vols., ed. Plinio Mendoza Neira, 1:62–100. Bogotá: Editorial Prag, 1946.

Gallón Giraldo, Gustavo, comp. *Entre movimientos y cuadillos: Cincuenta años de bipartidismo, izquierda, y alternativas populares en Colombia.* Bogotá: CINEP, 1989.

Galvis, Silvia, and Alberto Donadio. *El Jefe Supremo: Rojas Pinilla en la Violencia y el poder.* Bogotá: Editorial Planeta, 1988.

Galvis Galvis, Alejandro. *Memorias de un político centenarista.* 2 vols. Bucaramanga, 1975.

Galvis Gómez, Carlos. *Porqué cayó López.* Bogotá: Editorial ABC, 1946.

Galvis Salazar, Fernando. *Don Marco Fidel Suárez.* Bogotá: Editorial Kelly, 1974.

García, Antonio. *Gaitán y el problema de la revolución colombiana.* Bogotá: Cooperativa de Artes Gráficas, 1955.

———. *Hacia una teoría latinoamericana de las ciencias sociales del desarrollo.* Tunja: Publicaciones de la Universidad Pedagógica y Tecnológica de Colombia, 1972.

García, José Bernardo. *La explosión de mayo.* Cali: Imprenta Departamental, 1957.

García Cadena, Alfredo. *Unas ideas elementales sobre problemas colombianos.* Bogotá: Banco de la República, 1956.

García Márquez, Gabriel. *El coronel no tiene quien le escriba.* Buenos Aires: Editorial Sudamericana, 1972.

García Ortiz, Laureano. *Conversando.* Bogotá: Editorial Kelly, 1966.

———. *Estudios históricos y fisonomías colombianas.* Bogotá: Editorial ABC, 1939.

García Samudio, Nicolás. "La división departamental." *Boletín de Historia y Antigüedades* (Academia de Historia, Bogotá) 20:227 (February 1933): 1–14.

Gartner de la Cuesta, Jorge. *Mis memorias, o, Devaneos inútiles de un desocupado.* Manizales: Imprenta Departamental de Caldas, 1991.

Gilhodes, Pierre. "La cuestión agraria en Colombia, 1958–1985." In *Nueva Historia de Colombia,* 6 vols., ed. Alvaro Tirado Mejía, 3:339–70. Bogotá: Editorial Planeta, 1989.

———. "La cuestión agraria en Colombia, 1900–1946." In *Nueva Historia de Colombia,* 6 vols., ed. Alvaro Tirado Mejía, 3:307–38. Bogotá: Editorial Planeta, 1989.

Giraldo Londoño, Pedronel. *Don Fernando: Juicio sobre un hombre y una época.* Medellín: Editorial Granamerica, 1963.

Gómez, Eugenio J. *Problemas colombianos.* Vol. 2 of *Comunismo, socialismo, liberalismo.* Bogotá: Tipografía "Colón," 1942.

Gómez, Laureano. "Bodas de Plata." In *Recuerdo de las bodas de plata del Colegio Nacional de San Bartolomé.* Bogotá: Imprenta Eléctrica, 1910, 59–63.

———. *Comentarios a un régimen.* 3d ed. Bogotá: Editorial Minerva, 1934.

———. *El cuadrilátero.* 4th ed. Bogotá: Editorial Centro, 1935.

———. "Decadencia y grandeza España." *Revista colombiana* 9:105 (February 1, 1938): 257–63.

———. *Desde el exilio.* Bogotá: n.p., 1954.

———. *Los efectos de la Reforma de 1953.* Bogotá: Imprenta Nacional, 1953.

———. "La opresión del mundo moderno." In *Obras selectas.* ed. Bermúdez, 1:808–13.

———. *Interrogantes sobre el progreso de Colombia.* Bogotá: Populibro, 1970.

————. *El Mito de Santander.* 2 vols. 2d ed. Bogotá: Populibro, 1966.

————. *Obras completas.* 6 vols. Edited by Ricardo Ruiz Santos. Bogotá: Instituto Caro y Cuervo, 1984–89.

————. *Obra selecta, 1909–1956.* Bogotá: Imprenta Nacional, 1982.

————. *Obras selectas.* 2 vols. Edited by Alberto Bermúdez. Bogotá: Imprenta Nacional, 1981–89.

Gómez, Laureano, Eliseo Arango, Rafael Bernal Jiménez, Pedro María Carreño, Emilio Ferro, Esteban Jaramillo, Jesús Marulanda, Augusto Ramírez Moreno, José Domingo Rojas, and Oscar Terán. *La Constitución de 1886 y las reformas proyectadas por la República Liberal: Discursos, conferencias, y otros documentos.* Bogotá: Editorial Centro, 1936.

Gómez Botero, Alberto. Interviews by author. El Líbano, Tolima, March 4, 1971; August 9, 1973; July 11, 1974.

Gómez Hurtado, Alvaro. Interview by author. Washington, D.C., April 15–18, 1984.

Gómez Jurado, G. Luis. *Conflicto colombo-peruano.* Pasto: Javier Editores, 1981.

Gómez Martínez, Fernando. *Mordaza: Diario secreto de un escritor público, 1955–1957.* Medellín: Editorial El Colombiano, 1958.

Gómez Picón, Rafael. *Estampillas de timbre parroquial.* Bogotá: Editorial Renacimiento, 1936.

González, Fernán. *Educación y estado en la historia colombiana.* Bogotá: Centro de Investigación y Educación Popular, 1978.

————. "Iglesia católica y el estado colombiano, 1930–1985." In *Nueva Historia de Colombia,* 6 vols., ed. Alvaro Tirado Mejía, 2:271–396. Bogotá: Editorial Planeta, 1989.

González, Fernando. *Los negroides.* 4th ed. Medellín: Editorial Bedout, 1976.

González, José Jairo. *El estigma de las repúblicas independientes.* Bogotá: CINEP, 1993.

Guberik, Simón. *Yo vi crecer un país.* Bogotá: Tercer Mundo, 1974.

Guerra, José Joaquín. *Estudios históricos.* Biblioteca Popular de Cultura Colombiana. 4 vols. Bogotá: Editorial Kelly, 1952.

Guerrero, Javier. *Los años del olvido: Boyacá y los orígines de la Violencia.* Bogotá: Tercer Mundo, 1991.

Guillén Martínez, Fernando. *El poder político en Colombia.* Bogotá: Punta de Lanza, 1979.

Gutiérrez, José. *De la pseudo-aristocracia a la autenticidad: Psicología social colombiana.* Bogotá: Tercer Mundo, 1966.

————. *La rebeldía colombiana.* Bogotá: Editorial Anteres, 1962.

Gutiérrez, Rufino. *Monografías.* Biblioteca de Historia Nacional, vols. 28, 30. Bogotá: Imprenta Nacional, 1921.

Gutiérrez Girardot, Rafael. "La literatura colombiana en el siglo veinte." In *Manual de historia de Colombia,* 3 vols., ed. Jaime Jaramillo Uribe, 3:447–536. Bogotá: Instituto Colombiano de Cultura, 1980.

Gutiérrez Navarro, Isaac. *La luz de una vida.* Bogotá: Editorial ABC, 1949.

Guzmán Campos, Germán. *La violencia en Colombia: Parte descriptiva.* Cali: Ediciones Progreso, 1968.

Guzmán Campos, Germán, Orlando Fals Borda, and Eduardo Umaña Luna. *La violencia en Colombia: Estudio de un proceso social.* 2 vols. Bogotá: Tercer Mundo, 1962–64.

Hale, Charles A. "Political and Social Ideas, 1870–1930." In *The Cambridge History of Latin America*, vol. 5, ed. Leslie Bethel, 367–441. New York: Cambridge University Press, 1986.

Harker Valdivieso, Roberto, ed. *Otros autores santanderianos*. Bucaramanga: Impresos FRID, 1989.

———. *Quenientos años de lágrimas: Borbollones de sangre en Santander*. Bucaramanga: n.p., 1992.

Hartlyn, Jonathan. "Colombia: The Politics of Violence and Accommodation." In *Democracy in Developing Countries*, ed. Larry Diamond, 290–334. Boulder: Lynne Rienner, 1989.

———. *The Politics of Coalition Rule in Colombia*. New York: Cambridge University Press, 1988.

Hartwig, Richard E. *Roads to Reason: Transportation, Administration, and Rationality in Colombia*. Pittsburgh: University of Pittsburgh Press, 1983.

Helg, Aline. *Civiliser le peuple et former les élites: L'éducation en Colombie, 1918–1957*. Paris: Editions L'Harmattan, 1984.

———. "La educación en Colombia, 1946–1957." In *Nueva Historia de Colombia*, 6 vols., ed. Alvaro Tirado Mejía, 4:111–34. Bogotá: Editorial Planeta, 1989.

Helguera, J. León. "The Eighteenth and Nineteenth Century Ospinas." Paper presented at the annual meeting of the American Historical Association, New York, 1989.

Helguera, J. León, and Jo Ann Rayfield. "Adolfo León Gómez, 1858–1927: Colombian Literateur, Social Critic, and Nationalist." *SECOLAS Annals* 22 (March 1991): 5–16.

Henao, Jesús María, and Gerardo Arrubla. *Compendio de la historia de Colombia*. Bogotá: Editorial Voluntad, 1963.

Henao Ospina, Evelio. *Gilberto Alzate Avendaño, un hombre de carácter*. Armenia: Editorial Meridiano del Quindío, 1984.

Henderson, James D. *Conservative Thought in Twentieth-Century Latin America: The Ideas of Laureano Gómez*. Athens: Ohio University Press, 1988.

———. *Cuando Colombia de desangró: Una historia de la Violencia en metrópoli y provincia*. Bogotá: El Ancora, 1984.

———. "Latin American Conservative Parties." In *Encyclopedia of Latin American History*, ed. Barbara A. Tenenbaum. New York: Scribners, 1992.

———. *When Colombia Bled: A History of the Violencia in Tolima*. Tuscaloosa: University of Alabama Press, 1985.

Herrera, Martha, and Carlos Low. "La Escuela Normal Superior y la enseñanza de las ciencias sociales en Colombia." *Educación y Cultura* 11:61–65 (April 1987).

Herrera, Martha, Carlos Low, and Hernán Suárez. "Formar docentes con buen criterio." *Educación y Cultura* (Instituto Pedagógica Nacional, Bogotá) 7:20–26 (April 1986): 20–26.

Herrera Soto, Roberto. *La zona bananera del Magdalena*. Bogotá: Instituto Caro y Cuervo, 1979.

Hettner, Alfred. *Viajes por los andes colombianos*. Bogotá: Banco de la República, 1976.

Hilarión S., Alfonso. *Balas de la ley*. Bogotá: Editorial Santafé, 1953.

Hirschman, Albert O. *Journeys toward Progress: Studies of Economic Policy-Making in Latin America*. Garden City, N.Y.: Doubleday, 1965.

Hoenigsberg, Julio. *Las fronteras de los partidos en Colombia*. Bogotá: Editorial ABC, 1953.

Holguín, Jorge. *Desde cerca*. Paris: Librairie Génerale et Internationale, 1908.

Holguín Arboleda, Julio. *Mucho en serio y algo en broma*. Bogotá: Editorial Pio X, 1959.

Horgan, Terrence Burns. "The Liberals Come to Power, por debajo de la ruana: A Study of the Enrique Olaya Herrera Administration, 1930–1934." Ph.D. dissertation, Vanderbilt University, 1983.

Infante, Carlos J. *Dios y patria*. 2 vols. Bogotá: Editorial Minerva, 1938.

Ionescu, Ghiţa, and Ernest Gellner, eds. *Populism: Its Meaning and National Characteristics*. New York: Macmillan, 1969.

Iregüi, Antonio José. *Tercer conferencia*. Bogotá: Imprenta de la Crónica, 1898.

Iriarte, Alfredo. *Episodios bogotanos*. Bogotá: Editorial Oveja Negra, 1987.

Jaramillo, Carlos Eduardo. "Antecedentes generales de la guerra de los Mil Días y golpe de estado del 31 de julio de 1900." In *Nueva Historia de Colombia*, 6 vols., ed. Alvaro Tirado Mejía, 1:65–88. Bogotá: Editorial Planeta, 1989.

———. "La guerra de los Mil Días, 1899–1902." In *Nueva Historia de Colombia*, 1:89–112. Bogotá: Editorial Planeta, 1989.

Jaramillo, Estéban. *Memoria de hacienda, 1919, 1921, 1927, 1932, 1933, 1934*. Bogotá: Banco de la República, 1990.

Jaramillo Agudelo, Darío, comp. *La Nueva Historia de Colombia*. Bogotá: Colcultura, 1976.

Jaramillo Ocampo, Hernán. *1946–1950, de la unidad nacional a la hegémonia conservadora*. Bogotá: Editorial Pluma, 1980.

———. *Momentos estelares de la política colombiana*. Bogotá: Tercer Mundo, 1989.

Jaramillo Sierra, Bernardo. *Pepe Sierra: El método de un campesino millonario*. Medellín: Tipografía Bedout, 1947.

Jaramillo Uribe, Jaime, ed. *Manual de historia de Colombia*. 3 vols. Bogotá: Colcultura, 1978–80.

———. *El pensamiento colombiano en el siglo diecinueve*. Bogotá: Editorial Temis, 1964.

———. "El proceso de la educación del virreinato a la época contemporánea." In *Manual de historia de Colombia*, 3 vols., ed. Jaime Jaramillo Uribe, 3:249–342. Bogotá: Instituto Colombiano de Cultura, 1980.

Jeffreys-Jones, Rhodri. *The CIA and American Democracy*. New Haven: Yale University Press, 1989.

Jiménez, Michael F. "Class, Gender and Peasant Resistance in Central Colombia, 1900–1930." In *Everyday Forms of Peasant Resistance*, ed. Forrest D. Colburn, 122–50. New York: M. E. Sharp, 1989.

———. Interview by author. New York, December 30, 1989.

Jimeno Santoyo, Myriam. "Los procesos de colonización: Siglo veinte." In *Nueva Historia de Colombia*, 6 vols., ed. Alvaro Tirado Mejía, 3:371–95. Bogotá: Editorial Planeta, 1989.

Junguito, Roberto, and Diego Pizano, eds. *Producción de café en Colombia*. Bogotá: Ediciones Fondo Cultural Cafetero, 1991.

Kalmanovitz, Salomón. "Colombia: La industrialización a medias." *Cuadernos de Economía* (Universidad Nacional de Colombia, Bogotá) 9:12 (1988): 71–90.

———. *Economía y nación: Una breve historia de Colombia*. Bogotá: Siglo Veintiuno Editores, 1988.

Kesler, John C. "Spruille Braden as a Good Neighbor: The Latin American Policy of the United States, 1930–1947." Ph.D. dissertation, Kent State University, 1985.

Kurtz, Lester R. *The Politics of Heresy: The Modernist Crisis in Roman Catholicism.* Berkeley: University of California Press, 1986.

Lael, Richard. *Arrogant Diplomacy: U.S. Policy toward Colombia, 1903–1922.* Wilmington, Del.: Scholarly Resources, 1987.

Lame, Manuel Quintín. *Las luchas del indio que bajó de la montaña al valle de la "civilización."* Bogotá: Publicaciones de la Rosca, 1973.

Larteguy, Jean. *Los guerrilleros.* Barcelona: n.p., 1970.

Laserna, Mario. Interview by author. Bogotá, April 17, 1994.

Latorre Cabral, Hugo. *Dos reportajes de Alfonso López.* Bogotá: Editorial El Liberal, 1945.

———. *Mi novela: Apuntes autobiográficos de Alfonso López.* Bogotá: Editorial Mito, 1952.

Latorre Rueda, Mario. "1930–1934: Olaya Herrera: Un nuevo régimen." In *Nueva Historia de Colombia,* 6 vols., ed. Alvaro Tirado Mejía, 1:269–97. Bogotá: Editorial Planeta, 1989.

Leal Buitrago, Francisco. "La frustración política de una generación: La universidad colombiana y la formación de un movimiento estudiantil, 1958–1967." *Desarrollo y Sociedad* (CEDE, Universidad de los Andes, Bogotá) 6 (July 1981): 297–326.

———. "Surgimiento, auge, y crisis de la doctrina de seguridad nacional en América Latina y Colombia." *Análisis político* (Tercer Mundo, Bogotá) 15 (January-April 1992): 6–34.

Le Bot, Yvon. *Educación e ideología en Colombia.* 2d ed. Bogotá: La Carreta, 1985.

Lebret, Louis Joseph. *Estudio sobre las condiciones del desarrollo de Colombia.* Bogotá: Imprenta Nacional, 1958.

LeGrand, Catherine. "El Conflicto de las bananeros." In *Nueva Historia de Colombia,* 6 vols., ed. Alvaro Tirado Mejía, 3:183–218. Bogotá: Editorial Planeta, 1989.

———. *Frontier Expansion and Peasant Protest in Colombia, 1850–1936.* Albuquerque: University of New Mexico Press, 1986.

Lemaitre, Eduardo. *Rafael Reyes: Biografía de un gran colombiano.* 3d ed. Bogotá: Editorial Espiral, 1967.

León Gómez, Adolfo. *Secretos del Panóptico.* Bogotá: Imprenta de Medardo Rivas, 1905.

Liévano Aguirre, Indalecio. *Rafael Núñez.* Bogotá: Compañía Gran-Colombiana de Libros, 1946.

Lleras Camargo, Alberto. *Un año de gobierno, 1945–1946.* Bogotá: Imprenta Nacional, 1946.

———. *El primer gobierno del Frente Nacional.* 4 vols. Bogotá: Imprenta Nacional, 1962.

———. "Pasado y presente del liberalismo." In *El liberalismo en el poder,* 3 vols., ed. Plinio Mendoza Neira, 3:81–87. Bogotá: Editorial Minerva, 1946.

———. *Sus mejores páginas.* Bogotá: Compañía Grancolombia de Ediciones, 1959.

Lleras Restrepo, Carlos. *Borradores para una historia de la República Liberal.* Bogotá: Editora Nueva Frontera, 1975.

———. *Crónica de mi propia vida.* 11 vols. Bogotá: Stamato Editores, 1983–93.

———. *De la república a la dictadura: Testimonio sobre la política colombiana.* Bogotá: Editorial ARGRA, 1955.

———. *Hacia la restauración democrática y el cambio social: Nuevo testimonio sobre la política colombiana.* 2 vols. 2d ed. Bogotá: Editorial Argra, 1963.

———. "La obra económica y fiscal del liberalismo." In *El liberalismo en el poder,* 3 vols., ed. Plinio Mendoza Neira, 2:9–80. Bogotá: Editorial Minerva, 1946.

———. *Memoria de haciencda, 1939, 1940, 1942,* 2 vols. Bogotá: Banco de la República, 1990.

Londoño Botero, Rocío. "Crisis y recomposición del sindicalismo colombiano, 1946–1980." In *Nueva Historia de Colombia,* 6 vols., ed. Alvaro Tirado Mejía, 3:271–306.

Londoño Díaz, Oscar Gonzalo. *Colonización del Ariari, 1950–1970: Aproximación a una historia regional.* Villavicencio: CENESOLL, 1989.

Londoño Vega, Patricia. "La vida diaria: Usos y costumbres." In *Historia de Antioquia,* ed. Jorge Orlando Melo, 307–41. Medellín: Editorial Presencia, 1988.

Londoño Vega, Patricia, and Santiago Londoño Vélez. "Vida diaria en las ciudades colombianas." In *Nueva Historia de Colombia,* 6 vols., ed. Alvaro Tirado Mejía, 4:313–99. Bogotá: Editorial Planeta, 1989.

López, Alejandro. *Obras selectas.* Bogotá: Imprenta Nacional, 1982.

López de Mesa, Luis. *La crónica de los tres Comentadores.* Medellín: University de Antioquia, 1980.

———. *Escrutinio sociológico de la historia colombiana.* 2d ed. Bogotá: Editorial ABC, 1955.

———. *Historia de la Cancillería.* Bogotá: Imprenta del Estado Mayor General, 1942.

———. *Obras selectas.* Bogotá: Imprenta Nacional, 1981.

López Michelsen, Alfonso. *Colombia en la hora cero: Proceso y enjuiciamiento del Frente Nacional.* Bogotá: Tercer Mundo, 1963.

———. *Cuestiones colombianas.* Mexico City: Impresiones Modernas, 1955.

———. *Los elegidos.* 4th ed. Bogotá: Tercer Mundo, 1967.

———. *Los últimos días de López, y cartas íntimas de tres campañas políticas.* Bogotá: Editorial Mito, 1961.

López Pumarejo, Alfonso. *Alfonso López Pumarejo, polemista político.* Bogotá: Instituto Caro y Cuervo, 1986.

———. *Documentos relacionados con la renuncia de Alfonso López Pumarejo.* Bogotá: Imprenta Nacional, 1946.

———. *Obras selectas.* 2 vols. Compiled by Jorge Mario Eastman. Bogotá: Editorial Retina, 1979–80.

———. *La política oficial: Mensajes, cartas, y discursos del Presidente López.* 3 vols. Bogotá: Imprenta Nacional, 1935–37.

Loy, Jane Meyer. "Modernization and Educational Reform in Colombia, 1863–1886." Ph.D. dissertation, University of Wisconsin, 1968.

Lozano y Lozano, Juan. *Ensayos críticos.* Bogotá: Editorial Santafé, 1934.

———. *La patria y yo.* Bogotá: Editorial Litografía Colombia, 1933.

Machado, Absalón. *El café: De la aparcería al capitalismo.* Bogotá: Tercer Mundo, 1988.

Magraw, Roger. *France, 1815–1914: The Bourgeois Century.* London: Fontana, 1983.

Manrique, Ramón. *Bajo el signo de la hoz.* Bogotá: Editorial ABC, 1938.

Marroquín, Lorenzo. *Pax: Novela de costumbres latinoamericanas.* 2d ed. Bogotá: Imprenta de la Luz, 1907.

Martínez, Carlos, ed. *Bogotá reseñada por cronistas y viajeros ilustres.* Bogotá: Escala, 1978.

Martínez Delgado, Luis. *A propósito del Dr. Carlos Martínez Silva.* Bogotá: Editorial Marconi, 1930.

———. *Jorge Holguín, o, el político.* Editorial Creditario, 1980.

Martínez Silva, Carlos. *Capítulos de historia política de Colombia.* 3 vols. Bogotá: Banco Popular, 1973.

———. *Escritos políticos, literarios, y económicos.* 8 vols. Edited by Gustavo Otero Muñoz and Luis Martínez Delgado. Bogotá: Imprenta Nacional, 1937.

Martz, John D. *Colombia: A Contemporary Political Survey.* Chapel Hill: University of North Carolina Press, 1962.

Marulanda Alvarez, Elsy. *Colonización y conflicto: Las lecciones de Sumapaz.* Bogotá: Tercer Mundo, 1991.

Marulanda Vélez, Manuel. *Cuadernos de campaña.* 2d ed. Bogotá: Ediciones Abejón Mono, 1973.

Maya, Rafael. *Obra crítica.* Edited by Cristina Maya. 2 vols. Bogotá: Banco de la República, 1982.

Mayor Mora, Alberto. *Etica, trabajo, y productividad en Antioquia.* Bogotá: Tercer Mundo, 1984.

———. "Historia de la industria colombiana, 1886–1930." In *Nueva Historia de Colombia,* 6 vols., ed. Alvaro Tirado Mejía, 5:313–32. Bogotá: Editorial Planeta, 1989.

———. "Historia de la industria colombiana, 1930–1968." In *Nueva Historia de Colombia,* 6 vols., ed. Alvaro Tirado Mejía, 5:333–56. Bogotá: Editorial Planeta, 1989.

McFarlane, Anthony. "The Transition from Colonialism in Colombia, 1819–1875." In *Latin America, Economic Imperialism, and the State,* ed. Christopher Abel and Colin M. Lewis, 101–24. London: Athlone Press, 1985.

McGreevey, William Paul. *An Economic History of Colombia, 1845–1930.* New York: Cambridge University Press, 1971.

Mecham, J. Lloyd. *Church and State in Latin America.* Rev. ed. Chapel Hill: University of North Carolina Press, 1966.

Medhurst, Kenneth N. *The Church and Labor in Colombia.* Manchester, England: Manchester University Press, 1984.

Medina, Alvaro. *Procesos del arte en Colombia.* Bogotá: Colcultura, 1978.

Medina, Medófilo. *Historia del Partido Comunista de Colombia.* Bogotá: Editorial Colombia Nueva, 1980.

———. *La protesta urbana en colombia en el siglo veinte.* Bogotá: El Ancora Editores, 1984.

———. "Los terceros partidos en Colombia, 1900–1960." In *Nueva Historia de Colombia,* 6 vols., ed. Alvaro Tirado Mejía, 2:263–94. Bogotá: Editorial Planeta, 1989.

Meisel Roca, Adolfo. "El Banco de la República y la Reforma de 1951." In *El Banco de la República: Antecedentes, evolución, y estructura,* 405–41. Bogotá: Banco de la República, 1990.

———. "De la inflación de la posguerra a la bonanza cafetera." In *El Banco de la República,* 403–42. Bogotá: Banco de la República, 1989.

———. "La Reforma de 1951." In *El Banco de la República,* 243–62. Bogotá: Banco de la República, 1989.

Melo, Héctor, and Ivan López Botero. *El imperio clandestino del café.* Bogotá: Editorial Latina, 1976.

Melo, Jorge Orlando. "De Carlos E. Restrepo a Marco Fidel Suárez: Republicanos y gobiernos conservadores." In *Nueva Historia de Colombia,* 6 vols., ed. Alvaro Tirado Mejía, 1:215–31. Bogotá: Editorial Planeta, 1989.

———, ed. *Historia de Antioquia.* Medellín: Editorial Presencia, 1988.

———. "La evolución económica de Colombia, 1830–1900." In *Manual de Historia de Colombia,* 3 vols., ed. J. G. Cobo Borda and J. E. Ruiz, 2:135–210. Bogotá: Instituto Colombiano de Cultura, 1979.

———. "La República Conservadora, 1880–1930." In *Colombia, hoy.* 6th ed., ed. Mario Arrubla, 52–101. Bogotá: Siglo Veintiuno Editores, 1980.

———, ed. *Orígenes de los partidos políticos en Colombia.* Bogotá: Instituto Colombiano de Cultura, 1978.

———. *Sobre historia y política.* Bogotá: Editorial La Carreta, 1979.

Mendoza Neira, Plinio, ed. *El liberalismo en el gobierno.* 3 vols. Bogotá: Editorial PRAG, 1946.

Mesa, Darío. "La vida política después de Panamá." In *Manual de Historia de Colombia,* 3 vols., ed. Jaime Jaramillo Uribe, 3:83–178. Bogotá: Instituto Colombiano de Cultura, 1980.

Miranda Canal, Néstor José. "La medecina colombiana: De la Regeneración a los años de la segunda guerra mundial." In *Nueva Historia de Colombia,* 6 vols., ed. Alvaro Tirado Mejía, 4:257–84. Bogotá: Editorial Planeta, 1989.

Molano, Alfredo. *Los años del tropel: Crónicas de la violencia.* 2d ed. Bogotá: El Ancora Editores, 1991.

———. *Selva adentro: Una historia oral de la colonización del Guaviare.* Bogotá: El Ancora Editores, 1987.

Molina, Felipe Antonio. *Laureano Gómez: Historia de una rebeldía.* Bogotá: Librería Voluntád, 1940.

Molina, Gerardo. *Las ideas liberales en Colombia, 1915–1934.* Bogotá: Tercer Mundo, 1974.

Mollien, Gaspard. "Recorriendo la provincia de Socorro." In *Las maravillas de Colombia,* 1:17–36. Bogotá: Editorial Forja, 1979.

Moncada Abello, Alonso. *Un aspecto de la Violencia.* Bogotá: Promotora Colombiana de Ediciones, 1963.

Monsalve, Diego. *Colombia cafetera.* Barcelona: Artes Gráficas, 1927.

Montalvo, José Antonio. *Exposición hecha ante el honorable Senado en la sesión del 6 de noviembre de 1947.* Bogotá: Imprenta Nacional, 1947.

Montaña Cuellar, Diego. *Colombia: País formal y país real.* Buenos Aires: Editorial Platina, 1963.

Mora, Luis María. *Croniquillas de mi ciudad.* Bogotá: Banco Popular, 1972.

Morales Benítez, Otto. *Historias económicas del café y de don Manuel.* Bogotá: Ediciones Fondo Cultural Cafetero, 1990.

Morales Benítez, Otto, and Diego Pizano Salazar, eds. *Don Manuel: Mister Coffee.* 2 vols. Bogotá: Fondo Cultural Cafetero, 1989.

Murry, Pamela. "Feminizing the Fraternity: Colombia's First Women Engineers, 1941–1979." Paper presented at the annual meeting of the South Eastern Council on Latin American Studies, Charleston, S.C., 1992. Typescript.

Naranjo Villegas, Abel. Interview by author. Bogotá, June 18, 1986.

Navarro, Pedro Juan. *El parlamento en pijama.* Bogotá: Mundo al Día, 1935.

Navia Varón, Hernando. *Caudillo y gobernante: Dr. Ignacio Rengifo Borrero.* Cali: Imprenta Departamental, 1964.

————. *Yo ví cerrar el Congreso: La revolución de mayo de 1957 en el Palacio de San Carlos*. Popayán: Editorial Universidad del Cauca, 1960.

Nicholas, Francis C. *Across Panama and around the Caribbean*. 2d ed. New York: H. M. Caldwell, 1909.

Nieto Arteta, Luis Eduardo. *El café*. 1948. Bogotá: Litografía Villegas, 1958.

Nieto Caballero, Luis Eduardo. *Colombia joven*. Bogotá: Arboleda y Valencia, 1918.

————. *Escritos escogidos*. 5 vols. Compiled by Luis C. Adames Santos. Bogotá: Banco Popular, 1984.

————. *Vuelo al Amazonas*. Bogotá: Editorial Minerva, 1933.

Niles, Blair. *Colombia, Land of Miracles*. New York: Century, 1924.

Niño Murcia, Carlos. *Arquitectura y estado*. Bogotá: Universidad Nacional de Colombia, 1991.

Noguera Laborde, Rodrigo. Interview by author. Bogotá, November 18, 1992.

Noguera Mendoza, Aníbal, ed. *Aproximación a Alfonso López*. 2 vols. Bogotá: Banco de la República, 1986.

Núñez, Rafael. *La reforma política en Colombia*. 7 vols. Vol. 1, Bogotá: Imprenta Nacional, 1944; vols. 2–5, Bogotá: Editorial ABC, 1945–46; vols. 6–7, Bogotá: Editorial Iqueima, 1950.

Ocampo, José Antonio. "The Colombian Economy in the 1930s." In *Latin America in the 1930s, the Role of the Periphery*. ed. Rosemary Throp, 117–43. New York: St. Martin's Press, 1984.

————. *Colombia y la economía mundial, 1830–1910*. Bogotá: Siglo Veintiuno Editores, 1984.

————. "La consolidación de la industria cafetera, 1930–1958." In *Nueva Historia de Colombia*, 6 vols., ed. Alvaro Tirado Mejía, 5:233–62. Bogotá: Editorial Planeta, 1989.

————. "Los orígenes de la industria cafetera, 1830–1929." In *Nueva Historia de Colombia*, 6 vols., ed. Alvaro Tirado Mejía, 5:213–32. Bogotá: Editorial Planeta, 1989.

Ocampo, José Francisco. *Memorias inconclusas de un amnesico*. Editorial Cosmos, 1979.

Oquist, Paul. "Las elecciones presidenciales, 1930–1970." *Boletín Mensual de Estadística* 268–69 (1973): 63–334.

————. *Violencia, conflicto y política en Colombia*. Bogotá: Banco Popular, 1978.

Ortega Torres, Jorge. *Suárez*. Bogotá: Instituto Caro y Cuervo, 1956.

Ortiz Márquez, Julio. *El hombre que fue un pueblo*. Bogotá: Carlos Valencia Editores, 1978.

Ortiz Sarmiento, Carlos Miguel. *Estado y subversión en Colombia*. Bogotá: Editorial CEREC, 1985.

————. "Las guerrillas liberales de los años '50 y '60 en el Quindío." *Anuario colombiano de historia social y de la cultura* (Universidad Nacional de Colombia, Bogotá) 12 (1984): 103–53.

————. "The 'Business of Violence': The Quindío in the 1950s and 1960s." In *Violence in Colombia: The Contemporary Crisis in Historical Perspective*, ed. Charles Bergquist, Ricardo Peñaranda, Gonzalo Sánchez, 125–54. Wilmington, Del.: Scholarly Resources, 1992.

Osorio Lizarazo, José A. *La cosecha*. Manizales: Editorial Arturo Zapata, 1935.

————. *Gaitán. Vida, muerte, y permanente presencia*. 2d ed. Buenos Aires: Ediciones López Negri, 1952.

———. *Novelas y crónicas.* Bogotá: Instituto Colombiano de Cultura, 1978.

Osorio O., Iván Darío. "Historia del sindicalismo." In *Historia de Antioquia,* ed. Jorge Orlando Melo, 279–86. Medellín: Editorial Presencia, 1988.

Ospina, Joaquín. *Diccionario biográfico y bibliográfico de Colombia.* 3 vols. Bogotá: Editorial Aguila, 1927–39.

Ospina, Tulio. *Protocolo de urbanidad y del buen tono.* Medellín, 1919.

Ospina Pérez, Mariano. *El gobierno de Unión Nacional.* Bogotá: Imprenta Nacional, 1948.

Ospina Vásquez, Luis. *Industria y protección en Colombia, 1810–1930.* Bogotá: Editorial Santafé, 1955.

Osterling, Jorge P. *Democracy in Colombia: Clientelist Politics and Guerrilla Warfare.* New Brunswick, N.J.: Transaction Publishers, 1989.

Páez, Julián M. *Cartas a mi sobrina.* Bogotá: Librería Americana, 1912.

Palacio, Julio H. *Historia de mi vida.* Bogotá: Camacho Roldán, 1942.

Palacios, Marco. *Coffee in Colombia, 1850–1970: An Economic, Social, and Political History.* New York: Cambridge University Press, 1980.

———. *La delgada corteza de nuestra civilización.* Bogotá: Editorial Linotipa Bolívar, 1986.

———. *Estado y clases sociales en Colombia.* Bogotá: Editorial Linotipa Bolívar, 1986.

Pardo Umaña, Camilo. *Los toros en Bogotá: Historia y crítica de las corridas.* Bogotá: Editorial Kelly, 1946.

Parga Cortés, Rafael. Interview by author. Ibagué, March 24, 1971.

París Lozano, Gonzalo, ed. *Geografía económica de Colombia.* Vol. 5 of *Tolima.* Bogotá: Contraloría General de la República, 1948.

Parsons, James J. *Antioqueño Colonization in Western Colombia.* Berkeley: University of California Press, 1949.

Patiño Rosselli, Alfonso. *La prosperidad a debe y la gran crisis, 1925–1935: Capítulos de história ecónomica de Colombia.* Bogotá: Banco de la República, 1981.

Paxton, Virginia M. *Penthouse in Bogotá.* New York: Reynal and Hitchcock, 1943.

Pécaut, Daniel. *Orden y violencia: Colombia, 1930–1953.* 2 vols. Bogotá: Siglo Veintiuno, 1987.

Peña, Luis Davíd. *Gaitán íntimo.* Bogotá: Editorial Iqueima, 1948.

Pereira Gamba, F. *La vida en los Andes colombianos.* Quito: Imprenta de "El Progreso," 1919.

Pérez, Cleofas [Carlos Lleras Restrepo]. *Crónicas y coloquios.* Bogotá: Ediciones Mito, 1962.

Pérez, Felipe, ed. *Periodistas liberales.* Bogotá: Editorial Minerva, 1937.

Pérez, Santiago. *El manual del ciudadano.* Bogotá: Banco de Colombia, 1974.

Pérez Triana, Santiago. *Eslabones sueltos.* London: Imprenta de Wertheimer, 1910.

Perry, Oliverio, ed. *Quién es quién en Colombia.* Bogotá: Editorial Kelly, 1945.

Petre, Francis Loraine. *The Republic of Colombia: An Account of the Country, Its People, Its Institutions, and Its Resources.* London: Edward Stanford, 1906.

Pike, Fredrick B. *Hispanismo, 1898–1936: Spanish Conservatives and Liberals and Their Relations with Spanish America.* Notre Dame, Ind.: University of Notre Dame Press, 1971.

Pinzón, Martín Alonso. *Historia del conservatismo.* Bogotá: Tercer Mundo, 1979.

Pizarro Leongómez, Eduardo. *Las FARC: De la autodefensa a la combinación de todas las formas de lucha.* Bogotá: Tercer Mundo, 1992.

————. "Revolutionary Guerrilla Groups in Colombia." In *Violence in Colombia*, ed. Charles Bergquist, Gonzalo Sánchez, and Ricardo Peñaranda, 169–94. Wilmington, Del.: Scholarly Resources, 1992.

Plata Bermúdez, Francisco. Bogotá. Interview by author. May 14, 1989.

Pollock, John. "Evaluating Regime Performance in a Crisis: Violence, Political Demands, and Elite Accountability in Colombia." Department of Political Science, Stanford University, 1969. Typescript.

Pombo, Jorge, and Carlos Obregón. *Directorio general de Bogotá, año dos (1889–1890).* Bogotá: Imprenta de "La Luz," 1889.

Pombo, Miguel Antonio, and José Joaquín Guerra, eds. *Constituciones de Colombia.* Biblioteca Popular de Cultura Colombiana, vols. 143–47. Bogotá: Imprenta Nacional, 1951.

Posada, Eduardo, and Roberto Cortazar. *Instrucción cívica para escuelas y colegios.* Bogotá: Editorial Selecta, 1913.

Posada Callejas, Jorge, ed. *Libro azul de Colombia: Blue Book of Colombia.* New York: J. J. Little and Ives, 1918.

Posada Posada, Carlos Estéban. "La gran crisis en Colombia: El período 1928–1933." In *Nueva Historia de Colombia,* 6 vols., ed. Alvaro Tirado Mejía, 4:77–102. Bogotá: Editorial Planeta, 1989.

Poveda Ramos, Gabriel. "Cien años de ciencia colombiana." In *Nueva Historia de Colombia,* 6 vols., ed. Alvaro Tirado Mejía, 4:159–88. Bogotá: Editorial Planeta, 1989.

Powell, John Duncan. "Peasant Society and Clientelist Politics." *American Political Science Review* 64 (June 1970): 411–25.

Premo, Daniel Lawrence. "Alianza Nacional Popular: Populism and the Politics of Social Class in Colombia, 1961–1970." Ph.D. dissertation, University of Texas, Austin, 1972.

Quintana Pereyra, J. M. *La redención de la clase media.* Bogotá: Editorial ABC, 1936.

Quintero, Jaime. *Consacá.* Cali: Editorial EZA, 1944.

Ramírez Moreno, Augusto. *La crisis del partido conservador en Colombia.* Bogotá: Tipografía Granados, 1937.

Ramsey, Russell W. "The *Bogotazo:* Tentatively, as History." Gainesville: University of Florida, 1969. Mimeo.

————. "The Colombian Battalion in Korea and Suez." *Journal of Inter-American Studies* 9 (October 1967): 541–60.

————. *Guerrilleros y soldados.* Bogotá: Tercer Mundo, 1981.

————. "Internal Defense in the 1980s: The Colombian Model." *Comparative Strategy* 4:4 (1984): 349–67.

————. "The Modern Violence in Colombia, 1946–1965." Ph. D. dissertation. Gainesville: University of Florida, 1970.

Randall, Stephen J. *Colombia and the United States.* Athens: University of Georgia Press, 1992.

————. *The Diplomacy of Modernization: Colombian-American Relations, 1920–1940.* Toronto: University of Toronto Press, 1977.

Reclús, Eliseo. *Colombia.* 2d ed. Bogotá: Imprenta Nacional, 1958.

Regueros Peralta, Jorge. Interview by author. Bogotá, June 15, 26, 1993.

Reinhardt, Nola. *Our Daily Bread: The Peasant Question and Family Farming in the Colombian Andes.* Berkeley: University of California Press, 1988.

Restrepo, Antonio José. *El cancionero de Antioquia*. Medellín: Editorial Bedout, 1971.

Restrepo, Carlos E. *Orientación republicana*. 2d ed. 2 vols. Bogotá: Banco Popular, 1972.

Restrepo, Félix. *Colombia en la encrucijada*. Bogotá: Ministerio de Educación Nacional, 1951.

———. *Corporativismo*. Bogotá: Ediciones Revista Javeriana, 1939.

Restrepo Arango, Luis Antonio. "El pensamiento social en Antioquia." *Historia de Antioquia,* ed. Jorge Orlando Melo, 373–82.

———. "Literatura y pensamiento, 1958–1985." In *Nueva Historia de Colombia, 6* vols., ed. Alvaro Tirado Mejía, 6:89–108. Bogotá: Editorial Planeta, 1989.

Restrepo Piedrahita, Carlos. *Recopilación de actos legislativos, 1914–1986*. Bogotá: Banco Popular, 1986.

Restrepo Posada, José. *La Iglesia en dos momentos difíciles de la historia*. Bogotá: Editorial Kelly, 1971.

Restrepo Posada, José, and Bernardo Sanz de Santamaría. "Estudios Genealógicos: Familia Ospina y Ospina Rodríguez." *Boletín de Historia y Antigüedades* 61:635–45, 660–62.

Restrepo Yusti, Manuel. "Historia de la industria." In *Historia de Antioquia,* ed. Jorge Orlando Melo, 267–78. Medellín: Editorial Presencia, 1988.

Reveiz Roldán, Edgar, and María José Pérez Piñeros. "Algunas hipótesis sobre las formas de regulación de la economía y la estabilidad política colombiana entre 1950 y 1982." *Desarrollo y Sociedad* (CEDE, Facultad de Economía, Universidad de los Andes, Bogotá) 14 (May 1984): 31–58.

Reyes, Catalina. "El gobierno de Mariano Ospina Pérez, 1946–1950." In *Nueva Historia de Colombia, 6* vols., ed. Alvaro Tirado Mejía, 2:1–24. Bogotá: Editorial Planeta, 1989.

Reyes, Rafael. *Escritos varios*. Bogotá: Tipografía Arconvar, 1920.

Rincón Rozas, Saul. *Biografía de Gustavo Jiménez*. Bogotá: Coopanlgráficas, 1955.

Rippy, J. Fred. *The Capitalists and Colombia*. New York: Vanguard Press, 1931.

Rivera, Julius. *Latin America: A Sociocultural Interpretation*. New York: Houghton Mifflin, 1977.

Robles Bohórquez, Isabel. *La agricultura colombiana en la encrucijada*. 2d ed. Bogotá: Tercer Mundo, 1983.

Rodríguez, Amadco. *Caminos de guerra y conspiración*. Barcelona: Gráficas Claret, 1955.

Rodríguez, Gustavo Humberto. *Benjamín Herrera en la guerra y en la paz*. Bogotá: Imprenta de Eduardo Salazar, 1973.

———. *Olaya Herrera, político, estadista, y caudillo*. Bogotá: Presidencia de la República, 1979.

Rodríguez, Oscar. *Efectos de la gran depresión en la industria colombiana*. 2d ed. Bogotá: Oveja Negra, 1981.

Rodríguez Garavito, Agustín. *Gabriel Turbay, un solitario de la grandeza: Biografía de una generación infortunada*. Bogotá: Internacional de Publicaciones, 1965.

Rojas de Segura, Gladys Esther. "La violencia en Boyacá, 1946–1950: Protagonismo político del directorio departamental conservador." M.A. thesis, Universidad Pedagógica y Tecnológica de Colombia, Tunja, 1992.

Rojas Garrido, José María. *Empresarios y tecnología en la formación del sector azucarero en Colombia, 1860–1890*. Bogotá: Banco Popular, 1983.

Rojas Pinilla, Gustavo, ed. *Rojas Pinilla ante el Senado*. Bogotá: Editorial Excelsior, 1959.

———. *Seis meses de gobierno*. Bogotá: Imprenta Nacional, 1954.

Roldán, Mary. "La política de 1946 a 1958." In *Historia de Antioquia*, ed. Jorge Orlando Melo, 143–75. Medellín: Editorial Presencia, 1988.

Romero Aguirre, Alfonso. *Caída y aniquilamiento del liberalismo: El liberalismo en Cuba*. Bogotá: Editorial Iqueima, 1951.

Ronderos T., Carlos. *Rebelión en Colombia, 1930–1986*. Bogotá: FOCINE, 1986. Videocassette.

———. *Rebelión y amnestía en Colombia, 1930–1986*. Bogotá: FOCINE, 1986. Videocassette.

Rosales, José Miguel. *Colombia, tierra de humanidad: Reflexiones sobre su geografía física y económica*. Bogotá: Editorial Santafé, 1930.

Rosselli, Humberto. *Historia de la psiquiatría en Colombia*. 2 vols. Bogotá: Editorial Horizontes, 1968.

Rostow, Walt W. *The World Economy: History and Prospect*. Austin: University of Texas Press, 1978.

Roux, Rodolfo Ramón de. "Iglesia y sociedad en Colombia. 9 de abril de 1948. Funciones sociales y funcionamiento de la institución de la institución católica." Ph.D. thesis. Ecole des Hautes Etudes en Sciences Sociales, Paris, 1981.

Rubiano, Germán. "Las artes plásticas en el siglo veinte." In *Manual de historia de Colombia*, 3 vols., ed. Jaime Jaramillo Uribe, 3:415–44. Bogotá: Instituto Colombiana de Cultura, 1980.

Rueda Enciso, José Eduardo. "La antigua Facultad de Sociología de la Universidad Nacional y la creación de los departamentos de antropología." Facultad de antropología, Universidad Nacional de Colombia, Bogotá, 1992. Typescript.

Rueda Plata, José Olinto. "Historia de la población de Colombia, 1880–2000." In *Nueva Historia de Colombia*, 6 vols., ed. Alvaro Tirado Mejía, 5:357–96. Bogotá: Editorial Planeta, 1989.

Rueda Uribe, Pedro Nel. *El proceso Mamatoco, crímen de estado*. Bogotá: Editorial Hispana, 1984.

Rueda Vargas, Tomás. *Escritos*. Bogotá: Editorial Antares, 1963.

Rumazo González, Alfonso. *Enrique Olaya Herrera, un gran estadista*. Santiago: Editorial Zig-Zag, 1940.

Sáenz Rovner, Eduardo. "Documentos sobre el X Congreso Nacional de la CTC en 1950 y la persecución sindical en Colombia." *Anuario colombiano de historia social y de la cultura* (Universidad Nacional de Colombia, Bogotá) 18–19 (1990–1991): 309–35.

———. *La ofensiva empresarial: Industriales, políticos, y violencia en los años cuarenta en Colombia*. Bogotá: Tercer Mundo, 1992.

Salazar, J. A., and Ana María Jaramillo. *Medellín: Las subculturas del narcotráfico, 1975–1990*. Bogotá: CINEP, 1992.

Saldarriaga Betancur, Juan Manuel. *De sima a cima, o, Marco Fidel Suárez ante la conciencia colombiana*. Medellín: Imprenta Departamental, 1950.

Saldarriaga Roa, Alberto, and Lorenzo Fonseca M. "Un siglo de arquitectura colombiana." In *Nueva historia de Colombia*, ed. Alvaro Tirado Mejía, 6 vols. 6:181–212. Bogotá: Editorial Planeta, 1989.

Salgado, Cupertino. *Directorio general de Bogotá: Año cuatro (1893)*. Bogotá: Imprenta de "La Luz," 1893.

Samper, José María. *Ensayo sobre las revoluciones políticas y la condición social de las repúblicas colombianas.* 2d ed. Bogotá: Universidad Nacional de Colombia, 1963.

Samper, Miguel. *Escritos político-económicos.* 4 vols. Bogotá: Banco de la República, 1977.

Samper Gnecco, Andrés. *Cuando Bogotá no tuvo tranvía.* Bogotá: Instituto Colombiano de Cultura, 1973.

Sánchez, Gonzalo. *Los "Bolcheviques del Líbano" (Tolima): Crisis mundial, transición capitalista, y rebelión rural en Colombia.* Bogotá: Ecoe Ediciones, 1976.

———. *Ensayos de historia social y política del siglo veinte.* Bogotá: El Ancora, 1985.

———. "Rehabilitación y violencia bajo el Frente Nacional." *Análisis Político* 4 (May-August 1988): 21–42.

———. "La Violencia: De Rojas al Frente Nacional." In *Nueva Historia de Colombia,* 6 vols., ed. Alvaro Tirado Mejía, 2:153–78. Bogotá: Editorial Planeta, 1989.

———. "Violencia, guerrillas, y estructuras agrarias." In *Nueva Historia de Colombia,* 6 vols., ed. Alvaro Tirado Mejía, 2:127–54. Bogotá: Editorial Planeta, 1989.

Sánchez, Gonzalo, and Donny Meertens. *Bandoleros, gamonales, y campesinos: El caso de la Violencia en Colombia.* Bogotá: El Ancora Editores, 1983.

Sánchez, Ricardo. *Estado y planeación en Colombia.* Bogotá: Editorial La Rosa Rosa, 1984.

Sánchez Camacho, Jorge. *El General Ospina.* Bogotá: Editorial ABC, 1960.

———. *Marco Fidel Suárez.* Bucaramanga: Imprenta del Departamento, 1955.

Sánchez Juliao, David. *Un hombre a través de la anécdota.* Pereira: Universidad Simón Bolívar, 1979.

Sánchez Torres, Fabio. "Aspectos monetarios de la grán depresión en Colombia: Política y evidencia empírica, 1928–1936." *Cuadernas de Economía* (University Nacional, Bogotá) 10:14 (January 1990): 195–232.

Sanclemente Villalon, José Ignacio. *El 31 de julio: La otra historia de un cambio de gobierno.* Cali: Imprenta Departamental del Valle del Cauca, 1990.

Sandilands, Roger J. *The Life and Political Economy of Lauchlin Currie.* Durham: Duke University Press, 1990.

Sanmiguel, Luis J. *Recuerdos de un periodista.* Bucaramanga: Imprenta del Departamento, 1970.

Santa, Eduardo. *Arrieros y fundadores: Aspectos de la colonización antioqueña.* Bogotá: Editorial Cosmos, 1961.

———. *Rafael Uribe Uribe.* 4th ed. Bogotá: Instituto Colombiano de Cultura, 1974.

Santamaría S., Ricardo, and Gabriel Silva Luján. *Proceso político en Colombia: Del Frente Nacional a la Apertura Democrática.* Bogotá: Fondo Editorial CEREC, 1984.

Santos, Eduardo. *Las etapas de la vida colombiana: Discursos y mensajes, 1938–1942.* 13 vols. Bogotá: Imprenta Nacional, 1946.

———. *Obras selectas.* 2 vols. Bogotá: Imprenta Nacional, 1982.

Sardá y Salvany, Félix. *El liberalismo es pecado.* Bogotá: Imprenta de F. Torres Amaya, 1896.

Serrano Blanco, Manuel. *La vida es así.* Bucaramanga: Imprenta del Departamento, 1953.

———. *Las viñas del odio.* Bucaramanga: Imprenta del Departamento, 1949.

Serrano Camargo, Rafael. *En aquella ciudad.* Bogotá: Tercer Mundo, 1981.

———. *El General Uribe.* Bogotá: Tercer Mundo, 1976.

Sharpless, Richard E. *Gaitán of Colombia. A Political Biography.* Pittsburgh: University of Pittsburgh Press. 1977.

Silva Olarte, Renan. "La educación en Colombia, 1880–1930." In *Nueva Historia de Colombia,* 6 vols., ed. Alvaro Tirado Mejía, 4:61–86. Bogotá: Editorial Planeta, 1989.

Simmel, Georg. *The Philosophy of Money.* Translated by Tom Bottomore and David Frisby. 2d ed. London: Routledge, 1990.

Socarrás, José Francisco. *Laureano Gómez: Psicoanálisis de un resentido.* Bogotá: Ediciones Librería Siglo Veinte, 1942.

Solano, Armando. *Glosas y ensayos, 1923–1945.* Bogotá: Colcultura, 1982.

———. *Paipa, mi pueblo, y otros ensayos.* Bogotá: Banco de la República, 1983.

Solano Benítez, Guillermo. *Cincuenta años de vida nortesantanderiana.* 4 vols. Cúcuta: Imprenta Departamental, 1960.

Sowell, David Lee. "The Early Latin American Labor Movement: Artisans and Politics in Bogotá, Colombia, 1832–1919." Ph.D. dissertation, University of Florida, 1986.

———. "The Rise of the Worker's Labor Movement, 1899–1919." Department of History, Juniata College, 1991. Typescript.

Suárez, Marco Fidel. *Análisis gramatical de "Pax."* Bogotá: Imprenta de "La Luz," 1907.

———. *Doctrinas internacionales.* Bogotá: Imprenta Nacional, 1955.

———. *Obras.* 4 vols. Edited by José J. Ortega Torres, Horacio Bejarano Díaz, and Guillermo Hernández de Alba, Bogotá: Instituto Caro y Cuervo, 1958–1984.

———. *Sueños de Luciano Pulgar.* 12 vols. Bogotá: Librería Voluntad, 1927; Editorial ABC, 1954.

Téllez, Germán. "La arquitectura y el urbanismo en la época actual." In *Manual de historia de Colombia,* 3 vols., ed. Jaime Jaramillo Uribe, 3:343–412. Bogotá: Instituto Colombiano de Cultura, 1980.

———. "La arquitectura y el urbanismo en la época republicana, 1830–40/1930–35." In *Manual de historia de Colombia,* 3 vols., ed. Jaime Jaramillo Uribe, 2:466–564. Bogotá: Instituto Colombiano de Cultura, 1979.

Téllez, Pedro Claver. *Crónicas de la vida bandolera.* Bogotá: Editorial Planeta, 1987.

Téllez B., Hernando. *Cincuenta años de radiodifusión colombiana.* Bogotá: Caracol, 1974.

———. *Textos no recogidos en libro.* 2 vols. Bogotá: Instituto Colombiano de Cultura, 1979.

Thorp, Rosemary. *Economic Management and Economic Development in Peru and Colombia.* Pittsburgh: University of Pittsburgh Press, 1991.

Thorp, Rosemary, and Carlos Londoño. "The Effect of the Great Depression on the Economies of Peru and Colombia." In *Latin America in the 1930s: The Role of the Periphery,* ed. Rosemary Thorp, 81–116. New York: St. Martin's, 1984.

Tirado, Thomas. *Alfonso López Pumarejo, el conciliador.* Bogotá: Editorial Planeta, 1986.

Tirado Mejía, Alvaro. *Aspectos políticos del primer gobierno de Alfonso López Pumarejo, 1934–1938.* Bogotá: Gráficas Cabrera e Hijos, 1981.

———. "Del Frente Nacional al momento actual: Diagnóstico de una crisis." In *Nueva Historia de Colombia.* 6 vols., ed. Alvaro Tirado Mejía, 2:399–407. Bogotá: Editorial Planeta, 1989.

———. "El estado y la política en el siglo diecinueve." In *Manual de historia de Colombia,* 3 vols., ed. J. G. Cobo Borda and Jorge Eliécer Ruiz, 2:327–86. Bogotá: Instituto Colombiano de Cultura, 1980.

———. *El pensamiento de Alfonso López Pumarejo.* Bogotá: Banco de la República, 1986.

———. "El pensamiento de Alfonso López Pumarejo." Quinto Congreso de Historia de Colombia, Armenia, 1986.

———. "López Pumarejo: La Revolución en Marcha." In *Nueva Historia de Colombia.* Vol. 1, ed. Alvaro Tirado Mejía, 338–46. Bogotá: Editorial Planeta, 1989.

———, ed. *Nueva Historia de Colombia.* 6 vols. Bogotá: Editorial Planeta, 1989.

———. *Sobre historia y literatura.* Medellín: Editorial EALON, 1991.

Tirado Mejía, Alvaro, and Magdalena Velásquez. *La reforma constitucional de 1936.* Bogotá: La Oveja Negra, 1982.

Tobón Páramo, Julio. Interview by author. Bogotá, January 17, 1982.

Toro, Constanza. "Medellín: Desarrollo urbano, 1880–1950." In *Historia de Antioquia,* ed. Jorge Orlando Melo, 299–306. Medellín: Editorial Presencia, 1988.

Torres, Eddy. Interview by author. Bogotá, May 30, 1982.

Torres, Mauricio. *La naturaleza de la revolución colombiana.* Bogotá: Editorial Iqueima, 1959.

Torres de Restrepo, Lucía. Interview by author. Bogotá, April 20, 1993.

Torres García, Guillermo. *Nociones de economía política.* Bogotá: Siglo Veinte, 1942.

Torres Giraldo, Ignacio. *Los inconformes: Historia de la rebeldía de las masas en Colombia.* 5 vols. Bogotá: Editorial Latina, 1978.

———. *María Cano, mujer rebelde.* Bogotá: Publicaciones de la Rosca, 1972.

Torres Restrepo, Camilo. "Social Change and Rural Violence in Colombia." In *Masses in Latin America,* ed. Irving Louis Horowitz, 503–46. New York: Oxford University Press, 1970.

Tovar, Hermes. *El movimiento campesino en Colombia.* Bogotá: Ediciones Libres, 1975.

Tovar Zambrano, Bernardo. "La economía colombiana, 1886–1922." In *Nueva Historia de Colombia,* 6 vols., ed. Alvaro Tirado Mejía, 5:9–50. Bogotá: Editorial Planeta, 1989.

———. *La intervención económica del estado en Colombia, 1914–1936.* Bogotá: Banco Popular, 1984.

Triana y Antoveza, Humberto. *La acción comunal en Colombia: Resultados de una evulación en 107 municipios.* Bogotá: Imprenta Nacional, 1970.

United States of America. Department of State. National Archives. Spruille Braden to Secretary of State, December 9, 1940, DS821.00/1304.

United States of America. Department of State. National Archives. Spruille Braden to Secretary of State, December 19, 1940, DS821.00/1305.

———. Gerberich to Mills. 821.00/11–1549 (November 19, 1949).

———. Lankenau, R.F. 721.00/4–1553.

———. John F. Simmons to U.S. Embassy, Bogotá, Colombia, February 4, 1950. DS821.00/11–1549 (letter of November 29, 1949).

United States of America. Film Archives. National Archives. *Paramount Films,* April 21, 1948.

Urdaneta Arbeláez, Roberto. *Escritos y discursos.* Bogotá: Editorial Presencia, 1985.

———. *El materialismo contra la dignidad del hombre.* Bogotá: Editorial Lucrós, 1960.

Uribe, María Victoria. *Limpiar la tierra: Guerra y poder entre esmeralderos.* Santafé de Bogotá: CINEP, 1992.

Uribe Celis, Carlos. *Los años veinte en Colombia: Ideología y cultura.* Bogotá: Ediciones Aurora, 1985.

————. *La mentalidad del colombiano: Cultura y sociedad en el siglo veinte.* Santafé de Bogotá: Editorial Nueva America, 1992.

Uribe Holguín, Jaime. Interview by author. Bogotá, May 14, 1989.

Uribe Uribe, Rafael. "De cómo el liberalismo colombiano no es pecado." In *Obras selectas,* 2 vols., ed. Jorge Mario Eastman, 2:81–185. Bogotá: Imprenta Nacional, 1979.

————. *Obras selectas.* 2 vols. Compiled by Jorge Mario Eastman. Bogotá: Cámara de Representantes, 1979.

Urrutia, Miguel. *Cincuenta años de desarrollo económico colombiano.* Bogotá: La Carreta, 1979.

————. *Cuarenta años de desarrollo. Su impacto social.* Bogotá: FEDDESARROLLO, 1991.

————. "El desarrollo del movimiento sindical y la situación de la clase obrera." In *Manual de Historia de Colombia,* 3 vols., ed. Jaime Jaramillo Uribe, 3:179–246. Bogotá: Instituto Colombiano de Cultura, 1980.

————. *The Development of the Colombian Labor Movement.* New Haven: Yale University Press, 1969.

————. *Gremios, política económica, y democracia.* Bogotá: Fondo Cultural Cafetero, 1983.

————. *Historia del sindicalismo en Colombia.* Bogotá: Ediciones Universidad de los Andes, 1969.

————. "On the Absence of Economic Populism in Colombia." In *The Macroeconomics of Populism in Latin America,* ed. Rudiger Dornbusch and Sebastian Edwards, 369–87. Chicago: University of Chicago Press, 1991.

Urrutia, Miguel, and Mario Arrubla. *Compendio de estadísticas históricas de Colombia.* Bogotá: Universidad Nacional de Colombia, 1970.

Valderrama Andrade, Carlos, ed. *Epistolario del Beato Ezequel Moreno y otros Agustinos Recoletos con Miguel Antonio Caro y su familia.* Bogotá: Instituto Caro y Cuervo, 1983.

————. "Estudio preliminar." In *Miguel Antonio Caro: Discursos y otras intervenciones en el Senado de la República, 1903–1904,* ed. Carlos Valderrama Andrade, 19–146. Bogotá: Instituto Caro y Cuervo, 1979.

Valencia, Luis Emiro, ed. *Gaitán: Antología de su pensamiento social y economico.* Bogotá: Editorial Colombia Nueva, 1968.

Valencia Tovar, Alvaro. "Historia Militar Contemporanea." In *Nueva Historia de Colombia.* 6 vols., ed. Alvaro Tirado Mejía, 2:318–26. Bogotá: Editorial Planeta, 1989.

————. *Testimonio de una época.* Bogotá: Editorial Planeta, 1992.

Vallejo, Jorge Angel. *Cien años de Bavaria.* Medellín: Editorial Lealon, 1990.

Valois Arce, Daniel. *Enjuiciamiento de Laureano Gómez.* Bogotá: Editorial Pérez y Díaz, 1959.

————. *Itinerario espiritual.* Manizales: Editorial Zapata, 1937.

Vargas Lesmes, Julián, and Fabio Zambrano P. "Santa Fe y Bogotá: Evolución histórica y servicios públicos, 1600–1957." In *Bogotá cuatrocientos cincuenta años: Retos y realidades,* ed. Pedro Santana R., 11–92. Bogotá: Servigraphic, 1988.

Vargas Velásquez, Alejo. *Colonización y conflicto armado: Magdalena medio santanderiano.* Bogotá: CINEP, 1992.

Vargas Vila, José María. *Vargas Vila: Sufragio, selección, epitafio.* Edited by Malcolm Deas. Bogotá: Banco Popular, 1985.

Vásquez Carrizosa, Alfredo. *El poder presidencial en Colombia.* Bogotá: Editorial DOBRY, 1979.

Vázquez Cobo Carrizosa, Camilo. *El Frente Nacional, su origen y desarrollo. Memorias de Camilo Vázquez Cobo Carrizosa.* Cali: Carvajal, 1969.

Veatch, Arthur Clifford. *Quito to Bogotá.* London: Hodder and Stoughton, 1917.

———. *La federación en Colombia, 1810–1912.* Bogotá: Editorial ABC, 1952.

Vega Cantor, Renán. *Crisis y caída de la república liberal, 1942–1946.* Ibagué: Editorial Mohan, 1988.

Velasco A., Hugo. *Ecce Homo. Biografía de una tempestad.* Bogotá: Editorial ARGRA, 1950.

———. *Mariano Ospina Pérez.* Bogotá: Editorial Cosmos, 1953.

Velásquez, Atilio. *El padre de la Victoria Liberal y el autor de la derrota.* Bogotá: Editorial Kelly, 1946.

Velásquez Toro, Magdala. "Condición jurídica y social de la mujer." In *Nueva Historia de Colombia,* 6 vols., ed. Alvaro Tirado Mejía, 4:9–60. Bogotá: Editorial Planeta, 1989.

Velásquez Toro, Magdalena, and Alvaro Tirado Mejía. *Reforma Constitucional de 1936.* Colombia: Cámara de Representantes, 1986.

Vélez, Humberto. "Rafael Reyes: Quinquenio, régimen político, y capitalismo." In *Nueva Historia de Colombia,* 6 vols., ed. Alvaro Tirado Mejía, 1:187–214.

Villarreal, José María. Interview by author. Bogotá. July 9, 1971.

Villaveces, Jorge. *La Derrota. 25 años de historia, 1930–1955.* Bogotá: Editorial Jorvi, 1963.

Villegas, Jorge. *Petróleo colombiano, ganancia gringa.* Bogotá: El Ancora Editores, 1985.

Villegas, Jorge, and José Yunis. *Sucesos colombianos, 1900–1924.* Medellín: Universidad de Antioquia, 1976.

Villegas, Silvio. *No hay enemigos a la derecha.* Manizales: Editorial Zapata, 1937.

Walthour, Douglas Alan. "Laureano Gómez and Colombia in the Korean War: Internal and External Factors in Foreign Policy Decision-Making." M.A. thesis, University of Texas, Austin, 1990.

Wilde, Alexander Wiley. "Conversations among Gentlemen: Oligarchical Democracy in Colombia." In *The Breakdown of Democratic Regimes: Latin America,* ed. Juan J. Linz and Alfred Stepan, 28–81. Baltimore: Johns Hopkins University Press, 1978.

Woodruff, William. *The Emergence of an International Economy, 1700–1914.* London: Fontana, 1971.

Zalamea, Jorge. *El Gran Burundún Burundá ha muerto.* 1952. Bogotá: Editorial Colombia Nueva, 1966.

———. *Literatura, política, y arte.* Bogotá: Instituto Colombiano de Cultura, 1978.

———. *La metamórfosis de su excelencia.* Bogotá: n.p., 1949.

Zamudio, Lucero, and Norma Rubiano. *La nupcialidad en Colombia.* Bogotá: Universidad Externado de Colombia, 1991.

Zapata Isaza, Gilberto. *¿Patricios o asesinos?: Cincuenta años de cruda historia.* Medellín: Editorial Ital Torina, 1969.

Zapata Restrepo, Miguel. *La mitra azul: Miguel Angel Builes, el hombre, el obispo, el caudillo.* Medellín: Editora Beta, 1973.

Zuleta Angel, Eduardo. *El Presidente López.* Medellín: Editorial Albón, 1966.

Index

Abadía Méndez, Miguel, 26, 59, 70, 78, 98–99, 147, 154, 161–64, 167–69, 173–75, 191; labor legislation of, 217, 223
Abella, Arturo, 225, 392
Abello Salcedo, Rafael, 65
Academic societies: Academy of Caro (*see* Gómez Castro, Laureano); Colombian Academy of History, 52, 410; Colombian Academy of Jurisprudence, 64; Colombian Academy of Language, 163; Colombian Geographic Society, 52
Academy of Caro. *See* Gómez Castro, Laureano
Acción Comunal, 400–401
Acción Nacional Derechista. *See* Conservative Party
Adamo, Vicente, 158–59
Advanced School of Public Administration, 441
Afanador, Rafael, 286, 188–89
Agrarian counterreform (1944), 246–47
Agrarian movement (1925–36), 211–24; APEN (Asociación Patronal Económica Nacional), 219, 221, 230; Banco Agrícola, 222; Decree 1110 (1928), 223; land invasions, 220; Manifesto of Renters of El Chocho, 217–18, 223; PAN (Partido Agrarista Nacional), 220–21, 223; peasant leagues, 220; populist character of, 212; smallholder bias in, 242, 245–46; UNIR (Union Nacional Izquierdista Revolucionaria), 220–21; violence in, 219–20. *See also* Banks: Caja Agraria; Agrarian reform; Land tenancy
Agrarian reform
—of 1930s: Abadía Méndez and, 223; Law 200 of 1936 and, 211–12, 218, 221–23, 245–46; Laws 6 and 100 (1944) and, 246–47; smallholder bias in, 242, 245–46; Olaya Herrera and, 219. *See also* Land tenancy
—of 1960s. *See* Land reform
Agriculture, 50; agricultural bonds, 333–34; bananas, 117; commercialization of, 389; cotton, 334; Currie Report (1950) and, 333–34; earnings inequity, 389; economic protection of, 333; export, 59–60, 333; fertilizer use, 334; five-year plan (1945–50), 333; food imports (1930s–40s), 246; inequality of landholdings (1960s), 389; "integral protection" of cotton, 334; Instituto de Fomento Algodonero, 334; investment capital, 246–47; mechanization of, 246, 389; modernization of, 333–34; Ospina Pérez and, 334; prices (1940s), 246; production (1940s), 246, 334; rice, 334; sesame, 334; smallholders, 389; SAC, 60, 245–46 (*see also* Interest associations); sorghum, 334; sugar, 59, 334
Agua de Dios (leprosarium), 49
Aguirre, Adán de Jesús (El Aguila), 401
Airlines: Avianca, 248; SCADTA (Colombo-German Society of Air Transportation), 93, 240, 248, 275
Alcohol consumption, alcoholism, 91
Alcohol regulation, chicha prohibition (1949), 341
Alessandri, Arturo, 75
Alliance for Progress, 391, 400–401, 408
Alvarez, Juan, 214
Alvarez Restrepo, Antonio, 331–32, 378–79

Barco Contract. *See* Petroleum
Barrientos, José María, 98
Baseball, 253. *See also* Popular culture; Spectator sports
Bautista, Darío, 278
Bautista, Fulgencio, 391
Bautista, Tulio, 356
Bavaria Brewery. *See* Industrial concerns
Bayer, Tulio, 401
Beaulac, Willard, 313
Bejarano, Jesús A., 242, 343
Benavente, Toribio, 201
Benidorm Pact (1956). *See* National Front
Bentham, Jeremy, 33, 38
Berger [Julius] Consortium contract, 194–95, 198
Bergquist, Charles, 214, 250
Berrío, Gustavo, 361
Berrío, Pedro J., 196–98, 269
Berrío, Pedro María, 232
Berry, Albert, 405–6
Betancur Cuartas, Belisario, 368, 376, 392
Bipartisanship, 417–18; criticism of, 172; Darío Echandía and, 315–16; failure of (in 1930s), 178–82, 237–38; in 1940s, 320–21; interest associations and, 339; López Pumarejo and, 295, 320, 381; Olaya Herrera and, 196–97; Ospina Pérez and, 296, 315–16. *See also* National Front; Politics
Bogotá, 8–10, 18–24, 50, 52, 77, 141–42, 256; riot of April 9, 1948 (*see* Bogotazo); urban development, 94, 155, 252
Bogotazo (April 9, 1948), 288, 309–16; army and, 312–13; inflation and, 331; Liberal revolt in Antioquia, 315; Liberal revolt in Valle del Cauca, 315; Liberal revolt in Tolima, 315; looting, significance of 313–15; political utility of, 214–15; public to private transition and, 313; racism in, 312; radio in, 310–11, 314–16; reimbursement of commercial losses from, 332; revolutionary juntas, 314–16; U.S. interpretation of, 314
Bolívar, Simón, 31, 33, 141
Bolshevik Revolution (1917), 157–58
Bonitto, Eduardo, 278
Borda, Francisco de Paula, 73–74
Botero, Fernando, 258, 345

Botero, Mauricio, 394
Bowles, Chester, 391
Braden, Spruille, 273–74
Bradshaw, Thomas, 166
Braudel, Fernand, 121
Braun, Herbert, 292, 296, 312–13
Bravo Pérez, Gonzalo, 169
Bretton Woods Conference (1944), 290
Britain, 102; influence on Colombian elites, 27–28
Brunner, Karl, 344
Builes, Miguel Angel, 85, 261, 347, 357
Bureaucracy, politicization of, 305
Business sector, government intervention in, 283
Bustamante, Paulo E., 170

Caballero, Carlos, 217–18, 223
Caballero, Lucas, 60, 90, 145
Caballero, Manuel, 217–18, 223
Caballero Calderón, Eduardo, 240, 345–46, 407–8
Caballero Escobar, Enrique, 281, 290
Cabrales, Eusebio, 318
CAFAM (Cajas de Cooperación Familiar), 341
Cafure de Turbay, Avinader, 294
Caja Agraria. *See* Banks
Cajiao, Isabel, 133
Caldas, Francisco José, 114
Calderón, Guillermo Quintero, 41
Calderón Reyes, Clímaco, 55
Cali munitions explosion (1956), 373
Camacho, Ana María, 201
Camacho, Nemesio, 170, 173
Camacho Carreño, José, 196–97, 261
Camacho Roldán, Salvador, 27
Cano, Angel María, 336
Cano, Luis, 25, 49, 209
Cano, María, 159, 163, 165, 168–69
Cañón, Heraclio, 190
Capital, investment. *See* Investment capital
Capitalism: capitalist ethos, 120, 123, 414, 418; coffee and, 123; Generation of the Centenary and, 418–19
Capitanejo voting violence (1930). *See* Violence, political
CARE. *See* Catholic Church
Carlyle, Thomas, 150

James D. Henderson is professor of international studies at Coastal Carolina University, and the author of *Las ideas de Laureano Gómez* (1985), *Conservative Thought in Twentieth Century Latin America. The Ideas of Laureano Gómez* (1988), *When Colombia Bled: A History of the Violencia in Tolima* (1985; Spanish edition *Cuando Colombia se desangró, una historia de la Violencia en metrópoli y provincia,* 1984), *Meals by Fred Harvey, a Phenomenon of the American West* (1969). He is co-author of *A Reference Guide to Latin American History* (2000), and *Ten Notable Women of Latin America* (1978).